Compliments of
Charles B. Hoeven, M. C.
8th District of Iowa.

Papers Relating to the
Foreign Relations
of the
United States
1924

(In Two Volumes)

Volume I

United States
Government Printing Office
Washington : 1939

DEPARTMENT OF STATE

PUBLICATION 1366

For sale by the
Superintendent of Documents, Washington, D. C.
Price $1.50 (cloth)

CONTENTS

MESSAGE OF THE PRESIDENT OF THE UNITED STATES TO CONGRESS, DECEMBER 3, 1924

To THE CONGRESS OF THE UNITED STATES: The present state of the Union, upon which it is customary for the President to report to the Congress under the provisions of the Constitution, is such that it may be regarded with encouragement and satisfaction by every American. Our country is almost unique in its ability to discharge fully and promptly all its obligations at home and abroad, and provide for all its inhabitants an increase in material resources, in intellectual vigor and in moral power. The Nation holds a position unsurpassed in all former human experience. This does not mean that we do not have any problems. It is elementary that the increasing breadth of our experience necessarily increases the problems of our national life. But it does mean that if we will but apply ourselves industriously and honestly, we have ample powers with which to meet our problems and provide for their speedy solution. I do not profess that we can secure an era of perfection in human existence, but we can provide an era of peace and prosperity, attended with freedom and justice and made more and more satisfying by the ministrations of the charities and humanities of life.

Our domestic problems are for the most part economic. We have our enormous debt to pay, and we are paying it. We have the high cost of government to diminish, and we are diminishing it. We have a heavy burden of taxation to reduce, and we are reducing it. But while remarkable progress has been made in these directions, the work is yet far from accomplished. We still owe over $21,000,000,-000, the cost of the National Government is still about $3,500,000,000, and the national taxes still amount to about $27 for each one of our inhabitants. There yet exists this enormous field for the application of economy.

In my opinion the Government can do more to remedy the economic ills of the people by a system of rigid economy in public expenditure than can be accomplished through any other action. The costs of our national and local governments combined now stand at a sum close to $100 for each inhabitant of the land. A little less than one-third of this is represented by national expenditure, and a little more than two-thirds by local expenditure. It is an ominous fact that only the National Government is reducing its debt. Others are increasing theirs at about $1,000,000,000 each year. The depression that overtook business, the disaster experienced in agriculture, the lack of employment and the terrific shrinkage in all values which our country experienced in a most acute form in 1920, resulted in no small measure from the prohibitive taxes which were then levied on all productive effort. The establishment of a system of drastic economy in public expenditure, which has enabled us to pay off about one-fifth of the national debt since 1919, and almost cut in two the national tax burden since 1921, has been one of the main causes in reestablishing a prosperity which has come to include within its benefits almost every one of our inhabitants. Economy reaches everywhere. It carries a blessing to everybody.

The fallacy of the claim that the costs of government are borne by the rich and those who make a direct contribution to the National Treasury cannot be too often exposed. No system has been devised, I do not think any system could be devised, under which any person living in this country could escape being affected by the cost of our government. It has a direct effect both upon the rate and the purchasing power of wages. It is felt in the price of those prime necessities of existence, food, clothing, fuel and shelter. It would appear to be elementary that the more the Government expends the more it must require every producer to contribute out of his production to the Public Treasury, and the less he will have for his own benefit. The continuing costs of public administration can be met in only one way—by the work of the people. The higher they become, the more the people must work for the Government. The less they are, the more the people can work for themselves.

The present estimated margin between public receipts and expenditures for this fiscal year is very small. Perhaps the most important work that this session of the Congress can do is to continue a policy of economy and further reduce the cost of government, in order that we may have a reduction of taxes for the next fiscal year. Nothing is more likely to produce that public confidence which is the forerunner and the mainstay of prosperity, encourage and enlarge business opportunity with ample opportunity for employment at good wages, provide a larger market for agricultural products, and put our country in a stronger position to be able to meet the world competition in trade, than a continuing policy of economy. Of course necessary costs must be met, proper functions of the Government performed, and constant investments for capital account and reproductive effort must be carried on by our various departments. But the people must know that their Government is placing upon them no unnecessary burden.

TAXES

Everyone desires a reduction of taxes, and there is a great preponderance of sentiment in favor of taxation reform. When I approved the present tax law, I stated publicly that I did so in spite of certain provisions which I believed unwise and harmful. One of the most glaring of these was the making public of the amounts assessed against different income-tax payers. Although that damage has now been done, I believe its continuation to be detrimental to the public welfare and bound to decrease public revenues, so that it ought to be repealed.

Anybody can reduce taxes, but it is not so easy to stand in the gap and resist the passage of increasing appropriation bills which would make tax reduction impossible. It will be very easy to measure the strength of the attachment to reduced taxation by the power with which increased appropriations are resisted. If at the close of the present session the Congress has kept within the budget which I proposed to present, it will then be possible to have a moderate amount of tax reduction and all the tax reform that the Congress may wish for during the next fiscal year. The country is now feeling the direct stimulus which came from the passage of the last revenue bill, and under the assurance of a reasonable system of taxation there is every prospect of an era of prosperity of unprecedented proportions. But it would be idle to expect any such results unless business can continue free from excess profits taxation and be accorded a system of surtaxes at rates which have for their object not the punishment of success or the discouragement of business, but the production of the greatest amount of revenue from large incomes. I am convinced that the larger incomes of the country would actually yield more revenue to the Government if the basis of taxation were scientifically revised downward. Moreover the effect of the present method of this taxation is to increase the cost of interest on productive enterprise and to increase the burden of rent. It is altogether likely that such reduction would so encourage and stimulate investment that it would firmly establish our country in the economic leadership of the world.

WATERWAYS

Meantime our internal development should go on. Provision should be made for flood control of such rivers as the Mississippi and the Colorado, and for the opening up of our inland waterways to commerce. Consideration is due to the project of better navigation from the Great Lakes to the Gulf. Every effort is being made to promote an agreement with Canada to build the St. Lawrence waterway. There are pending before the Congress bills for further development of the Mississippi Basin, for the taking over of the Cape Cod Canal in accordance with a moral obligation which seems to have been incurred during the war, and for the improvement of harbors on both the Pacific and the Atlantic coasts. While this last should be divested of some of its projects and we must proceed slowly, these bills in general have my approval. Such works are productive of wealth and in the long run tend to a reduction of the tax burden.

RECLAMATION

Our country has a well-defined policy of reclamation established under statutory authority. This policy should be continued and made a self-sustaining activity administered in a manner that will meet local requirements and bring our arid lands into a profitable state of cultivation as fast as there is a market for their products. Legislation is pending based on the report of the Fact Finding Commission for the proper relief of those needing extension of time in which to meet their payments on irrigated land, and for additional amendments and reforms of our reclamation laws, which are all exceedingly important and should be enacted at once.

AGRICULTURE

No more important development has taken place in the last year than the beginning of a restoration of agriculture to a prosperous condition. We must permit no division of classes in this country, with one occupation striving to secure advantage over another. Each must proceed under open opportunities and with a fair prospect of economic equality. The Government can not successfully insure prosperity or fix prices by legislative fiat. Every business has its risk and its times of depression. It is well known that in the long run there will be a more even prosperity and a more satisfactory range of prices under the natural working out of economic laws than when the Government undertakes the artificial support of markets and industries. Still we can so order our affairs, so protect our own people from foreign competition, so arrange our national finances, so administer our monetary system, so provide for the extension of credits, so improve methods of distribution, as to provide a better working machinery for the transaction of the business of the Nation with the least possible friction and loss. The Government has been constantly increasing its efforts in these directions for the relief and permanent establishment of agriculture on a sound and equal basis with other business.

It is estimated that the value of the crops for this harvest year may reach $13,000,000,000, which is an increase of over $3,000,000,000 in three years. It compares with $7,100,000,000 in 1913, and if we make deduction from the figures of 1924 for the comparatively decreased value of the dollar, the yield this year still exceeds 1913 in purchasing power by over $1,000,000,000, and in this interval there has been no increase in the number of farmers. Mostly by his own effort the farmer has decreased the cost of production. A marked increase in the price of his products and some decrease in the price of his supplies has brought him about to a parity with the rest of the Nation. The crop area of this season is estimated at 370,000,000 acres, which is a decline of 3,000,000 acres from last year, and 6,000,000 acres from 1919. This has been a normal and natural application of economic laws, which has placed agriculture on a foundation which is undeniably sound and beginning to be satisfactory.

A decrease in the world supply of wheat has resulted in a very large increase in the price of that commodity. The position of all agricultural products indicates a better balanced supply, but we can not yet conclude that agriculture is recovered from the effects of the war period or that it is permanently on a prosperous basis. The cattle industry has not yet recovered and in some sections has been suffering from dry weather. Every effort must be made, both by Government activity and by private agencies, to restore and maintain agriculture to a complete normal relationship with other industries.

It was on account of past depression, and in spite of present more encouraging conditions, that I have assembled an Agricultural Conference made up of those who are representative of this great industry in both its operating and economic sides. Everyone knows that the great need of the farmer is markets. The country is not suffering on the side of production. Almost the entire difficulty is on the side of distribution. This reaches back, of course, to unit costs and diversification, and many allied subjects. It is exceedingly intricate, for our domestic and foreign trade, transportation and banking, and in fact our entire economic system, are closely related to it. In time for action at this session, I hope to report to the Congress such legislative remedies as the conference may recommend. An appropriation should be made to defray their necessary expenses.

MUSCLE SHOALS

The production of nitrogen for plant food in peace and explosives in war is more and more important. It is one of the chief sustaining elements of life. It is estimated that soil exhaustion each year is represented by about 9,000,000 tons and replenishment by 5,450,000 tons. The deficit of 3,550,000 tons is reported to represent the impairment of 118,000,000 acres of farm lands each year.

To meet these necessities the Government has been developing a water power project at Muscle Shoals to be equipped to produce nitrogen for explosives and fertilizer. It is my opinion that the support of agriculture is the chief problem to consider in connection with this property. It could by no means supply the present needs for nitrogen, but it would help and its development would encourage bringing other water powers into like use.

Several offers have been made for the purchase of this property. Probably none of them represent final terms. Much costly experimentation is necessary to produce commercial nitrogen. For that reason it is a field better suited to private enterprise than to Government operation. I should favor a sale of this property, or long-time lease, under rigid guaranties of commercial nitrogen production at reasonable prices for agricultural use. There would be a surplus of power for many years over any possibility of its application to a developing manufacture of nitrogen. It may be found advantageous to dispose of the right to surplus power separately with such reservations as will allow its gradual withdrawal and application to nitrogen manufacture. A subcommittee of the Committees on Agriculture should investigate this field and negotiate with prospective purchasers. If no advantageous offer be made, the development should continue and the plant should be dedicated primarily to the production of materials for the fertilization of the soil.

RAILWAYS

The railways during the past year have made still further progress in recuperation from the war, with large gains in efficiency and ability expeditiously to handle the traffic of the country. We have now passed through several periods of peak traffic without the car shortages which so frequently in the past have brought havoc to our agriculture and industries. The condition of many of our great freight terminals is still one of difficulty and results in imposing large costs on the public for inward-bound freight, and on the railways for outward-bound freight. Owing to the growth of our large cities and the great increase in the volume of traffic, particularly in perishables, the problem is not only difficult of solution, but in some cases not wholly solvable by railway action alone.

In my message last year I emphasized the necessity for further legislation with a view to expediting the consolidation of our railways into larger systems. The principle of Government control of rates and profits, now thoroughly embedded in our governmental attitude toward natural monopolies such as the railways, at once eliminates the need of competition by small units as a method of rate adjustment. Competition must be preserved as a stimulus to service, but this will exist and can be increased under enlarged systems. Consequently the consolidation of the railways into larger units for the purpose of securing the substantial values to the public which will come from larger operation has been the logical conclusion of Congress in its previous enactments, and is also supported by the best opinion in the country. Such consolidation will assure not only a greater element of competition as to service, but it will afford economy in operation, greater stability in railway earnings, and more economical financing. It opens large possibilities of better equalization of rates between different classes of traffic so as to relieve undue burdens upon agricultural products and raw materials generally, which are now not possible without ruin to small units owing to the lack of diversity of traffic. It would also tend to equalize earnings in such fashion as to reduce the importance of section 15A, at which criticism, often misapplied, has been directed. A smaller number of units would offer less difficulties in labor adjustments and would contribute much to the solution of terminal difficulties.

The consolidations need to be carried out with due regard to public interest and to the rights and established life of various communities in our country. It does not seem to me necessary that we endeavor to anticipate any final plan or adhere to any artificial and unchangeable project which shall stipulate a fixed number of systems, but rather we ought to approach the problem with such a latitude of action that it can be worked out step by step in accordance with a comprehensive consideration of public interest. Whether the number of ultimate systems shall be more or less seems to me can only be determined by time and actual experience in the development of such consolidations.

Those portions of the present law contemplating consolidations are not sufficiently effective in producing expeditious action and need amplification of the authority of the Interstate Commerce Commission, particularly in affording a period for voluntary proposals to the commission and in supplying Government pressure to secure action after the expiration of such a period.

There are other proposals before Congress for amending the transportation acts. One of these contemplates a revision of the method of valuation for rate-making purposes to be followed by a renewed valuation of the railways. The valuations instituted by the Interstate Commerce Commission 10 years ago have not yet been completed. They have cost the Government an enormous sum, and they have imposed great expenditure upon the railways, most of which has in effect come out of the public in increased rates. This work should not be abandoned or supplanted until its results are known and can be considered.

Another matter before the Congress is legislation affecting the labor sections of the transportation act. Much criticism has been directed at the workings of this section and experience has shown that some useful amendment could be made to these provisions. It would be helpful if a plan could be adopted which, while retaining the practice of systematic collective bargaining with conciliation and voluntary arbitration of labor differences, could also provide simplicity in relations and more direct local responsibility of employees and managers. But such legislation will not meet the requirements of the situation unless it recognizes the principle that the public has a right to the uninterrupted service of transportation, and therefore a right to be heard when there is danger that the Nation may suffer great injury through the interruption of operations because of labor disputes. If these elements are not comprehended in proposed legislation, it would be better to gain further experience with the present organization for dealing with these questions before undertaking a change.

Shipping Board

The form of the organization of the Shipping Board was based originally on its functions as a semijudicial body in regulation of rates. During the war it was loaded with enormous administrative duties. It has been demonstrated time and again that this form of organization results in indecision, division of opinion and administrative functions, which make a wholly inadequate foundation for the conduct of a great business enterprise. The first principle in securing the objective set out by Congress in building up the American merchant marine upon the great trade routes and subsequently disposing of it into private operation can not proceed with effectiveness until the entire functions of the board are reorganized. The immediate requirement is to transfer into the Emergency Fleet Corporation the whole responsibility of operation of the fleet and other property, leaving to the Shipping Board solely the duty of determining certain major policies which require deliberative action.

The procedure under section 28 of the merchant marine act has created great difficulty and threatened friction during the past 12 months. Its attempted application developed not only great opposition from exporters, particularly as to burdens that may be imposed upon agricultural products, but also great anxiety in the different seaports as to the effect upon their relative rate structures. This trouble will certainly recur if action is attempted under this section. It is uncertain in some of its terms and of great difficulty in interpretation.

It is my belief that action under this section should be suspended until the Congress can reconsider the entire question in the light of the experience that has been developed since its enactment.

NATIONAL ELECTIONS

Nothing is so fundamental to the integrity of a republican form of government as honesty in all that relates to the conduct of elections. I am of the opinion that the national laws governing the choice of members of the Congress should be extended to include appropriate representation of the respective parties at the ballot box and equality of representation on the various registration boards, wherever they exist.

THE JUDICIARY

The docket of the Supreme Court is becoming congested. At the opening term last year it had 592 cases, while this year it had 687 cases. Justice long delayed is justice refused. Unless the court be given power by preliminary and summary consideration to determine the importance of cases, and by disposing of those which are not of public moment reserve its time for the more extended consideration of the remainder, the congestion of the docket is likely to increase. It is also desirable that the Supreme Court should have power to improve and reform procedure in suits at law in the Federal courts through the adoption of appropriate rules. The Judiciary Committee of the Senate has reported favorably upon two bills providing for these reforms which should have the immediate favorable consideration of the Congress.

I further recommend that provision be made for the appointment of a commission, to consist of two or three members of the Federal judiciary and as many members of the bar, to examine the present criminal code of procedure and recommend to the Congress measures which may reform and expedite court procedure in the administration and enforcement of our criminal laws.

PRISON REFORM

Pending before the Congress is a bill which has already passed one House providing for a reformatory to which could be committed first offenders and young men for the purpose of segregating them from contact with hardened criminals and providing them with special training, in order to reestablish in them the power to pursue a law-abiding existence in the social and economic life of the Nation. This is a matter of so much importance as to warrant the early attention of the present session. Further provision should also be made, for a like reason, for a separate reformatory for women.

NATIONAL POLICE BUREAU

Representatives of the International Police Conference will bring to the attention of the Congress a proposal for the establishment of a national police bureau. Such action would provide a central point for gathering, compiling, and later distributing to local police authorities much information which would be helpful in the prevention and detection of crime. I believe this bureau is needed, and I recommend favorable consideration of this proposal.

DISTRICT OF COLUMBIA WELFARE

The welfare work of the District of Columbia is administered by several different boards dealing with charities and various correctional efforts. It would be an improvement if this work were consolidated and placed under the direction of a single commission.

FRENCH SPOLIATION CLAIMS

During the last session of the Congress legislation was introduced looking to the payment of the remaining claims generally referred to as the French spoliation claims. The Congress has provided for the payment of many similar claims. Those that remain unpaid have been long pending. The beneficiaries thereunder have every reason to expect payment. These claims have been examined by the Court of Claims and their validity and amount determined. The United States ought to pay its debts. I recommend action by the Congress which will permit of the payment of these remaining claims.

THE WAGE EARNER

Two very important policies have been adopted by this country which, while extending their benefits also in other directions, have been of the utmost importance to the wage earners. One of these is the protective tariff, which enables our people to live according to a better standard and receive a better rate of compensation than any people, any time, anywhere on earth, ever enjoyed. This saves the American market for the products of the American workmen. The other is a policy of more recent origin and seeks to shield our wage earners from the disastrous competition of a great influx of foreign peoples. This has been done by the restrictive immigration law. This saves the American job for the American workmen. I should like to see the administrative features of this law rendered a little more humane for the purpose of permitting those already here a greater latitude in securing admission of members of their own families. But I believe this law in principle is necessary and sound, and destined to increase greatly the public welfare. We must maintain our own economic position, we must defend our own national integrity.

It is gratifying to report that the progress of industry, the enormous increase in individual productivity through labor-saving devices, and the high rate of wages have all combined to furnish our people in general with such an abundance not only of the necessaries but of the conveniences of life that we are by a natural evolution solving our problems of economic and social justice.

THE NEGRO

These developments have brought about a very remarkable improvement in the condition of the negro race. Gradually, but surely, with the almost universal sympathy of those among whom they live, the colored people are working out their own destiny. I firmly believe that it is better for all concerned that they should be cheerfully accorded their full constitutional rights, that they should be protected from all of those impositions to which, from their position, they naturally fall a prey, especially from the crime of lynching, and that they should receive every encouragement to become full partakers in all the blessings of our common American citizenship.

CIVIL SERVICE

The merit system has long been recognized as the correct basis for employment in our civil service. I believe that first, second, and third class postmasters, and without covering in the present membership the field force of prohibition enforcement, should be brought within the classified service by statute law. Otherwise the Executive order of one administration is changed by the Executive order of another administration, and little real progress is made. Whatever its defects, the merit system is certainly to be preferred to the spoils system.

DEPARTMENTAL REORGANIZATION

One way to save public money would be to pass the pending bill for the reorganization of the various departments. This project has been pending for some time, and has had the most careful consideration of experts and the thorough study of a special congressional committee. This legislation is vital as a companion piece to the Budget law. Legal authority for a thorough reorganization of the Federal structure with some latitude of action to the Executive in the rearrangement of secondary functions would make for continuing economy in the shift of Government activities which must follow every change in a developing country. Beyond this many of the independent agencies of the Government must be placed under responsible Cabinet officials, if we are to have safeguards of efficiency, economy, and probity.

ARMY AND NAVY

Little has developed in relation to our national defense which needs special attention. Progress is constantly being made in air navigation and requires encouragement and development. Army aviators have made a successful trip around the world, for which I recommend suitable recognition through provisions for promotion, compensation, and retirement. Under the direction of the Navy a new Zeppelin has been successfully brought from Europe across the Atlantic to our own country.

Due to the efficient supervision of the Secretary of War the Army of the United States has been organized with a small body of Regulars and a moderate National Guard and Reserve. The defense test of September 12 demonstrated the efficiency of the operating plans. These methods and operations are well worthy of congressional support.

Under the limitation of armaments treaty a large saving in outlay and a considerable decrease in maintenance of the Navy has been accomplished. We should maintain the policy of constantly working toward the full treaty strength of the Navy. Careful investigation is being made in this department of the relative importance of aircraft, surface and submarine vessels, in order that we may not fail to take advantage of all modern improvements for our national defense. A special commission also is investigating the problem of petroleum oil for the Navy, considering the best policy to insure the future supply of fuel oil and prevent the threatened drainage of naval oil reserves. Legislative action is required to carry on experiments in oil shale reduction, as large deposits of this type have been set aside for the use of the Navy.

We have been constantly besought to engage in competitive armaments. Frequent reports will reach us of the magnitude of the military equipment of other nations. We shall do well to be little impressed by such reports or such actions. Any nation undertaking to maintain a military establishment with aggressive and imperialistic designs will find itself severely handicapped in the economic development of the world. I believe thoroughly in the Army and Navy, in adequate defense and preparation. But I am opposed to any policy of competition in building and maintaining land or sea armaments.

Our country has definitely relinquished the old standard of dealing with other countries by terror and force, and is definitely committed to the new standard of dealing with them through friendship and understanding. This new policy should be constantly kept in mind by the guiding forces of the Army and Navy, by the Congress and by the country at large. I believe it holds a promise of great benefit to humanity. I shall resist any attempt to resort to the old methods and the old standards. I am especially solicitous that foreign nations should comprehend the candor and sincerity with which we have adopted this position. While we propose to maintain defensive and supplementary police forces by land and sea, and to train them through inspections and maneuvers upon appropriate occasions in order to maintain their efficiency, I wish every other nation to understand that this does not express any unfriendliness or convey any hostile intent. I want the armed forces of America to be considered by all peoples not as enemies but as friends, as the contribution which is made by this country for the maintenance of the peace and security of the world.

VETERANS

With the authorization for general hospitalization of the veterans of all wars provided during the present year, the care and treatment of those who have served their country in time of peril and the attitude of the Government toward them is not now so much one of needed legislation as one of careful, generous and humane administration. It will ever be recognized that their welfare is of the first concern and always entitled to the most solicitous consideration on the part of their fellow citizens. They are organized in various associations, of which the chief and most representative is the American Legion. Through its officers the Legion will present to the Congress numerous suggestions for legislation. They cover such a wide variety of subjects that it is impossible to discuss them within the scope of this message. With many of the proposals I join in hearty approval and commend them all to the sympathetic investigation and consideration of the Congress.

FOREIGN RELATIONS

At no period in the past 12 years have our foreign relations been in such a satisfactory condition as they are at the present time. Our actions in the recent months have greatly strengthened the American policy of permanent peace with independence. The attitude which our Government took and maintained toward an adjustment of European reparations, by pointing out that it was not a political but a business problem, has demonstrated its wisdom by its actual results.

We desire to see Europe restored that it may resume its productivity in the increase of industry and its support in the advance of civilization. We look with great gratification at the hopeful prospect of recuperation in Europe through the Dawes plan. Such assistance as can be given through the action of the public authorities and of our private citizens, through friendly counsel and cooperation, and through economic and financial support, not for any warlike effort but reproductive enterprise, not to provide means for unsound government financing but to establish sound business administration, should be unhesitatingly provided.

Ultimately nations, like individuals, can not depend upon each other but must depend upon themselves. Each one must work out its own salvation. We have every desire to help. But with all our resources we are powerless to save unless our efforts meet with a constructive response. The situation in our own country and all over the world is one that can be improved only by hard work and self-denial. It is necessary to reduce expenditures, increase savings and liquidate debts. It is in this direction that there lies the greatest hope of domestic tranquillity and international peace. Our own country ought to furnish the leading example in this effort. Our past adherence to this policy, our constant refusal to maintain a military establishment that could be thought to menace the security of others, our honorable dealings with other nations whether great or small, has left us in the almost constant enjoyment of peace.

It is not necessary to stress the general desire of all the people of this country for the promotion of peace. It is the leading principle of all our foreign relations. We have on every occasion tried to cooperate to this end in all ways that were consistent with our proper independence and our traditional policies. It will be my constant effort to maintain these principles, and to reinforce them by all appropriate agreements and treaties. While we desire always to cooperate and to help, we are equally determined to be independent and free. Right and truth and justice and humanitarian efforts will have the moral support of this country all over the world. But we do not wish to become involved in the political controversies of others. Nor is the country disposed to become a member of the League of Nations or to assume the obligations imposed by its covenant.

INTERNATIONAL COURT

America has been one of the foremost nations in advocating tribunals for the settlement of international disputes of a justiciable character. Our representatives took a leading part in those conferences which resulted in the establishment of The Hague Tribunal, and later in providing for a Permanent Court of International

Justice. I believe it would be for the advantage of this country and helpful to the stability of other nations for us to adhere to the protocol establishing that court upon the conditions stated in the recommendation which is now before the Senate, and further that our country shall not be bound by advisory opinions which may be rendered by the court upon questions which we have not voluntarily submitted for its judgment. This court would provide a practical and convenient tribunal before which we could go voluntarily, but to which we could not be summoned, for a determination of justiciable questions when they fail to be resolved by diplomatic negotiations.

DISARMAMENT CONFERENCE

Many times I have expressed my desire to see the work of the Washington Conference on Limitation of Armaments appropriately supplemented by further agreements for a further reduction and for the purpose of diminishing the menace and waste of the competition in preparing instruments of international war. It has been and is my expectation that we might hopefully approach other great powers for further conference on this subject as soon as the carrying out of the present reparation plan as the established and settled policy of Europe has created a favorable opportunity. But on account of proposals which have already been made by other governments for a European conference, it will be necessary to wait to see what the outcome of their actions may be. I should not wish to propose or have representatives attend a conference which would contemplate commitments opposed to the freedom of action we desire to maintain unimpaired with respect to our purely domestic policies.

INTERNATIONAL LAW

Our country should also support efforts which are being made toward the codification of international law. We can look more hopefully, in the first instance, for research and studies that are likely to be productive of results, to a cooperation among representatives of the bar and members of international law institutes and societies, than to a conference of those who are technically representative of their respective governments, although, when projects have been developed, they must go to the governments for their approval. These expert professional studies are going on in certain quarters and should have our constant encouragement and approval.

OUTLAW OF WAR

Much interest has of late been manifested in this country in the discussion of various proposals to outlaw aggressive war. I look with great sympathy upon the examination of this subject. It is in harmony with the traditional policy of our country, which is against aggressive war and for the maintenance of permanent and honorable peace. While, as I have said, we must safeguard our liberty to deal according to our own judgment with our domestic policies, we can not fail to view with sympathetic interest all progress to this desired end or carefully to study the measures that may be proposed to attain it.

LATIN AMERICA

While we are desirous of promoting peace in every quarter of the globe, we have a special interest in the peace of this hemisphere. It is our constant desire that all causes of dispute in this area may be tranquilly and satisfactorily adjusted. Along with our desire for peace is the earnest hope for the increased prosperity of our sister republics of Latin America, and our constant purpose to promote cooperation with them which may be mutually beneficial and always inspired by the most cordial friendships.

FOREIGN DEBTS

About $12,000,000,000 is due to our Government from abroad, mostly from European Governments. Great Britain, Finland, Hungary, Lithuania and Poland have negotiated settlements amounting close to $5,000,000,000. This represents the funding of over 42 per cent of the debt since the creation of the special Foreign Debt Commission. As the life of this commission is about to expire, its term should be extended. I am opposed to the cancellation of these debts and believe it for the best welfare of the world that they should be liquidated and paid as fast as possible. I do not favor oppressive measures, but unless money that is borrowed is repaid credit can not be secured in time of necessity, and there exists besides a moral obligation which our country can not ignore and no other country can evade. Terms and conditions may have to conform to differences in the financial abilities of the countries concerned, but the principle that each country should meet its obligation admits of no differences and is of universal application.

It is axiomatic that our country can not stand still. It would seem to be perfectly plain from recent events that it is determined to go forward. But it wants no pretenses, it wants no vagaries. It is determined to advance in an orderly, sound and common-sense way. It does not propose to abandon the theory of the Declaration that the people have inalienable rights which no majority and no power of government can destroy. It does not propose to abandon the practice of the Constitution that provides for the protection of these rights. It believes that within these limitations, which are imposed not by the fiat of man but by the law of the Creator, self-government is just and wise. It is convinced that it will be impossible for the people to provide their own government unless they continue to own their own property.

These are the very foundations of America. On them has been erected a Government of freedom and equality, of justice and mercy, of education and charity. Living under it and supporting it the people have come into great possessions on the material and spiritual sides of life. I want to continue in this direction. I know that the Congress shares with me that desire. I want our institutions to be more and more expressive of these principles. I want the people of all the earth to see in the American flag the symbol of a Government which intends no oppression at home and no aggression abroad, which in the spirit of a common brotherhood provides assistance in time of distress.

CALVIN COOLIDGE

THE WHITE HOUSE,
December 3, 1924.

LIST OF PAPERS

[Unless otherwise specified, the correspondence is *from* or *to* officials in the Department of State.]

GENERAL

PROPOSALS FOR THE ADHERENCE OF THE UNION OF SOVIET SOCIALIST REPUBLICS TO THE SPITZBERGEN TREATY OF FEBRUARY 9, 1920

GENERAL

GENERAL

GENERAL

COOPERATION OF THE UNITED STATES WITH THE LEAGUE OF NATIONS IN THE
DRAFTING OF A CONVENTION FOR THE CONTROL OF THE TRAFFIC IN ARMS—
Continued

GENERAL

GENERAL

GENERAL

AMERICAN PARTICIPATION IN THE INTERNATIONAL CONFERENCE FOR CONTROL
OF THE TRAFFIC IN HABIT-FORMING DRUGS—Continued

GENERAL

AMERICAN PARTICIPATION IN THE INTERNATIONAL CONFERENCE FOR CONTROL OF THE TRAFFIC IN HABIT-FORMING DRUGS—Continued

GENERAL

AMERICAN PARTICIPATION IN THE INTERNATIONAL CONFERENCE FOR CONTROL OF THE TRAFFIC IN HABIT-FORMING DRUGS—Continued

GENERAL

REFUSAL BY THE UNITED STATES TO JOIN OTHER CREDITOR NATIONS IN FORMING
AN INTERNATIONAL COMMISSION TO LIQUIDATE RELIEF LOANS MADE TO
CERTAIN EUROPEAN STATES

GENERAL

NEGOTIATIONS ON BEHALF OF THE WORLD WAR FOREIGN DEBT COMMISSION FOR THE SETTLEMENT OF DEBTS OWED THE UNITED STATES BY FOREIGN GOVERNMENTS

GENERAL

Negotiations on Behalf of the World War Foreign Debt Commission for the Settlement of Debts Owed the United States—Continued

Agreement Between the United States and Austria and Hungary for the Establishment of a Claims Commission, Signed November 26, 1924

GENERAL

GENERAL

CONVENTIONS FOR THE PREVENTION OF LIQUOR SMUGGLING INTO THE UNITED STATES

GREAT BRITAIN, JANUARY 23, 1924

GENERAL

CONVENTIONS FOR THE PREVENTION OF LIQUOR SMUGGLING INTO THE UNITED
STATES—Continued

GENERAL

CONVENTIONS FOR THE PREVENTION OF LIQUOR SMUGGLING INTO THE UNITED STATES—Continued

DENMARK, MAY 29, 1924

ITALY, JUNE 3, 1924

GREAT BRITAIN IN RESPECT OF CANADA, JUNE 6, 1924

PANAMA, JUNE 6, 1924

GENERAL

CONVENTIONS FOR THE PREVENTION OF LIQUOR SMUGGLING INTO THE UNITED
STATES—Continued

GENERAL

CONVENTIONS FOR THE PREVENTION OF LIQUOR SMUGGLING INTO THE UNITED
STATES—Continued

REPRESENTATIONS BY SALVADOR, CUBA, RUMANIA, NORWAY, AND ITALY
REGARDING PROPOSED LEGISLATION TO RESTRICT IMMIGRATION INTO THE
UNITED STATES

GENERAL

REPRESENTATIONS BY SALVADOR, CUBA, RUMANIA, NORWAY, AND ITALY REGARDING PROPOSED LEGISLATION TO RESTRICT IMMIGRATION INTO THE UNITED STATES—Continued

ARRANGEMENTS WITH FOREIGN GOVERNMENTS FOR A FLIGHT AROUND THE WORLD BY UNITED STATES ARMY AIRPLANES

GENERAL

ARRANGEMENTS WITH FOREIGN GOVERNMENTS FOR A FLIGHT AROUND THE
WORLD—Continued

GENERAL

ARRANGEMENTS WITH FOREIGN GOVERNMENTS FOR A FLIGHT AROUND THE WORLD—Continued

GENERAL

ARRANGEMENTS WITH FOREIGN GOVERNMENTS FOR A FLIGHT AROUND THE WORLD—Continued

GENERAL

ARRANGEMENTS WITH FOREIGN GOVERNMENTS FOR A FLIGHT AROUND THE WORLD—Continued

REPRESENTATIONS BY THE UNITED STATES AGAINST THE EXCLUSION OF AMERICAN MORMON MISSIONARIES FROM CERTAIN EUROPEAN COUNTRIES

GENERAL

GENERAL

REPRESENTATIONS BY THE UNITED STATES AGAINST THE EXCLUSION OF AMERICAN
MORMON MISSIONARIES FROM CERTAIN EUROPEAN COUNTRIES—Continued

GENERAL

GENERAL

BOUNDARY DISPUTES—Continued

GENERAL

Boundary Disputes—Continued

GENERAL

BOUNDARY DISPUTES—Continued

ALBANIA

MAINTENANCE BY THE UNITED STATES OF UNOFFICIAL RELATIONS WITH THE
REVOLUTIONARY GOVERNMENT IN ALBANIA

ALBANIA

MAINTENANCE BY THE UNITED STATES OF UNOFFICIAL RELATIONS WITH THE
REVOLUTIONARY GOVERNMENT IN ALBANIA—Continued

ALBANIA

POSTPONEMENT OF NEGOTIATIONS FOR A TREATY BETWEEN THE UNITED STATES
AND ALBANIA

BOLIVIA

DISINCLINATION OF THE SECRETARY OF STATE TO OFFER THE GOOD OFFICES
REQUESTED BY BOLIVIA FOR MODIFICATION OF THE BOLIVIAN–CHILEAN
TREATY OF 1904

BRAZIL

EXPRESSION OF CONCERN BY THE DEPARTMENT OF STATE AT BRAZIL'S NAVAL
BUILDING PROGRAM

BRAZIL

Expression of Concern by the Department of State at Brazil's Naval
Building Program—Continued

CANADA

RATIFICATION OF THE FISHERIES CONVENTION—Continued

CANADA

RENEWED CONSIDERATION OF A JOINT PROJECT FOR THE IMPROVEMENT OF THE
ST. LAWRENCE WATERWAY

CANADA

PROTESTS BY THE CANADIAN GOVERNMENT AGAINST FURTHER DIVERSION OF
THE WATERS OF THE GREAT LAKES

CHILE

RESIGNATION OF PRESIDENT ALESSANDRI AND THE EXERCISE OF INFORMAL RELATIONS BETWEEN THE UNITED STATES EMBASSY AND THE NEW ADMINISTRATION AT SANTIAGO

CHINA

CIVIL WAR IN NORTHERN CHINA RESULTING IN THE OVERTHROW OF PRESIDENT
TSAO KUN AND THE ESTABLISHMENT OF A PROVISIONAL GOVERNMENT

CHINA

CIVIL WAR IN NORTHERN CHINA, ETC.—Continued

CHINA

CIVIL WAR IN NORTHERN CHINA, ETC.—Continued

CHINA

CIVIL WAR IN NORTHERN CHINA, ETC.—Continued

CHINA

CIVIL WAR IN NORTHERN CHINA, ETC.—Continued

CHINA

CIVIL WAR IN NORTHERN CHINA, ETC.—Continued

CHINA

CIVIL WAR IN NORTHERN CHINA, ETC.—Continued

CHINA

CIVIL WAR IN NORTHERN CHINA, ETC.—Continued

MAINTENANCE OF A UNITED FRONT BY THE POWERS IN OPPOSITION TO THE THREATENED SEIZURE OF CUSTOMS AT CANTON BY SUN YAT-SEN

CHINA

MAINTENANCE OF A UNITED FRONT BY THE POWERS IN OPPOSITION TO THE
THREATENED SEIZURE OF CUSTOMS AT CANTON—Continued

CHINA

MAINTENANCE OF A UNITED FRONT BY THE POWERS IN OPPOSITION TO THE
THREATENED SEIZURE OF CUSTOMS AT CANTON—Continued

RECOGNITION BY THE UNITED STATES AND OTHER POWERS OF THE PROVISIONAL
GOVERNMENT AS THE "DE FACTO" GOVERNMENT OF CHINA

CHINA

RECOGNITION BY THE UNITED STATES AND OTHER POWERS OF THE PROVISIONAL
GOVERNMENT AS THE "DE FACTO" GOVERNMENT OF CHINA—Continued

CHINA

RECOGNITION BY THE UNITED STATES AND OTHER POWERS OF THE PROVISIONAL
GOVERNMENT AS THE "DE FACTO" GOVERNMENT OF CHINA—Continued

CHINA

RECOGNITION BY THE UNITED STATES AND OTHER POWERS OF THE PROVISIONAL
GOVERNMENT AS THE "DE FACTO" GOVERNMENT OF CHINA—Continued

CHINA

NEGOTIATIONS LEADING TO THE OCCUPATION OF THE RUSSIAN LEGATION AT
PEKING BY THE NEWLY ACCREDITED SOVIET AMBASSADOR TO CHINA

CHINA

NEGOTIATIONS LEADING TO THE OCCUPATION OF THE RUSSIAN LEGATION AT
PEKING BY THE NEWLY ACCREDITED SOVIET AMBASSADOR TO CHINA—
Continued

CHINA

NEGOTIATIONS LEADING TO THE OCCUPATION OF THE RUSSIAN LEGATION AT PEKING BY THE NEWLY ACCREDITED SOVIET AMBASSADOR TO CHINA—Continued

CHINA

CHINA

Efforts To Obtain Unanimity Among the Powers Regarding the Proposal
To Raise the Diplomatic Rank of Their Representatives in China—
Continued

CHINA

EFFORTS TO OBTAIN UNANIMITY AMONG THE POWERS REGARDING THE PROPOSAL
TO RAISE THE DIPLOMATIC RANK OF THEIR REPRESENTATIVES IN CHINA—
Continued

CHINA

CHINA

RESERVATIONS BY THE UNITED STATES AND OTHER POWERS REGARDING DIS-
POSAL TO BE MADE OF THE CHINESE EASTERN RAILWAY UNDER THE SINO-
SOVIET AGREEMENT—Continued

CHINA

RESERVATIONS BY THE UNITED STATES AND OTHER POWERS REGARDING DIS-
POSAL TO BE MADE OF THE CHINESE EASTERN RAILWAY UNDER THE SINO-
SOVIET AGREEMENT—Continued

CHINA

RESERVATIONS BY THE UNITED STATES AND OTHER POWERS REGARDING DIS-
POSAL TO BE MADE OF THE CHINESE EASTERN RAILWAY UNDER THE SINO-
SOVIET AGREEMENT—Continued

CHINA

RESERVATIONS BY THE UNITED STATES AND OTHER POWERS REGARDING DIS-
POSAL TO BE MADE OF THE CHINESE EASTERN RAILWAY UNDER THE SINO-
SOVIET AGREEMENT—Continued

CHINA

CHINA

PROPOSAL BY THE CHINESE GOVERNMENT TO CONVENE A PRELIMINARY CUSTOMS CONFERENCE, ETC.—Continued

CHINA

PROPOSAL BY THE CHINESE GOVERNMENT TO CONVENE A PRELIMINARY CUSTOMS CONFERENCE, ETC.—Continued

CHINA

CONSENT BY THE UNITED STATES TO JOIN OTHER POWERS IN NEGOTIATIONS TO
RESTORE THE SHANGHAI MIXED COURT TO THE CHINESE—Continued

CHINA

FAILURE OF EFFORTS TO SECURE FROM THE INTERESTED POWERS A GENERAL ACCEPTANCE OF THE ARMS EMBARGO RESOLUTION PROPOSED AT THE WASHINGTON CONFERENCE

CHINA

FAILURE OF EFFORTS TO SECURE FROM THE INTERESTED POWERS A GENERAL
ACCEPTANCE OF THE ARMS EMBARGO RESOLUTION PROPOSED AT THE WASH-
INGTON CONFERENCE—Continued

CHINA

CHINA

JOINT RESOLUTION OF CONGRESS AUTHORIZING THE PRESIDENT TO REMIT FURTHER PAYMENTS ON THE BOXER INDEMNITY—Continued

CONCURRENCE BY THE UNITED STATES IN THE CONTENTION BY CERTAIN POWERS THAT THE BOXER INDEMNITY PAYMENTS SHOULD BE MADE IN GOLD CURRENCY

CHINA

CONCURRENCE BY THE UNITED STATES IN THE CONTENTION THAT THE BOXER
INDEMNITY PAYMENTS SHOULD BE MADE IN GOLD CURRENCY—Continued

CONTINUED SUPPORT BY THE UNITED STATES TO THE FEDERAL TELEGRAPH
COMPANY IN EFFORTS TO OBTAIN EXECUTION OF ITS CONTRACT WITH THE
CHINESE GOVERNMENT

CHINA

CONTINUED SUPPORT BY THE UNITED STATES TO THE FEDERAL TELEGRAPH
COMPANY—Continued

CHINA

CONTINUED SUPPORT BY THE UNITED STATES TO THE FEDERAL TELEGRAPH
COMPANY—Continued

EXPLANATIONS OF POLICY BY THE DEPARTMENT OF STATE RESPECTING QUESTIONS
OF TREATY RIGHTS RAISED BY AMERICANS IN CHINA

CHINA

PROTEST BY THE UNITED STATES AGAINST PARDON AND RESTORATION TO COMMAND OF THE CHINESE GENERAL HELD RESPONSIBLE FOR THE MURDER OF AN AMERICAN MISSIONARY

DOMINICAN REPUBLIC

THE ELECTION OF HORACIO VASQUEZ TO THE PRESIDENCY AND THE EVACUATION
OF THE FORCES OF THE UNITED STATES—Continued

DOMINICAN REPUBLIC

DOMINICAN REPUBLIC

APPROVAL BY THE UNITED STATES OF THE ISSUE OF $2,500,000 OF TWO-YEAR
NOTES BY THE DOMINICAN REPUBLIC—Continued

DOMINICAN REPUBLIC

APPROVAL BY THE UNITED STATES OF THE ISSUE OF $2,500,000 OF TWO-YEAR NOTES BY THE DOMINICAN REPUBLIC—Continued

DOMINICAN REPUBLIC

DOMINICAN REPUBLIC

PURCHASE OF THE PROPERTIES OF THE SANTO DOMINGO WATER, LIGHT AND POWER COMPANY BY THE DOMINICAN GOVERNMENT—Continued

DOMINICAN REPUBLIC

PURCHASE OF THE PROPERTIES OF THE SANTO DOMINGO WATER, LIGHT AND POWER COMPANY BY THE DOMINICAN GOVERNMENT—Continued

ECUADOR

RESUMPTION OF INTEREST PAYMENTS BY ECUADOR ON THE BONDS OF THE GUAYAQUIL AND QUITO RAILWAY COMPANY

ECUADOR

CLAIM OF THE MERCANTILE BANK OF THE AMERICAS AGAINST ECUADOR FOR
THE DEBT OF THE CACAO GROWERS ASSOCIATION—Continued

ECUADOR

CLAIM OF THE MERCANTILE BANK OF THE AMERICAS AGAINST ECUADOR FOR
THE DEBT OF THE CACAO GROWERS ASSOCIATION—Continued

EGYPT

REFUSAL BY THE UNITED STATES TO ASSENT TO THE COLLECTION OF THE GAFFIR
TAX FROM AMERICAN NATIONALS

EGYPT

EFFORTS BY THE UNITED STATES TO PROTECT THE INTERESTS OF AMERICAN
ARCHEOLOGISTS IN EGYPT

EGYPT

EFFORTS BY THE UNITED STATES TO PROTECT THE INTERESTS OF AMERICAN
ARCHEOLOGISTS IN EGYPT—Continued

FINLAND

EXTRADITION TREATY BETWEEN THE UNITED STATES AND FINLAND, SIGNED
AUGUST 1, 1924

FRANCE

CONVENTION BETWEEN THE UNITED STATES AND FRANCE REGARDING RIGHTS
IN SYRIA AND THE LEBANON, SIGNED APRIL 4, 1924

FRANCE

CONVENTION BETWEEN THE UNITED STATES AND FRANCE REGARDING RIGHTS
IN SYRIA AND THE LEBANON—Continued

CONSENT OF THE UNITED STATES TO INCREASED DUTIES ON IMPORTS INTO SYRIA
PENDING RATIFICATION OF THE SYRIAN MANDATE TREATY

FRANCE

FRANCE

FURTHER PROTESTS BY THE UNITED STATES AGAINST THE GRANT OF EXCLUSIVE PRIVILEGES TO FRENCH ARCHEOLOGISTS FOR RESEARCH IN ALBANIA AND AFGHANISTAN—Continued

FRANCE

DISCRIMINATION AGAINST AMERICAN SHIPPING BY FRENCH AUTHORITIES—
Continued

GENERAL

PROPOSALS FOR THE ADHERENCE OF THE UNION OF SOVIET SOCIALIST REPUBLICS TO THE SPITZBERGEN TREATY OF FEBRUARY 9, 1920 [1]

857h.01/14

The Norwegian Minister (Bryn) to the Secretary of State

[Translation [2]]

WASHINGTON, *March 20, 1924.*

MR. SECRETARY OF STATE: I have the honor by order of my Government to inform you that by a note dated February 16, last, the plenipotentiary representative of the Union of the Soviet Socialist Republics at Christiania notified the Ministry of Foreign Affairs of Norway that from now on the Government of the Union recognizes the sovereignty of Norway over Spitzbergen, including Bear Island, and therefore will not hereafter make any objection with respect to the Spitzbergen Treaty of February 9, 1920, and the mining regulations relative thereto.

In bringing the foregoing to Your Excellency's knowledge, I take the liberty of adding that the King's Government would attach value to having Russia allowed to adhere to the said treaty at the same time as the other powers which under the final provisions of the treaty will be asked by the Government of the French Republic to adhere to the treaty when it is duly ratified. The King's Government would therefore be thankful to know whether the Government of the United States of America would for its part raise any objection to Russia's being invited, together with the other nonsignatory powers, to adhere to the treaty concerning Spitzbergen.

Adding that a similar approach has been made by my Government to the other signatory governments parties to the Spitzbergen Treaty, I beg you to accept [etc.]

H. BRYN

---

[1] For text of treaty, see *Foreign Relations*, 1920, vol. I, p. 78.
[2] File translation revised.

1

857h.01/14

The Secretary of State to the Norwegian Minister (Bryn)

WASHINGTON, *April 30, 1924.*

SIR: I have the honor to acknowledge the receipt of your note of March 20, 1924, in which you bring up the question of Russian adherence to the Spitzbergen Treaty and ask whether the United States of America would raise any objection if Russia should be invited to adhere to this Treaty at the same time as the other powers not signatory to the Treaty are invited to adhere.

In reply I have the honor to inform you that, in the opinion of this Government, the question raised in your note appears to be covered by the provisions of Article 10 of the Spitzbergen Treaty as effective between the high contracting parties.[3]

Accept [etc.]   CHARLES E. HUGHES

857h.01/21½

Memorandum by the Secretary of State of a Conversation with the French Ambassador (Jusserand), June 21, 1924

[Extract]

The Ambassador said that he had been instructed to suggest a project of a protocol relating to the adhesion of Russia to the Spitzbergen Treaty. This protocol was to the effect that notwithstanding the stipulation of Article X of the Treaty Russia should be allowed to give her adhesion even though all the high contracting parties had not recognized the Russian Government. The Ambassador left with the Secretary a copy of this proposal.[4]

The Ambassador also left a memorandum giving a proposal of Mr. MacDonald. The memorandum is as follows:

"Mr. Ramsay MacDonald has proposed, and we agree that, in the protocol concerning Spitzbergen, wherever the word "Russie" appears, it be replaced by the expression: "Union des Républiques sovietiques socialistes".

---

[3] The pertinent clauses in the treaty read as follows:

"Until the recognition by the High Contracting Parties of a Russian Government shall permit Russia to adhere to the present Treaty, Russian nationals and companies shall enjoy the same rights as nationals of the High Contracting Parties.

.   .   .   .

"Third Powers will be invited by the Government of the French Republic to adhere to the present Treaty duly ratified. This adhesion shall be effected by a communication addressed to the French Government, which will undertake to notify the other Contracting Parties."

[4] Not printed.

The Secretary said that he did not care to comment on the matter at present; that it seemed to us that this question had been dealt with by Article X of the Spitzbergen Treaty and that this Government could not amend that Article without the consent of the Senate. The Secretary said that he would consider the question whether the suggestion of the French Government amounted to an amendment of the Article.

857h.01/24

The Norwegian Minister (Bryn) to the Secretary of State

AIDE-MÉMOIRE

In a note dated March 20, 1924, the Norwegian Minister, acting under instructions from his Government, asked whether the United States of America would raise any objection if Russia should be invited to adhere to the Spitsbergen Treaty at the same time as the other powers not signatory to the Treaty are invited to adhere.

In a note, dated April 30, 1924, His Excellency the Secretary of State replied that the question appears to be covered by the provisions of Article 10 of the Spitsbergen Treaty as effective between the high contracting parties.

As the Secretary's note seems not to give a definite reply, the Norwegian Government has instructed the Minister to approach again the Department of State informally, at the same time making the Department acquainted with the attitude taken by the other powers.

The Minister therefore begs to submit the following synopsis of the replies received by the Norwegian Government from the various powers interested:

France. In a note to the Norwegian Minister in Paris, dated March 22, 1924, the Minister of Foreign Affairs, Poincaré, states that the powers which have not yet recognized the Union of the Socialist Soviet Republics, could not without infringement of Article 10 of the Spitsbergen Treaty, actually admit Russia to adhere to the Treaty, but the French Government has, in deference to the desire of the Norwegian Government, sought a means to secure the adhesion of the Soviet Government without furnishing this one an opportunity to avail itself of Article 10 in order to pretend that it has been recognized by all the signatory powers. Monsieur Poincaré has therefore, so he further says, decided to confer on this point with those of the signatory powers which have not recognized the Soviet Government.

Netherlands. In a note dated April 14, the Dutch Foreign Minister states that Her Majesty's Government is disposed to render its co-operation in order that the desire of the Norwegian Government may be met, but an agreement to that effect cannot be concluded until after the ratification of the Spitsbergen Treaty. Monsieur van Karnebeek has notified the French Government accordingly.

Great Britain, Italy, Denmark, Sweden. The Governments of these countries have replied that they have no objection against inviting the Soviet Government to adhere to the Spitsbergen Treaty at the same time as the other non-signatory powers.

Japan. The Japanese Government is the only one from which nothing has been heard as yet.[5]

The Norwegian Minister will be thankful to know whether the Government of the United States in consideration of the above information might be disposed to reconsider the question raised by the Norwegian Government.

Mr. Bryn avails himself of this opportunity to renew to Mr. Hughes the assurances of his highest consideration.

WASHINGTON, *June 23, 1924.*

857h.01/24

The Secretary of State to the Norwegian Minister (Bryn)

WASHINGTON, *June 27, 1924.*

The Secretary of State presents his compliments to the Norwegian Minister and acknowledges the receipt of his *aide-mémoire* of June 23, 1924, in which the Minister, referring to previous correspondence with the Department, makes informal inquiry in behalf of his Government whether the Government of the United States would be disposed to reconsider the question whether it would raise any objection if Russia were invited to adhere to the Spitzbergen Treaty at the same time as other Powers not signatory to the same are invited to adhere thereto. In his *aide-mémoire* the Minister is good enough to submit a synopsis of replies received by the Norwegian Government from the Governments of France, Netherlands, Great Britain, Italy, Denmark and Sweden in relation to the matter.

---

[5] In a note dated June 26, 1924, the Norwegian Minister informed the Secretary of State that the Norwegian Government had received a communication from the Japanese Government to the effect that it had no objection to inviting the Russian Government to adhere to the Spitzbergen Treaty, provided all signatory powers agree on this point (file no. 857h.01/23).

The Secretary of State desires to make the following response:

First. The Treaty relating to Spitzbergen signed February 9, 1920, could not be modified save by agreement of all the Powers signatory thereto: and such modification in the case of the United States would not be effective without the approval of the Senate.

Second. As indicated in the Department's communication to the Norwegian Legation of April 30, 1924, the question raised must be regarded as covered by Article X of the Treaty. The provisions of the first paragraph thereof seem to have been designed primarily to safeguard the rights of Russian nationals and companies during a defined interval and until the recognition by the High Contracting Parties of a Russian Government.

Third. Should it be the desire of the States which have accepted the Spitzbergen Treaty to invite the adherence thereto of Russia through the medium of the régime now functioning therein, which has not been recognized by the United States, the Government of the United States would not raise an objection, provided it were clearly understood that the absence of such an objection should not be construed by any party to the Treaty or by the régime functioning in Russia as constituting the recognition of that régime by the Government of the United States.

857h.01/26a

The Department of State to the French Embassy [6]

PROPOSED DRAFT OF AGREEMENT RELATIVE TO THE ADHESION OF THE RÉGIME KNOWN AS THE UNION OF THE SOVIET SOCIALIST REPUBLICS TO THE SPITZBERGEN TREATY

The Governments of the United States of America, the British Empire, Denmark, France, Italy, Japan, Norway, the Netherlands, and Sweden, signatories to the Treaty concluded in Paris on February 9, 1920, concerning Spitzbergen, having found that some of them are recognizing the régime now functioning in Russia and known as the Union of the Soviet Socialist Republics and that those who do not recognize that régime are, under the following conditions, not opposed to the adherence of that régime to that Treaty,

Have agreed that, notwithstanding the stipulation in the first paragraph of Article 10, to permit the régime known as the Union of the Soviet Socialist Republics to adhere to the said Treaty, even though all of the High Contracting Parties may not have recognized

---

[6] Copy handed to the French Chargé by the Under Secretary of State, July 15, 1924.

that régime, on condition and with the definite understanding that the absence of objection to such adherence, on the part of the United States of America or of any other High Contracting Party shall not be construed by any party to said Treaty or to this Agreement or by the said régime known as the Union of the Soviet Socialist Republics as constituting the recognition thereof by any High Contracting Party which has not recognized that régime.

The present Agreement shall be ratified by all of the High Contracting Parties. Each High Contracting Party shall in the shortest possible time send its ratification to the French Government which will see to its being notified to His Majesty the King of Norway and to the other High Contracting Parties. The ratifications shall remain on deposit in the Archives of the French Government. The present Agreement shall go into effect for each High Contracting Party on the date of the deposit of its instrument of ratification.

Done at Paris . . . . . 1924, in duplicate originals, one of which will be transmitted to the Government of His Majesty the King of Norway, and the other deposited in the Archives of the Government of the French Republic, by which Government an authenticated copy thereof will be delivered to each of the other High Contracting Parties signatory to the said Treaty of February 9, 1920, or an adherent thereto.

REMONSTRANCE BY GREAT BRITAIN AGAINST A PROPOSED INCREASE IN GUN ELEVATION ON AMERICAN CAPITAL SHIPS RETAINED UNDER THE WASHINGTON NAVAL TREATY [7]

500.A4b/214

The British Chargé (Chilton) to the Secretary of State

No. 146   WASHINGTON, February 14, 1924.

SIR: It appears to His Majesty's Government from the extracts from the annual report of the Secretary of the Navy, which have been made public, that the United States naval authorities are again asking authority to utilise the large appropriation for the purpose of increasing the elevation of the turret guns of 13 capital ships already granted by Congress but on which action was suspended. In these circumstances His Majesty's Government think it desirable that their views on this important subject should at once be laid before the Government of the United States, especially as the fact that His Majesty's Government have not so far expressed their views on the subject is apparently regarded in some quarters as indicating

[7] For previous correspondence, see Foreign Relations, 1923, vol. I, pp. 24 ff.

that in their opinion the proposed action is not inconsistent with the terms of the Washington Naval Treaty.[8]

The relevant provision of the treaty is chapter II, Part 3, Section 1 (d), which prohibits, subject to certain exceptions, expressly provided for, any reconstruction of retained capital ships or aircraft carriers except for the purpose of providing means of defence against air and submarine attack. In the view of His Majesty's Government the words quoted govern the whole of the remainder of the paragraph, and the subsequent sentence dealing with alterations in side armour, in calibre, number or general type of mounting of main armament, does not in any way diminish the effect of these governing words, but merely develops them in certain respects, while also introducing certain exceptions which had been agreed on for special reasons. It follows that nothing which amounts to "reconstruction" may take place unless its object is to provide means of defence against air and submarine attack, as permitted by the above section.

It is clear that an increase in the elevation of turret guns of capital ships cannot be intended for the purpose of providing means of defence against air and submarine attack.

As regards the question whether such increase in the elevation involves any "reconstruction", the increase of the elevation of guns together with consequential alterations such as scrapping or replacement of existing fire-control systems, etc., involves considerable "reconstruction" in the fullest sense of that term. It is, therefore, the view of His Majesty's Government that an increase in the elevation of turret guns is not permissible under the terms of the treaty.

There is, however, a larger aspect of the question, and it is on this that His Majesty's Government desire to lay particular stress. One of the objects of the treaty, as expressed in the Preamble, is to reduce the burdens of competition in armament; and His Majesty's Government cannot but feel that the inevitable result of the action proposed by the United States naval authorities will be to defeat this object to a considerable extent. The proposal is to increase the elevation of the turret guns of 13 capital ships. His Majesty's Government are, of course, not aware of the exact amount of expenditure which this proposal would involve, but they note that the sum of $6,500,000 is proposed for that purpose, in addition presumably to any portion of the sum of $300,000 per ship per annum, regularly available for repairs without express congressional sanction, which may be employed. If, however, the proposal is carried out, it can hardly be doubted that public opinion in the United Kingdom will demand a corresponding increase in the elevation of

[8] *Ibid.*, 1922, vol. I, p. 247.

guns of the retained British capital ships, which will involve dealing with 17 or 18 ships, at an approximate cost of £116,000 per ship. The Japanese Government would probably feel compelled to take similar action, and the peoples of the three countries concerned would have to support the great expenditure involved, while the relative position of the three fleets would not be materially affected by the alterations. His Majesty's Government cannot doubt that the Government of the United States will agree that such a result would not only be deplorable in itself, but inconsistent with the objects of the Naval Treaty and the hopes which its conclusion inspired.

In these circumstances His Majesty's Government desire to make an earnest appeal to the Government of the United States not to impose upon the peoples of the countries concerned the burdens of the competition in armament, which will inevitably result from the execution of their present proposals. Those proposals are, in the opinion of His Majesty's Government, inconsistent with the provisions of the treaty, but even if arguments can be found in support of the contrary interpretation, it cannot be doubted that the effect of carrying them out would be entirely incompatible with its intentions. His Majesty's Government earnestly emphasize the psychological effect of such a departure as seems to be contemplated and the great disappointment it would cause to the people of all nations who regard the action of the United States Government at the Washington Conference as one of the most notable steps ever taken by any Government to establish conditions of world-peace.

In order to avoid any possibility of misconception, His Majesty's Government desire to repeat the assurance which has more than once been given to the United States Government that no alteration has been made in the elevation of the turret guns of any existing British capital ships since they were first placed in commission.

His Majesty's Government desire, therefore, to propose that the Government of the United States, the Japanese Government and His Majesty's Government (the Governments of France and Italy are not directly concerned in view of the special provision of the Treaty allowing them to increase the calibre of the guns of their retained capital ships), should each undertake not to make, during the term of the Treaty, any increase in the elevation of the turret guns of their existing capital ships.

In making this communication I am to explain that His Majesty's Government intend to make a similar proposal to the Japanese Government, but have thought it well to lay their views before the Government of the United States without delay.

I have [etc.]   H. G. CHILTON

500.A4b/226

The Secretary of the Navy (Denby) to the Secretary of State

WASHINGTON [*undated*].
[Received March 6, 1924.]

1. At the suggestion of The President I am writing this letter to inform you of the meaning and present status of the Gun-Elevation question in order that you may be in a position fully to advise The President regarding the rights and duties of the United States Government in the premises.

2. I desire first of all to state my very firm belief that a decision adverse to our right to increase the elevation of the turret guns of 13 of our present capital ships would permanently and irrevocably consign our present capital-ship fleet to a position of insuperable inferiority to the British capital-ship fleet. Such a position of inferiority was never contemplated by the terms or by the spirit of the Washington treaty. Equality in capital-ship strengths of the American and British fleets was the basis and backbone of that treaty. No other interpretation of the intent of the treaty is possible.

3. The following statement of the extreme ranges of British and American battleships and battle cruisers is official except as to the battleships *Rodney* and *Nelson* now building; these latter ships are expected to mount 16-inch guns; I assume they will have a maximum range equal to the range of the 16-inch guns on our *Maryland* class of ships:—

Name	Maximum Range	Name	Maximum Range
Nelson	34,300	West Virginia	34,500
Rodney	34,300	Colorado	34,500
Hood	30,300	Maryland	34,300
Royal Sovereign	24,300	California	35,000
Royal Oak	24,300	Tennessee	35,700
Resolution	24,300	Idaho	24,000
Ramillies	24,300	Mississippi	24,000
Revenge	24,300	New Mexico	24,000
Queen Elizabeth	24,300	Pennsylvania	21,000
Warspite	24,300	Arizona	20,900
Valiant	24,300	Nevada	21,000
Barham	24,300	Oklahoma	21,000
Malaya	24,300	Texas	21,000
Reknown	23,800	New York	21,000
Repulse	23,800	Arkansas	24,350
Benbow	23,800	Wyoming	23,500
Emperor of India	23,800	Utah	21,600
Iron Duke	23,800	Florida	22,000
Marlborough	23,800		
Tiger	23,800		

4. From the above table it will be seen that the British capital-ship fleet enjoys a very marked superiority in the number of ships that may be brought into action at the moderate and decisive ranges

between 21,000 and 24,000 yards. This superiority is shown in the following table:

Range in yards	No. of British ships in action	No. of American ships in action
24, 000	13	10
23, 000	20	10
22, 000	20	12
21, 000	20	18

I do not need to point out to you the very grave import of these comparisons.

5. I have been criticized in British papers for using the British navy for purposes of comparison. Such action is obviously unavoidable. Naval strengths are always relative, not absolute. We are strong or weak by comparison only. The friendly treaty that we made with Great Britain and other powers recognized our right to a parity in capital-ship strengths with Great Britain. We cannot determine if that parity is being attained or maintained unless definite comparisons are made. No criticism can justly lie against us or our motives if we strive towards a position definitely laid down in the treaty.

6. The table given in paragraph 4 above shows that at present there is no parity of the British and American fleets but rather a very great superiority of the British capital-ship fleet at vital and presumably decisive ranges. It is true that at ranges in excess of 25,000 yards advantage lies at present with American ships but the highest ranges are not decisive ranges. The consensus of present opinion is that decisive ranges in favorable weather are the very ranges where our inferiority is greatest, viz., between 20,000 and 25,000 yards. This fact makes the gun-elevation question one of commanding importance to the Navy.

7. Joined to the present British superiority of range of guns is a superiority in speed of their capital ships which enables the British fleet in comparison with our own to make full use of their superiority of range of guns. Nothing that we could do would bring our ships to an equality of speed with British ships so that should the unhappy event arise of the two fleets being engaged in battle under present conditions, the British fleet would by its superior speed be able to choose the range at which it would fight. Sound tactics would, of course, dictate the very ranges at which we are weakest, that is, the ranges between 20,000 and 25,000 yards. Illustration of the use of this advantage is to be had in the Battle of the Falkland Islands. Admiral Sturdee had under his command ships of speed superior to the speed of the German squadron under Von Spee. Admiral Sturdee deliberately chose to fight the German squadron at so great a range that the German fire was ineffective against the British ships. These sound tactics on Admiral Sturdee's part enabled him to achieve

victory with practically no injury to the personnel or ships under his command. I do not desire that the American Navy should ever be placed in a position at all corresponding to that of the German squadron at Falkland Islands.

8. I might elaborate farther upon the disadvantages under which our fleet suffers at present but will not do so. Such further information as you may desire on this subject will be gladly furnished.

9. The question of the legality of increasing the elevation of our turret guns has already been discussed in my Annual Report,[9] pages 75 and 76 and 114 to 117, to which reference is made above.[10] The views therein expressed are carefully considered views to which I ask your attention without repeating them here.

10. Some suggestions have appeared in the press to the effect that the elevation of our turret guns should be increased just sufficiently to equal the elevation of the British guns. This is an impracticable suggestion, first, because there is no treaty arrangement by which there is an exchange of information between the British and American navies on the subject of the extreme range of their guns; second, because there would be no assurance that equality once having been established would not be upset by still further increases either by one power or another; and third, our relations under the treaty are not only with Great Britain but also with three other signatory powers. My opinion is that there is only one satisfactory solution to the question and that is for each power to feel itself free and unhampered as to the extent to which it may increase the elevation of its turret guns. If each power gives to its turret guns the maximum elevation which it considers suitable and advisable, no other power can make any complaint or criticism regarding that act. But if one power increases to meet the elevations of another power and then after completing the work is again confronted with further increases of elevation, the task of maintaining a parity would be too complicated and expensive for all parties.

11. I have noted in the British Press statements to the effect that the treaty does not forbid increasing the elevation of our turret guns. I also have reason to believe that the professional opinion both in France and Italy is in agreement with this position, although in the case of France and Italy their interest is academic, those two powers being permitted under the treaty to re-arm their vessels with guns not exceeding 16 inches in caliber and, presumably, giving to those guns whatever elevation they deem most desirable. In order to illustrate more precisely the advantage which would accrue to our ships if the elevation of our turret guns were increased,

[9] For the fiscal year 1923.
[10] Annual report was listed on first page of letter as an enclosure.

I caused to be prepared a memorandum in which our fleet as at present is compared with our fleet as it might be if the elevation of the turret guns were increased. That memorandum is attached to this letter.[11]

12. I hope that a resolution will be introduced in Congress authorizing the use of the appropriation made by the 67th Congress of $6,500,000 for increasing the elevation of the turret guns of 13 United States capital ships and I further hope that that resolution will receive the support of the State Department. I believe that our national interests require a navy second to no other and that no steps should ever be taken that will bind us either directly or by implication to any line of conduct that hampers development of such a Navy.

EDWIN DENBY

500.A4b/262

The British Ambassador (Howard) to the Secretary of State

No. 718   MANCHESTER, MASS., *August 8, 1924.*
[Received August 11.]

SIR: In his note No. 146 of February 14th Mr. Chilton had the honour to draw the attention of the United States Government to the views of His Majesty's Government as to the bearing of the Washington Naval Treaty on the proposals published in the Annual Report of the Secretary of the Navy in regard to the increase of the elevation of the turret guns of thirteen capital ships of the United States Navy. At the same time Mr. Chilton drew attention to the larger aspects of the question and pointed out that whatever arguments might be put forward in support of the contention that such alterations are in accordance with the letter of the Treaty, it cannot be doubted that they would involve a renewal of competition in armaments, with the resultant burden upon the peoples of the countries concerned, and would thus be in direct opposition to the objects of the Naval Treaty as expressed in the Preamble.

It was added that His Majesty's Government therefore proposed that the United States Government and the Japanese Government and His Majesty's Government should each undertake not to make, during the term of the Naval Treaty, any increase in the elevation of the turret guns of their existing capital ships.

I have the honour, under instructions from my Government, to inform you that, in the absence of a reply on the part of the United States Government on this question, His Majesty's Government have now made a similar proposal to the Japanese Government, as fore-

[11] Not printed.

shadowed in the last paragraph of Mr. Chilton's note, and that His Majesty's Government have further suggested, in connection with the undertaking above referred to, that, should any increase in the elevation of the turret guns have already been made in any capital ship, by any of the signatories of the Washington Naval Treaty, the other signatories should be informed.

In this connection I would draw your attention to a statement which appeared in an editorial article in the *Washington Post* of July 31st in the following terms:

"It is asserted that both Great Britain and Japan have elevated some of their big guns since the Treaty became effective; but this has been denied and the point is in doubt".

In view of the explicit assurance contained in the seventh paragraph of Mr. Chilton's note, the latter part of the above quotation is a mis-statement of fact. Such statements by influential newspapers are all the more unfortunate in that they inspire other sections of the press with erroneous ideas. For instance, since the above article appeared in the *Washington Post* the *St. Louis Star* in its issue of August 4th has stated editorially in describing the Washington Conference and its results:

"Britain accepted the limitations as to the great line battleships and in a way persuaded the United States and Japan to make the most sacrifices. She then proceeded to modernize her fleet, and when the United States and Japan announced a similar programme raised numerous technical objections."

In acquainting you with the above, I have the honour to emphasize once more the unfortunate and widespread results which the elevation of turret guns on the 13 capital ships above referred to would have upon the competition in armaments, and to express the hope that you will be so good as to communicate to me in due course an expression of the views of the United States Government.

I have [etc.] ESME HOWARD

500.A4b/284a : Telegram

The Secretary of State to the Ambassador in Great Britain (Kellogg)

[Paraphrase]

WASHINGTON, *November 29, 1924—3 p. m.*

443. In view of current statements in the press I may state my attitude as follows regarding change of gun elevation on the capital ships which are retained under the Washington Treaty.

To the best of my knowledge there was nothing said at the Conference on the Limitation of Armaments concerning gun elevation. Subdivision (d), section I, part 3, chapter II of the naval treaty is in substance as drafted by agreement among the naval experts. It appears from detailed information supplied by the Navy Department that comparatively slight changes are involved in the proposals to elevate the guns on our ships and that these changes could not be considered either as alteration in the general type of mounting for the main armament or as a reconstruction of the ships. Assuming, however, that the proposed changes would not violate the treaty, a practical question remains involving economic considerations. We retain 18 capital ships. The guns of 5 of these now outrange the British. The difference with respect to 5 more is negligible. The remaining 8 capital ships have a shorter range than the British ships. These 8 ships will be replaced, however, within ten or a dozen years. Ships built to replace these may have any gun elevation desired. It is then a practical question whether the money required should be spent on the old ships or could be used more advantageously for other purposes.

In my campaign speeches I replied to misleading statements by Davis [12] by saying that the question was a practical one to be decided by Congress. I did not specifically state that in my opinion it would not violate the naval treaty to change the gun elevation. However, as I said it was a practical economic question it could readily be inferred that I did not believe that such changes would be in violation of the treaty. I have not replied to the British notes in opposition to a change in elevation as I thought that should Congress for economic reasons not think best to appropriate the funds for this purpose we might avoid joining an issue on this question under the treaty. I have explained the matter informally to the British Ambassador. It is probable that the question will be disposed of within a few weeks by the committees in Congress.[13] This telegram is sent simply in order that you may be informed should Chamberlain take the question up with you.

HUGHES

500.A4b/290

The Chairman of the House of Representatives Committee on Naval Affairs (Butler) to the Secretary of State

WASHINGTON, *December 30, 1924.*

DEAR MR. SECRETARY: I have the honor to transmit herewith on behalf of the Committee on Naval Affairs of the House of Repre-

---

[12] John W. Davis, Democratic candidate for President.
[13] In view of the failure of Congress to provide for gun elevation (see *Congressional Record*, vol. 66, pp. 2060–2061), no formal reply was made to the British notes.

sentatives (H. Res. 387) requesting certain information, and to request that same be furnished if not incompatible with the public interest.

Believe me [etc.] THOMAS S. BUTLER

[Enclosure]

Resolution 387 of the House of Representatives, December 20, 1924

Resolved, That the Secretary of State be, and he is hereby, authorized and directed, if not incompatible with the public interest, to furnish to the House of Representatives at the earliest date possible such data, information, or objections which he may have from any foreign government in connection with the modernization of certain capital ships of the United States Navy by increasing the elevation and range of turret guns.

500.A4b/290

The Secretary of State to the Chairman of the House of Representatives Committee on Naval Affairs (Butler)

WASHINGTON, *January 6, 1925.*

SIR: I have the honor to acknowledge the receipt of your communication on behalf of the Committee on Naval Affairs of the House of Representatives, transmitting House Resolution 387 and requesting that the information therein described should be furnished if not incompatible with the public interest.

The proposed resolution asks for "such data, information or objections" which the Secretary of State "may have from any foreign Government in connection with the modernization of certain capital ships of the United States Navy by increasing the elevation and range of turret guns".

While I understand that the resolution has not been passed there is no objection to giving to your Committee the information desired. The only "data, information and objections" which the Department of State has received from any foreign Government relating to the increase of the elevation and range of turret guns is as follows:

In a communication under date of March 15, 1923,[14] the British Ambassador at Washington reviewed the reports that had been made as to the increase in the elevation of the turret guns of British ships, and made the categorical declaration that no alteration had been made in the elevation of turret guns of any British capital ships since they were first placed in commission.

---

[14] *Foreign Relations*, 1923, vol. I, p. 26.

In subsequent communications from the British Ambassador at Washington it has been stated to be the view of His Majesty's Government that an increase in the elevation of turret guns is not permissible under the terms of the Naval Treaty, with special reference to Chapter II, Part 3, Section I (*d*) which prohibits, subject to certain exceptions expressly provided for, any reconstruction of retained capital ships or of aircraft carriers, except for the purpose of providing means of defense against air and submarine attack. As regards the question whether such increase in the elevation of turret guns involves any "reconstruction", it is stated to be the view of the British Government that the increase of the elevation of guns, together with consequential alterations such as scrapping or replacement of existing fire control systems, et cetera, involves considerable "reconstruction" in the fullest sense of the term. The British Government lay particular emphasis upon what is described as a larger aspect of the question, that is to say that one of the objects of the Treaty is to reduce the burdens of competition in armament, and the British Government feel that action by the United States in the elevation of turret guns would tend to defeat this object to a considerable extent. In these circumstances the British Government make an earnest appeal that the Government of the United States should not impose upon the peoples of the countries concerned the burdens of competition in armament which are deemed to result from the execution of the proposal to elevate the turret guns on retained capital ships of the United States, it being considered that even if arguments can be found in support of the contrary interpretation of the Treaty, the effect of carrying out such proposals would be incompatible with its intentions. The assurance is repeated that no alteration has been made in the elevation of the turret guns of any existing British capital ships since they were first placed in commission. It was further proposed that the Government of the United States, the Japanese Government and the British Government (the Governments of France and Italy not being deemed to be directly concerned in view of the exceptions of the Treaty) should undertake not to make during the term of the Treaty any increase in the elevation of the turret guns of their existing capital ships.

I have been informed by the Japanese Government that it was not the view of the Japanese Government that a change in the gun elevations, which did not require changes of the prohibited sort in the ships themselves, would be a violation of the Naval Treaty.[15]

---

[15] See memorandum by the Secretary of State of a conversation with the Japanese Ambassador, May 3, 1923, *Foreign Relations*, 1923, vol. I, p. 32.

I may add that, in view of the detailed description given by the Navy Department of the nature of the changes which would be necessary to elevate the turret guns on the capital ships retained by the United States, these changes appear to be of a minor sort and in my opinion would not constitute a reconstruction of the ships within the meaning which should be attributed to the provision of the Naval Treaty. I am of the opinion, however, that while such changes as would be contemplated in the case of American ships would not constitute a violation of the terms of the Treaty, they would tend to evoke the competition which it has been the policy of this Government to mitigate. It may also be stated that so far as the United States is concerned, the question appears to be of consequence only in relation to certain of the specified retained ships, and these ships under the replacement clauses of the Treaty are to be replaced within ten or twelve years.

I am [etc.]   CHARLES E. HUGHES

COOPERATION OF THE UNITED STATES WITH THE LEAGUE OF NATIONS IN THE DRAFTING OF A CONVENTION FOR THE CONTROL OF THE TRAFFIC IN ARMS [16]

511.3 B 1/138 : Telegram

The Minister in Switzerland (Grew) to the Secretary of State

BERNE, *January 22, 1924—3 p. m.*
[Received January 22—9:18 a. m.]

7. My despatch no. 1290 of December 15.[17] Secretariat of the League has informally inquired whether the United States Government has decided to accept the Council's invitation addressed to the Secretary of State by the Acting Secretary General in December, 1923,[18] to appoint representatives to cooperate with the Temporary Mixed Commission for the preparation of a new convention relating to traffic in arms, to be held at Geneva on February 4th. I am informed further that a draft convention has already been prepared for the consideration of the Commission to replace the Convention of Saint Germain [19] and has been drawn to overcome the objection previously raised by the United States.

GREW

---

[16] For previous correspondence, see *Foreign Relations*, 1923, vol. I, pp. 34 ff.
[17] *Ibid.*, p. 45.
[18] *Ibid.*, p. 43.
[19] *Ibid.*, 1920, vol. I, p. 180.

511.3 B 1/138 : Telegram

The Secretary of State to the Minister in Switzerland (Grew)

WASHINGTON, *February 1, 1924—6 p. m.*

8. Your No. 7, January 22, 3 P. M.

You may inform Secretariat in reply that you will attend the meeting of the Temporary Mixed Commission on February 4th for the purpose of being fully advised as to proposals and particularly to receive information respecting the draft convention which it is understood will be considered by the Commission. While you will have no authority to bind this Government, you will be in a position to explain its attitude as disclosed in correspondence relating to Convention of Saint Germain, and you will make immediate and full report. You may add that you will be glad to transmit any recommendations that may be formulated by the Commission, and that in case any appropriate plan is devised the question of securing necessary legislation will have proper consideration.

Further telegraphic instructions will follow.

HUGHES

511.3 B 1/138 : Telegram

The Secretary of State to the Minister in Switzerland (Grew)

WASHINGTON, *February 2, 1924—6 p. m.*

9. Reference Department's 8, February 1, 6 p. m.

In the event that you should be requested to express your views respecting the regulation of the traffic in arms you should refer to the Department's note to the British Embassy of August 5, 1922,[20] and the communication to the League of Nations dated September 12, 1923,[21] copies of both of which are in the files of the Legation. You may also in your discretion explain the scope of the joint resolutions mentioned in Department's telegram No. 53 of September 12. 1923,[22] as well as the policy of this Government not to encourage the sale of military supplies or the shipment of war material to the troubled areas of the world. (See Department's telegram No. 61 of September 27th last.[23]) You may point out that the Saint Germain Convention was not drawn on the theory of limitation of armament and that it imposed on the signatories no restriction on production or on the supply of arms *inter se*. You may also say that you understand that your Government would not be willing to restrict its

---

[20] *Foreign Relations*, 1922, vol. I, p. 554.
[21] See telegram no. 53, Sept. 12, 1923, to the Minister in Switzerland, *ibid.*, 1923, vol. I, p. 38.
[22] *Ibid.*
[23] *Ibid.*, p. 42.

entire freedom of action respecting the shipment of military supplies to countries of Latin America. In connection with matters of administration, the fact that the United States is not a member of the League of Nations should not be overlooked.

[Paraphrase.] It is the view of this Government that the Convention of Saint Germain is a political arrangement for the protection of existing governments, leaving them free to make and supply all the arms they wish as between themselves, and that it does not represent a bona fide effort to restrict the arms traffic. This Government has not been led to any different conclusion by the endeavor to arouse favor for such a convention by representing it as a genuine attempt to fulfill the wishes of those who are anxious to have the arms traffic restricted. Congress cannot be expected to pass legislation limiting the manufacture of arms in this country in the interest of any arrangement like that of Saint Germain. It should be observed in the meantime that the Government of the United States is doing very little in furnishing other countries with arms. Power vested in the President gives him strict control over such traffic with other countries in this hemisphere.

With the exception of one or two instances there is but a very small exportation of arms to countries in Europe. In 1922 the number of machine guns exported was 1,309, of which Sweden bought 749. With that exception, Great Britain and France have been the markets for the largest sales to Europe. The following statistics give the value of American sales of arms and ammunition to the territories which are indicated in the sixth article of the Convention of Saint Germain: Turkey, $1,334 in 1920, $260 in 1921, $32 in 1922; Hedjaz, $473 in 1922; Syria and Palestine, $1,917 in 1922; Persia, no sales during time under consideration; Belgian Congo, $64 in 1921, $187 in 1922; Egypt, $19,956 in 1920, $6,428 in 1921, $221 in 1922; British Africa, including British East and British West Africa, $15,547 in 1920, $7,629 in 1921, $17,692 in 1922; French Africa, $2,255 in 1920, $259 in 1921, $821 in 1922; Portuguese Africa, $10,136 in 1920, $2,441 in 1921, $2,506 in 1922; Abyssinia, $10,437 in 1921, the only sale apparently recorded for a number of years; Liberia, $896 in 1920, $1,705 in 1921, $846 in 1922. Statistics available for 9 months of 1923 do not give the country of destination. Statistics for the years mentioned do not indicate any exportation of machine guns or heavier armament to any of these territories. Items sold to the territories include pistols, rifles, shotguns, and cartridges.

Should it be the real intention of the Governments represented in the Temporary Mixed Commission to place a substantial restriction upon the production of and traffic in arms with the purpose of bringing about a reduction in the weapons of war, this Government will take any arrangement with that objective under most careful consideration and will find out as soon as possible whether Congress would pass such legislation as would be necessary to make it effective.

The above is for you to use discreetly in your discussions on this subject. [End paraphrase.]

HUGHES

511.3 B 1/140 : Telegram

The Minister in Switzerland (Grew) to the Secretary of State

GENEVA, *February 4, 1924—10 p. m.*
[Received February 5—6:34 a. m.]

1. Opening plenary session of Temporary Mixed Commission for the reduction of armaments took place this afternoon with Schanzer of Italy presiding. After initial business and announcement that the United States had sent representative, the chairman, followed by several of the delegates, made speeches eulogistical of the late President Wilson. It, therefore, became essential that I should respond. I said that as an American citizen I could not fail to acknowledge the tribute that had been paid to the memory of the late President and after speaking briefly of Mr. Wilson's personal qualities, I expressed my appreciation of the action of the Commission in thus participating in our national sorrow. At the desire of the chairman, I then defined my status precisely as outlined in the Department's number 8 to Berne, after which the meeting adjourned for 15 minutes in deference to the memory of Mr. Wilson.

The meeting then continued for 3 hours in a futile discussion of the mutual relation of functions as between Temporary Mixed Commission and the Permanent Advisory Commission. The next items on the agenda are the control of the traffic in arms and the private manufacture of arms and munitions. Although these items were originally listed separately, it is now proposed, on the motion of the French member, Colonel Fabri, to consider them simultaneously. If tomorrow it appears to be the intention of the Commission to combine these two subjects in a single convention, I shall make it clear that my instructions do not authorize me to entertain any subject other than that of the traffic in arms and munitions.

The texts of two draft conventions for the control of the traffic in arms have been circulated to the members of the Commission. One of them has clearly been drawn with a view to meeting our objections, although certain alterations would still have to be made. However, I consider it useless to telegraph it to the Department until the general attitude of the meeting towards its provisions is revealed.

[Paraphrase.] The indications are that the French members privately are opposed to any solution in which the questions of private manufacture of arms and the traffic in arms are not combined. Private information indicates the difficulty, and probably the impossibility, of obtaining consideration of any convention which will completely separate from the League of Nations the supervision of the control over the traffic in arms. [End paraphrase.]

GREW

511.3 B 1/141 : Telegram

The Minister in Switzerland (Grew) to the Secretary of State

GENEVA, *February 5, 1924—midnight.*
[Received February 6—2 : 14 a. m.]

2. At the opening of today's meeting it was tacitly agreed on the proposal of Lord Cecil that discussion on the traffic in arms and on the private manufacture of arms should be conducted simultaneously but that separate conventions should be drawn to cover the two subjects. Later developments indicated, however, that French members still hoped to conclude one convention combining the two subjects.

In a later address Cecil stated that "The League has the greatest amount of authority in the world," and that for this reason the machinery of the League should be used for the supervision of the control of the traffic in arms. This was obviously an attempt to dissuade the United States from insisting on the supervision of this control by any other body. With this object in view he quoted Congressman Porter as having said that for this same reason the control of the traffic in opium should be supervised by the League. These two subjects will be referred to a subcommittee tomorrow presided over by Lebrun, one of the French members.

Cecil then proposed the following draft resolution intended to cover the nonconflicting general principles in the Convention of Saint Germain and in addition two drafts already prepared in order to guide the subcommittee in its labors:

"1. It is desirable that the international traffic in arms should be controlled and for that purpose a distinction should be established between weapons and munitions of war and other weapons.

2. Weapons and munitions of war should only be sold to governments or bodies recognized as belligerents.

3. Whatever other steps may be taken for the control of the traffic in arms, full publicity should be secured for all international dealings.

4. Special regulations should apply to certain territory restricting or prohibiting altogether all traffic in arms."

This resolution evoked the opposition of the French members, the Italian member and the chairman and a serious effort was made by them to prevent a vote from taking place on the resolution. The vote was postponed.

The afternoon meeting was chiefly devoted to an inconclusive discussion of the duties which should devolve upon the subcommittee upon which I have been requested to sit. It will probably consider in detail the various drafts already laid before the commission after they have been [apparent omission] and freely discussed by the plenary commission tomorrow morning.

[Paraphrase.] I have received private information that the lengthy parliamentary discussion of today and yesterday has taken place because of the fact that members of the Permanent Advisory Commission are attempting to bring about the dissolution of the Temporary Mixed Commission, not wishing to cede to it any privilege.

Despite Cecil's emphatic statement that the League of Nations should have the supervision of the traffic in arms, apparently his resolution is an effort to meet our views. The reason for the French opposition to this proposal appears to be that France either does not wish any convention at all for the traffic in arms to be adopted or else wants to have one convention cover both the traffic in arms and the private manufacture of arms. [End paraphrase.]

GREW

511.3 B 1/143 : Telegram

The Minister in Switzerland (Grew) to the Secretary of State

GENEVA, February 6, 1924—3 p.m.
[Received 10: 17 p.m.]

3. The following draft convention for the international control of the traffic in arms and munitions has been submitted to the Temporary Mixed Commission by Admiral the Marquis Magaz, a Spaniard, in his personal capacity. This draft is now under general discussion in the Commission, after which it is proposed to refer it to the subcommittee for more detailed discussion. The comments of the Commission upon its provisions will be reported to the Department in separate telegrams. If the Department desires to express any opinions for my guidance in the subcommittee, it would be helpful to receive them immediately. This is the only draft submitted which would appear to tend to meet our views.

The explanatory preamble begins as follows:

"The Council, acting in pursuance of a recommendation of the Assembly, has invited our Commission to prepare draft conventions in such a form that they might be accepted by the governments of all countries which produce arms and munitions of war. We have also been asked to make alternative proposals for a convention or conventions which might be adopted by some of the producing powers, even if the others refused their cooperation.

In preparing the following draft, account has been taken of both the above recommendations. Care has been taken to avoid the insertion of any clause which might render it difficult for the Government of the United States to ratify the convention, while at the same time the draft has been conceived in such a way that it could if necessary be ratified by all the producing countries, even if the United States should refuse to adhere to it."

The text of the draft convention is as follows:

"The high contracting parties being desirous of establishing an international regime to control the traffic in arms, have agreed on the following provisions:

Article 1. The present convention shall apply to three categories of material, arms and munitions, namely,

Category 1. To war material, which term shall be understood for the purpose of this convention to include all arms, munitions, chemical products and other objects appearing in the list annexed to the present treaty. Modifications, in the form of a list, omissions from or interpretations of this list, may be made at any time at the request of a high contracting party and shall become binding on all the high contracting parties as soon as they have been ratified by two-thirds of them.

Category 2. To sporting weapons and ammunition, which expression shall be understood, for the purposes of this convention, to mean all arms, ammunition and similar materials which do not appear in the annex referred to in the last paragraph, and which are recognized as such by the national sporting associations recommended for this purpose by at least half the governments of the high contracting parties.

Category 3. To other arms, including, in particular, pocket firearms employed for personal defense, et cetera.

Article 2. A central international office shall be established for the purpose of collecting and preserving documents of all sorts exchanged by the high contracting parties with regard to the trade in and distribution of the arms and ammunition specified in the present convention.

Each of the high contracting parties shall publish an annual report showing the imports and exports of arms of all kinds which have taken place through its customs offices, specifying the place of departure and destination and the quantities and natures of the material thus imported or exported. Each of the high contracting parties shall send this report in triplicate to central international office.

FIRST CATEGORY, *Article 3.* The high contracting parties undertake not to permit the sale or export of material of the first category except to governments recognized by at least half of the high contracting parties.

Article 4. Material of the first category shall be exported by virtue of a license issued to the exporter by the exporting high contracting party. If the exporting high contracting party is not the state in whose territory the material has been manufactured, the export license must contain all the data necessary in order to trace, for the purposes of this convention, the movements of the material in question from the time of its leaving the factory until it was acquired by the exporter.

The export license must contain a certificate from the diplomatic or consular representatives of the purchasing government, granting the exporter official authorization to proceed with the export on behalf of the said government.

Article 5. With a view to rendering more effective the supervision of the limitations placed on export and sale by article 3, the high contracting parties undertake to prohibit the import of material of the first category, with the exception of material acquired for the government of the high contracting party concerned.

SECOND CATEGORY, *Article 6.* The high contracting parties undertake to prohibit the sale of material of the second category by any person not furnished with a license issued by the proper authorities. The latter shall only issue such licenses to persons who can show that they belong to sporting associations recognized by the competent authorities of the high contracting parties concerned.

Article 7. The high contracting parties undertake not to allow material of the second category to be exported except by persons holding a license issued by the competent authorities of the exporting high contracting parties. This license must include an authorization to import issued by the government which exercises sovereignty over the territory of destination.

Article 8. Each high contracting party shall draw up authentic copies of the export licenses referred to in the two preceding articles with a view to the transmission of copies to the high contracting party which exercises sovereignty over the territory of destination and to all the governments, whether of high contracting parties or not, through whose territory the material would have to pass in transit. These copies must be despatched in sufficient time to enable the governments to supervise the transport of the material.

THIRD CATEGORY, *Article 9.* The high contracting parties undertake to exercise supervision over the national and international traffic in arms of the third category and to take all necessary measures to prevent illicit stocks and traffic.

Article 10. With the above object in view, the high contracting parties undertake:

To provide for close cooperation among the respective national administrations and between these administrations and the international office referred to in article 2;

To institute a system of registration and licenses which shall make it possible at any time to trace arms which are in the possession of individuals;

To communicate to each other and to the international office referred to in article 2 any information calculated to facilitate this control.

Article 11. The high contracting parties undertake to apply to arms in the third category the regime laid down in articles 7 and 8 of the present convention in regard to arms of the second category.

GENERAL PROVISIONS, *Article 12.* The high contracting parties undertake to assist each other mutually in bringing to light any infractions of the rules of this convention. They recognize in advance the jurisdiction of the Permanent Court of International Justice for all international investigation concerning negligence or connivance on the part of a government administration concerned with these matters. They further undertake to impose penalties of a uniform character on their nationals (individuals, associations or firms) who may be found guilty of [violating] the national laws passed in execution of the provisions of the present convention. These penalties shall be codified by common agreement between the national administrations, and the code shall appear as an annex to the present convention.

Article 13. The present convention shall come into force when it has been ratified by 4 of the states mentioned in the Covenant of the League of Nations as permanent members of the Council and by 16 other states. The international office referred to in article [2] shall be organized by the Belgian Government as soon as the convention has been thus ratified.

Article 14. The duration of the present convention shall be for 15 years. It shall remain in force for all states which have not notified the international office of their intention to denounce it 2 years before the expiration of the above period, unless, as a result of successive denunciations, the number of high contracting parties shall have been reduced to 10, including 2 of the nations entitled, under the Covenant, to be permanently represented on the Council."

GREW

511.3 B 1/144 : Telegram

The Minister in Switzerland (Grew) to the Secretary of State

GENEVA, *February 6, 1924—7 p. m.*
[Received February 7—7 : 18 a. m.]

5. [Paraphrase.] I reminded the Commission today that I was not authorized to state views on any subject but the traffic in arms. I did this because of Department's 53 of September 12, 5 p. m., [24] which stated that the American Government was not in a position to secure the passage of legislation establishing effective control of the traffic in arms by imposing penalties applicable to private companies engaged in arms production. The occasion for my statement was the proposal that the subcommittee should discuss the private manufacture of arms with the idea of including both production of and traffic in arms in one convention. It seems to me difficult to reconcile the instruction referred to above with the reference in your telegram 9, February 2, 6 p. m., to "restriction on production." With this in

[24] *Foreign Relations,* 1923, vol. I, p. 38.

mind, and because the trend of discussion today indicates that it is possible that no distinction may be made between state and private manufacture of arms, I have left myself in a position to give a more detailed explanation of our views should I receive further instructions. It would be helpful to me to be informed whether any distinction is made by the Department between state and private production of arms. [End paraphrase.] In connection with the discussion of a central international office of control, I furthermore explained fully to the Commission the attitude of our Government towards the intertwining of the Convention of Saint Germain with the League of Nations, at the same time making it clear that other points of objection would be touched upon at the appropriate moment.

At the opening of the meeting this morning the Commission began the reading and discussion of the draft convention proposed by Magaz.[25] During my absence discussion of the first article Lebrun supported [26] Cecil expressed the view that he saw no reason why the objections raised by me should not be given satisfaction. Cecil added that I had explained the great objections of the United States to the ratification of the Convention of Saint Germain, whereupon I remarked that I did not wish to leave the impression that these were the only objections of the United States.

In the discussion on article 2 Cecil stated that to adopt an international bureau of control would be very difficult and unwise, particularly in that it would constitute a retrograde step in the principles of the League. In order to meet the views of the United States, however, he suggested the compromise that article 5 of the Convention of Saint Germain, omitting paragraph 1 thereof, should be used in lieu of article 2 of the draft convention under discussion and that the article should be complemented by the statement that a copy of this report should be sent to the League of Nations only by states members of the League, and that states not members should merely publish such reports. The Italian member, Lebrun, and Branting indicated support of this suggestion. The French labor member, Jouhaux, implied opposition, however. In explanation Cecil stated that the germ of his proposal was that it should be obligatory for all states signifying [sic] the convention to make public statistics regarding the traffic in arms, and added that "the final control of the traffic in arms is not the League of Nations but public opinion." The chairman stated that he believed the proposal of Cecil would satisfy the League as well as states not members of the League,

---

[25] Quoted in telegram no. 3, Feb. 6, from the Minister in Switzerland, *supra*.
[26] Opening phrases apparently garbled.

and expressed the hope that the suggestion would be adopted. Jouhaux then stated that he regretted to see the apparent tendency of certain opportunist elements of opinion in the League which are willing to make any sacrifice of the prestige of the League to secure the cooperation of the United States.

During the discussion of article 12 of the Magaz draft I furthermore took occasion to call the attention of the Commission to the fact that certain states were not members of the Permanent Court of International Justice.

GREW

511.3 B 1/145 : Telegram

The Minister in Switzerland (Grew) to the Secretary of State

GENEVA, *February 7, 1924—7 p. m.*
[Received February 7—6 p. m.]

6. Commission adjourned this evening. Subcommittee meets Paris, March 24. I return to Berne tomorrow and shall forward full written report with documents as soon as possible. In my final remarks today I reserved the decision of our Government regarding American participation in the subcommittee and in reply to a specific request for the objections of states which failed to ratify the Convention of Saint Germain I made a statement based on the Department's number 53, September 12, 5 p. m.,[27] and number 9, February 2, 6 p. m.

GREW

511.3 B 1/144 : Telegram

The Secretary of State to the Consul at Geneva (Haskell)

[Paraphrase]

WASHINGTON, *February 7, 1924—7 p.m.*

1. Please deliver the following immediately to Mr. Grew:

Your telegram no. 5 of February 6, 7 p.m. Reference in our 9, February 2, 6 p.m., does not conflict with our instruction no. 53, September 12, 1923.[27] It has not been my intention to suggest that only control of traffic in arms should be covered by the convention. Supposedly the control of manufacture would be in order to facilitate the control of traffic. The point I wish to make is that the American Government would not feel free to enter into any convention for the control of either the manufacture of or traffic in arms, or both, without being reasonably sure that Congress would pass the

---

[27] *Foreign Relations*, 1923, vol. I, p. 38.

necessary legislation. It was quite evident that Congress would not do so in the interest of a convention like that of Saint Germain. Whether it would do so in the interest of a new convention will depend upon the character of the convention, and this Government must reserve decision on this until it understands the full scope of the proposals and has an opportunity to consult leaders in Congress. The basic objections to the Saint Germain Convention would have been equally strong whether the control of traffic or of manufacture was intended. The wish of this Government was to have you in a position to learn the nature of the proposals, to explain the position of the American Government as previously expressed regarding the Saint Germain Convention, and to refer proposals to the Department with complete information for consideration. In this respect it was not intended to make a distinction between manufacture and traffic. Regarding the former a separate question might arise, of course, regarding the extent of control.

It has been stated in press reports that you have indicated that this Government's basic objection was to the proposal to vest administrative control in the League of Nations. This is incorrect. Although difficulties for this Government would arise through administration by the League of Nations, as the United States is not a member, the basic difficulties to which we called attention in our note regarding the Convention of Saint Germain would have existed had the League not been charged with its administration. Our basic objections were with respect to the freedom of parties to the convention to sell to each other and the prohibition against selling to others. After the extent and nature of control are decided upon, the question of administration is a subordinate one. We must reserve opinion as to whether any supervision satisfactory to the League authorities would be satisfactory to our Government until we see the actual plan. In the meantime, however, we do not want a mere question of administration given chief attention as if that were the difficulty in the way. It may well be that some form of administration acceptable to all could be found should the fundamental difficulties be removed.

As the Commission is probably about to adjourn, I shall not try to discuss the plan described in your telegram 3 of February 6, 3 p.m., except to say that it would be difficult, if not impossible, aside from other objections, for the United States to agree to refrain from selling arms to a government in this hemisphere not recognized by European powers but recognized by our Government.

Before giving further instructions as to attending meeting of the proposed subcommittee we will await your complete report and the text of the proposed convention or conventions.

HUGHES

511.3 B 1/146 : Telegram

The Minister in Switzerland (Grew) to the Secretary of State

BERNE, *February 8, 1924—8 p.m.*
[Received 11:10 p. m.]

11. I regret that the Temporary Mixed Commission had adjourned before your number 1, February 7, 7 p. m., was received.

With regard to the question of the private manufacture of arms, my statement to the Commission on February 6th was as follows:

"The second point that I have in mind was a reference in this Commission to the possible desirability of combining in one draft convention the two questions of the control of the traffic in arms and the control of the private manufacture of arms and of munitions of war. So far as my own position on this subject is concerned, I believe I should remind the members of this Commission that my instructions do not authorize me to entertain any subject other than the traffic in arms. It will be recalled that the invitation addressed to the Government of the United States on December 14th last [28] mentioned this subject only and that it was on this understanding that the Government accepted the invitation in question."

[Paraphrase.] I can inform the Commission that in view of the discussions on February 6 I asked for further instructions from my Government concerning its position with respect to the question of private production and as far as seems desirable I can set forth the views of the Department. There are two ways by which I suggest that this might be done: (1) I can write to the Secretary General of the League of Nations that my Government declines to participate in the meeting of the subcommittee on March 24 in Paris and in the same letter I can ask him to convey these further views of my Government; (2) we can be represented in the meeting of the subcommittee. When forwarding my complete written report I shall venture to include my recommendations on this point.

Second paragraph your 1, February 7, 7 p. m. I took care to explain to the Commission that administration of the control of the traffic in arms was but one of several objections of my Government. I clearly set forth the other objections at the final session. The question of administration came up at the start, which was the reason I raised objection on that point first. Lord Cecil remarked that I had presented the chief American objection to the Saint Germain Convention. Cecil added that this objection was entirely legitimate and that in his opinion it could be met. I arose at once and stated that I did not want to have an incorrect impression left and that I wished to have it clearly understood this was only one of the objections which had kept us from ratifying. I do not believe that the

---

[28] *Foreign Relations*, 1923, vol. I, p. 43.

members of the Commission retained the impression that this was
the all important objection.

I greatly regret that I misunderstood your no. 53, September 12,
1923,[29] and especially hope that the publicity given has not embarrassed you. The matter can be satisfactorily straightened out as far
as the Commission is concerned. [End paraphrase.]

GREW

511.3 B 1/149 : Telegram

The Secretary of State to the Minister in Switzerland (Grew)

[Paraphrase]

WASHINGTON, *March 7, 1924—5 p. m.*

22. Invitation extended to you to participate in the coming meeting of the Temporary Mixed Commission's first subcommittee has
been given careful consideration by the Department. You should
attend meeting of the subcommittee for the same purposes for which
you attended the meeting of the Commission, thus making it possible for our Government to be kept fully informed regarding proceedings in the subcommittee. You will not, of course, take part in
the actual drafting of the convention which is proposed. You should
inform M. Lebrun, therefore, that you will gladly attend the Paris
meeting to give information and appropriate explanations respecting the attitude of the United States as occasion may require.

With the above and previous instructions in mind you may use
the following as occasion arises:

1. Regarding the manufacture of arms. Production or manufacture in itself is not commerce and the interstate commerce power
does not give Congress the power to control mere production or
manufacture within a State. Congress, however, has power:

(*a*) To control the manufacture of arms in the Territories and
possessions of the United States and within the District of Columbia;

(*b*) To prohibit except under Federal license the shipment of arms
in foreign or interstate commerce.

2. Regarding the traffic in arms. Foreign or interstate commerce
is subject to the control of Congress. As a possible basis for cooperation with other powers the following points are suggested:

(*a*) Through a license system the Federal Government could control arms traffic in foreign commerce.

(*b*) Adequate publicity could be given.

---

[29] *Foreign Relations*, 1923, vol. I, p. 38.

(*c*) This Government could make or allow sales only to govern-ments or belligerents recognized by it.

3. The following are matters to be reserved:

(*a*) There must be no restriction upon this Government in sup-plying its own wants.

(*b*) The right of the United States Government in its discretion to sell or allow sales to other American governments whether such governments are parties to the convention or not must not be re-stricted.

(*c*) The American Government cannot place itself under the supervision or direction of the League of Nations, of which it is not a member, in any manner. It should also be noted that this country has not given its adherence to the protocol of the Permanent Court of International Justice.

(*d*) If the United States signed or adhered to a convention, legis-lation by Congress would be necessary to make it effective. For this reason this Government cannot finally commit itself without some reservation as to action by Congress or some assurance which will satisfy the President that Congress will pass the necessary legislation.

4. It is understood that in the above the word "arms" means arms and munitions of war, mere sporting or commercial munitions not being included.

Make a full report on proceedings of the subcommittee. Telegraph at your discretion.

HUGHES

511.3 B 1/155 : Telegram

The Ambassador in France (Herrick) to the Secretary of State

PARIS, *March 25, 1924—11 a. m.*
[Received March 25—8:35 a. m.]

143. From Grew. First day of subcommittee on traffic in arms was devoted to a general discussion of a new draft convention drawn up with the expressed view of amending and amplifying the con-vention of Saint Germain in order to secure the adhesion of the United States. Control of production or manufacture not included. In reply to a specific request for a statement I indicated our position on the basis of the Department's 22, March 7, 5 p. m., to Berne. The desire to meet our views appears to be almost unanimous.

HERRICK

511.3 B 1/156 : Telegram

The Ambassador in France (Herrick) to the Secretary of State

PARIS, *March 28, 1924—5 p. m.*
[Received March 28—3 : 49 p. m.]

158. From Grew. My 143, March 25, 11 a. m.

1. Subcommission adjourned today after eight meetings. Draft convention for the control of the traffic in arms and munitions has been revised substantially to meet the views expressed in the Department's several instructions. This effort culminated in the unanimous adoption of an amendment proposed by Cecil providing that,

"Any state may with the consent of the other High Contracting Parties notify its partial or conditional adherence to the provisions of the treaty provided that such conditions or partial adherences do not affect the effectiveness of the supervision of the traffic in arms."

This draft convention will be further considered and if necessary revised by the plenary session of the Temporary Mixed Commission which meets at Geneva on June [12?] before being submitted to the Council of the League and eventually to an international conference for the purpose of negotiating a final convention.

2. Separate draft convention for the control of private manufacture of arms and munitions was only briefly discussed. It was referred for further revision to a small drafting committee which will report to the Temporary Mixed Commission on June 30. During this brief discussion I explained our constitutional limitations as indicated in point 1 of the Department's 22 to Berne. Cecil asked if there were any constitutional difficulties which would prevent Federal legislation in the United States with a view to obtaining for publication statistical information respecting production by private manufacture in the various States of the Union. I replied that I should be glad to refer this question to my Government. If the Department considers it desirable to convey the requested information to the drafting committee through the legation at Berne it will be appreciated by the committee.

Full written report with documents follows.[30]

HERRICK

---

[30] Not printed.

511.3 B 1/170

The Chargé in Switzerland (Magruder) to the Secretary of State

No. 1504   BERNE, *May 12, 1924.*
L. N. No. 509   [Received May 26.]

SIR: With reference to Mr. Grew's despatch dated Paris, March 29, 1924,[31] reporting his attendance at the meetings of the first subcommittee of the Temporary Mixed Commission for the Reduction of Armaments of the League of Nations which met at Paris on March 24, 1924, to consider the control of the traffic in arms and ammunition, I have the honor to enclose herewith . . . the "Draft Convention amending the Convention signed at St. Germain-en-Laye September 10, 1919, for the Control of the trade in Arms and Ammunition" . . .

I have [etc.]   ALEXANDER R. MAGRUDER

[Enclosure]

Draft Convention Amending the Convention Signed at St. Germain-en-Laye September 10, 1919, for the Control of the Trade in Arms and Ammunition

PARIS, *March 27, 1924.*

(Here will follow the names of the H. C. P. signing the new Convention).

Whereas the Convention of St. Germain was signed by the H. C. P. therein mentioned

Whereas certain of them were not able to ratify such Convention.

Whereas for this and for other reasons it is desirable to amend such Convention;

Whereas it is necessary to exercise a general supervision over the trade in arms and ammunition, with the object of securing the fullest possible publicity in regard to such trade, thereby drawing attention to the danger of the accumulation, in peace time, of stocks of munitions;

Whereas it is necessary to institute a uniform procedure for the supervision over the trade in firearms and ammunition which are capable of both warlike and other uses;

Whereas the existing treaties and conventions, and particularly the Brussels Act of July 2, 1890, regulating the traffic in arms and ammunition in certain regions, no longer meet present conditions, which require more elaborate provisions applicable to a wider area in Africa

---

[31] Not printed.

and the establishment of a corresponding regime in certain territories in Asia;

Whereas a special supervision of the maritime zone adjacent to certain countries is necessary to ensure the efficacy of the measures adopted by the various Governments both as regards the importation of arms and ammunition into these countries and the export of such arms and ammunition from their own territory.

Have appointed as their Plenipotentiaries:

(Here will follow the names of the Plenipotentiaries of the new H. C. P.)

who, having communicated their full powers found in good and due form,

Have agreed as follows:—

ARTICLE 1

This Convention applies to the following arms and munitions:

Category I. Arms and munitions of war, as follows:

a) Ships of war of all kinds, including submarines and submersibles.

b) Airships, aeroplanes and seaplanes for use in war.

c) Tanks and armoured cars.

d) Artillery of all kinds.

e) Apparatus for the discharge of all kinds of projectiles, and for the discharge of all kinds of bombs, torpedoes and depth charges.

f) Flame throwers.

g) Mines whether for land or water.

h) Torpedoes and depth charges of all kinds.

i) Bombs and grenades of all kinds.

j) Machine guns and rifled smallbore breech-loading weapons of all kinds.

k) Pistols and revolvers of all kinds.

l) Ammunition of all kinds for use with any of the above.

m) Explosives and propellants of all kinds for use in war.

n) Component parts of any of the above including mountings.

Category II. Fire arms and ammunition for purposes of sport or personal defence.

In order to prevent the export and import of firearms and ammunition intended for warlike purposes though described and sold as articles of sport or personal defence and in order at the same time not to hamper unduly the legitimate trade in firearms and ammunition intended to be used only for sport and personal defence the H. C. P. hereby undertake that they will use their best endeavours to agree upon a uniform definition of

1) Military rifles, revolvers and pistols and the ammunition thereof.

2) Rifles, revolvers and pistols capable of use for both military and other purposes and the ammunition thereof.

3) Rifles, revolvers and pistols regarded as of no military value and the ammunition thereof.

ARTICLE 2

The H. C. P. undertake not to export themselves and to prohibit the export of arms and munitions of war in Category 1 except on the conditions mentioned in Article 3. This prohibition of exportation shall apply to all such arms and ammunition whether complete or in parts.

ARTICLE 3

Nevertheless, notwithstanding this prohibition, the H. C. P. reserve the right to grant in respect of arms and munitions of war whose use is not prohibited by international law licences for the export of arms and munitions of war in Category I, but such licences are only to be granted on the following conditions:

1. No licence is to be granted except for a direct supply to a Government recognised as such by the Government of the exporting territory.

The Form in which this licence shall be given shall, so far as practicable, resemble that given as an annex to the present Convention.

2. The Government acquiring the consignments must act through a duly accredited representative, who shall produce his credentials.

3. Such representative must produce a written authority from his Government for the acquisition of each consignment, which authority must state that the consignment is acquired for the use of that Government and not for transfer and will be delivered to them and to no one else.

4. Each licence must contain a full description of the arms and munitions of war to which it relates, and the names of the exporting and acquiring Governments, ports of embarkation and disembarkation, means of transport, route and destination.

5. A separate licence shall be required for each separate shipment which crosses the frontier of the exporting country whether by land, water or air.

ARTICLE 4

Without prejudice to any obligations to which they may have subscribed under international conventions dealing with transit, the H. C. P. undertake to take such steps as they reasonably can to supervise and prohibit the transit of the arms and munitions of war in Category I which are not accompanied by a licence made out in the proper form, as laid down in Article 3.

A copy of the licence shall be sent by the exporting State to the central international body referred to in Article 9 of the present Convention before the goods pass the frontier of the exporting country; a second copy shall be sent to the same international body by the importing country, if one of the H. C. P. within a month of the receipt of the consignment, mention being made of the heading under which the imported goods will appear in its imports statistics.

ARTICLE 5

Firearms and ammunition in Category II may, if the exporting country so desires, be exported without licence except to the prohibited areas and zone mentioned in Article 10. Provided nevertheless that in the case of firearms and ammunition adapted both to warlike and also to other purposes, the H. C. P. hereby undertake to determine from the size, destination and other circumstances of each shipment for what uses it is intended and to decide in each case whether such shipment falls properly under Category II, or whether it ought to be considered to belong to Category I and in the latter case they undertake that it shall become subject to Articles 2 and 3 hereof.

ARTICLE 6

The H. C. P. undertake in addition to prohibit the export both of arms and munitions of war in Category I and also of firearms and ammunition in Category II whether complete or in parts, to the areas and zone specified in Article 10. Nevertheless, notwithstanding this prohibition, the High Contracting Parties reserve the right to grant export licences on the understanding that such licences shall be issued only by the authorities of the exporting countries. Such authorities must satisfy themselves in advance that the arms or ammunition for which an export licence is requested are not intended for export to any destination or for disposal in any way contrary to the provisions of this Convention.

ARTICLE 7

Shipments to be effected under contracts entered into before the coming into force of the present Convention shall be governed by its provisions.

ARTICLE 8

The H. C. P. undertake to grant no export licences covering either Category I or Category II for delivery to any country which after having been placed under the tutelage of any Power, may endeavour to obtain from any other Power any of the arms or munitions of war in Category I or of the firearms or ammunition in Category II.

ARTICLE 9

A Central International Body shall be established by the Council of the League of Nations for the purpose of collecting and preserving documents of all kinds exchanged by the H. C. P. with regard to the trade in and distribution of the arms and ammunition in Category I and Category II specified in the present Convention, as well as the texts of all laws orders and regulations made for the carrying out of the present Convention.

Each of the H. C. P. shall publish an annual report showing the export licences which it may have granted in respect of arms and munitions in Category I or Category II together with the quantities and destination of the arms and munitions to which the export licences refer. A copy of this report shall be sent to the Central International Body.

Movements of arms and munitions made by a Power within territories placed under its sovereignty or authority, and for the use of its own military forces, will not be included in this report.

ARTICLE 10

The H. C. P. undertake, each as far as the territory under its jurisdiction is concerned, to prohibit the importation of arms and munitions of war in Category I and of firearms and ammunition in Category II into the following territorial areas, and also to prevent their exportation to, importation and transportation in the maritime zone defined below:

(Note:—The Commission is of opinion, in view of the new circumstances which have arisen since the Convention of St. Germain was drawn up, that the territories to be included in the restricted areas should form the subject of a fresh examination by the Council of the League of Nations).

Special licences for the import of arms and ammunition in Category I or Category II into the areas defined above may be issued. In the African area they shall be subject to the regulations specified in Articles 11 and 12 or to any local regulations of a stricter nature which may be in force.

In the other areas specified in the present Article, these licences shall be subject to similar regulations put into effect by the Governments exercising authority there.

ARTICLE[S] 11–25

Identical with Articles 7–21 of the Convention of St. Germain.
(Note :—These Articles are referred to the P. A. C. for technical
examination.)

ARTICLE 26

The H. C. P. who exercise authority over territories within the
prohibited areas and zone specified in Article 10 agree to take so
far as each may be concerned, the measures required for the enforcement of the present Convention, and in particular for the
prosecution and repression of offences against the provisions contained therein. They shall communicate these measures to the Central International Body and shall inform it of the competent
authorities referred to in the preceding Articles. Such of them as
are members of the League of Nations shall at the same time
transmit this information to the Secretary-General of the League.

ARTICLE 27

The H. C. P. will use their best endeavours to secure the accession
to the present Convention of other States whether members of the
League of Nations or not.

This accession shall be notified through the diplomatic Channel
to the Government of the French Republic, and by it to all the
signatory or adhering States. The accession will come into force
from the date of such notification to the French Government.

Any State may, with the consent of the H. C. P. notify its partial
or conditional adherence to the provisions of the present Convention,
provided that such conditions or partial adherence do not affect the
effectiveness of the supervision of trade in arms and ammunition.

ARTICLE 28

The H. C. P. agree that if any dispute whatever should arise between them relating to the application or interpretation of the present
Convention which cannot be settled by negotiation, this dispute shall
be submitted to the International Court of Justice, or alternatively
to a Court of Arbitration.

ARTICLE 29

All the provisions of former general international Conventions,
relating to the matters dealt with in the present Convention, shall

be considered as abrogated in so far as they are binding between the Powers which are Parties to the present Convention.

The present Convention shall in no way affect the rights and obligations which may arise out of the provisions either of the Covenant of the League of Nations or of the Treaties of Peace signed in 1919 and 1920 at Versailles, Neuilly, St. Germain and Trianon and the provisions of Agreements registered with the League of Nations and published by the League up to the date of the coming into force of the present Convention, so far as the Powers which are signatories of or benefit by the said Treaties or Agreements are concerned.

ARTICLE 30

The Council of the League of Nations shall cause to be published an annual report on the trade in arms and munitions of war, the licences issued by the different Governments and the situation of the trade in arms.

This report shall be submitted to the Assembly of the League of Nations.

ARTICLE 31

The present Convention shall be ratified as soon as possible.

Each Power will address its ratification to the French Government, who will inform all the other signatory Powers.

ARTICLE 32

The present Convention shall come into force when ratified by twelve Powers among whom shall be all of the following:—Belgium, United States of America, France, Great Britain, Italy, Japan and Russia.

ARTICLE 33

The present Convention shall remain in force for ten years. Thereafter it can be denounced by any H. C. P. by giving two years notice to the Government of the French Republic, who will inform all the other signatory Powers.

The H. C. P. agree that, at the conclusion of a period of five years, the present Convention shall, in the light of experience then gained, be subject to revision upon the request of . . . . of the said H. C. P.

511.3 B 1/169

The Acting Secretary of State to the Minister in Switzerland
(Gibson)

No. 16   WASHINGTON, *June 17, 1924.*

SIR: Under date of May 13th the Legation at Berne, in its despatch No. 1507 [32] advised the Department that information had been received from the Secretariat of the League of Nations that the first sub-committee as well as the Temporary Mixed Commission of the League of Nations, which is considering the control of the traffic in arms and ammunition, was to convene at Geneva on July 7th. The Department assumes that the Commission will also take up the question of the control of the private manufacture of munitions and implements of war on the basis of the report submitted with the Legation's despatch No. 1508 of May 13th.[32]

Pursuant to the invitation which was extended by the Acting Secretary General of the League of Nations in December 1923, the Department desires you to attend the meeting of the Commission on July 7th in the same capacity and for the same purpose as earlier meetings of this Commission and its sub-committee were attended by your predecessor.

In previous communications, as listed below, the Department has outlined in some detail its attitude with regard to the various proposals which have been considered by the T. M. C. for the control of traffic in, and the production of, arms and ammunition. It is desired that you should carefully review these instructions . . .

.   .   .   .

It is not the Department's desire that you should take an active part in the discussions of the T. M. C. or that you should directly participate in the framing of the Convention. The reasons for this are obvious. The Department cannot undertake to state at this time whether a Convention along the lines now being considered by the T. M. C. would be likely to receive the requisite approval of the Senate or whether legislation to put such a Convention into effect could be obtained. Such being the case the Department does not desire that the impression should be created as a result of your participation in the discussions at Geneva that a convention of the character proposed would necessarily be presented to the Senate by this Government or legislation to give it effect would be requested. Whether this action will be taken will depend in large measure upon the character which the Convention assumes as finally drafted.

After you have made this position clear to the Commission it is felt that it would be entirely appropriate, if inquiry is made of you

----
[32] Not printed.

as to the attitude of this Government, to point out to the T. M. C. the features of the Convention as indicated which might occasion difficulty in this country and thus render less probable the cooperation of the United States in this matter, a cooperation which this Government would be glad to be in a position to extend for the control of the improper traffic in arms in case a practical basis for such cooperation were presented; such a basis for example as is indicated in sub-headings (*a*), (*b*) and (*c*) under point 2 in the Department's telegram of March 7.

In indicating informally the Department's position with respect to certain points of the Convention which may come under discussion, it is not desired that you should press your views upon the Commission further than to make clear the position of this Government.

It is the Department's understanding that at its July meeting the T. M. C. of the League of Nations will devote its attention to the draft convention which was considered at Paris by the sub-committee and of which the revised text was submitted with the Legation's despatch No. 1504 of May 12, 1924. In the instructions which follow the Department will therefore take this draft as a basis and submit certain comments which may be helpful to you during the discussion of the draft convention.

PREAMBLE

It would appear unnecessary to refer in the Preamble to the Convention of St. Germain and to the fact that certain powers did not ratify this convention. It is the Department's understanding that the convention was not ratified by Great Britain, France, Italy or Japan, in addition to the United States. It seems both unnecessary and ambiguous to state that certain powers were not able "to ratify" this convention.

It is assumed that the sixth paragraph of the Preamble which relates to the barred zone will be subject to any modification necessary to bring it in line with the provisions of Article 10 of the Convention as finally determined, which is to define the zone. This article will be discussed in further detail below.

ARTICLE 1

Category I (*a*) of Article 1, which defines the arms and munitions to which the convention is to be applicable includes vessels of war. This provision taken in conjunction with Article 3 might be interpreted as sanctioning the export under license of naval vessels and as a result a case might be presented where there would be a conflict with the provisions of Article 18 of the Treaty on the

Limitation of Naval Armament, signed at Washington February 6, 1922.[33] This point will be further considered under the discussion of Article 3.

An obvious difficulty arises in connection with the definition of firearms and ammunition for sport or personal defense and the distinguishing of such arms from those essentially for war purposes. From the discussions of the Temporary Mixed Commission it appears that this difficulty has not been overlooked by the Commission and that the effort has been made not to interfere unduly with the legitimate trade in sporting arms.

ARTICLE 2

The Department assumes that the reference in Article 2 to the export of arms and munitions is designed to cover consignments of arms which may be presented by the government of one country as a subsidy or gift as well as the export of arms and munitions through purchase by the acquiring government. The Department would be glad if you could ascertain during the course of the discussions whether such is in fact the understanding of those who have drafted the convention.

ARTICLE 3

In order that the provisions of Article 3 should in no way conflict with the provisions of treaties drawn up at the Washington Conference of 1921–1922 (Treaty on the Limitation of Naval Armament and Treaty Relating to The Use of Submarines and Noxious Gases in Warfare), the Commission might find it desirable to insert after the words "International Law" in the first sentence of paragraph one of Article 3 the following words "or treaties, or of which the disposal by gift, sale or any mode of transfer has not been restricted by treaty, licenses for the export," etc., etc. This paragraph of Article 3 would then read in full as follows:

"Nevertheless, notwithstanding this prohibition, the H. C. P. reserve the right to grant in respect of arms and munitions of war whose use is not prohibited by international law or treaties or of which the disposal by gift, sale or any mode of transfer has not been restricted by treaty, licenses for the export of arms and munitions of war in Category I, but such licenses are only to be granted on the following conditions:"

In the following paragraph of Article 3 the Department considers it would be most desirable to add after "Government" the words "or belligerents" (see Department's telegram of March 7th). It appears from page 8 of your predecessor's report from Paris of

---

[33] *Foreign Relations*, 1922, vol. I, p. 247.

March 29 [34] that the insertion of this word was considered at the Paris meeting but not accepted by the Commission. Mr. Grew indicated, however, that if there had been further opportunity for the consideration of the point the change might have been made. It is therefore possible that this question may again be raised at Geneva and in this case, if an opportunity is presented, you should not fail to indicate this Government's view.

The Department has noted in the minutes of the discussion of the T. M. C. on Article 3 (see despatch No. 1458, April 4, enclosure pages 5 and 6, from the Legation at Berne [34]) that consideration was given to the effect upon neutrality of the issuance by a government of licenses for the export of arms to belligerents. This question would arise in a particularly acute form in a situation where, as during the World War, shipments to only one group of belligerents were possible.

The Department has also noted the statement of Lord Cecil "that he desired to allow sale in war time to belligerents without the violation of neutrality by the governments which granted the licenses." To this end Lord Cecil proposed the insertion of the following provision after Article 3:

"It is hereby declared that nothing in this article shall affect the rule of international law permitting the sale of munitions of war by the subject of a non-belligerent state to the Government of a belligerent state without breach of the neutrality of the non-belligerent state and the grant of a license under this article for such a sale shall not be deemed to be a breach of neutrality."

Lord Cecil also proposed the following "Questions for Decision" to the legal section of the Secretariat:

"(1) Would the grant of a license for export of arms to a belligerent be a breach of neutrality by the granting Power?
"(2) If the answer to the first question is in the affirmative, would this result be best prevented:

(i) By a declaration in the convention that such a breach of neutrality was not to occur, or
(ii) By a suspension of the operation of the convention during the war?"

The amendment suggested by Lord Robert Cecil would tend to meet the difficulty in so far as the parties to the Convention are concerned and would therefore be a desirable addition to Article 3.

The Department would be glad to have you report fully any discussion of this point, which it considers of particular importance, and one which should be given most careful consideration before any convention is concluded.

---

[34] Not printed.

ARTICLE 4

The first paragraph of Article 4 refers to the control of the transit of arms and ammunition and contains a reservation with respect to "international conventions" to which the H. C. P.'s may have subscribed. In order that there should be no misunderstanding as to the international conventions to which this Article has reference, it might be desirable that such international treaties and conventions respecting transit should be listed in the annex to the proposed convention. (See Legation's 1458, April 4, 1924, enclosure page 7 [36]).

In this connection the Department is enclosing for your information copies of two conventions to which the British Government is a party, one with Afghanistan [37] and one with Nepal,[38] which relate to the transit in arms and ammunition.

The second paragraph of Article 4 refers to the "exporting state." It would seem preferable that this expression should read "state from which the material originated," as it is understood that the convention contemplates that exports may be made by nationals of the H. C. P. under governmental license to recognized foreign governments (or belligerents) and that it is not intended that the exportation under license should be restricted to the export by governmental agencies or political divisions of the state from which the arms or ammunition are sent.

ARTICLE 5

Article 5 relates to the export without license of firearms and ammunition in Category II (sporting arms, etc.) "except to the prohibited areas and zones mentioned in Article 10." From Article 6, however, it would appear that the export to the prohibited areas of arms in Category II would be permitted under licenses and under the safeguards outlined in that article. Article 10 refers to "special licenses for the import of arms and ammunition in Category I or Category II" into the prohibited areas.

The Department does not find these various references entirely clear and does not fully understand the regime which it is contemplated should be applied to the export and import of sporting arms in the case of the prohibited areas. In reporting on the meeting of the T. M. C. it would be helpful to receive further information on this point.

In the consideration of Articles 1 and 8 the Department briefly referred to this government's view that the legitimate trade in

[36] Not printed.

[37] Great Britain, Cmd. 1786, Treaty Series No. 19 (1922) : *Treaty between the British and Afghan Governments, Signed at Kabul, November 22, 1921.*

[38] Great Britain, Cmd. 2453, Treaty Series No. 31 (1925) : *Treaty between the United Kingdom and Nepal . . . Signed at Katmandu, December 21, 1923.*

sporting arms should not be unduly restricted and that the principle of equality of opportunity should not be impaired in regulating such trade.

ARTICLE 6

The statement in this article that licenses for export to the 'barred' zone "shall be issued only by the authorities of the exporting countries" is not understood as the Department had assumed from earlier provisions of the draft convention that such licenses were in all cases to be issued only by authorities of the exporting state.

ARTICLE 7

This article appears to be retroactive in effect and as such might impair the obligation of contracts entered into in good faith by the nationals of the H. C. P. in the event that agreements for the shipments of arms by private agencies to private agencies abroad had been entered into. In such cases the requirement of export licenses might be considered. As now drawn the provision is too sweeping in character.

ARTICLE 8

In this article.

"The High Contracting Parties undertake to grant no export licenses covering either Category I or Category II for delivery to any country which after having been placed under the tutelage of any Power, may endeavor to obtain from any other Power any of the arms or munitions of war in Category I or of the firearms or ammunition in Category II."

The effect of this article would apparently be to limit the trade in arms and ammunition with states under mandate or "tutelage" to the mandatory power or to the power exercising the so-called "tutelage." The article is very similar to Article 4 of the St. Germain convention. In so far as this provision relates to the control of the export of arms and ammunition under Category II of which the export to private individuals without license, except with respect to certain defined areas, is to be permitted, the provision would appear to impair the freedom of economic opportunity and the equality of treatment as between the mandatory powers and other states. This equality of opportunity is guaranteed under the terms of the several mandates and should not be impaired by collateral agreements.

In so far as the article relates to the export of arms and ammunition in Category I the provision already contemplated under article 3, in limiting the export of arms and ammunition to recognized governments (or belligerents) tends to meet the purpose of the present article (Article 8) while avoiding its objectionable features.

For your personal and confidential guidance it may be added that in the view of this Department the provisions of Article 8 would be the subject of grave objection in this country. The primary purpose of the article appears to be to prevent the introduction of arms into certain areas and zones, including mandate regions, protectorates and territories occupied by backward peoples in which Great Britain, France, Italy and other countries are particularly interested. Such a provision might prevent this government from permitting the shipment of munitions of war to any oppressed peoples who might be endeavoring to free themselves from oppression, however worthy the cause or however desirable it might be that our market should be available to them. However remote the practical exigency may be, being ourselves a nation born of revolution this provision would, I believe, be open to serious objection and might, under given circumstances, prove to be unfortunate.

If such a provision had been in force at the time of the Cuban war of independence against Spain or for that matter at the time of the American Revolution it might have seriously affected the natural and proper development of large bodies of people. While it is recognized that conditions have very fundamentally changed since the events abovementioned, nevertheless the Department could not undertake to state that the present colonial situation is such that it should necessarily be continued indefinitely or that this Government should subscribe to a provision which would make it well nigh impossible for a change in the situation to be brought about should justice require. In this connection your attention is directed to the form of the Senate's approval of the Brussels Convention of 1890 for the repression of the African Slave-trade which contains in articles 8 to 13 certain provisions which were introduced with modifications into the St. Germain Convention and also into the present draft. You will find the Senate Resolution mentioned above on page 1991 of Malloy, Volume 2. Paragraph 3 of the Resolution reads as follows:

Resolved further, as a part of this act of ratification, That the United States of America, having neither possessions nor protectorates in Africa, hereby disclaims any intention, in ratifying this treaty, to indicate any interest whatsoever in the possessions or protectorates established or claimed on that Continent by the other powers, or any approval of the wisdom, expediency or lawfulness thereof, and does not join in any expressions in the said General Act which might be construed as such a declaration or acknowledgment; and, for this reason, that it is desirable that a copy of this resolution be inserted in the protocol to be drawn up at the time of the exchange of the ratifications of this treaty on the part of the United States.

ARTICLE 9

With respect to the provision in article 9 for the establishment of a Central International Body by the Council of the League of Nations, your attention is directed to Mr. Grew's statement on page 10 in his report of March 29 from Paris [39] to the sub-committee of the T. M. C. to the effect that while this government was already voluntarily and in a purely informal way furnishing the League of Nations with information and statistics on a variety of subjects neither he nor his government could undertake to indicate whether or not the Congress would bind itself to a treaty provision of this nature. The Department also desires to call your attention to its instruction to Mr. Grew, through the American Consul at Geneva, under date of February 7 with reference to the supervision of the League of Nations in the matter of arms traffic. Your attention is also directed to the statements in the Department's instruction of March 7 . . . that "this government cannot place itself in any manner under the direction or supervision of the League of Nations, of which it is not a member."

While the Department does not desire that objection in matters of administration should be given undue prominence, the provision in Article 9 that the "Central International Body shall be established by the Council of the League of Nations" would increase the opposition in this country to American adherence to the convention—opposition which might be obviated on this point by providing that the Central International Body in question should be established by agreement among the High Contracting Parties ratifying or adhering to the convention. (In this connection see Legation's 1458, April 4,[39] enclosure page 8).

The Department of course appreciates that if, as suggested, the Central International Body should be selected by the H. C. P. those powers would be free to designate the organization which they might consider best suited to perform the duties prescribed.

ARTICLE 10

In connection with this article, which relates to the prohibition of importation of arms and ammunition in the barred areas, as well as the prevention of such "exportation to, importation and transportation" in a certain maritime zone the Department calls your attention to the provisions of Article 6 under which the H. C. P. reserve the right to grant export licenses for the barred zone. The provisions of these two articles do not appear to be entirely consistent.

[39] Not printed.

It is difficult to submit detailed comments on Article 10, in view of the fact that the extent of the barred area is a matter for further examination. It may be suggested, however, that there are obvious objections to including in this area sovereign states.

Under the licensing system outlined in earlier articles of the Convention it would appear that means had been provided to deal with the situation of sovereign states which it might otherwise be contemplated to place in the barred zone. If conditions requiring more drastic treatment should be presented in a certain area, the powers could agree, if occasion arose, to put a stop to all shipments to such an area by declining to issue licenses for export to this destination.

As was indicated, however, in the Department's instruction of March 7th, this Government will give proper consideration to any proposal as to limitations in the shipment of armament respecting Europe, Asia and Africa to which the other governments declare themselves willing to submit. But this Government would hardly be disposed to undertake to participate in the enforcement of regulations within the barred area or in the waters contiguous thereto. Its action would be limited to the restriction which might be possible under law upon the export of arms and ammunition from this country to such an area.

With reference to the second paragraph of Article 10 it is not entirely clear to the Department in what respect "the special licenses" there mentioned differ, in so far as the exporting country is concerned, from the licenses referred to in Article 3.

ARTICLES 11 TO 26

Articles 11 to 14, deal particularly with supervision on land, articles 15 to 25 with ocean surveillance, within the so-called barred area. These articles particularly concern the powers which have possession either within these areas or immediately contiguous thereto, and relate chiefly to matters for domestic legislation or regulation on the part of the powers which have colonies, dependencies or which exercise mandates or supervision within the area.

Article 26 is of a general character relating to the adoption of the measures for the enforcement of the preceding articles.

Certain of the provisions contained in these articles are based on articles 8 to 13 of the General Act for the repression of the African Slave-trade signed at Brussels July 2, 1890 (see Malloy, Volume 2, pages 1964 ff.) As you will note, the United States was a party to this convention and the form of the Senate's concurrence therein has already been brought to your attention.

In a communication from the Navy Department of April 4, 1922,[41] in reply to an inquiry from this Department for an expression of views with regard to certain features of the convention of St. Germain, the Secretary of the Navy in dealing particularly with the articles of that Convention which have been taken over into the present draft states:

"The convention permits visit to certain classes of vessels in certain waters and provides that, the visit having been made, a definite obligation to bring in the vessel visited may follow. (See article 20). No other duty for vessels of the United States Navy is stated or implied in the convention.

"There is one other naval aspect of the convention. It extends in time of peace and for a new purpose the right of visit to certain classes of vessels on certain parts of the high seas."

In commenting on this extension of the "right of visit" the Secretary of the Navy (writing in April 1922) expressed the view that it was undesirable.

In view, however, of the treaties recently concluded by this Government with certain foreign powers for the prevention of the smuggling of intoxicating liquors, which permit the boarding of private vessels outside the limits of territorial waters for certain defined purposes, the Department does not consider that a provision along similar lines with respect to the prevention of the smuggling of arms and ammunition would be objectionable. In this connection, however, you will note that the limit within which such boarding of private vessels is permitted under the liquor smuggling treaties is defined (i. e. one hour's steaming distance from the shore in the British Treaty).[42] Such a limitation does not appear to be provided with respect to the boarding of private vessels to search for arms and ammunition. It would appear desirable that some limit should be placed upon this privilege which might otherwise lend itself to abuse.

Article 27

The last paragraph of this article, which provides that a state may, with the consent of the H. C. P., notify its partial or conditional adherence to the convention provided such partial adherence does "not affect the effectiveness of the supervision of trade in arms and ammunition," is doubtless intended to be a helpful provision and it may be one which would tend to make it more likely that the convention could be given full consideration by this Government.

---

[41] *Foreign Relations*, 1922, vol. I, p. 548.
[42] *Post*, p. 158.

Article 29

The second paragraph of this article, which relates to the Allied Peace Treaties with the Central Powers, was apparently added to the draft subsequent to the sub-committee meeting at Paris, and the discussions which led up to its adoption have not been found in the Department's files. However, in view of the concluding phrase of the second paragraph it is not considered that this provision affords any ground for objection.

Article 30

With reference to Article 30 your attention is called to the comments given above with respect to Article 9. It is suggested that the International Body which might be set up under Article 9 could publish the annual report which under the present draft is proposed should be published under the direction of the Council of the League of Nations.

Article 32

This article relates to the coming into force of the convention when ratified by certain powers among which figure the United States and, as now drawn, would appear to be inconsistent with Article 27 as now proposed, which provides for adherence as well as ratification.

Control of the Private Manufacture of Munitions and Implements of War

In addition to the draft convention relating to the traffic in arms and ammunition which has been discussed above, the Department has also given its attention to the report of the special committee appointed by the first sub-committee of the T. M. C. which met at Prague in April last. This report was transmitted with the Legation's despatch No. 1508 of May 13, 1924.[43] In connection with this report your attention is called to the Department's instruction of February 7th last to Mr. Grew, through the American Consul at Geneva, and to point one of the Department's instruction of March 7th . . .

The latest figures available to the Department do not indicate that this country is in any sense taking the lead in the production of arms and ammunition. In fact the figures given in the enclosed pamphlets issued by the Census Bureau [44] which contain comparative

[43] Not printed.

[44] *Census of Manufactures, 1921: Ammunition and Firearms* (Washington, Government Printing Office, 1923).

statements respecting the manufacture of arms and munitions in the United States for the period prior and subsequent to 1914, including the year 1921, indicate that in the number of establishments manufacturing arms, the number of persons employed in this trade and the value of the production, the United States in 1921 was substantially on the same basis as in 1909. It would be interesting if comparative figures of this character could also be obtained with respect to the important arms producing countries of Europe.

Further, with respect to the production of arms it should be recalled that the situation of this country differs from that of certain of the powers represented on the T. M. C. in view of the fact that there are in the United States no important government munition factories. The United States is therefore dependent for its needs both in time of peace and in time of war largely upon private manufacturers.

In view of the fact that the recommendations of the Committee which met at Prague, and which it is understood are to be considered by the T. M. C., have not assumed definite form, the Department does not consider that it is feasible to send you further instructions on this phase of the subject at the present time. As has already been pointed out in previous instructions (See telegram of March 7th) manufacture or production is not *per se* commerce and Congress under the power to regulate interstate commerce cannot control mere manufacture or production within the states. The power of Congress could, however, be exerted, if Congress were so disposed, to control production of arms in the District of Columbia and in the territories and possessions of the United States.

In a telegram from Paris of March 28 Mr. Grew reported that Lord Cecil had inquired whether there were any constitutional difficulties which would prevent federal legislation in the United States with a view to obtaining for publication statistical information respecting production by private manufacturers in the various states of the union.

The Department has given careful consideration to this question and while it cannot undertake to speak with finality on the constitutional question involved it is of the opinion that federal legislation to secure such statistics would be constitutional. In fact in paragraph 32 of the Act of the 65th Congress, approved March 3, 1919 to provide for the 14th and subsequent decennial censuses it is provided:

"That the Director of the Census be, and he is hereby, authorized and directed to collect and publish, for the years nineteen hundred and twenty-one, nineteen hundred and twenty-three, nineteen hundred and twenty-five, and nineteen hundred and twenty-seven, and for every tenth year after each of said years, statistics of the products of manufacturing industries; and the director is hereby authorized to prepare such schedules as in his judgment may be necessary."

Acting under the authority of this Act statistics covering the private manufacture of arms and ammunition have been compiled and the pamphlets mentioned above have been issued dealing specifically with such manufacture. Copies in duplicate of the pamphlet giving the figures for the year 1921, as well as a comparison with the figures of certain preceding years, are enclosed herewith in duplicate. You may, if you consider it desirable, file one copy with the T. M. C. The Department understands that the material for the publication of a similar pamphlet covering the year 1923 is now being collected and will be available in a comparatively short time. This information will also be sent you as soon as received by the Department.

From informal inquiry of the Census Bureau, which prepares these reports, the Department understands that the Bureau sends representatives to the various munition plants in this country to collect the information desired. An effort is made to reach every establishment having an annual production value of $5,000 or more and in the opinion of the Census Bureau no establishment of any consequence has been overlooked. As stated in the publication of the Census Bureau it is believed that the inclusion of all establishments having an annual production of less than $5,000 would affect the figures in the enclosed pamphlet to the extent of less than one-tenth of 1 percent.

The report of the Census Bureau does not include government establishments. With respect to such establishments the Department has informally obtained the following information through the courtesy of the War Department.

In 1914 the government owned and operated six plants and it has the same number of plants today. The production of military equipment in government owned and operated establishments is less than half of what it was in 1914. In 1914, for instance, the government employed approximately 7,500 people in its plants and today the Department understands the number employed is less than 4,000. Most of these persons, furthermore, are engaged in storage plants and not in the production of arms and ammunition as the only material manufactured by the Government today is a small quantity of small arms (rifles) and some experimental material for coast defense.

GENERAL CONSIDERATIONS

1. Experience has shown the difficulty of making effective any control of the arms traffic as long as there is over-production. It

does not appear that there is such over-production in the United States.

2. The United States has not contributed to any considerable extent in the traffic in arms with countries in Europe, Asia or Africa. Certain recent figures in this respect were included in Department's telegram No. 9, February 2. Shipments from the United States to countries in this hemisphere and to countries where the United States enjoys extraterritorial rights can, as occasion requires and as has often been done, be placed under strict control at the points of shipment. The shipments which have been made recently to Mexico and Cuba have been in the interest of the maintenance of peace and order and the results amply justified these shipments. (See enclosed statements with respect to the shipment of arms to Mexico [45]).

3. A licensing system and proper publicity are steps with which this Government is in general accord and if a convention giving effect to these principles should be drawn up which did not involve the supervision or control of the League of Nations and if other provisions of an objectionable character should not be included, this Government would give such a convention most careful consideration.

4. As a possible addition to the principles already included in the convention it is suggested that you might be in a position to suggest informally the inclusion of a provision to the effect that the High Contracting Powers agree to withhold diplomatic or other support from their nationals in respect to any claim against a foreign government or national based on an arms shipment which shall not have been made under proper license where such license is required and further that the High Contracting Powers serve notice upon other governments that they will not entertain any claim presented by another government with respect to any arms shipment which likewise shall not have been made under proper license.

There is enclosed, for convenient reference in connection with this instruction, a copy of the draft convention [45a] in the form in which, the Department understands from the reports of the Legation at Berne, mentioned above, it is to be considered by the T. M. C. on July 7th. In case the Department's understanding on this point is incorrect and if the draft which is to be considered by the T. M. C. differs in any material respects from that enclosed herewith the Department desires to be informed by telegraph.

The Department desires you to summarize by telegraph the discussions of the T. M. C. and to submit a full written report with the text of the minutes of the various meetings with your comments thereon.

---

[45] Not printed; see vol. II, pp. 428, ff.
[45a] *Ante,* p. 33.

Subsequent to the preparation of the foregoing instructions the Department has received your despatch No. 20 of May 27 [46] enclosing the minutes of the meeting of the Permanent Advisory Commission for military, naval and air questions of the League of Nations which, together with the Naval Sub-Committee of this Commission, considered certain features of the draft convention for the control of the traffic in arms and ammunition as prepared by the T. M. C. and as enclosed herewith. The Department understands from these minutes that the Permanent Advisory Commission has suggested certain modifications in the draft convention particularly with respect to the categories of arms and ammunition with which the convention is to deal. From the minutes it appears that three categories have been suggested to replace the two categories of the draft of the T. M. C. and in addition the instruments of warfare listed under these categories differ slightly from those listed under the two categories of the earlier draft. The Department has particularly noted that the enumeration under Category I of the list prepared by the P. A. C. does not appear to include naval vessels. If the Department's understanding on this point is correct and if the recommendations of the P. A. C. are adopted it might not be necessary for you to call the attention of the Commission to the possible effect of the convention upon the Treaty for the Limitation of Naval Armament which was discussed above under Article 1.

The Department has further noted recommendations of the P. A. C. with regard to Articles 11 to 26 which are taken from the St. Germain Convention. The proposed modifications in these articles do not appear to call for further comment at this time.

Finally the Department has noted the suggestion of the British delegation on the P. A. C. "that, instead of a single arms traffic convention of a general nature being prepared, two separate conventions should be drawn up: one dealing with the general or world-wide traffic in arms, and the other, of more limited scope, dealing with the supply of arms to certain territories such as are dealt with in Article 6 of the St. Germain Convention." (C. P. C.–47–1924, Annex 4, with the report of the P. A. C. to the Council of the League of Nations, dated Paris, May 20, 1924 [47]).

The Department considers that from the point of view of the United States the suggestion of the British delegation might have certain advantages. As already indicated the proposed regulations

---

[46] Not printed.
[47] League of Nations, *Conference for the Control of the International Trade in Arms, Munitions and Implements of War* (C.758.M.258.1924.ix), document 15, p. 141.

with regard to the "prohibited area" (area defined in Article 6 of the Treaty of St. Germain) particularly concern the countries possessing colonies or exercising authority within that area. It is believed that a convention containing the detailed provisions for supervision which are a part of the present draft convention would be more likely to meet with objection in this country than a convention of a more general and less technical character which would deal with the general question of the traffic in arms, which under the British proposal would be the subject of the first of the two conventions.

If therefore the suggestion of the British delegation is considered by the Temporary Mixed Commission the Department considers that you might appropriately express this view, should occasion arise.

I am [etc.]   JOSEPH C. GREW

511.3 B 1/184 : Telegram

The Minister in Switzerland (Gibson) to the Secretary of State

[Paraphrase]

BERNE, *July 14, 1924—11 a. m.*
[Received 2:55 p. m.]

58. On July 12 the Temporary Mixed Commission adjourned. The draft convention which the Commission drew up will be submitted in September to the Assembly of the League of Nations. The draft convention as approved by the Assembly will be submitted later to an international conference for negotiation. An invitation will be given to the interested governments to attend this conference.

The draft as approved by the Commission seems to be in harmony with the Department's views as indicated by its instructions.

GIBSON

511.3 B 1/189

The Minister in Switzerland (Gibson) to the Secretary of State

No. 79   BERNE, *July 23, 1924.*
L.N. No. 554   [Received August 5.]
SIR:

.   .   .   .

The draft convention as drawn up by the Commission, with textual corrections, has now been printed in final form by the Secretariat of the League as document C. T. A. 433 (1) entitled "The Draft Convention for the Control of the International Trade in Arms,

Munitions and Implements of War." Two copies of this document are transmitted herewith for the Department's information. . . .
I have [etc.]

> For the Minister:
> ALAN F. WINSLOW
> *2nd Secretary of Legation*

[Enclosure]

Draft Convention Adopted by the Temporary Mixed Commission for the Reduction of Armaments, July 12, 1924

PREAMBLE

Whereas the Convention of St. Germain signed by the H. C. P. therein mentioned has not entered into full force and effect,

Whereas it is necessary to exercise a general supervision over the international trade in arms, munitions and implements of war, with the object of securing the fullest possible publicity in regard to such trade,

Whereas the existing treaties and conventions, and particularly the Brussels Act of July 2nd, 1890 regulating the traffic in arms and munitions in certain regions, no longer meet present conditions,

Whereas a special supervision of the maritime zone adjacent to certain countries is necessary to ensure the efficacy of the measures adopted by the various Governments both as regards the import of arms, ammunition and implements of war into those countries and their export from their own territory
Have appointed:

CHAPTER I.—*Definition of the arms, munitions and implements of war the international trade of which is to be controlled*

ARTICLE 1

This Convention applies to the following arms, munitions and implements of war:

Category I.

1. Arms and munitions, assembled or component parts, exclusively designed for land, sea or aerial war, whatever their mode of employment.

(*a*)—All arms and ammunition which are or shall be comprised in the equipment of the armed forces of the different states, including:

—Pistols and revolvers, automatic or self-loading, and developments of the same, designed for single-handed use or fired from the shoulder, of a calibre greater than 6.5 mm. and length of barrel greater than 10 cm.

—rifles, muskets, carbines;

—machine guns, interrupter gears, mountings for machine guns;

—aerial gun sights;

—infantry apparatus for the discharge of projectiles;

—flame throwers;

—cannon, long or short, bomb throwers and mortars of all kinds and their carriages, mountings, recuperators, accessories for mounting and sighting apparatus;

—apparatus for the discharge of all kinds of projectiles, bombs, torpedoes, depth charges, etc;

—grenades, bombs, land mines, submarine mines fixed or floating torpedoes, depth charges;

—projectiles of all kinds;

—ammunition and appliances for the above arms and apparatus.

—bayonets, swords and lances;

—all arms and ammunition which, after having been employed in the service of the different States, are no longer part of their equipment but remain capable of being utilised for military purposes to the exclusion of any other utilisation.

2. Implements of war hereafter enumerated and component parts which are only capable of being utilised in the manufacture of the said material.

Ships of all kinds designed exclusively for war, including submarines and submersibles;

Airships, aeroplanes and seaplanes designed exclusively for war;

Tanks;

Armoured cars.

Category II. Arms and munitions, assembled or component parts, capable of use both for military and other purposes

(1) Firearms, designed or adapted for non-military purposes, that will fire cartridges that can be fired from firearms in Category I.

(2) All other rifles, or firearms, firing from the shoulder, of a calibre of 6 mm. or above, not included in Category I.

(3) Ammunition for the arms enumerated above.

(4) Gunpowder and explosives.

Category III. Arms and munitions having no military value.

All the arms and munitions other than those defined in Categories I and II such as:

—rifled weapons of a calibre of less than 6 mm. designed for firing from the shoulder;

—revolvers and automatic pistols of a calibre of 6.5 mm. or less and length of barrel of 10 cm. or less;

—smooth-bore shot guns;

—double-barrelled shot-guns of which one barrel is rifled, the other smooth-bore;

—single-shot pistols;

—firearms firing rimfire ammunition;

—muzzle loading firearms;

—life-saving rockets;

—guns for whaling or other fisheries;

—signal and saluting guns;

—humane cattle-killers of all sorts;

—ammunition for the above.

NOTE.—The above three categories do not include arms the use of which is prohibited by International Law, since it is clearly understood that all traffic in these arms must be prohibited and that no licence can be issued for such traffic.

CHAPTER II.—*Export and transit of arms, munitions and implements of war*

ARTICLE 2

The H. C. P.'s, undertake not to export themselves, and to prohibit the export of arms, munitions and other implements of war enumerated in Category I, whether complete or in parts, except on the conditions hereinafter mentioned.

ARTICLE 3

Notwithstanding this prohibition, the High Contracting Parties may grant in respect of arms, munitions and implements of war whose use is not prohibited by international law, licenses for the export of arms, munitions and implements of war enumerated in Category I, in the following conditions:—

1) Licenses are not to be granted except for a direct supply to a Government recognised as such by the Government of the exporting country.

2) The Government acquiring the consignment must act through a duly accredited representative.

3) Such representative must produce a written authority from the Government he represents for the acquisition of each consign-

ment, which authority must state that the consignment is required
for delivery to that Government for its own use.

4) The form in which this license shall be given shall, so far as
practicable, be that given as an annex to the present Convention.
(page . . .) Each license must contain a description sufficient for
the identification of the arms, munitions and implements of war to
which it relates and the names of the exporter and the acquiring
Government, ports, of embarkation and disembarkation, means of
transport, intended route and destination.

5) A separate licence shall be required for each separate consignment which crosses the frontier of the exporting country, whether by
land, water or air, and shall accompany each separate consignment.

6) A return of the licence granted shall be sent quarterly to the
Central International Office referred to in Article 8 of the present
Convention by the issuing Governments; importing Governments,
when H. C. P.'s, shall also forward quarterly to the C. I. O. a return
of the same licences enclosing particulars of the heading under
which the imported goods will appear in their imports statistics.

ARTICLE 4

Further, licences for the export to private individuals of component parts covered by Category I may be granted on the following
conditions:—

The said component parts must be exported direct to a recognised
manufacturer of war material, duly authorised by his own Government, on a declaration from him to the effect that the said component
parts are required by him.

The Government which grants the licence and the Government of
the importer's country shall take all adequate precautions to ensure
that the said component parts are sent direct to their destination.

The licences granted in the terms of the present Article shall, so
far as practicable, be drafted according to the form annexed to the
present Convention, and shall conform to the provisions of the present Convention, and particularly to those of Article 8.

ARTICLE 5

Without prejudice to any obligations to which they may have sub
scribed under international conventions dealing with transit, the
H. C. P., when they have reason to believe that any consignment of
arms, munitions or implements of war in transit through their territory does not conform to the provisions of the present Convention,
undertake to investigate the circumstances and if necessary to
prohibit the transit.

ARTICLE 6

Without prejudice to the provisions of Article 7, arms and munitions in Category II and III may, if the exporter's country so desires, be exported without licence. Provided, nevertheless, that in the case of arms and munitions of Category II the H. C. P.'s hereby undertake to determine from the size, destination and other circumstances of each consignment whether these arms and munitions are intended for war purposes. If such is the case, the H. C. P.'s undertake that the shipments shall become subject to Articles 2 to 5.

ARTICLE 7

The H. C. P. further undertake to prohibit the export of arms, munitions, and implements of war enumerated in Article 1, to the maritime or territorial zones specified in Article 9.

Nevertheless, the H. C. P. may grant export licences, notwithstanding this prohibition provided that they conform to the provisions of Articles 3 to 5. The competent authorities must satisfy themselves, before issuing them that the arms, munitions or implements of war are not intended for export to any destination or for disposal in any way contrary to the provisions of this Convention.

ARTICLE 8

A Central International Office shall be established by the Council of the League of Nations for the purpose of collecting, preserving and publishing documents of all kinds exchanged by the H. C. P.'s with regard to the trade in and the distribution of arms, munitions and implements of war, as well as the text of all laws, orders and regulations made for the carrying out of the present Convention.

Each of the H. C. P.'s shall publish an annual return of the export licences which each may have granted in respect of arms, munitions and implements of war in pursuance of the present Convention, mentioning the quantities and destination of the arms, munitions and implements of war to which the export licences refer. A copy of this return shall be sent to the Central International Office.

The H. C. P.'s further undertake to forward to the Central International Office all information which they will be in a position to provide relating to consignments under contracts entered into before the coming into force of the present Convention.

CHAPTER III.—*Import of Arms, Munitions and Implements of War,
Prohibited Zones*

ARTICLE 9

The H. C. P. undertake, each as far as the territory under its
jurisdiction is concerned, to prohibit the importation of arms, munitions and implements of war into the following territorial zones, and
also to prevent their exportation to, importation and transportation
in the territorial zones as well as in the maritime zones defined
below.

Special licences for the import of arms, munitions and implements of war into the zones defined above may be issued. In the
African zone they shall be subject to the regulations specified in
Article[s] 10 and 11 or to any local regulations of a stricter nature
which may be in force.

In the other zones specified in the present Article, these licences
shall be subject to similar regulations put into effect by the Governments exercising authority there.

CHAPTER IV.—*Supervision on Land*

ARTICLE 10

Arms, ammunition and implements of war exported under licence
into the prohibited zones shall be admitted only at ports, or other
places of entry, designated for this purpose by the authorities of
the State, Colony, Protectorate or territory under mandate concerned.

Such arms, ammunition and implements of war must be deposited
by the importer at his own risk and expense in a public warehouse
under the exclusive custody and permanent control of the Authority
and of its agents, of whom one at least must be a civil official or a
military or naval officer. No arms or ammunition shall be deposited or withdrawn without the previous authorisation of the
administration of the State, Colony, Protectorate or territory under
mandate, unless the arms, ammunition and implements of war to
be deposited or withdrawn are intended for the forces of the Government or the defence of the national territory.

The withdrawal of arms, ammunition or implements of war deposited in those warehouses shall be authorised only in the following cases:—

1. For despatch to places designated by the Government where
the inhabitants are allowed to possess arms, under the con-

trol and responsibility of the local Authorities, for the purpose of defence against robbers or rebels.

2. For despatch to places designated by the Government as warehouses and placed under the supervision and responsibility of the local Authorities.

3. For individuals who can show that they require them for their legitimate personal use.

ARTICLE 11

In the prohibited zones specified in Article 9, trade in arms, munitions and implements of war shall be placed under the control of officials of the Government and shall be subject to the following regulations:

1. No person may keep a warehouse for arms, munitions or implements of war without a licence.

2. Any person licenced to keep a warehouse for arms, munitions or implements of war must reserve for that special purpose enclosed premises having only one entry, provided with two locks, one of which can be opened only by the officers of the Government.

The person in charge of a warehouse shall be responsible for all arms, munitions or implements of war deposited therein and must account for them on demand. For this purpose all deposits or withdrawals shall be entered in a special register, numbered and initialled. Each entry shall be supported by references to the official documents authorising such deposits or withdrawals.

3. No transport of arms, munitions or implements of war shall take place without a special licence.

4. No withdrawal from a private warehouse shall take place except under licence issued by the local Authority on an application stating the purpose for which the arms or ammunition are required, and supported by a licence to carry arms or by a special permit for the purchase of ammunition. Every arm shall be registered and stamped, the Authority in charge of the control shall enter on the licence to carry arms the mark stamped on the weapon.

5. No one shall without authority transfer to another person either by gift or for any consideration any weapon or ammunition which he is licenced to possess.

ARTICLE 12

In the prohibited zones specified in Article 9 the manufacture and assembling of arms, munitions or implements of war, shall be prohibited, except at arsenals established by the local Government or, in the case of countries placed under tutelage, at arsenals established by the local Government, under the control of the Mandatory

Power, for the defence of its territory or for the maintenance of public order.

No arms shall be repaired except at arsenals or establishments licensed by the local Government for this purpose. No such licence shall be granted without guarantees for the observance of the rules of the present Convention.

ARTICLE 13

Within the prohibited zones specified in Article 9, a State which is compelled to utilise the territory of a contiguous State for the importation of arms or ammunition, whether complete or in parts, or of material or of articles intended for armament, shall be authorised on request to have them transported across the territory of such State.

It shall, however, when making any such request, furnish guarantees that the said articles are required for the needs of its own Government, and will at no time be sold, transferred or delivered for private use nor used in any way contrary to the interests of the High Contracting Parties.

Any violation of these conditions shall be formally established in the following manner:—

(a) If the importing State is a Sovereign independent Power, the proof of the violation shall be advanced by one or more of the Representatives accredited to it of contiguous States among the High Contracting Parties; After the Representatives of the other contiguous States have, if necessary, been informed, a joint enquiry into the facts by all these Representatives will be opened, and if need be, the importing State will be called upon to furnish explanations. If the gravity of the case should so require, and if the explanations of the importing State are considered unsatisfactory, the Representatives will jointly notify the importing State that all transit licences in its favour are suspended and that all future requests will be refused until it shall have furnished new and satisfactory guarantees.

The forms and conditions of the guarantees provided by the present Article shall be agreed upon previously by the Representatives of the contiguous States among the High Contracting Parties. These Representatives shall communicate to each other, as and when issued, the transit licences granted by the competent authorities.

(b) If the importing State has been placed under the mandatory system established by the League of Nations, the proof of the violation shall be furnished by one of the High Contracting Parties or on its own initiative by the Mandatory Power. The latter shall then notify or demand, as the case may be, the suspension and future refusal of all transit licences.

In cases where a violation has been duly proved, no further transit licence shall be granted to the offending State without the previous consent of the Council of the League of Nations.

If any proceedings on the part of the importing State or its disturbed condition should threaten the public order of one of the contiguous State signatories of the present Convention, the importation in transit of arms, ammunition, material and articles intended for armament shall be refused to the importing State by all the contiguous States until order has been restored.

CHAPTER V.—*Maritime Supervision*

ARTICLE 14

Subject to any contrary provisions in existing special agreements, or in future agreements, provided that in all cases such agreements otherwise comply with the provisions of the present Convention the Sovereign State or Mandatory Power shall carry out the supervision and police measures within Territorial waters in the prohibited zones specified in Article 9.

ARTICLE 15

Within the prohibited zones specified in Article 9, no native vessel of less than 500 tons (net tonnage) shall be allowed to ship, discharge or tranship arms, munitions or implements of war.

A ship shall be deemed to be native if she is either owned by a native, or fitted out, or commanded by a native, or if more than half of the crew are natives of the countries included in the prohibited zones specified in Article 9.

This provision does not apply to lighters or barges, nor to vessels which are engaged exclusively in the coasting trade between different ports of the same state, colony, protectorate or territory under Mandate, where warehouses are situated.

All cargoes of arms, munitions or implements of war shipped on the vessels specified in the preceding paragraph must obtain a special licence from the territorial authority, and all arms, munitions and implements of war so shipped shall be subject to the provisions of the present Convention.

This licence shall contain all details necessary to establish the nature and quantity of the items of the shipment, the vessel on which the shipment is to be loaded, the name of the ultimate consignee and the ports of loading and discharge. It shall also be specified thereon that the licence has been issued in conformity with the regulations of the present Convention.

The provisions of this Article do not apply

(*a*) to arms, munitions and implements of war conveyed on behalf of a Government either under that Government's authorisation or accompanied by a duly qualified official.

(*b*) to arms and munitions in the possession of persons provided with a licence to carry arms, provided such arms are for the personal use of the bearer and are accurately described on his licence.

ARTICLE 16

To prevent all illicit conveyance of arms, munitions and implements of war within the prohibited zones defined in Article 9, native vessels of less than 500 tons, net tonnage,

(*a*) if not exclusively engaged in the coasting trade between different ports of the same State, colony, protectorate or territory under Mandate

or

(*b*) if not engaged in carrying on behalf of a Government as permitted by Article 15, paragraph (*a*), and proceeding to or from any point within the said zones,

—must carry a manifest of their cargo or similar document specifying the quantities and nature of the goods on board, their origin and destination.

The provisions as to the above-mentioned document shall not apply to vessels only partially decked having a maximum crew of ten men and exclusively employed in fishing within territorial waters.

ARTICLE 17

Authority to fly the flag of one of the H. C. P. within the prohibited zones defined in Article 9, shall not be granted to native vessels of under 500 tons, net tonnage as defined in Article 15 unless they satisfy all the three following conditions:

(1) The owners must be nationals of the Power whose flag they claim to fly or a company duly registered under the laws of that Power.

(2) They must furnish proof that they possess real estate in the district of the authority to which their application is addressed or must supply a solvent security as a guarantee for any fines to which they may become liable.

(3) Such owners as well as the captain of the vessel must furnish proof that they enjoy a good reputation, and especially that they have never been convicted of illicit conveyance of the articles referred to in the present Convention.

The authorisation must be renewed every year. It shall contain the indications necessary to identify the vessel, the name, tonnage, type of rigging, principal dimensions, registered number and signal letters. It shall bear the date on which it was granted and the status of the official who granted it.

The initial letters of the port of registration of the native vessel followed by the vessel's registration number in the serial port numbers must be incised and painted in white on black ground on both quarters of each vessel.

The same marks may be painted in Black on the sails.

The net tonnage of the native vessel shall also, if practicable, be incised and painted in a conspicuous position inside the hull.

Article 18

The High Contracting Parties agree to apply the following rules in the maritime zone specified in Article 9.

(1) When a warship belonging to one of the H. C. P. encounters outside territorial waters a supposed native vessel of less than 500 tons burden (net tonnage)

    (*a*) Flying the flag of one of the H. C. P.
    (*b*) Flying the flag of a recognised nation.
    (*c*) Flying no flag.

and the Commander of the warship has good reason to believe that the supposed native vessel

    (*d*) is flying a flag without being entitled to do so
    (*e*) is not lawfully entitled to fly the flag of any recognised nation
    (*f*) is illicitly conveying arms or ammunition

he may proceed, subject to the conditions indicated in the paragraphs below to verify the nationality of the vessel by examining the document authorising the flying of the flag, if this document exists, and also the manifest referred to in Article 16.

Any vessel which presents the appearance of a native build or rig may be presumed to be a native vessel.

(2) With this object, a boat commanded by a commissioned officer in uniform, may be sent to visit the suspected vessel, after she had been hailed to give notice of such intention. The officer sent on board the vessel shall act with all possible consideration and moderation: before leaving the vessel the officer shall draw up a proces-verbal in the form and language in use in his own country. This proces-verbal shall state the facts of the case and shall be dated and signed by the officer.

Should there be on board the warship no commissioned officer, other than the commanding officer, the above-prescribed operations may be carried out by the warrant, petty or non-commissioned officer at the discretion of the commanding officer.

The captain or master of the vessel visited, as well as the witnesses, shall be invited to sign the proces-verbal, and shall have the right to add to it any explanations which they may consider expedient.

(3) In the cases referred to in para. 1 (*a*) and 1 (*b*) of this Article, unless the right to fly the flag can be established the vessel shall be conducted to the nearest port in the zone where there is a competent authority of the Power whose flag has been flown and shall be handed over to such authority.

Should the nearest competent authority representing the Power whose flag the vessel has flown be at some port at such a distance from the point of arrest that the warship would have to leave her station or patrol, to escort the detained vessel to that port, the foregoing regulation need not be carried out. In such a case, the vessel may be taken to the nearest port where there is a competent authority of one of the H. C. P. of nationality other than that of the warship, and handed over to such authority, and steps shall at once be taken to notify the detention to the competent authority representing the Power concerned.

No proceedings shall be taken against the vessel or her crew until the arrival of the representative of the Power whose flag the vessel was flying or without authority from him.

The suspected vessel may also be handed over to a warship of the nation whose flag she had flown, if the latter consents to take charge of her.

(4) The procedure laid down in Para. 3 may be followed if after the verification of the flag and in spite of the manifest being in order the Commander of the Warship continues to suspect the native vessel of engaging in the illicit conveyance of arms, munitions, or implements of war.

(5) In the cases referred to in para. 1 (*c*) of this Article, if it is ascertained as a result of the visit made on board the native vessel that whereas it flew no flag, it was also not entitled to fly the flag of a recognized State, the native vessel, shall, unless the innocent nature of her cargo can be established to the satisfaction of the Commanding Officer of the warship, be conducted to the nearest point in the zone where there is a competent authority of the Power to which the warship which effected the capture belonged, and shall be handed over to such authority.

If it is established that the vessel was engaged in the illicit conveyance of arms, munitions and implements of war, the vessel and all cargo carried in addition to the arms, munitions and implements of war shall be seized by such authority and disposed of according to its own laws—the destruction of the illicit cargo of arms, munitions and implements of war may be ordered according to the same laws.

ARTICLE 19

The authority before whom the suspected vessel has been brought shall institute a full enquiry in accordance with the laws of his country in the presence of an officer of the detaining warship.

If, however, owing to the duties upon which the warship is engaged it is not practicable for an officer of this warship to attend this enquiry, an affidavit sworn by the commanding officer of the warship shall be accepted by the authority holding the enquiry in place of the verbal evidence of an officer of the warship.

If it is proved at this enquiry that the flag has been illegally flown but that the vessel is entitled to fly the flag of a recognised State she shall, if that State is one of the H. C. P. be handed over to the nearest authority of that State and in all other cases shall be disposed of by agreement between the State responsible for her detention and the State whose flag she is entitled to fly, and pending such agreement shall remain in the custody of the authorities of the nationality of the detaining warship.

If it is established that the use of the flag by the detained vessel was correct, but that the vessel was engaged in the illicit conveyance of arms, munitions or implements of war, those responsible shall be brought before the courts of the State under whose flag the vessel sailed. The vessel herself and her cargo shall remain in charge of the authority directing the enquiry. The illicit cargo of arms, munitions or implements of war may be destroyed in accordance with the laws and regulations drawn up for the purpose.

ARTICLE 20

The H. C. P. agree to communicate to the Central International Office, specimen forms of the documents mentioned in Articles 15, 16, 17.

ARTICLE 21

Any illicit conveyance or attempted conveyance legally established against the captain or owner of a vessel authorised to fly the flag of one of the signatory Powers, or holding the licence provided for in Article 15, shall entail the immediate withdrawal of the said authorisation or licence.

The H. C. P. will take the necessary measures to ensure that their territorial authorities or their consuls shall send to the Central International Office certified copies of all authorisations granted under this Convention to fly their flag as soon as such authorisation shall have been granted, as well as notice of withdrawal of any such authorisation. They also undertake to communicate it to the said Office copies of the licences provided for under Article 15.

ARTICLE 22

The commanding officer of a warship who may have detained a vessel flying a foreign flag shall in all cases make a report thereon to his Government, stating the grounds on which he acted.

An extract from this report, together with a copy of the proces-verbal drawn up by the Officer, warrant officer, petty or non-commissioned officer sent on board the vessel detained shall be sent as soon as possible, to the Central International Office and at the same time to the Government whose flag the detained vessel was flying.

ARTICLE 23

If the authority entrusted with the enquiry decides that the detention and diversion of the vessel or the measures imposed upon her were irregular, he shall fix the amount of the compensation due. If the capturing officer or the authorities to whom he is subject, do not accept the decision or contest the amount of the compensation awarded, the dispute shall be submitted to a Court of Arbitration consisting of one arbitrator appointed by the Government whose flag the vessel was flying, one appointed by the Government of the capturing officer, and an umpire chosen by the two arbitrators thus appointed. The two arbitrators shall be chosen, as far as possible, from among the diplomatic, consular or judicial officers of the H. C. P. These appointments must be made with the least possible delay, and natives in the pay of the H. C. P. shall in no case be appointed. Any compensation awarded shall be paid to the person concerned within six months at most from the date of the award.

The decision shall be communicated to the Central International Office.

CHAPTER VI.—*General Provisions*

ARTICLE 24

The H. C. P. who exercise authority over territories within the prohibited areas and zones specified in Article 9, agree to take, so far as each may be concerned, the measures required for the enforcement of the present Convention, and in particular for the prosecution and repression of offences against the provisions contained therein and to appoint the necessary territorial and consular officers or special representatives competent for this purpose.

They shall communicate these measures to the Central International Body and shall inform them of the competent authorities referred to in the preceding Article.

ARTICLE 25

In time of war, Articles 2, 3, 4, 5, and 6, shall be considered as suspended from operation until the restoration of peace so far as concerns any export and transit of arms, munitions or implements of war to or on behalf of any of the belligerents recognised as such by the exporting country and the countries of transit, provided such recognition has been previously communicated to the other H. C. P.

ARTICLE 26

Any Government may on signing or adhering to the present Convention declare that it accepts its provisions partially or conditionally provided that the H. C. P. consent, and that it does not thereby affect the effectiveness of the supervision of the trade in arms, munitions, and implements of war.

Nevertheless the Convention shall only apply to Powers availing themselves of the option provided in the previous paragraph if within the period of one year from the notification by the French Government of the deposit of their ratification (or adherence), partial or conditional, no opposition to such ratification (or adherence) has been raised by any of the Contracting Parties.

ARTICLE 27

All the provisions of the former general international Conventions, relating to the matters dealt with in the present Convention included the convention for the control of the trade in arms and ammunition and the protocol signed at Saint Germain-en-Laye September 10th, 1919, shall be considered as abrogated in so far as they are binding between the Powers which are Parties to the present Convention.

The present Convention shall in no way affect the rights and obligations which may arise out of the provisions either of the Covenant of the League of Nations or of the Treaties of Peace signed in 1919 and 1920 at Versailles, Neuilly, St. Germain and Trianon or the Treaty limiting naval armaments signed at Washington on February 6th, 1922, and the provisions of Agreements registered with the

League of Nations and published by the League up to the date of the coming into force of the present Convention, so far as the Powers which are signatories of or benefit by the said Treaties or Agreements are concerned.

ARTICLE 28

The Council of the League of Nations shall cause to be published an annual report on the operation of the present Convention.

This report shall be presented to the Assembly of the League of Nations.

ARTICLE 29

The present Convention of which the French and English texts shall both be authentic, is subject to ratification. It shall bear to-day's date and shall be open for signature by the Powers until .... (date).

Each Power shall address its ratification to the French Government, which shall at once notify the deposit of ratification to each of the other signatory Powers.

The instruments of ratification shall then remain deposited in the archives of the French Government.

ARTICLE 30

The H. C. P. will use their best endeavours to secure the accession to the present Convention of the other States, whether Members of the League or not. On and after .... (date) the present Convention may be acceded to by any Power. Accession shall be effected by an instrument communicated to the French Government, which shall at once notify such deposit to all Powers which are signatories of or accede to the Convention.

The instruments of accession shall remain deposited in the archives of the French Government.

ARTICLE 31

Disputes between the parties relating to the interpretation or application of this Convention shall, if they cannot be settled by direct negotiation, be referred for decision to the Permanent Court of International Justice. In case either or both of the Parties to such a dispute should not be parties to the protocol of signature of the Permanent Court of International Justice, the dispute shall be referred, at the choice of the Parties, either to the Permanent Court of International Justice or to a court of arbitration.

ARTICLE 32

The present Convention will not come into force until it has been ratified by 12 Powers, among whom shall be the following: Belgium, the United States of America, France, Great Britain, Italy, Japan and Russia.

The date of its coming into force shall be the . . . . . day after the receipt by the French Government of the 12th ratification. Thereafter, the present Convention will take effect in the case of each Party . . . . . days after the receipt of its ratification or accession.

ARTICLE 33

The present Convention may be denounced by any Party thereto after the expiration of ten years from the date when it came into force in respect of that Party. Denunciation shall be effected by notification in writing addressed to the French Government which shall forthwith transmit copies of such notification to the other Parties, informing them of the date on which it was received.

A denunciation shall take effect two years after the date on which the notification thereof was received by the French Government, and shall operate only in respect of the notifying State.

ARTICLE 34

The H. C. P. agree that, at the conclusion of a period of 5 years, the present Convention shall, in the light of the experience then gained, be subject to revision upon the request of a third of the said H. C. P.

[Annex]

LICENCE TO EXPORT ARMS, MUNITIONS AND IMPLEMENTS OF WAR

(Name and Address of Exporter)
is hereby authorised to export the following Arms and Munitions of War.

(Here will follow a full description of the Arms and Munitions, their number, weight and other necessary data, including the heading under which the exported goods will appear in the export statistics of the exporting country).

To (Name of Importing Government)

The above Arms and Munitions of War will be sent by (Here state whether by sea, rail or air).

by the proposed following route or routes.

(Here give Port or Station of Embarkation and Disembarkation, Route and Destination, including last Port or Station of consignment).

(Name and address of Purchasing Agent of the Importing Government).

(Signature of Proper Authority of Government of Exporting country).

511.3 B 1/197 : Telegram

The Minister in Switzerland (Gibson) to the Secretary of State

BERNE, *August 29, 1924—5 p.m.*
[Received August 30—3:07 a.m.]

76. Drummond's communication to you dated August 18th is as follows:

"At its coming meeting the Council of the League of Nations will consider the report and draft convention prepared by the Temporary Mixed Commission for the reduction of armaments as a result of the following resolution of the Fourth Assembly:

'The Assembly recommends that the Temporary Mixed Commission should be invited to prepare a new convention or convention[s] to replace that of St. Germain for the control of the traffic in arms.

The Temporary Mixed Commission should be requested to draw up the draft convention or conventions in such a form that they might be accepted by the government[s] of all countries which produce arms or munitions of war.

The Temporary Mixed Commission should however also make alternative proposals for a convention or conventions which might be adopted by some of the producing powers even if others refused their cooperation.

The Assembly recommends that the Council should invite the United States Government to appoint representatives to cooperate with the Temporary Mixed Commission in preparing the draft convention or conventions.'

Following upon an invitation extended by the Acting President of the Council your Government was good enough to delegate its representative in Berne to attend the meeting of the Temporary Mixed Commission in order to receive information with regard to the proposals made respecting this draft convention.

The Temporary Mixed Commission in its report expressed their appreciation of the valuable assistance afforded to them by Mr. Grew and later by Mr. Gibson in the carrying out of the task entrusted to it by the Assembly and the Council. Special stress is laid in this report on the study given by the commission to the views of the Government of the United States with reference to the Convention of St. Germain and to the means by which, in the draft prepared by it, such views might be so far as possible met.

The draft convention prepared by the Temporary Mixed Commission together with the report at present under consideration by the Council will in due time be discussed at the Assembly with a view to considering whether the draft convention affords a sufficient basis to convoke an international conference for the purpose of adopting such a convention as has been contemplated. In view of the fact that the position of the United States in this matter has been considered as an important factor by the Assembly, the Council and its expert commissions, the members of the Council feel that the fullest opportunity should be afforded to your Government to follow every step in the development of this question and therefore that it would be of the greatest importance for the success of the work that a representative of the Government of the United States should be present during the meetings of the third committee of the coming Assembly which is to discuss the matter, and that his presence would be very highly appreciated by the third committee.

To this end, therefore, I am directed by the acting President of the Council to state that the members of the Council are in agreement that the presence of a representative of the United States Government at the time of the meetings of the third committee of the Assembly would be of great value, and to extend to the Government of the United States, an invitation in this sense.

I have the honor to enclose herewith for your information two copies of the report of the Temporary Mixed Commission to which reference is made above."

My reply to Drummond dated today is as follows:

"I beg leave to acknowledge the receipt of your note of August 18th and to inform you that I did not fail to transmit immediately to the Secretary of State the communication from the Council of the League of Nations inviting my Government to have a representative present at the meetings of the third committee of the forthcoming Assembly which is to discuss the question of the control of the traffic in arms.

I am now in receipt of a reply from the Secretary of State[48] desiring me to express, on behalf of my Government, its cordial appreciation of the courtesy shown by the Council in extending this invitation.

The Government of the United States has been happy to be represented at the meetings of the Temporary Mixed Commission and of its sub-committee. Its views have been fully explained on those occasions, and it is felt that they could not be usefully amplified by having a representative present at the meeting of the third committee.

It is observed from the invitation that the third committee will discuss this matter with a view to considering whether the draft convention affords a sufficient basis to convoke an international conference for the purpose of adopting such a convention as has been contemplated.

The Government of the United States, as is well known, is in cordial sympathy with efforts of supervisory power [suitably?] to restrict traffic in arms and ammunition of war, and it will be glad to cooperate in the formulation of any plan which would warrant the belief that necessary legislation could be obtained to give it effect.

To this end the United States would be disposed to give favorable consideration to an invitation to participate in an appropriate international conference of powers for the purpose of negotiating and concluding such a convention."

GIBSON

[48] Not printed.

511.3 B 1/229

The Minister in Switzerland (Gibson) to the Secretary of State

No. 170   BERNE, *October 14, 1924.*
L.N. No. 597   [Received October 28.]

SIR: I have the honor to refer to my despatch No. 153, of October 2, 1924 (L.N. No. 593),[49] enclosing a document (No. A.115.1924.IX) issued by the Secretariat of the League of Nations and embodying a resolution adopted by the Assembly and Council, requesting the interested governments to inform the Secretary General, before the Council meets in December 1924, whether they are prepared to take part in a conference to be convened in April or May 1925 for the purpose of discussing the Draft Convention for the Control of the International Traffic in Arms, Munitions and Implements of War.

I have now received a letter, dated October 9, 1924, from the Secretary General of the League, enclosing a communication (C.L.140.1924.IX) addressed to the Secretary of State in the sense of the above mentioned resolution. This communication, as well as a copy of Sir Eric Drummond's letter to me, is transmitted herewith.

I have [etc.]   HUGH GIBSON

[Enclosure]

The Secretary General of the League of Nations (Drummond) to the
Minister in Switzerland (Gibson)

GENEVA, *October 9, 1924.*

MY DEAR GIBSON: I am enclosing, herewith, an official letter to the Government of the United States, with reference to the proposed International Conference for the purpose of concluding a convention on the control of the international trade in arms and munitions.

The despatch of this letter is, of course, in execution of the general instructions of the Council, and you will, I am sure, understand that the Council did not overlook the fact that your Government has already, through your letter to me of August 29th, declared that it would be disposed to give favorable consideration to an invitation to participate in an appropriate international conference for this purpose.

As you will see, the suggestion now made is that the Conference should be held in April or May, 1925, and I hope to hear from you, in due course, that the proposed date is acceptable to Washington.

Believe me [etc.]   ERIC DRUMMOND

---

[49] Not printed.

[Subenclosure]

The Secretary General of the League of Nations (Drummond) to the Secretary of State

C.L.140.1924.IX   GENEVA [, *October 7, 1924*].

SIR: At its meeting held on September 30th, the Council adopted the following Resolution:—

"On the proposal of the Assembly the Council decides to authorise the Secretary-General to submit to the Governments of the States Members and non-Members of the League of Nations the draft Convention relating to the Control of the International Trade in Arms, Munitions and Implements of War drawn up by the Temporary Mixed Commission, and to request these Governments to inform him, before the Council meets in December, whether they are prepared to take part in a Conference to be convened in April or May, 1925, for the purpose of discussing the draft Convention.

"The Secretary-General will communicate to the various Governments the report of the Temporary Mixed Commission, the minutes of that Commission and the Minutes of the Permanent Advisory Commission relating to the discussion of Article 9, together with the minutes of the present meeting of the Council, in order that the representatives of the Governments on the International Conference may have the requisite information to enable them to come to a decision on the problems raised on this question during the present meeting."

In execution of this decision I have the honour to enclose herewith the draft Convention on the control of the International Trade in Arms, Munitions and Implements of War which was drawn up by the Temporary Mixed Commission (Document A.16.1924.IX, Annex IV.)[50]

The next meeting of the Council is to be held on December 8th 1924, and I should [be] grateful if you would kindly inform me, if possible before that date, whether the United States Government would be prepared to take part in an International Conference to be held in April or May 1925 for the purpose of discussing this draft and concluding a Convention on the control of the International Trade in Arms, Munitions and Implements of War.[51] The exact date of this Conference will be fixed by the Council at its December session.

In accordance with paragraph 2 of the Council's Resolution I am also enclosing herewith the report of the Temporary Mixed Commission for the reduction of armaments and the report of the 3rd Committee of the Assembly.[52]

---

[50] Same as draft convention printed *ante*, p. 56.

[51] On Dec. 7, 1924, Minister Gibson informed the Secretary General of the League of Nations that the United States was still favorably disposed to the proposed international conference and was agreeable to the suggestion that it be held in April or May 1925 (file no. 500.A14/34).

[52] Neither printed.

The report of the Temporary Mixed Commission contains that part of the Minutes of the Commission which relates to Article 9 (Document A.16.1924.IX. Annex V).

Further information relating to the preparations for the Conference will be forwarded to you as soon as possible.

I have [etc.]   ERIC DRUMMOND

511.3 B 1/231

The Secretary of War (Weeks) to the Secretary of State

WASHINGTON, *October 25, 1924.*

MY DEAR MR. SECRETARY: With reference to your letter of September 10, 1924, (NE 511.3 B 1/169 [*189*]),[53] inclosing for my consideration a copy of a draft convention of July 16, 1924, amending the Convention of St. Germain, I am pleased to advise you that in so far as the contents thereof concern matters properly within the purview of the War Department, a careful consideration of the same raises serious doubt as to the advisability of the United States being a party to the draft convention in its present form.

The international control of the trade in arms, munitions, and implements of war, along the lines indicated in the draft convention herewith, would result, in so far as the United States is concerned, in the international control of production and sources of supply of means vitally necessary to our national defense. This result would follow from the fact that the United States in time of war is almost wholly dependent upon the private manufacture of munitions. This private munitions industry, in time of peace, keeps munitions plants in existence, and holds together the trained technical personnel necessary for war time production. In time of peace, the private manufacture of munitions, in order to exist as an industry, must have a market for its production, which market, in so far as the United States is concerned, is found in:

a. Supply of the current needs of our military forces, which, on account of their small size, is comparatively negligible.

b. Supply of domestic needs.

c. Export to foreign countries, which, while not large, is an important factor in maintaining the existence of our munitions industry.

In this connection it should be noted that of the H. C. P. specifically mentioned in Article 32, the United States is the only nation that does not maintain government arsenals for the supply of its own war time needs, and in consequence the provisions of the convention as regards trade may place the United States in an extremely disadvantageous position in so far as the acquisition of items included

[53] Not printed.

in Category I are concerned, at a time when such procurement through normal trade channels may be vitally necessary for national defense, or for the preservation of our national sovereignty. While the United States maintains six so-called manufacturing arsenals, these plants are in reality little more than experimental laboratories, and in consequence the war time needs of our government must be supplied by private manufacture. The present state of our private manufacture is such that at the beginning of an emergency a portion of the raw materials and component parts of our munitions needs must be obtained from abroad through normal trade channels, in order to provide for the necessary expansion of our private munitions industry. It should further be noted that our present small private munitions plants are partially dependent for their peace time existence on foreign trade, namely, on exports to other nations. A limitation of these exports would inevitably result in the restriction of this industry in the United States and consequently in an alarming situation as regards the procurement of munitions in the event of a national emergency.

The provisions of Articles 1, 2, 3, 4, and 25, of the draft appear objectionable in that they might unduly hamper the United States in its preparations to meet a clearly foreseen national emergency. Article 9 is objectionable in not definitely defining and designating the zones and areas to which the draft convention is to be applicable.

The United States has already complied with the spirit of the Convention of St. Germain, and has gone further by drastically reducing its armed forces, by practically dismantling its war time munitions plants, by restricting the shipment of arms and ammunition to legitimate fields, and by prohibiting the sale of surplus war material to all foreign powers.

At present the United States maintains an extremely small and weak military force, our war reserves are entirely inadequate to meet war requirements under the General Mobilization Plan, and we possess no large government owned manufacturing arsenals. If we should be solely dependent upon newly constructed munitions plants in event of national emergency, it would require from twelve to twenty-four months before the rate of production would approximate our war time requirements.

The other great powers mentioned in Article 32 are in a totally different situation. They maintain comparatively large military forces, they possess large war reserves of materiel, and have large government owned or subsidized munitions plants. In event of an emergency, involving hostile action against this country, their situation in this regard alone is so infinitely superior to ours that we could not hope for even successful defensive operations, without the aid of our now existing private munitions industry.

Any acquiescence by the United States at this time in an international agreement to limit in any manner whatsoever the private or other manufacture of munitions, would in effect perpetuate the present disproportion existing between the munitions producing industry here and abroad, and this is a condition to which the War Department cannot in conscience subscribe. Any international agreement which would produce a universal proportional reduction or limitation, if based on present conditions, would quite naturally affect the United States more adversely than any other great power, since the United States, as stated above, has already so drastically cut down its defensive means. To reduce these or to limit them still further, by direct or by indirect action, would produce a situation in which I should be very loath to assume any responsibility for the national safety.

When the other great powers mentioned in Article 32 of the draft convention have given proof of their sincerity of purpose by reducing their armed forces, reserves of munitions, and munitions production capacity to the approximate level of that of the United States, the War Department would enthusiastically support any effort to solve on a universal and permanent basis, the problem of the limitation of the manufacture, storage, and traffic in arms, munitions, and implements of war. Until such action on the part of the other great powers mentioned is assured, it appears advisable, from the sole viewpoint of national defense, for the United States to reserve to itself full freedom of action as regards the control of the traffic in arms.

In view of the terms of the draft convention of July 16, 1924, I am constrained to reiterate the views expressed in my letter of September 26, 1923,[54] on the matter of private manufacture of arms and munitions and the international control of the arms traffic.

Sincerely yours,

JOHN W. WEEKS

UNFAVORABLE VIEWS OF THE UNITED STATES UPON A DRAFT TREATY OF MUTUAL ASSISTANCE SUBMITTED BY THE LEAGUE OF NATIONS

500.C117/21

The Secretary of State to the Minister in Switzerland (Gibson)

No. 14   WASHINGTON, *June 16, 1924.*

SIR: I enclose, for transmission by you in the usual manner, a communication to the Secretary General of the League of Nations, in reply to one addressed by him on January 9, 1924, to the Secre-

---

[54] *Foreign Relations*, 1923, vol. I, p. 40.

tary of State,[63] requesting, in conformity with a direction of the Council of the League, the views of the Government of the United States as a Government not a member of the League of Nations, respecting a draft Treaty of Mutual Assistance.[64]

I am [etc.]

For the Secretary of State:
JOSEPH C. GREW

[Enclosure]

The Secretary of State to the Secretary General of the League of Nations (Drummond)

The Secretary of State of the United States of America has the honor to acknowledge the receipt of a communication of the Secretary General of the League of Nations, submitting, by direction of the Council of the League of Nations, the draft Treaty of Mutual Assistance proposed by the Third Committee to the Fourth Assembly, and requesting the expression of the views of the Government of the United States.

In reply it may be said that the Government of the United States is most desirous that appropriate agreements should be reached to limit armament and thus to reduce the heavy burdens of expenditure caused by unnecessary and competitive outlays in providing facilities and munitions of war. The desire and purpose of this Government were fully manifested when the great military and naval Powers were invited by the President of the United States to send representatives to meet in conference at Washington in 1921, for the purpose of considering the limitation of armament. While that conference resulted in the conclusion of an important naval Treaty between the United States of America, the British Empire, France, Italy and Japan for the limitation of capital fighting ships, it was found to be impossible to obtain an agreement for the limitation of the tonnage of auxiliary naval craft or to make any progress in the direction of limitation of land forces. The Government of the United States, having reduced its own armament, continues to cherish the hope that the desired result in the case of other Powers may be achieved, and it notes with keen and sympathetic interest every endeavor to that end. In this spirit the draft Treaty submitted has been carefully considered.

It appears from the preamble of the Treaty that it has been formulated with the desire "of establishing the general lines of a scheme of mutual assistance with a view to facilitate the application of Articles 10 and 16 of the Covenant of the League of Nations, and of

[63] Not printed.
[64] For text of signed treaty, see *Monthly Summary of the League of Nations,* September 1923, vol. III, no. 9, p. 236.

a reduction or limitation of national armaments in accordance with Article 8 of the Covenant 'to the lowest point consistent with national safety and the enforcement by common action of international obligations.' "

The following provisions of the draft Treaty may be especially noted:

ARTICLE 2

"The High Contracting Parties, jointly and severally, undertake to furnish assistance, in accordance with the provisions of the Present Treaty, to any one of their number should the latter be the object of a war of aggression, provided that it has conformed to the provisions of the present Treaty regarding the reduction or limitation of armaments.

ARTICLE 3

In the event of one of the High Contracting Parties being of opinion that the armaments of any other High Contracting Party are in excess of the limits fixed for the latter High Contracting Party under the provisions of the present Treaty, or in the event of it having cause to apprehend an outbreak of hostilities, either on account of the aggressive policy or preparations of any State party or not to the present Treaty, it may inform the Secretary-General of the League of Nations that it is threatened with aggression, and the Secretary-General shall forthwith summon the Council.

The Council, if it is of opinion that there is reasonable ground for thinking that a menace of aggression has arisen, may take all necessary measures to remove such menace, and in particular, if the Council thinks right, those indicated in sub-paragraphs (a), (b), (c), (d) and (e) of the second paragraph of Article 5 of the present Treaty.

The High Contracting Parties which have been denounced and those which have stated themselves to be the object of a threat of aggression shall be considered as especially interested and shall therefore be invited to send representatives to the Council in conformity with Articles 4, 15 and 17 of the Covenant. The vote of their representatives shall, however, not be reckoned when calculating unanimity.

ARTICLE 4

In the event of one or more of the High Contracting Parties becoming engaged in hostilities, the Council of the League of Nations shall decide, within four days of notification being addressed to the Secretary-General, which of the High Contracting Parties are the objects of aggression and whether they are entitled to claim the assistance provided under the Treaty.

The High Contracting Parties undertake that they will accept such a decision by the Council of the League of Nations.

The High Contracting Parties engaged in hostilities shall be regarded as especially interested, and shall therefore be invited to send representatives to the Council (within the terms of Articles 4, 13 and 17 of the Covenant), the vote of their representative not being reckoned when calculating unanimity; the same shall apply to States signatory to any partial agreements involved on behalf of either of the two belligerents, unless the remaining Members of the Council shall decide otherwise.

ARTICLE 5

The High Contracting Parties undertake to furnish one another mutually with assistance in the case referred to in Article 2 of the Treaty in the form determined by the Council of the League of Nations as the most effective, and to take all appropriate measures without delay in the order of urgency demanded by the circumstances.

In particular, the Council may:

(*a*) decide to apply immediately to the aggressor State the economic sanctions contemplated by Article 16 of the Covenant, the Members of the League not signatory to the present Treaty not being, however, bound by this decision, except in the case where the State attacked is entitled to avail itself of the Articles of the Covenant;

(*b*) invoke by name the High Contracting Parties whose assistance it requires. No High Contracting Party situated in a continent other than that in which operations will take place shall, in principle, be required to co-operate in military, naval or air operations;

(*c*) determine the forces which each State furnishing assistance shall place at its disposal;

(*d*) prescribe all necessary measures for securing priority for the communications and transport connected with the operations;

(*e*) prepare a plan for financial co-operation among the High Contracting Parties with a view to providing for the State attacked and for the States furnishing assistance the funds which they require for the operations;

(*f*) appoint the Higher Command and establish the object and nature of his duty.

The representatives of States recognised as aggressors under the provisions of Article 4 of the Treaty shall not take part in the deliberations of the Council specified in this Article. The High Contracting Parties who are required by the Council to furnish assistance, in accordance with sub-paragraph (*b*), shall, on the other hand, be considered as especially interested, and, as such, shall be invited to send representatives, unless they are already represented, to the deliberations specified in sub-paras (*c*), (*d*), (*e*) and (*f*)."

Without attempting an analysis of these provisions, or of other provisions of the draft Treaty, it is quite apparent that its fundamental principle is to provide guarantees of mutual assistance and to establish the competency of the Council of the League of Nations with respect to the decisions contemplated, and, in view of the constitutional organization of this Government and of the fact that the

United States is not a member of the League of Nations, this Government would find it impossible to give its adherence.

The Government of the United States has not failed to note that under Article 17 of the draft Treaty "Any State may, with the consent of the Council of the League, notify its conditional or partial adherence to the provisions of this Treaty, provided always that such State has reduced or is prepared to reduce its armaments in conformity with the provisions of this Treaty", but it would not serve a useful purpose to consider the question of a conditional or partial adherence on the part of the Government of the United States when the conditions imposed would of necessity be of such a character as to deprive adherence of any substantial effect.

WASHINGTON, *June 16, 1924.*

ACCEPTANCE BY THE UNITED STATES OF CERTIFICATES OF IDENTITY ISSUED BY THE LEAGUE OF NATIONS TO RUSSIAN AND ARMENIAN REFUGEES IN LIEU OF PASSPORTS

511.1 C 1/1

The Russian Financial Attaché (Ughet) to the Chief of the Division of Eastern European Affairs, Department of State (Poole)

NEW YORK, *September 22, 1922.*
[Received September 23.]

MY DEAR MR. POOLE: I am in receipt of the text of the arrangement with regard to the issue of Certificates of Identity to Russian refugees, adopted by the Governmental Conference convened by Dr. Nansen, High Commissioner for Russian refugees at Geneva on July 3–5, 1922, a copy of which is herewith enclosed.[65]

It occurred to me that in case the procedure recommended by the Conference is going to be adopted by the European Governments, we may be confronted with the case of Russian citizens bearing these certificates and presenting them to be visa'ed for entrance into this country. Therefore, I take the liberty in writing to you informally to find out what in your opinion will be the attitude of the American Government towards this arrangement. This question is of a great practical importance, as it is quite probable that many Russian refugees will exchange their present passport for these Certificates, thinking that the possession of the latter will assure the protection of the League of Nations. It seems to me that it is our duty to prevent possible misunderstandings in this matter.

---

[65] Not printed.

Hoping that you will appreciate the reasons for my letter and will find it possible to fulfill my request, I remain [etc.]

S. UGHET

511.1 C 1/1

The Chief of the Division of Eastern European Affairs, Department of State (Poole) to the Russian Financial Attaché (Ughet)

WASHINGTON, *October 30, 1922.*

MY DEAR MR. UGHET: I am sorry that an answer to your letter of September 22, 1922, concerning the certificates of identity proposed to be issued to Russian refugees has been so long delayed. I postponed an answer in the thought that the question might be presented to the Department in some practical way. So far, however, the matter has not been brought before us except through your letter.

While the action of the Department cannot be anticipated with respect to such concrete cases as may arise, I believe that I am justified in saying to you that there is nothing in the situation to cause apprehension on behalf of the Russian refugees. I do not see how they can be placed in a worse situation with respect to travel and visas as a result of new provisions made in other countries on the suggestion of the League. There have been many cases since the war of persons holding no passports or the passports of non-recognized governments. To care for this the Department has provided a form (No. 228) which is in effect a declaration by the applicant for a visa as to the facts of his identity and nationality. If a regular passport is lacking, the visa, when granted, is affixed to this form.

I think that it is clear that under this procedure Russian refugees will not suffer any new or undue hardship in the matter of obtaining visas. Any document which they may have in the nature of certificates of identity of the kind proposed by the League of Nations will, presumably, only improve their situation by providing additional, though not necessarily conclusive, evidence of their identity and nationality.

I am [etc.]

D. C. POOLE

511.1 C 1/7

The Secretary General of the League of Nations (Drummond) to the Secretary of State

C.L. 72. 1924

GENEVA [, *June 10, 1924*].
[Received June 26.]

SIR: The Council of the League of Nations, at its meeting on September 28th last, had its attention called to the situation of some thousands of Armenian refugees in various countries who are gravely handicapped by the lack of any documents enabling them to establish their identity, or to travel freely in pursuance of their normal occupations.

In its desire to contribute towards the removal of this disability, the Council requested Dr. Nansen, the High Commissioner for refugees,

"to consider the possibility of having the necessary arrangements made for the issue of identity certificates to Armenian refugees."

Dr. Nansen has made a careful study of this problem, in consultation with the Secretariat of the League and with representatives of the refugees, and has reached the conclusion that effect could best be given to the Council's recommendation by the general adoption by interested governments of a form of certificate for Armenian refugees identical, *mutatis mutandis*, with the certificates established for Russian refugees under the Arrangement concluded at Geneva on July 3rd–5th, 1922.

The thirty-five States shown in the annexed list [66]—two of which, Germany and Mexico, are not Members of the League—are now parties to the Geneva Arrangement which has, in practice, yielded very satisfactory results. The principles laid down in the Arrangement would, it is thought, apply, with only minor modifications, to the proposed certificate for Armenian refugees.

In response to a communication enquiring whether, in the event of an inter-governmental conference being convened to consider the present question, it would be willing to send a representative, the Turkish Government has stated that there is no reason for it to take part in any arrangements concerning Armenian refugees as there are no such refugees from other countries in Turkey.

Dr. Nansen has prepared, and at his request I forward to you for consideration by your Government, a plan for the introduction, by agreement between interested governments, of an identity certificate for Armenian refugees.[67]

The plan contains similar rules to those laid down in the Geneva Arrangement relating to Russian refugees and the certificate is substantially identical with the certificate now employed for the latter. The only modification made is the insertion on the certificate of a space authorising its use for the purpose of returning to the country issuing it and the inclusion in the plan of a recommendation that such authorisation should be given if possible. This modification,

[66] Not printed.
[67] Plan not printed.

which in no way binds the hands of any government which may participate in the plan, is made because Dr. Nansen's experience has convinced him of the great importance of facilitating, as far as possible, free movement by refugees.

It has been found that if the refugee certificate authorises return to the issuing country, the economic position of the holder is improved by the facilities which he thus obtains for visiting temporarily other countries, which may offer him opportunities for employment or business, and his ultimate emigration to another country is in fact encouraged. It is thought that it would be very advantageous if governments felt themselves able to agree in principle to grant the right of return when issuing the refugee certificate. Dr. Nansen has not, however, ventured to make the certificate available for return in all cases.

The plan has been framed in a form which makes it possible for it to be brought into operation, without the convening of a special conference, through notification to me of the desire of individual governments to accede to it. If this method of solving the problem is found feasible, a saving of time and expense would be effected; and, in view of the practical identity of the present proposal with the Arrangement for Russian refugees made at Geneva, which was drawn up in careful consultation by a Conference of government representatives, and which has already secured the adhesion of so many States, it is thought possible that the governments interested will not consider a discussion necessary.

Should, however, the interested governments consider that the present matter requires discussion, no difficulty is anticipated in convening a meeting of representatives for this purpose.

Dr. Nansen desires me to emphasise that the object in view is solely to secure the provision to Armenian refugees of an identity certificate, and not in any way to prejudice any question as to their national status.

The Arrangement of Geneva relating to Russian refugees and the certificate issuable under that Arrangement was circulated in Document C. L. 79. 1922.

I have the honour to ask whether your Government would consider the present communication and the enclosed plan by Dr. Nansen and communicate to me, for Dr. Nansen's information, at an early date its decision as to whether it is disposed to adopt the plan submitted, without the convening of a special meeting or whether it thinks it necessary that such a meeting should be held.

I have [etc.]　　　　　　　　　　　　　　　ERIC DRUMMOND

511.1 C 1/7

The Acting Secretary of State to the Minister in Switzerland
(Gibson)

No. 41   WASHINGTON, *August 5, 1924.*

SIR: I enclose, for transmission in the usual informal manner, a communication to the Secretary General of the League of Nations in reply to a Note, dated June 10, 1924, concerning a plan for the issuance of certificates of identity to Armenian refugees in order that they might establish their identity and travel freely in pursuit of their normal occupations.

In transmitting this Note you should request the appropriate authorities of the League of Nations to inform you when the text of this communication will be released to the press. This information should be cabled to the Department in order that a simultaneous release may be effected here.

I am [etc.]

For the Acting Secretary of State:
LELAND HARRISON

[Enclosure]

The Acting Secretary of State to the Secretary General of the League of Nations (Drummond)

The Acting Secretary of State of the United States of America has received the communication of the Secretary General of the League of Nations, dated June 10, 1924, transmitting a plan for the issue of certificates of identity to Armenian refugees in order that they may establish their identity and travel freely in pursuance of their normal occupations.

The American Government is not in a position to issue travel documents to aliens. It does not require certificates of identity of aliens sojourning within its territory or of those desiring to depart therefrom. For entry into the United States alien immigrants are required to present an immigration visa issued by the appropriate American Consul. The American Consuls will accept from aliens unable to present passports in connection with their applications for immigration visas appropriate documents of identity in lieu of passports. The Nansen certificates issued to Russian refugees have been considered to fall within the category of documents in lieu of passports. Similarly, non immigrant aliens are granted passport visas upon personal affidavits or other documents in lieu of passports when they are unable to present passports. Aliens resident in the United

States who desire to depart temporarily, may obtain from the Commissioner General of Immigration, Washington, D. C., permits to return valid for six months, capable of further extension in the discretion of the Commissioner General of Immigration.

WASHINGTON, *August 5, 1924.*

511.1 C 1/11

The Minister in Switzerland (Gibson) to the Secretary of State

No. 142   BERNE, *September 24, 1924.*
                                          [Received October 6.]

SIR: I have the honor to refer to the Department's instruction No. 41, of August 5, 1924, enclosing a communication to the Secretary General of the League of Nations in reply to a note, dated June 10, 1924, concerning a plan for the issuance of certificates of identity to Armenian refugees in order that they might establish their identity and travel freely in pursuit of their normal occupations.

There is enclosed herewith the reply from the Secretary General of the League to the Department's communication referred to above.

With reference to the second paragraph of the Department's instruction under reference, I have the honor to transmit herewith a copy of a letter, dated September 19, 1924,[68] from Mr. Huntington Gilchrist, of the Secretariat of the League, stating that the Department's communication to the Secretary General would be released to the press in Geneva on October tenth next. My telegram No. 86, of September 20, 1924, 12 a. m.,[68] conveying this information to the Department, was based on this letter.

I have [etc.]   HUGH GIBSON

[Enclosure]

The Secretary General of the League of Nations (Drummond) to the Acting Secretary of State

The Secretary-General of the League of Nations has the honour to acknowledge with thanks the communication of the Acting Secretary of State of the United States of America, dated August 5th, 1924, relative to the identity certificates for refugees prepared by Dr. Nansen, High Commissioner for Refugees.

Dr. Nansen, to whom this communication has been transmitted, desires to record his high appreciation of the recognition by the Government of the United States of the Identity Certificate for Russian Refugees and ventures to assume that as the Identity Certificate for the Armenian Refugees is to all intents and purposes an analo-

---

[68] Not printed.

gous document, the Government of the United States of America will find it possible to afford recognition to that document also.

GENEVA, *September 12, 1924.*

511.1 C 1/11 : Telegram

The Secretary of State to the Minister in Switzerland (Gibson)

WASHINGTON, *October 9, 1924—5 p.m.*

75. Your despatch 142, September 24.

You may inform the Secretary General of the League of Nations that the Department of State will be willing for all practical purposes to consider the identity certificates for Armenian refugees as appropriate documents in lieu of passports.

HUGHES

AMERICAN PARTICIPATION IN THE INTERNATIONAL CONFERENCE FOR CONTROL OF THE TRAFFIC IN HABIT-FORMING DRUGS [69]

511.4 A 2/6

The Secretary General of the League of Nations (Drummond) to the Netherland Minister of Foreign Affairs (Van Karnebeek) [70]

[Translation [71]]

C.L.108(a).1923 XI   GENEVA, *October 18, 1923.*

MR. MINISTER: The Assembly of the League of Nations, at its recent session, considered and adopted the report of the Advisory Committee on Opium and Other Dangerous Drugs (A. 13) and passed certain resolutions in connection therewith. Of these, two resolutions, nos. 5 and 6, deal with the calling by the Council of the League of two conferences and read as follows:

RESOLUTION 5: The Assembly approves the proposal of the Advisory Committee that the governments concerned should be invited immediately to enter into negotiations with a view to the conclusion of an agreement as to the measures for giving effective application in the Far Eastern territories to part II of the Convention [72] and as to a reduction of the amount of raw opium to be imported for the purpose of smoking in those territories where it is temporarily

---

[69] For previous correspondence, see *Foreign Relations*, 1923, vol I, pp. 89 ff.
[70] Copy received from the Netherland Legation Nov. 27, 1923. A similar communication (C. L. 108, Oct. 18, 1923) was transmitted to the Department through the Legation in Switzerland Nov. 7.
[71] File translation revised.
[72] International Opium Convention signed at The Hague Jan. 23, 1912; *Foreign Relations*, 1912, p. 196.

continued, and as to the measures which should be taken by the Government of the Republic of China to bring about the suppression of the illegal production and use of opium in China, and requests the Council to invite those governments to send representatives with plenipotentiary powers to a conference for the purpose and to report to the Council at the earliest possible date.

RESOLUTION 6: The Assembly, having noted with satisfaction that, in accordance with the hope expressed in the fourth resolution adopted by the Assembly in 1922,[73] the Advisory Committee has reported that the information now available makes it possible for the governments concerned to examine, with a view to the conclusion of an agreement, the question of the limitation of the amounts of morphine, heroin, or cocaine and their respective salts to be manufactured; of the limitation of the amounts of raw opium and the coca leaf to be imported for that purpose and for other medicinal and scientific purposes; and of the limitation of the production of raw opium and the coca leaf for export to the amount required for such medicinal and scientific purposes: requests the Council, as a means of giving effect to the principles submitted by the representatives of the United States of America,[74] and to the policy which the League, on the recommendation of the Advisory Committee, has adopted, to invite the governments concerned to send representatives with plenipotentiary powers to a conference for this purpose, to be held, if possible, immediately after the conference mentioned in Resolution 5.

The Assembly also suggests, for the consideration of the Council, the advisability of enlarging this conference so as to include within its scope all countries which are members of the League or parties to the Convention of 1912, with a view to securing their adhesion to the principles that may be embodied in any agreement reached.

The Council, at its meeting on September 29th, considered these two resolutions, and adopted the following resolution, which decides the place where the Conference is to be held and fixes the provisional date:

The Council of the League of Nations, while reserving until its December session the final fixing of the conferences provided for by the Assembly in connection with the traffic in opium and other dangerous drugs, decides, provisionally, that the first conference of countries having possessions where the smoking of opium is still continued should be convoked at Geneva in July 1924, the second conference to follow immediately afterwards.

The Secretary General has the honor to request the Government of the Netherlands to bring this information to the notice of the Governments of the United States of America, the Dominican Republic, Ecuador, and Mexico, with a view to enabling them to make such preliminary arrangements as they may deem advisable to obtain

---

[73] Sept. 19; League of Nations, *Resolutions and Recommendations Adopted by the Assembly During Its Third Session (September 4th to 30th, 1922)*, p. 31.

[74] See statement of the position of the United States, *Foreign Relations, 1923*, vol. I, p. 100.

the data which they may wish to place at the disposal of the conference.

The question as to whether the conference should be enlarged so as to include within its scope all countries which are members of the League or parties to the Convention of 1912 will be considered at the coming meeting of the Council in December next.

I have [etc.]   ERIC DRUMMOND

511.4 A 2/18

The Secretary General of the League of Nations (Drummond) to the Secretary of State

12A/32738/32738   GENEVA, *January 14, 1924.*
C.L.5.1924.XI   [Received January 30.]

SIR: With reference to my letter C.L. 108, dated October 18th, 1923, I have the honour to inform you that the following Resolution was adopted by the Council at its meeting on December 13th, last:—

"The Council notes the adoption by the Assembly of the Report and Resolutions of the Advisory Committee on Traffic in Opium and the Resolutions of the Fourth Assembly.[75] It instructs the Secretary-General to take all the action required by these Resolutions and decides that the First Conference consisting of countries having possessions where the smoking of opium is continued should be convoked at Geneva on the 1st Monday in November 1924 and the Second Conference in Geneva on the 3rd Monday in November 1924".

The special purpose of the Second Conference is set forth in Assembly Resolution VI, a copy of which is attached for purposes of reference.[76]

As regards the question of what States should be invited to take part in this Conference, the Council after considering the suggestion of the Assembly adopted the following further Resolution:—

"The Council is convinced that the extension of the Second Conference to include all countries which are members of the League or Parties to the Convention of 1912 would result in a correspondingly wider acceptance of the principles embodied in any agreement reached. It therefore instructs the Secretary-General to invite to this Conference all Members of the League and Parties to the Convention of 1912"

I accordingly have the honour, on behalf of the Council, to invite your Government to be represented at the Second Conference, which will take place on the 3rd Monday in November 1924, by a delegate, or delegates, having plenipotentiary powers.

---

[75] Sept. 28, 1923.
[76] See the Secretary General's note of Oct. 18, 1923, *supra.*

I have the honour further, to inform you that at its meeting on December 13th, the Council decided that a preparatory Committee should be set up to prepare a draft programme for the Conference in question. This Committee is to be nominated by the Advisory Committee on Traffic in Opium, and will consist of six members, including one representative of the United States and the two European Assessors on the Advisory Committee.

The Council further resolved as follows:—

"The Council feeling that the success of the Conference depends on the cooperation of the Governments, instructs the Secretary-General to invite the Governments to make proposals for the carrying out of Assembly Resolution VI; such proposals to be considered by the preparatory Committee."

This Resolution was adopted by the Council in the earnest hope that the Governments, by their cooperation, would make it possible to bring about the suppression of the abuse of Opium and other dangerous drugs.

I accordingly have the honour, on behalf of the Council, to invite the Government of the United States of America to forward to the Secretariat any relevant proposals it may be disposed to make for the consideration of the preparatory Committee, which is being entrusted with the preliminary work of the Conference.

I have [etc.]   ERIC DRUMMOND

511.4 A 2/25 : Telegram

The Minister in Switzerland (Grew) to the Secretary of State

BERNE, *February 9, 1924—1 p.m.*
[Received 9 : 08 p.m. (?)]

12. Reference Legation's 3, January 7, 2 p.m.[77] I am informally advised by League of Nations that the Preparatory Committee on Opium will be summoned within the next few days to meet on March 5th, and that it is regarded as essential to have the American delegation in Geneva at that time especially as the foundations laid by the Preparatory Committee will greatly influence the work of the later conference.

I am asked to inform the Department that the Advisory Committee has selected by ballot the representatives of France, Great Britain, and the Netherlands as members of the Preparatory Committee. In addition the two European assessors, Sir John Jordan and Monsieur Brenier have accepted the invitation to serve. There thus remains for the full constitution of the Committee only that

---

[77] Not printed.

representative to be nominated by the United States. The opinion in Geneva seems to be that the success of this Preliminary Committee lies largely in the choice of the American delegate and that if the program of the later conference and the tentative draft agreement is to be thoroughly comprehensive it is highly desirable that the Preparatory Committee as at present constituted be aided by the very best technical experts available in the United States. While no official suggestion was made it was clear in conversation that it was felt that the best could be secured, particularly from the point of view represented by the United States, if the first American delegate were a man thoroughly familiar with the opium situation and highly trained in negotiation aided by an internal enforcement officer from the Federal Narcotic Board and a customs officer who has had experience pertaining to customs, steamers, bonded warehouses, et cetera.

GREW

511.4 A 2/31b

The Secretary of State to the American Representative on the Preparatory Committee (Neville [78])

WASHINGTON, *February 21, 1924.*

SIR: The United States has been invited to send a representative to attend the meetings of a Preparatory Committee at Geneva, Switzerland, which has been called by the League of Nations to prepare a draft program for the Narcotics Conference in November, 1924. You are instructed to proceed to Geneva, Switzerland, and attend these meetings in a consultative capacity.

There are enclosed certain suggestions, the international adoption of which, this Government believes, would be of material value in lessening the world-wide traffic in harmful drugs. You are authorized to bring these suggestions to the notice of the Preparatory Committee and to explain that the suggestions are tentative in character and are intended to serve as a basis for discussion.

You will be careful to avoid any attempt to commit this Government in your discussion, as the Department understands that the work of this Committee is purely suggestive and not final. Any recommendations or conclusions which may be reached by the Committee will, therefore, not be binding on the Governments which are represented there.

It is assumed that much of the work will be of a technical character and will involve discussion of the narcotics laws of many na-

---

[78] Edwin L. Neville, consular officer, representative on Advisory Board to U. S. Federal Narcotics Control Board, 1922.

tions of the world. The Department has, therefore, requested the Treasury Department to allow an officer from the Narcotics Section who is familiar with the actual operation of the several Statutes of the United States on this subject to proceed with you. That Department has also been requested to authorize the presence of the Treasury agent in Switzerland at Geneva during your stay there, as it is probable that the discussions will involve questions affecting the shipment, trans-shipment and bonding practices of the nations concerned. In view of the questions of hygiene which may arise, the Department is requesting the Public Health Service to authorize the Surgeon in charge at Paris to proceed to Geneva in case of necessity.

I am [etc.]　　　　　　　　　　　　　　　CHARLES E. HUGHES

[Enclosure]

Suggestions of the United States To Be Presented to the Preparatory Committee

The Resolution calling the Narcotics Conference reads as follows:

"The Assembly, having noted with satisfaction that in accordance with the hope expressed in the fourth resolution adopted by the Assembly in 1922, the Advisory Committee has reported that the information now available makes it possible for the Governments concerned to examine with a view to the conclusion of an agreement, the question of the limitation of the amounts of morphine, heroin or cocaine and their respective salts to be manufactured; of the limitation of the amounts of raw opium and the coca leaf to be imported for that purpose and for other medicinal and scientific purposes, and of the limitation of the production of raw opium and the coca leaf for export to the amount required for such medicinal and scientific purposes.

"Requests the Council, as a means of giving effect to the principles submitted by the representatives of the United States of America and the policy which the League, on the recommendation of the Advisory Committee has adopted, to invite the Governments concerned to send representatives with plenipotentiary powers to a Conference for this purpose, to be held, if possible, immediately after the Conference mentioned.

"The Assembly also suggests for the consideration of the Council, the advisability of enlarging this Conference so as to include within its scope all countries which are Members of the League, or Parties to the Convention of 1912, with a view to securing their adhesion to the principles that may be embodied in any agreement arrived at."

It is assumed that all suggestions for the practical application thereof should be in accordance with its terms.

The Government of the United States believes that the following suggestions should be considered, but does not commit itself thereby to a definite plan, reserving the right to add to, alter or propose other suggestions in the light of proposals from other Powers.

A. Production

1. The cultivation of the opium poppy and the coca leaf plant to be reduced to the amount required for the production of opium and coca leaves sufficient for medicinal and scientific requirements only, as determined by proper authority. As a preliminary measure no increase of poppy or coca leaf plant to be permitted, and those nations in whose territory these articles are not produced to prevent their introduction.

2. No encouragement to be given to poppy or coca leaf cultivators by the State.

3. The acceptance of the principle that no state should rely upon the revenue from the control of opium and the coca leaf for purposes of operating the Government, beyond the expenses incident to controlling the narcotics traffic.

4. Consideration of difficulties arising out of treaty obligations which prevent certain states from raising increased revenues from Customs taxes as a substitute for the tax on opium or coca leaf and their derivatives.

5. The provisions of Articles 1, 2, 3, 4 and 5 of the Hague Opium Convention to be applied to coca leaves.

B. Transportation

1. Opium to be exported only upon license from the importing country which must be party to The Hague Opium Convention, issued upon prescribed rules and regulations showing that it is imported either for purposes temporarily permissible under Chapter II of the Convention or for medicinal purposes. The exportation of opium of less than 9% morphine content, or for purposes under Chapter II of the Convention to cease after a fixed period, say ten years.

2. Coca leaves to be exported only upon permit issued upon prescribed rules and regulations for medicinal purposes, from the importing country, which must be party to the Hague Opium Convention.

3. Derivatives or preparations of opium and the coca leaf to be exported solely for medicinal or scientific purposes.

4. No vessel or other common carrier to receive for transport any opium, coca leaf or derivative of either, which is not accompanied by a certificate from the country of destination showing that it may be lawfully imported, and, by a document from the country of export showing that it may lawfully be exported. Reciprocal right of search on the high seas in regions agreed upon from time to time, to enforce this provision.

5. Transshipment and bonding privileges to be restricted, to the end that, as a general rule, there shall be no re-export of opium, coca leaf or their derivatives and preparations.

C. Manufacture

1. The provisions of Articles 9, 10, 11, 12 and 13 of The Hague Opium Convention to apply to all derivatives or preparations of opium and coca leaf with suitable exceptions for small quantities in medicines.

2. Countries with well developed chemical and pharmaceutical facilities to prohibit the importation of narcotic drugs, derivatives of opium and the coca leaf, permitting only raw opium and the coca leaves to be imported, except small quantities for scientific purposes.

3. The export of manufactured drugs preparations or derivatives of opium or the coca leaf to be permitted only to nations which are party to The Hague Opium Convention and which have adequate systems of domestic control, except that medicines in small quantities may be exported.

D. Administration

1. A consideration of the administrative features of the Convention with a view to prescribing definite powers for a permanent central organization.

2. Annual Reports to be submitted by all Powers party to the Convention. The reports should show the amount of opium and coca leaves produced, imported, exported or used for local consumption; the amounts of derivatives or preparations made therefrom, imported, exported or used for local consumption, and should cover the same periods of time.

3. Illegal possession of opium coca leaf or their preparations or derivatives to be a penal offense.

E. General Provisions

1. The foregoing provisions to be applied to all drugs which might, after generally recognized scientific investigations give rise to similar abuses and result in the same injurious effects.

Management of Conference

1. Day for hearing petitions and suggestions.
2. Order of business.
3. Place of Conference.

511.4 A 2/55 : Telegram

The Secretary of State to the Ambassador in France (Herrick)

WASHINGTON, *May 13, 1924—5 p. m.*

153. The British Embassy has left an *aide memoire* [79] at the Department asking whether this Government would be willing to join with the British Government in making representations at Paris in regard to proposals made at the Committee of preparation for the forthcoming international opium conference.

This Government is of the opinion that international measures must be taken which will have the effect of limiting the quantities of opium and coca leaves in international traffic and the quantities of drugs manufactured therefrom if the present illicit traffic in dangerous drugs is to be dealt with in an effective manner.

You may informally invite the attention of the French Government to the views expressed above, adding that it is hoped that the Government will find it possible to cooperate upon that basis.

Repeat to London for its information.

HUGHES

511.4 A 2/58 : Telegram

The Ambassador in France (Herrick) to the Secretary of State

PARIS, *May 21, 1924—noon.*
[Received 9:20 a. m.]

271. On carrying out instructions contained in your 153, May 13, 5 p. m., I was informed by Péan, who has charge of these matters at the Foreign Office, that the French proposals were now ready and would be submitted as soon as possible to the different governments so as to give the latter time to examine them before the next preparatory meeting at The Hague.

The French experts are apparently of the opinion that it would be very difficult if not impossible to limit the production of raw opium throughout the world. They seem to think that if the powers principally interested agree on a limitation of production it will merely incite other countries not parties to the agreement to increase their production. The French proposals are therefore presumably designed to overcome this objection.

I had already on May 2 after a conversation with Neville discussed the French attitude with Péan and obtained assurances then

[79] Not printed.

that we could continue to count on French support. He renewed these assurances yesterday saying that there was every reliance desired on the part of the French Government to cooperate with the other powers. Copy to European Information Center.[80]

HERRICK

511.4 A 2/90a : Telegram

The Secretary of State to the Ambassador in Peru (Poindexter)[81]

WASHINGTON, September 11, 1924—10 p. m.

41. There will be an international conference in Geneva in November, 1924, to consider measures for the further restriction of the traffic in opium and other dangerous drugs. It is the hope of this Government that the participation in the work of this conference be very general, and particularly that those countries which produce the raw product from which morphine and cocaine are made will be adequately represented. The Department understands that the Government of Peru has been invited to attend the Conference, and trusts that it will be represented there.

One of the vital questions for consideration is the problem of controlling the production of coca leaves. This Government believes that it is only by reducing the quantity of the raw material produced that effective control can be obtained. Accordingly the Government of the United States hopes that the Government of Peru will find it possible to prevent the cultivation of the coca leaf plant in quantities larger than are required for medicinal or scientific purposes. Unrestricted production means uncontrollable consumption, especially when the product enters into international channels.

You should invite the attention of the Government of Peru to this question, and ask for a frank statement of its views, and an exposition of any difficulties which are anticipated in putting a program of this character into effect. The complete acceptance of the Hague Convention by the Government of Peru leads this Government to believe that Peru will be willing to cooperate further in the suppression of the traffic in dangerous drugs.

Repeat *mutatis mutandis* to La Paz as No. 19.

HUGHES

---

[80] An office established Apr. 1, 1924, at the Embassy in Paris, to which copies of telegrams and despatches from the chiefs of missions in Europe to the Department were sent for distribution to other interested missions.
[81] See last paragraph for instructions to repeat to Bolivia.

511.4 A 2/90b : Telegram

The Secretary of State to the High Commissioner in Turkey (Bristol)

WASHINGTON, *September 11, 1924—10 p. m.*

163. The Department hopes that the Government of Turkey will be represented at the forthcoming opium Conference at Geneva in November next. The question of production of raw opium is one of prime importance and without the cooperation of the producing countries, it will be difficult to reach a satisfactory conclusion. The Department suggests, therefore, that you communicate the views of this Government to the Government of Turkey through appropriate channels in substantially the following form:

"As the Government of Turkey is undoubtedly aware, a conference to consider measures to restrict the traffic in opium and other dangerous drugs will be held in Geneva in November of this year. This is a humanitarian question of world wide importance in which the Government of the United States has always been deeply interested, and it is hoped that the Turkish Government will find it possible to participate in the work of the Conference.

One of the principal questions to be considered is the production of raw opium and its transportation in international commerce. It is the earnest hope of this Government that the Government of Turkey will cooperate in an international effort to terminate the production and transportation of raw opium in quantities over and above those needed for medicinal purposes, thereby attacking the problem at its source.

The Government of the United States would be glad to have the views of the Government of Turkey in this regard, and hopes that the delegates at the Conference will be prepared to discuss sympathetically this fundamental point, with a view to accepting the principle." [82]

HUGHES

511.4 A 2/93a : Telegram

The Secretary of State to the Chargé in Persia (Murray)

[Extract [83]]

WASHINGTON, *September 15, 1924—5 p. m.*

83. 1. The Department hopes that the Government of Persia will be represented at the forthcoming opium conference at Geneva in November next. The question of production of raw opium is one of prime importance and without the cooperation of the producing countries it will be difficult to reach a satisfactory conclusion. The

[82] An undated telegram from the High Commissioner, received Oct. 24, 8:37 a. m., informed the Department that the Turkish Under Secretary of State for Agriculture had been appointed delegate to the Conference (file no. 511.4A2/120).
[83] The telegram is printed in full in vol. II, p. 586.

13330

Department suggests, therefore, that you communicate the views of this Government to the Government of Persia through appropriate channels in substantially the following form:

"As the Government of Persia is undoubtedly aware, a conference to consider measures to restrict the traffic in opium and other dangerous drugs will be held in Geneva in November of this year. This is a humanitarian question of world-wide importance in which the Government of the United States has always been deeply interested, and it is hoped that the Persian Government will find it possible to participate in the work of the conference.

One of the principal questions to be considered is the production of raw opium and its transportation in international commerce. It is the earnest hope of this Government that the Government of Persia will cooperate in an international effort to terminate the production and transportation of raw opium in quantities over and above those needed for medicinal purposes, thereby attacking the problem at its source.

The Government of the United States would be glad to have the views of the Government of Persia in this regard, and hopes that the delegates at the conference will be prepared to discuss sympathetically this fundamental point, with a view to accepting the principle."

.   .   .   .

HUGHES

511.4 A 2/92 : Telegram

The Minister in Bolivia (Cottrell) to the Secretary of State

LA PAZ, *September 17, 1924—9 a. m.*
[Received 11: 35 a. m.]

28. Department's telegram no. 19, September 11, 10 p. m.[84]   Foreign Office informs me delegate has been appointed to opium conference but impossible to restrict cultivation of coca leaf plant. Full report by mail.[85]

COTTRELL

511.4 A 2/91 : Telegram

The Chargé in Persia (Murray) to the Secretary of State

TEHERAN, *September 17, 1924—2 p. m.*
[Received 10: 31 a. m.]

120. Department's 65, August 13, 4 p. m.[86] and 83, September 15, 5 p. m.   I learned informally this morning from Dr. Millspaugh that the Persian Government has decided to send Mirza Eissa Khan to represent Persia at the forthcoming opium conference at Geneva in

---

[84] See footnote 81, p. 98.
[85] Not printed.
[86] Not printed; see despatch no. 652, Sept. 23, from the Chargé in Persia, vol. II, p. 588.

November. This Persian is at present the Persian Government Commissioner with the Anglo-Persian Oil Company in London.

Legation will transmit by next pouch to the Department full report on the opium situation in Persia based on data Dr. Millspaugh has kindly offered to supply me.[87]

MURRAY

511.4 A 2/110 : Telegram

The Secretary General of the League of Nations (Drummond) to the Secretary of State

GENEVA [*undated*].
[Received October 15, 1924—12 : 36 p. m.]

Reference my letter C. L. 5, 14th January, 1924. Would remind you no reply yet received. Answer would facilitate preliminary arrangements conference.

DRUMMOND

511.4 A 2/110 : Telegram

The Acting Secretary of State to the Minister in Switzerland (Gibson)

WASHINGTON, *October 15, 1924—6 p. m.*

78. You may inform the Secretary General of the League of Nations in reply to his telegram received today that the United States accepts the invitation to be represented at the Opium Conference on the third Monday in November, 1924.

GREW

511.4 A 2/158

The Ambassador in Peru (Poindexter) to the Secretary of State

No. 300   LIMA, *October 23, 1924.*
[Received November 18.]

SIR: I have the honor to refer to the Department's cablegram No. 41 of September 11, 10 p. m., and to transmit herewith in Spanish and translation copy of a note just received from the Foreign Office,[88] in response to representations made by the Embassy as directed in the cabled instruction under acknowledgment.

The Foreign Office note states that Don Glicerio Camino, Peruvian Chargé d'Affaires at Prague, will represent Peru at the forthcoming conference in Geneva for the further restriction in the traffic of narcotic drugs; and that that part of the Embassy's note relating

---

[87] The report, prepared by Col. D. W. MacCormack of the American Financial Mission in Persia and submitted to the Second Opium Conference by the Persian delegation, is printed in League of Nations, *Records of the Second Opium Conference, Geneva, November 17th, 1924–February 19th, 1925*, vol. II, p. 194.

[88] Note not printed.

to restriction in the cultivation of the coca leaf plant has been communicated to the Ministry of Hacienda with a request for appropriate action.

I have [etc.]   MILES POINDEXTER

511.4 A 2/121b : Telegram

The Acting Secretary of State to the Minister in Switzerland
(Gibson)

WASHINGTON, *October 25, 1924—4 p. m.*

84. American Delegation to Opium Conference at Geneva will consist of Honorable Stephen G. Porter, chairman, Right Reverend Charles H. Brent, Assistant Surgeon General Rupert Blue, Mrs. Hamilton Wright, Mr. Edwin L. Neville, delegates, with five assistants and clerks. Please notify Secretary General of League of Nations and the appropriate Swiss authorities.

GREW

511.4 A 2/173

The British Ambassador (Howard) to the Secretary of State

No. 1118   WASHINGTON, *November 19, 1924.*

SIR: I have the honour to inform you, by direction of Mr. Secretary Chamberlain, and with reference to previous correspondence regarding the international control of narcotic drugs, that the Japanese delegation at the Geneva Opium Conference have proposed that the Powers should be obliged to allow the export or transhipment of opium on production of import certificates, and have attacked His Majesty's Government for refusing to honour suspicious certificates for export from Hong Kong to Formosa.

When the British delegate of the Conference above mentioned declared that His Majesty's Government could not abandon their right to refuse to sanction the export of opium at their discretion, the Japanese delegation stated that they had positive instructions not to sign the Convention unless their demand was satisfied. The Conference has accordingly been adjourned until November 21st and is in grave danger of breaking down altogether.

In these circumstances, His Majesty's representative at Tokio has been instructed to express to the Japanese Government the surprise which my Government feel at the attack referred to above and, at the same time, to urge that the matter is one for negotiation between the two Governments concerned and not for submission to the Conference. His Majesty's Government cannot abandon their right to refuse to sanction the export or transhipment of drugs in cases where such action is deemed advisable, especially in view of the unfortunate incidents which have occurred in the past at Formosa and in Mongolia. My Government realize, however, that the question of the prestige of the Japanese Government may be thought to be involved and the former are therefore prepared to consider a compromise on the following lines.

While reserving their right to scrutinise permits in special cases, His Majesty's Government might be disposed to agree to accept such permits as a matter of usual routine up to a yearly maximum to be decided upon by mutual agreement, if necessary with the approval of the League of Nations. This procedure would be an extension of the "Direct Sales Agreements" which the Government of India already make with other countries and which His Majesty's Government have endeavoured to negotiate with Japan, their efforts in this direction having failed owing to the refusal of the Japanese Government to furnish information regarding the opium and morphia industry in Formosa. In bringing this suggestion to the notice of the Japanese Government, His Majesty's representative at Tokio has been instructed to emphasize that, if the plan in question should be adopted, His Majesty's Government would require full information on all such matters.

My Government feel that the present opium conference at Geneva cannot, however, be held up for such negotiations, and the attention of the Japanese Government is being drawn to the deplorable impression that will be created if the latter wreck the said conference on such a question, when their record in regard to the control of drugs remains open to certain criticisms.

In communicating to you the substance of the instructions which have been despatched to His Majesty's representative at Tokio, I am directed to express the hope that the United States Government will be disposed to support both at Tokio and at Geneva the attitude of His Majesty's Government in regard to this question, as Mr. Secretary Chamberlain feels that American public opinion could justly criticise His Majesty's Government were they to contract out of their responsibilities in the manner desired by the Imperial Japanese Government.

I have [etc.]

(For the Ambassador)
H. G. CHILTON

511.4 A 2/173

The Secretary of State to the British Ambassador (Howard)

WASHINGTON, *November 25, 1924.*

EXCELLENCY: I have the honor to acknowledge the receipt of your note of November 19, 1924, concerning certain phases of the opium question now under discussion at the International Narcotics Conference at Geneva.

In reply it affords me pleasure to inform Your Excellency that the pertinent portion of your note has been telegraphed to the Chairman of the American Delegation at Geneva and to the American Ambassador at Tokyo with the information that since the United States produces no raw opium or coca leaves, the question of exportation for which import certificates may have been issued by other governments does not directly concern this country except as it might involve reexportation in American territory. It has also been pointed out by the Department that under the construction of existing law hitherto adopted and embodied in regulations the reexportation of crude opium from the United States has not been permitted by the Federal Narcotics Control Board. It was further stated that since this Government has always taken a leading part in the international control of narcotics, it is greatly concerned with the success of the Geneva Conference and would view with deep regret any controversy which might arise there threatening the success of the Conference and nullifying the efforts of this and other participating governments towards negotiating an agreement which would effectively regulate the traffic in narcotic drugs. The hope was expressed that the Japanese and British Governments would resolve the question which now threatens to impair the success of the Conference and it was suggested that a solution might be found through negotiation between the two governments rather than through an attempt to settle the controversy in the Conference itself. The American Ambassador at Tokyo was instructed to take early occasion to intimate the viewpoint set forth above to the Japanese Foreign Minister and to advise the British Ambassador at Tokyo of his action.

Accept [etc.]   CHARLES E. HUGHES

511.4 A 2/258

Suggestions of the United States Presented to the Second Opium Conference [89]

CHAPTER I—RAW OPIUM *AND COCA LEAVES*

Definitions. By "raw opium" is understood:

The spontaneously coagulated juice obtained from the capsules of the papaver somniferum, which has only been submitted to the necessary manipulation for packing and transport.

By "coca leaves" is understood:

The leaves of Erythroxylon Coca and its varieties from which cocaine may be extracted.

---

[89] Printed from *International Control of the Traffic in Habit-Forming Narcotic Drugs, Fourth International Conference, Geneva, Switzerland, November, 1924.* Deletions from International Opium Convention of 1912 indicated by canceled type; amendments printed in italics.

ARTICLE 1

The Contracting ~~Powers~~ *Parties* shall enact effective laws or regulations for the control of the production and distribution of raw opium ~~unless laws or regulations on the subject are already in existence~~ *and coca leaves so that there will be no surplus available for purposes not strictly medical or scientific.**

The foregoing provision shall not operate to prevent the production for exportation, or exportation, of raw opium for the purpose of making prepared opium into those territories where the use of prepared opium is still temporarily permitted under Chapter II of this Convention, so long as such exportation is in conformity with the provisions of this Convention.

ARTICLE 2

Due regard being had to the differences in their commercial conditions, the Contracting ~~Powers~~ *Parties* shall limit the number of towns, ports, or other localities through which the export or import of raw opium *and coca leaves* shall be permitted.

Article 2-A

The Contracting Parties shall require that a separate import license must be obtained for each importation of raw opium or coca leaves. The license may allow the importation of the amount for which the license is given in one or more consignments within a period to be specified in the license.

ARTICLE 3

~~The Contracting Powers shall take measures:~~

~~(a) To prevent the export of raw opium to countries which shall have prohibited its entry; and~~

~~(b) To control the export of raw opium to countries which restrict its import, unless regulations on the subject are already in existence.~~

The Contracting Parties shall require that a separate export license must be obtained for each exportation of raw opium or coca leaves. The Contracting Party before issuing such license shall require an import certificate issued by the authorities having jurisdiction over the territory into which the importation is made and certifying that the importation is approved, to be presented by the person applying for the license.

---

*See the report of the Advisory Committee on Traffic in Opium and Other Dangerous Drugs, Fifth Session, Appendix page. [Footnote in the original. Report not printed.]

The license may allow the exportation of the amounts for which the license is given in one or more consignments within a period to be specified in the license.

Unless a copy of the export license accompanies the consignment, the authorities issuing the export license shall send a copy to the authorities having jurisdiction over the territory into which the importation is made.

The authorities having jurisdiction over the territory into which the importation is made, when the importation has been effected, shall return the export license with an endorsement to that effect to the Contracting Party issuing such export license.

In the case of an application to export a consignment to any place for the purpose of being placed in a bonded warehouse in that place, the production of a special certificate from the authorities having jurisdiction over that place, certifying that they have approved the introduction of the consignment for the said purpose, may be accepted by the Contracting Party permitting the export in place of the import certificate provided for above.

ARTICLE 4

The Contracting ~~Powers~~ *Parties* shall make regulations requiring that every package containing raw opium *or coca leaves* intended for export shall be marked in such a way as to indicate its contents, ~~provided that the consignment exceeds 5 kilograms.~~

~~ARTICLE 5~~

~~The Contracting Powers shall not allow the import and export of raw opium except by duly authorized persons.~~

CHAPTER II—PREPARED OPIUM

Definition. By "prepared opium" is understood:

The product of raw opium, obtained, by a series of special operations, especially by dissolving, boiling, roasting, and fermentation, designed to transform it into an extract suitable for consumption.

Prepared opium includes dross and all other residues remaining when opium has been smoked.

ARTICLE 6

The Contracting ~~Powers~~ *Parties* shall take measures for the gradual and effective suppression of the manufacture of, internal trade in, and the use of, prepared opium.

Article 7

The Contracting ~~Powers~~ Parties shall prohibit the import and export of prepared opium~~; these Powers, however, which are not ready to prohibit immediately the export of prepared opium shall prohibit it as soon as possible.~~

Article 8

~~The~~ Each Contracting ~~Powers~~ Party ~~which are not as yet ready to prohibit immediately the export of prepared opium:~~

~~(a) Shall restrict the number of towns, ports, or other localities through which prepared opium may be exported;~~

~~(b) Shall prohibit the export of prepared opium to countries which now forbid, or which may hereafter forbid, the import thereof;~~

~~(c) Shall, in the meanwhile, prohibit the consignment of prepared opium to a country which desires to restrict its entrance, unless the exporter complies with the regulations of the importing country;~~

~~(d) Shall take measures to ensure that every package exported, containing prepared opium bears a special mark indicating the nature of its contents;~~

~~(e) Shall not permit the export of prepared opium except by specially authorized persons.~~

*in whose territory the use of prepared opium is now temporarily permitted agrees to reduce its imports of raw opium for the purpose of making prepared opium by 10 percent of its present importation each year for a period of 10 years beginning with the date of ratification of this Convention by it, and further agrees not to supplement the reduction by domestically produced opium; and further agrees that at the end of such period of 10 years it will prohibit the importation of raw opium for the purpose of making prepared opium. By "present importation" is understood the importation during the 12 months immediately preceding the date the Contracting Party ratifies this Convention.**

CHAPTER III—MEDICINAL OPIUM, MORPHINE, COCAINE, ETC.

Definitions.—By "medicinal opium" is understood:
Raw opium which has been heated to 60° Centigrade and contains not less than 10 per cent. of morphine, whether or not it be powdered or granulated or mixed with indifferent materials.

---

*See speech of the Right Rev. Charles H. Brent on "The opium problem in the Philippine Islands." (Hearings of the Congress of the United States, p. 91, accompanying this document.) [Footnote in the original.]

By "morphine" is understood:

The principal alkaloid of opium having the chemical formula $C_{17}H_{19}NO_3$.

By "cocaine" is understood:

~~The principal alkaloid of the leaves of Erythroxylon Coca, having the formula $C_{17}H_{21}NO_4$.~~

The methylbenzoyl derivatives of ecgonine ($C_9H_{15}O_3N$) of the chemical formula $C_{17}H_{21}O_4N$, whether occurring naturally or prepared synthetically; and all other derivatives of ecgonine, whether occurring naturally or prepared synthetically, which possess the property of creating addiction by their use.

By "heroin" is understood:

Diacetyl-morphine, having the formula $C_{21}H_{23}NO_5$.

ARTICLE 9

The Contracting ~~Powers~~ *Parties* shall enact ~~pharmacy~~ *effective* laws or regulations to limit exclusively to medical and ~~legitimate~~ *scientific* purposes the manufacture, sale, and use of morphine, cocaine, and their respective salts *and derivatives*, ~~unless laws or regulations on the subject are already in existence~~. They shall cooperate with one another to prevent the use of these drugs for any other purpose.

Article 9–A

The Contracting Parties shall enact effective laws or regulations prohibiting the manufacture and distribution of heroin.[*]

ARTICLE 10

The Contracting ~~Powers~~ *Parties* shall ~~use their best endeavours to control, or to cause to be controlled,~~[90] all persons manufacturing, importing, selling, distributing, ~~and~~ *or* exporting morphine, cocaine, ~~and~~ *or* their respective salts *or derivatives*, as well as the buildings in which these persons carry on such industry or trade.

With this object, the Contracting Parties shall ~~use their best endeavours to adopt, or cause to be adopted, the following measures, unless regulations on the subject are already in existence:~~

(a) ~~To~~ Confine the manufacture of morphine, cocaine, and their respective salts *and derivatives* to those establishments and premises

---

[*] (See Hearings of the Congress of the United States accompanying this document.) [Footnote in the original.]

[90] No explanation is given for the deletion of these words which obscures the meaning of the paragraph.

alone which have been licensed for the purpose, or ~~to~~ obtain information respecting the establishments and premises in which these drugs are manufactured and ~~to~~ keep a register of them;

(b) ~~To~~ Require that all persons engaged in the manufacture, import, sale, distribution, or export of morphine, cocaine, ~~and~~ *or* their respective salts *or derivatives* shall ~~be furnished with~~ *obtain* a license or permit to engage in these operations~~, or shall make to the competent authorities an official declaration that they are so engaged~~;

(c) ~~To~~ Require that such persons shall enter in their books the quantities manufactured, imports, sales, and all other distribution, and exports of morphine, cocaine, and their respective salts *and derivatives.* ~~This rule shall not necessarily apply to medical prescriptions and to sales by duly authorized chemists.~~

ARTICLE 11

The Contracting ~~Powers~~ *Parties* shall take measures to prohibit, as regards their internal trade, the delivery of morphine, cocaine, and their respective salts *and derivatives* to any unauthorized persons~~, unless regulations on the subject are already in existence.~~

ARTICLE 12

~~Due regard being had to the differences in their conditions, the Contracting Powers shall use their best endeavours to restrict to authorized persons the import of morphine, cocaine, and their respective salts.~~ *The Contracting Parties shall require that a separate import license must be obtained for each importation of morphine, cocaine, or their respective salts or derivatives. The license may allow the importation of the amount for which the license is given in one or more consignments within a period to be specified in the license.*

ARTICLE 13

~~The Contracting Powers shall use their best endeavours to adopt, or cause to be adopted, measures to ensure that morphine, cocaine, and their respective salts shall not be exported from their countries, possessions, colonies, and leased territory to the countries, possessions, colonies, and leased territories of the other Contracting Powers except when consigned to persons furnished with the licenses or permits provided for by the laws or regulations of the importing country.~~

~~With this object each government may communicate from time to time to the governments of the exporting countries lists of the persons~~

to whom licenses or permits for the import of morphine, cocaine, and their respective salts have been granted.

The Contracting Parties shall require that a separate export license must be obtained for each exportation of morphine, cocaine, or their respective salts or derivatives. The Contracting Party before issuing such license shall require an import certificate issued by the authorities having jurisdiction over the territory into which the importation is made and certifying that the importation is approved, to be presented by the person applying for the license.

The license may allow the exportation of the amounts for which the license is given in one or more consignments within a period to be specified in the license.

Unless a copy of the export license accompanies the consignment, the authorities issuing the export license shall send a copy to the authorities having jurisdiction over the territory into which the importation is made.

The authorities having jurisdiction over the territory into which the importation is made, when the importation has been effected, shall return the export license with an endorsement to that effect to the Contracting Party issuing such export license.

In the case of an application to export a consignment to any place for the purpose of being placed in a bonded warehouse in that place, the production of a special certificate from the authorities having jurisdiction over that place, certifying that they have approved the introduction of the consignment for the said purpose, may be accepted by the Contracting Party permitting the export in place of the import certificate provided for above.

ARTICLE 14

The Contracting Powers *Parties* shall apply the laws and regulations, respecting the manufacture, import, sale, *distribution, delivery,* or export of morphine, cocaine, and their respective salts and their derivatives;

(a) To medicinal opium;

(b) To all preparations (officinal and non-officinal, including the so-called anti-opium remedies) containing more than 0.2 per cent. of morphine, or more than 0.1 per cent. of cocaine, *morphine, cocaine, or their salts or derivatives;*

(c) To heroin, its salts and preparations containing more than 0.1 per cent of heroin;

(d) To all new derivatives of morphine, of *or* cocaine, or of their respective salts, and to every other alkaloid of opium or *coca leaves, and to any habit-forming drug* which may be shown by scientific research, generally recognized, to be liable to similar abuse and productive of like ill-effects.

CHAPTER IV

CHAPTER V

ARTICLE 20

The Contracting ~~Powers~~ *Parties* shall ~~examine the possibility of enacting~~ *enact* laws or regulations making it a penal offense to be in illegal possession of ~~raw opium, prepared opium, morphine, cocaine, and their respective salts, unless laws or regulations on the subject are already in existence.~~ *any of the substances to which this Convention applies.*

Article 20–A

The Contracting Parties shall furnish annually to the Central Board hereinafter constituted, not later than April 1st, for the calendar year beginning January 1st following, in respect of raw opium; coca leaves; morphine, its salts, derivatives, and preparations containing morphine; and cocaine, its salts, derivatives, and preparations containing cocaine, estimates of:

> *(1) Their import requirements for medical and scientific purposes, whether for domestic consumption, manufacture, or commerce;*
> *(2) Their total production and requirements:*
>> *(a) For all purposes,*
>>> *(1) For domestic consumption for all purposes,*
>>> *(2) For domestic consumption for medical and scientific purposes,*
>>> *(3) For export for all purposes,*
>>> *(4) For export for medical and scientific purposes.*

Article 20–B

The Contracting Parties undertake to prohibit the importation into their territory of any of the substances mentioned in Article 20–A in excess of the quantities specified in the estimates furnished in pursuance of Article 20–A (1) or fixed by the Central Board in pursuance of Article 20–E. The foregoing provision shall not operate to prevent the importation of raw opium for the purpose of making prepared opium into those territories where the use of prepared opium is still temporarily permitted under Chapter II of this Convention, so long as such importation is in conformity with the provisions of this Convention.

Article 20-C

A permanent Central Board shall be constituted consisting of one representative each from _____, _____, _____, _____, _____, _____, _____, _____, _____, _____, _____; _____, _____, _____, _____, _____, and _____.*

The Board shall fix its headquarters, shall determine its procedure, and shall meet at least once annually beginning the first Monday in May. The decision of all questions coming before the Board shall be by a majority vote of those present, but two-thirds of the Board shall be necessary to constitute a quorum.

The Board may appoint an Executive Committee of not more than five persons who shall perform such of the Board's duties as it may delegate to the Committee. The members of the Executive Committee need not be members of the Board.

The expenses of the members of the Board shall be defrayed by the Parties they represent. The expenses of the Executive Committee and its clerical staff shall be divided among the Contracting Parties in proportion to their total imports and exports of raw opium and coca leaves.

Article 20-D

The Contracting Parties, in addition to the estimates called for in Article 20-A, agree to send to the Central Board:

(1) In respect of each of the substances mentioned in Article 20-A:

(a) Within three months after the end of each quarter statistics of their imports, specifying their source, and of their exports and re-exports, specifying their destination, during that quarter;

(b) If possible, within three months after the end of each half year the wholesale stocks, whether in Government or in private hands, at the end of that half year;

(2) In respect of morphine and cocaine and their salts and derivatives, within three months after the end of each half year, the statistics of their manufacture during that half-year;

(3) In respect of raw opium and coca leaves, within three months after the end of each year, the total quantity produced and consumed during that year.

The Central Board shall communicate periodically to all the parties to this Convention the situation as regards the quantity and destination of all exports and re-exports of the substances mentioned in

---

* The nations having representatives shall be selected by this Conference. [Footnote in the original.]

Article 20–A, calling to their particular attention the fact that, in the case of any territory, the imports have already reached the amounts to which such territory is entitled under this Convention.

Article 20–E

If any Contracting Party furnishes no estimate of its import requirements in pursuance of Article 20–A or furnishes an estimate which appears to the Central Board upon investigation undertaken on its own motion or on complaint of any of the Contracting Parties, to be greatly in excess of its reasonable requirements, the Board shall immediately ascertain the amount of the reasonable requirements of that Contracting Party for the calendar year beginning January first following, after taking into account its population, climatic and hygienic conditions and all other factors which appear to the Board to be relevant as well as any other special circumstances which such Contracting Party may be at liberty to submit to the Board.

The Board shall notify to all Contracting Parties its conclusion as to the amount so ascertained by it. The Board shall recommend that each Contracting Party other than that Contracting Party the extent of whose import requirements has been ascertained by the Board, shall prohibit the exportation from their respective territories to the territory of that Contracting Party, amounts of substances specified in Article 20–A which, taken in conjunction with other exports thereto, will exceed the amount ascertained as aforesaid by the Board to be the reasonable annual import requirements of such Party. Due consideration shall be given to the recommendation of the Board.

Article 20–F

Each Contracting Party shall make it a penal offense for any person within its jurisdiction to procure or assist the commission, in any place outside its jurisdiction, of any offense against the laws in force in such place for controlling or regulating the manufacture, sale, delivery, distribution, use, possession, export, or import of any of the substances covered by this Convention.

Article 20–G

Each Contracting Party shall forbid the conveyance in any vessel sailing under its flag of any consignment of the substances covered by this Convention,

(*1*) *Unless an export license has been issued in respect of such consignment in accordance with the provisions of this convention and the consignment is accompanied by an official copy of such license;*

(*2*) *To any destination other than the destination mentioned in the license.*

Article 20–H

For the purpose of ensuring the full application and enforcement of the provisions of this Convention in Free Ports and Free Zones, the Contracting Parties undertake to apply in Free Ports and Free Zones situated within their territories the same laws and regulations, and to exercise the same supervision and control in respect of the substances covered by this Convention as in other parts of their territories.

Article 20–I

The Contracting Parties shall enact effective laws and regulations to prohibit the transportation through their territory from a place outside thereof to another place outside thereof, of any of the substances covered by this Convention unless such Contracting Party is advised of the contents and the destination of the consignment.

Article 20–J

The Contracting Parties shall enact effective laws and regulations to prohibit the transshipment within their territories of a consignment of any of the substances covered by this Convention unless such consignment is accompanied by an official copy of the export license issued by the authorities having jurisdiction over the territory from which exported or by an official copy of the import certificate issued by the authorities having jurisdiction over the territory to which destined. The Contracting Parties shall also enact effective laws and regulations to prohibit in the territory of transshipment the diversion of, or attempt to divert, a consignment of any of the substances covered by this Convention to any destination other than that named in the official copy of the export license or import certificate, unless an export license is first obtained from the authorities of the territory where the transshipment occurs.

Article 20–K

The Contracting Parties shall enact effective laws and regulations to prohibit a consignment of any of the substances covered by this Convention which is landed in their territory and placed in a bonded warehouse from being withdrawn from such warehouse for export,

*unless an import certificate issued by the authorities having juris-
diction over the territory to which the consignment is destined, certifying that the importation is approved, is presented to the authorities having jurisdiction over the bonded warehouse.*

*A special certificate shall be issued by the Contracting Parties in
respect of each consignment so withdrawn and shall take the place
of the export license for the purpose of the preceding provisions of
this Convention.*

Article 20–L

*In the case of a geographical area the Government of which is
not a party to this Convention the Contracting Parties undertake
to allow the export to such geographical area of any of the substances covered by this Convention only in such amounts as may be
fixed by the Central Board as being reasonably required for the
medical and scientific needs of such area. The Central Board shall
communicate periodically to all the Parties to this Convention the
amount fixed in respect of each geographical area and the situation
as regards the exports and re-exports thereto.*

Article 20–M

~~The present Convention shall come into force three months after
the date mentioned in the notification by the Government of the
Netherlands, referred to in the last paragraph of the preceding
Article.~~

*This Convention shall come into force between the Contracting
Parties who have ratified it as soon as it has been ratified by four
of the Contracting Parties.*

511.4 A 2/179 : Telegram

The Consul at Geneva (Tuck) to the Secretary of State

GENEVA, *December 4, 1924*—11 a.m.
[Received 12 : 11 p.m.]

From Porter. All the American suggestions except chapter 2 have
been presented and referred to committees. Article 1 was objected
to by India as being outside the call of the conference but on vote
of the conference the objection of India was overruled.

When the agenda of the conference was adopted American delegation reserved the right to move to amend it in case no agreement
or an unsatisfactory agreement was reached by the first conference.
As the first conference has not yet formally concluded its labors
or definitely adopted an agreement the American delegation has

not so far presented its suggestion for the carrying out of chapter 2 of the Hague Convention. I understand however that the first conference has confessed itself unable to set any date for the eventual suppression of the use of prepared opium. I further understand that the British and Japanese have reached an agreement in regard to the transit of opium through Hong Kong.

It seems probable that the second conference will not conclude its labors before the 15th or 20th of December.

Tuck

511.4 A 2/178 : Telegram

The Secretary of State to the Consul at Geneva (Tuck)

Washington, *December 5, 1924—4 p. m.*

Your December 4, 11 A. M. For Porter.

The Department has received an *Aide Memoire* from the British Embassy at Washington dated December 3, reading as follows:

"The American Delegation to the Second Opium Conference which is now proceeding at Geneva have submitted a number of proposals including two which the British Delegate considers to be outside the scope of the Conference.

The object of the Conference is to consider measures to limit— (1) the manufacture of morphine, heroin, cocaine, etc., (2) the amounts of raw opium and coca leaf to be imported for manufacture and for other medicinal and scientific purposes and (3) the production of raw opium and coca leaf for export to the amount required for medicinal and scientific purposes.

The American proposals in question are—(1) that the contracting parties shall control the production and distribution of raw opium so that there will be no surplus available for purposes not strictly medical or scientific; and (2) that the contracting parties, in whose territories the use of prepared opium is temporarily permitted, shall agree to reduce the importation by 10 per cent each year so as to bring the use of opium to an end within 10 years.

Of these proposals the first raises questions of domestic consumption in India and His Majesty's Government fear that unless it is withdrawn a difficult situation will arise. The question will be raised whether the Conference is competent to discuss a matter not specified on the agenda and the decision taken on this point will have a bearing on the second American proposal above referred to.

If the American delegates bring forward their second proposal the course of the proceedings at the Conference will probably be as follows: The Netherlands Delegation will refuse to take part in the discussion and some of the other Powers with Far Eastern territories, if not all, will do the same. The British Delegate will take the line that the matter is outside the scope of the Conference and that it was considered by the first Conference (on the control of opium smoking in the Far East) which reached an agreement as to the further measures to be taken. The position in British territories was then fully set out and, apart from the question as to the competence of the Conference, no useful purpose will be served by re-opening the matter.

The British Delegate will then propose that the Council of the League of Nations should be invited to appoint a small impartial Commission with an American Chairman to visit the territories concerned of all nationalities as well as any other countries, such as China, that may be necessary in order to investigate and report on all relevant facts as affecting further measures of repression. In the opinion of His Majesty's Government this Commission should include no nationals of Powers possessing Far Eastern territories.

His Majesty's Government feel that the adoption of this proposal would disarm criticism in the United States, where British administrative difficulties in the Far East are naturally not widely known, and would also convince public opinion generally that His Majesty's Government neither shirk impartial investigation nor desire to take up an obstructive attitude.

In the circumstances His Majesty's Government hope that the above proposal will be acceptable to the United States Government and that they will be disposed to instruct the American Delegation at Geneva to co-operate with the British Delegate when he puts it forward, with a view to its being carried into effect."

The Department proposes to reply to the British that in view of the conditions set forth in the preamble of the House Joint Resolution approved May 15, 1924, authorizing an appropriation for the participation of this Government in the International Narcotics Conference, and in view of the further fact that the representatives of the United States are not authorized to sign any agreement which does not fulfill the conditions necessary for the suppression of the habit-forming narcotic drug traffic, as set forth in the preamble of the Joint Resolution in question, it finds itself unable to acquiesce in the suggestions made by the British Government as set forth in the *Aide Memoire*. The Department may further suggest to the British that since all the other participating Governments in the Geneva Conference are likewise interested in the questions at issue, it would perhaps be better to have the questions determined by the Conference itself.

The Department is hopeful that no issues will arise at Geneva which will jeopardize the success of the Conference and with that in mind it suggests that you may find it advisable not to rigidly adhere to a fixed term of 10 years within which the importation of raw opium for the purpose of making prepared opium should be discontinued. The Department feels that some flexibility in this period of time might afford an avenue through which a compromise might be reached if the differences foreseen by the British Government, as set forth in its *Aide Memoire*, should arise.

The Department desires your comment on the *Aide Memoire* and the proposed reply.

HUGHES

511.4 A 2/185 : Telegram

The Consul at Geneva (Tuck) to the Secretary of State

GENEVA, *December 8, 1924—4 p. m.*
[Received 11 : 58 a. m.]

From Porter. Your December 4[5], 4 p. m. Department's proposed reply to the British note would materially strengthen our position. I am not disposed to insist upon a 10-year limit for the suppression of the traffic in prepared opium but it seems essential that a time limit of some kind should be placed upon this phase of the general traffic in opium. It is true that conditions in the Far East are different from an administrative point of view but it seems essential that something more definite should be agreed upon than appears from the results of the first conference which makes no provision for progressive suppression. We hope to obtain a definite recognition of the necessity of carrying out chapter 2 of the Hague Convention within some specific time limit. If administrative measures are impossible immediately, they can be promised upon any improvement of the situation in regard to illicit production.

I share the Department's hope that the success of the conference will not be jeopardized and am prepared to accept any reasonable arrangement which would prevent compromise our plan, in spite of the technical objection of jurisdiction which may be raised against bringing up the question of prepared opium in the second conference.

TUCK

511.4 A 2/178

The Department of State to the British Embassy

MEMORANDUM

The Department of State has received the British Embassy's memorandum of December 3, 1924, concerning certain proposals which are to be advanced by the British delegate to the International Narcotics Conference, now sitting at Geneva, on the subject of the domestic consumption of prepared opium in India.

In view of the conditions set forth in the Preamble of the House Joint Resolution approved May 15, 1924, a copy of which is enclosed herewith for the British Embassy's information,[91] authorizing an appropriation for the participation of the United States in the International Narcotics Conference, the Government of the United States finds itself unable to acquiesce in the suggestions communicated by the British Government in the memorandum under ac-

---

[91] Not printed.

knowledgment. It would seem also that, since there are a large number of governments participating in the Geneva Conference, presumably with a divergence of views on the question at issue, it would perhaps be advisable to leave the matter entirely to the determination of the Conference itself.

The Chairman of the American Delegation to the Geneva Conference has been informed that the Department of State entertains the hope that no issues will arise at Geneva which will jeopardize the success of the Conference, and, with that in mind, the Department of State ventures to assure the British Embassy that the Chairman of the American Delegation will accord the utmost consideration to any proposals which may be made by the British delegates at the Conference.

WASHINGTON, *December 12, 1924.*

511.4 A 2/221

The Chairman of the American Delegation (Porter) to the Secretary of State

GENEVA, *December 17, 1924.*
[Received January 2, 1925.]

SIR: Referring to my telegram of this date,[92] I have the honor to enclose a copy of the agreement which was reached by the First Conference, but which has not yet been signed, together with commentaries on this document by Bishop Brent and myself.[93]

I do not feel that this agreement can be considered as a strict compliance with the intent of Chapter II of The Hague Convention, and I am fearful that an acquiescence in its terms on the part of the United States would be construed to mean that we are prepared to accept an interpretation of Chapter II, which will mean an almost indefinite postponement of the period when the use of prepared opium should terminate.

For these reasons I feel that our Government should adopt a determined attitude in this connection. The Japanese have informed me privately that they do not like this agreement and that it represents much less than they are already doing, and that they are prepared to accept and enforce complete prohibition within a definite period of years. The British also were prepared to go much further than the terms of the document indicate, and the Dutch occupy a

---

[92] Not printed.
[93] Enclosures not printed. The copy of the agreement transmitted was the same as the text signed at Geneva, Feb. 11, 1925, by the British Empire (with India), China, France, Japan, the Netherlands, Portugal, and Siam; League of Nations Treaty Series, vol. LI, p. 337.

position, so far as their Far Eastern colonies are concerned, midway between that of the Japanese and British. The document apparently represents all that the French and the Portuguese were prepared to accede to.

The presentation of the American Suggestions under Chapter II of the Convention caused much controversy, particularly among those nations which were represented at the First Conference and who insisted that the questions affecting prepared opium were outside the scope of the present Conference. More than this, they insisted that they had been instructed by their Governments on this point and that they were not prepared to repudiate a convention which they had just completed and which, they stated, they had authority to sign. I brought up the question in plenary session on the 12th, and it was obvious that the parties to the agreement reached at the First Conference were in a hopeless minority, and that they would lose if a vote were taken as to the competence of the Conference to consider the question of prepared opium. Discussion was adjourned to yesterday, when a proposal was laid before the Conference by the President to adjourn until the 12th of January, when the American proposal would be the first item on the program.

In the meantime, when the First Conference agreement was ready for signature the British and French representatives announced that they were not in a position to sign the document, which they have never attempted to justify in public. I am inclined to believe that the agreement will be disavowed and the principles outlined in our own suggestions in regard to Chapter II will be accepted if we insist sufficiently upon our point of view.

In conclusion, I wish to reiterate that the attitude of the South American states represented at the Conference has been consistently friendly, and that they have supported us in every public meeting at which any issue or principle has been at stake. I feel it would be desirable to acknowledge our appreciation through appropriate channels.

I have [etc.] STEPHEN G. PORTER

511.4 A 2/263 : Telegram

The Consul at Geneva (Tuck) to the Secretary of State

GENEVA, *February 1, 1925—4 p. m.*
[Received February 2—7 : 02 a. m.[94]]

From Porter. I do not consider that the conference can reach an agreement satisfactory to us or which will be an improvement over the Hague Convention.

---

[94] Telegram in four sections.

1. A vital part of our program—the limitation of production to medicinal and scientific needs—seems unlikely to be embodied in the convention. However, if inserted in convention little if any useful purpose would be served, as producing countries which are disinclined to assume any further obligations to restrict production have indicated they will record nullifying reservations. Persia has at every opportunity made it clear that production cannot for economic reasons be limited except upon the unique conditions: (a) Loan of 10 million toman for 20 years. No interest charges for first 5 years, thereafter at 5 percent. (b) Moratorium to be granted by foreign countries having claims against Persia during period of transition—that is until substitution of other crops for opium had proven feasible. (c) Removal of restrictions on Persia's liberty of action in tariff questions—that is revision of tariff treaties so as to provide increased [revenue?]. Representatives of Servia and Turkey state that they have received definite instructions not to agree to limit productions but when pressed add that they will ask for further instructions. No change in their instructions has as yet been reported. China, the largest producer, which is admittedly powerless owing to internal chaotic condition to fulfill obligation, has had for some time laws against the cultivation of poppy but they are not nor are they likely soon to be enforced. India refuses to accept the principle and asks that the words "for export" be added. This would not affect the situation so far as other producers are concerned and India now avows strict supervision over exports is maintained. The result of any effort under present conditions to strike at the source of the evil—production of raw material—I regard as negligible.

2. It is proposed that a central board shall be established consisting of seven members to be appointed by representatives of the United States, Germany, France, Great Britain, Italy, Japan and those nations having nonpermanent seats on the Council of the League of Nations from a list upon which each of the signatory parties to the convention may place one name. While not in final form the following provision seems not unlikely to be adopted.

"The Council shall in consultation with the board make the necessary arrangements for the organization and working of the board with the object of assuring the full technical independence of the board in carrying out their duties under the present convention while providing for the control of the staff in administrative matters by the Secretary General.

The Council shall also in consultation with the governments of any contracting parties who are not members of the League take the necessary measures to allocate the expenses of the board among the contracting parties.

The board shall, subject to the approval of the Council, appoint their secretary and staff".

The British delegation is urging the acceptance of the following amendment against which no objections have been raised except our own.

"The Secretary General shall appoint the secretary and staff of the board on the nomination of the board and subject to the approval of the Council".

To the board are to be sent statistics of production, manufacture, consumption, import and export of substances covered by convention. The board shall have the right in case the information at its disposal leads it to conclude that excessive quantities are accumulating in any country to ask for explanations and in the case of no explanations or an unsatisfactory explanation to call the attention of the governments and the Council of the League to the matter and to recommend that no further exports be made to the country in question until the board reports that it is satisfied with the situation [in?] the country concerned and any exporting country has the right to appeal to the Council of the League against any decision of the board. A government not prepared to act on the recommendation shall notify the board; the board may publish a report on the matter and communicate it to the Council which shall forward it to the governments. Any decision by the board with respect to complaints shall be by an absolute majority.

The right of making representations to the board is to be given to any signatory power. The board has been granted certain limited powers to make regulations principally regarding the furnishing of information but it has been impossible to obtain consent that the board be granted power to make sufficient regulations to carry out its duties, it being generally believed that such authority should be exercised jointly by board and Council of the League. The board is so closely connected with the organization of the League of Nations as to make it practically subservient to the Council of the League, as [a?] result which if it will not defeat ratification certainly will provoke a bitter fight in the Senate. In striving to preserve the full independence of the board I have been repeatedly advised that unless the board tied up with the League the object for which the board was created could not be accomplished. Any further attempt to preserve the independence of the board seems futile.

3. There is no prospect of obtaining a control [of] opium and coca-leaf derivatives extensive as that provided by our own legislation. No agreement can be obtained which would immediately include as dangerous drugs any derivative of opium other than those specified in the Hague Conference although coca leaves and ecgonine and possibly Indian hemp may be added. Some additional restrictions are to be placed upon the sale of heroin but no agreement to prevent

manufacture is possible. Machinery for the determination of dangerous drugs under article 14 is proposed.

4. After repeated conferences with the representatives of the interested governments I do not believe that there is any prospect of obtaining more definite assurances regarding the suppression of prepared opium than are contained in the Hague Convention. The British, French and Dutch proposals are in substance that 15 years after the producing countries limit production and prevent smuggling they will abolish the traffic. The time when period shall begin to run is to be determined by Council whose decision shall be final.

While acknowledging their obligations under the Hague Convention they insist that owing to increased production and smuggling they are powerless to take any further measures than those contemplated by agreement concluded by first conference. The well-known disinclination of producing countries to limit production [and?] their seeming inability to stop smuggling do not strengthen the belief that the governments interested in prepared opium are seriously considering suppressing the traffic. On the contrary the acceptance of the proposals offered would in my judgment weaken chapter 2 of the Hague Convention, a result which must be avoided, as the main protection we have against leakage from the ordinary traffic in hundreds of tons of raw and prepared opium is the right to demand suppression of traffic in prepared opium under article 6 of this chapter. It should be mentioned that the central board while entitled to receive statistics regarding prepared opium would be expressly [denied?] the right to question them in any way or to file or receive any complaint against countries engaged in the traffic until the board has found that illicit international transactions are taking place on an appreciable scale. I fear that it would be extremely unwise for any action to be taken which would postpone the date for the suppression of this traffic and which could be regarded as placing it upon a more secure foundation.

5. While statistical information to be given the board represents decided improvement over present situation, this information and the import [and?] export certificate which it is proposed to make of general application can be obtained otherwise than by treaty.

Under all circumstances I am reluctantly forced to the conclusion that it would be inadvisable for the delegation to continue to participate in the conference. Perhaps I have been remiss in not making the recommendation sooner but despite repeated adjournments to which I reluctantly consented I have held on in the hope that some way might be found out of the difficulties encountered. The political aspect of the proposed agreement, the small gain to be hoped for over the control of the traffic and the terms of the resolution of Congress under which the delegation proceeded to Geneva, prompt me respectfully to suggest that the delegation be instructed to withdraw.

I am aware of the seriousness of the steps suggested but I am forced to the conclusion in the light of all the circumstances that perhaps greater stride[s] in the control of the traffic may be hoped for if the United States in accordance with its traditional policy did not through the present agreement associate itself with the League but reserving entirely its freedom of action should stand ever ready to assert its rights under the Hague Convention and if necessary to demand [that?] the obligations there undertaken be promptly and completely performed.

It is of the utmost importance that I receive word by Tuesday noon, Geneva time, as to the course to be followed, as a most important meeting of the conference is scheduled for that day. If you concur I would suggest that owing to faulty news service here an announcement of the reason for withdrawal should be made public in Washington immediately following a telegraphic communication from the delegation advising that withdrawal had actually taken place.

TUCK

511.4 A 2/263 : Telegram

The Secretary of State to the Consul at Geneva (*Tuck*)

WASHINGTON, *February 2, 1925—5 p. m.*

For Porter. If as appears from your telegram of February 1, 4 P. M., you are convinced that there is no possibility the Conference can agree upon a convention satisfactorily carrying out the purposes of the Hague Opium Convention of 1912 and of the Joint Resolution of Congress of May 15 last, the American Delegation is authorized in your discretion to withdraw from the Conference.

Upon receiving word of your withdrawal, the Department will, in pursuance of your suggestion, give out a brief explanatory statement to the following effect:

"This Government has received from the American Delegation to the Opium Conference now in session at Geneva a report to the effect that that Conference cannot be expected to reach an agreement which would be satisfactory to this Government as carrying out the purposes of the Hague Opium Convention of 1912, or acceptable to it as according with the purposes set forth in the Joint Resolution of Congress of May 15 last, which authorized the participation of this Government in the present Conference.

The President has therefore, to his regret, found it necessary to authorize the American Delegation to withdraw from further participation in the Conference at the discretion of its chairman, the Honorable Stephen G. Porter."

It is assumed that in announcing the withdrawal of our Delegation you will make a statement of the reasons for that action substantially as set forth in your telegram though of course with the modifications appropriate to a public statement likely to have reactions upon our relations with other governments and therefore requiring to be drawn up in a way to avoid all unnecessary occasion for irritation. You will please telegraph to the Department as soon as possible the text of your statement.

Hughes

511.4 A 2/271 : Telegram

The Chairman of the American Delegation (Porter) to the Secretary of State

Geneva [undated].
[Received February 6, 1925—10:48 a. m.]

I propose to enclose following in letter to president of conference tomorrow morning. Do not release pending my telegram announcing withdrawal.[95]

"On October 18, 1923, the League of Nations extended an invitation to the powers signatory to the Hague Convention including the United States to participate in an international conference which was called for the purpose of giving effect to the following principles subject to reservations made by certain nations regarding smoking opium.

1. If the purpose of the Hague Opium Convention is to be achieved according to its spirit and true intent it must be recognized that the use of opium products for other than medical and scientific purpose is an abuse and not legitimate.

2. In order to prevent the abuse of these products it is necessary to exercise the control of the production of raw opium in such a manner that there will be no surplus available for nonmedical and nonscientific purpose. The joint resolution adopted by the Congress of the United States May 15, 1924, authorizing our participation in the present conference, quoted the principles referred to in the preamble and expressly stipulated that the representatives of the United States shall sign no agreement which does not fulfill the conditions necessary for the suppression of the narcotic drug traffic as set forth in the preamble. Despite more than 2 months of discussion and repeated adjournments it now clearly appears that the purpose for which the conference was called cannot be accomplished.

[95] An undated telegram from Mr. Porter received Feb. 6, 6:44 a. m., stated that the letter of withdrawal had been presented at 10:35 Geneva time (file no. 511.4 A 2/270).

The reports of the various committees of the conference plainly indicate that there is no likelihood under present conditions that the production of raw opium and coca leaves will be restricted to the medicinal and scientific needs of the world. In fact the nature of the reservations made show[s] that no appreciable reduction in raw opium may be expected. It was hoped that if the nations in whose territories the use of smoking opium is temporarily permitted would, in pursuance of the obligation undertaken under chapter 2 of the Hague Convention, adopt measures restricting the importation of raw opium for the manufacture of smoking opium or would agree to suppress the traffic within a definite period, such action would materially reduce the market for raw opium and an extensive limitation of production would inevitably follow. Unfortunately however these nations with the exception of Japan are not prepared to reduce the consumption of smoking opium. Unless the producing nations agree to reduce production and prevent smuggling from their territories, and then only in the event of an adequate guarantee being given that the obligations undertaken by the producing nations would be effectively and promptly fulfilled, no restriction of the production of raw opium under such conditions can be expected. In the matter of manufactured drugs and the control of transportation an improvement over the Hague Convention is noticeable. There is however no likelihood of obtaining a complete control of all opium and coca-leaf derivatives irrespective of the measure of control provided. For manufactured drugs it is believed that by reason of the very small bulk, the ease of transportation with minimum risk of detection, and the large financial gains to be obtained from their illicit handling such drugs and their derivatives can only be effectively controlled if the production of the raw opium and coca leaves from which they are obtained is strictly limited to medical and scientific purposes. This the conference is unable to accomplish. In the circumstances the delegation of the United States in pursuance of instructions received from its Government has no alternative under terms of the joint resolution authorizing participation in the conference other than to withdraw, as it could not sign the agreement which it is proposed to conclude. We desire to make it clear that withdrawal from the present conference does not mean that the United States will cease its efforts through international cooperation for the suppression of the illicit traffic in opium and other dangerous drugs. The United States recognizes that the world-wide traffic in habit-forming drugs can be suppressed only by international cooperation but believes that for the present at least greater strides in the control of the traffic may be hoped for if it should continue to work towards this end upon the basis of the Hague Convention of 1912".

PORTER

REFUSAL BY THE UNITED STATES TO JOIN OTHER CREDITOR NATIONS IN FORMING AN INTERNATIONAL COMMISSION TO LIQUIDATE RELIEF LOANS MADE TO CERTAIN EUROPEAN STATES

551.A1a/8

The French Chargé (Laboulaye) to the Secretary of State

[Translation [96]]

WASHINGTON, *September 26, 1923.*

[Received September 28.]

MR. SECRETARY OF STATE: As Your Excellency knows, an international committee was appointed in Paris in 1920 to settle the question of the credits needed by certain countries such as Austria, Hungary, Poland, Rumania, Czechoslovakia, the Baltic and the Caucasian states, to insure their economic recuperation. The United States of America, England, Denmark, Norway, the Netherlands, Sweden, and Switzerland gave their assistance to this undertaking in various forms.[97]

In October 1921, on the eve of adjourning, the International Commission on "Relief Credits" had offered the advice that a coordinating agency should be maintained between the lending and borrowing countries. The French Government, for its part, thought that in accordance with the suggestions of several members of the Commission, Mr. de Haller, former president of the Swiss National Bank and a delegate to the conference, was particularly well qualified to take that part of intermediary or "trustee", but it does not seem that any action was ever taken on the suggestion. The fact that there is no special appropriation to compensate even in a meager way the person who would take charge of those duties, obviously adds to the difficulties that the question carries.

However, considering the propositions that have been received separately by a number of the lending states from certain borrowing states in the last few months, with a view either to determining how the payment of their debts should be made or to obtaining postponements, and owing, on the other hand, to the difficulties and delays which unavoidably spring from the exchange of correspondence between the several governments concerned, the Government of the Republic deems it more and more indispensable, if a practical solution is to be reached, to create a centralizing organ which would

---

[96] File translation revised.
[97] See "Relief in Central Europe," *Foreign Relations,* 1920, vol. I, pp. 235 ff.

coordinate the steps taken toward the settlement of the claims flowing from the relief credits.

Among these several institutions now in existence capable of performing the task above referred to, the financial committee of the League of Nations would appear, in my Government's opinion, to be particularly well fitted for its successful accomplishment. It would, however, have no objection to offer to having such an organization as the Control Committee of the Austrian Loan, for instance, charged with the same duties, but it may be remarked in this connection that in order to perform its duties with greater judgment it would be advisable for such a committee to have among its members the largest possible number of representatives of the borrowing as well as the lending states.

The question as to who will assume the comparatively simple part of the contemplated intermediary is besides of minor importance. So the French Government is ready to concur in any other suggestion which would make it possible to apply the principle laid down in 1921 by the International Conference on Relief Credits.

In making the foregoing suggestions known to Your Excellency I should be much obliged to you if you would kindly let me know as soon as you can the views of the Government of the United States on this question.

Be pleased to accept [etc.]   André de Laboulaye

551.A1a/9

The Secretary of State to the French Ambassador (Jusserand)

Washington, *December 14, 1923.*

Excellency: I have the honor to refer to the note addressed to me on September 26, 1923, by M. de Laboulaye and to inform Your Excellency that careful consideration has been given to the request contained therein for an expression of the views of the Government of the United States respecting the desirability of establishing a coordinating agency, to deal with questions arising out of the relief credits advanced by the United States and other governments to certain European countries. I desire also to acknowledge the receipt of your communication of November 30, 1923, bearing on the same subject.[98]

While this Government was happy to cooperate with the other interested governments with a view to providing the necessary credits for the purchase of the relief supplies which were so urgently needed in order to facilitate the prompt and practical solution of

---

[98] Not printed.

the pressing relief problems arising in Europe after the conclusion
of the war, it has never been the opinion of the Government of the
United States that it would be necessary to establish any international agency for the settlement of questions arising out of its advances to foreign governments for the purpose of relief or for other
purposes, as this Government has believed and still believes that
any questions that may arise in this regard are susceptible of adjustment through existing channels. As the French Government
has already been informed, the World War Foreign Debt Commission was created by act of the Congress to negotiate with respect to
the debts owed to the United States Government by foreign Governments,[99] and under existing legislation that Commission could
not undertake to execute its authority through any international
agency.

I regret, therefore, to have to inform Your Excellency that the
Government of the United States finds itself unable to acquiesce in
the suggestion that an international agency be created to deal with
questions arising out of these relief credits and that the United
States participate in such an agency.

Accept [etc.]   CHARLES E. HUGHES

551.A1a/11

The British Chargé (Chilton) to the Secretary of State

No. 129   WASHINGTON, *February 9, 1924.*

SIR: I have the honour to inform you that His Majesty's Government, in conjunction with the French Government, have lately had
under consideration the advisability of setting up some centralizing
organ to deal with questions arising out of the liquidation of the
Relief Credits granted in 1920 and 1921 by certain Allied and Neutral Governments to other Governments in Central and Eastern
Europe, and to transmit to you herewith, for facility of reference, a
memorandum explaining the steps taken to furnish these credits to the
countries concerned. The French Government, while favouring the
utilisation of the Financial Committee of the League of Nations for
the purpose of dealing with the questions referred to above, has declared that it would have no difficulty in agreeing to any other suggestion embodying the same principle.

His Majesty's Government entirely share the view of the French
Government that the interests of the creditor states will best be
served, when the date for repayment of the advances approaches, by
acting in unison and dealing with individual debtor states according

[90] *Foreign Relations,* 1922, vol. I, p. 396.

to the circumstances of each. At the same time, they doubt whether the Financial Committee of the League of Nations would be a suitable body to deal with these credits, even if it were willing to undertake the work. The Committee is a purely advisory body, with no administrative functions; and it is neither intended nor suited for carrying out routine administration demanding constant attention.

A further disadvantage is that its members do not correspond in nationality with all the creditor countries concerned and include at least one member of a debtor nationality. Moreover, the members do not represent the governments of their countries, and have always regarded themselves as entirely independent experts. It appears essential that where decisions with regard to government advances have to be taken, the deciding body must be strictly representative of the governments concerned.

His Majesty's Government have therefore suggested that the best course would be for a Relief Credits Committee to be formed, which might meet in London, to whom all applications by debtor governments with regard to their liabilities under the Relief Credits should be referred. The committee would consist of the representatives of the credit-giving governments and would be furnished by those governments with full particulars of the present position of such credits. It would probably be sufficient for the committee to meet occasionally, and it might possibly be formed in the main from representatives already in London.

The Committee (after settling its procedure) would naturally be chiefly concerned with the arrangements to be made with the debtor countries in view of the maturity of a considerable portion of the original bonds on the 1st of January, 1925.

All proposals received by any creditor Government as regards the relief credits would, of course, be referred to the committee, who would be in a position to undertake oral discussions with representatives of each debtor country.

The Committee could also consider whether there would be any advantage in appointing a Trustee as suggested in 1921, though there would seem to be little need for this proposal at this stage.

While His Majesty's Government suggest that the Committee should consist primarily of the European credit-giving countries, they would naturally welcome the presence of an American representative and, inasmuch as they are aware that, under the United States laws, only the Debt Funding Commission can deal with American Credits, I am instructed to express the hope that, in the event of the United States Government being willing to share in the work of the Committee, a representative of the Debt Funding Commission might be delegated to attend the meetings of the Committee in London. I should be glad to receive in due course an expression of the views of the United States Government in regard to this matter for communication to my Government.

I have the honour to add that His Majesty's representatives at Christiania and the Hague have been instructed to bring these proposals to the notice of the Norwegian and Netherlands Governments.

I have [etc.] H. G. CHILTON

[Enclosure]

Memorandum on Relief Credits

The Relief Credits grew out of the Relief Missions organised in 1919 under the Supreme Economic Council, the successor to the short-lived Supreme Council of Supply and Relief. These two bodies had been the result of negotiations for the formation of some allied organization for the prevention of starvation and disorder in Central, Eastern and Southern Europe. The principal contributors to the Relief thus administered were the United States, Great Britain, (with Canada and Newfoundland) France and Italy. By the end of 1919 it had become evident that in order to cope with the economic needs of Eastern and Southern Europe it was urgently necessary to substitute for "Relief" some comprehensive form of credits in order to remedy the situation in those regions. "To continue to provide food without at the same time providing raw materials on which to re-establish industry would merely be to aggravate the problem of Europe". It seemed improbable that any group of American, French, Italian or British bankers, would make a long-term contract with governments whose political existence and whose assets and liabilities were from day to day of doubtful duration. There was therefore little likelihood of credits being provided on a scale and on terms likely to be effective unless the allied and associated governments and also the neutral governments intervened with some scheme to minimise the political risk preventing the introduction of private foreign capital into such countries.

Negotiations with this in view accordingly took place with the result that the International Committee for Relief Credits was set up in Paris in April 1920. It consisted of representatives of Argentine, Belgium, Canada, (unofficial), Denmark, France, Italy, Netherlands, Norway, Sweden, Switzerland, United Kingdom and United States, (unofficial). The object of the committee was to administer, in consultation with the representatives of the debtor countries, the relief and reconstruction credits which had been granted by the governments of some of the above-mentioned creditor countries and to arrange for new credits.

Each lending country reserved complete liberty as to the country to which its credits should be extended but agreed to accept a common form of bond as security. In the case of Austria-Hungary these bonds were accorded priority over reparation payments, this having been a condition as to participation made by several neutral governments.

This committee sat until the winter of 1921, when it was dissolved. It had during that time arranged for credits for Poland, Czecho-Slovakia, Hungary, Servia, Roumania, Baltic States, Armenia and Austria. The United States of America advanced the largest sum— approximately £63,000,000, the United Kingdom coming next with £17,000,000, followed by Italy and France with £4¾ millions and £3½ millions respectively. After them the two most substantial creditors are Holland and Norway. These sums do not include the relief advances made prior to the beginning of 1920.

551.A1a/11

The Secretary of State to the British Ambassador (Howard)

WASHINGTON, *March 13, 1924.*

EXCELLENCY: I have the honor to acknowledge the receipt of Mr. Chilton's note of February 9, 1924, stating that His Majesty's Government, in conjunction with the French Government, have lately had under consideration the advisability of setting up some centralizing organ to deal with questions arising out of the liquidation of the relief credits granted in 1920 and 1921, by certain allied and neutral Governments to other Governments in central and eastern Europe.

While the Government of the United States was happy to cooperate with the other interested Governments with a view to providing the necessary credits for the purchase of the relief supplies which were so urgently needed in order to facilitate the prompt and practical solution of the pressing relief problems arising in Europe after the conclusion of the war, it has never been the opinion of this Government that it would be necessary to establish any international agency for the settlement of questions arising out of its advances to foreign Governments for the purposes of relief as this Government has believed and still believes that any questions that may arise in this regard are susceptible of adjustment through existing channels. Furthermore, as pointed out in your note under acknowledgment, under existing legislation the World War Foreign Debt Commission alone is competent to deal with the question of refunding the indebtedness of other Governments to the Government of the United States, and that Commission has no authority to execute its powers through any international agency.

It is the understanding of the Government of the United States, however, that your Government is suggesting not that an international agency with plenary powers be established for the purpose of settling questions arising out of the liquidation of the above mentioned relief credits, but that a committee be appointed for ancillary purposes only.

I have noted the suggestion of your Government that the committee should consist primarily of the European credit-giving countries, but that they would welcome the presence of an American representative, and that in the event that the Government of the United States were willing to share in the work of the committee, a representative of the World War Foreign Debt Commission might be delegated to attend the meetings of the committee.

This suggestion has been transmitted to the Chairman of the World War Foreign Debt Commission and upon the receipt of a reply from him, I shall take pleasure in communicating with you further on this subject.

Accept [etc.]   CHARLES E. HUGHES

551.A1a/15

The British Ambassador (Howard) to the Secretary of State

No. 396

His Britannic Majesty's Ambassador presents his compliments to the Secretary of State, and with reference to Mr. Hughes' note of March 13th last, regarding the proposal to set up a centralizing organ to deal with questions arising out of the liquidation of relief credits granted by certain allied and neutral Governments to other Governments in Central and Eastern Europe, has the honour to request that he may be informed whether it is yet possible to furnish an expression of the views of the United States Government on the question of delegating a representative of the Debt Funding Commission to attend the meetings of the Relief Credits Committee to be formed in this connection.

WASHINGTON, *May 3, 1924.*

551.A1a/15

The Secretary of State to the British Ambassador (Howard)

WASHINGTON, *June 3, 1924.*

EXCELLENCY: I have the honor to acknowledge the receipt of your note of May 3, 1924, in which you refer to this Department's reply of March 13, 1924, to Mr. Chilton's note of February 9, 1924, regarding the establishment of a centralizing organ to deal with questions arising out of the liquidation of relief credits granted by certain

Allied and Neutral Governments to other Governments in central and eastern Europe and possible participation therein by a representative of the World War Foreign Debt Commission.

Appropriate inquiries have been made in connection with the proposal of His Majesty's Government and it has been found that it would be impracticable to have a representative of the World War Foreign Debt Commission attend the meetings of the proposed committee. I take pleasure in advising you, however, that if the committee in question should be constituted, the American Ambassador at London will be instructed to keep in close touch with its work. I should be pleased, therefore, to be informed as to the decision that may be finally taken regarding the creation of such a committee and the time and place of its meetings.

Accept [etc.]   CHARLES E. HUGHES

551.A1a/10

The Secretary of State to the Ambassador in Great Britain (Kellogg)

No. 236   WASHINGTON, *June 17, 1924.*

SIR: The Department transmits herewith for your information a copy of each of the following documents regarding a proposal that an Interallied Agency be constituted to deal with questions arising out of the relief credits extended to certain European governments:[1]

1. Translation of note dated September 26, 1923, from the French Chargé at Washington.
2. Translation of note dated November 30, 1923, from the French Ambassador at Washington.
3. Department's note dated December 14, 1923, to the French Ambassador at Washington.
4. Note dated February 9, 1924, from the British Chargé at Washington, and the memorandum transmitted therewith.
5. Department's note dated March 13, 1924, to the British Ambassador at Washington.
6. Department's note dated June 3, 1924, to the British Ambassador at Washington.

As you will observe, the Department's note of June 3, 1924, to the British Ambassador states that "if the committee in question should be constituted, the American Ambassador at London will be instructed to keep in close touch with its work." The Department feels that it is highly important that this Government be kept closely and fully informed of the proceedings of the proposed committee. The United States is a large creditor on account of the relief loans

---

[1] All the documents listed, except the French Ambassador's note of Nov. 30, 1923, are printed *supra.*

in question and is entitled to as favorable treatment, both as to payment of interest and of principal, as any other creditor government. In several instances, however, debtor governments have made payments to other creditor governments on account of these relief loans without making corresponding payments to the United States. When attention has been called to this discrimination the reply has been made that the omission was an oversight, or that the amounts due to the United States were so much greater than those due to other governments that it was impossible for the debtor governments to pay them under existing conditions.

The Department does not desire that the activities of the proposed committee should in any way result in prejudicing the position of the United States. The Department will advise you promptly of any further information received on this subject from the British Government, and in the meantime you are requested to telegraph any significant developments in connection with the proposed committee which may come to your notice in London.

I am [etc.] CHARLES E. HUGHES

551.A1a/22 : Telegram

The Acting Secretary of State to the Ambassador in Great Britain (Kellogg)

WASHINGTON, *July 18, 1924—7 p. m.*

226. Department's 171, June 21, 2 p. m.,[2] regarding relief credits committee.

Meeting of Committee postponed to July 29. Please have representative attend at that time.

GREW

NEGOTIATIONS ON BEHALF OF THE WORLD WAR FOREIGN DEBT COMMISSION FOR THE SETTLEMENT OF DEBTS OWED THE UNITED STATES BY FOREIGN GOVERNMENTS[3]

800.51 W 89 Lithuania/23

The Lithuanian Chargé (Bizauskas) to the Secretary of State

WASHINGTON, *May 1, 1924.*

SIR: I have the honor to inform you that I have been telegraphically instructed by my Government to communicate to you that I am authorized by my Government to enter into negotiations with the

---

[2] Not printed.
[3] Continued from *Foreign Relations*, 1923, vol. I, pp. 272–277.

Government of the United States with regard to the settlement of the indebtedness of Lithuania to the United States.

I should be very grateful if you will cause this to be communicated to the World War Foreign Debt Commission.

Please accept [etc.]   K. BIZAUSKAS

800.51 W 89 Lithuania/23

The Secretary of State to the Lithuanian Chargé (Bizauskas)

WASHINGTON, *May 12, 1924.*

SIR: I have the honor to acknowledge the receipt of your note of May 1, 1924, stating that you have been authorized by your Government to enter into negotiations with the Government of the United States with regard to the settlement of the indebtedness of Lithuania to the United States and requesting that this information be communicated to the World War Foreign Debt Commission.

I take pleasure in informing you that the substance of your note under acknowledgment has been communicated to the Honorable A. W. Mellon, Secretary of the Treasury and Chairman of the World War Foreign Debt Commission, with whom it will be proper for you to enter into direct negotiations.

Accept [etc.]

For the Secretary of State:
LELAND HARRISON

800.51 W 89 Lithuania/26 : Telegram

The Minister in Estonia, Latvia, and Lithuania (Coleman) to the Secretary of State

RIGA, *July 30, 1924—3 p. m.*
[Received 3 : 15 p. m.]

118. *In re* Lithuanian debt to the United States, Lithuanian Government inquires whether the United States Government would protest the ratification by the Lithuanian Assembly of the trade agreement with Germany which provides for the mutual cancelation of all claims arising out of the war, the German occupation, reparations and *post-bellum* supplies, etc. Agreement now before the Assembly. Prompt reply desired.

COLEMAN

800.51 W 89 Lithuania/26 : Telegram

The Acting Secretary of State to the Minister in Estonia, Latvia, and Lithuania (Coleman)

WASHINGTON, *August 8, 1924—4 p.m.*

38. Your 118, July 30, 3 p. m. Please hand to the appropriate Lithuanian official the following memorandum:

"The American Minister to Lithuania did not fail promptly to communicate to the Government of the United States the inquiry of the Lithuanian Government whether the Government of the United States would protest the ratification by the Lithuanian Assembly of the trade agreement with Germany now before the Assembly which provides for the mutual cancellation of all claims arising out of the war, the German occupation, reparations, and *post-bellum* supplies etc. The Minister has now been advised that neither the Treasury nor the World War Foreign Debt Commission has authority to consent to a release of the securities provided for in Lithuania's obligations held by the Government of the United States except in connection with a refunding of the indebtedness of the Lithuanian Government under existing American legislation. The Government of the United States is gratified that the Lithuanian Minister at Washington has been instructed by his Government to inform the World War Foreign Debt Commission that it is ready and willing, subject to ratification by the Assembly of Lithuania, to enter into an agreement providing for the refunding of its indebtedness to the United States upon terms similar to those set forth in the agreement previously concluded by the Government of the United States with the Government of Finland, and the Minister of the United States is authorized to state that, if assurance be given that such an agreement will in fact be concluded, the Government of the United States would not be disposed to raise any objection to the ratification of the proposed agreement with Germany."

[Paraphrase.] The following is for your information: In view of the provision that Lithuania's obligations shall be entitled to security of and shall be charge upon any payments or property received from Germany or from its allies by way of reparation or cession equally with all other notes which represent similar advances to Lithuania since the Armistice by other Allied and Associated Powers, the Treasury thinks that the suggested ratification of the trade agreement with Germany seems to release the security definitely provided for these obligations. In view, moreover, of the theory advanced informally by Mr. Narushkevich that payments were to be made the United States only from reparations received by Lithuania, a theory which has not, as far as the Department is aware, been discarded by Lithuania, although it is wholly inacceptable to the Government of the United States, it is obvious that should the Lithuanian Government adopt this view as its position the ratification of the proposed agreement with Germany would preclude the possibility of recovery by the United States upon obligation in question. The release of this security, furthermore, by the United States seems all the more inappropriate if any payments have been made to the British Government on obligations similar to those held by this Government unless it is understood definitely that Lithuania's indebtedness to the United States be refunded at once.

Department observes from your despatch no. 1540, December 7, 1923,[4] that you expected to inform Mr. Narushkevich of the views of this Government in the matter but the Department does not have a record that you have yet done so. The Department presumes, however, that you did, and that the Lithuanian Government is fully aware of the views of this Government in the matter as stated in the Department's instruction no. 78, November 7, 1923,[5] and concurs in them. If you have not taken up this matter, consult Department before taking action in regard to it. [End paraphrase.]

GREW

800.51 W 89 Latvia/25 : Telegram

The Secretary of State to the Minister in Estonia, Latvia, and Lithuania (Coleman)

[Paraphrase]

WASHINGTON, *September 11, 1924—4 p. m.*

43. The Debt Commission has informed Department that several of the Governments indebted to the United States have, in the course of negotiations for refunding, requested inclusion of a most-favored-nation clause in one form or another, but that to date the Commission has denied all requests of this sort. This statement is for your confidential guidance in any conversations you may have with Latvian officials on Latvia's indebtedness to the United States.

Please advise Department promptly of any developments in regard to designation of representative by Latvia to negotiate with Debt Commission.

HUGHES

---

[4] *Foreign Relations*, 1923, vol. I, p. 277.
[5] *Ibid.*, p. 276.

800.51 W 89 Latvia/31 : Telegram

The Chargé in Estonia, Latvia, and Lithuania (White) to the Secretary of State

[Paraphrase]

RIGA, *November 20, 1924—noon.*
[Received 1:24 p. m.]

183. Minister of Finance has informed me that the Cabinet of Ministers has decided to inaugurate funding negotiations through the Latvian consul at New York.[6]

WHITE

868.51 Refugee Loan, 1924/48 : Telegram

The Secretary of State to the Minister in Greece (Laughlin)

[Paraphrase]

WASHINGTON, *December 6, 1924—3 p. m.*

88. Department informed by Guaranty Trust Company of New York that it has been approached by certain London banks on matter of participating to extent of $10,000,000 to $15,000,000 in loan of £12,500,000, the flotation of which is projected for the Refugee Settlement Commission.[7] Banker's inquiry as to Department's attitude was pursuant to course usually followed in accordance with Department's statement of March 3, 1922;[8] Department replied that in light of information before it no objection was offered to the flotation of this amount of Greek refugee loan in the American market.[9] Department has not been informed whether Guaranty Trust Company has decided to proceed with the matter and has requested that for time being its possible participation be not divulged.[10]

In view of humanitarian interests involved, Department did not condition its prompt and favorable reply to the company's inquiry upon action to be taken by Greece to regulate any of the outstanding

---

[6] Minister Coleman informed the Department by despatch of Jan. 28, 1925, that Mr. Ringold Kalning, formerly Latvian Minister of Finance, would proceed to the United States as Commissioner to assist the consul in the funding negotiations (file no. 800.51 W 89 Latvia/36).

[7] Letter from Guaranty Trust Co. not printed. For other correspondence concerning the Greek Refugee Loan, see vol. II, pp. 282 ff.

[8] *Foreign Relations*, 1922, vol. I, p. 557.

[9] Department's reply not printed.

[10] On Dec. 13 the Department informed Minister Laughlin that the Guaranty Trust Co. had turned the negotiations for the issue in the United States of the proposed loan over to Speyer & Co., New York City (file no. 868.51 Refugee Loan, 1924/53).

questions between Greece and the United States, including question of Greek financial obligations to this Government. Nor did this Government make its consent to the pledging by Greece of fresh security for an external loan contingent to the performance of any act by Greece herself. Not only in dealing with these questions but in regard to all matters which have in any way been related to the amelioration of the refugee problem, the Government of the United States has acted with marked consideration towards Greece.

Department thinks it would be only proper and right, therefore, that Greece on her part show a spirit of willingness to settle the few questions of importance between the two countries, especially at the present time when it is planned that a Greek loan be floated in the American market. The outstanding questions are:

(1) The exchange of notes in regard to most-favored-nation treatment.[11]

(2) The loan agreement of 1918.[12]

(3) Funding of the Greek indebtedness to the United States.

The Government of the United States does not think that it is under any further obligation to make advances to the Hellenic Government under the agreement of 1918, and feels that in candor and fairness to that Government it should be informed of this view. If Greece will make satisfactory arrangements for the funding of the Greek debt to this country, the Treasury will be willing to recommend that Greece be relieved of the obligation to obtain consent of the United States to the pledging of any new security for external loans. A helpful effect upon the position of Greek securities in the American market would undoubtedly follow the prompt announcement of Greece's intention to initiate the negotiations referred to. In view, furthermore, of the Greek–Canadian Agreement[13] and the interest which Greece is paying to Canada, it seems only just and proper that action should be taken at an early date to regulate Greek indebtedness to this Government.

In the Department's opinion any attempt by the Hellenic Government to insist upon further advances under the agreement of 1918, in the light of the agreement made with Canada in 1923 as well as for other reasons, would be unjustified, and, in the light of present circumstances, would necessarily be met by the statement that in the agreement between Greece and Canada the former Government appears to have violated the agreement of 1918 and that the Government of the United States is under no obligation to make further advances.

---

[11] See vol. II, p. 273.
[12] See *Greek Debt Settlement:* Hearings before the House Committee on Ways and Means, 70th Cong., 1st sess., on H. R. 10760 (Washington, Government Printing Office, 1928).
[13] See *ibid.*, p. 56.

Department desires you to broach this whole matter promptly to the Hellenic Government through informal conversations, unless you feel that the present moment is not favorable, with the object of effecting an early settlement of the three questions listed above. To the extent that you deem wise under the circumstances you may make use of the foregoing in your conversations, refraining, however, from referring to the Guaranty Trust Company by name.

You are to telegraph Department should situation arise in which a written communication to the Hellenic Government appears to be desirable in your opinion, or if further instructions are needed.

HUGHES

868.51 War Credits/461 : Telegram

The Minister in Greece (Laughlin) to the Secretary of State

ATHENS, December 15, 1924—10 p. m.
[Received December 16—12 : 32 a. m.]

116. Your 88, December 6, 3 p. m., and 93, December 13, 8 p. m.,[14] both confidential. As I was already engaged upon the most pressing item of the former instruction before it reached me I thought it wise to exercise the discretion allowed me and delayed further conversations until today when I communicated to Roussos orally the substance of the whole instruction.

He replied that his Government felt the deepest gratitude for the humanitarian disposition you had shown toward Greece but that he was unable to renounce Greek claims to the remainder of the 1918 credits. He did not consider that the Canadian agreement affected these claims as it covered materials purchased in Canada.

He said that he wished to go to Washington to discuss the question of the credits and that he would start early in January; meanwhile, he has authorized me to announce to you for publication Greece's intention to take up the regulation of the funding of Greek debts to the United States which he would discuss with you at the same time.

[Paraphrase.] He told me that in urging the reopening of the credits he would propose that no money be turned over to Greece, but that entire balance be used to pay for public works that would be executed by American firms; these works would include the reclamation of large areas of land near Saloniki, which must be drained in order to protect refugee colonies and population there from malaria. [End paraphrase.]

LAUGHLIN

---

[14] Latter not printed.

868.51 War Credits/461 : Telegram

The Secretary of State to the Minister in Greece (*Laughlin*)

WASHINGTON, *December 31, 1924—5 p. m.*

99. Your 116, December 15, 10 p. m. This Government is unable to perceive that the fact that Greece expended in Canada the proceeds of the loan refunded by the Greek-Canadian Agreement of December, 1923, in any way affects the situation. Under the refunding agreement Greece pledged additional revenues for the service of an external loan without obtaining the consent of the United States, as required by the 1918 agreement. This appears to be a substantial breach of the latter's agreement and even in the absence of other considerations it would seem to follow that the United States is relieved from further obligation in the matter.

While this Government would be glad to receive Mr. Roussos or any other representative of the Greek Government duly authorized to negotiate with the World War Foreign Debt Commission for the funding or other settlement of the debt of Greece to the United States, the Department feels that the Greek Government should be aware of the fact that, in the light of this Government's view that the 1918 Loan Agreement has been violated, this Government considers that discussion in Washington with a representative of the Greek Government with respect to the making of further advances under this Agreement would serve no useful purpose.

The use of the proceeds of further advances for the purposes indicated by Mr. Roussos instead of those contemplated under the original agreement would not change the position of this Government in the matter.

You may convey the foregoing informally and orally to Mr. Roussos so that in connection with his contemplated visit he may be under no misapprehension as to the views of this Government.

HUGHES

AGREEMENT BETWEEN THE UNITED STATES AND AUSTRIA AND HUNGARY FOR THE ESTABLISHMENT OF A CLAIMS COMMISSION, SIGNED NOVEMBER 26, 1924

463.11 W 891/12

The Secretary of State to the Minister in Austria (*Washburn*)

No. 610   WASHINGTON, *February 1, 1924.*

SIR: As you are aware, the treaty to establish friendly relations between the United States and Austria, signed at Vienna, August 24, 1921,[15] and the treaty between the United States and Hungary, signed at Budapest on August 29, 1921,[16] contemplate the concluding of agreements for the satisfaction of claims of the United States and its nationals against the Austro-Hungarian Government or its successors. You reported in your telegram, No. 45 of December 14, 1923, 6 P. M.,[17] that the Austrian Minister for Foreign Affairs had no objection to the early conclusion of an agreement providing for the settlement of claims. The Hungarian Government has indicated its willingness to negotiate such an agreement.

There is enclosed herewith draft of a proposed tripartite agreement [17] in which it is proposed to make what the Government of the United States regards as suitable provisions for the determination of the amounts to be paid by Austria and Hungary in satisfaction of their obligations under the treaties concluded by the United States with Austria on August 24, 1921, and with Hungary on August 29, 1921. The draft agreement, as you will observe, is similar in purport to the agreement concluded August 10, 1922, between the United States and Germany.[18] It differs from the agreement with Germany mainly in that it is to be signed by representatives of three governments instead of two, and that it provides that the obligations of Austria and Hungary shall be determined by one commissioner instead of two commissioners and an umpire, as provided by the agreement between the United States and Germany.

It is deemed desirable to have any agreement which provides means for determining the obligations of Austria and Hungary under the treaties establishing friendly relations between the United States and those countries, signed by representatives of both Austria and Hungary as well as the United States, for the reason that many claims of American citizens which have been filed and which are in prospect arose out of acts of the former Austro-Hungarian Government for which, as successors to the Austro-Hungarian Government and by applicable treaty provisions, Austria and Hungary assumed responsibility. Both Austria and Hungary are, therefore, interested in any agreement which provides means of determining their respective obligations under the treaties to the United States and its nationals.

The Government of the United States considers that the purposes of the agreement could be accomplished with greater expedition and with less expense if provision were made for a single commissioner instead of two commissioners and an umpire for which provision was made in the agreement with Germany. Such a commissioner would perform the judicial functions of an arbitrator in behalf of the several litigants.

---

[15] *Foreign Relations,* 1921, vol. I, p. 274.
[16] *Ibid.,* vol. II, p. 255.
[17] Not printed.
[18] *Foreign Relations,* 1922, vol. II, p. 262.

At the time the agreement between the United States and Germany was signed, the German Chancellor addressed to the American Ambassador at Berlin, a note requesting that the President of the United States designate a suitable American to act as umpire.[19] The two governments selected the Honorable William R. Day, formerly an Associate Justice of the United States, as umpire and upon his retirement, the Honorable Edwin B. Parker was selected in the same manner to serve as umpire. The Government of the United States understands that the manner in which Judge Parker has performed the duties of umpire is a source of satisfaction to the Government of Germany no less than to the Government of the United States. It has occurred to me, therefore, that possibly the Government of Austria and the Government of Hungary might agree to the selection of Judge Parker as sole commissioner or arbitrator to determine the obligations of Austria and of Hungary to the United States and its nationals under the treaties establishing friendly relations and under the proposed agreement.

You will please communicate with the Foreign Office in the sense of the foregoing, expressing the hope that the plan proposed by the Government of the United States for the determination of the obligations of the Governments of Austria and of Hungary under the treaties establishing friendly relations will commend itself to the Austrian Government. It is desired that you endeavor to obtain a reply from the Austrian Government as promptly as possible, and that you advise the Department by telegraph of developments. It is desired to have the agreement concluded at an early date in order that the appropriation to carry out the provisions of the agreement may be obtained before the adjournment of Congress. It is the view of the Department that the agreement should be signed in Washington where the representatives of the three Governments can be conveniently assembled.

Similar instructions have been sent to the Legation at Budapest.[20] I am [etc.]

For the Secretary of State:

WILLIAM PHILLIPS

463.11 W 891/13 : Telegram

The Minister in Austria (Washburn) to the Secretary of State

VIENNA, *February 23, 1924*—2 p. m.
[Received February 24—6 : 35 p. m.]

7. Department's instruction no. 610, February 1st, received yesterday. Had a conference during the day with Dr. Schüller who is

---

[19] See telegram no. 159, Aug. 7, 1922, from the Ambassador in Germany, *Foreign Relations*, 1922, vol. II, p. 259.
[20] Department's no. 833, Feb. 1, 1924 ; not printed.

charged with negotiations. As a matter of first impressions, I think there will be no objection to tripartite agreement to be signed at Washington and I believe that Judge Parker will be acceptable. Schüller is, however, somewhat concerned over the proposal to make the Austrian Government liable for debts due American citizens by Austrian nationals. He apparently fears that this proposal may bridge over some connection with property of Austrian nationals in the hands of alien property custodian and that foundation is possibly being laid to satisfy judgments out of the proceeds of such property. Since, however, our treaty with Germany contains similar clause, he presumes that provision is working satisfactorily in practice and if Berlin should confirm this, he would personally withdraw all objection to draft as it now stands. I am supplying him with a copy of the draft today and he promises prompt consideration.

WASHBURN

463.11 W 891/15 : Telegram

The Minister in Austria (Washburn) to the Secretary of State

VIENNA, April 3, 1924—7 p.m.
[Received April 4—8 : 05 p. m.]

17. Department's telegram 15, March 28, 5 p.m.[21] As a result of two extended Foreign Office conferences during the last fortnight and note received today, I can definitely state that Austrian Government accepts submitted draft of the proposed claims convention in principle and agrees to request the President of the United States to select a single commissioner. Austrian Government makes the following suggestions:

1. The question against which party or nationals a special claim should be properly made is in each instance a legal question which the agreement to a tripartite convention should not be construed as prejudicing. A future official communication will be made to me upon this point.

2. Proposed claims convention modified the question for mixed arbitral tribunal provided for in the treaty between the United States and Austria August 24, 1921, and article 256 of the Treaty St. Germain, which treaties have force of law here. Austrian Government is without sufficient power to make new convention operative by simple decree but must secure ratification by Parliament and Federal President. German Constitution gives more latitude in this respect. Suggestion is therefore made that article 6 of proposed draft should be amended to read as follows: "The present convention shall be ratified in accordance with the constitutional forms of the high contracting parties and shall take effect immediately on the exchange of ratifications which shall take place as soon as possible at (blank)."

---

[21] Not printed.

3. Proposed convention does not invest single commissioner with all the jurisdiction conferred upon mixed arbitral tribunal by section 6 of part 10 of St. Germain Treaty (see especially article 256, subsection *b*). Government desires to avoid expense of two tribunals operating possibly on diverging legal principles, and therefore suggests investing single commissioner with absolute and exclusive competency to exercise all jurisdiction contemplated by the peace treaty.

I am asked to ascertain whether these suggestions are acceptable. I infer that understanding here is that Hungarian Government has not subscribed to any specific text. Certainly the two Governments are in an advantageous position and since tripartite agreement is proposed, Austrian Foreign Office is preparing to hand to the resident Hungarian Minister a memorandum embodying substance of its views as above outlined.

WASHBURN

463.11 W 891/15 : Telegram

The Secretary of State to the Minister in Austria (Washburn)

WASHINGTON, *April 9, 1924—4 p.m.*

20. Your 17, April 3, 7 P. M. Significance of first suggestion of Austrian Government is not clear to Department. It will probably be necessary to await receipt of official communication promised before definitely answering this suggestion. It may be said, however, that purpose of tripartite agreement is to confer on arbitrator authority to determine party which is obligated on any claim presented for adjudication.

Department has no objection to adopting second suggestion of Austrian Government to include provision regarding ratification.

As to third suggestion terms of proposed tripartite agreement clearly indicate that purpose of agreement is to provide means of determining amounts to be paid by Austria and Hungary in satisfaction of their obligations under our treaties of August 24, 1921 with Hungary [*Austria*] and of August 29, 1921 with Austria [*Hungary*]. Department considers jurisdiction of arbitrator as defined in proposed agreement to be sufficiently comprehensive to determine amounts due by Austria and Hungary under treaties mentioned. In making suggestion for tripartite agreement United States Government did not contemplate establishment of two tribunals. While Department does not perceive purpose or necessity of enlarging jurisdiction of arbitrator it will be glad to receive and consider concrete suggestion as to language which Austrian Government considers should be employed in amending draft to enlarge jurisdiction.

In order that appropriation for purposes of convention may be obtained before adjournment of Congress it is necessary that convention be signed as soon as possible. Endeavor expedite action and telegraph developments and substance any communication received from Austrian Government.

HUGHES

463.11 W 891/17 : Telegram

The Minister in Austria (Washburn) to the Secretary of State

VIENNA, *April 18, 1924—3 p. m.*
[Received April 21(?)—8:21 p. m.]

20. Department's telegram 20, April 9, 4 p. m. As main illustration of first suggestion, if public claim be decided adversely to old dual monarchy Austrian Government does not believe Commissioner can decide in what respective proportion judgment shall be satisfied by Austria and Hungary but thinks that this is a question of interior relations to be settled by these two powers. Basis of settlement hitherto two-thirds Austria and one-third Hungary but negotiations in progress to readjust ratio. America holds excess of security and it is pointed out that Austria and Hungary would have every inducement to effect speedy amicable arrangement in this respect. Foreign Office states that anyway this first suggestion is only a reservation and need not call for change of phraseology in submitted draft.

For class of possible cases covered by third suggestion see my despatch number 446 mailed April 5th.[22] I believe these more or less hypothetical cases can be provided for by protocol or supplemental agreement if necessary. Schüller has been ill with influenza and left last evening for Rome on urgent business back in 10 days and he promises me on his return to wind up this matter speedily. I am convinced that in the last analysis with some understanding about cases embraced in suggestion 3, the submitted draft amended only by ratification clause of suggestion 2 can, provided Hungary assents, be signed before May 15th.

WASHBURN

463.11 W 891/20 : Telegram

The Minister in Austria (Washburn) to the Secretary of State

VIENNA, *May 5, 1924—11 a. m.*
[Received May 6—3:33 a. m.]

23. My 20, April 18, 3 p. m. Provisional, but for all purposes complete, draft of communication mentioned under the first suggestion my telegram no. 16 [17], April 3, 7 p. m., forwarded with full

---

[22] Not printed.

explanation in my despatch 455, May 2nd.[24] Said draft too intricate for detailed synopsis, but the substance of argument is that dual citizenship under the old monarchy did not exist. One was either Austrian subject or Hungarian subject. Excepting limited classes of public property enumerated in the draft, all other property, whether public or private, must be solely Austrian or Hungarian. Main point made is that Austrian property cannot be held as security for or used to satisfy a Hungarian claim. The above may conveniently be termed a reservation regarding nationality.

Am advised that instructions are being forwarded by mail early this week to Prochnik, Austrian Chargé d'Affaires, authorizing him to sign original draft of tripartite agreement as submitted by the Department, amended articles only to be article 6 by ratification language contained in second suggestion of my aforesaid telegram 16 [17]. Simultaneously with signing, Prochnik is instructed to address letter to the American Government formulating above-mentioned reserve regarding nationality and also making concrete suggestions for enlarging jurisdiction, should the necessity later arise, along lines set forth under the suggestion 3, my telegram no. 16 [17], and also my despatch no. 446, April 4th.[24]

WASHBURN

464.11 W 89/8 : Telegram

The Minister in Hungary (Brentano) to the Secretary of State

BUDAPEST, *May 21, 1924*—4 *p. m.*
[Received May 22—1 : 17 a.m.]

27. Referring to the Department's instruction no. 833 of February 1st.[25] Minister of Foreign Affairs on behalf of the Government makes the following comments regarding the draft of proposed agreement:

1. Proposes that since the purpose is identical the text of the introductory paragraph of article 1 be verbally identical with that of corresponding paragraph of the German-American agreement.
2. Since the provisions of the Treaty of Trianon included in the treaty of peace permit legal claims between nationals of the two countries to be submitted to a tribunal even by a Hungarian, it is suggested but not insisted that a clause be inserted in article 1 conferring exclusive jurisdiction upon the Commissioner so that he alone shall have authority to pass upon claims submitted even by nationals of Hungary and/or Austria against citizens of the [United States?] arising from the peace treaties.

---

[24] Not printed.
[25] Not printed; see instruction no. 610, Feb. 1, to the Minister in Austria, p. 142.

3. Proposes the inclusion of a clause providing a 6 month's limit for filing claims.

4. Considering the depressed economic conditions here the Hungarian Government would consider it only fair that article 5 provide that the expenses be borne one-half by the United States and one-quarter by each of the other countries instead of one-third by each of the three.

5. As Hungarian laws provide that important international agreements shall be effective only after ratification or after exchange of ratifications the Hungarian Government proposes that article 6 be changed to provide for ratification and exchange of ratifications and that the agreement be effective from say 15 days after or, at the earliest, from the date of exchange of ratifications. Copy to European Information Center.

BRENTANO

463.11 W 891/20 : Telegram

The Secretary of State to the Minister in Austria (Washburn)

WASHINGTON, *May 31, 1924—1 p.m.*

25. Your No. 23, May 5, 11 A. M. Department is gratified that Austrian Government is disposed to sign tripartite agreement in form submitted by Department with amendment to Article VI as already agreed upon. With respect to reservation of question of liability and of the division of responsibility between Austria and Hungary, which Austrian Government apparently intends to make in note to be delivered when agreement is signed, it may be stated that the Hungarian Government as well as the Austrian Government is concerned in the question of liability and the division of responsibility, and that the Commissioner would be competent under the terms of the proposed agreement to determine whether there was liability to indemnify in any given case and how the burden of indemnifying should be divided between Austria and Hungary. The United States would prefer that this question be not raised by the Austrian Government, and if it is raised in the note as proposed, the United States would be obliged to answer as indicated.

The Austrian Government apparently intends to make in its note a further reservation regarding the enlargement of the jurisdiction of the Commissioner. The purpose of the tripartite agreement is, as indicated in the terms of the draft submitted by the Department, to provide means for determining the amounts to be paid by Austria and by Hungary to the United States or to its nationals. Austria and Hungary are committed in the treaties establishing friendly relations to make suitable provision for satisfaction of claims of American nationals and the American Government. The agreement with Germany made no provision for the adjudication of any claims against the United States and its nationals, and the discussions with Austria and Hungary have proceeded on the understanding that the agreement was to be along the lines of agreement between United States and Germany. The Department considers it preferable that there be no reservations made in the note to be delivered by Austrian Government when agreement is signed.

HUGHES

464.11 W 89/8 : Telegram

The Secretary of State to the Minister in Hungary (Brentano)

WASHINGTON, *May 31, 1924—5 p.m.*

25. Your telegram No. 27, May 21, 4 P. M. First suggestion of Minister for Foreign Affairs is believed to be impracticable. Tripartite character of proposed agreement, different plan for adjudication and fact that different treaties are involved render it necessary to employ different language in the first paragraph of Article I than was employed in the corresponding paragraph of agreement with Germany. Except as to parenthetical expression in first paragraph of Article I, it is considered that the language of that paragraph is adequate and necessary to accomplish desired purposes. Department willing to omit parenthetical expression if desired.

Second suggestion. Purpose of proposed tripartite agreement is to provide means for determining amounts due by Austria and Hungary to United States or its nationals. Austria and Hungary are committed in treaties establishing friendly relations to make suitable provision for satisfaction of claims of United States and its nationals. Agreement with Germany made no provision for adjudication of any claims against United States or its nationals and discussions with Austria and Hungary regarding proposed agreement have proceeded on understanding that agreement was to be along lines of agreement with Germany. Department gratified Hungary will not insist on this suggestion.

Third suggestion. Department regards 6 months' period for filing claims inadequate. Would agree to provision that claims must be filed within 1 year from date of exchange of ratifications.

Fourth suggestion. Department agrees.

Fifth suggestion. Similar suggestion made by Austrian Government and agreed to by Department.

Legation Vienna reports Austrian Government is instructing Austrian Chargé d'Affaires at Washington to sign agreement as submitted by Department, but to make reservations in note delivered on signing agreement. Department replied stating it was deemed undesirable to have reservations made. Inasmuch as Austrian Government has instructed Chargé d'Affaires here to take matter up with Department, and since views of Austrian and Hungarian Governments have now been ascertained, Department believes conclusion of agreement satisfactory to all parties would be expedited if Hungarian Government would instruct its Minister here to discuss matter with Department.

You may answer Minister for Foreign Affairs as above.

HUGHES

464.11 W 89/12

The Chief of the Division of Western European Affairs, Department of State (Castle) to the Acting Secretary of State

[Extract]

[WASHINGTON,] *August 11, 1924.*

MR. GREW: Mr. Pelenyi, Hungarian Chargé, came to see me this morning to say that he had received authorization from his Government for the signing of the agreement for a mixed claims commission. He said, however, that this authorization to sign was made out in the name of the Minister and Count Szechenyi will not be back in this country before the end of October. He said, therefore, that instead of sending the papers to us he was at the moment merely informing us that the authorization had arrived so that, if the Department so desired, the papers could be ready when the Minister reaches Washington.

.   .   .   .

W. R. C[ASTLE]

463.11 W 891/28 : Telegram

The Minister in Austria (Washburn) to the Secretary of State

VIENNA, *September 5, 1924—1 p.m.*
[Received 4:23 p.m.]

52. Department's telegram number 25, May 31, 1 p.m. I spoke to Foreign Office about this matter on Monday last and received satisfactory assurances. Prochnik has now been authorized by cable to sign tripartite agreement in form already agreed upon without any reservations whatever. His instructions dated 3d instant should now be in Washington.

WASHBURN

Treaty Series No. 730

Agreement between the United States of America and Austria and Hungary, Signed at Washington, November 26, 1924 [26]

The United States of America and the Republic of Austria, hereafter described as Austria, and the Kingdom of Hungary, hereafter described as Hungary, being desirous of determining the amounts to be paid by Austria and by Hungary in satisfaction of their obligations under the treaties concluded by the United States with Austria on August 24, 1921, and with Hungary on August 29, 1921, which secure to the United States and its nationals rights specified under a Joint Resolution of the Congress of the United States of July 2, 1921, including rights under the Treaties of St. Germain-en-Laye and Trianon, respectively, have resolved to submit the questions for decision to a commissioner and have appointed as their plenipotentiaries to sign an agreement for that purpose:

The President of the United States of America, Charles Evans Hughes, Secretary of State of the United States of America,

The President of the Federal Republic of Austria, Mr. Edgar L. G. Prochnik, Chargé d'Affaires of Austria in Washington, and

The Governor of Hungary, Count László Széchényi, Envoy Extraordinary and Minister Plenipotentiary of Hungary to the United States,

Who, having communicated their full powers, found to be in good and due form, have agreed as follows:

ARTICLE I

The three governments shall agree upon the selection of a Commissioner who shall pass upon all claims for losses, damages or injuries suffered by the United States or its nationals embraced within the terms of the Treaty of August 24, 1921, between the United States and Austria and/or the Treaty of August 29, 1921, between the United States and Hungary, and/or the Treaties of St. Germain-en-Laye and/or Trianon, and shall determine the amounts to be paid to the United States by Austria and by Hungary in satisfaction of all such claims (excluding those falling within paragraphs 5, 6 and 7 of Annex I to Section I of Part VIII of both the Treaty of St. Germain-en-Laye and the Treaty of Trianon) and including the following categories:

(1) Claims of American citizens arising since July 31, 1914, in respect of damage to or seizure of their property, rights and inter-

---

[26] Ratified by the President, Aug. 4, 1925; ratified by Austria, Aug. 25, 1925; ratified by Hungary, Nov. 5, 1925; ratifications exchanged at Washington, Dec. 12, 1925.

ests, including any company or association in which they are interested, within the territories of either the former Austrian Empire or the former Kingdom of Hungary as they respectively existed on August 1, 1914;

(2) Other claims for loss or damage to which the United States or its nationals have been subjected with respect to injuries to or death of persons, or with respect to property, rights and interests, including any company or association in which American nationals are interested, since July 31, 1914, as a consequence of the war;

(3) Debts owing to American citizens by the Austrian and/or the Hungarian Governments or by their nationals.

ARTICLE II

Should the Commissioner for any cause be unable to discharge his functions, a successor shall be chosen in the same manner that he was selected. The Commissioner shall hold a session at Washington within two months after the coming into force of the present agreement. He may fix the time and the place of subsequent sessions according to convenience. All claims shall be presented to the Commissioner within one year from the date on which he holds the first session required by the foregoing provision.

ARTICLE III

The Commissioner shall cause to be kept an accurate record of the questions and cases submitted and correct minutes of proceedings. To this end each of the Governments may appoint a secretary, and these secretaries shall act together as joint secretaries and shall be subject to the direction of the Commissioner.

ARTICLE IV

The three Governments may designate agents and counsel who may present oral or written arguments to the Commissioner under such conditions as he may prescribe.

The Commissioner shall receive and consider all written statements or documents which may be presented to him, in accordance with rules which he may prescribe, by or on behalf of the respective Governments in support of or in answer to any claim.

The Governments of Austria and Hungary shall be notified of all claims filed with the Commissioner and shall be given such period of time as the Commissioner shall by rule determine in which to answer any claim filed.

The decisions of the Commissioner shall be accepted as final and binding upon the three Governments.

ARTICLE V

Each Government shall pay its own expenses, including the compensation of the secretary appointed by it and that of its agent and counsel. All other expenses which by their nature are a charge on the three Governments, including the compensation of the Commissioner and such employees as he may appoint to assist him in the performance of his duties, shall be borne one-half by the Government of the United States and one-half by the Governments of Austria and Hungary in equal moieties.

ARTICLE VI

This agreement shall be ratified in accordance with the constitutional forms of the contracting parties and shall come into force on the date of the exchange of ratifications.

IN FAITH WHEREOF, the above named plenipotentiaries have signed the present agreement and have hereunto affixed their seals.

Done in triplicate at the City of Washington this twenty-sixth day of November, one thousand nine hundred and twenty-four.

CHARLES EVANS HUGHES [SEAL]
EDGAR PROCHNIK [SEAL]
LÁSZLÓ SZÉCHÉNYI [SEAL]

INTEREST OF THE UNITED STATES IN THE DISPOSITION OF THE PROPOSED LIBERATION BONDS OF THE AUSTRO-HUNGARIAN SUCCESSION STATES

463.00 R 29/156 : Telegram

The Ambassador in France (Herrick) to the Secretary of State

PARIS, *February 9, 1924—3 p. m.*
[Received 5 p. m.]

64. L-89. 1st. In connection with apportionment and distribution of liberation debt of the Austrian states of Austro-Hungarian Monarchy, Finance Service recommends following repartition to Commission all gold francs: Poland 225,000,000, Roumania 235,000,000, Servia 178,-000,000, Czechoslovakia 750,000,000, Italy 59,000,000; and also recommends notification of repartition to Great Britain, France and Italy with a request for their views as to whether the issue of the liberation bonds should be called for and if so "whether the United States of America should be consulted."

2d. Last suggested question arises from the fact that by article 4 of liberation debt agreement of September 10, 1919 signed by the powers and by United States delegates to Peace Conference [27] it was provided that the bonds should be delivered "to such person or body as the Governments of the United States of America, the British Empire, France and Italy may designate." A similar provision in article 4 of amendatory agreement of December 20[8], 1919.[28]

3d. In practice understand that only Poland and Czechoslovakia may be called upon to issue bonds, because reparation claims of other states involved more than offset the liberation bond indebtedness. However this point is not quite clear.

4th. By article 2 Spa Agreement [29] and paragraph 3 of annex of Finance Ministers' Agreement of March 1922 [30] provided that the issue of liberation bonds is to be divided among the powers in the ratio of their participation in Austro-Hungarian reparation payments and credited on Austro-Hungarian account.

5th. Finance Service intimates view that United States probably not interested in delivery or division of present bonds in view of non-ratification of peace treaties and nonparticipation in Spa Agreement. Furthermore it does not appear that United States ratified liberation bond agreement of September 10, 1919.

6th. Am sending this advance outline of situation so that you may decide upon appropriate attitude of United States and instruct me whether I should take any action or make any reserves when the subject of transmitting the repartition problem to the powers is discussed in the Reparation Commission. Inasmuch as we probably will, and have had no participation in these bonds [it] seems immaterial to what body bonds are delivered. Present suggestion is Reparation Commission. Logan.

HERRICK

463.00 R 29/156 : Telegram

The Secretary of State to the Ambassador in France (Herrick)

[Paraphrase]

WASHINGTON, *February 29, 1924—6 p. m.*

67. L–54 for Logan. Your February 9, 3 p. m., L–89. When question comes up in the Reparation Commission in regard to the person or body to whom delivery of bonds shall be made under the provisions of article 4, Liberation Debt Agreement of September 10, 1919, as

---

[27] William M. Malloy, *Treaties, Conventions, etc., between the United States of America and Other Powers,* 1910–1923 (Washington, Government Printing Office, 1923), vol. III, p. 3299.
[28] *Ibid.,* p. 3303; the amended agreement was held open for signature until Dec. 20, 1919.
[29] *Foreign Relations,* 1920, vol. II, p. 406.
[30] *British and Foreign State Papers,* 1922, vol. CXVI, pp. 612, 621.

amended December, 1919, you may state that this Government would not object to the delivery of these bonds to the Reparation Commission.

The Department does not perceive that the Government of the United States has an interest in the disposition of the liberation bonds such as to preclude the above expression of its attitude, although as long as our Army cost claim remains unsatisfied [31] and no procedure is decided upon for payment of American claims adjudicated by the Mixed Claims Commission,[32] this Government has an interest in reparation credits.

You will advise the Department of your opinion whether a claim could properly be made under the Army Costs Agreement [33] for share in cash realized from the liberation bonds.

HUGHES

463.00 R 29/159 : Telegram

The Ambassador in France (Herrick) to the Secretary of State

[Paraphrase]

PARIS, March 6, 1924—3 p. m.
[Received 5:23 p. m.[33a]]

102. L–102. Department's L–54.

1. I have noted instructions about liberation bonds and when question comes up before Commission shall take position directed.

2. In answer to question last paragraph your telegram regarding applicability of ultimate cash payments on bonds to Army Costs Agreement, the date of maturity is not yet clearly fixed, but it is possible that this will be so remote as to fall beyond period of operation of Army Costs Agreement. Amortization beginning in 1931 and running to 1956 is now being considered.

3. I am inclined to the view that proceeds of liberation bonds may not on a proper construction of the Army Costs Agreement be claimed as subject to it. Our proper charges are: (1) against all payments made by German Government or for Germany's account where they are deliveries or transfers made by her except for items excluded in section 4 of article 2; and (2) for payments credited to reparation account of Germany which are made as or for accounts of another country from which a similar payment may be exacted. It is my opinion that true intent of that proviso was to cover payments made by former enemy countries like Austria-Hungary and Bulgaria.

[31] See *Foreign Relations*, 1923, vol. II, pp. 218 ff.
[32] See *ibid.*, 1922, vol. II, pp. 240 ff.
[33] *Ibid.*, 1923, vol. II, p. 180.
[33a] Telegram in two sections.

This construction is in words "similar" and "exacted". The liberation bonds are not cash payments and are made by Allied countries instead of former enemy powers; and they are made as part of cost of liberation of certain territory to them. It is true that there is canceled on the reparation claim against Austria and on the German C bonds an amount equivalent to the bonds, but I do not think that this cancelation constitutes a payment of reparations by a country from whom a reparation payment may be exacted as required by Army Costs Agreement.

4. If we have any claim to cash which may flow ultimately from these bonds, there would be probability that we may have claim against the bonds by and by, for they are a mode of payment which does not fall within the excluded classes; i. e., deliveries in kind, British Recovery Act,[34] etc., which are not applicable to the Army Costs Agreement. Claim could only be based on cancelation of C bonds provided for in annex to Finance Ministers' Agreement of March 11, 1922. I shall not put forward any such claim, however, for reasons above stated, unless I am instructed to contrary. Logan.

HERRICK

CONVENTIONS FOR THE PREVENTION OF LIQUOR SMUGGLING INTO THE UNITED STATES [35]

Great Britain, January 23, 1924

711.419/95 : Telegram

The Ambassador in Great Britain (Kellogg) to the Secretary of State

[Paraphrase]

LONDON, *March 1, 1924—11 a.m.*
[Received March 1—10:55 a.m.]

77. A note I have just received from the Prime Minister states that to his regret he had misinformed me yesterday in regard to the status of the liquor treaty. He now states that definite assurance has been given Canada that ratification binding on the Dominion will not take place until Canadian Parliament has had opportunity to discuss the matter. In regard to the other Dominions, Imperial Conference decided at its last meeting that each Government will decide whether approval of Parliament or legislation is required before it indicates concurrence in ratification. Prime Minister adds

---

[34] *British and Foreign State Papers*, 1921, vol. cxiv, p. 26.
[35] For previous correspondence, see *Foreign Relations*, 1923, vol. i, pp. 133 ff.

that he has telegraphed Dominion Governments urging as prompt action as possible, and he hopes to have replies immediately.[36]

KELLOGG

Treaty Series No. 685

Convention between the United States of America and Great Britain, Signed at Washington, January 23, 1924 [37]

The President of the United States of America;

And His Majesty the King of the United Kingdom of Great Britain and Ireland and of the British Dominions beyond the Seas, Emperor of India;

Being desirous of avoiding any difficulties which might arise between them in connection with the laws in force in the United States on the subject of alcoholic beverages;

Have decided to conclude a Convention for that purpose;

And have appointed as their Plenipotentiaries:

The President of the United States of America:

Charles Evans Hughes, Secretary of State of the United States;

His Majesty the King of the United Kingdom of Great Britain and Ireland and of the British Dominions beyond the Seas, Emperor of India:

The Right Honorable Sir Auckland Campbell Geddes, G. C. M. G., K. C. B., His Ambassador Extraordinary and Plenipotentiary to the United States of America;

Who, having communicated their full powers found in good and due form, have agreed as follows:

ARTICLE I

The High Contracting Parties declare that it is their firm intention to uphold the principle that 3 marine miles extending from the coast-line outwards and measured from low-water mark constitute the proper limits of territorial waters.

ARTICLE II

(1) His Britannic Majesty agrees that he will raise no objection to the boarding of private vessels under the British flag outside the limits of territorial waters by the authorities of the United States,

---

[36] The Department was informed on Mar. 15 that the Governments of Australia, Newfoundland, New Zealand, and South Africa had concurred in ratification, and on Apr. 10 that Canada and the Irish Free State had assented (file nos. 711.419/100, 108, and 109).

[37] Ratification advised by the Senate, Mar. 13, 1924; ratified by the President, Mar. 21, 1924; ratified by Great Britain, Apr. 30, 1924; ratifications exchanged at Washington, May 22, 1924; proclaimed by the President, May 22, 1924.

its territories or possessions in order that enquiries may be addressed to those on board and an examination be made of the ship's papers for the purpose of ascertaining whether the vessel or those on board are endeavoring to import or have imported alcoholic beverages into the United States, its territories or possessions in violation of the laws there in force. When such enquiries and examination show a reasonable ground for suspicion, a search of the vessel may be instituted.

(2) If there is reasonable cause for belief that the vessel has committed or is committing or attempting to commit an offense against the laws of the United States, its territories or possessions prohibiting the importation of alcoholic beverages, the vessel may be seized and taken into a port of the United States, its territories or possessions for adjudication in accordance with such laws.

(3) The rights conferred by this article shall not be exercised at a greater distance from the coast of the United States its territories or possessions than can be traversed in one hour by the vessel suspected of endeavoring to commit the offense. In cases, however, in which the liquor is intended to be conveyed to the United States its territories or possessions by a vessel other than the one boarded and searched, it shall be the speed of such other vessel and not the speed of the vessel boarded, which shall determine the distance from the coast at which the right under this article can be exercised.

Article III

No penalty or forfeiture under the laws of the United States shall be applicable or attach to alcoholic liquors or to vessels or persons by reason of the carriage of such liquors, when such liquors are listed as sea stores or cargo destined for a port foreign to the United States, its territories or possessions on board British vessels voyaging to or from ports of the United States, or its territories or possessions or passing through the territorial waters thereof, and such carriage shall be as now provided by law with respect to the transit of such liquors through the Panama Canal, provided that such liquors shall be kept under seal continuously while the vessel on which they are carried remains within said territorial waters and that no part of such liquors shall at any time or place be unladen within the United States, its territories or possessions.

Article IV

Any claim by a British vessel for compensation on the grounds that it has suffered loss or injury through the improper or unreasonable exercise of the rights conferred by Article II of this Treaty or on the ground that it has not been given the benefit of Article III shall be referred for the joint consideration of two persons, one of whom shall be nominated by each of the High Contracting Parties.

Effect shall be given to the recommendations contained in any such joint report. If no joint report can be agreed upon, the claim shall be referred to the Claims Commission established under the provisions of the Agreement for the Settlement of Outstanding Pecuniary Claims signed at Washington the 18th August, 1910, but the claim shall not, before submission to the tribunal, require to be included in a schedule of claims confirmed in the manner therein provided.

ARTICLE V

This Treaty shall be subject to ratification and shall remain in force for a period of one year from the date of the exchange of ratifications.

Three months before the expiration of the said period of one year, either of the High Contracting Parties may give notice of its desire to propose modifications in the terms of the Treaty.

If such modifications have not been agreed upon before the expiration of the term of one year mentioned above, the Treaty shall lapse.

If no notice is given on either side of the desire to propose modifications, the Treaty shall remain in force for another year, and so on automatically, but subject always in respect of each such period of a year to the right on either side to propose as provided above three months before its expiration modifications in the Treaty, and to the provision that if such modifications are not agreed upon before the close of the period of one year, the Treaty shall lapse.

ARTICLE VI

In the event that either of the High Contracting Parties shall be prevented either by judicial decision or legislative action from giving full effect to the provisions of the present Treaty the said Treaty shall automatically lapse, and, on such lapse or whenever this Treaty shall cease to be in force, each High Contracting Party shall enjoy all the rights which it would have possessed had this Treaty not been concluded.

The present Convention shall be duly ratified by the President of the United States of America, by and with the advice and consent of the Senate thereof, and by His Britannic Majesty; and the ratifications shall be exchanged at Washington as soon as possible.

IN WITNESS WHEREOF, the respective Plenipotentiaries have signed the present Convention in duplicate and have thereunto affixed their seals.

DONE at the city of Washington this twenty-third day of January, in the year of our Lord one thousand nine hundred and twenty-four.

[SEAL] CHARLES EVANS HUGHES
[SEAL] A. C. GEDDES

Germany, May 19, 1924

711.629/1

The German Ambassador (Wiedfeldt) to the Secretary of State

[Translation [38]]

WASHINGTON, *April 28, 1924.*

MR. SECRETARY OF STATE: I have the honor most respectfully to return herewith to Your Excellency the draft for a convention between the United States and Germany concerning the regulation of liquor traffic, sent to me on March 24, giving a few amendments proposed by my Government. I wish to remark in this connection that these changes are of form and agree with the text of the American-British treaty. They are underscored in red ink in the enclosure.[39] The German translation is given on the right side opposite the English text.

I also enclose the German text with the English translation opposite.[39]

Accept [etc.] O. WIEDFELDT

711.629/2

The Secretary of State to the German Ambassador (Wiedfeldt)

WASHINGTON, *May 1, 1924.*

EXCELLENCY: I have the honor to refer to suggested changes in the draft of the proposed convention to prevent the smuggling of intoxicating liquors into the United States as set forth in a communication from Doctor von Lewinski [40] to the Solicitor for this Department under date of April 26, 1924.[41] In accordance with

---

[38] File translation revised.
[39] Not printed.
[40] Counselor of the German Embassy.
[41] Not printed; the suggested changes, all of which were accepted by the Department, were indicated in the draft submitted with the German Ambassador's note of Apr. 28, *supra*.

your suggestions, the following changes in the draft are acceptable to this Government:

PREAMBLE.

". . . have appointed as their Plenipotentiaries:
   The President of the United States of America, Mr. Charles Evans Hughes, Secretary of State of the United States of America,
   The President of the German Empire, Dr. Otto Wiedfeldt, German Ambassador to the United States of America."

ARTICLE II. (1)
   "The President of the German Empire agrees that Germany will raise no objection".

ARTICLE VI, PARAGRAPH 2:
   "The present Convention shall be duly ratified by the President of the United States of America, by and with the advice and consent of the Senate thereof, and by the President of the German Empire in accordance with the requirements of the German Constitution".

I have the honor to attach hereto a text of the proposed draft incorporating the changes above noted.[42]

Accept [etc.]   CHARLES E. HUGHES

Treaty Series No. 694

Convention between the United States of America and Germany, Signed at Washington, May 19, 1924[43]

The President of the United States of America and the President of the German Empire being desirous of avoiding any difficulties which might arise between them in connection with the laws in force in the United States on the subject of alcoholic beverages have decided to conclude a Convention for that purpose, and have appointed as their Plenipotentiaries:

The President of the United States of America, Mr. Charles Evans Hughes, Secretary of State of the United States of America; and

The President of the German Empire, Dr. Otto Wiedfeldt, German Ambassador to the United States of America;

Who, having communicated their full powers found in good and due form, have agreed as follows:

[42] See signed convention, *infra.*
[43] In English and German; German text not printed. Ratification advised by the Senate, May 26, 1924; ratified by the President, Aug. 9, 1924; ratified by Germany, July 8, 1924; ratifications exchanged at Washington, Aug. 11, 1924; proclaimed by the President, Aug. 11, 1924.

Article I

The High Contracting Parties declare that it is their firm intention to uphold the principle that 3 marine miles extending from the coastline outwards and measured from low-water mark constitute the proper limits of territorial waters.

Article II

(1) The President of the German Empire agrees that Germany will raise no objection to the boarding of private vessels under the German flag outside the limits of territorial waters by the authorities of the United States, its territories or possessions, in order that enquiries may be addressed to those on board and an examination be made of the ship's papers for the purpose of ascertaining whether the vessel or those on board are endeavoring to import or have imported alcoholic beverages into the United States, its territories or possessions in violation of the laws there in force. When such enquiries and examination show a reasonable ground for suspicion, a search of the vessel may be initiated.

(2) If there is reasonable cause for belief that the vessel has committed or is committing or attempting to commit an offense against the laws of the United States, its territories or possessions prohibiting the importation of alcoholic beverages, the vessel may be seized and taken into a port of the United States, its territories or possessions for adjudication in accordance with such laws.

(3) The rights conferred by this article shall not be exercised at a greater distance from the coast of the United States its territories or possessions than can be traversed in one hour by the vessel suspected of endeavoring to commit the offense. In cases, however, in which the liquor is intended to be conveyed to the United States its territories or possessions by a vessel other than the one boarded and searched, it shall be the speed of such other vessel and not the speed of the vessel boarded, which shall determine the distance from the coast at which the right under this article can be exercised.

Article III

No penalty or forfeiture under the laws of the United States shall be applicable or attach to alcoholic liquors or to vessels or persons by reason of the carriage of such liquors, when such liquors are listed as sea stores or cargo destined for a port foreign to the United States, its territories or possessions on board German vessels voyaging to or from ports of the United States, or its territories or possessions or passing through the territorial waters thereof, and such carriage shall be as now provided by law with respect to the transit of such liquors through the Panama Canal, provided that such liquors shall be kept under seal continuously while the vessel on which they are carried remains within said territorial waters and that no part of such liquors shall at any time or place be unladen within the United States, its territories or possessions.

ARTICLE IV

Any claim by a German vessel for compensation on the grounds that it has suffered loss or injury through the improper or unreasonable exercise of the rights conferred by Article II of this Treaty, or on the ground that it has not been given the benefit of Article III shall be referred for the joint consideration of two persons, one of whom shall be nominated by each of the High Contracting Parties.

Effect shall be given to the recommendations contained in any such joint report. If no joint report can be agreed upon, the claim shall be referred to the Permanent Court of Arbitration at The Hague described in the Convention for the Pacific Settlement of International Disputes, concluded at The Hague, October 18, 1907. The Arbitral Tribunal shall be constituted in accordance with Article 87 (Chapter IV) and with Article 59 (Chapter III) of the said Convention. The proceedings shall be regulated by so much of Chapter IV of the said Convention and of Chapter III thereof (special regard being had for Articles 70 and 74, but excepting Articles 53 and 54) as the Tribunal may consider to be applicable and to be consistent with the provisions of this agreement. All sums of money which may be awarded by the Tribunal on account of any claim shall be paid within eighteen months after the date of the final award without interest and without deduction, save as hereafter specified. Each Government shall bear its own expenses. The expenses of the Tribunal shall be defrayed by a ratable deduction of the amount of the sums awarded by it, at a rate of five per cent. on such sums, or at such lower rate as may be agreed upon between the two Governments; the deficiency, if any, shall be defrayed in equal moieties by the two Governments.

ARTICLE V

This Treaty shall be subject to ratification and shall remain in force for a period of one year from the date of the exchange of ratifications.

Three months before the expiration of the said period of one year, either of the High Contracting Parties may give notice of its desire to propose modifications in the terms of the Treaty.

If such modifications have not been agreed upon before the expiration of the term of one year mentioned above, the Treaty shall lapse.

If no notice is given on either side of the desire to propose modifications, the Treaty shall remain in force for another year, and so on, automatically, but subject always in respect of each such period of a year to the right on either side to propose as provided above three months before its expiration modifications in the Treaty, and to the provision that if such modifications are not agreed upon before the close of the period of one year, the Treaty shall lapse.

ARTICLE VI

In the event that either of the High Contracting Parties shall be prevented either by judicial decision or legislative action from giving full effect to the provisions of the present Treaty the said Treaty shall automatically lapse, and, on such lapse or whenever this Treaty shall cease to be in force, each High Contracting Party shall enjoy all the rights which it would have possessed had this Treaty not been concluded.

The present Convention shall be duly ratified by the President of the United States of America, by and with the advice and consent of the Senate thereof, and by the President of the German Empire in accordance with the requirements of the German Constitution; and the ratifications shall be exchanged at Washington as soon as possible.

In witness whereof, the respective Plenipotentiaries have signed the present Convention in duplicate and have thereunto affixed their seals.

Done at the city of Washington, this nineteenth day of May in the year of our Lord one thousand nine hundred and twenty-four.

[SEAL]   CHARLES EVANS HUGHES
[SEAL]   DR. OTTO WIEDFELDT

Sweden, May 22, 1924

711.589/7

The Secretary of State to the Minister in Sweden (Bliss)

No. 17   WASHINGTON, *January 3, 1924.*

SIR: The Department has received your despatch No. 72 dated November 21, 1923,[44] enclosing a memorandum dealing with the

---

[44] *Foreign Relations, 1923, vol. I, p. 211.*

extent of territorial jurisdiction claimed by Sweden.[45] You refer to
Article 7 of the Treaty of Friendship, Commerce and Navigation
between Sweden and Mexico, ratified on the 28th day of May, 1886, at
Stockholm, and on the first of July, 1886, at Mexico, which contains
the following provision:

"Both parties agree to consider as limit of territorial waters on
their respective coast for everything pertaining to the application of
customs regulations and to measures taken to prevent smuggling, a
distance of three sea leagues from the line of the low water."

You state that three sea leagues is approximately ten miles from
shore.

The information you have furnished is considered important.
Reference is made to the request contained in the Department's instruction of September 10, 1923,[46] for a report setting forth information concerning the views held by Swedish officials with respect
to the proposal for a treaty dealing with the enforcement of prohibition on Swedish vessels within American territorial waters and measures for stopping liquor smuggling operations outside the three-mile
limit. The Department will be glad to receive a report dealing with
this matter at your early convenience.

You are informed that the British Government has submitted a
counter-draft for the proposed treaty dealing with the subject referred to in the Department's telegram dated June 12, 1923, 3 p. m.,
forwarded to you from the American Embassy at Paris.[47] The Department has suggested certain modifications in the counter-draft
which are now under consideration by the British Government.
Negotiations for a treaty have also been started with the Netherlands Government and a communication commenting upon the American draft for the proposed treaty has been received from the Foreign
Office of the Netherlands Government.[48]

I am [etc.]   CHARLES E. HUGHES

711.589/8

The Minister in Sweden (Bliss) to the Secretary of State

No. 135   STOCKHOLM, *February 20, 1924.*
                                          [Received March 8.]

SIR: I have the honor to acknowledge the receipt of the Department's Instruction No. 17, of January 13 [*3*], in further reference

[45] Not printed.
[46] *Foreign Relations*, 1923, vol. I, p. 184.
[47] See *ibid.*, p. 152.
[48] See telegram no. 66, Dec. 5, 1923, from the Minister in the Netherlands,
ibid., p. 219.

to the question of the jurisdiction claimed by Sweden over territorial waters. In that instruction I am directed to report "the views held by Swedish officials with respect to the proposal for a treaty dealing with the enforcement of prohibition on Swedish vessels within American territorial waters and measures for stopping liquor smuggling operations outside of the three mile limit."

On receipt of this instruction, I took the first opportunity which was presented to speak informally with Baron Marks von Würtemberg, the Minister for Foreign Affairs, on the matter. I told him that I was desirous of learning the views of the Swedish Government officials on this subject, but explained that my inquiry was made informally and should not be considered as a proposal to negotiate a treaty. The Minister stated that he could not reply immediately, as the matter was a subject which required consideration and the necessity of talking with his colleagues, but that he would give me an answer as soon as possible.

Not having the text of the treaty then being negotiated between our Government and that of Great Britain on this same subject, I was unable to accede to the Minister's request to supply him with a copy thereof.

He asked several questions, especially wishing to know what advantage it would be to Swedish vessels and Swedish commerce if his Government were to recognize the jurisdiction of the United States beyond the three mile limit for the purpose of suppressing liquor smuggling operations. I replied that according to the treaty we were then discussing with England, Swedish vessels would obtain the privilege of carrying liquor as sealed stores within the territorial waters of the United States and cargoes of liquors, not destined for disembarkation within the confines of the United States. I also pointed out that a somewhat similar provision for extending the limits of jurisdiction over territorial waters was contained in the treaty between Sweden and Mexico, whereby it was provided, for the purpose of enforcement of customs regulations, that the territorial waters of the two contracting parties would be extended to a distance of about ten miles.

A fortnight ago Baron von Würtemberg told me that he had received a copy of the American-English treaty, which was being examined by his colleagues, and that he hoped to have something to say to me shortly. Yesterday, at the weekly diplomatic reception, he said that he had examined that treaty with much interest and that Sweden would be quite disposed to enter into negotiations with the United States looking to the conclusion of a treaty of that nature.

He expressed the desire that whatever agreement might be reached for extending the territorial waters beyond the three mile limit would be a reciprocal arrangement. I told the Minister that I could make no rejoinder to that request other than to say that I would acquaint my Government with the desire that he expressed, for my inquiry to him having been of an informal nature, I could not enter into a discussion of the subject with him.

I have [etc.]   ROBERT WOODS BLISS

711.589/8b : Telegram

The Secretary of State to the Minister in Sweden (Bliss)

WASHINGTON, *March 28, 1924—5 p. m.*

11. Treaty with Great Britain to aid in the prevention of the smuggling of intoxicating liquors into the United States was approved by the Senate March 13. A similar text has been submitted to Swedish Minister at this capital, as likewise to diplomatic representatives here of Netherlands, Japan, Denmark, Germany, Italy and Norway.[49] Expect copy by pouch. Take no action without further instructions.

There is a substitute Article 1 in Treaty given to Italian Ambassador as follows:

"The High Contracting Parties respectively retain their rights and claims, without prejudice by reason of this agreement, with respect to the extent of their territorial jurisdiction."

Department prefers Article 1 as contained in Treaty with Great Britain and that no question be raised as to any change in text. Department is willing, however, if insisted upon, to give same Article as that proposed to the Italian Government which was unwilling to assent to three-mile limit.

HUGHES

711.589/9

The Swedish Legation to the Department of State

MEMORANDUM

Before signing the proposed so-called liquor treaty with the United States the Swedish Government desires to know if the American Government would be willing to have article 1 omitted or, if not that, to have inserted in this article or in the introduction to the treaty provisions to the effect that the treaty shall not be considered

---

[49] Draft texts not printed. Negotiations with Japan did not take place until 1928.

as establishing a precedent with regard to the territorial limits hitherto upheld by the contracting parties.

Further, the Swedish Government desires to know if the American Government would be willing to agree to reciprocal rights of boarding smuggling vessels outside the limits of the territorial waters. It is thought that such reciprocal rights might be of importance in the event Sweden should wish to make similar treaties with other powers.

In passing the Swedish Government should like to know if there may be a possibility of having the treaty ratified by the Senate during the present session of Congress, if the treaty were to be signed in the middle of this month.

[WASHINGTON,] *May 3, 1924.*

711.589/9

The Department of State to the Swedish Legation

MEMORANDUM

Referring to the memorandum handed by the Counselor of the Swedish Legation to the Solicitor of the Department of State on May 3 last, in relation to the proposed treaty to aid in the prevention of the smuggling of intoxicating liquors into the United States, the Secretary of State begs to say:

First. The Government of the United States is not disposed to omit Article I but will be willing to accept as a substitute therefor the following:

"The High Contracting Parties respectively retain their rights and claims, without prejudice by reason of this agreement, with respect to the extent of their territorial jurisdiction."

Second. With respect to the other provisions of the proposed treaty, the Government of the United States desires to have the treaty conform to the draft handed to the Swedish Minister on March 20, 1924, for the reason that the provisions of the draft are those of the treaty already concluded with Great Britain.

Third. The treaty if concluded with the Swedish Government would be at once submitted to the Senate of the United States and, as the Senate has already approved the treaty with Great Britain, it is not expected that there would be any great delay in its action upon the treaty in question.

[WASHINGTON,] *May 5, 1924.*

Treaty Series No. 698

Convention between the United States of America and Sweden, Signed at Washington, May 22, 1924 [50]

The President of the United States of America and His Majesty the King of Sweden being desirous of avoiding any difficulties which might arise between them in connection with the laws in force in the United States on the subject of alcoholic beverages have decided to conclude a Convention for that purpose, and have appointed as their Plenipotentiaries:

The President of the United States of America, Mr. Charles Evans Hughes, Secretary of State of the United States;

His Majesty the King of Sweden, Mr. V. Assarsson, Counselor of His Legation at Washington;

Who, having communicated their full powers found in good and due form, have agreed as follows:

ARTICLE I

The High Contracting Parties respectively retain their rights and claims, without prejudice by reason of this agreement, with respect to the extent of their territorial jurisdiction.

ARTICLE II

(1) His Majesty agrees that he will raise no objection to the boarding of private vessels under the Swedish flag outside the limits of territorial waters by the authorities of the United States, its territories or possessions in order that enquiries may be addressed to those on board and an examination be made of the ship's papers for the purpose of ascertaining whether the vessel or those on board are endeavoring to import or have imported alcoholic beverages into the United States, its territories or possessions in violation of the laws there in force. When such enquiries and examination show a reasonable ground for suspicion, a search of the vessel may be initiated.

(2) If there is reasonable cause for belief that the vessel has committed or is committing or attempting to commit an offense against the laws of the United States, its territories or possessions prohibiting the importation of alcoholic beverages, the vessel may be seized and taken into a port of the United States, its territories or possessions for adjudication in accordance with such laws.

---

[50] In English and Swedish; Swedish text not printed. Ratification advised by the Senate, May 26, 1924; ratified by the President, Aug. 15, 1924; ratified by Sweden, June 13, 1924; ratifications exchanged at Washington, Aug. 18, 1924; proclaimed by the President, Aug. 18, 1924.

(3) The rights conferred by this article shall not be exercised at a greater distance from the coast of the United States its territories or possessions than can be traversed in one hour by the vessel suspected of endeavoring to commit the offense. In cases, however, in which the liquor is intended to be conveyed to the United States its territories or possessions by a vessel other than the one boarded and searched, it shall be the speed of such other vessel and not the speed of the vessel boarded, which shall determine the distance from the coast at which the right under this article can be exercised.

Article III

No penalty or forfeiture under the laws of the United States shall be applicable or attach to alcoholic liquors or to vessels or persons by reason of the carriage of such liquors, when such liquors are listed as sea stores or cargo destined for a port foreign to the United States, its territories or possessions on board Swedish vessels voyaging to or from ports of the United States, or its territories or possessions or passing through the territorial waters thereof, and such carriage shall be as now provided by law with respect to the transit of such liquors through the Panama Canal, provided that such liquors shall be kept under seal continuously while the vessel on which they are carried remains within said territorial waters and that no part of such liquors shall at any time or place be unladen within the United States, its territories or possessions.

Article IV

Any claim by a Swedish vessel for compensation on the grounds that it has suffered loss or injury through the improper or unreasonable exercise of the rights conferred by Article II of this Treaty or on the ground that it has not been given the benefit of Article III shall be referred for the joint consideration of two persons, one of whom shall be nominated by each of the High Contracting Parties.

Effect shall be given to the recommendations contained in any such joint report. If no joint report can be agreed upon, the claim shall be referred to the Permanent Court of Arbitration at The Hague described in the Convention for the Pacific Settlement of International Disputes, concluded at The Hague, October 18, 1907. The Arbitral Tribunal shall be constituted in accordance with Article 87 (Chapter IV) and with Article 59 (Chapter III) of the said Convention. The proceedings shall be regulated by so much of Chapter IV of the said Convention and of Chapter III thereof (special regard being had for Articles 70 and 74, but excepting Articles 53 and 54) as the Tribunal may consider to be applicable and to be consistent with the provisions of this agreement. All sums of money which may be awarded by the Tribunal on account of any claim shall be paid within eighteen months after the date of the final award without interest and without deduction, save as hereafter specified. Each Government shall bear its own expenses. The expenses of the Tribunal shall be defrayed by a ratable deduction of the amount of the sums awarded by it, at a rate of five per cent. on such sums, or at such lower rate as may be agreed upon between the two Governments; the deficiency, if any, shall be defrayed in equal moieties by the two Governments.

Article V

This Treaty shall be subject to ratification and shall remain in force for a period of one year from the date of the exchange of ratifications.

Three months before the expiration of the said period of one year, either of the High Contracting Parties may give notice of its desire to propose modifications in the terms of the Treaty.

If such modifications have not been agreed upon before the expiration of the term of one year mentioned above, the Treaty shall lapse.

If no notice is given on either side of the desire to propose modifications, the Treaty shall remain in force for another year, and so on automatically, but subject always in respect of each such period of a year to the right on either side to propose as provided above three months before its expiration modifications in the Treaty, and to the provision that if such modifications are not agreed upon before the close of the period of one year, the Treaty shall lapse.

Article VI

In the event that either of the High Contracting Parties shall be prevented either by judicial decision or legislative action from giving full effect to the provisions of the present Treaty the said Treaty shall automatically lapse, and, on such lapse or whenever this Treaty shall cease to be in force, each High Contracting Party shall enjoy all the rights which it would have possessed had this Treaty not been concluded.

The present Convention shall be duly ratified by the President of the United States of America, by and with the advice and consent of the Senate thereof, and by His Majesty the King of Sweden; and the ratifications shall be exchanged at Washington as soon as possible.

In Witness whereof, the respective Plenipotentiaries have signed the present Convention in duplicate in the English and Swedish languages and have thereunto affixed their seals.

Done at the city of Washington this twenty-second day of May, in the year of our Lord one thousand nine hundred and twenty-four.

[SEAL]   CHARLES EVANS HUGHES

[SEAL]   V ASSARSSON

711.579/6½

Norway, May 24, 1924

Memorandum by the Secretary of State of a Conversation with the Norwegian Minister (Bryn), March 20, 1924

[Extract]

Liquor Treaty.—The Secretary referred to the request of the Minister to be informed in case a liquor treaty were concluded with Great Britain and stated that such a treaty had been concluded and as it had been approved by the Senate he was at liberty to hand the Minister a copy. The Secretary said he was ready to conclude a similar treaty with Norway and handed to the Minister a draft of a treaty which was identical with the treaty with Great Britain (with the change of name) except in the second paragraph of Article 4 where he had incorporated in the draft provisions substantially as those contained in the Convention of 1910 with Great Britain.[51] The Minister said that his Government might not be willing to sign a provision upholding the three-mile limit and hence might object to Article 1. The Secretary said he would be glad to substitute for Article 1 the following:

"The High Contracting Parties respectively retain their rights and claims, without prejudice by reason of this agreement with respect to the extent of their territorial jurisdiction."

711.579/10

The Norwegian Legation to the Department of State

AIDE-MÉMOIRE

The Norwegian Government is willing to negotiate a Liquor Treaty on the basis of the draft submitted by the Government of the United States, Article I being substituted by the alternative text delivered by the Secretary of State, and providing that the provisions of the Treaty be made reciprocal. The Norwegian Government prefers that instead of the rules for computation of the distance contained in Article II, Paragraph 3, there be agreed upon a

---

[51] *Foreign Relations*, 1911, p. 266.

fixed distance from the coast within which boarding of vessels etc. can take place, preferably 10 nautical miles, which is the distance established by Norwegian Law for the police activities of the customs authorities. With regard to the expenses of the Tribunal mentioned in Article IV the Norwegian Government should prefer, instead of the provisions of the draft, that the provision of Article 85 of The Hague Convention,[52] according to which each Government shall bear an equal share of the expenses of the Tribunal, be adopted.

In the last paragraph of the last Article the words "in English and Norwegian language" should be inserted.

WASHINGTON, *May 8, 1924.*

711.579/10

The Department of State to the Norwegian Legation

MEMORANDUM

Referring to the *aide-mémoire* handed by the Norwegian Minister to the Secretary of State on May 8, 1924, in relation to the proposed treaty to aid in the prevention of the smuggling of intoxicating liquors into the United States, the Secretary of State begs to say:

First. It is noted that the Norwegian Government accepts the alternative text for Article I submitted by the Secretary of State.

Second. The Government of the United States finds it impossible to agree to the proposals of the Norwegian Government amendatory of paragraph (3), Article II respecting the distance from the coast within which the boarding of vessels, etc., can take place. The Government of the United States desires to have the treaty conform in this regard to the draft submitted to the Norwegian Minister for the reason that the provisions of the Article are those of the treaty recently concluded between the United States and Great Britain.

Third. After consideration of the Norwegian proposal for the substitution of Article 85 of The Hague Convention of 1907 for the Pacific Settlement of International Disputes respecting the payment of the expenses of the Tribunal mentioned in Article IV of the treaty, the Government of the United States prefers to retain the provisions which it has submitted to the Norwegian Government.

Fourth. The Government of the United States accepting the proposal of the Norwegian Government that the final Article should

---

[52] *Foreign Relations*, 1907, pt. 2, p. 1181.

refer to the two languages in which the treaty is expressed, suggests that after the words "in duplicate" in Article VI there be incorporated the words "in the English and Norwegian languages".

[WASHINGTON,] *May 14, 1924.*

711.579/10

The Secretary of State to the Norwegian Minister (Bryn)

WASHINGTON, *May 21, 1924.*

SIR: With further reference to your *aide-mémoire* of May 8th last, in regard to the proposed treaty to aid in the prevention of the smuggling of intoxicating liquor into the United States, I have to confirm my verbal statement to you of May 8th that this Government would be unwilling to agree to the proposal of your Government that the provisions of the treaty be made reciprocal and so differ from those of the treaty recently concluded between the United States and Great Britain. It is desired that the treaties on this subject should be of the same tenor.

Accept [etc.]   CHARLES E. HUGHES

711.579/11

The Norwegian Minister (Bryn) to the Secretary of State

WASHINGTON, *May 22, 1924.*

MY DEAR MR. SECRETARY OF STATE: Referring to your notes of the 14th and 21st instant I have the pleasure to state that I have been authorized to sign with you a liquor treaty as the one recently concluded between the United States and Great Britain with the alternative text for Article I submitted by you and with the words "in the English and Norwegian languages" to be incorporated in Article VI after the words "in duplicate."

I enclose the text in Norwegian language.[53]

I beg to add that in signing the treaty my Government, which maintains its desire with regard to reciprocity and to 10 miles distance from the shore as limit within which the boarding of vessels etc. can take place, ventures to hope that in a possible revision of the treaty in accordance with Article V the Government of the United States will meet my Government's desire in those respects.

Believe me [etc.]   H. BRYN

---

[53] Not printed.

711.579/11

The Secretary of State to the Norwegian Minister (Bryn)

WASHINGTON, *May 23, 1924.*

MY DEAR MR. MINISTER: Permit me to acknowledge the receipt of your communication of May 22nd, in which you inform me that you have been authorized by your Government to sign a liquor treaty such as that recently concluded between the United States and Great Britain, with the alternative text for Article I which I submitted to you and also with the words "in the English and Norwegian languages" to be incorporated in Article VI after the words "in duplicate".

With your note you were good enough to enclose a text in the Norwegian language.

I take note of your further statement that your Government maintains its desire with regard to reciprocity and to ten miles from the shore as the limit within which the boarding of vessels, etc. can take place and that it ventures to hope that in a possible revision of the treaty in accordance with Article V, the Government of the United States will meet the desires of the Norwegian Government in those respects.

By way of response to this suggestion, permit me to renew the expression of my opinion that the treaties of the United States to aid in the prevention of the smuggling of intoxicating liquors into the United States should, so far as possible, be of the same tenor and that, therefore, this Government might find difficulty in accepting provisions differing with respect to what you refer from those in the treaty recently concluded between the United States and Great Britain.

I am [etc.]   CHARLES E. HUGHES

Treaty Series No. 689

Convention between the United States of America and Norway, Signed at Washington, May 24, 1924 [54]

The President of the United States of America and His Majesty the King of Norway being desirous of avoiding any difficulties which might arise between them in connection with the laws in force in the United States on the subject of alcoholic beverages have decided to

---

[54] In English and Norwegian; Norwegian text not printed. Ratification advised by the Senate, May 31, 1924; ratified by the President, June 20, 1924; ratified by Norway, June 20, 1924; ratifications exchanged at Washington, July 2, 1924; proclaimed by the President, July 2, 1924.

conclude a Convention for that purpose, and have appointed as their Plenipotentiaries:

The President of the United States of America, Charles Evans Hughes, Secretary of State of the United States;

His Majesty the King of Norway, Helmer H. Bryn, His Envoy Extraordinary and Minister Plenipotentiary to the United States of America;

Who, having communicated their full powers found in good and due form, have agreed as follows:

ARTICLE I

The High Contracting Parties respectively retain their rights and claims, without prejudice by reason of this agreement with respect to the extent of their territorial jurisdiction.

ARTICLE II

(1) His Majesty agrees that he will raise no objection to the boarding of private vessels under the Norwegian flag outside the limits of territorial waters by the authorities of the United States, its territories or possessions in order that enquiries may be addressed to those on board and an examination be made of the ship's papers for the purpose of ascertaining whether the vessel or those on board are endeavoring to import or have imported alcoholic beverages into the United States, its territories or possessions in violation of the laws there in force. When such enquiries and examination show a reasonable ground for suspicion, a search of the vessel may be initiated.

(2) If there is reasonable cause for belief that the vessel has committed or is committing or attempting to commit an offense against the laws of the United States, its territories or possessions prohibiting the importation of alcoholic beverages, the vessel may be seized and taken into a port of the United States, its territories or possessions for adjudication in accordance with such laws.

(3) The rights conferred by this article shall not be exercised at a greater distance from the coast of the United States its territories or possessions than can be traversed in one hour by the vessel suspected of endeavoring to commit the offense. In cases, however, in which the liquor is intended to be conveyed to the United States its territories or possessions by a vessel other than the one boarded and searched, it shall be the speed of such other vessel and not the speed of the vessel boarded, which shall determine the distance from the coast at which the right under this article can be exercised.

Article III

No penalty or forfeiture under the laws of the United States shall be applicable or attach to alcoholic liquors or to vessels or persons by reason of the carriage of such liquors, when such liquors are listed as sea stores or cargo destined for a port foreign to the United States, its territories or possessions on board Norwegian vessels voyaging to or from ports of the United States, or its territories or possessions or passing through the territorial waters thereof, and such carriage shall be as now provided by law with respect to the transit of such liquors through the Panama Canal, provided that such liquors shall be kept under seal continuously while the vessel on which they are carried remains within said territorial waters and that no part of such liquors shall at any time or place be unladen within the United States, its territories or possessions.

Article IV

Any claim by a Norwegian vessel for compensation on the grounds that it has suffered loss or injury through the improper or unreasonable exercise of the rights conferred by Article II of this Treaty or on the ground that it has been given the benefit of Article III shall be referred for the joint consideration of two persons, one of whom shall be nominated by each of the High Contracting Parties.

Effect shall be given to the recommendations contained in any such joint report. If no joint report can be agreed upon, the claim shall be referred to the Permanent Court of Arbitration at The Hague described in the Convention for the Pacific Settlement of International Disputes, concluded at The Hague, October 18, 1907. The Arbitral Tribunal shall be constituted in accordance with Article 87 (Chapter IV) and with Article 59 (Chapter III) of the said Convention. The proceedings shall be regulated by so much of Chapter IV of the said Convention and of Chapter III thereof (special regard being had for Articles 70 and 74, but excepting Articles 53 and 54) as the Tribunal may consider to be applicable and to be consistent with the provisions of this agreement. All sums of money which may be awarded by the Tribunal on account of any claim shall be paid within eighteen months after the date of the final award without interest and without deduction, save as hereafter specified. Each Government shall bear its own expenses. The expenses of the Tribunal shall be defrayed by a ratable deduction of the amount of the sums awarded by it, at a rate of five per cent. on such sums, or at such lower rate as may be agreed upon between the two Governments; the deficiency, if any, shall be defrayed in equal moieties by the two Governments.

ARTICLE V

This Treaty shall be subject to ratification and shall remain in force for a period of one year from the date of the exchange of ratifications.

Three months before the expiration of the said period of one year, either of the High Contracting Parties may give notice of its desire to propose modifications in the terms of the Treaty.

If such modifications have not been agreed upon before the expiration of the term of one year mentioned above, the Treaty shall lapse.

If no notice is given on either side of the desire to propose modifications, the Treaty shall remain in force for another year, and so on automatically, but subject always in respect of each such period of a year to the right on either side to propose as provided above three months before its expiration modifications in the Treaty, and to the provision that if such modifications are not agreed upon before the close of the period of one year, the Treaty shall lapse.

ARTICLE VI

In the event that either of the High Contracting Parties shall be prevented either by judicial decision or legislative action from giving full effect to the provisions of the present Treaty the said Treaty shall automatically lapse, and, on such lapse or whenever this Treaty shall cease to be in force, each High Contracting Party shall enjoy all the rights which it would have possessed had this Treaty not been concluded.

The present Convention shall be duly ratified by the President of the United States of America, by and with the advice and consent of the Senate thereof, and by His Majesty the King of Norway; and the ratifications shall be exchanged at Washington as soon as possible.

In witness whereof, the respective Plenipotentiaries have signed the present Convention in duplicate in the English and Norwegian languages and have thereunto affixed their seals.

Done at the city of Washington this twenty-fourth day of May, in the year of our Lord one thousand nine hundred and twenty-four.

[SEAL] CHARLES EVANS HUGHES
[SEAL] HELMER H. BRYN

Denmark, May 29, 1924

711.599/13

The Danish Chargé (Helmer-Petersen) to the Secretary of State

No. 99   WASHINGTON, *May 26, 1924.*

SIR: I have the honor to inform you that the Danish Government is prepared to sign a Treaty with the United States Government concerning the Regulations of the Liquor Traffic similar to that signed between the United States and Great Britain on January 25th [*23d*], 1924.

As I have already had the honor to communicate verbally to the Honorable the Undersecretary of State, the Danish Government proposes that in the English text of the Treaty, after the word "between" in *alinea* three of the preamble, instead of the word "them" the words "the United States of America and Denmark" should be inserted.

Furthermore the Danish Government proposes the following text of Article I of the Treaty: *The high contracting Parties respectively retain their rights and claims without prejudice by reason of this agreement with respect to the extent of their territorial jurisdiction.*

It is also desired that the full title of His Majesty the King, to wit: *His Majesty the King of Denmark and Iceland,* be inserted in the text, wherever the King is mentioned.

As I have understood that the United States Government will have no objections to these modifications, I beg to enclose a draft of the Danish text of the proposed treaty.[55]

I beg to add that, according to a cablegram received today from the Ministry of Foreign Affairs, it is expected that the full power for me can be ready for verification by the American Minister in Copenhagen on Wednesday next.

I have [etc.]   HELMER-PETERSEN

711.599/13

The Secretary of State to the Danish Chargé (Helmer-Petersen)

WASHINGTON, *May 28, 1924.*

SIR: I have the honor to acknowledge the receipt of your communication No. 99 of May 26, in which you inform me of the readiness of your Government to conclude a treaty with the United States to aid in the prevention of the smuggling of intoxicating liquors into the United States similar to that concluded between the United States and Great Britain on January 23, 1924, subject, however, to certain modifications which you specify and which are acceptable to this Government.

[55] Not printed.

You have been good enough to enclose a draft of the Danish text of the proposed treaty.

With reference to your full powers to sign the treaty, I have to inform you that the American Minister at Copenhagen has telegraphed the Department that he has inspected the same.

Permit me to suggest the hour of ten forty-five A. M. on Thursday, May 29th, as an appropriate one for the signature of the treaty, if agreeable to yourself.

Accept [etc.] CHARLES E. HUGHES

Treaty Series No. 693

Convention between the United States of America and Denmark, Signed at Washington, May 29, 1924 [56]

The President of the United States of America and His Majesty the King of Denmark and Iceland being desirous of avoiding any difficulties which might arise between the United States and Denmark in connection with the laws in force in the United States on the subject of alcoholic beverages have decided to conclude a Convention for that purpose, and have appointed as their Plenipotentiaries:

The President of the United States of America, Mr. Charles Evans Hughes, Secretary of State of the United States; and

His Majesty the King of Denmark and Iceland, Mr. Kai Helmer-Petersen, His Majesty's Chargé d'Affaires at Washington,

Who, having communicated their full powers found in good and due form, have agreed as follows:

ARTICLE I

The High Contracting Parties respectively retain their rights and claims, without prejudice by reason of this agreement, with respect to the extent of their territorial jurisdiction.

ARTICLE II

(1) His Majesty the King of Denmark and Iceland agrees that he will raise no objection to the boarding of private vessels under the Danish flag outside the limits of territorial waters by the authorities of the United States, its territories or possessions in order that enquiries may be addressed to those on board and an examination be made of the ship's papers for the purpose of ascertaining whether the vessel or those on board are endeavoring to import or have im-

---

[56] In English and Danish; Danish text not printed. Ratification advised by the Senate, June 3, 1924; ratified by the President, July 11, 1924; ratified by Denmark, July 8, 1924; ratifications exchanged at Washington, July 25, 1924; proclaimed by the President, July 25, 1924.

ported alcoholic beverages into the United States, its territories or possessions in violation of the laws there in force. When such enquiries and examination show a reasonable ground for suspicion, a search of the vessel may be initiated.

(2) If there is reasonable cause for belief that the vessel has committed or is committing or attempting to commit an offense against the laws of the United States, its territories or possessions prohibiting the importation of alcoholic beverages, the vessel may be seized and taken into a port of the United States, its territories or possessions for adjudication in accordance with such laws.

(3) The rights conferred by this article shall not be exercised at a greater distance from the coast of the United States its territories or possessions than can be traversed in one hour by the vessel suspected of endeavoring to commit the offense. In cases, however, in which the liquor is intended to be conveyed to the United States its territories or possessions by a vessel other than the one boarded and searched, it shall be the speed of such other vessel and not the speed of the vessel boarded, which shall determine the distance from the coast at which the right under this article can be exercised.

ARTICLE III

No penalty or forfeiture under the laws of the United States shall be applicable or attach to alcoholic liquors or to vessels or persons by reason of the carriage of such liquors, when such liquors are listed as sea stores or cargo destined for a port foreign to the United States, its territories or possessions on board Danish vessels voyaging to or from ports of the United States, or its territories or possessions or passing through the territorial waters thereof, and such carriage shall be as now provided by law with respect to the transit of such liquors through the Panama Canal, provided that such liquors shall be kept under seal continuously while the vessel on which they are carried remains within said territorial waters and that no part of such liquors shall at any time or place be unladen within the United States, its territories or possessions.

ARTICLE IV

Any claim by a Danish vessel for compensation on the grounds that it has suffered loss or injury through the improper or unreasonable exercise of the rights conferred by Article II of this Treaty or on the ground that it has not been given the benefit of Article III shall be referred for the joint consideration of two persons, one of whom shall be nominated by each of the High Contracting Parties.

Effect shall be given to the recommendations contained in any such joint report. If no joint report can be agreed upon, the claim shall be referred to the Permanent Court of Arbitration at The Hague described in the Convention for the Pacific Settlement of International Disputes, concluded at The Hague, October 18, 1907. The Arbitral Tribunal shall be constituted in accordance with Article 87 (Chapter IV) and with Article 59 (Chapter III) of the said Convention. The proceedings shall be regulated by so much of Chapter IV of the said Convention and of Chapter III thereof (special regard being had for Articles 70 and 74, but excepting Articles 53 and 54) as the Tribunal may consider to be applicable and to be consistent with the provisions of this agreement. All sums of money which may be awarded by the Tribunal on account of any claim shall be paid within eighteen months after the date of the final award without interest and without deduction, save as hereafter specified. Each Government shall bear its own expenses. The expenses of the Tribunal shall be defrayed by a ratable deduction of the amount of the sums awarded by it, at a rate of five per cent. on such sums, or at such lower rate as may be agreed upon between the two Governments; the deficiency, if any, shall be defrayed in equal moieties by the two Governments.

Article V

This Treaty shall be subject to ratification and shall remain in force for a period of one year from the date of the exchange of ratifications.

Three months before the expiration of the said period of one year, either of the High Contracting Parties may give notice of its desire to propose modifications in the terms of the Treaty.

If such modifications have not been agreed upon before the expiration of the term of one year mentioned above, the Treaty shall lapse.

If no notice is given on either side of the desire to propose modifications, the Treaty shall remain in force for another year, and so on automatically, but subject always in respect of each such period of a year to the right on either side to propose as provided above three months before its expiration modifications in the Treaty, and to the provision that if such modifications are not agreed upon before the close of the period of one year, the Treaty shall lapse.

Article VI

In the event that either of the High Contracting Parties shall be prevented either by judicial decision or legislative action from giving full effect to the provisions of the present Treaty the said Treaty shall automatically lapse, and, on such lapse or whenever this Treaty shall cease to be in force, each High Contracting Party shall enjoy all the rights which it would have possessed had this Treaty not been concluded.

The present Convention shall be duly ratified by the President of the United States of America, by and with the advice and consent of the Senate thereof, and by His Majesty the King of Denmark and Iceland; and the ratifications shall be exchanged at Washington as soon as possible.

In witness whereof, the respective Plenipotentiaries have signed the present Convention in duplicate in the English and Danish languages and have thereunto affixed their seals.

Done at the city of Washington this twenty-ninth day of May one thousand nine hundred and twenty-four.

[SEAL]   CHARLES EVANS HUGHES
[SEAL]   HELMER-PETERSEN

Italy, June 3, 1924

711.659/10½

Memorandum by the Secretary of State of a Conversation with the Italian Ambassador (Caetani), March 20, 1924

[Extract]

Liquor Treaty.—The Secretary referred to the request of the Ambassador to be advised in case a liquor treaty were concluded with Great Britain and stated that such a treaty had been concluded and had been approved by the Senate. The Secretary handed a copy to the Ambassador. The Secretary said that he had prepared the draft of a proposed treaty with Italy to the same effect. This was the same (with the names changed) with the exception of Article 1 and Article 4. For Article 1 of the British Treaty the Secretary had substituted in the draft treaty with Italy, in accordance with the Ambassador's suggestion at a recent conference, the following:

"The High Contracting Parties respectively retain their rights and claims, without prejudice by reason of this agreement, with respect to the extent of their territorial jurisdiction."

In the second paragraph of Article 4 the Secretary said he had inserted the substance of the provisions of the Convention of 1910 with Great Britain.[57]

---

[57] *Foreign Relations*, 1911, p. 266.

Treaties Series No. 702

Convention between the United States of America and Italy, Signed at Washington, June 3, 1924 [58]

The President of the United States of America and His Majesty the King of Italy being desirous of avoiding any difficulties which might arise between them in connection with the laws in force in the United States on the subject of alcoholic beverages have decided to conclude a Convention for that purpose, and have appointed as their Plenipotentiaries:

The President of the United States of America, Charles Evans Hughes, Secretary of State of the United States;

His Majesty the King of Italy, Signor Augusto Rosso, Counselor of His Embassy at Washington;

Who, having communicated their full powers found in good and due form, have agreed as follows:

Article I

The High Contracting Parties respectively retain their rights and claims, without prejudice by reason of this agreement, with respect to the extent of their territorial jurisdiction.

Article II

(1) The Italian Government agrees that it will raise no objection to the boarding of private vessels under the Italian flag outside the limits of territorial waters by the authorities of the United States, its territories or possessions in order that enquiries may be addressed to those on board and an examination be made of the ship's papers for the purpose of ascertaining whether the vessel or those on board are endeavoring to import or have imported alcoholic beverages into the United States, its territories or possessions in violation of the laws there in force. When such enquiries and examination show a reasonable ground for suspicion, a search of the vessel may be initiated.

(2) If there is reasonable cause for belief that the vessel has committed or is committing or attempting to commit an offense against the laws of the United States, its territories or possessions prohibiting the importation of alcoholic beverages, the vessel may be seized and taken into a port of the United States, its territories or possessions for adjudication in accordance with such laws.

---

[58] In English and Italian; Italian text not printed. Ratification advised by the Senate, June 4, 1924; ratified by the President, Oct. 16, 1924; ratified by Italy, July 7, 1924; ratifications exchanged at Washington, Oct. 22, 1924; proclaimed by the President, Oct. 22, 1924.

(3) The rights conferred by this article shall not be exercised at a greater distance from the coast of the United States its territories or possessions than can be traversed in one hour by the vessel suspected of endeavoring to commit the offense. In cases, however, in which the liquor is intended to be conveyed to the United States its territories or possessions by a vessel other than the one boarded and searched, it shall be the speed of such other vessel and not the speed of the vessel boarded, which shall determine the distance from the coast at which the right under this article can be exercised.

ARTICLE III

No penalty or forfeiture under the laws of the United States shall be applicable or attach to alcoholic liquors or to vessels or persons by reason of the carriage of such liquors, when such liquors are listed as sea stores or cargo destined for a port foreign to the United States, its territories or possessions on board Italian vessels voyaging to or from ports of the United States, or its territories or possessions or passing through the territorial waters thereof, and such carriage shall be as now provided by law with respect to the transit of such liquors through the Panama Canal, provided that such liquors shall be kept under seal continuously while the vessel on which they are carried remains within said territorial waters and that no part of such liquors shall at any time or place be unladen within the United States, its territories or possessions.

ARTICLE IV

Any claim by an Italian vessel for compensation on the grounds that it has suffered loss or injury through the improper or unreasonable exercise of the rights conferred by Article II of this Treaty or on the ground that it has not been given the benefit of Article III shall be referred for the joint consideration of two persons, one of whom shall be nominated by each of the High Contracting Parties.

Effect shall be given to the recommendations contained in any such joint report. If no joint report can be agreed upon, the claim shall be referred to the Permanent Court of Arbitration at The Hague described in the Convention for the pacific Settlement of International Disputes, concluded at The Hague, October 18, 1907. The Arbitral Tribunal shall be constituted in accordance with Article 87 (Chapter IV) and with Article 59 (Chapter III) of the said Convention. The proceedings shall be regulated by so much of Chapter IV of the said Convention and of Chapter III thereof (special regard being had for Articles 70 and 74, but excepting Articles 53 and

54) as the Tribunal may consider to be applicable and to be consistent with the provisions of this agreement. All sums of money which may be awarded by the Tribunal on account of any claim shall be paid within eighteen months after the date of the final award without interest and without deduction, save as hereafter specified. Each Government shall bear its own expenses. The expenses of the Tribunal shall be defrayed by a ratable deduction of the amount of the sums awarded by it, at a rate of five per cent. on such sums, or at such lower rate as may be agreed upon between the two Governments; the deficiency, if any, shall be defrayed in equal moieties by the two Governments.

Article V

This Treaty shall be subject to ratification and shall remain in force for a period of one year from the date of the exchange of ratifications.

Three months before the expiration of the said period of one year, either of the High Contracting Parties may give notice of its desire to propose modifications in the terms of the Treaty.

If such modifications have not been agreed upon before the expiration of the term of one year mentioned above, the Treaty shall lapse.

If no notice is given on either side of the desire to propose modifications, the Treaty shall remain in force for another year, and so on automatically, but subject always in respect of each such period of a year to the right on either side to propose as provided above three months before its expiration modifications in the Treaty, and to the provision that if such modifications are not agreed upon before the close of the period of one year, the Treaty shall lapse.

Article VI

In the event that either of the High Contracting Parties shall be prevented either by judicial decision or legislative action from giving full effect to the provisions of the present Treaty the said Treaty shall automatically lapse, and, on such lapse or whenever this Treaty shall cease to be in force, each High Contracting Party shall enjoy all the rights which it would have possessed had this Treaty not been concluded.

The present Convention shall be duly ratified by the President of the United States of America, by and with the advice and consent of the Senate thereof, and by His Majesty the King of Italy; and the ratifications shall be exchanged at Washington as soon as possible.

In witness whereof, the respective Plenipotentiaries have signed the present Convention in duplicate, in the English and Italian languages, and have thereunto affixed their seals.

Done at the city of Washington this third day of June in the year of our Lord one thousand nine hundred and twenty-four.

[SEAL]   CHARLES EVANS HUGHES
[SEAL]   AUGUSTO ROSSO

Great Britain in Respect of Canada, June 6, 1924

811.114 Ottawa Conference/72

The Secretary of State to the British Ambassador (Howard)

WASHINGTON, *June 4, 1924.*

EXCELLENCY: I have the honor to acknowledge the receipt of your communication No. 478 of May 28, 1924,[59] with which you were good enough to submit to me a draft of the proposed treaty between the United States and the Dominion of Canada for the purpose of suppressing the illicit liquor traffic across the international boundary between the two countries and for other purposes, and which you inform me was drawn up as a result of recommendations agreed upon by representatives of the United States and Canada in the conference held at Ottawa November last.[60]

You add that Lord Byng of Vimy feels confident that the terms of the treaty will be agreeable to this Government and requests you to emphasize the mutual advantages which would accrue to both the governments concerned if the treaty should be signed and ratified during the present session of the Congress. You request, moreover, to be furnished with an expression of my views as soon as possible.

The text of the Canadian draft has been examined with care by the appropriate authorities of this Government. Save with respect to a few minor details which it is believed might be capable of adjustment in conference, this Government is prepared to accept the Canadian draft.

Inasmuch as the interval is very brief before the adjournment of Congress, I am hopeful that the Honorable Ernest Lapointe, K. C. who, I am advised by your Embassy has been empowered to conclude the treaty proposed with this Government and to sign the same in behalf of His Majesty the King in respect to the Dominion of Canada, may be good enough to come to Washington at the earliest possible moment. Through his presence here the treaty might be signed and submitted to the Senate before its adjournment.

Accept [etc.]   CHARLES E. HUGHES

---

[59] Not printed.
[60] See *Foreign Relations*, 1923, vol. I, pp. 228 ff.

Treaty Series No. 718

Convention between the United States of America and Great Britain in Respect of Canada, Signed at Washington, June 6, 1924 [61]

The United States of America and His Majesty the King of the United Kingdom of Great Britain and Ireland and of the British Dominions beyond the Seas, Emperor of India, in respect of the Dominion of Canada, being desirous of suppressing smuggling operations along the boundary between the United States of America and the Dominion of Canada, and of assisting in the arrest and prosecution of persons violating the narcotic laws of either Government, and of providing as to the omission of penalties and forfeitures in respect to the carriage of alcoholic liquors through Alaska into the Yukon territory, have agreed to conclude a Convention to give effect to these purposes and have named as their Plenipotentiaries:

The President of the United States of America: Charles Evans Hughes, Secretary of State of the United States; and

His Britannic Majesty, in respect of the Dominion of Canada: The Honorable Ernest Lapointe, K. C., a member of His Majesty's Privy Council for Canada and Minister of Justice in the Government of that Dominion;

Who, having communicated to each other their respective full powers, which were found to be in due and proper form, have agreed upon the following articles:

ARTICLE I

The High Contracting Parties agree that the appropriate officers of the Governments of the United States of America and of Canada respectively shall be required to furnish upon request to duly authorized officers of the other Government, information concerning clearances of vessels or the transportation of cargoes, shipments or loads of articles across the international boundary when the importation of the cargo carried or of articles transported by land is subject to the payment of duties; also to furnish information respecting clearances of vessels to any ports when there is ground to suspect that the owners or persons in possession of the cargo intend to smuggle it into the territory of the United States or of Canada.

[61] Ratification advised by the Senate, Dec. 10, 1924; ratified by the President, Dec. 17, 1924; ratified by Great Britain, May 7, 1925; ratifications exchanged at Washington, July 17, 1925; proclaimed by the President, July 17, 1925.

Article II

The High Contracting Parties agree that clearance from the United States or from Canada shall be denied to any vessel carrying cargo consisting of articles the importation of which into the territory of the United States or of Canada, as the case may be, is prohibited, when it is evident from the tonnage, size and general character of the vessel, or the length of the voyage and the perils or conditions of navigation attendant upon it, that the vessel will be unable to carry its cargo to the destination proposed in the application for clearance.

Article III

Each of the High Contracting Parties agrees with the other that property of all kinds in its possession which, having been stolen and brought into the territory of the United States or of Canada, is seized by its customs authorities shall, when the owners are nationals of the other country, be returned to such owners, subject to satisfactory proof of such ownership and the absence of any collusion, and subject moreover to payment of the expenses of the seizure and detention and to the abandonment of any claims by the owners against the customs, or the customs officers, warehousemen or agents, for compensation or damages for the seizure, detention, warehousing or keeping of the property.

Article IV

The High Contracting Parties reciprocally agree to exchange information concerning the names and activities of all persons known or suspected to be engaged in violations of the narcotic laws of the United States or of Canada respectively.

Article V

It is agreed that the customs and other administrative officials of the respective Governments of the United States and of Canada shall upon request be directed to attend as witnesses and to produce such available records and files or certified copies thereof as may be considered essential to the trial of civil or criminal cases, and as may be produced compatibly with the public interest.

The cost of transcripts of records, depositions, certificates and letters rogatory in civil or criminal cases, and the cost of first-class transportation both ways, maintenance and other proper expenses involved in the attendance of such witnesses shall be paid by the nation requesting their attendance at the time of their discharge by the court from further attendance at such trial. Letters rogatory and commissions shall be executed with all possible despatch and copies of official records or documents shall be certified promptly by the appropriate officials in accordance with the provisions of the laws of the respective countries.

ARTICLE VI

The following offenses are added to the list of offenses numbered 1 to 3 in Article I of the Treaty concluded between the United States and Great Britain on May 18, 1908,[62] with reference to reciprocal rights for the United States and Canada in the matters of conveyance of prisoners and wrecking and salvage, that is to say:

4. Offenses against the narcotic laws of the respective Governments.

ARTICLE VII

No penalty or forfeiture under the laws of the United States shall be applicable or attached to alcoholic liquors or to vessels, vehicles or persons by reason of the carriage of such liquors when they are in transit under guard by Canadian authorities through the territorial waters of the United States to Skagway, Alaska, and thence by the shortest route, via the White Pass and Yukon Railway, upwards of twenty miles to Canadian territory, and such transit shall be as now provided by law with respect to the transit of alcoholic liquors through the Panama Canal or on the Panama Railroad, provided that such liquors shall be kept under seal continuously while the vessel or vehicle on which they are carried remains within the United States, its territories or possessions, and that no part of such liquors shall at any time or place be unladen within the United States, its territories or possessions.

ARTICLE VIII

This Convention shall be ratified, and the ratifications shall be exchanged at Washington as soon as possible. The Convention shall come into effect at the expiration of ten days from the date of the exchange of ratifications, and it shall remain in force for one year. If upon the expiration of one year after the Convention shall have been in force no notice is given by either party of a desire to terminate the same, it shall continue in force until thirty days after either party shall have given notice to the other of a desire to terminate the Convention.

---

[62] *Foreign Relations,* 1908, p. 397.

IN WITNESS WHEREOF, the respective Plenipotentiaries have signed the present Convention in duplicate and have thereunto affixed their seals.

DONE at the city of Washington this sixth day of June, one thousand nine hundred and twenty-four.

[SEAL]   CHARLES EVANS HUGHES
[SEAL]   ERNEST LAPOINTE

Panama, June 6, 1924

711.199/orig.

The Chief of the Division of Latin American Affairs, Department of State (White) to the Secretary of State

WASHINGTON, *May 28, 1924.*

DEAR MR. SECRETARY: The Panaman Minister has just telephoned to say that he had received instructions from his Government to sign the liquor treaty as given to him the other day (I gave him an exact copy of the German treaty, *mutatis mutandis*). His Government desired, however, to have reference made to the special conditions existing between the Canal Zone and Panama and the question of the three mile limit. Certain waters three miles from the Canal Zone limits are Panaman territorial waters, and he suggests an exchange of notes at the time of the signing of the treaty making reservations on this point. He would also like to have it stated in the exchange of notes that the article which we have agreed upon on the subject of the carriage of liquors, under seal and certificate by the Panaman authorities from the terminal ports of the Canal to the cities of Panama and Colon and from those cities to other ports in the Republic, for inclusion in the treaty to take the place of the Taft Agreement [63] will in no manner be prejudiced by the signing of this special liquor treaty. Mr. Baker is drafting the proposed exchange of notes.

WHITE

Treaty Series No. 707

Convention between the United States of America and Panama, Signed at Washington, June 6, 1924 [64]

The President of the United States of America and the President of the Republic of Panama being desirous of avoiding any difficulties

---

[63] For correspondence on inconclusive negotiations for a convention to replace the Taft Agreement, see vol. II, pp. 521 ff.

[64] In English and Spanish; Spanish text not printed. Ratification advised by the Senate, Dec. 12, 1924; ratified by the President, Jan. 15, 1925; ratified by Panama, Dec. 30, 1924; ratifications exchanged at Washington, Jan. 19, 1925; proclaimed by the President, Jan. 19, 1925.

which might arise between them in connection with the laws in force in the United States on the subject of alcoholic beverages have decided to conclude a Convention for that purpose, and have appointed as their Plenipotentiaries:

The President of the United States of America, Charles Evans Hughes, Secretary of State of the United States of America, and

The President of Panama, Ricardo J. Alfaro, Envoy Extraordinary and Minister Plenipotentiary of the Republic of Panama in Washington,

Who, having communicated their full powers found in good and due form, have agreed as follows:

Article I

The High Contracting Parties declare that it is their firm intention to uphold the principle that three marine miles extending from the coast line outwards and measured from low-water mark constitute the proper limits of territorial waters.

Article II

(1) The President of Panama agrees that Panama will raise no objection to the boarding of private vessels under the Panaman flag outside the limits of territorial waters by the authorities of the United States, its territories or possessions, in order that enquiries may be addressed to those on board and an examination be made of the ship's papers for the purpose of ascertaining whether the vessel or those on board are endeavoring to import or have imported alcoholic beverages into the United States, its territories or possessions in violation of the laws there in force. When such enquiries and examinations show a reasonable ground for suspicion, a search of the vessel may be initiated.

(2) If there is reasonable cause for belief that the vessel has committed or is committing or attempting to commit an offense against the laws of the United States, its territories or possessions prohibiting the importation of alcoholic beverages, the vessel may be seized and taken into a port of the United States, its territories or possessions for adjudication in accordance with such laws.

(3) The rights conferred by this article shall not be exercised at a greater distance from the coast of the United States its territories or possessions than can be traversed in one hour by the vessel suspected of endeavoring to commit the offense, and shall not be exercised in waters adjacent to territorial waters of the Canal Zone. In cases, however, in which the liquor is intended to be conveyed to the United States its territories or possessions by a vessel other than the

one boarded and searched, it shall be the speed of such other vessel and not the speed of the vessel boarded, which shall determine the distance from the coast at which the right under this article can be exercised.

ARTICLE III

No penalty or forfeiture under the laws of the United States shall be applicable or attach to alcoholic liquors or to vessels or persons by reason of the carriage of such liquors, when such liquors are listed as sea stores or cargo destined for a port foreign to the United States, its territories or possessions on board Panaman vessels voyaging to or from ports of the United States, or its territories or possessions or passing through the territorial waters thereof, and such carriage shall be as now provided by law with respect to the transit of such liquors through the Panama Canal, provided that such liquors shall be kept under seal continuously while the vessel on which they are carried remains within said territorial waters and that no part of such liquors shall at any time or place be unladen within the United States, its territories or possessions.

ARTICLE IV

Any claim by a Panaman vessel for compensation on the grounds that it has suffered loss or injury through the improper or unreasonable exercise of the rights conferred by Article II of this Treaty or on the ground that it has not been given the benefit of Article III shall be referred for the joint consideration of two persons, one of whom shall be nominated by each of the High Contracting Parties.

Effect shall be given to the recommendations contained in any such joint report. If no joint report can be agreed upon, the claim shall be referred to the Permanent Court of Arbitration at The Hague described in the Convention for the Pacific Settlement of International Disputes, concluded at The Hague, October 18, 1907. The Arbitral Tribunal shall be constituted in accordance with Article 87 (Chapter IV) and with Article 59 (Chapter III) of the said Convention. The proceedings shall be regulated by so much of Chapter IV of the said Convention and of Chapter III thereof (special regard being had for Articles 70 and 74, but excepting Articles 53 and 54) as the Tribunal may consider to be applicable and to be consistent with the provisions of this agreement. All sums of money which may be awarded by the Tribunal on account of any claim shall be paid within eighteen months after the date of the final award without interest and without deduction, save as hereafter specified. Each Government shall bear its own expenses. The expenses of the Tribunal shall be defrayed by a ratable deduction of the amount of the sums awarded by it, at a rate of five per cent. on such sums, or at such lower rate as may be agreed upon between the two Governments; the deficiency, if any, shall be defrayed in equal moieties by the two Governments.

ARTICLE V

This Treaty shall be subject to ratification and shall remain in force for a period of one year from the date of the exchange of ratifications.

Three months before the expiration of the said period of one year, either of the High Contracting Parties may give notice of its desire to propose modifications in the terms of the Treaty.

If such modifications have not been agreed upon before the expiration of the term of one year mentioned above, the Treaty shall lapse.

If no notice is given on either side of the desire to propose modifications, the Treaty shall remain in force for another year, and so on automatically, but subject always in respect of each such period of a year to the right on either side to propose as provided above three months before its expiration modifications in the Treaty, and to the provision that if such modifications are not agreed upon before the close of the period of one year, the Treaty shall lapse.

ARTICLE VI

In the event that either of the High Contracting Parties shall be prevented either by judicial decision or legislative action from giving full effect to the provisions of the present Treaty the said Treaty shall automatically lapse, and, on such lapse or whenever this Treaty shall cease to be in force, each High Contracting Party shall enjoy all the rights which it would have possessed had this Treaty not been concluded.

The present Convention shall be duly ratified by the President of the United States of America, by and with the advice and consent of the Senate thereof and by the President of Panama in accordance with the requirements of the Panaman Constitution; and the ratifications shall be exchanged at Washington as soon as possible.

In witness whereof, the respective Plenipotentiaries have signed the present Convention in duplicate and have thereunto affixed their seals.

Done at the city of Washington, this sixth day of June in the year of our Lord one thousand nine hundred and twenty-four.

[SEAL]   CHARLES EVANS HUGHES
[SEAL]   R. J. ALFARO

711.199/3b

The Secretary of State to the Panaman Minister (Alfaro)

WASHINGTON, *June 6, 1924.*

SIR: I have the honor to confirm to you the understanding developed in the conversations that took place during the negotiation of the treaty signed by us today to aid in the prevention of the smuggling of intoxicating liquors into the United States, that the signing of this treaty will in no wise affect the inclusion in the treaty now under negotiation to take the place of the Taft Agreement of an article in the terms of Exhibit 8 of the American Commissioners reading as follows:

It is agreed that no penalty or forfeiture under the laws of the United States shall be applicable or attach to alcoholic liquors or to vehicles or persons by reason of the carriage of such liquors when they are transported under seal and under certificate by Panaman authority from the terminal ports of the Canal to the cities of Panama and Colon and between those cities and any other point of the Republic and between any two points of the territory of the Republic when in either case the direct or natural means of communication is through Canal Zone territory and provided that such liquors remain under said seal and certificate while they are passing through Canal Zone territory.

Accept [etc.]   CHARLES E. HUGHES

711.199/6

The Panaman Minister (Alfaro) to the Secretary of State

[Translation]

No. D. 360   WASHINGTON, *July 7, 1924.*

MR. SECRETARY: I have the honor to inform Your Excellency that my Government informs me that it has received a copy of the treaty signed by Your Excellency and by me to prevent the smuggling of alcoholic beverages in the United States of America. I have also received the note sent by Your Excellency to this Legation about the explanation offered by Your Excellency that the treaty does not in any way interfere with the insertion of the clause already agreed on in the new treaty to take the place of the Taft Agreement concerning the enforcement of the Volstead law in the Canal Zone. My Government also informs me that as soon as the National Assembly meets again the treaty will be referred to it for its approval.

I avail myself [etc.]   R. J. ALFARO

857H.01/21½

France, June 30, 1924

Memorandum by the Secretary of State of a Conversation with the French Ambassador (Jusserand), June 21, 1924

[Extract]

The Ambassador submitted a draft of a treaty to prevent the smuggling of intoxicating liquors. He said that the French Government preferred Article I as it had appeared in the treaties with Norway, Sweden and Italy. The Secretary said that that was satisfactory. The Ambassador said that his Government proposed a modification in order to make more efficacious the provision for an agreement under Article IV, that is, it was proposed to insert a line to the effect that if the two persons selected to make the inquiry failed to agree there should be one other step before it went to the Permanent Court at the Hague, that is, that the two Governments should choose a third arbitrator and should go to the Hague if they were unable to agree upon a choice. The Secretary said that he would give the matter consideration.[65]

Treaty Series No. 755

Convention between the United States of America and France, Signed at Washington, June 30, 1924 [66]

The President of the United States of America and the President of the French Republic being desirous of avoiding any difficulties which might arise between them in connection with the laws in force in the United States on the subject of alcoholic beverages have decided to conclude a Convention for that purpose, and have appointed as their Plenipotentiaries:

The President of the United States of America: Mr. Charles Evans Hughes, Secretary of State of the United States; and

The President of the French Republic: Mr. J. J. Jusserand, Ambassador of the French Republic to the United States;

Who, having communicated their full powers found in good and due form, have agreed as follows:

ARTICLE I

The High Contracting Parties respectively retain their rights and claims, without prejudice by reason of this agreement, with respect to the extent of their territorial jurisdiction.

---

[65] The modification proposed was made in the treaty as signed.

[66] In English and French; French text not printed. Ratification advised by the Senate, Dec. 12, 1924; ratified by the President, Dec. 30, 1924; ratified by France, Mar. 1, 1927; ratifications exchanged at Washington, Mar. 12, 1927; proclaimed by the President, Mar. 12, 1927.

Article II

(1) The President of the French Republic agrees that France will raise no objection to the boarding of private vessels under the French flag outside the limits of territorial waters by the authorities of the United States, its territories or possessions in order that enquiries may be addressed to those on board and an examination be made of the ship's papers for the purpose of ascertaining whether the vessel or those on board are endeavoring to import or have imported alcoholic beverages into the United States, its territories or possessions in violation of the laws there in force. When such enquiries and examination show a reasonable ground for suspicion, a search of the vessel may be effected.

(2) If there is reasonable cause for belief that the vessel has committed or is committing or attempting to commit an offense against the laws of the United States, its territories or possessions prohibiting the importation of alcoholic beverages, the vessel may be seized and taken into a port of the United States, its territories or possessions for adjudication in accordance with such laws.

(3) The rights conferred by this article shall not be exercised at a greater distance from the coast of the United States its territories or possessions than can be traversed in one hour by the vessel suspected of endeavoring to commit the offense. In cases, however, in which the liquor is intended to be conveyed to the United States its territories or possessions by a vessel other than the one boarded and searched, it shall be the speed of such other vessel and not the speed of the vessel boarded, which shall determine the distance from the coast at which the right under this article can be exercised.

Article III

No penalty or forfeiture under the laws of the United States shall be applicable or attach to alcoholic liquors or to vessels or persons by reason of the carriage of such liquors, when such liquors are listed as sea stores or cargo destined for a port foreign to the United States, its territories or possessions on board French vessels voyaging to or from ports of the United States, or its territories or possessions or passing through the territorial waters thereof, and such carriage shall be as now provided by law with respect to the transit of such liquors through the Panama Canal, provided that such liquors shall be kept under seal continuously while the vessel on which they are carried remains within said territorial waters and that no part of such liquors shall at any time or place be unladen within the United States, its territories or possessions.

Article IV

Any claim by a French vessel for compensation on the grounds that it has suffered loss or injury through the improper or unreasonable exercise of the rights conferred by Article II of this Treaty or on the ground that it has not been given the benefit of Article III shall be referred for the joint consideration of two persons, one of whom shall be nominated by each of the High Contracting Parties. Effect shall be given to the recommendations contained in any such joint report. If no joint report can be agreed upon, the claim shall be referred to an umpire selected by the two Governments; should they fail to agree on the choice of that umpire, it shall be referred to the Permanent Court of Arbitration at The Hague described in the Convention for the Pacific Settlement of International Disputes, concluded at The Hague, October 18, 1907. The Arbitral Tribunal shall be constituted in accordance with Article 87 (Chapter IV) and with Article 59 (Chapter III) of the said Convention. The proceedings shall be regulated by so much of Chapter IV of the said Convention and of Chapter III thereof (special regard being had for Articles 70 and 74, but excepting Articles 53 and 54) as the Tribunal may consider to be applicable and to be consistent with the provisions of this agreement. All sums of money which may be awarded by the Tribunal on account of any claim shall be paid within eighteen months after the date of the final award without interest and without deduction, save as hereafter specified. Each Government shall bear its own expenses. The expenses of the Tribunal shall be defrayed by a ratable deduction of the amount of the sums awarded by it, at a rate of five per cent. on such sums, or at such lower rate as may be agreed upon between the two Governments; the deficiency, if any, shall be defrayed in equal moieties by the two Governments.

Article V

This Treaty shall be subject to ratification and shall remain in force for a period of one year from the date of the exchange of ratifications.

Three months before the expiration of the said period of one year, either of the High Contracting Parties may give notice of its desire to propose modifications in the terms of the Treaty.

If such modifications have not been agreed upon before the expiration of the term of one year mentioned above, the Treaty shall lapse.

If no notice is given on either side of the desire to propose modifications, the Treaty shall remain in force for another year, and so on automatically, but subject always in respect of each such period of a year to the right on either side to propose as provided above three months before its expiration modifications in the Treaty, and to the provision that if such modifications are not agreed upon before the close of the period of one year, the Treaty shall lapse.

ARTICLE VI

In the event that either of the High Contracting Parties shall be prevented either by judicial decision or legislative action from giving full effect to the provisions of the present Treaty the said Treaty shall automatically lapse, and, on such lapse or whenever this Treaty shall cease to be in force, each High Contracting Party shall enjoy all the rights which it would have possessed had this Treaty not been concluded.

The present Convention shall be duly ratified by the President of the United States of America, by and with the advice and consent of the Senate thereof, and by the President of the French Republic in accordance with the constitutional laws of France; and the ratifications shall be exchanged at Washington as soon as possible.

In witness whereof, the respective Plenipotentiaries have signed the present Convention in duplicate in the English and French languages and have thereunto affixed their seals.

Done at the city of Washington this thirtieth day of June, one thousand nine hundred and twenty-four.

[SEAL]   CHARLES EVANS HUGHES
[SEAL]   JUSSERAND

The Netherlands, August 21, 1924

711.569/16

The Netherland Minister (De Graeff) to the Secretary of State

No. 1595

The Minister of The Netherlands presents his compliments to the Honorable, the Secretary of State and acting upon instructions received from the Minister for Foreign Affairs in The Hague, has the honor to inform him, that the Royal Government having taken cognizance of the draft of a convention to regulate the traffic of alcoholic beverages, proposed to Her by the United States Government, suggests the following modifications in the text of that document.

1. The Royal Government proposes to insert in the first paragraph of the Article 2 the words: "hovering off the coasts of the United States" after the word: "flag", so as to read this paragraph as it was originally drawn up in the draft treaty submitted to the Royal Government by the American Minister at The Hague in November

1923. By the insertion of these words the right of boarding, etc. will be limited to those cases whereto the treaty in fact pertains and will not be extended to regular mail steamers in normal course, which if necessary can be examined after their arrival within American territorial waters.

2. The wording of the third paragraph of the Article 2 seeming complicated and apt to give rise to controversies the Royal Government recommends the substitution in the paragraph's first sentence of the words: "at a distance greater than 12 geographical miles (each 1/60 equatorial degree) from the coast of the United States, its territories or possessions" for the words: "at a greater distance from the coast of the United States, its territories or possessions than can be traversed in an hour by the vessel suspected of endeavoring to commit the offense", and the striking out of the paragraph's second sentence.

In case the United States Government should not be able to agree with this modification, it seems at any rate desirable to add a clause to this article, stipulating that the rights conferred by it can never be exercised at a distance greater than 12 geographical miles from the coast of the United States, its territories or possessions.

3. It seems further desirable to make an exception on the stipulation in Article 3 prohibiting the unloading of liquor within the United States, in so far that unloading for transhipment in another Netherland vessel may be possible. The addition to the end of the article 3 of the words: "unloading for transhipment in another Netherland vessel is allowed" is therefore proposed.

It be moreover well understood that by "seastores" not only the liquor destined for the use of the crew and the passengers is meant but also the provisions for medical purposes.

4. The Royal Government agrees with the provisions of the first part of the Article 4, ruling that claims for compensation will be referred to the joint consideration of two persons nominated for the purpose and that in case no joint report can be agreed upon, these claims shall be submitted to the Permanent Court of Arbitration. The arrangement however prescribed in the second part of this article seems hardly to be acceptable. The latter part of this article is evidently taken from the "special agreement for the submitting to arbitration of pecuniary claims outstanding between Great Britain and the United States" of August 18, 1910.[67] This agreement existing between the Union and the United Kingdom, it is a matter of course that the claims arising eventually from any new agreement concluded between these two Powers be submitted to the same special procedure. As, however, no such a special

---

[67] *Foreign Relations*, 1911, p. 266.

agreement exists between the United States and The Netherlands it will be difficult to the Royal Government to accept the special arrangement, mentioned in the second part of the Article 4, the more so as this arrangement greatly differs from the way generally adopted for settling claims by arbitration and as it does not harmonize with the system adopted in other treaties concluded by the Netherlands. The Royal Government suggests therefore to replace the last part of this article beginning with the words: "All sums of money etc. . . . ["] by the sentence: "Each Government shall bear its own expenses and half of the expenses of the tribunal". So the stipulation shall be in harmony with the tenor of the article 57 of the Convention of 1899 (Art. 85 of the Convention of 1907),[68] which article is declared applicable by the Arbitration Convention, concluded between the United States and The Netherlands.[69] It does further seem unnecessary to exclude the applicability of the articles 53 and 54 of the Convention of 1907. In case the High Contracting Parties might not succeed in agreeing upon a compromise, it is not clear why a solution should not be found in the way prescribed by the aforesaid articles.

5. To the opinion of the Royal Government the meaning of the second and subsequent paragraphs of the Article 5 does not seem very clear. According to the letter of these paragraphs a simple denunciation of the convention by one party is not allowed; in case such party wishes to terminate the convention the only way for her is to propose a modification unacceptable for the other party. On the other side each proposed but not accepted modification automatically does terminate the whole convention even in case such modification may not be of such a nature that the party which made the proposal wishes such consequence. It being obvious that this would not be in accordance with the intentions of the United States Government the Royal Government proposes to read these paragraphs as follows: "If neither of the High Contracting Parties has given notice three months before the expiration of the said period of its intention to terminate the treaty, it shall be deemed to be renewed for a further period of a year and so on automatically, each party being free to terminate it by giving notice at least three months before the expiration of each period. If either of the High Contracting Parties has given notice of its desire to terminate the treaty it shall lapse at the end of that period".

6. The Royal Government recommends an exchange of notes at the time of the conclusion of this convention regarding the substitution of the Permanent Court of Arbitration by the Permanent

---

[68] *Foreign Relations*, 1907, pt. 2, p. 1181.
[69] *Ibid.*, 1909, p. 442.

Court of International Justice, in case the United States adhere to the Protocol of the latter Court.

7. The Royal Government wishes the convention to be concluded in the English and Dutch languages.

WASHINGTON, *June 12, 1924.*

711.569/16

The Secretary of State to the Netherland Minister (De Graeff)

The Secretary of State presents his compliments to the Netherlands Minister and acknowledges the receipt of his communication of June 12, 1924, in which there are set forth certain modifications proposed by the Netherlands Government of the draft of the convention submitted by the Government of the United States with respect to the prevention of smuggling of intoxicating liquors into the United States.

The Government of the United States deems it of great importance that the treaties of the United States on this subject should not substantially differ. Uniformity is regarded as desirable as a means of establishing one set of regulations for the guidance of the appropriate authorities charged with the duty of enforcement of prohibitions against smuggling, and who could not without great confusion consider differences with respect to vessels of different flags. Uniformity of tenor is deemed important also with respect to other matters, such as privileges of foreign vessels in American waters, the adjustment of differences by arbitration, and the mode of amendment or termination of the treaty. Treaties similar to that submitted to the Netherlands Government have been concluded with certain other Governments; and one with Great Britain is now in force. It is, therefore, the hope of the Secretary of State that the Netherlands Government may understand that, while the Government of the United States has every disposition to conclude a treaty with the Netherlands Government similar to the British treaty and the conventions recently signed in behalf of Germany, Sweden, Norway, Denmark, and Italy, it finds obstacles in the way of the acceptance of a convention embracing the modifications proposed by the Netherlands Government in its recent communication, save with respect to the matter of languages. The Government of the United States is, of course, happy to accede to the wish of the Netherlands Government that the treaty be concluded in the Dutch and English languages.

WASHINGTON, *June 20, 1924.*

711.569/17

The Netherland Minister (De Graeff) to the Secretary of State

No. 1939   WASHINGTON, *July 10, 1924.*

SIR: I have the honor to acknowledge receipt of your note dated June 20, 1924 in which you state that the United States Government cannot agree with the modifications which the Royal Government has proposed with regard to the draft of the convention submitted by your Government with respect to the preventing of smuggling of intoxicating liquors into the United States.

After having taken cognizance of the contents of your note the Foreign Minister at The Hague feels somewhat disappointed by this decision of your Government. Jonkheer van Karnebeek is inclined to concede that for practical reasons it is desirable to establish one set of regulations for the guidance of the authorities charged with the duty of enforcement of prohibitions against smuggling. He understands that for that reason substantial differences between the treaties of the United States on this subject with one Government and with another Government are not acceptable to the United States Government as far as such differences should occur in stipulations wherewith the said authorities are concerned.

The Minister, however, regrets that in your note no further explanation has been given why also with respect to other stipulations as f. i. the adjustment of differences by arbitration and the mode of amendment or termination of the treaty, uniformity of tenor of the different treaties is deemed of so great importance that the United States Government had to object also against the modifications proposed sub 4° and 5° of my communication of June 12, 1924. It seems to my Government, also after further consideration, that strong arguments have been brought forward to support these proposals, and that there is no sufficient reason to fear confusion if matters of this kind are arranged between the United States and our country in a different way as between the United States and other countries.

Furthermore, in sub 6° of the said note I suggested an exchange of notes regarding the substitution of the Permanent Court of Arbitration by the Permanent Court of International Justice in case the United States should adhere to the Protocol of the latter Court. In your note no special mention has been made of this suggestion, which seems to my Government a logical consequence of the notes I had the pleasure to exchange with you on the occasion of the renewal of the Arbitration treaty between the United States and The Netherlands.

Being desirous to bring the negotiations about the treaty in question to a conclusion, the Royal Government, although reluctantly, has decided to abandon further discussion on the modifications proposed sub 4° and 5° of my note of June 12, 1924, but feels obliged to emphasize once more the great importances She attaches to the suggested exchange of notes and to express the hope that the United States Government as yet could be found willing to accede to this proposal. In order to make clear the intentions of the Royal Government I take the liberty to enclose herewith a draft of the note that eventually I could sign simultaneously with the signature of the Convention.[71]

In expectation of your answer, I beg to inform you that I am in possession of a formal authorization to sign on behalf of the Royal Government a treaty in conformity with the draft which you handed to me on March 22, 1924, provided that in the penultimate paragraph the words "in the English and Dutch languages" are inserted between the words "in duplicate" and "and".

The Dutch text of the drafted convention has been mailed to me but has not yet reached me.

Accept [etc.] De Graeff

711.569/17

The Acting Secretary of State to the Netherland Minister (De Graeff)

Washington, *July 29, 1924.*

Sir: I have the honor to acknowledge the receipt of your note dated July 10, 1924 and to express gratification that you have been authorized to sign a convention relating to the prevention of the smuggling of intoxicating liquors into the United States in the form of a draft submitted to your Government, provided that it is executed in the Dutch and English languages.

The Government of the United States will be glad to accede to your request that notes be exchanged expressing the understanding that if the United States adheres to the protocol establishing the Permanent Court of International Justice, the Government of the United States will not be averse to considering a modification of the convention to provide that claims arising under the convention shall be referred to the Permanent Court of International Justice instead of to the Permanent Court of Arbitration.

Upon the receipt of the Dutch text, which you state has been mailed to you, the Department will be prepared to proceed to the signature of the treaty.

Accept [etc.] Joseph C. Grew

---

[71] Draft note not printed; same as signed note no. 2330, Aug. 21, 1924, *post,* p. 210.

711.569/20

The Netherland Minister (De Graeff) to the Acting Secretary of State

WASHINGTON, *August 6, 1924.*

MY DEAR MR. GREW: In connection with the so called liquor treaty that soon will be concluded between the United States and the Royal Government I take liberty to ask you whether it would be possible that the provisions of that treaty practically are put in force already from the date of signature of the treaty. My Government is quite willing to accept the consequences of that treaty pending the exchange of ratifications and we hope sincerely that the American Government could do the same, so that the American authorities from the date of signature are entitled to board and to search our ships outside the 3-mile limit and on the other side our ships may carry alcoholic beverages under seal within that limit.

As on account of the recess of the Senate ratification of the treaty cannot be expected before the beginning of next year both parties for purely formal reasons still for several months would be deprived of the benefits of the treaty and in the opinion of my Government this would be regrettable and useless as there is no reasonable doubt whether the treaty will have the approval of the Senate and of our Parliament.

The question is for us of special importance as after the decision of the Supreme Court [72] our steamship companies had to abandon the carrying of alcoholic beverages in transit to our West Indian colonies and they are anxious to resume this profitable business as soon as possible.

I would highly appreciate if you could let me know at your earliest convenience if the American Government could agree with this proposal and eventually would be willing to issue instructions to the authorities concerned so that the carrying of alcoholic beverages under seal will be allowed to our ships from the date of signature of the treaty.

While offering you my anticipated thanks I avail myself [etc.]

DE GRAEFF

711.569/20

The Secretary of State to the Netherland Minister (De Graeff)

WASHINGTON, *August 21, 1924.*

MY DEAR MR. MINISTER: I beg to acknowledge the receipt of your note dated August 6, 1924, in which you inquire whether it will be

---

[72] See letter of May 3, 1923, to the chiefs of foreign missions in the United States, *Foreign Relations*, 1923, vol. I, p. 133.

possible that the so-called liquor treaty between the United States and the Netherlands be put in force from the date of the signature of the treaty without awaiting its ratification, so that the American authorities would be entitled from the date of signature to board and search Netherlands ships outside of the three mile limit and Netherlands ships would be entitled to carry alcoholic beverages under seal within that limit from the same date.

By way of response I am obliged to inform you that this Government finds itself unable to give application to the treaty prior to the exchange of ratifications and proclamation thereof.

I am [etc.]   CHARLES E. HUGHES

Treaty Series No. 712

Convention between the United States of America and the Netherlands, Signed at Washington, August 21, 1924 [73]

The President of the United States of America and Her Majesty the Queen of the Netherlands being desirous of avoiding any difficulties which might arise between them in connection with the laws in force in the United States on the subject of alcoholic beverages have decided to conclude a Convention for that purpose, and have appointed as their Plenipotentiaries:

The President of the United States of America: Charles Evans Hughes, Secretary of State of the United States; and

Her Majesty the Queen of the Netherlands: Jonkheer Dr. A. C. D. de Graeff, Her Envoy Extraordinary and Minister Plenipotentiary to the United States of America;

Who, having communicated their full powers found in good and due form, have agreed as follows:

ARTICLE I

The High Contracting Parties declare that it is their firm intention to uphold the principle that 3 marine miles extending from the coastline outwards and measured from low-water mark constitute the proper limits of territorial waters.

ARTICLE II

(1) Her Majesty agrees that she will raise no objection to the boarding of private vessels under the Netherlands flag outside the limits of territorial waters by the authorities of the United States,

---

[73] In English and Dutch; Dutch text not printed. Ratification advised by the Senate, Dec. 12, 1924; ratified by the President, Feb. 26, 1925; ratified by the Netherlands, Mar. 31, 1925; ratifications exchanged at Washington, Apr. 8, 1925; proclaimed by the President, Apr. 8, 1925.

its territories or possessions in order that enquiries may be addressed to those on board and an examination be made of the ship's papers for the purpose of ascertaining whether the vessel or those on board are endeavoring to import or have imported alcoholic beverages into the United States, its territories or possessions in violation of the laws there in force. When such enquiries and examination show a reasonable ground for suspicion, a search of the vessel may be initiated.

(2) If there is reasonable cause for belief that the vessel has committed or is committing or attempting to commit an offense against the laws of the United States, its territories or possessions prohibiting the importation of alcoholic beverages, the vessel may be seized and taken into a port of the United States, its territories or possessions for adjudication in accordance with such laws.

(3) The rights conferred by this article shall not be exercised at a greater distance from the coast of the United States its territories or possessions than can be traversed in one hour by the vessel suspected of endeavoring to commit the offense. In cases, however, in which the liquor is intended to be conveyed to the United States its territories or possessions by a vessel other than the one boarded and searched, it shall be the speed of such other vessel and not the speed of the vessel boarded, which shall determine the distance from the coast at which the right under this article can be exercised.

Article III

No penalty or forfeiture under the laws of the United States shall be applicable or attach to alcoholic liquors or to vessels or persons by reason of the carriage of such liquors, when such liquors are listed as sea stores or cargo destined for a port foreign to the United States, its territories or possessions on board Netherlands vessels voyaging to or from ports of the United States, or its territories or possessions or passing through the territorial waters thereof, and such carriage shall be as now provided by law with respect to the transit of such liquors through the Panama Canal, provided that such liquors shall be kept under seal continuously while the vessel on which they are carried remains within said territorial waters and that no part of such liquors shall at any time or place be unladen within the United States, its territories or possessions.

Article IV

Any claim by a Netherlands vessel for compensation on the grounds that it has suffered loss or injury through the improper or unreasonable exercise of the rights conferred by Article II of this

Treaty or on the ground that it has not been given the benefit of Article III shall be referred for the joint consideration of two persons, one of whom shall be nominated by each of the High Contracting Parties.

Effect shall be given to the recommendations contained in any such joint report. If no joint report can be agreed upon, the claim shall be referred to the Permanent Court of Arbitration at The Hague described in the Convention for the Pacific Settlement of International Disputes, concluded at The Hague, October 18, 1907. The arbitral tribunal shall be constituted in accordance with Article 87 (Chapter IV) and with Article 59 (Chapter III) of the said Convention. The proceedings shall be regulated by so much of Chapter IV of the said Convention and of Chapter III thereof (special regard being had for Articles 70 and 74, but excepting Articles 53 and 54) as the tribunal may consider to be applicable and to be consistent with the provisions of this agreement. All sums of money which may be awarded by the Tribunal on account of any claim shall be paid within eighteen months after the date of the final award without interest and without deduction, save as hereafter specified. Each Government shall bear its own expenses. The expenses of the Tribunal shall be defrayed by a ratable deduction of the amount of the sums awarded by it, at a rate of five per cent on such sums, or at such lower rate as may be agreed upon between the two Governments; the deficiency, if any, shall be defrayed in equal moieties by the two Governments.

Article V

This Treaty shall be subject to ratification and shall remain in force for a period of one year from the date of the exchange of ratifications.

Three months before the expiration of the said period of one year, either of the High Contracting Parties may give notice of its desire to propose modifications in the terms of the Treaty.

If such modifications have not been agreed upon before the expiration of the term of one year mentioned above, the Treaty shall lapse.

If no notice is given on either side of the desire to propose modifications, the Treaty shall remain in force for another year, and so on automatically, but subject always in respect of each such period of a year to the right on either side to propose as provided above, three months before its expiration, modifications in the Treaty, and to the provision that if such modifications are not agreed upon before the close of the period of one year, the Treaty shall lapse.

ARTICLE VI

In the event that either of the High Contracting Parties shall be prevented either by judicial decision or legislative action from giving full effect to the provisions of the present Treaty the said Treaty shall automatically lapse, and, on such lapse or whenever this Treaty shall cease to be in force, each High Contracting Party shall enjoy all the rights which it would have possessed had this Treaty not been concluded.

The present Convention shall be duly ratified by the President of the United States of America, by and with the advice and consent of the Senate thereof, and by Her Majesty the Queen of the Netherlands; and the ratifications shall be exchanged at Washington as soon as possible.

In witness whereof, the respective Plenipotentiaries have signed the present Convention in duplicate in the English and Dutch languages and have thereunto affixed their seals.

Done at the city of Washington this twenty-first day of August, in the year of our Lord one thousand nine hundred and twenty-four.

CHARLES EVANS HUGHES [SEAL]

DE GRAEFF   [SEAL]

711.569/21

The Netherland Minister (De Graeff) to the Secretary of State

No. 2330   WASHINGTON, *August 21, 1924.*

SIR: In connection with the signing today of a convention pertaining to avoid difficulties which might arise between our two Governments in connection with the laws in force in the United States on the subject of alcoholic beverages and in pursuance of our previous correspondence on the subject, I have the honor to inform you that the Royal Government understands that in the event of the adhesion by the United States to the Protocol of December 16, 1920 under which the Permanent Court of International Justice has been created at The Hague,[74] the Government of the United States will not be averse to considering a modification of the said Convention, or the making of a separate agreement, providing that claims as mentioned in Article IV of that Convention, which cannot be settled in the way as indicated in the first paragraph of that article, shall be referred to the Permanent Court of International Justice instead of the Permanent Court of Arbitration.

---

[74] *Foreign Relations*, 1920, vol. I, p. 17.

I shall be glad to have you confirm this understanding on behalf of your Government.

Accept [etc.]   DE GRAEFF

711.569/21

The Secretary of State to the Netherland Minister (De Graeff)

WASHINGTON, *August 21, 1924.*

SIR: I have the honor to acknowledge the receipt of your note of today's date, in which you were so good as to inform me, in connection with the signing this day of the Convention between the United States and the Netherlands to aid in the prevention of the smuggling of intoxicating liquors into the United States, that the Government of the Netherlands understands that in the event of the adhesion by the Government of the United States to the Protocol of December 16, 1920, under which the Permanent Court of International Justice has been created at The Hague, the Government of the United States will not be averse to considering a modification of the said Convention, or the making of a separate Agreement, providing that claims mentioned in Article IV of that Convention which can not be settled in the way indicated in the first paragraph of that Article, shall be referred to the Permanent Court of International Justice instead of to the Permanent Court of Arbitration.

Complying with your request for confirmation of this understanding, I have the honor to state that the Netherlands Government's understanding of the attitude of the Government of the United States in this respect is correct, and that in the event that the Senate gives its assent to the proposal made by the President on February 24, 1923,[75] that it consent under certain stated conditions to the adhesion by the United States to the Protocol of December 16, 1920, under which the Permanent Court of International Justice has been created at The Hague, the Government of the United States will not be averse to considering a modification of the Convention this day signed, or the making of a separate Agreement, providing for the reference of claims mentioned in Article IV of the Convention which can not be settled in the way indicated in the first paragraph of that Article, to the Permanent Court of International Justice instead of to the Permanent Court of Arbitration.

Accept [etc.]   CHARLES E. HUGHES

---

[75] *Foreign Relations*, 1923, vol. I, p. 17.

REPRESENTATIONS BY SALVADOR, CUBA, RUMANIA, NORWAY, AND ITALY REGARDING PROPOSED LEGISLATION TO RESTRICT IMMIGRATION INTO THE UNITED STATES

150.01/758

The Salvadoran Chargé (Castro) to the Secretary of State

[Translation [77]]

DE–2　　　　　　　　　　WASHINGTON, *January 4, 1924.*

MR. SECRETARY: I learn through the press that the Department of Labor has sent to the Committees on Immigration of the Senate and House of Representatives a bill relative to immigration which provides for the extension of the provisions concerning the quota of immigration to the American countries.

I regret that it becomes my duty to say to Your Excellency that if a measure like that contemplated were adopted, it would greatly concern my Government as it appears to be inconsistent with the special policy followed by the Government of the United States towards the other republics of America, a policy which has always manifested itself in acts which show that the relations of the United States with its sister republics are above all inspired by the strong ties of interest which are born of neighborhood. I will not fail to assure Your Excellency that I greatly indulge the hope that the contemplated measure will not be adopted insofar as it tends to restrict immigration from Salvador, which has always found the doors of the territory of the United States widely open to it.

I renew [etc.]　　　　　　　　HÉCTOR DAVID CASTRO

150.01/806

The Cuban Ambassador (Torriente) to the Secretary of State

[Translation [77]]

WASHINGTON, *January 14, 1924.*

MOST EXCELLENT SIR: My Government having heard of the amendment which the Honorable the Secretary of Labor, Mr. Davis, has proposed to make in the immigration law to the effect of setting a quota of admission into this country for Cuban immigrants,[78] I have the honor, in compliance with instructions received, to apply to Your Excellency and represent that the institution of such restric-

---

[77] File translation revised.
[78] Communicated by Secretary Davis to Senator Colt, Chairman of the Senate Committee on Immigration, Dec. 31, 1923, and made public in the press, Jan. 2, 1924; it advocated application of the quota arrangement to Canada, Mexico, and South and Central America.

tions with regard to Cuba might affect the commercial relations of the two countries and would greatly hamper the coming to the United States of thousands of Cuban citizens who are not immigrants, without any advantage at all in the way proposed by the Department of Labor inasmuch as very few Cubans do emigrate to this country.

In support of this statement I beg leave to call the attention of Your Excellency's Government to the fact that in Cuba letters of citizenship are not issued to any but the foreigners who become naturalized in accordance with the laws and must add that the cases of fraud that have been brought before the courts have given rise to sentences in some cases and will surely lead to the same result in others.

I avail myself [etc.]   Cosme de la Torriente

150.01/799

The Rumanian Chargé (Nano) to the Secretary of State

The Chargé d'Affaires ad interim of Roumania presents his compliments to the Secretary of State and, acting under instructions from his Government, has the honour to inform him that the bill known as the "Johnson Bill", now pending in Congress, is viewed with much concern by the Government of Roumania. While conceding absolutely the undoubted right of the United States of America to limit or even to entirely suppress immigration, the Roumanian Government cannot but be painfully surprised when it contemplates the possibility of a bill becoming law, the undisguised purpose of which is not only the reduction in the total number of admissible immigrants, but more particularly the practical elimination of immigration from southern and southeastern Europe, including Roumania. Under the terms of the bill now before Congress, which adopts as a basis for the quota the census of 1890, the quota of certain countries of northern and northeastern Europe would be but slightly modified, whereas the Roumanian quota would be reduced to a wholly negligible figure, probably around 10 to 15 percent of the present one. No attempt is even made to justify the selection of the census of 1890 as a basis for the immigration quota.

The Roumanian Government feels compelled to draw the attention of the Secretary of State to the painful impression and the disappointment which would be caused in Roumania should the bill above referred to become law in its present form, the more so as the United States of America have always expressed their determined opposition and aversion to discriminatory policies. Further, it should be considered that the adoption of the census of 1890 would not only deeply wound the pride of the Roumanian people but also strongly affect their material interests, inasmuch as Roumanian immigrants by their savings increase the amount of stable currencies available for commercial and financial purposes in Roumania. This, in turn, would not fail to have a detrimental effect on the chances of Roumania to speedily attain its goal, economic recuperation, an aim which cannot be indifferent to any Government interested in assisting the world to recover from the consequences of the world war.

[WASHINGTON,] *February 2, 1924.*
[No.] 535/1

150.01/778

The Secretary of State to the Chairman of the Committee on Immigration and Naturalization of the House of Representatives (Johnson)

WASHINGTON, *February 8, 1924.*

MY DEAR MR. JOHNSON: I have received your letter of January 28 [79] enclosing copies of "Committee Print No. 1, Selective Immigration Act," requesting any recommendations the Department of State may desire to submit with respect to this measure. I have also received a copy of H. R. 6540 introduced by you on February 1, 1924 and my comments will be made with respect to it.

I fully appreciate the importance of removing present hardships by the issue of immigration certificates to those who would normally come under immigration laws. I endorse this policy. Assuming that treaties were not violated and immigration certificates were demanded of those who normally would be classed as immigrants, I should not object to the giving of authority to Consular Officers to issue immigration certificates, provided, of course, that Consular Offices were properly equipped with the requisite staff to carry out the provisions of the law. It seems to me that the granting of such immigration certificates might be treated as so analogous to the granting of visas as properly to come within a broad description of consular functions. In the absence of the violation of any treaty, I assume that the admission of immigrants to this country could be conditioned upon their receiving an immigration certificate in the manner required by our laws; although, of course, if independent machinery through special immigration officials were sought to be set up in foreign countries such officials would have to be properly accredited to the foreign governments and could not function with-

---

[79] Not printed.

out the consent of the foreign State in whose territory they would act.

It is hardly necessary for me to say that I am in favor of suitable restrictions upon immigration. The questions which especially concern the Department of State in relation to the international effects of the proposed measure are these: (1) the question of treaty obligations; (2) the provision excluding Japanese; (3) the establishment of the quotas upon the basis of the Census of 1890.

 First. Treaties.—According to the terms of the proposed measure "immigrant" is defined (Sec. 3) as "any alien departing from any place outside the United States destined for the United States, except (1) a government official, his family, attendants, servants, and employees, (2) an alien visiting the United States as a tourist or temporarily for business or pleasure, (3) an alien in continuous transit through the United States, (4) an alien lawfully admitted to the United States who later goes in transit from one part of the United States to another through foreign contiguous territory, and (5) a bona fide alien seaman serving as such on a vessel arriving at a port of the United States and seeking to enter temporarily the United States solely in the pursuit of his calling as a seaman."

The result is that under this definition of "immigrant" all aliens are subject to the restrictions of the proposed measure unless they fall within the stated exceptions. The question at once arises whether there would be aliens, not falling within these exceptions who would be entitled to be admitted under our treaties.

Article I of the Treaty between the United States and Japan, concluded in 1911,[80] provides:

"The citizens or subjects of each of the High Contracting Parties shall have liberty to enter, travel and reside in the territories of the other to carry on trade, wholesale and retail, to own or lease and occupy houses, manufactories, warehouses and shops, to employ agents of their choice, to lease land for residential and commercial purposes, and generally to do anything incident to or necessary for trade upon the same terms as native citizens or subjects, submitting themselves to the laws and regulations there established."

There appears to be no such exception in the proposed measure as that contained in subdivision (5) of paragraph (*a*) of Section 2 of the quota act of 1921,[81] and hence the proposed restrictions would apply to Japan not simply in relation to laborers or other classes falling outside of our treaty but with respect to those who come directly within the provisions of our treaty as above set forth.

---

[80] *Foreign Relations,* 1911, p. 315. For correspondence on Japanese immigration in 1924, see vol. II, pp. 333 ff.
[81] 42 Stat. 5.

Reference may also be made to our treaties with Great Britain of 1815, with Denmark of 1826, with Norway of 1827, with Italy of 1871, and with Spain of 1902. (See Malloy's *Treaties, Conventions,* etc.) In view of the provisions of Section 4 (*c*) I have omitted reference to clauses, similar to that above quoted, in our treaties with Latin American countries.

In my opinion the restrictions of the proposed measure, in view of their application under the definition of "immigrant", are in conflict with treaty provisions. The exception in subdivision (2) of Section 3 with respect to aliens visiting the United States "temporarily for business or pleasure" would not meet the treaty requirements to which I have referred, for this phrase would seem to indicate a stay more temporary than that permitted by these provisions and the right established by a treaty can not be cut down without a violation of the treaty so long as it is maintained in force. Accordingly, I take the liberty of suggesting that there be included in Section 3 of the proposed measure an additional exception to read as follows:

"an alien entitled to enter the United States under the provisions of a treaty."

I should add that the persons entitled to enter and reside here under the terms of our treaties for the purposes of trade and commerce are not those against whom immigration restrictions are deemed to be necessary.

Second.—Section 12 (*b*) provides as follows:

"No alien ineligible to citizenship shall be admitted to the United States unless such alien (1) is admissible as a non-quota immigrant under the provisions of sub-divisions (*b*), (*d*) or (*g*) of section 4, or (2) is the wife or unmarried child under 18 years of age of an immigrant admissible under such sub-division (*d*), and is accompanying or following to join him, or (3) is not an immigrant as defined in section 3."

In determining the effect of this provision it should be noted that sub-division (*b*) of Section 4 relates to "an immigrant previously lawfully admitted to the United States, who is returning from a temporary visit abroad." Sub-division (*d*) of the same section relates to immigrants who seek to enter the United States solely to carry on "the vocation of minister of any religious denomination, or professor of a college, academy, seminary, or university." And sub-division (*g*) of the same section relates to immigrants who are bona fide students seeking to enter the United States for the purpose of study at an accredited college, academy, seminary, or university approved by the Secretary of Labor.

It is apparent that Section 12, sub-division (*b*) taken in connection with Sections 3 and 4 of the proposed measure, operates to exclude Japanese. This is inconsistent with the provision of the Treaty of 1911 above-mentioned, and, with respect to those defined as immigrants who do not come within the treaty, it establishes a statutory exclusion.

So far as the latter class is concerned, the question presented is one of policy. There can be no question that such a statutory exclusion will be deeply resented by the Japanese people. It would be idle to insist that the provision is not aimed at the Japanese, for the proposed measure (Sec. 25) continues in force the existing legislation regulating Chinese immigration and the Barred Zone provisions of our immigration laws which prohibit immigration from certain other portions of Asia. The practical effect of Section 12 (*b*) is to single out Japanese immigrants for exclusion. The Japanese are a sensitive people and unquestionably would regard such a legislative enactment as fixing a stigma upon them. I regret to be compelled to say that I believe such legislative action would largely undo the work of the Washington Conference on Limitation of Armament, which so greatly improved our relations with Japan. The manifestation of American interest and generosity in providing relief to the sufferers from the recent earthquake disaster in Japan would not avail to diminish the resentment which would follow the enactment of such a measure, as this enactment would be regarded as an insult not to be palliated by any act of charity. It is useless to argue whether or not such a feeling would be justified; it is quite sufficient to say that it would exist. It has already been manifested in the discussions in Japan with respect to the pendency of this measure and no amount of argument can avail to remove it.

The question is thus presented whether it is worth while thus to affront a friendly nation with whom we have established most cordial relations and what gain there would be from such action. Permit me to suggest that the legislation would seem to be quite unnecessary even for the purpose for which it is devised. It is to be noted that if the provision of subdivision (*b*) of Section 12 were eliminated, and the quota provided in Section 10 of the proposed measure were to be applied to Japan, there would be a total of only 246 Japanese immigrants entitled to enter under the quota as thus determined. That is to say, this would be the number equal to two per cent. of the number of residents in the United States as determined by the Census of 1890 plus 200. There would remain, of course, the non-quota immigrants, but if it could possibly be regarded that the provisions of Section 4 would unduly enlarge the number admitted, these provisions could be modified without involving a statutory discrimination aimed at the Japanese. We now have an understanding with the Japanese Government whereby Japan undertakes to prevent the immigration of laborers from Japan to the United States except the parents, wives and children of those already resident here. Furthermore, the Japanese Government, incidentally to this undertaking, now regulates immigration to territory contiguous to the United States with the object of preventing the departure from Japan of persons who are likely to obtain surreptitious entry into this country. If the provision of Section 12 (b) were to be deleted and the provision in regard to certificates for immigrants to this country were to become applicable to Japan, we should with the present understanding with the Japanese Government be in a position to obtain active cooperation by the Japanese authorities in the granting of passport and immigration certificates. We could in addition be assured that the Japanese Government would give its assistance in scrutinizing and regulating immigration from Japan to American territory contiguous to the United States. It is believed that such an arrangement involving a double control over the Japanese quota of less than 250 a year would accomplish a much more effective regulation of unassimilable and undesirable classes of Japanese immigrants than it would be practicable for us, with our long land frontier lines on both North and South to accomplish by attempting to establish a general bar against Japanese subjects to the loss of cooperation with the Japanese Government in controlling the movement of their people to the United States and adjacent territories.

I am unable to perceive that the exclusion provision is necessary and I must strongly urge upon you the advisability, in the interest of our international relations, of eliminating it. The Japanese Government has already brought the matter to the attention of the Department of State and there is the deepest interest in the attitude of Congress with respect to this subject.

Third.—There remains the question of the adoption of the Census of 1890 as the basis of quota restriction. This has evoked representations from European countries, and especially from Italy, which regards the choice of such a basis as a discrimination against her. On December 31, 1923 I communicated to you a memorandum presented to the Department of State by the Italian Ambassador [82] and, as I have no doubt that your committee will examine these representations attentively, I shall not attempt to add any further recital of facts. In appropriately providing for a restriction of immigration, the importance of which I fully recognize, I hope that it will be possible to find some basis which will be proof against the charge of discrimination.

---

[82] Italian *pro memoria* of Dec. 15, 1923; printed in H. Rept. 350, 68th Cong., 1st sess., p. 15.

In addition to the questions considered above, permit me to direct your attention to the following:

Section 4 (c) of the proposed measure does not appear to provide for immigrants from British Honduras and British, French and Dutch Guiana as they would seem not to be "countries of Central or South America" within the meaning of the bill (See sec. 11 (a)). It is also not clear from the provisions of Section 4 (c) that it would provide for Haiti, the Dominican Republic, the British, French and Dutch islands of the West Indies, St. Pierre and Miquelon, and Greenland.

It is also to be noted that Section 4 (c) applies only to residents of the countries named and makes no provision for persons born in these countries, and citizens of them, but residing abroad. In view of the fact that under Section 11 (a), for the purposes of the Act, nationality is to be determined by country of birth, it would appear that such persons would still be referred to the country of birth and yet could not come in as non-quota immigrants. This would apparently make necessary the establishing of quotas to cover such classes, but it is not clear that this is the intention of the measure, or, on the other hand, that there is any reason why such persons should not be able to come in as "non-quota immigrants" as well as those who are described in Section 4 (c). I therefore suggest that you consider amending Section 4 (c) to read as follows:

"(c) An immigrant who was born in or has resided continuously for at least 10 years immediately preceding the time of his application for admission to the United States in the Dominion of Canada, Newfoundland, the Republics of Mexico, Cuba, and Haiti, the Dominican Republic, countries of Central America and of South America, colonies and dependencies of European countries in Central America, South America, the West Indies, or other islands adjacent to the American continents, and his wife, and his unmarried children under 18 years of age, if accompanying or following to join him."

I desire to invite your attention to the fact that under the provisions of Section 6 (f) the only copy of the application for an immigration certificate is attached to the immigration certificate, and would therefore be delivered to the alien with the immigration certificate and surrendered to the immigration officer at the port of arrival in the United States. This would leave the Government without a copy of the application and without any record of the facts upon which the immigration certificate was issued. It would seem that difficulties might arise on account of lost certificates or that copies of the applications might be desired for use in prosecutions where false statements were made, or where the certificate was altered while in the immigrant's possession. I therefore believe that it would be desirable to provide that a copy of the application for an immigration certificate should be kept on file in the Consular Office.

Section 8 (*e*) provides that if the Commissioner General finds the fact stated in the petition to be true and the immigrant is entitled to admission as a non-quota immigrant, he shall, through the Secretary of State, authorize the Consular Officer to issue an immigration certificate. I consider it important that Consular Officers shall continue to be under the direction and control of the Department of State and I assume that it is not the intention to divert this control which is important in order that there may be retained for such Officers the recognition which they should receive from the foreign governments concerned. I suggest the advisability, in order to avoid any possible question, of amending Section 8 (*e*) by striking out the words "he shall, through the Secretary of State, authorize the Consular Officer with whom the application for the immigration certificate has been filed to issue the immigration certificate" and by inserting in lieu thereof the following:

"he shall inform the Secretary of State of his decision and the Secretary of State shall then authorize the Consular Officer with whom the application for the immigration certificate has been filed to issue the immigration certificate."

With regard to Section 11 (*a*), I may state that some question has arisen under the present Quota Act whether the words "treating as separate countries the colonies or dependencies for which separate enumeration was made in the United States census" were sufficient to authorize the granting of a separate quota to Australia, which is a self-governing dominion under the British Empire. In order that this doubt may be removed, I suggest that in line 17, page 14, after the word "countries", the words "the self-governing dominions," be inserted.

With respect to Section 11 (*a*) (1) which provides that the nationality of a minor child accompanied by its alien parent not born in the United States shall be determined by the country of birth of such parent, if such parent is entitled to an immigration certificate, I may observe that in case the minor child is accompanied by both parents it is not clear whether the nationality of the minor child shall be determined by the place of birth of the father or of the mother. I suggest that the following provision be added:

"If the minor child is accompanied by both parents its nationality shall be determined by the country of birth of the father."

With respect to Section 11 (*a*) (2), I desire to invite attention to the fact that apparently this Section creates a class of immigration certificates that are not to be counted as quota certificates and are also not issued as non-quota certificates. The issuance of such certificates may cause difficulties in the regulation of the number of immigration certificates to be issued by Consular Officers. I believe that a more definite provision on this subject should be included in the Act.

Section 11 (*b*) incorporates provisions contained in the present Quota Act. In administering these provisions certain difficulties have arisen which, I believe, it would be advisable to remedy in the proposed legislation, as follows:

Section 11 (*b*) (1) refers to changes in political boundaries in foreign countries occurring subsequent to 1890 and resulting in the creation of new countries, the governments of which are recognized by the United States. This provision does not deal with the establishment of a new self-governing dominion within the British Empire since 1890. Under the provisions of the present law consideration was given to the matter of establishing a separate quota for the Irish Free State which is a new self-governing dominion. It appeared, however, that such a separate quota was not warranted by the terms of the law. For administrative reasons it would be helpful if separate quotas could be given the self-governing dominions. Reference is made in this connection to the fact that the census of 1890 does not contain a separate enumeration for New Zealand or the Union of South Africa. It is therefore believed that the following amendment should be added after the word "States" in line 18, page 15, the words "or in the establishment of self-governing dominions".

I may also observe that questions have arisen under the provisions of the present law, which are incorporated in Section 11 (*b*) (2) concerning the establishment of quotas covering the territories which had been transferred by the government exercising sovereignty therein in 1910 but where formal recognition of a new sovereign had not been extended by the Government of the United States. Cases of this character have arisen with respect to Palestine, Syria, Fiume, and other territories involved in settlements arising out of the World War. I believe that this situation could be dealt with by adding after Section 11 (*b*) (2) a new section numbered (3) to read as follows:

"in the surrender of territory by one country but the transfer of which to another country has not been recognized by the United States."

Your attention is also invited to the fact that several small countries recognized by the United States in 1890 were not clearly given a separate enumeration in the census of 1890. A similar situation arose under the present Act with respect to the granting of a separate quota to San Marino which had been recognized by the United States prior to 1910. With a view to making it proper for the United States to provide for a separate quota for such countries, I suggest that the following sentence be added after the word "boundary" in line 25, page 15, of the proposed measure:

"Such officials jointly are authorized to prepare a separate statement for countries recognized by the United States before 1890, but to which a separate enumeration was not given in the census of 1890."

With respect to Section 15 (*b*), it is observed that provision is made for the clearance of a vessel involved upon the deposit of an amount sufficient to cover such sums. The present law contains a similar provision, and it was construed that the foreign ship owner was obliged to deposit money and that a bond with sufficient surety could not be accepted. Such a provision, it seems, would work an undue hardship in cases where a serious question of fact was involved and the sum of money required to be deposited was very large. I therefore suggest that it would be desirable to provide that the Secretary of Labor may, in his discretion, accept a bond with sufficient sureties thereon to guarantee the payment of such sums.

The same observations apply to Section 19 (*f*).

With respect to Section 24, which provides that the Commissioner General shall prescribe rules and regulations for the enforcement of the provisions of the Act, so far as its administration by Consular Officers is concerned, subject to the approval of the Secretary of State, I desire to refer to my comments with respect to Section 8 (*e*). For the reasons there stated, I am of the opinion that the rules and regulations, so far as they relate to Consular Officers should be prescribed by the Secretary of State upon the recommendation of the Commissioner General.

I remain [etc.]   CHARLES E. HUGHES

150.01/799

The Secretary of State to the Rumanian Chargé (Nano)

The Secretary of State presents his compliments to the Chargé d'Affaires ad interim of Rumania and has the honor to acknowledge the receipt of his *note verbale* (535/1) of the 2d instant, in which under instructions of his Government he protests against certain immigration legislation now pending in the Congress of the United States.

In reply the Secretary of State begs to say that copies of the note of the Chargé d'Affaires have been referred to the appropriate authorities.

WASHINGTON, *February 19, 1924.*

150.01/784

The Secretary of State to the Salvadoran Chargé (Castro)

WASHINGTON, *February 19, 1924.*

SIR: I have the honor to acknowledge the receipt of your note, dated January 4, 1924, in which you refer to reports in the press respecting proposals to extend to the American countries the provisions establishing quotas for immigration. You state that if a measure of this character were adopted, it would greatly concern your Government and you express the hope that the proposals will not be adopted insofar as they tend to restrict immigration from Salvador.

I forwarded copies of your note to the appropriate authorities of this Government for consideration, and I am pleased to state that I have been informed that the Immigration Bill reported by the Committee on Immigration and Naturalization to the House of Representatives does not contain a provision establishing immigration quotas applicable to Salvador.

Accept [etc.] CHARLES E. HUGHES

150.01/802

The Norwegian Minister (Bryn) to the Secretary of State

WASHINGTON, *February 20, 1924.*

MR. SECRETARY OF STATE: The new Immigration Bill (H. R. 6540) introduced in the House of Representatives on February 1, 1924, contains in Section 3 a definition of the term "Immigrant" and provides in Section 10 (*a*) for percentage limitations on immigration **to the United States.**

The Treaty of Commerce and Navigation between Norway and the United States, concluded on July 4, 1827, contains in its Article I a provision which in the English translation reads as follows:

"The citizens and subjects of each of the two high contracting parties may, with all security for their persons, vessels, and cargoes, freely enter the ports, places, and rivers of the territories of the other, wherever foreign commerce is permitted. They shall be at liberty to sojourn and reside in all parts whatsoever of said territories; to rent and occupy houses and warehouses for their commerce; and they shall enjoy, generally, the most entire security and protection in their mercantile transactions, on condition of their submitting to the laws and ordinances of the respective countries."

On this occasion I have the honor, acting under instructions from my Government, to apply for Your Excellency's good offices in order that such steps as Your Excellency deem appropriate, may be taken with a view to secure that the right which Norwegian subjects and citizens under the terms of the treaty have to enter, sojourn and reside in the United States, may not be curtailed or made illusory by the law.

Hoping that Your Excellency will deem it expedient to intervene so that a possible conflict between the law and the treaty be avoided, I avail myself [etc.]

H. BRYN

150.01/806 supplemental

The Secretary of State to the Cuban Ambassador (*Torriente*)

WASHINGTON, *February 21, 1924.*

EXCELLENCY: I have the honor to refer to your note, dated January 14, 1924, concerning a proposed amendment to the immigration law by which a quota for Cuba would be established, and to state that I have received a communication from the Chairman of the Committee on Immigration and Naturalization of the House of Representatives, from which it appears that the Immigration Bill that has been reported to the House of Representatives by that Committee does not contain such a provision.

Accepted [etc.]　　　　CHARLES E. HUGHES

150.01/802

The Secretary of State to the Norwegian Minister (*Bryn*)

WASHINGTON, *March 19, 1924.*

SIR: I have the honor to acknowledge the receipt of your note dated February 20, 1924, with respect to certain provisions of the new immigration bill (H. R. 6540) introduced in the House of Representatives on February 1, 1924.

You may be assured that all questions relating to the appropriate recognition of the treaty provisions to which you refer are having proper consideration.

Accept [etc.]　　　　CHARLES E. HUGHES

150.01/852

The Italian Embassy to the Department of State

PRO-MEMORIA

Congress is now taking into consideration two important bills on restrictive and selective immigration, one presented by Senator D. A. Reed and the other by representative Albert Johnson; more so a number of other bills and amendments have been presented and there is every indication that Congress will soon take some final decision with regard to the immigration policy of the United States.

The Italian Government has always manifested by words and by action, its sincere desire of cooperating in a friendly way with the Government of the United States in all matters concerning emigration; in venturing therefore to express its point of view on some of the contemplated provisions of law, the Italian Government is animated solely by the desire of avoiding any possible motives of discussion and any eventual difficulties in the practical application of the United States Immigration laws.

The principal provisions to be considered are:

1) On the 15th of December 1923 the Italian Ambassador has already fully expressed to the Secretary of State [83] his government's point of view with regard to the question of basing the quota law on the 1890 census; there is no need therefore to go further at present into this matter.

2) Some members of Congress have considered, implicitly or explicitly, the opportunity of granting immigration certificates independently from the fact whether passports are obligatory in the country to which the immigrants owe allegiance.

This would practically invalidate the sovereign right of the Italian Government to control the emigration of its citizens and interfere with the necessary national measure to safeguard public order and with the regulations relating to passports.

If American consular certificates should be issued before the prospective immigrant has obtained an indispensable Italian passport this would doubtlessly lead towards encouraging and facilitating the exit of certain individuals to the departure of whom the Italian authorities may oppose themselves for reasons of public order or on account of unfulfilled military service.

3) The issuance of numbered certificates or visa certificates may be an efficient means for maintaining the number of emigrants within the quota limits and of reducing the number of rejections of immigrants from the United States.

In accordance to the sovereign rights of every state to regulate the admittance of aliens within its territory, the United States government has doubtlessly the faculty to subordinate the admittance of an immigrant to certain requisites and formalities. But the exertion of such right must not come into contrast with the Italian Government's exclusive right of jurisdiction over its own subjects in Italy.

---

[83] *Pro memoria* printed in H. Rept. 350, 68th Cong., 1st sess., p. 15.

Therefore the American consuls in the fulfilment of their customary functions should not broaden these out with reference to the certificates into an extraordinary investigation that would become a jurisdictional act exceeding the recognized consular functions.

The proper selection of immigrants as desired by the United States can only be efficiently accomplished by a friendly cooperation between the United States consular officers and the Italian Authorities, due regard being taken toward the legitimate requirements and the unquestionable prerogative of one and the other country. The Italian Commissariat of Emigration has constantly given proof of its willingness in such direction.

4) The Johnson bill contemplates the admittance, extra quota, of children, wives and parents of American citizens, but the Reed bill only grants them a preference in obtaining the visa certificates. There seems to be every good reason to believe that the free admittance into the United States should be a privilege accruing to the family of every citizen through his constitutional right to cohabitate with his wife and children and to be unhampered in the enjoyment of family life.

5) The provision of laying the burden of proof on the alien in case of refusal of admittance or of deportation from the United States, contained in both the Reed and the Johnson bills, is in contradiction to the recognized procedure of law the world over; in the original Reed bill N. 2576 it was applicable to all individuals but in the amended bill the word "individual" has been substituted by the word "alien" thereby refusing to aliens an equitable safeguard granted to any citizen.

It should also be considered that in accordance to Section 2 (*e*) of the Reed bill the visa certificate is to be surrendered by the immigrant to the immigration officer at the port of entry so that he finds himself deprived of the most important document with which to prove that he has been lawfully admitted into the United States.

The Italian Government sincerely hopes that the preceding remarks may be taken into serious consideration by the United States Government with the aim of suggesting such forms in the drafting of the immigration law and regulations as will harmonize the rightful interests and the friendly feelings of their respective countries.[84]

WASHINGTON, *April 5, 1924.*

---

[84] The Department appears to have made no reply.

ARRANGEMENTS WITH FOREIGN GOVERNMENTS FOR A FLIGHT AROUND THE WORLD BY UNITED STATES ARMY AIRPLANES

811.2300/– : Telegram

The Secretary of State to the Minister in Denmark (Prince)

WASHINGTON, *July 17, 1923—2 p.m.*

20. Army Air Service plans around the world flight of several airplanes to commence early in spring of 1924. Itinerary includes Iceland. War Department has detailed an officer to investigate conditions there as soon as possible in order to secure data necessary for plan of flight.

Please inquire whether Danish Government will grant permission for this investigation. Report by cable.

HUGHES

811.2300/–

The Secretary of State to the Chargé in Japan (Wilson)[85]

WASHINGTON, *July 18, 1923.*

SIR: The Department is in receipt of a letter, dated July 5, 1923, from the Acting Secretary of War, stating that the Army Air Service is preparing for a flight of several airplanes around the world to commence early in the spring of 1924. The letter added that it will be necessary to collect data concerning various portions of the route and, consequently, requested that permission be obtained from the Governments whose territories are to be crossed for two officers who have been detailed to make a path-finding expedition to investigate conditions and secure the data necessary for the complete plan of the flight.

A copy of this letter is enclosed,[86] for your information, and you are requested to obtain the permission sought by the War Department and report by cable in so far as concerns the territories mentioned in the proposed itinerary which belong to the Government to which you are accredited.

I am [etc.]

For the Secretary of State:
WILLIAM PHILLIPS

---

[85] The same instruction was sent to the Embassies in France, Great Britain, and Italy.
[86] Not printed.

811.2300/1 : Telegram

The Minister in Denmark (Prince) to the Secretary of State

COPENHAGEN, *August 1, 1923—5 p.m.*
[Received August 1—1:53 p.m.]

26. Department's telegram 20, July 17, 2 p.m. Danish Foreign Office informs me that Icelandic Government has granted permission for proposed investigation by War Department.

PRINCE

811.2300/1 : Telegram

The Acting Secretary of State to the Chargé in Japan (Caffery)

[Paraphrase]

WASHINGTON, *August 30, 1923—5 p.m.*

102. Refer to Department's mail instruction of July 18 in regard proposed air flight around the world.

You will advise Department by cable whether proposed flight over Japanese territory could be arranged for under present law, and whether request could, in your judgment, be made without antagonizing Japanese opinion, both official and popular.

PHILLIPS

811.2300/2 : Telegram

The Ambassador in Italy (Child) to the Secretary of State

ROME, *September 18, 1923—noon.*
[Received 3:11 p.m.]

118. Department's unnumbered instructions July 18.[88] Foreign Office advises Italian Government will be glad to furnish American officer with all information and data he may require for fulfillment of mission in connection with preparations for round-the-world flight of Army aeroplanes.

CHILD

811.2300/3

The Chargé in France (Whitehouse) to the Secretary of State

No. 3490   PARIS, *September 19, 1923.*
[Received October 2.]

SIR: With reference to the Department's instruction of July 18, 1923, File No. 811.2300/-,[88] I have the honor to report that by a note

---

[88] See footnote 85, p. 227.

dated September 15, 1923, the French Foreign Office informs me that the "Central Aeronautical Service" of the Ministry of Marine, will give our officers all possible information and that such of this information as concerns climatology, meteorology, tides, etc., will be given by Major Lefranc, of the Hydrographic Service.

I have [etc.]   SHELDON WHITEHOUSE

811.2300/5 : Telegram

The Ambassador in Great Britain (Harvey) to the Secretary of State

LONDON, *October 9, 1923—5 p. m.*
[Received October 9—4:47 p. m.]

430. Your instruction number 879, July 18th.[89] The Admiralty will give Major Davidson, our air attaché here, all information desired. The Air Ministry is expected to take the same attitude.

Canada will assist the pathfinding officers in every way. There is no objection to their Canadian itinerary as outlined in the above-named instruction.

HARVEY

811.2300/7 : Telegram

The Secretary of State to the Chargé in Japan (Caffery)

[Paraphrase]

WASHINGTON, *November 27, 1923—5 p. m.*

258. Department is repeating text of its telegram no. 102 of August 30, 5 p. m.

[Here follows text of telegram printed on page 228.]

The Department wishes you to take the matter up immediately as the War Department must have a reply by November 30 because of contracts for construction work in connection with the flight.

For your discreet use you are confidentially informed that of all the Governments from which permission for flight across territory was requested, the Japanese Government is the only one which has not yet replied.

HUGHES

[89] Copy in Department file is unnumbered ; see footnote 85, p. 227.

811.2300/9 : Telegram

The Chargé in Japan (Caffery) to the Secretary of State

[Paraphrase]

TOKYO, *November 30, 1923—5 p. m.*
[Received November 30—3 : 28 p. m.]

179. Department's no. 258, November 27, 5 p. m., was received last night. About a week ago, having noted that no reply had ever been made to the Embassy's note carrying out Department's mail instruction of July 18, I informally requested the Vice Minister for Foreign Affairs to give me his frank personal opinion on the probable attitude of the Japanese authorities in connection with the proposed air flight around the world insofar as it concerned Japan. The Vice Minister told me quite frankly, a few days later, that the War Department did not look with favor on the particular flights proposed, but if the American Government would not urge the Government of Japan to grant permission for American officers to visit Japan on such an expedition it was his personal belief that the Japanese War Department would not raise objections to the projected flight across Japanese territory. He inquired if the American authorities had in mind a route across Japanese territory. After I had talked with the military attaché of this Embassy I handed the Vice Minister the information prepared by the War Department at Washington, showing the tentative route. He promised to expedite the decision, and I hope that I may receive a definite answer tomorrow.

CAFFERY

811.2300/15

The Chargé in Japan (Caffery) to the Secretary of State

No. 134–E   TOKYO, *December 14, 1923.*
[Received January 7, 1924.]

SIR: With reference to my telegram, Number 189, December 8th, 6 p. m.,[90] reporting that the Japanese authorities stated that they would offer no objection to American army aircraft flying over or landing in Japanese territory, but imposing certain conditions; I have the honor to transmit herewith copies of a memorandum [90] on the subject handed to me by the Vice-Minister for Foreign Affairs.

It is to be noted that the following three conditions are imposed:

1. The only landing place permitted on the flight from the Aleutian Islands to the Island of Hon-shu is one on the Island of Shumushu.

---

[90] Not printed.

2. Certain details relating to fortified zones and naval stations shall be settled by agreement between the Japanese military authorities and an American officer detailed for that purpose.

3. In case of a similar request being made by the Japanese authorities, the United States shall permit Japanese military or naval aircraft to fly over or land in American territory.

I have [etc.] JEFFERSON CAFFERY

811.2300/11

The Secretary of State to the British Chargé (Chilton)

WASHINGTON, *December 19, 1923.*

SIR: I beg to inform you that the War Department is contemplating a flight around the world of five aeroplanes leaving the United States about April 1, 1924 and completing the circuit in the early autumn. It is proposed to divide the flight into five divisions, assigning one advance officer to each division of the route and a sixth advance officer to coordinate all the divisions by travelling over the entire route. The Embassy at London has been instructed to bring this project to the attention of His Majesty's Government,[90a] at the same time requesting permission for the advance officers to cross British territory as outlined in the tentative route, requesting permission for the flight to cross British territory, and to land at such points on British territory as may be subsequently agreed upon. The Embassy was further directed to request the waiver of any special restrictions in regard to aerial photography except insofar as they related to fortifications or such other areas as might be specified.

The following is the tentative itinerary of the flight:

Washington, D. C.		Aomori (Honshu) Japan	245 miles
Dayton, Ohio	400 miles	Tokyo, Japan	410 miles
St. Joseph, Missouri or Fort		Nagasaki, Japan	610 miles
Cook, Nebraska	560–675 miles	Chemulpo (Jinsen)	440 miles
Cheyenne, Wyoming	500–455 miles	Tsingtau (Shantung) China	350 miles
Salt Lake City, Utah	400 miles	Shanghai (Woosung) China	350 miles
Seattle, Washington	770 miles	Amoy, China	555 miles
Prince Rupert, British Co-		Hongkong	300 miles
lumbia	650 miles	Haipong, French Indo-China	500 miles
Sitka, Alaska	300 miles	Tourane, French Indo-China	395 miles
Cordova, Alaska	475 miles	Saigon, French Indo-China	530 miles
Seward, Alaska	135 miles	Bangkok, Siam	675 miles
Chignik, Alaska	450 miles	Rangoon, Burma	450 miles
Akutan or Dutch Harbor,		Akyab, Burma	445 miles
Unalaska	380–400 miles	Calcutta, India	400 miles
Hazan, Island of Atka	350 miles	Allahabad, India	475 miles
Chicagoff, Island of Attu	530 miles	Delhi, India	380 miles
Paramushiru Island		Multan, India	425 miles
(Kuriles)	878 miles	Karachi, India	475 miles
Bettobu, Yetorofu (Kuriles)	495 miles	Charbar, Persia	395 miles
Akkeshie (Yezo) Japan	250 miles	Bandar Abbas, Persia	330 miles

[90a] Telegram no. 385, *infra.*

Bushire, Persia	400 miles	Thorshavn, Faroe Islands	275 miles
Bagdad (Mesopotamia)	475 miles	Baykjaviki, Iceland	550 miles
Aleppo, Syria	480 miles	Angmagsalik, Greenland	500 miles
Konia, Turkey	285 miles	Avigtut, Greenland	500 miles
San Stefano, Turkey [91]	300 miles	Rigolet, Labrador (Indian	
Belgrade, Yugoslavia	525 miles	Harbor)	700 miles
Vienna, Austria	340 miles	Mingan, Quebec	525 miles
Strassbourg, France	400 miles	Quebec, Quebec	450 miles
Paris, France	250 miles	Montreal, Quebec	175 miles
London, England	225 miles	Keyport, New Jersey	400 miles
Hull, England	155 miles	Washington, D. C.	200 miles
Kirkwall, Orkney Islands	370 miles		

The Chief of the Air Service is desirous of sending Lieutenant Clayton Bissell over the proposed route of the projected flight through British Columbia from Victoria to Prince Rupert as soon after January 1, 1924 as the weather will permit, the purpose of his trip being to make all necessary arrangements in connection with the flight relative to supplies, transportation facilities, et cetera.

I should greatly appreciate it if you would be so good as to inform me whether or not Lieutenant Bissell's trip would be agreeable to the Dominion Authorities.

Accept [etc.]

For the Secretary of State:
WILLIAM PHILLIPS

811.2300/5 : Telegram

The Secretary of State to the Ambassador in Great Britain (Kellogg) [92]

WASHINGTON, *December 19, 1923—2 p. m.*

385. Your 430, October 9, 4 [5] p. m.

War Department contemplating flight around the world of five aeroplanes leaving the United States about April 1, 1924 and completing the circuit in the early autumn. It is proposed to divide the flight into five divisions, assigning one advance officer to each division of the route and a sixth advance officer to coordinate all the various divisions by travelling over the entire route. Address Note immediately to Foreign Office:

1. Requesting permission for advance officers to cross British territory as outlined in proposed route;

---

[91] On Dec. 29 the Legations in Bulgaria and Yugoslavia and the High Commissioner at Constantinople were informed that the itinerary had been changed to "San Stefano to Bucharest to Belgrade."

[92] The same telegram, *mutatis mutandis* and with appropriate changes of itinerary in point 5 of the note to be addressed to the Foreign Offices, was sent, on Dec. 22, 1923, to the Embassies in France (no. 474) and Germany (no. 107) ; the Legations in Austria (no. 23), Bulgaria (no. 17), China (no. 255), Denmark (no. 31), Hungary (no. 31), Persia (no. 34), Siam (no. 17), and Yugoslavia (no. 19) ; the High Commissioner in Turkey (no. 236) with the last sentence of the first paragraph changed to read, "In case you see no objection, communicate with appropriate Turkish authorities in following sense"; and on Dec 29 to the Legation in Rumania (no. 49). (File no. 811.2300/11.)

2. Requesting permission for flight to cross territory;

3. Requesting permission for flight to land at points on British territory to be subsequently agreed upon;

4. Requesting the waiver of any special restrictions in regard to aerial photography except as to fortifications or such other areas as may be specified. Personnel will conform strictly to restrictions imposed;

5. Following are pertinent portions of tentative itinerary which would be of particular interest to British authorities: Seattle to Prince Rupert to Sitka (Alaska); Bangkok (Siam) to Rangoon to Akyab to Calcutta to Allahabad to Delhi to Multan to Karachi to Charbar (Persia); Bushire (Persia) to Bagdad to Aleppo (Syria); Paris to London to Hull to Kirkwall (Orkney Islands) to Thorshavn (Faroe Islands); Greenland to Rigolet to Mingan, to Quebec, to Montreal, to Keyport, New Jersey.

Tentative itinerary of entire flight is being forwarded to you by mail.[93]

HUGHES

811.2300/18

The British Chargé (Chilton) to the Secretary of State

No. 34   WASHINGTON, *January 10, 1924.*

SIR: With reference to the note which you were so good as to address to me on the 19th ultimo regarding the contemplated flight around the world of five American aeroplanes, I have the honour to state that, according to a communication which I have received from His Excellency the Governor-General of Canada, the Canadian Government has no objection to the projected visit of Lieutenant Clayton Bissell over the proposed route of this flight through British Columbia from Victoria to Prince Rupert.

Lord Byng of Vimy has also requested me to state, for the information of the appropriate United States authorities, that officers of the Royal Canadian Air Force who have flown between Victoria and Prince Rupert, and who may be able to advise and assist Lieutenant Bissell, are stationed at the Royal Canadian Air Flight Station, Vancouver, British Columbia. Lord Byng adds that the Officer Commanding that Station has been instructed to render every possible assistance to Lieutenant Bissell.

I have [etc.]

(For His Majesty's Chargé d' Affaires)
HERBERT W. BROOKS

---

[93] See note of Dec. 19 to the British Chargé, *supra.*

811.2300/15 : Telegram

The Secretary of State to the Chargé in Japan (Caffery)

WASHINGTON, *January 10, 1924—5 p. m.*

8. Department's 2, January 4, 3 p m [94]
Your despatch 134–E of December 14, 1923. Reference second condition imposed.

As Japanese Government has of its own accord brought up desirability of itinerary and other details being settled by Japanese military authorities and American officer detailed for that purpose, please inform Foreign Office that visit of advance officer was contemplated in order that details connected with itinerary and technical requirements of flight might be adjusted between him and Japanese officials. It would appear therefore that there has been misapprehension on part of Japanese Government as to object of officer's visit.

Reference condition No. 3. In case Japan should make a specific request for a similar flight over United States territory this Department would be glad to recommend to the Governors of the States and to the Executive Departments administering the territories over which the flight was contemplated that permission to fly over and to land be granted to the Japanese. Department has no reason to believe that permission would not be readily accorded and all facilities extended. You will of course appreciate that because of constitutional requirements reference to appropriate state authorities is essential.

You may make such use of information contained in preceding paragraph as you deem advisable.

HUGHES

811.2300/19 : Telegram

The Chargé in Japan (Caffery) to the Secretary of State

TOKYO, *January 12, 1924—3 p. m.*
[Received January 12—1 : 55 p. m.]

10. Department's 8, January 10, 5 p. m. Japanese authorities now state they have no objection to visit to Tokyo of an officer to discuss details and technical requirements of flight but as hitherto reported they do object to pathfinding expedition described in Department's instruction of July 18, 1923, and enclosure from War Department dated July 5, which had been communicated to Foreign Office on August 14th.

.   .   .   .

CAFFERY

---

[94] Not printed.

811.2300/22 : Telegram

The Chargé in Japan (Caffery) to the Secretary of State

Tokyo, *January 17, 1924—9 p. m.*
[Received 9:45 p. m.]

13. My 10, January 12, 3 p. m. War Office has notified me informally this evening that the Japanese authorities consent to landing at Bettobu and will be prepared to receive advance officer here in Tokyo to discuss details. Navy Department is disposed to send war vessel to Kurile Islands for "protection purposes" during flight. Naval hydrographic bureau offers suggestion that flight should take place between latter part of April and middle of May on account of floating ice before that period and dense fogs thereafter.

CAFFERY

811.2300/22 : Telegram

The Secretary of State to the Chargé in Japan (Caffery)

Washington, *January 18, 1924—1 p. m.*

13. Your 13, January 17, 9 p. m.

Express gratification to appropriate authorities for informal consent. Telegraph promptly as soon as written confirmation is received.[95] Lieutenant Nutt, Advance Officer, has been instructed to leave Philippines for Tokyo to arrange details. War Department would be glad if Japanese Officer would accompany him on pathfinding expedition and believes that Japanese objection to expedition as stated in your 10, January 12, 3 p. m., will now be withdrawn.

HUGHES

811.2300/25 : Telegram

The Minister in Persia (Kornfeld) to the Secretary of State

Teheran, *January 21, 1924—12 noon.*
[Received January 22—1:25 a. m.]

4. Department's January 18, 5 p. m.[96] Persian Government consents to flight. See Legation's telegram 2, January 10, 12 noon.[96]

KORNFELD

---

[95] On Jan. 25, the Chargé informed the Department that he had received formal written confirmation from the Minister for Foreign Affairs of the informal consent previously given by the War Office (file no. 811.2300/35).
[96] Not printed.

811.2300/27 : Telegram

The Minister in Austria (Washburn) to the Secretary of State

VIENNA, *January 21, 1924—1 p. m.*
[Received January 22—7: 07 a. m.]

3. Department's telegram 3, January 18, 7 a. m. [*p. m.*] [97] Foreign Office states that requests made by Legation in pursuance of Department's telegram 23, December 22, 3 p. m.,[98] will be granted and that written reply to Legation's note will be forthcoming without delay.

WASHBURN

811.2300/24 : Telegram

The Minister in Siam (Brodie) to the Secretary of State

BANGKOK, *January 21, 1924—3 p. m.*
[Received January 21—2: 42 p. m.]

1. Department's telegram 17, December 22, 3 p. m.[98] Permission granted in accordance with Department's telegram covering all requests. Mail despatch following.[97]

BRODIE

811.2300/26 : Telegram

The Minister in the Kingdom of the Serbs, Croats and Slovenes (Dodge) to the Secretary of State

BELGRADE, *January 21, 1924—5 p. m.*
[Received 11: 50 p. m.]

6. Your January 18, 7 p. m.[97] Minister of War has just informed me that he is happy to grant all requests your 19, December 22, 3 p. m.,[98] and will shortly send me confirmation in writing.

DODGE

811.2300/29 : Telegram

The Minister in Bulgaria (Wilson) to the Secretary of State

SOFIA, *January 22, 1924—3 p. m.*
[Received January 23—12: 18 a. m.]

5. Department's telegram 17, December 22, 3 p. m.[98] Permission granted.

WILSON

---

[97] Not printed.
[98] See footnote 92, p. 232.

811.2300/30 : Telegram

The Minister in Denmark (Prince) to the Secretary of State

COPENHAGEN, *January 23, 1924—noon.*
[Received January 23—9:20 a. m.]

6. Department's 3, January 18, 7 p. m.[99] Am informed verbally by Director General of Foreign Office that permission will be granted for requests as outlined. Written confirmation to follow.

PRINCE

811.2300/32 : Telegram

The Minister in Hungary (Brentano) to the Secretary of State

BUDAPEST, *January 23, 1924—6 p. m.*
[Received January 24—12:07 a. m.]

5. Your December 22, 3 p. m.[1] and January 18, 7 p. m.[99] Foreign Office writes that the Government authorizes the aviators to fly over and land in Hungary and that it will inform me later regarding landing points and restrictions against photography.

BRENTANO

811.2300/38 : Telegram

The Minister in China (Schurman) to the Secretary of State

PEKING, *January 26, 1924—noon.*
[Received January 26—6:37 a. m.]

46. Your 19, January 18, 7 p. m.[99] Aviation Department object to granting permission on the ground that, whereas, when in other instances permission given for experimental flights across Chinese territory, governments concerned had stated machines to be of non-military character and flights made for scientific purposes, in present instance no such information given. Foreign Office states Chinese regulations prohibit military aeroplanes of foreign nations flying over Chinese territory. Aviation Department holding conference with representatives of general staff and Ministry of War on January 30th to decide question.

I suggest you telegraph that aeroplanes to be used are of non-military character and flight for scientific purposes if such is the case.

SCHURMAN

[99] Not printed.
[1] See footnote 92, p. 232.

811.2300/37 : Telegram

The Ambassador in Germany (Houghton) to the Secretary of State

BERLIN, *January 28, 1924—4 p. m.*
[Received 9:45 p. m.]

30. Your 12, January 18, 7 p. m. My 26, January 25, noon.[9] Have just received a note from Foreign Office stating that Government permits the proposed crossing of German territory and possible landings in Germany during the flight around the world. German Government likewise permits carriage and use of photographic apparatus over German territory on condition (1) course and time of flight be notified in advance to the German Government, (2) that no photographs be made of fortifications at Ingolstadt and Ulm, and (3) that a copy of each photograph made during flight over German territory be supplied to German Government. Government adds that it will be glad to support and facilitate undertaking in other respects also.

HOUGHTON

811.2300/39 : Telegram

The Secretary of State to the Minister in China (Schurman)

WASHINGTON, *January 28, 1924—6 p. m.*

28. Your 46, January 26, noon. Following is extract from letter from War Department:

"The purpose of the flight is to demonstrate the feasibility with which aerial communication may be established between the various continents and to obtain desired information concerning the operation of present type aircraft in various climates of the world. It is hoped also to increase our scientific knowledge of aeronautics and to advance the art of aviation. Naturally, this government is also desirous of being the first to circumnavigate the globe by air.

The type of aircraft to be used is a transcript called the *Douglas Cruiser*. This is a modification of a commercial airplane which has been used for some time as a commercial air transport along our east coast. The plane is in no way a military type. It was built only for the purpose of the accomplishment of this flight."

Bring foregoing to the attention of appropriate authorities and in your discretion state that replies have been received from majority of governments to whom requests were addressed for permission to cross territory and that all replies received have been favorable with the exception of that from Government at Peking.

HUGHES

_____

[9] Neither printed.

811.2300/40 : Telegram

The High Commissioner in Turkey (Bristol) to the Secretary of State

CONSTANTINOPLE, *January 30, 1924—noon.*
[Received 1 : 55 p. m.]

22. Referring to the Department's 236, December 22, 3 p. m.[10] and 15, January 18, 7 p. m.[11] Treat [12] reports from Angora as follows:

"January 29, 3 p. m. In a conversation with the Under Secretary today he states that a reply to your request for permission for United States aeroplanes to include Turkey in their world flight itinerary had been given on January 21 to the effect that the Government is desirous of having Turkey omitted from the itinerary, giving as reasons that safety to machines and crews could not be assured, or that the flight over Turkey should be postponed until appropriate arrangements could be made. The Under Secretary was informed that the personnel of the expedition would strictly observe regulations concerning [omission] et cetera, it was furthermore pointed out that the Turks would be deriving distinct benefits from such visit. The Under Secretary conveyed the impression that the question might be subjected to further examination, but brought to my attention in the conversation that an identical refusal has been given to a British request of similar nature."

The fact that I have not received this message officially from Adnan Bey as yet gives me hope he is still endeavoring to persuade Angora to meet our request. I will telegraph further information as soon as possible.

BRISTOL

811.2300/43 : Telegram

The Ambassador in Great Britain (Kellogg) to the Secretary of State

LONDON, *February 5, 1924—5 p. m.*
[Received February 5—2 : 57 p. m.]

51. Your 10, January 18, 7 p. m.[11] Foreign Office informs me that Canada has granted permission for flight over her territory; will give all facilities asked for.

KELLOGG

---

[10] See footnote 92, p. 232.
[11] Not printed.
[12] R. A. Wallace Treat, consul at Smyrna, detailed to Angora Jan. 7, 1924.

811.2300/45 : Telegram

The Ambassador in France (Herrick) to the Secretary of State

PARIS, *February 7, 1924—5 p. m.*
[Received February 7—3 : 40 p. m.]

59. Your 474, December 22, 3 p. m.[14] The French Government has given permission for facilities requested by the Department.[15] I am transmitting copy of note received from the Foreign Office in pouch tomorrow.[16]

HERRICK

811.2300/48 : Telegram

The Chargé in Rumania (Dennis) to the Secretary of State

BUCHAREST, *February 9, 1924—3 p. m.*
[Received 9 : 10 p. m.]

7. My telegram no. 5, January 22, 10 a. m.[16] Note received today from the Roumanian Government grants all permissions requested but makes no mention of aerial photography.[17] Foreign Office desires details of the expedition in due time.

DENNIS

811.2300/40 : Telegram

The Secretary of State to the High Commissioner in Turkey (Bristol)

WASHINGTON, *February 9, 1924—6 p. m.*

26. Your 22, January 30, noon and 24, February 7, 11 a. m.[18] Following is extract from letter from War Department:

[Here follow the two paragraphs quoted in the Department's telegram no. 28, January 28, to the Minister in China, printed on page 238.]

[Paraphrase.] You may, if you deem it advisable, bring the paragraphs quoted from the letter of the War Department to the attention of the appropriate Turkish authorities and communicate them to Treat for similar action by him at Angora.

You may, in your discretion, with regard to the statement that an identical refusal was given to the British request of similar nature,

---

[14] See footnote 92, p. 232.
[15] On Apr. 8, 6 p. m., the Ambassador telegraphed that the French Government had requested the Governor General of Syria to waive photographic restrictions in the mandated territory (file no. 811.2300/88).
[16] Not printed.
[17] On June 14, 3 p. m., the Minister telegraphed that permission for aerial photography was included in the note (file no. 811.2300/135).
[18] Latter not printed.

point out that no state of war has existed between Turkey and the United States of America.

Although the Department still hopes that the Government of Turkey will grant permission, it is recommending to the War Department that the advance officer now in Paris be sent immediately to Constantinople to discuss the situation with you. The itinerary as now proposed includes passage through Bulgaria, Rumania, Yugoslavia, Hungary, Austria, Germany, France, Great Britain, Denmark, Canada, Japan, Siam, and Persia. Favorable replies have been received from all above-mentioned countries. It would be most difficult and embarrassing if it were now found necessary, due to the failure of Turkey to grant permission, to change itinerary as now arranged.

HUGHES

811.2300/50 : Telegram

The Minister in China (Schurman) to the Secretary of State

PEKING, *February 14, 1924—3 p. m.*
[Received February 14—7 : 30 a. m.]

57. Your 28, January 28, 6 p. m. Note from Minister for Foreign Affairs received 11th grants permission for flight to cross Chinese territory and land at points therein subject to certain regulations. None of these appear onerous except provision that no photographic or wireless apparatus may be carried. I delayed telegraphing Department in order to discuss this matter as well as the regulations generally with Minister for Foreign Affairs yesterday. I explained to him that we wanted all the regulations interpreted in a reasonable way and the specified prohibition of photographic or wireless apparatus eliminated, since these were necessary for the personal safety of aviators and the scientific objects of the flight. Koo seemed very receptive and sympathetic to these arguments and promised he would seek to have the undesirable regulations modified as the Chinese Government would not want to do anything prejudicial [to] the object of the flight.

Koo told me that the regulations were "for general application", and I believe that they are merely perfunctory in the present instance and that no serious effort will be made to carry them into effect. Full report by mail in the pouch giving text of regulations.[19]

SCHURMAN

[19] Despatch no. 2086, Feb. 19, not printed; the Chinese Government granted permission to enter Chinese territory.

811.2300/51 : Telegram

The Ambassador in Great Britain (Kellogg) to the Secretary of State

LONDON, *February 15, 1924—4 p. m.*
[Received 11:47 p. m.]

61. Your 32, February 9, 6 p. m.,[21] *re* world aeroplane flight. A note was received from the Foreign Office today to the following effect:

1. His Majesty's Government will be glad to facilitate the flight and to afford any advice or assistance on land portions of the route in which establishments of the Royal Air Force exist.

2. Canada will give every assistance. There is no objection on the part of the Iraq Government. The reply of India is still awaited.[22]

3. In view of the amount of work which flight will entail on the Royal Air Force authorities as regards route between Karachi and western frontier of Iraq, full and early information should be supplied to the air officer commanding Iraq concerning proposed arrangement for flight between these two limits.

4. Question of waiver of photographic restrictions is under consideration and the decision will be made known at an early date.

KELLOGG

811.2300/64a : Telegram

The Secretary of State to the Chargé in Japan (Caffery)

WASHINGTON, *March 3, 1924—6 p. m.*

33. Reference War Department World Flight. War Department has received telegram from Nutt stating that Japanese destroyers will transport gasoline and oil for aeroplanes to Kurile Islands, but will not permit Nutt to go as passenger. Chartering boat to Kurile Islands requiring 30 days time would cost $300 gold per day.

War Department states that it is necessary for Nutt to proceed to Kurile Islands to arrange for details regarding fueling, landings, et cetera, but expense of chartering vessel prohibitive. It is hoped that arrangements may be made with Japanese authorities to permit Nutt to proceed on destroyer, in which case he would comply absolutely with any restrictions. If this not practicable, would Jap-

---

[21] Not printed.
[22] On Feb. 18, 2 p. m., the Ambassador telegraphed that the Government of India would permit the planes to cross and land in India at prearranged points. Permission to take aerial photographs was granted except in certain specified areas and the native states (file no. 811.2300/52). Permission to take photographs while passing over Iraq was telegraphed on May 27 (file no. 811.2300/113).

anese authorities object to Nutt's proceeding to Kurile Islands on United States Navy destroyer? Japanese Naval Attaché and Assistant Naval Attaché have on several occasions been taken on board United States Naval vessels to witness bombing tests, et cetera.

HUGHES

811.2300/70 : Telegram

The High Commissioner in Turkey (Bristol) to the Secretary of State

CONSTANTINOPLE, *March 6, 1924—noon.*
[Received March 7—11 p. m.]

39. Department's 35, February 28, 4 p. m.[23] Permission received for flight to cross Turkish territory under following conditions:

1. The American aviators should be advised that there do not exist in Turkey specially prepared landing places.
2. Excepting in case of *force majeure* aeroplanes shall only land at the places which the inspectors of the Turkish air service shall designate.
3. The aeroplanes shall follow after Aleppo the line Adana, Konia, Afion Karahissar, Ismet, San Stephano.
4. As has been agreed upon officers in the Turkish air service shall be permitted to make a study of the American machines.

BRISTOL

811.2300/66 : Telegram

The Ambassador in Japan (Woods) to the Secretary of State

TOKYO, *March 6, 1924—6 p. m.*
[Received March 6—9 : 10 a. m.]

46. Department's telegram no. 33, March 3, 6 p. m. Japanese authorities have promised to send two destroyers to the Kurile Islands for flight which will carry 1,000 gallons gasoline which is about half supply required. Lieutenant Nutt informs me remainder must be carried on a chartered boat. He adds that, assisted by both Japanese authorities and Standard Oil, he has made every effort to get bids on transportation of gasoline to Kuriles and has canvassed thoroughly Japanese shipping firms but on account hazardous nature of the undertaking due to climates in April, May, it is almost impossible to find shipping captain willing to undertake trip. Their attitude is set out in letter from one firm reading: "This journey must be undertaken by those who are prepared to die." However, a very few bids have finally been received ranging from 18 to 20 thousand yen for the trip.

[23] Not printed.

Thus far Japanese military authorities have been unwilling to consent to Nutt's proceeding to Kuriles as they say Japanese air service officials will look after all details regarding fueling, landings, etc., as well as provide accommodation on destroyers for American flight officers arriving in aeroplanes.

In view of consistent and insistent reference of Japanese War Office to fact that there is no open port in Kuriles, it is my opinion that they would regard suggestion that Nutt proceed there on United States destroyer with disapproval and suspicion. I understand informal British request for similar privileges already refused.

WOODS

811.2300/68 : Telegram

The Ambassador in Great Britain (Kellogg) to the Secretary of State

LONDON, *March 6, 1924—6 p. m.*
[Received March 6—2 : 42 p. m.]

87. My telegram no. 61, February 15, 4 p. m., *re* world aeroplane flight. The British Government agrees to waive usual restrictions on aerial photography in the case of the five aeroplanes, provided they do not fly over or photograph any of prohibited areas named in schedule 7 of Air Navigation Order 1923, copy of which I am forwarding you,[24] or the areas in which armament depots are situated at Woolwich, Bedenham, Marchwood, Bandeath and Wrabness.

KELLOGG

811.2300/66 : Telegram

The Secretary of State to the Ambassador in Japan (Woods)

WASHINGTON, *March 8, 1924—6 p. m.*

37. Your 46, March 6, 6 p. m. Navy Department authorizing Commander of Asiatic Squadron to place destroyer if desired at disposal of Lieutenant Nutt to transport him to Kurile Islands. Please request Japanese authorities to grant permission to Nutt to proceed on Japanese destroyer. At the same time state that if such an alternative course would be more acceptable to the Japanese Government, arrangements could be made to have him proceed along route aboard an American naval vessel, with the approval of the Japanese Government, in order to arrange for details regarding fueling, landings, et cetera. War Department advises that in order to insure carrying out of technical arrangements, it is essential that these details be handled by American officer familiar with flight. In approaching

---

[24] Not printed.

Japanese authorities in the above sense, refer to last sentence of Department's 33, March 3, 6 p. m.

HUGHES

811.2300/86 : Telegram

The Ambassador in Japan (Woods) to the Secretary of State

TOKYO, *March 22, 1924—2 p. m.*
[Received March 23—12 : 15 p. m.]

54. Department's 37, March 8, 6 p. m. Vice Minister of Foreign Affairs notified me informally this morning that he had finally succeeded in securing the consent of the Japanese military and naval authorities to allow one American destroyer to proceed to Bettobu and another destroyer to Kashiwabara as desired by our War Department under following conditions:

"1. This expedition to be solely for the purpose of taking essential supplies.

2. The destroyers are to stop at Yokohama to take on board one Japanese Army and one Japanese naval officer who are to remain on board during the trip to the Kurile Islands."

I desire to emphasize the fact that this permission has been secured solely through the personal intervention of the Vice Minister of Foreign Affairs and that throughout these negotiations the Embassy had had to contend with the vigorous opposition of the Japanese military and naval authorities who had been opposed in principle to the flight and categorically opposed to allowing any foreign warship to enter the ports of the Kurile Islands which they say have always been regarded as closed territory, as set forth in my telegram number 200, December 21, 8 p. m.[25] The Japanese War Office had definitely declared to the military attaché at this Embassy that the only flight the War Office would consent to would be a nonstop flight from the Aleutian Islands to Aomori. In view of this attitude of the Army and Navy Departments it was found necessary to appeal to Vice Minister for Foreign Affairs who through his personal influence has been able finally to have the wishes of our War Department carried out.

WOODS

811.2300/87b : Telegram

The Secretary of State to the Ambassador in Great Britain
(Kellogg)

WASHINGTON, *April 3, 1924—5 p. m.*

84. World Flight. Through inadvertence Department did not request permission from British Government for flight to pass through

---

[25] Not printed.

Hongkong. Please endeavor to obtain permission immediately and telegraph reply.[26]

HUGHES

REPRESENTATIONS BY THE UNITED STATES AGAINST THE EXCLUSION OF AMERICAN MORMON MISSIONARIES FROM CERTAIN EUROPEAN COUNTRIES

354.116 M 82/1

Senator Reed Smoot [27] to the Secretary of State

WASHINGTON, *March 24, 1921.*

MY DEAR MR. SECRETARY: I desire to bring to your attention by letter a question of very great importance affecting the missionary work of the Church of Jesus Christ of Latter-day Saints (commonly called the Mormon Church), and kindly ask you to direct that steps be taken by the State Department to secure the removal of certain restrictions imposed upon the missionaries of said Church from entering the following countries to carry on missionary work, a privilege enjoyed for over fifty years preceding the recent war: Denmark, Norway, Sweden, Switzerland, Holland, and South Africa.

Shortly after the breaking out of the war most of the European countries requested that American citizens return to their own country, principally on account of the shortage of food. The Church immediately complied with the request as soon as it was suggested to them. The armistice was signed twenty-eight months ago, and yet these countries named above are refusing to visa American passports issued to the missionaries of said Church. The work of the Church requires that missionaries be sent to these countries, not only to direct the missionary work but to look after the property interests of the Church.

There can be no possible reason for discriminating against this class of American citizens. I explained to you yesterday more in detail the situation as it exists, and I now ask you to direct the proper American representatives to the above named countries to secure an order from the proper officials of each country named to their American representatives, authorizing them to visa the American passports issued to members of said Church when called to do missionary work therein. The recent and present policy has been very embarrassing and burdensome to the work of the Church, and I ask you to endeavor to have it corrected.

[26] The Ambassador telegraphed on Apr. 25, 1 p. m., that permission had been granted (file no. 811.2300/96).
[27] Senator from Utah and Apostle in the Church of Jesus Christ of Latter-day Saints.

Do not hesitate to call upon me at any time for any information touching this question.

Sincerely yours,

REED SMOOT

358.116 M 82/28 : Telegram

The Minister in Sweden (Morris) to the Secretary of State

STOCKHOLM, *April 2, 1921—2 p. m.*
[Received 3: 30 p. m.]

38. The Swedish Government has recently assumed an unfriendly attitude toward the missionaries of the Mormon Church in Sweden and has to date ordered the expulsion of 4 of the 11 American missionaries here as was done in 1914. See my number 8, September 17th.[28] At the instance of Mr. Oscar W. Soderberg, vice president of this church in Sweden, I took the matter up with the Foreign Minister who informed me that the case had been decided in Crown Council meeting and that the attitude of the Government on this point was firm. However, at my request he would allow Mr. Soderberg himself to remain a month to wind up the affairs of the church here.

MORRIS

358.116 M 82/28a : Telegram

The Secretary of State to the Minister in Sweden (Morris)

WASHINGTON, *April 2, 1921—5 p. m.*

17. Department informed Mormon missionaries who are American citizens being forced out of Sweden by authorities and obliged abandon their missionary work and valuable property. Department is unaware of reasons for this action. Ask that nothing drastic be done until matter can be fully investigated. Reply by telegraph.

HUGHES

358.116 M 82/29 : Telegram

The Minister in Sweden (Morris) to the Secretary of State

STOCKHOLM, *April 4, 1921—4 p. m.*
[Received April 4—3: 55 p. m.]

40. My number 38, of April 2nd, 2 p. m., Department's number 17, of April 2nd, 5 p. m., also please refer Department's mail instruction number 4 of November 6th 1914.[29] Have again pressed

---

[28] Not printed.
[29] Instruction of 1914 not printed.

matter of Mormon missionaries to Minister for Foreign Affairs as instructed. Count Wrangel informs me that decision was arrived at by Crown Council and regrets inability to alter attitude of Government regarding expulsion of Mormons but that Mr. Soderberg will be allowed to remain 1 month to wind up affairs of church. Foreigners are not allowed to purchase or sell property in Sweden without permission of the King which in this case has not been granted. Property here claimed by the Mormon Church is in the name of Swedish citizens adhering to Mormon faith.

MORRIS

354.116 M 81/1 : Circular telegram

The Secretary of State to the Chargé in Great Britain (Wright)[30]

WASHINGTON, April 5, 1921—1 p. m.

Department advised that British diplomatic and consular officers here refuse visas to American Mormon missionaries going to South Africa. Investigate and report.

Repeat *mutatis mutandis* to The Hague, Copenhagen, Christiania, and Berne.

HUGHES

358.116 M 82/29 : Telegram

The Secretary of State to the Minister in Sweden (Morris)

WASHINGTON, April 7, 1921—6 p. m.

20. Department's No. 17, April 2, 5 p. m. Your No. 40 April 4, 4 p. m.

Telegraph Swedish Government's reasons for expelling Mormons. Request no drastic action be taken until matter can be fully investigated.

HUGHES

358.116 M 82/30 : Telegram

The Minister in Sweden (Morris) to the Secretary of State

STOCKHOLM, April 9, 1921—11 a. m.
[Received 2:35 p. m.]

43. Your 20, April 7, 6 p. m. In taking up the matter again with the Foreign Office Count Wrangel informed me that the Crown Council met yesterday to consider the petition of all the Swedish Mormons in this country and decided to maintain the

---

[30] See last paragraph for instructions to repeat to The Hague, Copenhagen, Christiania, and Berne.

decisions already arrived at by the Government. He also told me that he had again consulted with the Archbishop of Sweden and the Minister of Public Instructions and that the matter had been thoroughly investigated and decided upon and it was further pointed out that they did not consider the action drastic as it was the result of the decision of the Swedish Government which does not consider the presence of Mormons desirable because they are proselytizing in favor of church community which holds public services without having had granted its application to be recognized by the Swedish State in accordance with the Royal ordinance of October 31st, 1873, transmitted in our unnumbered despatch of October 3rd, 1914,[31] and likewise for inducing proselytes to leave the Swedish State Church without the requisite permission of the King as provided by section 3 of the same act.

The Swedish law provides (as set forth in the Foreign Office's note of November 7th, 1914 enclosed in Legation's number 19 [*29*] of November 10th [32]) that as the right of expulsion is a sovereign prerogative exercised by the King in council, that is to say in supreme instance [*sic*], there can be no appeal against a such [*sic*] decree.

The present status of the case is that visas enabling the missionaries to remain in Sweden have been withdrawn and will not be renewed. However a formal order of expulsion from the Kingdom will not be made unless they do not leave the country within a reasonable length of time which in practice is considered to be about 10 days.

In relation to this matter I would say that I have done everything possible to have the Swedish Government postpone action pointing out to them, as set forth in your telegram, the desirability of a thorough investigation before any drastic action should take place. In connection with this the Foreign Minister stated that the question was not a new one and that the Government had gone into this question very thoroughly and had come to their decision regarding same in Crown Council which was unanimous and therefore were averse to our request that no drastic action be taken until the matter could be fully investigated.

I have also spoken several times and had a conference with the leaders of the American Mormons in Sweden and they assure me they feel and they are satisfied that the Legation is doing everything possible regarding the matter.

MORRIS

---

[31] Original in Department file is numbered 13; not printed.
[32] Neither printed.

357.116 M 82/1 : Telegram

The Minister in Norway (Schmedeman) to the Secretary of State

CHRISTIANIA, *April 9, 1921—3 p. m.*
[Received April 9—1:31 p. m.]

11. Department's circular of April 5, 1 p. m.[34] Norwegian Foreign Office states informally that the question of Mormon missionaries has not been seriously discussed in recent years, that the Department of Justice is firmly convinced that they are undesirable and the police are satisfied that they lead young girls astray and that the efforts of conversion are centered upon them. It was intimated that an official request by the Legation would result in careful reconsideration of the matter but I did not feel justified in requesting this without further instructions.

SCHMEDEMAN

357.116 M 82/1 : Telegram

The Secretary of State to the Minister in Norway (Schmedeman)

WASHINGTON, *April 9, 1921—6 p. m.*

14. Department's circular April 5, 1 p. m.[34] Your No. 11, April 9, 3 p. m. Mormon case.

Request careful reconsideration of matter, and ask no drastic action be taken until case can be fully investigated.

HUGHES

358.116 M 82/31 : Telegram

The Secretary of State to the Minister in Sweden (Morris)

WASHINGTON, *April 9, 1921—6 p. m.*

21. Department's No. 20, April 7, 6 p. m. Inform Swedish Government Mormon Church invites any investigation Swedish Government may desire to make and will be glad to pay expenses both to and from Utah of any investigator the Swedish Government may desire to send.

HUGHES

358.116 M 82/32 : Telegram

The Minister in Sweden (Morris) to the Secretary of State

STOCKHOLM, *April 28, 1921—3 p. m.*
[Received April 28—1:56 p. m.]

46. Your 21, April 9, 6 p. m. and 23, April 26, 6 p. m.[35] Since my report, telegram number 43, April 9, 11 a. m., no change in condi-

_____

[34] See footnote 30, p. 248.
[35] Latter not printed.

tions. The two missionaries who had received notice of the cancellation of their visas are still here although the period of their original permission to remain in Sweden has expired and they have not been asked to leave the country. Have today received following note from Foreign Office in reply to request to send investigator to Utah.

"In response to this communication I have the honor to call to your attention that the Royal Government does not believe that it should accept this invitation as the conditions to be looked into are already sufficiently known from reports of persons worthy of credence who have been sent there by the Government for the purpose of giving an account of the state of affairs in the Mormon Church and community."

MORRIS

356.116 M 82/1 : Telegram

The Minister in the Netherlands (Phillips) to the Secretary of State

THE HAGUE, *April 30, 1921—noon.*
[Received 12 : 10 p. m.]

54. Your 22, April 13, 5 p. m.[36] Visa questions are generally left to the discretion of consular officers but Dutch Government has no objection in principle to the entrance of Mormon missionaries. About 60 and their families were refused admission last year because of housing shortage. As this condition is not improved request for admission on a large scale will not meet with favorable reception.

PHILLIPS

359.116 M 82/1 : Telegram

The Minister in Denmark (Grew) to the Secretary of State

COPENHAGEN, *May 3, 1921—7 p. m.*
[Received May 3—6 : 15 p. m.]

36. Department's 19, April 30, 2 p. m.[36] Foreign Office states that no definite policy on question of granting visas to American Mormon missionaries as such has as yet been formulated. Danish Legation at Washington generally refused such occasional applications until at the request of Senator Smoot last summer it was decided to grant visas to a limited number to proceed to Denmark to look after property interests, et cetera. There were seven applications during the past year all at Washington of which four were granted and three refused.

---

[36] Not printed.

I gather that Ministry of Ecclesiastical Affairs is opposed in principle to their admission. Shall await further instructions before pressing for a definite ruling.

GREW

357.116 M 82/2

The Minister in Norway (Schmedeman) to the Secretary of State

No. 1845   CHRISTIANIA, *May 28, 1921.*
[Received June 22.]

SIR: Referring to the Department's cable instruction No. 14 of April 9th, 6 p. m., relative to permission for Mormon missionaries to enter Norway, and instructing me to request of the Norwegian Government that no drastic action be taken in this matter, I have the honor to report that immediately upon receipt of the instruction I called on the Minister for Foreign Affairs in order to obtain an expression from him regarding permission for Mormon missionaries to enter the country.

I told His Excellency that I believed that certain reports circulated regarding the missionaries were untrue and that, as far as I knew, the Mormon missionaries in this country had always conducted themselves in a proper manner; that I had been informed by the Presiding Elder of that denomination in this country that no efforts on their part had been made to have the converts emigrate to the United States and that, as Norway permitted missionaries of other faiths to freely enter the country and carry on religious propaganda, I believed it was unfair for the Norwegian Government to discriminate against the Mormons. The Minister for Foreign Affairs informed me that complaints had reached him from the Police and the Department of Justice that the efforts of the missionaries were especially directed towards influencing young women to join the church, but added that he knew comparatively little about the matter and suggested that I address a Note to him on the subject and he would then refer the matter to the Department of Justice.

I accordingly addressed such a Note to His Excellency on April 12th last (a copy of which is enclosed herewith),[38] and under date of May 24th I received a reply (a copy and translation of which is also enclosed herewith)[38] in which it is stated that the Norwegian Government has issued no general instructions to its diplomatic and consular officers to refuse visas to Mormon missionaries, but that the Department of Justice maintains that questions of this character must be submitted to the Central Passport Bureau for its decision

---

[38] Not printed.

and that that Bureau will very likely refuse all or the majority of such requests.

I have [etc.] A. G. SCHMEDEMAN

341.116 M 82/17 : Telegram

The Ambassador in Great Britain (Harvey) to the Secretary of State

LONDON, *May 28, 1921—1 p. m.*
[Received May 28—10 : 39 a. m.]

440. My 306, April 13, 6 p. m.[39] I am reliably informed that South African Government do not desire to encourage the entry of Mormon missionaries into that country.

HARVEY

354.116 M 82/12

The Secretary of State to the Chargé in Switzerland (Lane)

No. 162 WASHINGTON, *December 26, 1922.*

SIR: The receipt is acknowledged of your despatches, number 680 of November 23, and number 694 of November 29, 1922,[40] concerning the difficulties experienced by Mr. and Mrs. Ripplinger and Mr. Hugh J. Ford, American Mormon missionaries, in their attempts to secure permission to reside in certain of the Swiss Cantons.

You suggest, as a result of conversations with an official of the Political Department, concerning the matter, that you be instructed to inform the Swiss Government that, so far as is known, the countenance of polygamy is no longer tolerated by the Church of the Latter Day Saints. You further suggest that the Swiss authorities might be willing to interpret Article I of the Convention of Friendship, Commerce and Extradition, concluded between the United States and Switzerland on November 25, 1850,[41] pertaining to the rights of citizens of the United States in the matter of residence in Switzerland, and to the rights of Swiss citizens in the matter of residence in the United States, in favor of the missionaries, who are requesting the assistance of the Legation.

The Department does not consider it advisable that representations be made to the Swiss Government in favor of the missionaries on the ground that Article I of the Convention of Friendship, Commerce, and Extradition entitles them to the privilege of residence in Switzerland.

---

[39] Not printed.
[40] Neither printed.
[41] Miller, *Treaties*, vol. 5, p. 845.

You may, however, inform the Political Department, unofficially, that polygamy is forbidden not only by the laws of the United States but as well by the Mormon Church, and that this Government hopes that the Swiss authorities will accord to Mormon missionaries the same privileges that are granted to missionaries of other faiths.

I am [etc.]

For the Secretary of State:
WILLIAM PHILLIPS

348a.116 M 82/22

The Secretary of State to Senator Reed Smoot

WASHINGTON, January 22, 1923.

MY DEAR SENATOR SMOOT: I wish to refer to my letter of August 10, 1922,[43] relating to the refusal of the South African railway authorities to allow reduced rates to elders of the Church of Jesus Christ of Latter Day Saints.

I have now received a despatch from the American Consulate General at Cape Town [43] stating that as a result of the Consulate General's representations the South African Railway Administration has now recognized the elders of the Church of Jesus Christ of Latter Day Saints as entitled to the usual travel concessions granted to Ministers of the Gospel and Missionaries under the new regulations which were effective January 1, 1923.

I am [etc.]

CHARLES E. HUGHES

357.116 M 82/4

The Minister in Norway (Swenson) to the Secretary of State

No. 286   CHRISTIANIA, October 19, 1923.

[Received November 6.]

SIR: I have the honor to enclose herewith copies of correspondence exchanged with the Foreign Office,[43] relative to the refusal of Norwegian visaes to Mormon missionaries holding passports issued to them as citizens of the United States.

Senator Reed Smoot, who visited Norway last summer, called my attention to this discrimination against members of the Church of Jesus Christ of Latter-Day Saints and asked that I take the matter up with the Norwegian Government. I did so, requesting that the present practice be changed and that hereafter visaes be granted to Mormons desiring to enter Norway.

---

[43] Not printed.

The Department of Justice and Police has now taken favorable action on my note, reversing its previous decision, when the question was submitted through the Norwegian Legation at Washington.

I have [etc.]   LAURITS S. SWENSON

358.116 M 82/35

The Minister in Sweden (Bliss) to the Secretary of State

No. 101   STOCKHOLM, *January 3, 1924.*
[Received January 22.]

SIR: I have the honor to enclose herewith copies of correspondence exchanged between this Legation and the Minister for Foreign Affairs [44] regarding the refusal by the Swedish consuls at Chicago and Copenhagen to visa the American passport of Darcey U. Wright to enter Sweden, on the ground that he was a missionary of the Mormon Church.

This question of Mormon missionaries in Sweden was the subject of telegraphic correspondence between the Department and this Legation in April, 1921, since which time I find no record in the files that the matter has been taken up by this Legation. In April of 1921, the expulsion from Sweden of missionaries of the Mormon church was ordered, but through the intervention of Mr. Morris it was apparently never fully carried out, as it would seem that some missionaries were permitted to remain in Sweden. There is a record in the Legation files that one of the missionaries was permitted to continue for a limited period his sojourn in Sweden on his engaging to "abstain from all preaching and propaganda on behalf of the Mormon Church during his stay in Sweden" (Foreign Office third person note, May 28, 1921).

Last July, two or three days after my arrival in Stockholm, Senator Reed Smoot of Utah came to Stockholm and at that time I presented him to the Prime Minister, Mr. Trygger. During the interview which followed, Senator Smoot referred to the difficulties of entering Sweden that were placed in the way of Mormon missionaries by the Swedish authorities and expressed the hope that the Government might be disposed to examine the matter further with a view to satisfying itself that there were grounds to warrant a change in its attitude towards the representatives of the Church of Jesus Christ of Latter Day Saints.

Since my arrival here, however, no concrete case has arisen to give an opportunity for me to make representations to the Foreign

[44] Not printed.

Office in this matter until the one which is the subject of this report to the Department.

In handing to Baron Marcks von Wurtemberg my note of December 17th, 1923,[45] regarding the case of Mr. Wright, I went into the subject as fully as the information on file at the Legation would permit. I mentioned, in the course of our conversation, that the restrictions in Norway, somewhat similar to those in Sweden, had recently been removed.

Last evening I dined with the Minister for Foreign Affairs, and after dinner he referred to this matter of the Mormon missionaries. He said that it presented considerable difficulty to his Government, as the information which it has regarding the Mormon Church was not favorable. He spoke of a report to the Swedish Government which had been made some years ago, promising to send me a copy, which I shall forward to the Department as soon as possible.

I learned that the Minister has instructed the Swedish Legation at Washington and the Swedish Consulate at San Francisco to make new investigation of the activities and standing of the Mormon Church. In view of this instruction, the Minister said it would be some time before he could make an answer to the note which I sent to him on December 17th last.

Should the Department see no objection, I beg that the information contained in this despatch be brought to the attention of Senator Smoot, in order that he may be acquainted with the present situation regarding the entrance of Mormon missionaries into Sweden and, also, that he may inform the competent authorities of the Mormon Church of the investigation which is to be made by the Swedish diplomatic and consular officers in order that they may facilitate such investigation if the proper opportunity presents itself.

In this respect, it is my opinion that it would not be advisable for the Mormon Church to repeat the invitation that an investigation be made nor to offer to pay the expenses of an investigator of the Swedish Government, as its previous offer of this nature was rejected in terms which do not counsel repetition (see Department's telegram No. 21, April 9, 1921, 6 p. m. and Legation's cabled answer No. 46, April 28, 1921, 3 p. m.)

I should be obliged if the Department would indicate what further action it desires taken in this case, should the Minister's answer to my note refuse the request that a visa be given to Mr. Wright.

I have [etc.]   ROBERT WOODS BLISS

---

[45] Not printed.

359.116 M 82/7

The Minister in Denmark (Prince) to the Secretary of State

No. 666   COPENHAGEN, *February 6, 1924.*
[Received February 20.]

SIR: Referring to my despatch No. 631, of December 21, 1923,[46] I have the honor to report that Count Reventlow, Director General of the Danish Foreign Office, has informed me unofficially that the Church Ministry of Denmark from now on will exercise the utmost leniency with regard to the admission of Mormon preachers, as it is highly probable that all visa restrictions between Denmark and the United States are soon to be abolished. The Church Ministry, therefore, regards it as not worth while to insist upon strict visa observation at the present moment. This means practically free entry for all Mormon clergy, unless, as Count Reventlow pointed out, half jestingly, "a shipload were to come at once", which I assured him would not be the case. I believe that the problem is practically solved so far as Denmark is concerned.

I have [etc.]   JOHN DYNELEY PRINCE

358.116 M 82/38 : Telegram

The Minister in Sweden (Bliss) to the Secretary of State

STOCKHOLM, *June 7, 1924—1 p. m.*
[Received June 7—11: 50 a. m.]

19. With reference to my despatch number 115, January 25,[46] Foreign Office informs me that hereafter visas for Mormons will be subject to the same regulations as applied to all foreigners.

BLISS

354.116 M 82/21

The Secretary of State to the Consul at Zürich (Wilkinson)

WASHINGTON, *October 7, 1924.*

SIR: The Department has received your confidential despatch No. 1911 of August 16, 1924,[46] concerning the opposition of the Swiss authorities to the continued presence of Mormon missionaries in Switzerland.

There would appear to be no action which you could take in this matter other than to render to Mormon missionaries who may be American citizens, such assistance as may be warranted with a view

[46] Not printed.

to seeing that they are accorded the protection to which they may be entitled under the laws of Switzerland.

With reference to your statement that the police at Zurich appear to be under the impression that your office has been over-zealous in the action which it has taken in behalf of Mormon missionaries, it is suggested that should you have reason to believe that the local authorities share this view you may be able to convince them that you have merely rendered to Mormon missionaries the assistance to which as American citizens they are entitled. With reference to the extent to which you should intervene in behalf of Mormon missionaries who are American citizens, it may be observed that this is a matter depending largely upon the facts and circumstances of the individual case. You should, however, be convinced that the facts are such as to warrant you in taking up a particular case with the local authorities. In general, it may be stated that you should render to Mormon missionaries who are American citizens the same degree of assistance that should properly be rendered to any other class of American citizens.

You may upon an appropriate occasion informally express to the local authorities the hope that so long as American citizens professing the Mormon faith do not violate the Swiss laws or preach any doctrine that is contrary to law or morality, they will be granted the same privileges and protection as are accorded to other aliens and will not be discriminated against merely because of their religion. However, should the Swiss authorities insist upon enforcing the laws of Switzerland bearing upon the stay of Mormon missionaries in that country, the Department considers that you would not be warranted in intervening in behalf of any American citizens who may be affected by such laws unless in enforcing the regulations governing the departure of such missionaries from Swiss territory, American citizens should be subjected to harsh or arbitrary treatment.

A copy of this instruction has been sent to the Legation at Berne for its information.

I am [etc.]

For the Secretary of State:
Joseph C. Grew

354.116 M 82/22

The Minister in Switzerland (Gibson) to the Secretary of State

No. 166   Berne, *October 7, 1924.*

[Received October 18.]

Sir: During the past few years this Legation has frequently been called upon to deal with the cases of American Mormon missionaries resident in Switzerland, who are refused renewals of residence permits by the cantonal authorities.

These cases are usually referred to rather loosely as "deportations" or "expulsions" and I venture to point out at once the inaccuracy of this description. The residence of foreigners in Switzerland is a matter regulated by the cantons and is subject to residence permits granted for short periods. The cantonal authorities have complete power to grant or withhold renewals of these residence permits and while the Federal Government is usually prepared to use its good offices in seeing that justice is done to foreigners, it cannot, constitutionally, enforce its views upon the cantonal authorities.

The customary procedure is for the cantonal authorities to send a notice to the individual concerned informing him that his residence permit will expire at some future date, usually some weeks or months in advance and that the canton does not see its way to granting an extension. The foreigner is informed that he will be expected to leave the canton or the Confederation on or before the date of the expiration of his existing permit. The procedure in this matter is entirely different from that of deportations which are effected by the police and with much less consideration of the individual's convenience and with less warning. I have entered into this rather detailed explanation of the question in the belief that it has a considerable importance in considering the rights of the American citizens who frequently appeal to the Legation for protection and assistance.

In the past it has been the practice of the Legation to deal with each case as it arose, to endeavor to secure the statement of the reasons for the action taken by the cantonal authorities and frequently to secure an extension of the time limit fixed by the local authorities. It has recently become increasingly evident, however, that the cantonal authorities, notably those of the canton of Zurich, where most of the Mormon missionaries reside, have adopted a definite policy of eliminating them gradually from the canton through a refusal to renew their residence permits. Several of the missionaries have recently been informed that their present permits will not be renewed and that they will be expected to leave the canton of Zurich before the end of the year. I am further informed that a number of other missionaries expect such notification in due course. In view of this the Department may wish to consider the entire question and to give the Legation and consular officers in Switzerland some general instructions to govern their action in dealing with this case.

.   .   .   .

It would be very helpful to me to have the Department's instructions on the following points:

1. Whether the Department is disposed to take exception to the Swiss contention that those provisions of the Constitution bearing upon religious liberty concern Swiss citizens only and cannot be invoked by the missionaries as specifically covering their proselytizing. If it is desired that I take exception to the Swiss position I should like a statement of the Department's views for my guidance.

2. Whether the Department is disposed to contest the Swiss contention that Article III of the Convention of Friendship, Commerce and Extradition gives full warrant for refusing residence permits to American citizens whose presence is considered undesirable by the Swiss authorities; if so on what grounds.

3. What action the Department desires me to take on behalf of these missionaries. If it is desired that I support the contention of these missionaries that they should be allowed to remain indefinitely I should like a statement of the arguments to be advanced on their behalf. In deciding this question the Department will doubtless wish to bear in mind the possibility that serious pressure on behalf of these people may compromise the ability of the Legation to support the interests of other Americans who are in need of its assistance.

Pending receipt of the Department's instructions, I shall continue to deal with each case individually, to seek an explanation of the reasons for refusing to renew residence permits and where such action by me appears warranted, to request that suitable extensions be granted.

In submitting the foregoing I venture to point out that action in some of the cases now pending is contemplated not later than October 31st. I should be glad, therefore, if I might be given full telegraphic instructions as soon as possible.

I have [etc.]   HUGH GIBSON

354.116 M 82/22 : Telegram

*The Acting Secretary of State to the Minister in Switzerland
(Gibson)*

WASHINGTON, *October 27, 1924—4 p. m.*

85. Your 166, October 7. Department's attitude concerning Mormon missionaries is indicated in its instruction of October 7 to Consul at Zurich, copy of which was sent to you by Department October 10.

See Department's 162, December 26, 1922, stating that it did not consider it advisable to make representations to Swiss authorities in favor of Mormon missionaries on ground that Article I of the Convention of Friendship, Commerce and Extradition of 1850 entitles them to privilege of residence in Switzerland.

You would not be warranted in objecting to denial by appropriate Swiss authorities of residence permits to Mormon missionaries found to have been engaged in practices objectionable under laws of Switzerland. You may, however, exercise good offices to prevent expulsion being accompanied by undue hardship in individual cases.

If, as would appear from your despatch, it is intention of cantonal authorities of Zurich gradually to refuse renewal of residence permits in cases of all Mormon missionaries as a class, irrespective of whether they have violated the laws of Switzerland, you should inform Foreign Office that this Government considers that they should not be denied residence permits merely because of their religious belief.

Department does not consider it advisable to discuss with Swiss authorities question whether provisions in Article 49 of Swiss Constitution guaranteeing religious freedom apply to Mormon missionaries, in view of other provisions in Articles 50 and 51 placing limitations upon such guarantee.

GREW

354.116 M 82/23

The Minister in Switzerland (Gibson) to the Secretary of State

No. 206 BERNE, *November 5, 1924.*
[Received November 18.]

SIR: I have the honor to refer to my despatch No. 166 of October 7th requesting instructions with regard to the case of American Mormon missionaries, resident in Switzerland, who have been refused renewal of residence permits by certain cantonal authorities.

Upon receipt of the Department's telegram No. 85, of October 27, 4 p. m., embodying instructions in the nature requested, I immediately drew up an *aide-memoire* based on these instructions which I left personally with Mr. Dinichert, Chief of the Division of Foreign Affairs of the Federal Political Department, on October 28, 1924. A copy of this *aide-memoire* is transmitted herewith.[49] It will be noted that as the residence permits of certain of these missionaries were to expire on October 31, 1924, I specifically called attention to this fact in my *aide-memoire* in the hope that a reply might be received prior to that date.

Accordingly, on October 31, 1924, I received a memorandum from the Political Department, a copy and translation of which are enclosed,[49] in answer to my *aide-memoire* under reference. It will be noted that this memorandum states that the question of religious freedom in Switzerland is absolutely independent of the question of the residence of foreigners in this country. Religious freedom does

---

[49] Not printed.

not carry with it the right of foreigners to travel or to establish themselves in Switzerland. The exercise of this right lies within the sovereignty of the cantons as expressly provided for by federal legislation. It is therefore the cantons alone which, in each particular case, are capable of deciding on questions of residence. Their decisions in these matters are without appeal and the Federal authorities have no means at their disposal to bring about a modification of the cantonal decisions. The memorandum adds that, in view of the foregoing, the missionaries in this country have never been disturbed in any way on account of their personal religious convictions. The refusal of certain cantons to prolong the residence permits of the missionaries in question has, on the contrary, been especially necessitated by their proselytizing methods which have caused trouble and disturbances in many Swiss families, disturbances which in turn have led to general complaints. In view of these frequent unfortunate experiences, the memorandum declares that there is nothing surprising in the action of the cantonal authorities.

In discussing this matter with the appropriate official of the Political Department, the Legation was clearly informed that the portion of this memorandum which concerns the measures taken by the cantonal authorities, alone relates to the missionaries the prolongation of whose residence permits has at this time been refused—and in no way applies to Mormon missionaries as a class. He went on to say that there were a large number of missionaries residing in Switzerland whose activities had caused no criticism whatsoever and so long as no complaints were generally directed against these remaining missionaries they would be allowed to reside undisturbed in Switzerland.

It would not appear that the Legation has grounds for making further representations to the Federal authorities on behalf of the missionaries whose prolongation of residence permits has been refused in view of the nature of the foregoing memorandum. It has been definitely stated that the cantonal authorities are supreme in matters of this sort; that their decisions are without appeal; that their action in these cases under reference has in no way been influenced by their religious beliefs, and that their decisions in each case to refuse the prolongation of residence permits were solely based on the fact that complaints had been generally directed against these particular missionaries for having caused disturbances in various families. In emphasizing this portion of the memorandum, the official of the Political Department with whom this matter was discussed made the following observation: He said that only a few days ago a member of the National Council had come to his office with the request that representations be made to this Legation with a view to securing for him permission to remain in the United States on his proposed visit for a longer period than is provided for by the immigration act with respect to the residence in America of non-immigrants. The official in question told the deputy that, as the question of the residence of foreigners in the United States was purely a matter of national sovereignty, he must decline to make the representations requested.

The fact that it has not been possible to extend the residence permits of the missionaries in question has been communicated to them and I understand that their departure from Switzerland has taken place in accordance with the limit of time placed upon their residence.

I have [etc.]   Hugh Gibson

362.116 M 82/31

The Acting Secretary of State to the Chargé in Germany (*Robbins*)

No. 3839   Washington, *April 27, 1925.*

Sir: The Department has received your despatch No. 1015, of March 16, 1925,[50] together with the enclosures thereto concerning the refusal of the local authorities in East Prussia to permit Mr. Carvel M. James, an American citizen, to remain in the province on the ground that his activities as a Mormon missionary disturb the peace.

It appears that the Prussian authorities base their action on the ground that Mr. James' proselytizing was a source of disturbance in a number of families in Selbogen. It also appears that the authorities declined to give Mr. James a hearing and refused to accept the testimony of witnesses who were prepared to testify in Mr. James' defense.

You advise the Department that in bringing this case to the Embassy's attention, Mr. Nathaniel P. Davis, American Consul in Charge at Berlin, stated that, though he felt that the provincial authorities were within their rights in refusing Mr. James permission to remain in East Prussia, it was felt nevertheless that if the latter's statements were correct, that he had not been given an opportunity to defend himself or to produce witnesses in his defense, it might be considered advisable for the Embassy to make some representations to the Foreign Office in order that this case might not be quoted later as a precedent for similar action in the future. You request to be instructed in the matter.

.   .   .   .

While this Government does not contest the right of the authorities of East Prussia to request an American citizen to leave the territory under their jurisdiction in case he proves himself a cause

---

[50] Not printed.

of serious disturbance, it is considered, however, that he should be given an opportunity to defend himself respecting charges brought against him and that a failure of the authorities to accord him a hearing constitutes an arbitrary exercise of the right of expulsion. This Government considers, moreover, that the reasons given by the local authorities for refusing to allow Mr. James to defend himself against the charges, namely that he could not have disproved them and that the witnesses produced by him would not be willing to testify against him, are not convincing and, in fact, are contradictory. If the report of this case as received by the East Prussian authorities is correct, they might, it would seem, have been able to obtain the testimony of witnesses to substantiate the charges and refute the defense set up by Mr. James and his supporters.

In bringing the foregoing considerations to the attention of the German Foreign Office, you will advise it that it is not sought to obtain a reversal of the decision in this case since it appears that Mr. James does not desire to return to East Prussia but that this Government has no doubt that the German Government will readily agree that the expulsion of American citizens without an opportunity to defend themselves against charges brought against them constitutes an arbitrary procedure. You will further advise the Foreign Office that this Government confidently hopes that the necessary steps will be taken by the German Government to insure American citizens in the future an opportunity to defend themselves before an impartial authority against charges which, if established, would warrant their expulsion from German territory under the appropriate German laws.

You are requested to transmit to the Consulate General at Berlin and the Consulate at Koenigsberg for their information copies of this instruction, which are enclosed.

I am [etc.]   JOSEPH C. GREW

STATEMENTS BY THE SECRETARY OF STATE THAT THE QUESTION OF PHILIPPINE INDEPENDENCE IS EXCLUSIVELY A DOMESTIC PROBLEM OF THE UNITED STATES

811b.01/63

The Chairman of the Committee on Insular Affairs of the House of Representatives (Fairfield) to the Secretary of State

WASHINGTON, *March 25, 1924.*

DEAR SIR: The Insular Affairs Committee of the House of Representatives has directed me to inquire of the State Department as to whether the granting of Independence at this time to the

Philippine Islands would be contrary to any provisions of the Four
Power Pact.[51]

An early reply would be very much appreciated.

Very sincerely yours,

LOUIS W. FAIRFIELD

811b.01/63

*The Secretary of State to the Chairman of the Committee on
Insular Affairs of the House of Representatives (Fairfield)*

WASHINGTON, *April 3, 1924.*

SIR: I have the honor to acknowledge the receipt of your letter
of March 25, 1924, in which you inquire whether the granting of
independence at this time to the Philippine Islands would be contrary to any provisions of the Four Power Pact.

The controversies referred to in paragraph two of Article I of
the Treaty concluded December 13, 1921 at Washington between
the United States, the British Empire, France and Japan, relating
to their insular possessions and insular dominions in the region of the
Pacific Ocean do not, as indicated in the declaration accompanying
the Treaty,[52] embrace questions which, under the principles of international law, lie exclusively within the domestic jurisdiction of
the respective powers. The question whether independence shall be
granted to the Philippine Islands is one which lies exclusively
within the domestic jurisdiction of the United States. I, therefore,
do not consider that the Treaty mentioned, the declaration accompanying the Treaty, or the Treaty supplementary thereto, concluded
February 6, 1922,[53] in any manner affect the exclusive right of this
Government to withhold or to grant independence to the Islands
in question.

I have [etc.] CHARLES E. HUGHES

811b.01/64

The Secretary of War (Weeks) to the Secretary of State

WASHINGTON, *May 7, 1924.*

DEAR MR. SECRETARY: Do you think it advisable to make a suggestion or to ask for a suggestion from foreign governments,
particularly Great Britain, France and Holland, relative to any
action we may take in giving independence or future independence
to the Philippine Islands. Of course, the dependencies of those

---

[51] *Foreign Relations*, 1922, vol. I, p. 33.
[52] *Ibid.*, p. 36.
[53] *Ibid.*, p. 46.

countries are watching our action with a great deal of interest because their people will naturally want about the same privileges as we will give the Filipinos, and it may add greatly to their troubles.

On the other hand, you may conclude that it is really no affair of theirs what we do, which is probably the case, but it seemed to me that I had better have an expression of opinion from you about the desirability of making a representation of that kind to them.

Sincerely yours,

JOHN W. WEEKS

811b.01/64

The Secretary of State to the Secretary of War (Weeks)

WASHINGTON, *May 8, 1924.*

MY DEAR MR. SECRETARY: I have received your letter of May seventh asking whether I think it advisable to make a suggestion, or to ask for a suggestion from foreign governments, particularly Great Britain, France and Holland, relative to any action we may take in giving independence or future independence to the Philippine Islands. While I fully realize that our action in this matter may be of considerable interest to the Powers, I do not think that we should invite any suggestions from them as to what we should do with our own possessions. It seems to me that any action inviting a suggestion from the other Powers on this subject would easily give rise to misapprehensions and would involve us in needless difficulties.

Faithfully yours,

CHARLES E. HUGHES

SANITARY CONVENTION BETWEEN THE UNITED STATES AND OTHER AMERICAN REPUBLICS, SIGNED NOVEMBER 14, 1924

Treaty Series No. 714

Convention between the United States of America and Other American Republics, Signed at Habana, November 14, 1924 [54]

The Presidents of Argentine, Brazil, Chile, Colombia, Costa Rica, Cuba, Dominican Republic, Guatemala, Haiti, Honduras, Mexico, Salvador, Panama, Paraguay, Peru, United States of America, Uruguay and Venezuela, being desirous of entering into a sanitary

---

[54] In English and Spanish; Spanish text not printed. Ratification advised by the Senate, Feb. 23, 1925; ratified by the President, Mar. 28, 1925; ratification of the United States deposited with the Government of Cuba, Apr. 13, 1925; proclaimed by the President, Apr. 28, 1925.

convention for the purpose of better promoting and protecting the public health of their respective nations, and particularly to the end that effective cooperative international measures may be applied for the prevention of the international spread of the communicable infections of human beings and to facilitate international commerce and communication, have appointed as their plenipotentiaries, to-wit:

The Republic of Argentine:
Dr. Gregorio Araoz Alfaro.
Dr. Joaquín Llambías.

The United States of Brazil:
Dr. Nascimento Gurgel.
Dr. Raúl Almeida Magalhaes.

The Republic of Chile:
Dr. Carlos Graf.

The Republic of Colombia:
Dr. R. Gutiérrez Lee.

The Republic of Costa Rica:
Dr. José Varela Zequeira.

The Republic of Cuba:
Dr. Mario G. Lebredo.
Dr. José A. López del Valle.
Dr. Hugo Roberts.
Dr. Diego Tamayo.
Dr. Francisco M. Fernández.
Dr. Domingo F. Ramos.

The Republic of El Salvador:
Dr. Leopoldo Paz.

The United States of America:
Dr. Hugh S. Cumming.
Dr. Richard Creel.
Mr. P. D. Cronin.
Dr. Francis D. Patterson.

The Republic of Guatemala:
Dr. José de Cubas y Serrate.

The Republic of Haiti:
Dr. Charles Mathon.

The Republic of Honduras:
Dr. Arístides Agramonte.

The Republic of Mexico:
Dr. Alfonso Pruneda.

The Republic of Panama:
  Dr. Jaime de la Guardia.
The Republic of Paraguay:
  Dr. Andrés Gubetich.
The Republic of Peru:
  Dr. Carlos E. Paz Soldán.
The Dominican Republic:
  Dr. R. Pérez Cabral.
The Republic of Uruguay:
  Dr. Justo F. González.
The United States of Venezuela:
  Dr. Enrique Tejera.
  Dr. Antonio Smith.

Who, having exchanged their full powers, found in good and due form, have agreed to adopt, *ad referendum*, the following

PAN AMERICAN SANITARY CODE

CHAPTER I.—OBJECTS OF THE CODE AND DEFINITIONS OF TERMS USED THEREIN

ARTICLE 1. The objects of this code are:

(*a*) The prevention of the international spread of communicable infections of human beings.

(*b*) The promotion of cooperative measures for the prevention of the introduction and spread of disease into and from the territories of the signatory Goverments [*sic*].

(*c*) The standardization of the collection of morbidity and mortality statistics by the signatory Governments.

(*d*) The stimulation of the mutual interchange of information which may be of value in improving the public health, and combating the diseases of man.

(*e*) The standardization of the measures employed at places of entry, for the prevention of the introduction and spread of the communicable diseases of man, so that greater protection against them shall be achieved and unnecessary hindrance to international commerce and communication eliminated.

ART. 2. *Definitions.* As herein used, the following words and phrases shall be taken in the sense hereinbelow indicated, except as a different meaning for the word or phrase in question may be given in a particular article, or is plainly to be collected from the context or connection where the term is used.

Aircraft.—Any vehicle which is capable of transporting persons or things through the air, including aeroplanes, seaplanes, gliders, helocopters, air ships ballons and captive ballons [*sic*].

Area.—A well determined portion of territory.

Disinfection.—The act of rendering free from the causal agencies of disease.

Fumigation.—A standard process by which the organisms of disease or their potential carriers are exposed to a gas in lethal concentrations.

Index, Aedes Aegypti.—The percentage ratio determined after examination between the number of houses in a given area and the number in which larvae or mosquitoes of the *Aedes aegypti* are found, in a fixed period of time.

Inspection.—The act of examining persons, buildings, areas, or things which may be capable of harboring, transmitting or transporting the infectious agents of disease, or of propagating or favoring the propagation of such agents. Also the act of studying and observing measures put in force for the suppression or prevention of disease.

Incubation, Period of.—For plague, cholera and yellow fever, each 6 days, for smallpox, 14 days, and for typhus fever 12 days.

Isolation.—The separation of human beings or animals from other human beings or animals in such manner as to prevent the interchange of disease.

Plague.—Bubonic, septicemic, pneumonic or rodent plague.

Port.—Any place or area where a vessel or aircraft may seek harbor, discharge or receive passengers, crew, cargo or supplies.

Rodents.—Rats, domestic and wild, and other rodents.

CHAPTER II

SECTION 1. NOTIFICATION AND SUBSEQUENT COMMUNICATIONS TO OTHER COUNTRIES

ART. 3. Each of the signatory Governments agrees to transmit to each of the other signatory Governments and to the Pan-American Sanitary Bureau, at intervals of not more than two weeks, a statement containing information as to the state of its public health, particularly that of its ports.

The followings [*sic*] diseases are obligatorily reportable:

Plague, cholera, yellow fever, smallpox, typhus, epidemic cerebropinal [*sic*] meningitis, acute epidemic poliomyelitis, epidemic lethargic encephalitis, influenza or epidemic la grippe, typhoid and paratyphoid fevers, and such other diseases as the Pan American Sanitary Bureau may, by resolution, add to the above list.

ART. 4. Each signatory Government agrees to notify adjacent countries and the Pan American Sanitary Bureau immediately by the most rapid available means of communication, of the appearance in its territory of an authentic or officially suspected case or cases of plague, cholera, yellow fever, small pox, typhus or any other dangerous contagion liable to be spread through the intermediary agency of international commerce.

ART. 5. This notification is to be accompanied, or very promptly followed, by the following additional information:

1. The area where the disease has appeared.
2. The date of its appearance, its origin, and its form.
3. The probable source or country from which introduced and manner of introduction.
4. The number of confirmed cases, and number of deaths.
5. The number of suspected cases and deaths.
6. In addition, for plague, the existence among rodents of plague, or of an unusual mortality among rodents; for yellow fever, the *Aedes aegypti* index of the locality.
7. The measures which have been applied for the prevention of the spread of the disease, and its eradication.

ART. 6. The notification and information prescribed in Articles 4 and 5 are to be addressed to diplomatic or consular representatives in the capital of the infected country, and to the Pan American Sanitary Bureau at Washington, which shall immediately transmit the information to all countries concerned.

ART. 7. The notification and the information prescribed in Articles 3, 4, 5, and 6 are to be followed by further communications in order to keep other Governments informed as to the progress of the disease or diseases. These communications will be made at least once weekly, and will be as complete as possible, indicating in detail the measures employed to prevent the extension of the disease. The telegraph, the cable, and the radio will be employed for this purpose, except in those instances in which the data may be transmitted rapidly by mail. Reports by telegraph, cable or radio will be confirmed by letter. Neighboring countries will endeavor to make special arrangements for the solution of local problems that do not involve widespread international interest.

ART. 8. The signatory Governments agree that in the event of the appearance of any of the following diseases, namely: cholera, yellow fever, plague, typhus fever or other pestilential diseases in severe epidemic form, in their territory, they will immediately put in force appropriate sanitary measures for the prevention of the international carriage of any of the said diseases therefrom by passengers, crew, cargo and vessels, and mosquitoes, rats and vermin that may be carried thereon, and will promptly notify each of the other signatory Governments and the Pan American Sanitary Bureau as to the nature and extent of the sanitary measures which they have applied for the accomplishment of the requirements of this article.

SECTION 2. PUBLICATION OF PRESCRIBED MEASURES

ART. 9. Information of the first non-imported case of plague, cholera, or yellow fever justifies the application of sanitary measures against an area where said disease may have appeared.

ART. 10. The Government of each country obligates itself to publish immediately the preventive measures which will be considered necessary to be taken by vessels or other means of transport, passengers and crew at any port of departure or place located in the infected area. The said publication is to be communicated at once to the accredited diplomatic or consular representatives of the infected country, and to the Pan American Sanitary Bureau. The signatory Government [sic] also obligate themselves to make known in the same manner the revocation of these measures, or of modifications thereof that may be made.

ART. 11. In order that an area may be considered to be no longer infected, it must be officialy [sic] established:

1. That there has neither been a death nor a new case as regards plague or cholera for ten days; and as regards yellow fever for twenty days, either since the isolation, or since the death or recovery of the last patient.

2. That all means for the eradication of the disease have been applied and, in the case of plague, that effective measures against rats have been continuously carried out, and that the disease has not been discovered among them within six months; in the case of yellow fever, that Aedes aegypti index of the infected area has been maintained at an average of not more than 2 per cent for the 30-day period immediately preceding, and that no portion of the infected area has had an index in excess of 5 per cent for the same period of time.

SECTION 3. MORBIDITY AND MORTALITY STATISTICS

ART. 12. The international classification of the causes of death is adopted as the Pan American Classification of the Causes of Death, and shall be used by the signatory nations in the interchange of mortality and morbidity reports.

ART. 13. The Pan American Sanitary Bureau is hereby authorized and directed to re-publish from time to time the Pan American Classification of the Causes of Death.

ART. 14. Each of the signatory Governments agrees to put in operation at the earliest practicable date a system for the collection and tabulation of vital statistics which shall include:

1. A central statistical office presided over by a competent official.
2. The establishment of regional statistical offices.
3. The enactment of laws, decrees or regulations requiring the prompt reporting of births, deaths and communicable diseases, by health officers, physicians, midwives and hospitals, and providing penalities [sic] for failure to make such reports.

ART. 15. The Pan American Sanitary Bureau shall prepare and publish standard forms for the reporting of deaths and cases of communicable disease, and all other vital statistics.

CHAPTER III.—SANITARY DOCUMENTS

SECTION 1. BILLS OF HEALTH

ART. 16. The master of any vessel or aircraft which proceeds to a port of any of the signatory Governments, is required to obtain at the port of departure and ports of call, a bill of health, in duplicate, issued in accordance with the information set forth in the appendix and adopted as the standard bill of health.

ART. 17. The bill of health will be accompanied by a list of the passengers, and stowaways if any, which shall indicate the port where they embarked and the port to which they are destined, and a list of the crew.

ART. 18. Consuls and other officials signing or countersigning bills of health should keep themselves accurately informed with respect to the sanitary conditions of their ports, and the manner in which this code is obeyed by vessels and their passengers and crews while therein. They should have accurate knowledge of local mortality and morbidity, and of sanitary conditions which may affect vessels in port. To this end, they shall be furnished with information they request pertaining to sanitary records, harbors and vessels.

ART. 19. The signatory Governments may assign medical or sanitary officers as public health attaches to embassies or legations, and as representatives to international conferences.

ART. 20. If at the port of departure there be no consul or consular agent of the country of destination, the bill of health may be issued by the consul or consular agent of a friendly Government authorized to issue such bill of health.

ART. 21. The bill of health should be issued not to exceed forty eight hours before the departure of the ship to which it is issued. The sanitary visa should not be given more than twenty-four hours before departure.

ART. 22. Any erasure or alteration of a bill of health shall invalidate the document, unless such alteration or erasure shall be made by competent authority, and notation thereof appropriately made.

ART. 23. A clean bill of health is one which shows the complete absence in the port of departure of cholera, yellow fever, plague, typhus fever, or of other pestilential disease in severe epidemic form, liable to be transported by international commerce. Provided, that the presence only of *bona fide* imported cases of such disease, when properly isolated, shall not compel the issuance of a foul bill of health, but notation of the presence of such cases will be made under the heading of "Remarks" on the Bill of health.

ART. 24. A foul bill of health is one which shows the presence of non-imported cases of any of the diseases referred to in Art. 23.

ART. 25. Specific bill of health are [*sic*] not required of vessels which, by reason of accident, storm or other emergency condition, including wireless change of itinerary, are obliged to put into ports other than their original destinations but such vessels shall be required to exhibit such bills of health as they possess.

ART. 26. It shall be the duty of the Pan American Sanitary Bureau to publish appropriate information which may be distributed by port health officers, for the purpose of instructing owners, agents and master [*sic*] of vessels as to the methods which should be put in force by them for the prevention of the international spread of disease.

SECTION 2. OTHER SANITARY DOCUMENTS

ART. 27. Every vessel carrying a medical officer will maintain a sanitary log which will be kept by him, and he will record therein daily: the sanitary condition of the vessel, and its passengers and crew; a record showing the names of passengers and crew which have been vaccinated by him; name, age, nationality, home address, occupation and nature of illness or injury of all passengers and crew treated during the voyage; the source and sanitary quality of the drinking water of the vessel, the place where taken on board, and the method in use on board for its purification; sanitary conditions, observed in ports visited during the voyage; the measures taken to prevent the ingress and egress of rodents to and from the vessel; the measures which have been taken to protect the passengers and crew against mosquitoes, other insects, and vermin. The sanitary log will be signed by the master and medical officer of the vessel, and will be exhibited upon the request of any sanitary or consular officer. In the absence of a medical officer, the master shall record the above information in the log of the vessel, in so far as possible.

ART. 28. Equal or similar forms for Quarantine Declarations, Certificate of Fumigation, and Certificate of Vaccination, set forth in the appendix, are hereby adopted as standard forms.

CHAPTER IV.—CLASSIFICATION OF PORTS

ART. 29. An infected port is one in which any of the following diseases exist, namely, plague, cholera, yellow fever, or other pestilential disease in severe epidemic form.

ART. 30 A suspected port, is a port in which, or in the areas contiguous thereto, a non imported case or cases of any of the disesases [sic] referred to in Art. 23, have occurred within sixty days, or which has not taken adequate measures to protect itself against such diseases, but which is not known to be an infected port.

ART. 31. A clean port, Class A, is one in which the following conditions are fulfilled:

1. The absence of non-imported cases of any of the diseases referred to in Art. 23, in the port itself and in the areas contiguous thereto.

2. (a) The presence of a qualified and adequate health staff.

(b) Adequate means of fumigation.

(c) Adequate personnel and material for the capture or destruction of rodents.

(d) An adequate bacteriological and pathological laboratory;

(e) A safe water supply.

(f) Adequate means for the collection of mortality and morbidity data;

(g) Adequate facilities for the isolation of suspects and the treatment of infectious diseases.

(h) Signatory Governments shall register in the Pan-American Sanitary Bureau those places that comply with these conditions.

ART. 32. A clean port, Class B, is one in which the conditions described in Art. 31, 1 and 2 (a) above, are fulfilled, but in which one or more of the other requirements of Art. 31, 2 are not fulfilled.

ART. 33. An unclassified port is one with regard to which the information concerning the existence or non-existence of any of the diseases referred to in Art. 23, and the measures which are being applied for the control of such diseases, is not sufficient to classify such port.

An unclassified port shall be provisionally considered as a suspected or infected port, as the information available in each case may determine, until definitely classified.

ART. 34. The Pan American Sanitary Bureau shall prepare and publish, at intervals, a tabulation of the most commonly used ports of the Western Hemisphere, giving information as to sanitary conditions.

Chapter V.—Classification of Vessels

Art. 35. A clean vessel is one coming from a clean port, Class A or B, which has had no case of plague, cholera, yellow fever, small pox or typhus aboard during the voyage, and which has complied with the requirements of this code.

Art. 36. An infected or suspected vessels [*sic*] is:

1. One which has had on board during the voyage a case or cases of any of the diseases mentioned in Art. 35.
2. One which is from an infected or suspected port.
3. One which is from a port where plague or yellow fever exists.
4. Any vessel on which there has been mortality among rats.
5. A vessel which has violated any of the provisions of this code.

Provided that the sanitary authorities should give due consideration in applying sanitary measures to a vessel that has not docked.

Art. 37. Any master or owner of any vessel, or any person violating any provisions of this Code or violating any rule or regulation made in accordance with this Code, relating to the inspection of vessels, the entry or departure from any quarantine station, grounds or anchorages, or trespass thereon, or to the prevention of the introduction of contagious or infectious disease into any of the signatory countries, or any master, owner, or agent of a vessel making a false statement relative to the sanitary condition of a vessel, or its contents, or as to the health of any passenger, or person thereon, or who interferes with a quarantine or health officer in the proper discharge of his duty, or fails or refuses to present bills of health, or other sanitary document, or pertinent information to a quarantine or health officer, shall be punished in accordance with the provisions of such laws, rules or regulations, as may be or may have been enacted, or promulgated, in accordance with the provisions of this Code, by the Government of the country within whose jurisdiction the offense is committed.

Chapter VI.—The Treatment of Vessels

Art. 38. Clean vessels will be granted pratique by the port health authority upon acceptable evidence that they properly fulfill the requirements of Art. 35.

Art. 39. Suspected vessels will be subjected to necessary sanitary measures to determine their actual condition.

Art. 40. Vessels infected with any of the diseases referred to in Art. 23 shall be subjected to such sanitary measures as will prevent the continuance thereon, and the spread therefrom, of any of said diseases to other vessels or ports. The disinfection of cargo, stores and personal effects shall be limited to the destruction of the vectors of disease which may be contained therein, provided that things which have been freshly soiled with human excretions capable of transmitting disease, shall always be disinfected. Vessels on which there is undue prevalence of rats, mosquitoes, lice, or any other potential vector of communicable disease, may be disinfected irrespective of the classification of the vessel.

ART. 41. Vessels infected with plague shall be subjected to the following treatment.

1. The vessel shall be held for observation and necessary treatment.

2. The sick, if any, shall be removed and placed under appropriate treatment in isolation.

3. The vessel shall be simultaneously fumigated throughout for the destruction of rats. In order to render fumigation more effective, cargo may be wholly or partially discharged prior to such fumigation, but care will be taken to discharge no cargo which might harbor rats,* except for fumigation.

4. All rats recovered after fumigation should be examined bacteriologically.

5. Healthy contacts, excepts [sic] those actually exposed to cases of pneumonic plague, will not be detained in quarantine.

6. The vessel will not be granted pratique until it is reasonably certain that it is free from rats and vermin.

ART. 42. Vessels infected with cholera shall be subjected to the following treatment.

1. The vessels shall be held for observation and necessary treatment.

2. The sick, if any, shall be removed and placed under appropriate treament [sic] in isolation.

3. All persons on board shall be subjected to bacteriological examination, and shall not be admitted to entry until demonstrated free from cholera vibrios.

4. Appropriate disinfection shall be performed.

ART. 43. Vessels infected with yellow fever shall be subjected to the following treatment.

1. The vessel shall be held for observation and necessary treatment.

2. The sick, if any, shall be removed and placed under appropriate treatment in isolation from *Aedes aegypti* mosquitoes.

3. All persons on board non immune to yellow fever shall be placed under observation to complete six days from the last possible exposure to *Aedes aegypti* mosquitoes.

---

*Explanatory Footnote:—The nature of the goods or merchandise likely to harbor rats (plague suspicious cargo), shall, for purpose of this section, be deemed to be the following, namely; rice or other grain (exclusive of flour); oilcake in sacks, beans in mats or sacks; goods packed in crates with straw or similar packing material; matting in bundles; dried vegetables in baskets or cases; dried and salted fish; peanuts in sacks; dry ginger; curios, etc., in fragile cases, copra, loose hemp in bundles; coiled rope in sacking kapok, maize in bags, sea grass in bales; tiles, large pipes and similar articles; and bamboo poles in bundles. [Footnote in the original.]

4. The vessel shall be freed from *Aedes aegypti* mosquitoes.

ART. 44. Vessels infected with small pox shall be subjected to the following treatment.

1. The vessels shall be held for observation and necessary treatment.

2. The sick, if any, shall be removed and placed under appropriate treatment in isolation.

3. All persons on board shall be vaccinated. As an option the passenger may elect to undergo isolaton [*sic*] to complete fourteen days from the last possible exposure to the disease.

4. All living quarters of the vessels shall be rendered mechanically clean, and used clothing and bedding of the patient desinfected [*sic*].

ART. 45. Vessels infected with typhus shall be subjected to the following treatment.

1. The vessel shall be held for observation and necessary treatment.

2. The sick, if any, shall be removed and placed under appropriate treatment in isolation from lice.

3. All persons on board and their personal effects shall be deloused.

4. All persons on board who have been exposed to the infection shall be placed under observation to complete twelve days from the last possible exposure to the infection.

5. The vessel shall be deloused.

ART. 46. The time of detention of vessels for inspection or treatment shall be the least consistent with public safety and scientific knowledge. It is the duty of port health officers to facilitate the speedy movement of vessels to the utmost compatible with the foregoing.

ART. 47. The power and authority of quarantine will not be utilized for financial gain, and no charges for quarantine services will exceed actual cost plus a reasonable surcharge for administrative expenses and fluctuations in the market prices of materials used.

CHAPTER VII.—FUMIGATION STANDARDS

ART. 48. Sulphur dioxide, hydrocyanic acid and cyanogen chloride gas mixture shall be considered as standard fumigants when used in accordance with the table set forth in the appendix, as regards hours of exposure and of quantities of fumigants per 1,000 cubic feet.

ART. 49. Fumigation of ships to be most effective should be performed periodically and preferable [*sic*] at six months intervals, and should include the entire vessel and its lifeboats. The vessels should be free of cargo.

Art. 50. Before the liberation of hydrogen cyanide or cyanogen chloride, all personnel of the vessel will be removed, and care will be observed that all compartments are rendered as nearly gas tight as possible.

Chapter VIII.—Medical Officers of Vessels

Art. 51. In order to better protect the health of travelers by sea, to aid in the prevention of the international spread of disease and to facilitate the movement of international commerce and communication, the signatory Governments are authorized in their discretion to license physicians employed on vessels.

Art. 52. It is recommended that license not issue unless the applicant therefor is a graduate in medicine from a duly chartered and recognized school of medicine, is the holder of an unrepealed license to practice medicine, and has successfully passed an examination as to his moral and mental fitness to be the surgeon or medical officer of a vessel. Said examination shall be set by the directing head of the national health service, and shall require of the applicant a competent knowledge of medicine and surgery. Said directing head of the national health service may issue a license to an applicant who successfully passes the examination, and may revoke said license upon conviction of malpractice, unprofessional conduct, offenses involving moral turpitude or infraction of any of the sanitary laws or regulations of any of the signatory Governments based upon the provisions of this code.

Art. 53. When duly licensed as aforesaid, said surgeons or medical officers of vessels may be utilized in aid of inspection as defined in this code.

Chapter IX.—The Pan American Sanitary Bureau

Functions and Duties

Art. 54. The organization, functions and duties of the Pan American Sanitary Bureau shall include those heretofore determined for the International Sanitary Bureau by the various International Sanitary and other Conferences of American Republics, and such additional administrative functions and duties as may be hereafter determined by Pan American Sanitary Conferences.

Art. 55. The Pan American Sanitary Bureau shall be the central coordinating sanitary agency of the various member Republics of the Pan American Union, and the general collection and distribution center of sanitary information to and from said Republic. For this purpose it shall, from time to time, designate representatives to visit and confer with the sanitary authorities of the various signatory Governments on public health matters, and such representatives shall be given all available sanitary information in the countries visited by them in the course of their official visits and conferences.

ART. 56. In addition, the Pan American Sanitary Bureau shall perform the following specific functions:

To supply to the sanitary authorities of the signatory Governments through its publications, or in other appropriate manner, all available information relative to the actual status of the communicable diseases of man, new invasions of such diseases, the sanitary measures undertaken, and the progress effected in the control or eradication of such diseases; new methods for combating disease; morbidity and mortality statistics; public health organization and administration; progress in any of the branches of preventive medicine, and other pertinent information relative to sanitation and public health in any of its phases, including a bibliography of books and periodicals on public hygiene.

In order to more efficiently discharge its functions, it may undertake cooperative epidemiological and other studies; may employ at headquarters and elsewhere, experts for this purpose; may stimulate and facilitate scientific researches and the practical application of the results therefrom; and may accept gifts, benefactions and bequest [sic], which shall be accounted for in the manner now provided for the maintenance funds of the Bureau.

ART. 57. The Pan American Sanitary Bureau shall advise and consult with the sanitary authorities of the various signatory Governments relative to public health problems, and the manner of interpreting and applying the provisions of this Code.

ART. 58. Officials of the National Health Services may be designated as representatives, ex-officio, of the Pan American Sanitary Bureau, in addition to their regular duties, and when so designated they may be empowered to acts [sic] as sanitary representatives of one or more of the signatory Governments when properly designated and accredited to so serve.

ART. 59. Upon request of the sanitary authorities of any of the signatory Governments, the Pan American Sanitary Bureau is authorized to take the necessary preparatory steps to bring about an exchange of professors, medical and health officers, experts or advisers in public health of any of the sanitary sciences, for the purpose of mutual aid and advancement in the protection of the public health of the signatory Governments.

ART. 60. For the purpose of discharging the functions and duties imposed upon the Pan American Sanitary Bureau, a fund of not less than $50,000 shall be collected by the Pan American Union, apportioned among the signatory Governments on the same basis as are the expenses of the Pan American Union.

Chapter X.—Aircraft

Art. 61. The provisons [*sic*] of this Convention shall apply to aircraft, and the signatory Governments agree to designate landing places for aircraft which shall have the same status as quarantine anchorages.

Chapter XI.—Sanitary Convention of Washington

Art. 62. The provisions of Articles 5, 6, 13, 14, 15, 16, 17, 18, 25, 30, 32, 33, 34, 37, 38, 39, 40, 41, 42, 43, 44, 45, 49, and 50, of the Pan American Sanitary Convention concluded in Washington on October 14, 1905,[55] are hereby continued in full force and effect, except in so far as they may be in conflict with the provisions of this Convention.

Chapter XII

Be is understood that this Code does not in any may [*sic*] abrogate or impair the validity or force of any existing treaty convention or agreement between any of the signatory governments and any other government.

Chapter XIII.—Transitory Disposition

Art. 63. The Governments which may not have signed the present Convention are to be admitted to adherence thereto upon demand, notice of this adherence to be given through diplomatic channels to the Government of the Republic of Cuba.

Made and signed in the city of Havana, on the fourteenth day of the month of November, 1924, in two copies, in English and Spanish, respectively, which shall be deposited with the Department of Foreign Relations of the Republic of Cuba, in order that certified copies thereof, in both English and Spanish, may be made for transmission through diplomatic channels to each of the signatory Governments.

By the Republic of Argentine:
Gregorio Araoz Alfaro
Joaquin Llambias

By the United States of Brazil:
Nascimento Gurgel
Raul Almeida Magalhaes

By the Republic of Chile:
Carlos Graf

---

[55] Malloy, *Treaties*, 1776–1909, vol. ii, p. 2144.

By the Republic of Colombia:
R. GUTIERREZ LEE

By the Republic of Costa Rica:
JOSE VARELA ZEQUEIRA

By the Republic of Cuba:
MARIO G. LEBREDO
JOSE A. LOPEZ DEL VALLE
HUGO ROBERTS
DIEGO TAMAYO
FRANCISCO M. FERNANDEZ
DOMINGO F. RAMOS

By the Republic of El Salvador:
LEOPOLDO PAZ

By the United States of America:
HUGH S. CUMMING
RICHARD CREEL
P. D. CRONIN

By the Republic of Guatemala:
JOSE DE CUBAS Y SERRATE

By the Republic of Haiti:
CHARLES MATHON

By the Republic of Honduras:
ARISTIDES AGRAMONTE

By the Republic of Mexico:
ALFONSO PRUNEDA

By the Republic of Panama:
JAIME DE LA GUARDIA

By the Republic of Paraguay:
ANDRES GUBETICH

By the Republic of Peru:
CARLOS E. PAZ SOLDAN

By the Dominican Republic:
R. PEREZ CABRAL

By the Republic of Uruguay:
JUSTO F. GONZALEZ

By the United States of Venezuela:
ENRIQUE TEJERA
ANTONIO SMITH

[An appendix to the convention, containing forms of certificates and other documents, and an annex are not printed here; but may be found in Treaty Series No. 714 published by the Department of State in 1925.]

BOUNDARY DISPUTES

Bolivia and Paraguay

724.3415/51

The Acting Secretary of State to the Chargé in Paraguay (Southworth)

No. 247   WASHINGTON, *July 25, 1924.*

SIR: The Department is in receipt of your confidential telegram No. 14, of June 12, 6 p. m., and your confidential despatch No. 1397, dated June 14,[56] with reference to the recrudescence of the boundary dispute between Paraguay and Bolivia concerning the sovereignty over a portion of the Chaco Boreal. You state that the Bolivian Government has protested to the Paraguayan Foreign Office against the grant reported to have been made by the Government of Paraguay to Canadian Mennonites of certain land in this territory, and you add that the Chargé d'Affaires of Bolivia at Asuncion has inquired whether you would not submit to him a memorandum containing suggestions in regard to a possible intervention of the United States in this problem, which he might transmit to his Government.

The Department desires to inform you in this connection that the Government of the United States would not be willing to intervene in this boundary dispute until it is requested to do so by both of the countries in question.

I am [etc.]   JOSEPH C. GREW

724.3415/59

The Ambassador in Argentina (Riddle)[57] to the Secretary of State

ASUNCIÓN, *August 20, 1924.*
[Received September 17.]

SIR: This afternoon the Minister for Foreign Affairs sent word he would like to call on me at 4.30 and on his arrival at that hour he handed me a short document in Spanish—a copy and translation of which are herewith enclosed. This memorandum constitutes a summing up of the communications exchanged between the governments

---

[56] Neither printed.
[57] Temporarily at Asunción.

of Bolivia and Paraguay relative to the disputed question of the limitation of their frontiers and indicates a disposition on the part of both governments to submit the question to the arbitration of the United States.

The Foreign Minister in handing me this paper said that the President of Paraguay requested me to forward it to my government at Washington.

I have [etc.]   J. W. RIDDLE

[Enclosure—Translation [58]]

Draft of an Agreement between Paraguay and Bolivia

ARTICLE 1. The Governments of Paraguay and Bolivia, not having been able to reach a direct agreement in former negotiations, agree to ask the Government of the United States of America to act as arbiter in the arbitration of right (*arbitraje de derecho*) to which they must submit their boundary dispute according to the protocol of April 5, 1913,[59] still in force.

ARTICLE 2. If before the arbitration is commenced any intervening circumstance should permit a new direct negotiation between the parties, they may request the mediation of the designated arbiter in the negotiations which would be initiated in Washington by the respective representatives duly empowered for this purpose.

ARTICLE 3. The present agreement confirms the abrogation of all boundary treaties formerly concluded. Until the arbitral award is made the *status quo* of the Agreement of January 12, 1907 [60] now in force by virtue of the extensions stipulated in the later protocols, shall alone continue in force.

ARTICLE 4. A special protocol will establish the remaining conditions and formalities tending to facilitate the early and effective execution of the arbitration agreement.

ASUNCIÓN, *August 20, 1924.*

724.3415/60

The Chargé in Paraguay (Southworth) to the Secretary of State

No. 1422   ASUNCIÓN, *September 4, 1924.*
                                          [Received October 1.]

SIR: I have the honor to acknowledge the Department's instruction No. 247 of July 25, 1924 concerning the Paraguay-Bolivia bound-

[58] File translation revised.
[59] *Foreign Relations*, 1915, p. 33.
[60] *Ibid.*, 1907, vol. I, p. 87.

ary dispute; in which I am informed that the government of the United States would not be willing to intervene in this dispute until it is requested to do so by both of the countries in question.

Referring also to Ambassador Riddle's despatch in this regard from Asuncion, of August 20, 1924, enclosing a draft of an agreement between Paraguay and Bolivia requesting the acceptance by the United States of the rôle of judge, I would now inform the Department that it seems the above draft is a copy of a counter-proposal made to Bolivia by President Ayala in answer to one essentially similar, submitted just after the inauguration by the Bolivian Special Ambassador, Señor Diez de Medina, who has since returned to his regular post at Buenos Aires.

This information was offered me today by the new Minister of Foreign Affairs, Dr. Manuel Peña; he continued by relating frankly the present status of negotiations with Bolivia in the boundary dispute.

The protest recently made by the Bolivian Chargé against the grants of land in the Chaco to Canadian Mennonites, and referred to in my telegram No. 14 of June 12th, 5 P.M. [*6 p.m.*],[61] has now been fully answered, I was informed, by the observation that the Paraguayan government had no part in the concession to the Mennonites beyond passing a law requested by them exempting them from compulsory military service and granting other similar favors; and moreover that Señor Casado, of the Company which sold them their lands, had personally demonstrated on the map that these lands were not only not in Bolivian territory, but were between Parallels 59 and 60 of West Longitude.

Dr. Peña touched on historical aspects of this case, declaring— as Dr. Manuel Gondra, ex-President and Foreign Minister has also recently assured me—that since about 1911 it has been the Paraguayan desire to have this question arbitrated by the United States. The language of the Ayala-Mujía protocol of April 5, 1913, providing for the present *status-quo*, bears this out to some extent in its use of precisely the same verbiage, "arbitraje de derecho", employed in the present draft agreement. The President of Argentina had at that time declined to serve as arbiter.

Dr. Peña then referred to the representations telegraphed by the Department in December, 1914 [62] at the time that a Paraguayan military incursion into the Chaco was reported; and stated that proofs of its non-existence were immediately furnished to President Wilson. Paraguay could not but desire American intervention in this problem, he continued, in view of the happy settlement by

---

[61] Not printed.
[62] See note of Nov. 30, 1914, to the Bolivian Minister, *Foreign Relations, 1914.* p. 29.

President Hayes of the territorial dispute with Argentina also involving a portion of the Chaco.[63]

Negotiations with Bolivia will continue for the present in La Paz the Minister stated; adding that what his government contemplates after signing such an agreement as that drafted, is, first, direct conversations between representatives of Bolivia and Paraguay in Washington, "with the friendly aid of President Coolidge"; and later, in case no decision is reached in this way, the consummation of the proposed "arbitration of right", with the President as umpire. I am informed that since Manuel Gondra has declined the appointment as Minister to the United States on account of his health, this will probably go to ex-President Eusebio Ayala; who will accordingly be the Paraguayan negotiator if the proposed agreement with Bolivia is reached.

In this regard I note from the President of Bolivia's reply to Minister Guggiari's recent speech on presenting his credentials, furnished me by Minister Cottrell, that Señor Saavedra declared his government was "disposed to open immediate negotiations" on the boundary question; and referred also to the possibility of arbitration.

Public interest in Paraguay in this question has steadily grown, especially since it has become known that the United States may be asked to arbitrate. The Colorado (opposition) party has attempted to capitalize the situation by some extravagant nationalistic propaganda; a sample of which is transmitted herewith in the form of a handbill[64] urging attendance at a demonstration of "Colorado Youth" in favor of radical action against Bolivia, held in a public square of this city on August 24th. This demonstration, however, passed off without disorder; and President Ayala considered it politic to appear on a balcony of the Palace on the approach of the demonstrants, and address them with the assurance that measures would be taken to preserve the Fatherland intact. On the whole the calm and considered attitude that the government has taken in this regard toward the rabid element has been admirable.

I have [etc.]   WILLIAM B. SOUTHWORTH

724.3415/59

The Secretary of State to the Chargé in Paraguay (Southworth)

No. 258   WASHINGTON, *October 13, 1924.*

SIR: The Department is in receipt of the despatch dated Asunción, Paraguay, August 20, 1924, from the American Ambassador to the

---

[63] *Ibid.*, 1878, p. 711.
[64] Not printed.

Argentine Republic referred to in your despatch No. 1422, dated September 4, the receipt of which is hereby acknowledged, stating that the Minister for Foreign Affairs of Paraguay had handed him a memorandum in relation to the Paraguayan-Bolivian boundary dispute and had added that the President of Paraguay requested the Ambassador to forward it to Washington. Mr. Riddle encloses a copy and translation of this document, copies of which are transmitted herewith for your information.[65]

You are instructed to inform the Minister for Foreign Affairs, orally and informally, that the Department has received from Mr. Riddle a copy of the memorandum in question. You should indicate to him, however, in the same informal manner, the position of the Government of the United States in regard to this boundary question, as described in the Department's instruction No. 247 of July 25, 1924.

I am [etc.]

For the Secretary of State:
JOSEPH C. GREW

724.3415/68

The Chargé in Bolivia (Barker) to the Secretary of State

No. 596   LA PAZ, *November 26, 1924.*
                                      [Received December 18.]

SIR: I have the honor to refer to the Department's instruction No. 136, dated October 13, 1924,[66] with regard to the possibility of American arbitration of the Bolivian-Paraguayan boundary dispute. I am informed by Dr. Germán Costas R., Acting Under-Secretary for Foreign Affairs, that since the departure last September of Doctor Guggiari, former Paraguayan Minister to Bolivia, there have been no further negotiations of any importance in connection with the boundary dispute between Bolivia and Paraguay. It is expected, however, that with the arrival of Señor Deconel, the newly appointed Paraguayan Minister to Bolivia, Chile and Peru, negotiations will again enter upon an active phase.

Doctor Costas today repeated to me his previous statement, reported in the Legation's Report No. 30, dated August 19, 1924,[67] that Bolivia is desirous of having the United States chosen as arbitrator of the boundary dispute and that his Government has approached the Paraguayan Government in this sense. The Government of Paraguay has intimated to the Bolivian Government that

---

[65] See draft agreement, *ante,* p. 283.
[66] Not printed; see instruction no. 258, Oct. 13, to the Chargé in Paraguay, *supra.*
[67] Not printed.

it also desires the selection of the United States as arbitrator. The divergence in the views of the two Governments on this boundary question which still exists has no connection with the choice of the arbitrator, Doctor Costas states, but is a question of what matters the arbitrator shall be called upon to decide and the form in which the protocol of arbitration is to be drawn up.

I may add that there is at present no evidence of any intention on the part of the Foreign Office here to recede from its previous uncompromising position, which would reduce Paraguayan claims to be arbitrated to territory which has long been in the full military and economic control of the latter.

I have [etc.] W. Roswell Barker

Colombia and Panama [68]

719.2115/23½

Memorandum by the Secretary of State of a Conversation with the Colombian Minister (Olaya), March 13, 1924

[Extract]

The Minister then referred to relations with Panama as his Government was most anxious to have an adjustment. He hoped the Secretary would examine into the situation to see if something could not be done along the lines that had been suggested before for the purpose of securing a resumption of relations between Panama and Colombia. The Minister said that from what he had heard he believed Panama would at this time be very much disposed to listen to any suggestions the Secretary would make. The Secretary referred to what had already been done and to the protocol that had been arranged and to the difficulty that had arisen with respect to the boundary question. The Secretary said he would look into the matter to see if there would be any prospect of success if the matter were taken up again.

719.21/52

Procès-Verbal of a Meeting between the Secretary of State, the Colombian Minister (Olaya), and the Panaman Minister (Alfaro), May 8, 1924

Doctor Enrique Olaya and Doctor Ricardo J. Alfaro, Envoys Extraordinary and Ministers Plenipotentiary of the Republics of Colombia and Panama, respectively, having on the invitation of the

---

[68] Continued from *Foreign Relations*, 1923, vol. I, pp. 328–351.

Secretary of State of the United States, met with him in his office at the Department of State, Washington, at 2:30 o'clock on May 8, 1924:

Mr. Hughes stated that he had invited Messrs. Olaya and Alfaro to his office to confer with them regarding the institution of diplomatic relations between the two Republics which is so cordially desired by the Government of the United States.

The Secretary of State added that it would be most gratifying indeed for the two neighboring Republics of Colombia and Panama to enter into regular diplomatic relations, and he, therefore, asked the Minister of Colombia whether, by reason of the recognition of Panama by Colombia as an independent nation, he did not think the moment opportune for establishing such relations and inquired whether it would please the Government of Colombia to receive the representative that the Government of Panama would accredit for that purpose to negotiate and conclude with the Government of Colombia a boundary convention and a treaty of peace and friendship and to adjust all questions of pecuniary liability as between the two countries, in accordance with recognized principles of law and precedents. He further inquired whether Colombia would also be prepared to accredit a Minister to Panama.

Doctor Olaya replied that he was authorized by his Government to state officially to the Panaman Minister that the Republic of Colombia recognizes Panama as an independent nation and that his Government would be pleased to receive the duly accredited agent whom the Republic of Panama would despatch to negotiate and conclude with the Government of Colombia a boundary convention and a treaty of peace and friendship and to adjust all questions of pecuniary liability as between the two countries, in accordance with recognized principles of law and precedents. He added that the Government of Colombia would also be pleased to accredit a Minister to the Republic of Panama.

Thereupon, the Secretary of State, addressing the Panaman Minister, expressed the hope that the Panaman Government was ready to enter into diplomatic relations with the Government of Colombia and inquired whether his Government would be inclined, with a view to instituting official relations between the two Republics, to accredit a diplomatic agent to the Republic of Colombia, for the purposes mentioned, and to receive the Minister whom the Republic of Colombia might accredit.

Doctor Alfaro replied that he was authorized by his Government to express its gratification at the recognition of Panama by Colombia as an independent nation and added that his Government would despatch a duly accredited agent to negotiate and conclude with the Government of Colombia a boundary convention and a treaty of peace and friendship and to adjust all questions of pecuniary liability as between the two countries, in accordance with recognized principles of law and precedents. He added that his Government would be pleased to receive the Minister accredited by the Government of Colombia.

The Secretary of State then stated that he desired to avail himself of that opportunity to offer to serve as a medium for the request of the *agrément* of the Ministers who should be accredited by the Republics of Colombia and Panama, respectively, if Messrs. Olaya and Alfaro had instructions on the subject.

The Panaman Minister stated that he was authorized by his Government to inquire, in case the Minister of Colombia should have been instructed to answer, whether Mr. Nicolas Victoria J. would be *persona grata* to the Colombian Government.

The Colombian Minister replied that he was authorized by his Government to accept as *persona grata* anyone whose name should have been suggested by the Government of Panama, and he added that he was authorized by his Government, in reciprocation, to inquire whether Doctor José Maria González Valencia would be *persona grata* to the Government of Panama.

The Panaman Minister replied that he was authorized by his Government to accept as *persona grata* anyone whose name should have been suggested by the Government of Colombia.

The Secretary of State then expressed his appreciation of the good-will and friendly attitude thus shown by the Governments of Colombia and Panama towards each other, and his gratification that the sister Republics were to establish regular diplomatic relations and undertake formally to adjust their relations in accordance with recognized principles of law and precedents. It was, he said, his understanding that both Governments earnestly desired the establishment of regular diplomatic relations as soon as possible and to that end it might be agreeable to both Governments to set a date for the appointment of Mr. Victoria J. as Panaman Minister to Colombia and Doctor González Valencia as Colombian Minister to Panama. If so, he would suggest May 15, 1924, as a suitable date, it being mutually agreed that both representatives shall thereupon proceed forthwith to their respective posts.

The Panaman and Colombian Ministers both replied that they were authorized by their respective Governments to state that Messrs. Victoria J. and González Valencia would be appointed respectively as Panaman Minister to Colombia and Colombian Minister to Panama on May 15, 1924, and that they would thereupon proceed forthwith to their posts.

This procès verbal of the meeting, drawn up in triplicate in English and Spanish, was signed by the Secretary of State and the Ministers of Colombia and Panama. One copy will be retained by the Secretary of State, who will send of the remaining two copies, one each to the Ministers of Colombia and Panama respectively.

CHARLES E. HUGHES

R. J. ALFARO   ENRIQUE OLAYA

719.2115A/110

The Panaman Minister (Alfaro) to the Secretary of State

[Translation]

No. 253   WASHINGTON, *May 8, 1924.*

MR. SECRETARY: Referring to the conversations that have been held between this Legation and the Department of State with regard to establishing diplomatic relations between the Republic of Panama and the Republic of Colombia, it affords me pleasure to inform Your Excellency that my Government, after giving due consideration to a study of the different phases of the subject, has reached the conclusion that the question of limits between the two countries must be settled by establishing in a final manner the boundary line existing now *de facto* and described as follows:

"From Cape Tiburón to the headwaters of the Rio de la Miel and following the mountain chain by the ridge of Gandi to the Sierra de Chugargun and that of Mali going down by the ridges of Nigue to the heights of Aspave and from thence to a point on the Pacific half way between Cocalito and La Ardita."

Although the Government of Panama in the negotiations set on foot through the powerful mediation of the Department of State had made a proposition which implied the acceptance of the frontier above described as far as the heights of Aspave, leaving open for future negotiation the small part of the line lying between that point and the Pacific Ocean, it believes that there are considerations of the highest order which make for a final immediate agreement on the boundary question. I therefore have the honor to express to Your Excellency in communicating to you the wish of Panama to agree on the border line above described that the Minister Plenipotentiary that my Government may accredit to the Government of Colombia under the terms signed this day will carry instructions to sign as soon as it may be agreeable to the Government of Colombia a special boundary convention establishing the boundary as expressed in this note.

I avail myself [etc.]   R. J. ALFARO

719.21/52

The Secretary of State to the Panaman Minister (Alfaro)

WASHINGTON, *May 8, 1924.*

SIR: I have the honor to acknowledge the receipt of your note of today by which you were so good as to inform me that your Government having studied the question of establishing regular diplomatic relations between Panama and Colombia has decided that the boundary question between Panama and Colombia should be settled by establishing definitively the frontier line existing in fact today and which is described as follows:

"From Cape Tiburón to the headwaters of the Rio de la Miel and following the mountain chain by the ridge of Gandi to the Sierra de Chugargun and that of Mali going down by the ridges of Nigue to the heights of Aspave and from thence to a point on the Pacific half way between Cocalito and La Ardita".

You add that in order to bring this about the Minister Plenipotentiary who[m] your Government is accrediting near the Government of Colombia by virtue of the Procès Verbal signed today will bear instructions to sign as soon as may be agreeable to the Government of Colombia a special boundary convention which will fix the boundary as defined in your note quoted above.

In expressing to you the satisfaction which it has afforded this Government to learn that your Government has decided to settle this matter in the manner stated I take this opportunity to inform you that a copy of your note under acknowledgment is being transmitted by me today to the Colombian Minister.

Accept [etc.]   CHARLES E. HUGHES

719.21/52

The Secretary of State to the Colombian Minister (Olaya)

WASHINGTON, *May 8, 1924.*

SIR: I have the honor to send you herewith English and Spanish original copies of the Proces Verbal of the meeting between you and the Panaman Minister held in my office today.[69] I likewise take pleasure in enclosing herewith a certified copy of a note dated May 8, 1924, from the Panaman Minister [70] in which he informs me that the Government of Panama accepts as the boundary between Colombia and Panama the following, which you will note is the

---

[69] *Ante,* p. 287.
[70] *Ante,* p. 290.

boundary provided in Article III of the Treaty between the United States and Colombia signed April 6, 1914:

"From Cape Tiburón to the headwaters of the Rio de la Miel and following the mountain chain by the ridge of Gandi to the Sierra de Chugargún and that of Mali going down by the ridges of Nigue to the heights of Aspave and from thence to a point on the Pacific half way between Cocalito and La Ardita."

The note from the Panaman Minister adds that in consequence of the acceptance of this boundary Señor Nicolas Victoria J. who will be appointed Panaman Minister to Colombia will have specific instructions to conclude as soon as may be agreeable to the Government of Colombia a special boundary convention fixing the boundary as above provided.

This Government is not only mindful of its engagement under Article III of the Treaty between the United States and Colombia signed at Bogotá April 6, 1914, but will also be prepared to contribute to the final solution of the boundary question through the ratification by the Congress of Panama of the boundary convention provided for in the note from the Panaman Minister enclosed herewith.

It affords me great pleasure to transmit to you the two documents above mentioned embodying the agreement of the Government of Panama on the boundary between the Republics of Colombia and Panama as well as the latter Government's engagement to despatch a duly accredited agent to negotiate and conclude with the Government of Colombia a treaty of peace and friendship with a view to bring about the establishment of regular diplomatic relations between the two countries and the adjustment of all questions of pecuniary liability.

Accept [etc.]   CHARLES E. HUGHES

719.2115/27½

Memorandum by the Secretary of State of a Conversation with the Colombian Minister (Olaya), September 18, 1924

The Minister said that a treaty had been concluded with Panama in accordance with the arrangement that had been stated in the procès verbal which had been signed through the Secretary's mediation. The Minister left a copy of the treaty. The Minister said that this was to be submitted at once to the Colombian Congress and that he understood the Congress of Panama was now in session and he hoped that it would be submitted there promptly as he understood that they would not have another session for two years. He hoped the Secretary would use his friendly offices to have the treaty considered at an early date by the Panaman Congress. The Secretary said that we were gratified at the conclusion of the treaty and that it was hoped that it would be ratified at an early date. The Secretary said that he would inquire with respect to the situation in Panama.

The Minister spoke of the American Economic Mission to Colombia [71] and of its success. His Government was very much pleased and important measures had resulted.

Colombia and Peru [72]

721.2315/121

The Ambassador in Peru (Poindexter) to the Secretary of State

No. 107 LIMA, *January 15, 1924.*
[Received January 30.]

SIR: Reference is made to my despatch No. 88 of December 1, 1923.[73]

I have the honor to report that Congress adjourned the 11th instant.

The signed treaty of March 24, 1922,[73a] fixing the Colombian-Peruvian frontier, was not submitted to Congress for ratification. This long-standing controversy thus has no prospect of settlement for the present; probably not before 1925. The new Congress, I understand, is not to convene until October next, the time fixed for the celebration of the Ayacucho Centenary.

Since last reporting to the Department regarding the status of this treaty, I had occasion again to see the President and, in the spirit of the Department's instructions on the subject, I once more raised the subject of ratification—deeming this opportune in view of the Colombian Minister's categoric denial and representations to the Peruvian Government following President Leguía's statement that Mr. Lozano [74] had acquiesced in postponing ratification until the convening of the next Congress.

President Leguía again spoke of Brazilian opposition but volunteered the information—in the form of a definite assurance—that he would submit the treaty to Congress during the session which has just ended. The President has not as yet offered me any explanation for not having carried out his announced intention.

---

[71] Kemmerer Financial Mission; see *Foreign Relations*, 1923, vol. I, p. 831.
[72] Continued from *Foreign Relations*, 1923, vol. I, pp. 351–353.
[73] Not printed; see telegram no. 46, Nov. 16, from the Ambassador in Peru, *Foreign Relations*, 1923, vol. I, p. 353.
[73a] League of Nations Treaty Series, vol. LXXIV, p. 9.
[74] Colombian Minister to Peru.

It may be opportune to add that though I have had several conversations with the Colombian Minister, I have taken pains to avoid giving the Peruvian Government any impression that there has been cooperation between us. I limited my actions to that inspired by the disinterested friendship of my Government for both countries and its desire to see the adjudication of this Continent's long-standing controversies.

.   .   .   .

I have [etc.]   MILES POINDEXTER

721.2315/122

The Minister in Colombia (Piles) to the Secretary of State

No. 355   BOGOTÁ, *February 1, 1924.*
                                           [Received March 8.]

SIR: I have the honor to acknowledge copy of despatch No. 88 of December 1, 1923 of the American Ambassador at Lima [75] reviewing the efforts the Ambassador has made to bring about an early ratification of the boundary treaty between Colombia and Peru. Feeling that the knowledge of this interest in Colombia's welfare as well as the salient facts contained in the despatch would be most welcome news to President Ospina, I called at the Palace and informed the President as far as discretion would permit, of course omitting all reference to the attitude of Brazil, relative to the extent of the informal good offices of the United States in the matter.

The President appeared worried relative to the fate of the treaty and stated how much the negotiations mean to his administration. He was particularly concerned over the obligatory absence from Lima at this juncture for motives of health of the Colombian Minister and the necessity of leaving representations in the hands of a young and relatively inexperienced Chargé d'Affaires ad interim. I therefore ventured to suggest that the Chargé d'Affaires, when he felt in need, have recourse to the advice of the American Ambassador who is thoroughly conversant with all the angles of the situation. President Ospina ended by expressing his profound gratification for the sincere interest my Government is taking in the settlement of this long standing frontier dispute and stated that it constitutes one of the most friendly acts of one Government towards another that has come within his experience.

I have [etc.]   SAMUEL H. PILES

---

[75] Not printed.

721.2315/122

The Secretary of State to the Minister in Colombia (Piles)

No. 657   WASHINGTON, *March 28, 1924.*

SIR: The receipt is acknowledged of your despatch No. 355, dated February 1, 1924, in which you state that you had informed President Ospina as far as discretion would permit of the substance of certain parts of despatch No. 88, dated December 1, 1923, from the American Ambassador at Lima regarding the boundary dispute and Treaty of 1922 between Colombia and Peru.

As you are aware, the good offices of this Government are frequently extended to assist in bringing about a settlement of a controversy between two parties when both sides so request. In the case of the boundary dispute between Colombia and Peru its friendly offices were extended at the request of one of the parties after some assurance was had that such action would not be unfavorably received by the other.

The Department has noted your statement that in the conversation with President Ospina on this subject you suggested that the Colombian Chargé d'Affaires at Lima, when he felt in need, have recourse to the advice of the American Ambassador who is thoroughly conversant with all angles of the situation. While the Department is gratified to learn of the President's appreciation as expressed to you, it trusts that the Colombian Government fully realizes that this Government's attitude in the matter is one of the strictest impartiality, and that President Ospina has not been led by your suggestion to believe that the efforts of this Government to be of assistance to the Colombian and Peruvian Governments in this question might extend beyond the informal and friendly acts already performed. The Department does not desire to appear as the agency suggesting or initiating measures which, if brought to the attention of the other party, might incline it to view further informal action with disfavor. For that reason, the Department considers that suggestions such as that made by you to the President of Colombia should in the future be avoided.

I am [etc.]   CHARLES E. HUGHES

721.2315/121

The Secretary of State to the Ambassador in Peru (Poindexter)

No. 127   WASHINGTON, *October 7, 1924.*

SIR: Reference is made to your confidential despatch No. 107 of January 15, 1924, regarding the boundary treaty of March 24, 1922, between Peru and Colombia, and to report No. 16 dated July

24, 1924, from the American Minister at Bogotá,[76] a copy of which was sent you on September 2, 1924, giving translations of telegrams exchanged between President Leguía and President Ospina, of Colombia, on the occasion of the Colombian national holiday. In view of the statement of President Leguía in the above mentioned telegram that the approval of the Peruvian–Colombian boundary treaty will be requested of the Peruvian Congress during the forthcoming session, the Department suggests that you may be able to express again to the President and to the Minister for Foreign Affairs, orally and informally, the friendly interest and hope of this Government that action may be taken to bring this long-standing boundary dispute to a successful termination.

I am [etc.]

For the Secretary of State:
JOSEPH C. GREW

721.2315/139

The Ambassador in Peru (Poindexter) to the Secretary of State

No. 312   LIMA, *November 17, 1924.*
[Received December 3.]

SIR: Referring to the Department's confidential instruction No. 127 of October 7, 1924, I beg to say, confirming my cablegram No. 61 of this date,[76] that from a conversation which I have had today with Doctor Salomón, Peruvian Minister of Foreign Relations, I have formed the conclusion that it is not likely that the Peruvian Congress will ratify the treaty which has been formulated and signed by the executive representatives of Colombia and Perú, fixing the boundary line between the two countries.

Doctor Salomón showed me a copy of a formal memorandum which had been submitted by the Minister of Foreign Affairs of Brazil to the Peruvian Minister at Rio de Janeiro, supplementing a conversation which the Brazilian Minister had with the Peruvian representative. This memorandum raised two points of objection by Brazil to the ratification of the treaty:

First. It pointed out that in the agreement which Brazil had made with Perú,—fixing a line running due south from the Caquetá River to the Amazon River, as the boundary line, in that section, between Brazil and Perú,—Brazil did not contemplate that an area of land contiguous to this boundary line, and which, by the said agreement, came under the sovereignty of Perú, would be transferred voluntarily or at all by the latter country to an entirely new and different sov-

---

[76] Not printed.

ereignty. The memorandum also stated that in agreeing to the provision of the treaty between Brazil and Perú, that in case Colombia should be the winner in the controversy existing between that country and Perú in regard to the identical territory lying west of and contiguous to the said boundary line, then Brazil would negotiate with Colombia in regard to the respective rights of the two countries thereto,—it did not contemplate the cession of this territory by Perú to Colombia, by treaty stipulation, but did suppose that the controversy would be submitted to an arbitral or juridical decision by some impartial tribunal. In support of this last statement, the memorandum called attention to the fact that in the agreement between Perú and Brazil, in regard to this point, the language used was "ganar la causa", which, the Brazilian Minister of Foreign Affairs argues, necessarily implied a cause to be tried before an arbitral or juridical tribunal. The Brazilian Minister further stated, in the memorandum, that Brazil was induced to make this agreement because of the implicit confidence which it had that any impartial arbitral or juridical tribunal to which the case might be submitted would necessarily decide in favor of Perú, because of the incontrovertible merits and justice of the latter's claim to the territory in question;—the memorandum proceeding to state that it was never conceived by Brazil that Perú would voluntarily cede its jurisdiction over territory which was occupied by Peruvian citizens, and over which its actual jurisdiction was daily enforced without interruption or interference.

The memorandum then calls attention to the substantial interest which Brazil has in the question as to whether Perú or Colombia shall exercise sovereign jurisdiction over this strip of territory lying contiguous to her boundary line, and that while Brazil is entirely willing, and has agreed, that Peru should exercise sovereign jurisdiction over this territory, Brazil would be compelled to protest against the transfer of it to Colombia.

Second. The memorandum of the Brazilian Minister pointed out that the treaty between Colombia and Perú, which has just been submitted to the Peruvian Congress for ratification, would, by its distribution of territory, give Colombia access to the main, navigable stream of the Amazon River; and proceeds to state that this is a vital point with Brazil,—and that Brazil would strenuously oppose the acquisition by a third sovereignty of territory bordering upon this great river, whose banks were now controlled exclusively by Brazil and Perú. The memorandum expressed surprise that the treaty had been submitted to the Peruvian Congress for ratification.

Doctor Salomón stated to me that, aside from the memorandum, the Peruvian Minister in Rio had been informed by the Brazilian Minister for Foreign Relations that the Government of the latter country had learned through its secret service that, if the pending treaty should be ratified before the approaching Centenary of the Battle of Ayacucho, Colombia would send a distinguished Mission to the Centenary; but that, on the contrary, if the treaty should not be ratified, Colombia would send no Mission. *Vis-à-vis* to this, the Brazilian Minister stated that, while Brazil expected to send a Mission to do honor to Peru in the Centenary of the Battle of Ayacucho; that in case the treaty referred to above, which concerns its interests so vitally, should be ratified by the Peruvian Congress, Brazil would be compelled to refrain from sending such a Mission. I judged from the tone and manner of Dr. Salomón in stating this latter circumstance that he regarded it as of the utmost importance and concern. The Peruvian Foreign Minister stated to me, in quite a lengthy conversation on the subject, that he himself had never approved of the terms of the treaty aforesaid, although he had signed it. Upon my questioning he stated that he had signed it because of its approval by President Leguía. He stated that Perú, by the unfortunate circumstances in which it had been involved, in order to bring an end to controversies with its neighbors and restore harmonious relations with them, had been compelled to cede to Bolivia and Brazil large areas of land to which it had a clear right; that it had agreed to an arbitration with Ecuador of the dispute involving great areas of territory to which the Minister believed the title of Perú was indisputable; and that, for the same reason, Perú had formulated, signed, and submitted for ratification, to the Peruvian Congress, the pending treaty with Colombia. He stated, however, that if the ratification of this treaty, which had for its object the gaining of the friendship of Colombia, and the establishment of harmonious relations with that country, should have the result of alienating Brazil and "making an enemy while gaining a friend", it would be of no profit to Perú. Throughout the conversation of the Foreign Minister I gained the impression that the protest of Brazil had been so pointed, and that either the hope of gaining favor with Brazil by refraining from the ratification of the treaty in question, or the fear of creating the enmity of that country by its ratification, had made such a lively impression upon the Peruvian Government that the latter would bring no pressure to bear upon Congress to secure favorable action. Doctor Salomon stated to me that he showed me the memorandum and gave me the information which I have related above under the direction of President Leguía, which I am apprehensive tends to indicate that the latter also regards both the circumstance and manner of the opposition and protest of Brazil as an insuperable obstacle to the ratification of the treaty. In forming this impression I have in mind also the significant intimations and inquiries of President Leguía on the subject of the opposition of Brazil to the ratification of the treaty,

which I took occasion to report to the Department in Despatch No.
62 of August 25, 1923,[78] Cablegram No. 46, Nov. 16, 12 m.,[79] Despatch
No. 88, December 1, 1923.[78]

In addition to the foregoing, Doctor Salomón informed me that
the Administration was compelled to respect the independence, and
jealousy of its rights, of the Peruvian Congress in the consideration
of a treaty, and that the Congress, in his opinion, would vigorously
oppose the cession to Colombia of land bordering upon the Amazon
River. Dr. Salomón stated specifically that he, himself, was also
opposed to this, and that it was upon this point that he had disagreed
with President Leguía, and had disapproved of the treaty, although
signing it.

He stated, nevertheless, that the treaty had been submitted to
Congress with a recommendation for its ratification, and that, notwithstanding his personal objections to some of the terms of the
treaty, he would be entirely content should Congress see fit to ratify
it; but that, as Minister of Foreign Relations, he would be compelled
to submit to Congress full information as to the protest of the Brazilian Government, and the grounds upon which it is based. . . .

.   .   .   .

I expressed to Minister Salomón, as I have heretofore done to
President Leguía, the lively interest of the United States as a friendly
sister American nation, in the ratification of the treaty, and the
profound regret which I knew would be felt by the Government and
people of the United States, if this settlement of a long-standing
controversy between two neighboring South American countries,
which had come so near to a peaceable solution, should fail. I ventured to call the Minister's attention to the fact that the entire trend
of modern international policy was towards the opening of great
navigable rivers to international navigation, and that a sound economic and international policy should promote the accessibility of the
interior, for the purpose of its development and communication, to
such a continental stream as the Amazon.

I suggested to the Minister that Perú had profited a great deal
in prestige, as well as in economic stability, by the concessions which
it had made in the settlement of its boundary disputes with Bolivia
and Brazil, and in the prospective adjustment by arbitration, if necessary, of a similar dispute with Ecuador; and the immense benefit
that would accrue to the country by the settlement of its dispute with
Colombia,—a dispute which would undoubtedly be reopened in an
intensified form if the treaty should be rejected.

From all I can learn, especially through conversations with the
Minister of Colombia in Perú, the rejection of the treaty by the Peru-

---

[78] Not printed.
[79] *Foreign Relations,* 1923, vol. I, p. 353.

vian Congress, or the failure of that body to ratify it, would cause very intense, hostile feeling in the former country.

I have [etc.]   MILES POINDEXTER

721.2315/139½

Memorandum by the Secretary of State of a Conversation with the Colombian Minister (Olaya), November 26, 1924

The Minister left a confidential memorandum dated November twenty-sixth [81] with respect to the Boundary Treaty signed in March, 1922, between Colombia and Peru and the action which had been taken by Brazil in relation thereto. The Minister explained the memorandum by saying that if the Government of Brazil would withdraw its memorandum in opposition to the ratification of the Treaty between Colombia and Peru he was authorized to say that the Colombian Government would be glad to take up the questions that might exist with Brazil in order to find an immediate solution.

The Secretary said that he was already conversant to some extent with the matter but that he would like to study the memorandum left with him by the Minister of Colombia and such data as he had at hand and he would then have an interview in two or three days with the Minister and would see whether some method of solution could be suggested. The Secretary said that while this Government did not wish to intrude into controversies to which it was not a party it was always glad, at the request of the parties concerned, to use its friendly offices to promote an amicable settlement.

721.2315/198

The Colombian Legation to the Department of State

Supplementing the confidential memorandum of November 26, 1924,[81] the Minister of Colombia permits himself to emphasize the importance of the friendly solution reached by the Governments of Colombia and Peru with the signing of the Treaty of March, 1922.

The boundary question has been the cause of bitter disputes between the two Republics for nearly a century, occasioning sharp diplomatic correspondence and creating constantly a dangerous situation which in 1829 turned into war. Subsequently, this dispute has kept the two countries in a state of prolonged anxiety. In 1907 and 1908 certain conflicts between Colombian and Peruvian officials

---

[81] Not printed.

caused armed encounters. In 1911 this state of things was repeated, armed forces of both governments compromising themselves in the Caquetá region in a struggle of such an alarming character that the diplomatic representatives of Brazil and Venezuela in Colombia found it opportune, with the previous authorization of their Governments, to offer their good offices. The continuous clashes between Colombian and Peruvian colonists have been a cause of unrest and anxiety on the part of the two Governments. In later years the negotiations which culminated in the Boundary Treaty produced a favorable and well marked change in the situation, but if the Treaty fails, that situation will again assume its former deplorable character.

The said prolonged state of dispute created—as it could not fail to do—a state of insecurity in that territory, particularly for the indian tribes, which in consequence have been reduced to a state of actual slavery due to the fact that the protection of the two governments does not fully reach them, in zones of disputed sovereignty, thus making it easy for those guilty of such slavery to elude and evade the action of justice. These are facts known by the name of Atrocities and Crimes of the Putumayo, which have attracted the attention of the world and concerning which there exists an extensive correspondence from United States Consular officials to the Department of State, published in *Foreign Relations* for 1913.

Aside from the international and humanitarian aspects involved, there are also considerations of an economical character. Any foreign capital destined to the exploitation of the Caquetá and Putumayo regions naturally meets with protests from Peru, if the concession is granted by Colombia, and from the latter if the concession is granted by Peru. Foreign capital already invested, or that is about to be invested, in the exploitation of that territory can only find safe and stable conditions through a Treaty exactly fixing the boundary limit of each country and recognizing the properties there established, or to be established, in good faith. This is provided by the Treaty of Colombia and Peru in Article IX which reads as follows:

"Artículo 9°—Las Altas Partes Contratantes se obligan a mantener y respetar todas las concesiones de terrenos de que estuvieren en posesión antes de la fecha del presente Tratado los nacionales de la otra y, en general, todos los derechos adquiridos por nacionales y extranjeros, conforme a las legislaciones respectivas, sobre las tierras que por efecto de la determinación de fronteras constante en el Artículo Primero del presente Tratado, quedan reconocidas como pertenecientes, respectivamente, a Colombia y al Perú".

All these considerations serve to set forth the great and exceptional value, in benefit of the entire Continent, which would result from the friendly cooperation of the Government of the United States on behalf of a treaty which would not only definitely fix the limits of this line between Colombia and Peru, but would also open the way for a prompt fixation of the boundary line between Colombia and Brazil in the section left undetermined in the Boundary Treaty of 1907. The Government of Colombia, in a spirit of conciliation and of sincere good will, is ready to collaborate to this end.

WASHINGTON, *November 28, 1924.*

721.2315/139½

Memorandum by the Secretary of State of a Conversation with the Colombian Minister (Olaya), December 4, 1924

Mr. Hughes stated that he had examined the memorandum which had been handed to him by the Colombian Minister on November 26, 1924,[83] and the supplementary memorandum of November 28, 1924, and that he had given careful attention to the matters presented therein; that he would be glad to see an amicable solution of this boundary problem and that while the United States Government did not desire to intervene in the matter he was disposed to offer such friendly advice as might tend to expedite a settlement of the question.

Mr. Hughes said that he had noted from Doctor Olaya's memoranda and from other available information on the subject that the pending treaty between Peru and Colombia, signed in 1922, provided for the cession by Peru to Colombia of certain territory to the west of the line agreed upon by Peru and Brazil in their Treaty of 1851 as the boundary between the two countries. Mr. Hughes suggested that it might be a practicable solution of the present difficulty if Colombia should agree to recognize the line specified in the Treaty of 1851 between Peru and Brazil as the boundary between Colombia and Brazil, in the event that the latter should withdraw its objections to the Peruvian-Colombian Treaty of 1922 and the latter Treaty should be ratified by Peru.

Mr. Hughes added that he was prompted to make this suggestion in view of the fact that he understood that line had already been accepted by the Executive branch of the Colombian Government in the unratified treaty signed with Brazil at Bogotá July 25, 1853.

In conclusion Mr. Hughes stated that he would be pleased to communicate this proposal informally to the Government of Brazil, should he be advised that it would be acceptable to the Colombian Government.

---

[83] Not printed.

721.2315/141a

The Secretary of State to the Ambassador in Brazil (Morgan)

No. 955   WASHINGTON, *December 11, 1924.*

SIR: There is enclosed for your information an English translation of a memorandum presented to the Government of Peru by the Brazilian Legation in Lima [84] expressing the objections of Brazil to the boundary convention signed by Peru and Colombia in 1922. The Portuguese text of this document was left at the Department on November 14, 1924, by the Brazilian Chargé d'Affaires.

In this connection the Department desires to refer to its strictly confidential instruction No. 850, dated January 22, 1924.[85] Your comments on this matter are awaited with interest.

I am [etc.]

For the Secretary of State:
JOSEPH C. GREW

721.2315/139¾

Memorandum by the Secretary of State of a Conversation with the Peruvian Ambassador (Velarde), December 12, 1924, 3 p. m.

The Ambassador said that a difficulty had arisen with respect to this boundary. Peru and Colombia had made a treaty in 1922 fixing the boundary but Brazil had taken exception to this treaty upon the ground that it affected her rights. Peru was very desirous that the whole matter should be harmoniously adjusted and knowing the wish of the Government of the United States to do all in its power to promote friendly relations in Latin America, the Ambassador asked if the Secretary would look into the question and see if some suggestion could be made which would provide an harmonious solution.

The Secretary said that he greatly appreciated the Ambassador's suggestion; that the Government of the United States did not desire to intrude in matters in which it was not concerned, but that the Government was always desirous to aid by its friendly offices in the settlement of differences when other Governments so desired. The Secretary said he would be glad to look into the matter with which he was already to some extent conversant, and that within a short time he would ask the Ambassador to come in and talk it over. The Ambassador expressed his appreciation.

---

[84] Not printed; for substance of memorandum, see despatch no. 312, Nov. 17, from the Ambassador in Peru, p. 296.
[85] Not printed.

721.2315/139½

Memorandum by the Secretary of State of a Conversation with the Brazilian Chargé (Gracie), December 12, 1924, 3: 30 p. m.

Mr. Gracie, the Chargé d'Affaires, called under instructions by his Government, to leave a memorandum [86] relating to the question that had arisen with respect to the treaty between Peru and Colombia defining their boundaries. Reference was made to the note already sent to the Peruvian Government by the Brazilian Government stating that this treaty affected Brazilian interests and their desire that it should not be ratified. The Brazilian Government desired an harmonious settlement between Peru, Colombia and Brazil, and suggested that the matter might be disposed of by arbitration. The Government of the United States was asked to consider the question to see if some helpful suggestion in the direction of the settlement could be made. The Secretary responded to Mr. Gracie's statement, expressing his appreciation of the attitude of the Brazilian Government. The Secretary said that this Government was always desirous to use its good offices to aid in promoting settlements in Latin America when this was agreeable to the Governments concerned. The Secretary said that he had already studied this question somewhat and he would be glad to give the memorandum and the subject further consideration and within a few days he would ask Mr. Gracie to come in and talk this matter over.

Ecuador and Peru

722.2315/632 : Telegram

The Ambassador in Peru (Poindexter) to the Secretary of State

LIMA, *June 24, 1924—5 p. m.*
[Received June 25—10 : 42 a. m.]

35. See my despatch No. 62, August 25, 1923.[86] Protocol signed June 21, between Peru and Ecuador at Quito, provides for submission boundary settlement to arbitration in Washington. Delegates meet there immediately after Tacna-Arica decision. Text follows by next pouch.[87] Minister for Foreign Affairs categorically states that above agreement in no way prejudices Peruvian-Colombian treaty which will be submitted to Congress for ratification immediately on convening.[88]

POINDEXTER

---

[86] Not printed.
[87] See telegram no. 7, June 24, from the Minister in Ecuador, *infra*.
[88] See pp. 293 ff.

722.2315/633 : Telegram

The Minister in Ecuador (Bading) to the Secretary of State

QUITO, *June 24, 1924—11 a. m.*
[Received June 26—12:21 p. m.]

7. Referring to Legation's number 327, May 13, 1924, and 162, August 14, 1923.[89] The following protocol has been signed by the Ecuadorean Minister for Foreign Affairs and the Peruvian Minister, preamble omitted:

"1st. The two Governments, with the previous assent of that of the United States of America, shall send to Washington their respective delegations to discuss there in a friendly manner the boundary question, in order that, if they do not succeed in fixing a definite line, they may determine by common agreement the zones which each of the parties reciprocally recognize and the zone which will have to be submitted to the arbitral award of the President of the United States of America;

"2d. When one or the other of the above-mentioned ends is obtained, the delegations shall sign a protocol thereof which will be submitted to the approval of the Congresses of both nations;

"3d. The delegations must be constituted in Washington immediately after the question submitted to the arbitration of the President of the United States by the Governments of Peru and Chile has been decided. As far as the appointment of the delegates is concerned, both Governments shall have the power of appointing at any time, but in any case, the delegations should be organized at Washington within the term mentioned in this article;

"4th. Regardless of what is established in the preceding clauses, the two Governments, through their respective Ministers shall try to anticipate the settlement of the controversy.

"Signed in duplicate, in Quito, June 21st of the year 1924. Signed N. Clemente Ponce [90] and E. Castro Oyanguren." [91]

Details by mail.[92]

BADING

---

[89] Neither printed.
[90] Ecuadoran Minister for Foreign Affairs.
[91] Peruvian Minister in Ecuador.
[92] Despatch no. 356, June 30; not printed. No further action in fulfillment of the protocol was taken by the Governments of Ecuador and Peru until 1934.

ALBANIA

MAINTENANCE BY THE UNITED STATES OF UNOFFICIAL RELATIONS WITH THE REVOLUTIONARY GOVERNMENT IN ALBANIA

811.111 Rustem, Avni : Telegram

The Minister in Albania (Grant-Smith) to the Secretary of State

> TIRANA, *May 4, 1924—noon.*
> [Received 11:25 p. m.]

40. My 35, April 20, 6 p.m.[1] The opposition has profited [by] assassination of Avni Rustem [2] to launch agitation which may result in revolution. Deputies attending funeral at Valona made speeches and telegraphed majority party here demanding that Assembly meet elsewhere, alleging lack of personal safety in Tirana. Receiving negative reply, they declared intention not to return for the session opening 7th. Battalion moved to Valona. The Prime Minister made a proclamation warning that revolting would probably result in dissolution of country. Fear of continued influence of late Prime Minister [3] of reactionary leanings and desire to force removal of seat of government apparent actuating motives.

Copy to European Information Center.

> GRANT-SMITH

875.00/122 : Telegram

The Minister in Albania (Grant-Smith) to the Secretary of State

> TIRANA, *May 18, 1924* [*—12 noon*].
> [Received 5:20 p. m.]

43. My telegram number 40 of May 4, noon. . . .

Arms are being distributed here to reserves and others. Movement on Scutari planned for this week. A portion of Tirana garrison of doubtful loyalty. Should south join rebels, which seems probable, telegraph lines would be cut. I recommend that a destroyer be sent to Durazzo for communication purposes. Copy to European Information Center.

> GRANT-SMITH

---

[1] Not printed.
[2] A prominent delegate to the Constituent Assembly who was shot on a street in Tirana Apr. 20 and died Apr. 22.
[3] Ahmed Bey Zogu.

875.00/124 : Telegram

The Minister in Albania (Grant-Smith) to the Secretary of State

TIRANA, *May 19, 1924—3 p. m.*
[Received 9:25 p. m.]

44. My 43, May 18, 12 noon. Officers of Tirana garrison have notified the Government their objection to precipitating civil war by moving on Scutari. The Assembly has sent delegation to confer with recalcitrant members at Scutari. Prospects for peaceful solution brighter.

Destroyer not needed unless foreign communications with central Albania interrupted. I recommend the Embassy at Rome be instructed to communicate direct with Admiral in such case. Copy to European Information Bureau.

GRANT-SMITH

875.00/122 : Telegram

The Secretary of State to the Minister in Albania (Grant-Smith)

WASHINGTON, *May 20, 1924—5 p. m.*

31. Your 43, May 18 and 44, May 19, 3 p. m. Department has informed Navy of substance of your telegrams and in accordance with your recommendation has expressed desire that the Commander of United States Naval Forces in European waters be authorized to despatch a destroyer to Durazzo upon receipt of a request to that effect from you or the Embassy at Rome. Embassy at Rome has been advised in the premises by telegraph.

HUGHES

875.00/133 : Telegram

The Ambassador in Italy (Fletcher) to the Secretary of State

ROME, *June 2, 1924—8 p. m.*
[Received 8:45 p. m.]

104. I am just notified by the Foreign Office that as communication with Durazzo is interrupted an Italian destroyer is being sent immediately to Durazzo. In accordance with desire of Minister Tirana I have just relayed his request for a destroyer to the naval attaché at Athens.

FLETCHER

875.00/134 : Telegram

The Ambassador in Italy (Fletcher) to the Secretary of State

ROME, *June 5, 1924—11 a. m.*
[Received June 5—8:15 a. m.]

105. Albanian revolution seems to be succeeding. Details as far as known here are fully covered in Associated Press reports. Copy to European Information Center.

FLETCHER

875.00/136 : Telegram

The Minister in Albania (Grant-Smith) to the Secretary of State

TIRANA, *June 6, 1924—7 p. m.*
[Received June 7—9:50 a. m.]

49. Armistice declared evening 4th at the instance of the Government. Beys fearful confiscation of estates. The same day the majority of the Government deputies, a number of officials and families, fled to Durazzo. Tirana garrison immediately took effective measures to insure public safety. Force of tribesmen raised by Ahmed Zogu dissolving, carrying off arms. Nationalists insist upon immediate exile of Ahmed Bey . . . Destroyer *Bulmer* arrived at Durazzo Wednesday afternoon. Copy to European Information Center.

GRANT-SMITH

875.00/138 : Telegram

The Ambassador in Italy (Fletcher) to the Secretary of State

[Paraphrase]

ROME, *June 7, 1924—3 p. m.*
[Received 6:38 p. m.]

111. Following information regarding Albanian situation is confidential. I have been requested by the Secretary General of the Foreign Office to inform you that the Governments of Italy and Yugoslavia have no intention of interfering in the internal affairs of Albania in any way and that on this point the two Governments are completely in accord.[4]

FLETCHER

---

[4] In despatch no. 78, June 9, the Ambassador in Italy reported that the Italian Foreign Office had issued a communiqué to the press of similar purport to the statement reported in this telegram.

875.00/140 : Telegram

The Ambassador in Italy (Fletcher) to the Secretary of State

ROME, *June 11, 1924—noon.*
[Received 2 : 06 p. m.]

114. Following from Grant-Smith:

"Repeat to Department: 51, June 8, 4 p. m. The Prime Minister, War Minister and Commander of Gendarmerie fled to Durazzo today. Some hundreds of armed tribesmen still in Tirana. Local authorities will probably be able to maintain order.

Government forces in south routed. Insurgent forces expected to enter Tirana tomorrow."

FLETCHER

875.002/10 : Telegram

The Minister in Albania (Grant-Smith) to the Secretary of State

[Paraphrase]

TIRANA, *June 19, 1924—8 a. m.*
[Received 8 : 41 p. m.]

56. The following Cabinet was announced the day before yesterday: Prime Minister, Fan Noli; Foreign Affairs, Suleiman Delvino; War, Colonel Kiafzezi; Finance, Gurakuchi; Interior, Colonel Shala; Public Works, Kotsuli; Justice, Vinyau.

Foreign representatives were given the announcement formally in writing. I have not answered. It is very questionable whether Peci, the one remaining regent, has legal authority to authorize the formation of a cabinet.

The Italians much desire that the present regime be given support by the admission of its legality. If this is not given they wish nevertheless that it receive the support of early recognition. Of course the British Minister, who left June 15 for London, is very much opposed to recognition. My French colleague is not inclined to admit the legality of the regime and expresses doubts regarding its stability. The Greeks and Servians may be expected to seek the overthrow of the regime, though not openly.

The present regime is a minority in the Parliament which has gained power with the help of the Army and is [not?] considered a legal government under the present constitution until it has received a vote of confidence from the reassembled Assembly or until new elections have been held. It would appear that American interests would be served by the continuance of the new regime, which is favorably inclined toward us at present and is committed against the pretensions of the British. Until I receive instructions I intend to refrain from any act which rightly could be construed as recognition but I shall keep up friendly though informal relations with the leaders.

GRANT-SMITH

875.002/11 : Telegram

The Minister in Albania (Grant-Smith) to the Secretary of State

[Paraphrase]

TIRANA, *June 21, 1924—4 p. m.*
[Received June 22—11 : 10 a. m.]

58. Legation's 56, June 19, 8 a. m. Mussolini [5] has answered a telegram which was sent to him direct from Fan Noli, and the notes which the Albanian Prime Minister and Minister for Foreign Affairs addressed to my Italian colleague have been formally acknowledged in terms which are usual after there has been a normal change of Ministry. The question of recognition was not mentioned. I have been informed by the Secretary General of the Ministry of Foreign Affairs that a reply to Fan Noli's telegram has been received from the Yugoslav Prime Minister in similar terms. The French Chargé has not received instructions as yet.

GRANT-SMITH

875.01/244 : Telegram

The Minister in Albania (Grant-Smith) to the Secretary of State

[Paraphrase]

TIRANA, *June 22, 1924—6 p. m.*
[Received June 23—2 : 05 p. m.]

59. Legation's 56, June 19, 8 a. m. Fan Noli called upon me today and made a plea for recognition by the United States. His plea was expressed in the same terms as transmitted through the Albanian consul at New York.[6] He caused telegrams to be given to me which had been received from the League of Nations and from the Greek, Italian, and Yugoslav Prime Ministers acknowledging his announcement of the formation of a new Albanian Government. The Greek and Yugoslav replies were cordial and did not raise the question of recognition. The Italian Government had Fan Noli notified of a fact yesterday which he did not mention to me, that the telegram from Mussolini could not be construed as

---

[5] Benito Mussolini, President of the Council of Ministers and Minister for Foreign Affairs of Italy.
[6] See telegram no. 41, June 25, to the Minister in Albania, p. 311.

recognition should the Allied Powers find serious reasons for withholding it.

I mentioned our policy of avoiding the impression of hasty actions regarding recognition, especially in Europe, and reminded Fan Noli that the late regime had failed to fulfill its promises as to equality of opportunity and bringing the murderers to justice.[7] He replied that his stand regarding the former was so well known that he need not repeat it and that an early favorable answer would be given regarding the punishment of the murderers.

My recommendation is that we obtain from the new Government formal engagements respecting the two matters mentioned above. Do I have authority to take any action constituting recognition?

GRANT-SMITH

875.01/243 : Telegram

The Secretary of State to the Minister in Albania (Grant-Smith)

[Paraphrase]

WASHINGTON, *June 24, 1924—1 p.m.*

39. Legation's 56 of June 19 and 58 of June 21. Unless the head of the State has been changed, the question of recognition does not seem to arise. There is no objection to your continuing to carry on with the present Government the relations which you had with the preceding one if in your opinion it is properly constituted, stable, and in control of the country. You are authorized at your discretion to continue such relations. Department desires telegraphic report of your action.

HUGHES

875.01/244 : Telegram

The Secretary of State to the Minister in Albania (Grant-Smith)

[Paraphrase]

WASHINGTON, *June 25, 1924—6 p.m.*

41. Legation's 59, June 22, and Department's 39, June 23 [*24*]. Department records do not show receipt of any message from Fan Noli either through consul of Albania at New York or from any other source.

Your suggestion that you should impress upon present regime the importance attached by this Government to prompt and vigorous action for the punishment of those responsible for the murder of Coleman and De Long is approved.

---

[7] Robert Lewis Coleman and George B. de Long, Americans, were murdered by bandits in Albania, Apr. 6, 1924.

In its telegram 39 of June 23 [*24*], the Department answered inquiry in final sentence of your telegram. Telegraph promptly if you feel that additional instructions are needed on this point.

HUGHES

875.01/245 : Telegram

The Minister in Albania (Grant-Smith) to the Secretary of State

[Paraphrase]

TIRANA, *July 2, 1924—9 a.m.*
[Received July 3—10:30 a.m.]

62. Department's 39 of June 24. Greece is the only country which has given unconditional recognition to Fan Noli's government. The only failure to reply to his direct telegram was by the British Prime Minister. The Greek and Italian representatives have established formal relations with the government, but in the latter case with the reservations previously reported. The Servians will doubtless delay recognition. They are much concerned over the Irredentist influence which is apparent in the new regime, and Ahmed Zogu is at Belgrade. The French express [omission]. The only remaining regent, whose term expires next fall, has gone on indefinite leave, ostensibly for reasons of health, and his functions have been professedly transferred to the Prime Minister who states that there will be no elections before March 1925. Under these circumstances there is no remaining head of the State and the government proposes to start its program of much-needed agrarian and social reform unhampered by a legislative body. There is no longer any pretension that the government has a legal status under the constitution.

I shall not address any formal communications to the Minister of Foreign Affairs. I propose to hand to him impersonal memoranda of important conversations if such action is needed.

GRANT-SMITH

875.00/157 : Telegram

The Chargé in Albania (Kodding) to the Secretary of State

[Paraphrase]

TIRANA, *September 16, 1924—8 a.m.*
[Received September 17—4:12 a.m.]

71. I am mailing a report [8] giving details of the alleged dissatisfaction which is accumulating with respect to the present Government of Albania. The opposition here and abroad is aided in accentuating differences between the regions and parties which united to over-

---

[8] Not printed.

throw the former Government by the uncompromising attitude of the present regime on land-tenure reforms in contrast with its inability to pay salaries and its vacillating policy concerning appointments. The British Minister does not conceal his belief that a revolution will occur within two weeks. In other quarters, however, the feeling is that a crisis will not develop, at least until after the harvest, because of the work and contentment resulting from a very good crop.

Since the departure of Minister Grant-Smith there has been at no time such a change of conditions as would justify my reopening the question of recognition. . . .

KODDING

875.1123 Coleman and De Long/89 : Telegram

The Chargé in Albania (Kodding) to the Secretary of State

[Paraphrase]

TIRANA, *October 10, 1924—4 p. m.*
[Received October 11—3 : 52 p. m.]

78. Your 48, September 22, 4 p. m.[9] There is no improvement in the weakened position of the Albanian head of State and Cabinet, which Legation indicated in its 71, September 16, 8 a. m., and despatch 327 of September 20.[9a] Both the Prime Minister and Finance Minister remain abroad. An example of the failure to assure public safety is the throwing of a rock yesterday into the state hospital here. Our expectations as to action regarding the murder of the Americans have not been fulfilled.

I do not believe that it will serve American interests to take up formal relations at present with the Nationalist regime, in view of all the facts and considering that Greece is the only nation represented here which is not reserving recognition for a more favorable time.

KODDING

875.00/163

The Minister in Albania (Grant-Smith) to the Secretary of State

No. 355　　　　　　　　　TIRANA, *November 20, 1924.*
[Received December 10.]

SIR: I have the honor to report that after protracted negotiations between the various political groups M. Peci, acting as the "High Council of Regency" signed on the 13th instant a decree calling for elections for a legislative body to be held from December 20th to Jan-

---

[9] Not printed.
[9a] Despatch not printed.

uary 20th next. Notwithstanding the fact that the Constituent Assembly which adjourned in May last had constituted itself into a "regular" Parliament [which?] has never been dissolved, nor [and] that none of the acts of the present régime nor [or] of the sole Regent remaining since the last revolution have been legal according to the terms of the Provisional Constitution of Lushnia, they go merrily along choosing such phrases from the Constitution as suits their purposes for the moment and ignoring the rest.

It is a provisional government sitting at a provisional capital acting illegally under a provisional constitution. The anomaly will be further accentuated after [apparent omission] through the expiration on that date of the term of office of H. E. M. Sotir Peci, sole remaining Regent acting as the High Council of Regency, whereupon all the honors and powers pertaining thereto will devolve, according to the Constitution, of course, upon the Prime Minister, Mgr. Fan Noli who will bear and discharge them until such time as others are duly elected. This will doubtless be the first act of the new "Parliament"; the second to overthrow Mgr. Fan Noli who has failed, they complain, to execute the twenty points set forth in his programme announced in June last.

I have [etc.]   U. GRANT-SMITH

875.00/164 : Telegram

The Minister in Albania (Grant-Smith) to the Secretary of State

[Paraphrase]

TIRANA, *December 12, 1924—2 p. m.*
[Received 7 : 55 p. m.]

91. Threats of incursion by refugees from Yugoslav territory increase as the date for the election approaches. Reports in the foreign press that a revolution has started in Albania are premature.

GRANT-SMITH

875.00/165 : Telegram

The Minister in Albania (Grant-Smith) to the Secretary of State

TIRANA, *December 16, 1924—5 p. m.*
[Received December 17—12 : 28 a. m.]

93. My telegram number 91, December 12, 2 p. m. Incursions of armed bands announced in the south from Greece and near Ochrida and Prizren, the latter bands reported well armed; also number Wrangel's Russian and Stambouliski Bulgarian refugees participating. Strategic points to the east reported occupied by Ahmed Bey's

forces. Fighting has occurred along Yugoslav border. Public demonstrations Yugoslavia held yesterday in Tirana and Durazzo and League of Nations and Great Powers appealed to by telegraph.

GRANT-SMITH

875.00/167 : Telegram

The Minister in Albania (Grant-Smith) to the Secretary of State

TIRANA, *December 25, 1924—6 p. m.*
[Received December 26—9:16 a. m.]

100. Ahmed Bey Zogu entered Tirana this morning. Quiet reigns. No signs of Servians or Russian refugees among his ragged followers. Total casualties not greater than last revolution. Zogu's opponents may continue show of resistance in south for the short time. Scutari and Koushidacha [*sic*] reported in hands of his partisans.

GRANT-SMITH

POSTPONEMENT OF NEGOTIATIONS FOR A TREATY BETWEEN THE UNITED STATES AND ALBANIA

765.752/1

The Secretary of State to the Minister in Albania (Grant-Smith)

No. 83   WASHINGTON, *March 25, 1924.*

SIR: Your despatch No. 208 of January 23, 1924 [10] reporting that on the same date a Treaty of Commerce and Navigation was signed at Rome between Italy and Albania [11] has been received.

The Department desires your opinion as to the advisability of undertaking the negotiation of a treaty in the near future to define and regularize the relations between the United States and Albania. Your views as to the points which it might eventually be desirable to cover in such a treaty would also be helpful. In this connection a copy of the Albanian Treaty with Italy, which you say you will forward to the Department as soon as it can be obtained, would be useful.

I am [etc.]

For the Secretary of State:
WILLIAM PHILLIPS

---

[10] Not printed.
[11] For text of treaty, which was signed Jan. 20, see League of Nations Treaty Series, vol. XLIV, p. 359.

765.752/4

The Minister in Albania (Grant-Smith) to the Secretary of State

No. 274   TIRANA, *June 2, 1924.*
                                             [Received June 24.]

SIR: I have the honor to acknowledge the receipt of the Department's instruction No. 83 of March 25th last, with regard to the advisability of undertaking the negotiation of a treaty in the near future to define and regularize the relations between the United States and Albania.

The relations between the two Governments are now based on the notes exchanged on June 23rd and 25th, 1922, between the American Commissioner, the Honorable Maxwell Blake, and the Albanian President of the Council (of Ministers)—Minister for Foreign Affairs, H. E. Monsieur Xhafer Ypi, copies of which were transmitted to the Department with the former's despatch No. 3 of August 2, 1922.¹² As will be seen from them the Albanian Government engaged itself, in return for official recognition on the part of the Government of the United States, to

(1) "recognize the passports given by the authorities of the United States of America to persons of Albanian origin, who are naturalized Americans in conformity with the American laws concerning nationalities"

and,

(2) in case a commercial treaty should be concluded between the Government of the United States and that of Albania, to insert in the said treaty, the ' "most favored nation clause" ' . . . and, pending the conclusion of the treaty above mentioned, the American interests in Albania will receive the most favored nation treatment. Furthermore, the Albanian Government is ready to show all kinds of facilities to the installation of American capital in Albania, as well as to accord concessions to American concerns".

The Department is aware of the difficulties which have been encountered in our efforts to insure most-favored-nation treatment for American corporations in Albania in spite of the fact that certain ones were invited by the Albanian Government to submit offers for the development of the petroleum resources of the country. On several occasions the representatives of those corporations have been on the point of withdrawing from the field but on each occasion the Albanian Government has urged them to remain. . . .

·   ·   ·   ·   ·   ·   ·   ·

---

¹² Not printed.

The terms of the notes above referred to, reinforced by the declarations made by the United States on March 2, 1923,[13] in support of the principle of the "open door", and accepted by the Albanian Government without demur, would seem to afford the United States a sufficient basis for carrying on the relations between the two countries until a more propitious moment should arrive. In order that the Government of Albania might have no shadow of excuse on account of frequent changes of Ministry, lack of organization, inexperience or otherwise, for not giving due weight to the claims of the United States in their negotiation of treaties with the other Powers, I ventured to address a note to the Minister for Foreign Affairs under date of April 17, 1924, (a copy of which is herewith enclosed) wherein was quoted that portion of his predecessor's note of June 25, 1922, relative to most-favored-nation treatment.[14] I took this precaution after the present incumbent, Ilias Bey Vrioni, had expressed to me the opinion that "no one" had a right to see the text of a treaty until it had been ratified by the legislative body.

The enclosed copy of the Albano-Italian Treaty of Commerce and Navigation,[15] with accompanying protocol and supplementary declarations was given me privately by my Italian Colleague. The Italian aim at economic penetration is clearly shown, especially in Articles 6 (establishment of bonded warehouses), 9 (right of Italian companies to operate in Albania), 10 (monopolies), 13 (equal rights for imports, exports, transit or warehousing goods, transportation in national bottoms), 14 (rights of captains and boats or barges to navigate interior waters), 16 (use of interior means of communication, ports, etc.), 17 (coastal shipping), 18 (fishing).

The Yugoslav Government is opposed to the treaty on this account and may cause serious opposition to be raised against its ratification by the Constituent Assembly or subsequent legislative body. The British, it is said, object especially to the provision covering monopolies and have succeeded in focussing public attention on Article 10. The Italians, however, have countered by expressing a willingness to fix the interpretation of that article by an exchange of notes. My Italian colleague desired me to support him with regard to Article 10 on the ground that it was in consonance with the demands put forward by the American, Italian, and French Governments on March 2nd, 3rd and 4th, of last year for conformity by the

---

[13] See telegram no. 10, Feb. 27, 1923, to the Minister in Albania and telegram no. 20, Mar. 2, from the Minister, *Foreign Relations*, 1923, vol. I, pp. 373 and 375.
[14] This quotation does not appear in the only note to the Minister for Foreign Affairs enclosed, which is printed *infra*.
[15] Not printed.

Albanian Government to the policy of the open door. In reply I pointed out that the article, as now phrased, might be interpreted in the sense that no concession of any character whatsoever might be accorded to foreigners by the Albanian Government unless Italian capital participated therein; that, for example, telephone service, the country was too small to admit of more than one operating company. The American view would be met, I thought, if open and fair international competition were assured for all concessions, whether monopolistic or otherwise. Doubtless, certain of the Italian negotiators hoped that Article 10 might pass unchallenged which would have given Italy a veritable "strangle hold" on Albania. My Italian colleague did not, however, combat my criticisms with much vigor and mentioned the proposals, referred to above, to fix the interpretation of that article by an exchange of notes with the Albanian Government.

.   .   .   .

Should the revolution which is now in progress result in a decisive victory for either side a longer period of calm might follow and consequently of [a?] more stable government which would be more favorable for negotiations suggested. The Italian treaty and those concluded with Turkey are still unratified and there would seem no prospect of their being acted on at the earliest before the coming winter.

I have [etc.]   U. GRANT-SMITH

[Enclosure]

The American Minister (Grant-Smith) to the Albanian Minister for Foreign Affairs (Vrioni)

No. 62   TIRANA, *April 17, 1924.*

EXCELLENCY: I have the honor to transmit herewith, for the information of your Excellency's Government, a copy, with translation into Albanian of a letter addressed to me by Mr. E. S. Sheffield, the representative of the Standard Oil Company of New York.[16] After carrying on negotiations, on behalf of his company, with the Ministry of Public Works over a period of several months, he finally, under date of February 25, 1923, deposited with that Ministry signed proposals for a concession for the development of the petroleum resources of certain areas in Albania.

It is with some surprise that I learn that these proposals have been held at the Ministry of Public Works since that date without having been brought before the Council of Ministers for considera-

---

[16] Not printed.

tion with a view to their being submitted, in the regular course, to the legislative body for final action.

It can be readily understood, in consequence, that the representative of the Standard Oil Company of New York should have gained the impression of a "lack of any serious intention on the part of the Albanian Government as regards the business in question". Such delay whether due to administrative neglect or to other causes, has operated to the serious detriment of the company above mentioned and would also be in contravention of the rights and treatment formally guaranteed to American citizens and companies by the Government of Albania.

In bringing the foregoing to the attention of your Excellency I have the honor to request that the necessary remedial steps may be taken without further delay and avail myself [etc.]

U. Grant-Smith

BOLIVIA

DISINCLINATION OF THE SECRETARY OF STATE TO OFFER THE GOOD OFFICES REQUESTED BY BOLIVIA FOR MODIFICATION OF THE BOLIVIAN-CHILEAN TREATY OF 1904

723.2515/1246

Memorandum by the Chief of the Division of Latin American Affairs, Department of State (White)

[WASHINGTON,] *May 5, 1924.*

The Bolivian Minister called on the Secretary of State at twelve o'clock on Monday, May 5. The Secretary stated that he had invited the Minister to come in as Mr. White had told him that the Minister desired to speak with him regarding his note [1] asking the United States to use its good offices to bring about a modification of the Treaty of 1904 between Bolivia and Chile [2] in order that the former might obtain an outlet to the sea.

The Minister stated that if the Department's reply to his note was to be favorable he merely desired to thank the Department but if however the Secretary could not see his way clear to giving a favorable answer he would like to discuss the matter with him. The Secretary replied that it is the desire of this Government to be helpful to the other countries of America in composing and settling their difficulties and that it is very glad to do so when asked by all parties concerned which in this case would be Bolivia and Chile; that this Government of course cannot take such action unless it is requested to do so by all concerned and in this case Chile had not yet asked this Government to take any action in the matter and the Secretary must therefore to his regret decline to take the action requested.

The Minister stated that he was sure that the desire existed in Chile for a settlement of this question; that he had been told so by President Alessandri himself and also by the Minister of Foreign Affairs and other Cabinet officers of Chile. The Secretary stated that while this Government was glad at all times to be of help it would soon fritter away the helpful position which it now has should it

[1] Not printed.
[2] *British and Foreign State Papers*, 1904–1905, vol. XCVIII, p. 763.

320

intervene in questions between two foreign governments without knowing that it was agreeable to both sides; that it was not sufficient for one party to say that it desired the intervention of the United States and it felt sure that the other side would also; that if this desire existed in Chile it would be very easy for the Chilean Government to inform us thereof or it could be made evident in the correspondence comprising the negotiations between Bolivia and Chile and that until this Government was informed by both parties it could not take the action requested. The Secretary added that in the Tacna-Arica case this Government had taken no action until it had been assured that both parties to the dispute would welcome the assistance of the United States. The Minister stated that in the Tacna-Arica case he had seen, as he was then Minister for Foreign Affairs of Bolivia, in the interchange of telegrams between Chile and Peru that the negotiations fell through and that the United States had inquired of both Governments whether an invitation to come to Washington to carry on the negotiations would be acceptable and that both parties had agreed.[3] There was evidence he said in the direct exchange of telegrams between the Chilean and Peruvian Foreign Offices that such a meeting would be acceptable to both parties; that what Bolivia now wants is the United States to inquire of Bolivia and Chile whether an invitation from the United States for those Governments to send representatives to Washington to discuss the matter would be agreeable.

The Secretary replied that in the Tacna-Arica case the inquiry as to whether an invitation would be acceptable had been sent only after this Government had been informally advised by both parties that such action on the part of the United States would be agreeable to the two parties to the dispute. The Secretary added that even after the Peruvian and Chilean delegates had arrived in Washington the United States took no part in bringing about agreements or arrangements between them except when asked to use its good offices by both parties.

The Minister then inquired whether this statement by the Secretary was to be taken as a definite statement of policy of the United States for all time, in other words could he take it that the United States would never enter into a discussion between two Latin American countries or in his country's case between Bolivia and any of its neighbors unless requested to do so by both parties. The Secretary replied that he was not formulating any rules of law nor could he of course prescribe what action his successors in office might adopt nor could he discuss any suppositional or hypothetical questions;

---

[3] *Foreign Relations*, 1922, vol I, pp. 447 ff.

that this Government dealt with each question as it came up as wisdom and friendship would seem to dictate and that it could not permit the discussion to take the phase of binding the United States to any definite policy in the future in cases which had not arisen. The Minister said that he understood the Secretary's point of view; that in this case if the United States would not take action his Government had misinterpreted the addresses of the Secretary and President Coolidge which had expressed a desire to be helpful to Latin American countries. The Secretary replied that of course this Government as President Coolidge had stated desired to be helpful in any way it properly could but that it could not take action without the request of both parties.

Referring back to the question of policy the Minister stated that he was talking purely and simply of the matter connected with his note which dealt with the ardent desire of Bolivia to have an outlet to the sea. Bolivia was now moved with a great feeling in this regard, the question had been taken up in the League of Nations and then directly with Chile and now with the United States and he wanted to know whether the determination of the United States not to take part in this discussion meant that the United States as far as this question was concerned would in its future developments refuse to take any part whatsoever.

The Secretary replied that he would not bind this Government's action for the future; that the case before him was the note of the Bolivian Minister dealing with the situation that actually exists; that in the case as it now is the United States has not been requested by Chile to intervene in the matter and he very much regretted that this Government could not at this time intervene as requested by Bolivia. The Secretary could not foresee what the situation might be in the future or what later developments might occur and he therefore would do nothing now which might hamper the action of this Government in dealing in the future with a case which might arise, that in the actual case the United States could not meet the Bolivian Minister's desires. As the Minister was leaving the Secretary expressed his regret to him that he was unable to comply with his wishes in the matter.

WHITE

BOUNDARY DISPUTE WITH PARAGUAY

(See pages 282 ff.)

BRAZIL

EXPRESSION OF CONCERN BY THE DEPARTMENT OF STATE AT BRAZIL'S NAVAL BUILDING PROGRAM

832.20/35 : Telegram

The Chargé in Brazil (Crosby) to the Secretary of State

[Extract—Paraphrase]

RIO DE JANEIRO, *June 6, 1924—3 p. m.*
[Received 6 : 30 p. m.]

24. . . . . Rear Admiral Vogelgesang, the head of the American Naval Mission in Brazil,[1] has just informed me that his recommendations to the Minister of Marine on proposed naval building for the next 10 years, which provide for destroyers 15,000 tons, submarines 6,000 tons, cruisers 60,000 tons, and battleships 70,000 tons, will be submitted immediately to the President.

CROSBY

832.34/182 : Telegram

The Secretary of State to the Chargé in Brazil (Crosby)

[Paraphrase]

WASHINGTON, *June 11, 1924—6 p. m.*

18. Reference your telegram no. 24, June 6, 3 p. m. The proposed naval building plan submitted by Rear Admiral Vogelgesang is most disturbing to the Department. While from a purely naval technical point of view this program may be justifiable, the outlay appears to be exorbitant and out of all proportion to the necessities of a country like Brazil that is menaced from no quarter. This Government's cardinal policy in Latin America is peace and the promotion among the Latin American countries of the most friendly relations. Severe criticism has been directed against this Government's Naval Mission to Brazil. The motive of the Mission was friendship to Brazil, for if an American mission had not been sent a similar mission from some European country would have been contracted for instead and this Government would in consequence

---

[1] For correspondence concerning the agreement providing for an American Naval Mission to Brazil, see *Foreign Relations*, 1922, vol. I, pp. 651 ff.

have lost the opportunity to exert its influence for moderation in naval armaments. To carry out a program on the scale proposed would afford ample justification for the criticism which has already been directed against the Mission. Please explain the views of the Secretary of State under these premises to Rear Admiral Vogelgesang and express to him the grave concern with which the Department has received this information; request him to give you a full explanation regarding the matter for transmission to the Department by cable. If possible you will also request him to stop any further steps from being taken in this matter while it is under the Department's consideration.

HUGHES

832.34/185 : Telegram

The Chargé in Brazil (Crosby) to the Secretary of State

[Paraphrase]

RIO DE JANEIRO, *June 15, 1924—10 a. m.*
[Received 6:32 p. m.]

27. I have just had an interview with Rear Admiral Vogelgesang who has been confined to his bed with a fever but is better. Neither the chief nor any other member of the Naval Mission is pushing the naval construction program. The Admiral informed me that the President wishes to initiate a program of replacement for old and worn-out units and that at the request of the Minister of Marine a replacement program covering a period of 10 years was submitted. There has been no new construction since 1912; existing submarines are no longer useful and only 5 of the 11 destroyers are now in service; the others are undergoing extensive overhauling and are of little military value. Battleships have not been contemplated or recommended except that battleship tonnage should be utilized for the replacement of the *São Paulo* and the *Minas Geraes*, the two existing battleships. Construction will be governed by the financial situation in any event, and there has been no materialization of the rumored loan reported in my despatch no. 2206, May 28.[2] This year, in any event, submarines only are likely to be provided for. The Admiral informs me that Ambassador Morgan, now in the United States, has a copy of the recommendations which were made to the Minister of Marine relative to the replacement building program and in which was outlined the Mission's attitude on general naval policy of Brazil in response to a request of the Minister of Marine. Admiral Vogelgesang has stated to me that the attitude of the Mission to new construction is to harmonize as nearly as pos-

---

[2] Not printed.

sible the views of the Secretary of State as known to him and the desires of the Brazilian Government to modernize strong naval defense.

CROSBY

832.34/185 : Telegram

The Secretary of State to the Chargé in Brazil (Crosby)

[Paraphrase]

WASHINGTON, *June 26, 1924—4 p. m.*

27. Your no. 27, June 15, 10 a. m. Admiral Vogelgesang's recommendations to Minister of Marine relative to Brazilian naval program shown to Department by Ambassador Morgan. The Department fully understands that it is unlikely that any new construction will be undertaken in the immediate future but it desires to point out to Admiral Vogelgesang that the existence of such a program as the one proposed will make it necessary for Argentina and Chile to elaborate likewise their naval programs and thus there may be started a competition in naval construction. The Brazilian building program is spoken of as a program of defense. The Department does not know by what power Brazil is threatened that she should need such a large defensive fleet. 6,000 tons of submarines, of which 5,000 are to be new and 1,000 eventual replacement, are called for by the program; of the 15,000 tons for destroyers 10,000 are new construction and 5,000 replacement; 50,000 of the 60,000 tons for cruisers are new construction; and the *Minas Geraes* is to be replaced in 1929 and the *São Paulo* in 1930 by battleships each of 35,000 tons, or a total of 70,000 tons.

As the *Minas Geraes* and the *São Paulo* and other units in the Brazilian Navy are practically obsolete, it is true that Brazil is now in an inferior position compared with Argentina and Chile, but the new program instead of putting Brazil on a footing of equality with those countries will place her in a very superior position which will necessitate new naval construction by them for the same reason which now moves Brazil to desire new construction; namely, the desire not to be left in a position of inferiority. Any such result as this would be most unfortunate and there would be brought about a condition of rivalry in armaments in this hemisphere which up to the present has happily not existed.

The Department's feeling about this matter is so strong that it would rather recall the Naval Mission than assume the responsibility for the naval program that the Mission has proposed. Explain the Department's position to Admiral Vogelgesang and request him to take the first opportunity to revise the naval program on the principle of no new construction or replacement of tonnage in any category that will be greater than the maximum which exists at present in any one of the three states, Argentina, Brazil, or Chile.

Ambassador Morgan has been made fully aware of the Department's position in the matter, and immediately upon the Ambassador's return to Rio de Janeiro he will discuss it with Admiral Vogelgesang.

HUGHES

832.34/186 : Telegram

The Chargé in Brazil (Crosby) to the Secretary of State

[Paraphrase]

RIO DE JANEIRO, *July 1, 1924—noon.*
[Received 3 p. m.]

38. Your no. 27, June 26, 4 p. m. Admiral Vogelgesang has requested me to inform the Secretary of State that in accordance with the Secretary's wishes the recommendations for a naval program for Brazil made by the Naval Mission were withdrawn for revision. In the revised recommendations all reference to a concrete building program and any suggestions in regard to tonnage, types, or number of units have been canceled and omitted.

CROSBY

832.34/188a : Telegram

The Secretary of State to the Ambassador in Brazil (Morgan)

WASHINGTON, *December 9, 1924—4 p. m.*

77. The *New York Times* this morning carries despatch from Buenos Aires, dated December 8, stating that the Naval Committee of the Brazilian Chamber of Deputies adopted a resolution recommending the construction of 12 warships. The resolution provides for 2 cruisers of approximately 10,000 tons each, 4 destroyers of 1,440 tons each, 1 destroyer of 1,800 tons and 5 submarines of between 1,300 and 1,500 tons each. The report adds that further aviation development is also recommended. Please cable facts.

HUGHES

832.34/189 : Telegram

The Ambassador in Brazil (Morgan) to the Secretary of State

RIO DE JANEIRO, *December 10, 1924—4 p. m.*
[Received December 10—3:49 p. m.]

103. Department's 77, December 9, 4 p. m. Resolution adopted by Naval Committee of Chamber corresponds to information con-

tained in Department's telegram 77 following Minister of Marine's recommendation renewed frequently in recent years. Naval Mission in no wise responsible. Unlikely that national resources will make it possible to carry out any such program. Attaché Glenn Howell, who leaves today, will fully report. Orders will probably be placed abroad if at all in several countries with the firms which grant long-time payments irrespective of cost.

MORGAN

BULGARIA

EXTRADITION TREATY BETWEEN THE UNITED STATES AND BULGARIA, SIGNED MARCH 19, 1924

Treaty Series No. 687

Treaty between the United States of America and Bulgaria, Signed at Sofia, March 19, 1924 [1]

The United States of America and Bulgaria desiring to promote the cause of justice, have resolved to conclude a treaty for the extradition of fugitives from justice between the two countries and have appointed for that purpose the following Plenipotentiaries:

The President of the United States of America,

Charles S. Wilson, Envoy Extraordinary and Minister Plenipotentiary of the United States of America to Bulgaria, and

His Majesty, the King of the Bulgarians,

Christo Kalfoff, Minister for Foreign Affairs and Worship of Bulgaria,

Who, after having communicated to each other their respective full powers, found to be in good and due form, have agreed upon and concluded the following articles:

ARTICLE I

It is agreed that the Government of the United States and the Government of Bulgaria shall, upon requisition duly made as herein provided, deliver up to justice any person, who may be charged with, or may have been convicted of, any of the crimes specified in Article II of the present Treaty committed within the jurisdiction of one of the High Contracting Parties, and who shall seek an asylum or shall be found within the territories of the other; provided that such surrender shall take place only upon such evidence of criminality, as according to the laws of the place where the fugitive or person so charged shall be found, would justify his apprehension and commitment for trial if the crime or offense had been there committed.

[1] In English and Bulgarian; Bulgarian text not printed. Ratification advised by the Senate, May 12, 1924; ratified by the President, May 15, 1924; ratified by Bulgaria, June 10, 1924; ratifications exchanged at Sofia, June 24, 1924; proclaimed by the President, June 26, 1924.

Article II

Persons shall be delivered up according to the provisions of the present Treaty, who shall have been charged with or convicted of any of the following crimes:

1. Murder, comprehending the crimes designated by the terms parricide, assassination, manslaughter when voluntary, poisoning or infanticide.

2. The attempt to commit murder.

3. Rape, abortion, carnal knowledge of children under the age of twelve years.

4. Abduction or detention of women or girls for immoral purposes.

5. Bigamy.

6. Arson.

7. Wilful and unlawful destruction or obstruction of railroads, which endangers human life.

8. Crimes committed at sea:

(a) Piracy, as commonly known and defined by the law of nations, or by statute;

(b) Wrongfully sinking or destroying a vessel at sea or attempting to do so;

(c) Mutiny or conspiracy by two or more members of the crew or other persons on board of a vessel on the high seas, for the purpose of rebelling against the authority of the Captain or Commander of such vessel, or by fraud or violence taking possession of such vessel.

(d) Assault on board ship upon the high seas with intent to do bodily harm.

9. Burglary, defined to be the act of breaking into and entering the house of another in the night time with intent to commit a felony therein.

10. The act of breaking into and entering the offices of the Government and public authorities, or the offices of banks, banking houses, savings banks, trust companies, insurance and other companies, or other buildings not dwellings with intent to commit a felony therein.

11. Robbery, defined to be the act of feloniously and forcibly taking from the person of another goods or money by violence or by putting him in fear.

12. Forgery or the utterance of forged papers.

13. The forgery or falsification of the official acts of the Government or public authority, including Courts of Justice, or the uttering or fraudulent use of any of the same.

14. The fabrication of counterfeit money, whether coin or paper, counterfeit titles or coupons of public debt, created by National, State, Provincial, Territorial, Local or Municipal Governments, bank notes or other instruments of public credit, counterfeit seals, stamps, dies and marks of State or public administrations, and the utterance, circulation or fraudulent use of the above mentioned objects.

15. Embezzlement or criminal malversation committed within the jurisdiction of one or the other party by public officers or depositaries, where the amount embezzled exceeds one hundred dollars or Bulgarian equivalent.

16. Embezzlement by any person or persons hired, salaried or employed, to the detriment of their employers or principals, when the crime or offense is punishable by imprisonment or other corporal punishment, by the laws of both countries, and where the amount embezzled exceeds one hundred dollars or Bulgarian equivalent.

17. Kidnapping of minors or adults, defined to be the abduction or detention of a person or persons, in order to exact money from them, their families or any other person or persons, or for any other unlawful end.

18. Larceny, defined to be the theft of effects, personal property, or money, of the value of twenty-five dollars or more, or Bulgarian equivalent.

19. Obtaining money, valuable securities or other property, by false pretences or receiving any money, valuable securities or other property knowing the same to have been unlawfully obtained, where the amount of money or the value of the property so obtained or received exceeds one hundred dollars or Bulgarian equivalent.

20. Perjury or subornation of perjury.

21. Fraud or breach of trust by a bailee, banker, agent, factor, trustee, executor, administrator, guardian, director or officer of any company or corporation, or by any one in any fiduciary position, where the amount of money or the value of the property misappropriated exceeds one hundred dollars or Bulgarian equivalent.

22. Crimes and offenses against the laws of both countries for the suppression of slavery and slave trading.

23. Wilful desertion or wilful non-support of minor or dependent children.

24. Extradition shall also take place for participation in any of the crimes before mentioned as an accessory before or after the fact; provided such participation be punishable by imprisonment by the laws of both the High Contracting Parties.

ARTICLE III

The provisions of the present Treaty shall not import a claim of extradition for any crime or offense of a political character, nor for acts connected with such crimes or offenses; and no person surrendered by or to either of the High Contracting Parties in virtue of this Treaty shall be tried or punished for a political crime or offense. When the offense charged comprises the act either of murder or assassination or of poisoning, either consummated or attempted, the fact that the offense was committed or attempted against the life of the Sovereign or Head of a foreign State or against the life of any member of his family, shall not be deemed sufficient to sustain that such crime or offense was of a political character; or was an act connected with crimes or offenses of a political character.

ARTICLE IV

No person shall be tried for any crime or offense other than that for which he was surrendered.

ARTICLE V

A fugitive criminal shall not be surrendered under the provisions hereof, when, from lapse of time or other lawful cause, according to the laws of the place within the jurisdiction of which the crime was committed, the criminal is exempt from prosecution or punishment for the offense for which the surrender is asked.

ARTICLE VI

If a fugitive criminal whose surrender may be claimed pursuant to the stipulations hereof, be actually under prosecution, out on bail or in custody, for a crime or offense committed in the country where he has sought asylum, or shall have been convicted thereof, his extradition may be deferred until such proceedings be determined, and until he shall have been set at liberty in due course of law.

ARTICLE VII

If a fugitive criminal claimed by one of the parties hereto, shall be also claimed by one or more powers pursuant to treaty provisions, on account of crimes committed within their jurisdiction, such criminal shall be delivered to that State whose demand is first received.

ARTICLE VIII

Under the stipulations of this Treaty, neither of the High Contracting Parties shall be bound to deliver up its own citizens.

ARTICLE IX

The expense of arrest, detention, examination and transportation of the accused shall be paid by the Government which has preferred the demand for extradition.

ARTICLE X

Everything found in the possession of the fugitive criminal at the time of his arrest, whether being the proceeds of the crime or offense, or which may be material as evidence in making proof of the crime, shall so far as practicable, according to the laws of either of the High Contracting Parties, be delivered up with his person at the time of surrender. Nevertheless, the rights of a third party with regard to the articles referred to, shall be duly respected.

ARTICLE XI

The stipulations of the present Treaty shall be applicable to all territory wherever situated, belonging to either of the High Contracting Parties or in the occupancy and under the control of either of them, during such occupancy or control.

Requisitions for the surrender of fugitives from justice shall be made by the respective diplomatic agents of the High Contracting Parties. In the event of the absence of such agent from the country or its seat of Government, or where extradition is sought from territory included in the preceding paragraphs, other than the United States or Bulgaria, requisitions may be made by superior consular officers. It shall be competent for such diplomatic or superior consular officers to ask and obtain a mandate or preliminary warrant of arrest for the person whose surrender is sought, whereupon the judges and magistrates of the two Governments shall respectively have power and authority, upon complaint made under oath, to issue a warrant for the apprehension of the person charged, in order that he or she may be brought before such judge or magistrate, that the evidence of criminality may be heard and considered and if, on such hearing, the evidence be deemed sufficient to sustain the charge, it shall be the duty of the examining judge or magistrate to certify it to the proper executive authority, that a warrant may issue for the surrender of the fugitive.

In case of urgency, the application for arrest and detention may be addressed directly to the competent magistrate in conformity to the statutes in force.

The person provisionally arrested shall be released, unless within three months from the date of arrest in Bulgaria, or from the date of commitment in the United States, the formal requisition for surrender with the documentary proofs hereinafter prescribed be made as aforesaid by the diplomatic agent of the demanding Government or, in his absence, by a consular officer thereof.

If the fugitive criminal shall have been convicted of the crime for which his surrender is asked, a copy of the sentence of the court before which such conviction took place, duly authenticated, shall be produced. If, however, the fugitive is merely charged with crime, a duly authenticated copy of the warrant of arrest in the country where the crime was committed, and of the depositions upon which such warrant may have been issued, shall be produced, with such other evidence or proof as may be deemed competent in the case.

Article XII

In every case of a request made by either of the High Contracting Parties for the arrest, detention or extradition of fugitive criminals, the appropriate legal officers of the country where the proceedings of extradition are had, shall assist the officers of the Government demanding the extradition before the respective judges and magistrates, by every legal means within their power; and no claim whatever for compensation for any of the services so rendered shall be made against the Government demanding the extradition; provided, however, that any officer or officers of the surrendering Government so giving assistance, who shall, in the usual course of their duty, receive no salary or compensation other than specific fees for services performed, shall be entitled to receive from the Government demanding the extradition the customary fees for the acts or services performed by them, in the same manner and to the same amount as though such acts or services had been performed in ordinary criminal proceedings under the laws of the country of which they are officers.

Article XIII

The present Treaty shall be ratified by the High Contracting Parties in accordance with their respective constitutional methods and shall take effect on the date of the exchange of ratifications which shall take place at Sophia, as soon as possible.

ARTICLE XIV

The present Treaty shall remain in force for a period of ten years, and in case neither of the High Contracting Parties shall have given notice one year before the expiration of that period of its intention to terminate the Treaty, it shall continue in force until the expiration of one year from the date on which such notice of termination shall be given by either of the High Contracting Parties.

In witness whereof the above-named Plenipotentiaries have signed the present Treaty and have hereunto affixed their seals.

Done in duplicate at Sophia this nineteenth day of March nineteen hundred and twenty-four.

[SEAL]   CHARLES S. WILSON
[SEAL]   CHR. KALFOFF

CANADA

RATIFICATION OF THE FISHERIES CONVENTION SIGNED ON MARCH 2, 1923, BETWEEN THE UNITED STATES AND GREAT BRITAIN [1]

711.428/778

The Under Secretary of State (Phillips) to the Canadian Deputy Minister of Marine and Fisheries (Johnston)

WASHINGTON, *January 10, 1924.*

My DEAR MR. JOHNSTON: I have received from the Consul General at Ottawa a copy of your courteous letter of December 28, 1923,[2] communicating the opinion of the Deputy Minister of Justice on certain questions in regard to the interpretation of the Northern Pacific Halibut Fishery Act passed by the Canadian Parliament in June, 1923.

The views of the Deputy Minister of Justice were communicated to Senator Lodge, Chairman of the Foreign Relations Committee of the Senate, and also your statement that there is no intention on the part of Canada to relieve British vessels from seizure and forfeiture for breach of any of the provisions of the treaty and that if reasonable doubt arises in the mind of anyone that this would be possible under the Act of 1923, steps will be taken to remedy it during the next session of Parliament. I have also had a conversation with Senator Lodge in regard to the matter.

The President has referred the Halibut Fisheries Convention to the Senate for further consideration. Confidentially I may say that Senator Lodge desires to bring it up for action and it is believed that there is no disposition on the part of Senators to insist on the understanding which was made a part of the resolution of March 4, 1923, advising and consenting to ratification.[3] Senator Lodge is apprehensive, however, that the provisions of Section 9 of the Act of the Canadian Parliament under which vessels of the United States would be liable to seizure and forfeiture for the causes to which that Section relates whereas vessels navigated according to the laws of the United Kingdom or of Canada would expressly not be so liable

---

[1] For previous correspondence concerning the convention, see *Foreign Relations.* 1923, vol. I, p. 467.
[2] *Ibid.*, p. 480.
[3] See note of Mar. 5, 1923, to the British Ambassador, *ibid.*, p. 471.

335

under that Section will make it difficult to obtain the approval of the Senate to the Convention without a reservation.

Senator Lodge said to me personally that he would be willing to endeavor to obtain the advice and consent of the Senate to the ratification of the convention without a reservation if he could first have an assurance from the Premier of Canada that the Canadian Government would construe and enforce the Act as the Deputy Minister of Justice stated in his letter to you it should in his opinion be construed. I cannot but believe, however, that as a permanent measure it would be more satisfactory to this Government if the Act of Parliament were amended so that the ambiguity which arises out of Section 9 would be removed. If I may be permitted to make a specific suggestion I should say that this might be accomplished by eliminating Section 9.

As favorable action on the Convention by the Senate seems to depend on an adjustment with reference to Section 9 of the Canadian Act, I should be appreciative of any action which you could take either in the direction of obtaining an expression of the views of the Premier or of putting the matter in course to obtain an amendment of the Act at the next session of Parliament. I should also be grateful for any information which you could furnish me as to progress in either direction.

I am [etc.]   WILLIAM PHILLIPS

711.428/784

The Prime Minister of Canada (Mackenzie King) to the Secretary of State

OTTAWA, *January 30, 1924.*
[Received February 2.]

MY DEAR MR. SECRETARY: I have had an opportunity quite recently of perusing the letters and telegrams that have been exchanged between Mr. Phillips, the Under-Secretary of State at Washington and the Deputy Minister of Marine and Fisheries in the matter of the North Pacific Halibut Treaty.

I am in entire agreement with the view outlined by the Department of Marine and Fisheries and by the Department of Justice that section 9 of the Act passed last session of Parliament should be eliminated. It has therefore been decided that the Minister of Marine and Fisheries will, on behalf of the Government, introduce as early as opportunity will permit after the opening of the forthcoming session of Parliament, the necessary legislation to that end.

In this connection I may be permitted to observe that I am exceedingly anxious that the Treaty should at as early a date as it will be convenient to do so, be ratified in its present form by the Senate of the United States. The Canadian Parliament has been summoned to meet on the 28th of February next. If I were put in a position to announce either at the opening of Parliament or very shortly thereafter, that the Treaty had been ratified, it would go a very long way towards calming the apprehension of those who are more directly interested in the industry on the Pacific Coast. I need scarcely say that anything that can be done to expedite final consideration of the matter will be very sincerely appreciated.

Yours sincerely,

W. L. MACKENZIE KING

711.428/786

The Canadian Deputy Minister of Marine and Fisheries (Johnston)
to the Under Secretary of State (Phillips)

721–19–8   OTTAWA, *31 January, 1924.*
[Received February 2.]

MY DEAR MR. PHILLIPS: This will confirm my telegram to you of the 21st instant which read:—

"Regret delay replying your letter January tenth. Act of last session has received further consideration law officers with result that amending Act will be submitted to Parliament forthcoming Session repeal section nine. Will obtain confirming letter from Department Justice and will forward to you. Suggested also that we amend section six by inserting after the word 'waters' in line seven the words 'during the close season'."

I now attach a copy of the letter received from the Department of Justice [4] in which, you will observe, it is explained that there is no objection to the repealing of section 9 of the Northern Pacific Halibut Fishery Protection Act of last session. You will also observe that the Department concurs in the view that section 6 of the Act should be amended by adding the obviously omitted words 'during the close season' at the appropriate place.

Legislation making these two changes will be submitted to Parliament as soon after the opening of the forthcoming session as possible. There will go forward today or tomorrow a letter addressed to Mr. Secretary Hughes from the Prime Minister, with reference to this matter, which I trust will be accepted as an assurance of our determination to act in such a way as to meet the views of your Department and your Senate.

Yours very truly,

A. JOHNSTON

---

[4] Not printed.

711.428/784

The Secretary of State to the Prime Minister of Canada (Mackenzie King)

WASHINGTON, *February 26, 1924.*

MY DEAR MR. MACKENZIE KING: I have not failed to consider most carefully the questions relating to the ratification of the North Pacific Halibut Treaty and I was highly gratified to receive your letter of January thirtieth stating that you were in entire agreement with the view outlined by the Dominion Department of Marine and Fisheries and by the Department of Justice that section 9 of the Act passed at the last session of the Dominion Parliament should be eliminated. From the advices that I have received from the Chairman of the Committee on Foreign Relations of the Senate I am convinced that it will not be possible for this Government to proceed to the ratification of the treaty until the legislation repealing section 9 has been enacted. I am glad to be advised of the intention of your Government to introduce a bill to that effect and I am quite confident that as soon as the bill has been passed the United States Senate will give its assent to the treaty and it may then promptly be ratified by the President.

With assurance [etc.]   CHARLES E. HUGHES

711.428/800

The British Ambassador (Howard) to the Secretary of State

No. 408   WASHINGTON, *May 8, 1924.*

SIR: In his note of October 4th, 1923,[5] Mr. Phillips was so good as to inform Mr. Chilton that the President of the United States had expressed his readiness to re-submit to the Senate the Convention, concluded between the United States and Great Britain on March 2nd, 1923 for the protection of the Northern Pacific halibut fishery, with a view to obtaining the advice and consent of the Senate to the ratification of the Convention as signed, that is to say, without the reservation made by the Senate on March 3rd,[6] 1923.

As the Government of Canada are taking steps to pass legislation in connection with the Convention, I have the honour to ask you to be so good as to inform me at the earliest possible moment whether this Convention has been re-submitted to the Senate and whether the Senate has agreed to its ratification without the reservation above referred to.

I have [etc.]   ESME HOWARD

---

[5] See *Foreign Relations*, 1923, vol. I, p. 478.
[6] Legislative day.

711.428/800

The Secretary of State to the British Ambassador (Howard)

WASHINGTON, *May 12, 1924.*

EXCELLENCY: I have the honor to acknowledge the receipt of your note No. 408 of May 8, 1924, relating to the Convention for the preservation of the halibut fishery of the northern Pacific Ocean signed by representatives of the United States and Great Britain on March 2, 1923, and to legislation which the Government of Canada is taking steps to enact in connection with the Convention.

The President resubmitted the Convention to the Senate on December 11, 1923, for determination by that body whether it would reconsider its resolution of March 4, 1923, and advise and consent to the ratification of the Convention as signed.

I understand that it is the purpose of the Chairman of the Committee on Foreign Relations to bring the matter up for consideration as soon as advices have been received that the legislation under consideration by the Canadian Government to amend the Northern Pacific Halibut Fishery Protection Act of 1923 has become law.

Accept [etc.]   CHARLES E. HUGHES

711.428/804

The British Ambassador (Howard) to the Secretary of State

No. 439   WASHINGTON, *May 16, 1924.*

SIR: I have the honour to acknowledge the receipt of your note of the 12th instant, regarding the Northern Pacific Halibut Fishery, in which you were good enough to inform me that as soon as he is informed that the Canadian Parliament has passed the legislation, which it has lately been considering on this subject, the Chairman of the Committee on Foreign Relations proposes to resubmit to the Senate the Convention referred to it by the President on December 11th, 1923.

I am happy to be in a position to inform you that the bill, of which I have the honour to enclose a copy,[7] has been passed by both Houses of the Canadian Parliament, by the House of Commons on the 3rd ultimo and by the Senate on the 10th ultimo, and that it only requires the formal assent of His Excellency the Governor-General (which can and will be given at any convenient time) before it becomes law. There appears to be therefore no reason why the Chairman of the Committee on Foreign Relations should

---

[7] Not printed.

not now proceed to secure the necessary action by the Senate and I shall be glad to be informed as soon as this action has been taken. I have [etc.]

(For the Ambassador:)

H. G. CHILTON

711.428/804

The Secretary of State to the British Ambassador (Howard)

WASHINGTON, *May 21, 1924.*

EXCELLENCY: I have the honor to acknowledge the receipt of your note No. 439, of May 16, 1924, in further reference to the Convention for the preservation of the Halibut Fishery of the Northern Pacific Ocean signed by representatives of the United States and Great Britain on March 2, 1923, and to legislation which the Government of Canada has under consideration in connection with the protection of the halibut fishery.

The reference in the first paragraph of your note to the purpose of the Chairman of the Committee on Foreign Relations of the Senate to bring the Halibut Fishery Convention up for reconsideration by the Senate as soon as he is informed that the Canadian Parliament has passed the legislation represents inaccurately the circumstance as stated in my note of May 12 that the Chairman of the Committee will take such action as soon as the legislation has become law. It may be that this discrepancy of statement is of little practical importance since from the statements in your note it appears that the Royal assent is regarded as a formality of the execution of which there is no uncertainty.

I am bringing your statement of the situation to the attention of the Chairman of the Committee on Foreign Relations for his consideration.

Accept [etc.]   CHARLES E. HUGHES

711.428/807

The Secretary of State to the British Ambassador (Howard)

WASHINGTON, *May 27, 1924.*

EXCELLENCY: With further reference to the convention for the preservation of the Halibut Fishery of the Northern Pacific Ocean, signed by the United States and Great Britain on March 2, 1923, which is now before the Committee on Foreign Relations of the Senate and the legislation which the Government of Canada has under consideration in connection with the protection of the Halibut Fishery, I have the honor to state that the Chairman of the Committee on Foreign Relations has informed me that he cannot expect the committee to act on the convention until the Royal assent shall have been given to the Canadian legislation.

The Chairman desires to bring the convention up for final action at the earliest possible moment. Unless approval of the convention is given by the Senate during the present session of Congress, which probably will adjourn within a short time, it may not be possible to bring the convention into operation before the beginning of the proposed close season in November next, the effective operation of the convention thereby being postponed for another year.

This Government is hopeful that the Governor General will find it convenient to give his formal assent at an early date to the Halibut Fishery Amendment Act recently passed by the two houses of the Canadian Parliament.

Accept [etc.]   CHARLES E. HUGHES

711.428/813

The British Ambassador (Howard) to the Secretary of State

No. 479   WASHINGTON, *May 28, 1924.*

SIR: I have the honour to refer to the note which you were so good as to address to me on the 27th instant regarding the convention for the preservation of the Halibut Fishery of the Northern Pacific, signed on March 2nd, 1923, and to inform you that I am in receipt of a communication from the Government of Canada to the effect that the Halibut Fishery Amendment Act, recently passed by the two Houses of the Canadian Parliament, received the Royal assent on the evening of the 27th instant. The Bill in question thus becomes effective as law.

I have [etc.]   ESME HOWARD

711.428/813a

The Secretary of State to the British Ambassador (Howard)

WASHINGTON, *June 4, 1924.*

EXCELLENCY: I have the honor and the pleasure to inform you that the Senate, by its Resolution of May 31, 1924, gave its advice and consent to the ratification of the Convention between the United States and His Britannic Majesty for the preservation of the halibut fisheries of the northern Pacific Ocean and including Bering Sea, signed at Washington on March 2, 1923, and that I shall be prepared to effect the exchange of ratifications [8] at your convenience.

Accept [etc.]   CHARLES E. HUGHES

---

[8] Ratifications exchanged at Washington, Oct. 21, 1924, by the Secretary of State and the Minister of Justice for Canada; proclaimed by the President, Oct. 22, 1924.

RENEWED CONSIDERATION OF A JOINT PROJECT FOR THE IMPROVEMENT OF THE ST. LAWRENCE WATERWAY [9]

711.42157 Sa 29/106

The Secretary of State to the British Chargé (Chilton)

WASHINGTON, *November 17, 1923.*

SIR: The Ambassador informed me by his note No. 431 of June 3, 1922 [10] that the Canadian Government had not had opportunity to give to the report of the International Joint Commission in regard to the St. Lawrence River improvement scheme and the accompanying report of the engineers the careful consideration which the importance of the subject merits and that on account of the magnitude of the project and the large outlay of public money involved the Canadian Government was of the opinion that it was not expedient to deal with the matter at that time.

Because of the interest which continues among the people of the United States in the project for the improvement of the St. Lawrence River, I have the honor to inquire whether the Canadian Government would now be inclined to give consideration to the matter and to enter into negotiations along the lines suggested in my note of May 17, 1922.[11]

Accept [etc.]   CHARLES E. HUGHES

711.42157 Sa 29/150

The British Chargé (Chilton) to the Secretary of State

No. 97   WASHINGTON, *January 30, 1924.*

SIR: I have the honour to refer to the note which you were so good as to address to me on November 17th last, regarding the St. Lawrence River improvement scheme and to inform you, by request of His Excellency the Governor-General of Canada, that the Dominion Government have had under consideration the contents of your note addressed to Sir Auckland Geddes on May 17th, 1922. In that note you suggested either the immediate conclusion of a treaty looking to the development of the St. Lawrence waterway along the lines recommended by the International Joint Commission in its report and providing for the constitution of a Joint Commission charged with the formulation of a complete plan which would be subject to the approval of the two Governments, or, alternatively, the constitution of a Joint Commission of experts to make preliminary studies and investigations and to frame the draft of a treaty.

---

[9] For previous correspondence concerning the St. Lawrence Waterway, see *Foreign Relations*, 1922, vol. I, pp. 677 ff.

[10] *Ibid.*, p. 679.

[11] *Ibid.*, p. 677.

The Dominion Government point out that the report of the International Joint Commission recommended that, before any work was carried out, the Joint Engineering Board, whose proposals it generally approved, should be enlarged, and that once so enlarged the said Board should further consider the technical aspects of the problems in detail and decide upon the plan which should be adopted.

While the Government of Canada desire to give further consideration to the suggestions put forward in your note of May 17th, 1922, they are of opinion that the proposal made by the International Joint Commission should be acted upon without further delay. The Dominion Government are accordingly prepared to appoint additional engineers to enlarge the Joint Engineering Board with a view to the Board undertaking the preparation of a final report covering the engineering features of the whole project, including its cost. The Government of Canada intend, further, to form a committee which will, in consultation with the Canadian members of the Joint Engineering Board, enquire fully from a national standpoint into the wide questions involved, and they hope shortly to be in a position to take further action on the proposals made by the United States Government.

Meanwhile the Government of Canada would be glad to learn the views of the United States Government in regard to the number of additional engineers who should be appointed by each Government to the Joint Engineering Board. The Dominion Government are also ready to nominate one or more technical officers to discuss with similar United States officers the form which the instructions to the enlarged Joint Engineering Board should take, and the time within which the Board should be directed to report.

In expressing the hope of the Government of Canada that the above proposals will be agreeable to the United States Government, I have the honour to inform you that Lord Byng of Vimy would be grateful if arrangements could be made by telegraph for their publication simultaneously in Washington and Ottawa.

I have [etc.] H. G. Chilton

711.42157 Sa 29/150

The Secretary of State to the British Chargé (Chilton)

Washington, *February 27, 1924.*

Sir: In your note of January 30, 1924, in regard to the project for joint action by the United States and Canada for the improvement of the St. Lawrence River between Montreal and Lake Ontario for navigation and the development of water power, you informed me that while the Government of the Dominion of Canada desires to give further consideration to the suggestions brought forward in my note of May 17, 1922, to Sir Auckland Geddes with a view to carrying out the recommendations made by the International Joint Commission, the Dominion Government is nevertheless prepared to act without delay on the recommendation for the enlargement of the Joint Engineering Board which assisted the Commission in making the investigation of the project and to appoint additional engineers to the Board with a view to having it undertake the preparation of a final report covering the engineering features of the whole project, including its cost.

You informed me also that the Government of Canada intends to form a committee which will in consultation with the Canadian members of the Joint Engineering Board, inquire fully from a national standpoint into the wide questions involved in the project.

In reply permit me to say that this Government is gratified to learn that the Canadian Government hopes shortly to be in a position to take further action on the proposals made in my note of May 17, 1922, and meanwhile is especially pleased to be advised that the Government of Canada intends to create a committee for the, purpose described in your note. This Government, similarly, will immediately constitute a national committee which will in consultation with the American members of the Joint Engineering Board make adequate inquiry from a national standpoint into the questions involved to the end that the project for the improvement of the St. Lawrence River for navigation and the development of its water power may be carried forward as speedily as possible.

This Government is glad to give its assent to the suggestion that the Joint Engineering Board should be enlarged and, in response to the request of the Canadian Government for its view as to the number of additional engineers which should be appointed, suggests that two engineers be added to the Board by each Government, the membership of the Board thus being increased to six, three of whom would be representatives of the United States and three would be representatives of Canada. In connection with this enlargement of the Board it may be noted that the first of the recommendations made by the International Joint Commission was that the Governments of the United States and Canada enter into an arrangement by way of treaty for a scheme of improvement of the St. Lawrence River between Montreal and Lake Ontario. It would appear that the Commission did not contemplate that negotiations for a treaty should be postponed until after a report should be made by an enlarged board of engineers but that negotiations should forthwith be opened, that the proposed works between Montreal and Lake

Ontario should "be based upon the report of the Engineering Board" accompanying the report of the Commission, and that the Governments should have the benefit of the advice of an enlarged Board of Engineers before a "final decision" should be reached.

This Government would propose that the instructions to the enlarged Engineering Board should be prepared in joint conference by the two advisory committees which the Governments of Canada and the United States intend to establish, as indicated in your note and this reply, and that the two committees should accordingly be empowered to meet in joint conference for the purpose of formulating such instructions. However, the instructions would be given to the Board of Engineers by the Governments and the report of the engineers would be made to the Governments.

As it appears that the report of the Board of Engineers of June 24, 1921, while of a preliminary character, as contemplated in their instructions, nevertheless presented a general plan believed to be practicable in its main features, this Government would desire to have included in the first instructions to the enlarged Board the two fundamental questions whether the scheme for the improvement of the St. Lawrence Waterway which the Board presented in its report of June 24, 1921, is practicable and whether the estimates of costs made by it require revision. The time within which the Board should make its report should, as was suggested by the Canadian Government, be determined in advance and stated in the instructions. It is believed that the fundamental questions can be reported upon within a short time. If the suggestion that the instructions to the Joint Engineering Board be prepared by the two advisory committees in joint conference be acceptable to the Canadian Government the appointment of technical officers especially for this purpose as proposed by the Canadian Government would not be necessary.

This Government further suggests that the two committees be empowered to meet from time to time in joint session in order to prepare supplemental instructions for the Board of Engineers as occasion may require, and to consider and develop the broader aspects of the whole matter so that each committee may be as helpful to the other as possible.

This Government is hopeful that the foregoing proposals will be acceptable to the Government of Canada and I should be pleased if arrangements can be made by telegraph for publishing them simultaneously at Washington and Ottawa.

Accept [etc.]   CHARLES E. HUGHES

711.42157 Sa 29/164

The British Ambassador (Howard) to the Secretary of State

No. 228   WASHINGTON, *March 12, 1924.*

SIR: I have the honour to inform you that the Government of Canada have had under consideration the contents of the note which you were so good as to address to Mr. Chilton on the 27th ultimo in connection with the proposed improvement of the St. Lawrence River Waterway, and they concur in the suggestion of the Government of the United States that two additional engineers be appointed by each Government to the Joint Engineering Board whose membership will thus be increased to six, three members thereof representing the United States and three representing the Dominion of Canada. The Canadian Government desire me to express regret, however, that, owing to the death on the 3rd ultimo of Mr. W. A. Bowden, the late Canadian member of the Board, all three Canadian representatives will have to be new appointees.

The Dominion Government have noted the proposal of the United States Government that the national committees to be appointed by the two Governments concerned should meet from time to time for the purpose of formulating the terms in which the matters to be enquired into by the enlarged Joint Engineering Board should be defined. In this connection I would point out that the intention of the Dominion Government in constituting a national committee is that the body in question should be advisory to the Government of Canada, and it is felt that to impose upon this body, at all events at the outset, the duties suggested would be inconsistent with the purpose which it is intended to serve and would change the character of the said body from one primarily national to one of international significance. The Government of Canada consider that the terms of reference can, at least in the first instance, be settled quite adequately and in all probability more promptly in the manner set forth in the note which Mr. Chilton had the honour to address to you on January 30th last, and they desire me to express the hope that the Government of the United States will concur in this view. Immediately upon being advised to that effect the Government of Canada will be ready to appoint a technical officer for the purpose named, and in the event of the Government of the United States considering the appointment of more than one such officer to be desirable, they would have no objection to making an additional appointment.

The Government of Canada are entirely agreeable to the inclusion in the first instructions to the enlarged Joint Engineering Board of the two fundamental questions referred to in your note under reply,

namely, whether the scheme for the improvement of the St. Lawrence Waterway which the Engineering Board submitted in their
report of June 24th, 1921, is practicable and whether the estimates
of the costs put forward by the Board require revision. On their
part, the Dominion Government would suggest that amongst other
matters, the Board should be directed to enquire into the extent to
which the water levels in the River at and below Montreal, as well
as the River and lake levels generally may be affected.

The Dominion Government desire me to suggest that, subject
to the concurrence of the United States Government, this correspondence may be released on the night of Friday the 14th instant
for publication simultaneously in Washington and in Ottawa on the
morning of Saturday the 15th instant, and in these circumstances, I
have the honour to request that I may be favoured with the views of
the United States Government on this matter as soon as possible.

    I have [etc.]   Esme Howard

711.42157 Sa 29/179

The Secretary of State to the British Ambassador (Howard)

Washington, *April 28, 1924.*

Excellency: In your note of March 12, 1924, you informed me
further in regard to the views of the Canadian Government with
reference to the proposal for joint action by the United States and
Canada for the improvement of the St. Lawrence River between
Montreal and Lake Ontario for navigation and the development of
water power.

In pursuance of the intention of this Government, as stated in
my note of February 27, 1924, the President has appointed a national
committee of nine members having as its Chairman the Honorable
Herbert Hoover, Secretary of Commerce, which will act as an advisory committee to this Government on all questions that may arise
in the consideration of the project.

While regretting that the Canadian Government does not desire
that the committees for the two Governments shall meet in joint
conferences, at least at the outset, to prepare instructions for the
enlarged joint engineering board and to consider the broader aspects
of the project for the proposed development of the St. Lawrence
waterway, this Government would be grateful if you would inform
the Canadian Government that the National Committee for the
United States will be prepared at all times to meet in conference
with the Canadian Committee in the event that circumstances should
develop which in the view of the Canadian Government would cause
it to appear that joint conferences by the two committees or by rep-

resentatives of the committees might be desirable for the consideration of any questions arising in connection with the project.

This Government is pleased to note that the Canadian Government concurs in its suggestion that the enlarged Joint Engineering Board shall consist of six members, three representing the United States and three representing Canada, and to accept the proposal of the Canadian Government that two technical officers be appointed by each Government for the purpose of formulating the terms in which the matters to be inquired into by the Board shall be defined.

The United States will be represented on the Joint Engineering Board by Colonel Edgar Jadwin, Colonel William Kelly, and Lieutenant Colonel George B. Pillsbury, Corps of Engineers, United States Army. Colonel Jadwin and Lieutenant Colonel Pillsbury will also act as technical officers for the United States to formulate in collaboration with the technical officers to be designated by the Canadian Government the instructions which will be given to the engineers.

This Government is also pleased to note the acceptance by the Government of Canada of the proposal of this Government that there shall be included in the first instructions to the Joint Engineering Board the two fundamental questions, whether the scheme for the improvement of the St. Lawrence River waterway which the Engineering Board submitted in its report of June 24, 1921, is practicable and whether the estimates of the costs of the project made by the Board require revision, and to agree to the suggestion made by the Dominion Government that amongst other matters the enlarged Board shall be directed to inquire into the extent to which the water levels in the St. Lawrence River at and below Montreal, as well as the river and lake levels generally, will be affected by the execution of the project.

It will, of course, be understood that the instructions drafted by the technical officers will be subject to review and approval by the appropriate officials of the respective Governments before they would be given to the Board of Engineers by the Governments in conformity with the remark made on that point in my note of February 27, 1924. In connection with such review and approval, the instructions drafted by the technical officers will be submitted by the officers for the United States to the National Committee for this Government.

This Government would be pleased to be informed at the early convenience of the Canadian Government of the names of the technical officers appointed by that Government in order that the officers for the two Governments may make arrangements with as little delay as possible to collaborate in the drafting of the instructions for the joint engineering Board. This Government would also be pleased to be informed in due course of the names of the Canadian members of the Joint Engineering Board.[12]

Accept [etc.] CHARLES E. HUGHES

PROTESTS BY THE CANADIAN GOVERNMENT AGAINST FURTHER DIVERSION OF THE WATERS OF THE GREAT LAKES

711.4216 M 58/20

The British Chargé (Chilton) to the Secretary of State

No. 1111 WASHINGTON, *December 29, 1923.*

SIR: My attention has been drawn by the Government of Canada to the fact that about the month of June last the Government of the United States were granted an injunction restraining the Sanitary District of Chicago from diverting water from Lake Michigan, but that this injunction would not take effect for a period of six months in order to allow time for the Sanitary District of Chicago to appeal to the Supreme Court of the United States. I understand that such an appeal has been lodged but that the Supreme Court has not yet acted upon it.

I have the honour to inform you that the Government of Canada have received numerous communications from various bodies and interests directly concerned with this question, protesting against this diversion of water from Lake Michigan and I would further explain that, owing to the injurious effects of such diversion both upon navigation and water power, the Dominion Government still maintain their attitude of opposition as already explained to the United States Government in Sir Auckland Geddes' note No. 285 of April 22nd, 1921,[13] and previous correspondence.

In these circumstances, the Governor General of Canada has asked me to enquire the present status of the legal proceedings instituted by the Government of the United States with a view to preventing any increase in the diversion of water from Lake Michigan, and to add that the Dominion Government confidently hope that these legal proceedings will be vigorously pressed by the United States Government.

I have [etc.] H. G. CHILTON

---

[12] For further details, see *Report of Joint Board of Engineers on St. Lawrence Waterway Project* (Ottawa: F. A. Acland, printer to the King's Most Excellent Majesty, 1927).

[13] Not printed; see *Correspondence Relating to Diversion of the Waters of the Great Lakes by the Sanitary District of Chicago, from March 27, 1912, to October 17, 1927* (Ottawa: F. A. Acland, printer to the King's Most Excellent Majesty, 1928), p. 21.

711.4216 M 58/22

The British Chargé (Chilton) to the Secretary of State

No. 144   WASHINGTON, *February 13, 1924.*

SIR: I have the honour to inform you that the Government of
Canada have recently noted that a special Committee of the United
States Senate has been appointed by the Vice-President to investigate the problem of a nine-foot channel in the waterway from the
Great Lakes to the Gulf of Mexico and to enquire into the navigability of the Mississippi, Ohio and Missouri rivers, with a view presumably to exploring the possibility of establishing direct maritime
communication between the Great Lakes and the South Atlantic and
Pacific Oceans. The Dominion Government further understand that
certain legislation now before Congress proceeds, after defining the
nature of the work to be undertaken in the stretch above mentioned,
to confer upon the Sanitary District of Chicago the legal right to
divert for sewage dilution and navigation purposes, 10,000 cubic feet
of water per second from Lake Michigan upon condition that the
said district shall pay into the Treasury of the United States such
sums as may be estimated to be its reasonable share of the cost of
constructing compensating works at several points for the purpose
of controlling and restoring to the lakes in question the levels lost
by reason of this diversion of water.

In this connection, the Dominion Government observe that no provision is made for the restoration of the levels of the St. Lawrence
River from its head to tidewater. In other words, the restoration to
be provided in the legislation above-named is to be in the waters
where United States navigation predominates but no such restoration is provided for the waters so extensively used by Canadian
shipping.

Reports submitted to the Canadian Government during recent
months refer not only to the loss of levels that affect navigation, but
also to the diversion of water for power purposes both in the international stretches where compensation may be determined and in the
international stretches below Cornwall in the Province of Quebec.
In that regard, Lord Byng of Vimy desires me to point out that the
limit of 10,000 cubic feet of water per second, as contemplated by
the proposed legislation, is about 1,500 cubic [feet] per second more
than is being diverted at present, and His Excellency considers it
possible that the proposed legislation may mean that 10,000 cubic
feet per second is allowed for diversion and power at Lockport,
while additional water power will doubtless be required for lockages.

In view of the above, I have the honour to inform you that the Government of Canada are unalterably opposed to the proposed diversion of water from the Great Lakes watershed to that of the Mississippi, to the great detriment of navigation from Sault Ste. Marie to tidewater. The diversion that has already taken place at Chicago has lowered the waters of the Great Lakes to an extent that is now common knowledge. This affects harbours upon which many million dollars have been expended in deepening operations. It also affects the locksills of the Sault Ste. Marie Canals, the Welland Canal and the St. Lawrence Canals and, further, this diversion of water has a most injurious effect upon the ocean shipping channel between Montreal and the sea, where the Government of the Dominion have spent many more millions of dollars in dredging operations. How great have been the injuries sustained by navigation interests may be seen from the fact that every inch of navigable water means an additional 60 to 80 tons of carrying capacity. The waters of the Great Lakes are the heritage of both the people of the United States and the people of Canada, and the Dominion Government are of opinion that it is quite obvious that these waters should be conserved for the interests of both peoples. The Government of Canada, therefore, sincerely hope that the Government of the United States will not only not permit any further diversion of water from Lake Michigan, but will intimate to, and if necessary insist upon, the Sanitary District of Chicago adopting some more scientific method of sewage disposal than is foreshadowed at present.

I have the honour to request that I may in due course be furnished with an expression of the views of the United States Government upon the contents of this note, for communication to His Excellency the Governor-General of Canada.

I have [etc.]   H. G. CHILTON

711.4216 M 58/21

The Secretary of State to the British Chargé (Chilton)

WASHINGTON, *February 16, 1924.*

SIR: With further reference to your note of December 29, 1923, in regard to the legal proceedings instituted by the Government of the United States against the Sanitary District of Chicago to prevent the unauthorized diversion of water from Lake Michigan, I have the honor to inform you that the Department has been advised by the Solicitor General of the United States that an appeal has been taken by the Sanitary District of Chicago from the decision of the

United States District Court in favor of the Government and that the appeal is still pending in the Supreme Court of the United States. The Solicitor General further stated that as soon as the record of the case shall have been printed a motion will be submitted to the court to advance the case for early argument.

Accept [etc.]

For the Secretary of State:
LELAND HARRISON

711.4216 M 58/25

The British Ambassador (Howard) to the Secretary of State

No. 256   WASHINGTON, *March 21, 1924.*

SIR: I have the honour to refer to the note which you were so good as to address to Mr. Chilton on February 16th last and to inform you, by request of His Excellency the Governor-General of Canada, that the question of the diversion of water from the St. Lawrence River watershed into that of the Mississippi continues to cause grave concern to the Government and people of Canada, more especially in view of the provisions of the bill which has been introduced into Congress in regard to this matter. The Dominion Government desire me to express the hope that no action will be taken either to confirm or permit the claim of the Sanitary District of Chicago to continue the diversion of water referred to above, inasmuch as this would adversely affect navigation on the Great Lakes and the St. Lawrence River as well as the actual or prospective development of power upon river and inter-lake connecting waters.

The attitude of the Government of Canada in opposition to and in protest against the most injurious effects of this proposed diversion of water has been consistently maintained throughout and has been made known to the United States Government. The Dominion Government feel that it would be most unfortunate if, now that the development of the St. Lawrence Waterway for navigation and power purposes is under consideration, any action should be taken which might adversely affect the possibility of such development, and they trust that these views will meet with the agreement of the United States Government.

In this connection I would draw your particular attention to the contents of Mr. Chilton's note No. 144 of February 13th, the receipt of which you were good enough to acknowledge on the 15th ultimo,[14] and to enquire whether you are yet in a position to inform me of the attitude of the United States authorities in this matter. At the same time it would be a matter of convenience both to myself and to the

---

[14] Not printed.

Government of Canada to learn whether the time has yet been fixed for the hearings of the Committee, which you foreshadowed in your note of the 18th ultimo,[15] and if so whether Mr. Stewart[16] will be at liberty to attend them.

I have [etc.] ESME HOWARD

711.4216 M 58/25

The Secretary of State to the British Ambassador (Howard)

WASHINGTON, *April 2, 1924.*

EXCELLENCY: Further reference is made to the note from your Embassy No. 130 of February 9, 1924,[15] in which it was stated that the Government of the Dominion of Canada desired to send Mr. W. J. Stewart, Chief Hydrographer of the Dominion Government to be present in its behalf at hearings of a special committee of the Senate appointed to investigate the problem of a nine foot channel in the proposed waterway from the Great Lakes to the Gulf of Mexico, and to the inquiry made in your note No. 256 of March 21, 1924, in regard to the date on which these hearings will be held, and whether Mr. Stewart will be at liberty to be present.

The Committee of the Senate to which reference was made in the Embassy's note of February 9, 1924, has not held hearings during the present session of Congress or yet arranged to hold them.

I am informed by the Chairman of the Committee on Rivers and Harbors of the House of Representatives that this Committee has arranged to resume hearings on April 15, on bills dealing with the diversion of waters from Lake Michigan, the most important one, I understand, being known as the Hull Bill (H. R. 5475). The Committee desires to obtain all the information it can which will be helpful towards a correct determination of the matters which it has under consideration. It will welcome the help of all who have information of value relating to these matters, and will be glad to have Mr. Stewart attend the hearings.

Accept [etc.] CHARLES E. HUGHES

711.4216 M 58/43

The British Ambassador (Howard) to the Secretary of State

No. 533 WASHINGTON, *June 13, 1924.*

SIR: I have the honour to refer to my note No. 256 of the 21st of March and to other correspondence on the subject of the diversion

---

[15] Not printed.
[16] W. J. Stewart, chief hydrographer of the Canadian Government.

of water from the Great Lakes as a result of the Chicago drainage system, and at the request of His Excellency the Governor General of Canada to call your attention to the fact that this matter has come up for discussion in the Canadian Parliament on several different occasions during the current session.

On each occasion, and with increasing emphasis amounting to unanimity, demands have been made upon the Dominion Government to renew the protests which have already been lodged against the action of the Sanitary District of Chicago, in continuing and seeking to extend their claim to diversion of water from the St. Lawrence Watershed into that of the Mississippi, with consequent adverse effect upon important interests in the navigation both of the Great Lakes and of the St. Lawrence River, and the development of power, actual and prospective, upon the River itself and upon the waters connecting the Lakes.

The Dominion Government are constrained to believe that unless some reassuring message can be made to the people of Canada that favourable progress is being made in the matter, public opinion throughout the Dominion will become so aroused as to render exceedingly difficult the amicable consideration and discussion of the far less-reaching problem and issue incident to the Great Lakes and the International Waterway. The Government of Canada are fully aware that in many parts of the United States public opinion is similarly being aroused, and are not ignorant of the fact that the United States Government is not less anxious than they are to see a settlement speedily effected.

It is for these reasons, therefore, while unwilling to prefer any request or take any steps which might add to the existing embarrassment, the Dominion Government feel that they must once again direct the attention of the United States Government to the serious situation, which has developed, and in doing so express the hope that it may be possible now to obtain an expression of the views of the United States Government on the points raised in my note of March 21st. The Government of Canada feel that it would be most advantageous for them to obtain a statement from the competent United States authorities which will definitely define the position as it now stands, and they trust that such a statement will be of a reassuring character as to probable future developments.

In bringing these facts to your notice, I venture to hope that I may receive an expression of the views of the United States Government at your earliest convenience for communication to the Dominion Government.

In this connection I would add that the Dominion Government propose to publish forthwith the note No. 256 which I addressed to you on March 21st.

I have [etc.]

(For the Ambassador)
HERBERT W. BROOKS [17]

711.4216 M 58/43

The Secretary of State to the British Ambassador (Howard)

WASHINGTON, *June 28, 1924.*

EXCELLENCY: I have the honour to acknowledge the receipt of your note No. 533 of June 13, 1924, in further reference to the diversion of water from Lake Michigan at Chicago.

In previous correspondence in regard to this matter reference was made to the suit brought by this Government to restrain the Sanitary District of Chicago from diverting a larger quantity of water from Lake Michigan than is authorized by the permit issued to the Sanitary District by the Secretary of War and to bills introduced in Congress during the past session with reference to the construction of the proposed waterway from Lake Michigan to the Mississippi River and the sewage disposal system of Chicago.

The suit for an injunction, which is now pending on appeal in the Supreme Court of the United States, has been assigned for argument on November 10, 1924, early in the next term of the court. The position of the United States as plaintiff in this litigation is evidence of the interest which this Government has in the preservation of the navigability of the Great Lakes system of waterways. Until the Court has rendered an opinion in the case this Department will not be in a position to furnish the Canadian Government with further information in regard to the views of this Government concerning the questions involved in the litigation.

Hearings were held in March, April and May, 1924, by the Committee on Rivers and Harbors of the House of Representatives on the several bills introduced in Congress. In order that the Committee might be fully informed of the views of the Canadian Government in regard to the diversion of water from Lake Michigan I sent copies of your notes of February 13, 1924, and March 21, 1924, to the Chairman of the Committee. I have also sent him a copy of your note of June 13, 1924. In my note of April 2, 1924, I informed you that the Committee would be glad to have Mr. W. J. Stewart,

[17] Secretary of Embassy.

Chief Hydrographer of the Canadian Government attend the hearings. The bills were still before the Committee on the adjournment of the session of Congress on June 7, 1924.

I regret that the formulation of a comprehensive statement of the views of this Government concerning the diversion of water from Lake Michigan will have to be deferred for a time because certain of the questions involved are under consideration by Congress and the Supreme Court both of which are at the present time in recess. This Government is prepared, however, to include consideration of the diversions of water from Lake Michigan among the questions to be referred by the United States and Canada to the Joint Board of Engineers appointed for the further investigation of the proposed Saint Lawrence Waterway,[18] as will be fully explained in my note in regard to the instructions to be given to the engineers. It would be understood, of course, that the submission of this question to the Joint Board of Engineers would be without prejudice to the rights of this Government with reference to the diversion of water from Lake Michigan or the position which it may take concerning questions that may arise because of such diversions.

In connection with the statement made in your note under acknowledgment that it is the purpose of the Canadian Government to publish forthwith your note No. 256 of March 21, 1924, I invite your attention to the release of my note of April 2, 1924, given in my note of April 9, 1924.[19]

Accept [etc.]   CHARLES E. HUGHES

---

[18] See note of Apr. 28, 1924, to the British Ambassador, p. 347.
[19] Latter not printed.

CHILE

RESIGNATION OF PRESIDENT ALESSANDRI AND THE EXERCISE OF INFORMAL RELATIONS BETWEEN THE UNITED STATES EMBASSY AND THE NEW ADMINISTRATION AT SANTIAGO

825.001 A1 2/6 : Telegram

The Ambassador in Chile (Collier) to the Secretary of State

SANTIAGO, *September 9, 1924—3 p. m.*
[Received September 9—10:10 a. m.]

53. Alessandri resigned last night rather than accede to Junta's demands.[1] He dissolved Congress. He arrived at Embassy accompanied by various members of his immediate family at 3 a. m. seeking asylum which was granted for the night. General Altamirano, head of the Government and now acting President, was duly informed. I gave out the following statement to the press:

"Don Arturo Alessandri came to the American Embassy after midnight accompanied by members of his family stating that he has resigned as President of Chile. He asked the hospitality of the Embassy. It was granted to him. No Chilean ever asked the hospitality of the Embassy and was refused."

.   .   .   .

COLLIER

825.00/282 : Telegram

The Ambassador in Chile (Collier) to the Secretary of State

[Paraphrase]

SANTIAGO, *September 9, 1924—4 p. m.*
[Received 8:30 p. m.]

55. Foreign Minister in his personal capacity and in the name of the Government called to express thanks for the hospitality which I extended to Alessandri; also for the form of press statement included in my number 53, September 9. Several hundred people, including many of the opposition, have visited the Embassy with full permission of the Government to pay their respects to Alessandri. All appeared deeply touched by the fact that I had refrained from

---

[1] La Junta de Gobierno de Septiembre.

saying that I had afforded him asylum and instead had stated that I had extended him hospitality thereby avoiding the implication that his life was in danger. Complete calm and order prevail.

COLLIER

825.00/284 : Telegram

The Ambassador in Chile (Collier) to the Secretary of State

[Paraphrase]

SANTIAGO, *September 10, 1924—7 p. m.*
[Received September 11—9 : 20 a. m.]

56. Tonight Alessandri and family depart for Buenos Aires with Europe as their ultimate destination. I shall accompany them to Mendoza, returning Friday evening. I am taking this course at the request of the family and with the full permission of the Government. On two occasions Alessandri tendered his resignation but each time it was rejected by Congress. The latter, however, under the Constitution has granted him a leave of 6 months. He stated to me that he intends again to resign when he crosses the frontier, inasmuch as he believes it to be inconsistent with his self-respect and dignity to remain in office when he is not permitted by the military junta to perform the duties of his office. In a sense his resignation is absolutely voluntary although his departure from Chile is a result of his knowledge that if he did not depart he would be forced to by the junta. The junta wants him to accept the leave granted and not resign. In keeping with the Constitution General Altamirano as Minister of the Interior assumed full power as Acting President. The Cabinet offered to send in their resignations but the members have all been retained. No other faction or party claims to be the Government. Thousands of people throughout Chile undoubtedly do not approve of what has happened. However, I have learned of no protests, especially by organized factions. Everything has been done according to constitutional forms. The exertion of pressure has been by intimation rather than by direct threats. No act of violence has yet occurred, but if compliance had not been given force would undoubtedly have been used. The nation as a whole seems inclined to accept the present Government at least until a new Constitution is adopted or until new elections bring about a change. The legality of the Government is not challenged by the press. Under the existing situation I believe that the new Cabinet must be recognized as legal and General Altamirano as constitutionally selected. I believe most and possibly all members of the diplomatic corps hold this view. It is practically certain, however, that the present Congress will be done away with. . . . It cannot be constitu-

tionally dissolved but the junta will certainly ask its members to resign and if necessary dissolve it by force. Please instruct me concerning the recognition of the new Government.

COLLIER

825.00/285 : Telegram

The Secretary of State to the Ambassador in Chile (*Collier*)

[Paraphrase]

WASHINGTON, *September 12, 1924—2 p. m.*

40. Since you have stated that constitutional forms have been observed in the executive branch of the Government, the Government of the United States does not desire to raise the question of recognition.

Department believes it advisable to avoid discussion of recognition and to let relations continue as at present without making public statements which seemingly are not called for.

HUGHES

825.00/285 Suppl. : Telegram

The Secretary of State to the Ambassador in Chile (*Collier*)

[Paraphrase]

WASHINGTON, *September 13, 1924—1 p. m.*

42. Refer to my September 12, 2 p. m. According to press reports military junta has accepted Alessandri's resignation. It is reported from Buenos Aires that Alessandri has made statement that he was banished and that there is no constitutional government in Chile.

You are instructed to avoid any formal relations with the new regime until the situation clears up, but do not make your course conspicuous. Should a situation arise where it would be impossible to remain noncommittal telegraph Department at once.

HUGHES

825.00/287 : Telegram

The Secretary of State to the Ambassador in Chile (*Collier*)

[Paraphrase]

WASHINGTON, *September 15, 1924—5 p. m.*

43. Department appreciates desirability of avoiding any steps which might have an unfavorable reaction on the local situation. However, the attitude of the Government of the United States so far as the recognition of the new regime is concerned must be guided not simply by the sincerity and objectives of those in control but

also by those general principles which must govern our policy in extending recognition to any administration which may come into power in another nation by extra-constitutional means. At the present time it does not seem clear that the Government of the United States would be justified in assuming that the new regime was sufficiently established to warrant formal relations. For the present you will maintain frank, friendly, but informal relations, and you may make it clear that the United States is only pursuing that course which it invariably takes in like cases in other parts of the world.

HUGHES

825.01/21

The Secretary of State to the Chilean Ambassador (Mathieu)

WASHINGTON, *October 9, 1924.*

EXCELLENCY: While it is not the intention of this Government to discontinue dealing with you as Ambassador of Chile, I desire to state in order to avoid misapprehension that it should be understood that this Government's action in so doing is not to be construed as a recognition of the régime now functioning in Chile as other than the *de facto* authorities in control of the administration of Chile.

Accept [etc.]   CHARLES E. HUGHES

825.01/13 : Telegram

The Secretary of State to the Ambassador in Chile (Collier)

WASHINGTON, *October 9, 1924—5 p. m.*

52. Your 72, October 6, 6 p. m., paragraph 2.[2] You may legalize documents issued by officials mentioned and authenticate their signatures indicating that the officials in question are the *de facto* authorities now functioning in Chile. Such legalization with such indication does not constitute recognition of a new government. It is the policy of the United States either to recognize or not to recognize a new government as such. It does not now recognize a régime functioning in a country as a so-called *de facto* government. Until circumstances impel it to recognize a régime as the government of a country the dealings with that régime are to be deemed merely dealings with the authorities actually in control and as having no other significance. Their character should therefore be made clear in order to prevent misconstruction.

HUGHES

---

[2] Not printed; it requested instructions with regard to authentication of documents bearing signatures of officers of new regime.

CHINA

CIVIL WAR IN NORTHERN CHINA RESULTING IN THE OVERTHROW OF PRESIDENT TSAO KUN AND THE ESTABLISHMENT OF A PROVISIONAL GOVERNMENT [1]

893.00/5481 : Telegram

The Chargé in China (Bell) to the Secretary of State

PEKING, *August 26, 1924—3 p. m.*
[Received August 26—10:10 a. m.]

304. For past month rumors have been current of possibilities of conflict involving Wu Pei-fu; Chi Hsieh-yuan, Inspector General of Kiangsu, Anhui and Kiangsi; Lu Yung-hsiang, Anfu leader and Tuchun of Chekiang in control of Shanghai; and ultimately Chang Tso-lin. Lately and especially within the past few days rumors have crystallized and reports now to hand from reliable sources to the effect that war is quite probable between Chekiang and Kiangsu, men and stores being mobilized and warlike activity increasingly evident in those regions. Real cause for apprehension is not conflict between above Provinces but that if clash occurs there it will almost inevitably bring on a Chihli-Fengtien war.

Factors against present conflict are flood conditions, lack of funds, and mutual jealousies. As however it is impossible to gauge ramifications of Chinese politics which may actuate Wu, Chi, Lu and Chang at any given time, it is impossible to say with any degree of certainty what course events will take although optimistic tone seems to prevail that armed clash will be averted.

Am keeping in as close touch as possible with situation and will report further if and when it seems expedient.

BELL

893.00/5483 : Telegram

The Chargé in China (Bell) to the Secretary of State

PEKING, *August 28, 1924—3 p. m.*
[Received August 28—9:30 a. m.]

312. My 304, August 26, 3 p. m. Following from consul general Shanghai:

"August 27, 6 p. m. Conditions becoming graver hourly. Military took charge of the railway stations, closing gates this morning,

---

[1] For previous correspondence concerning political affairs in China, see *Foreign Relations*, 1923, vol. I, pp. 503 ff.

but through intervention of British consul general, General Ho was induced to allow existing foreign and Chinese staff to continue operating trains, they accepting requests for required transportation for the military and promising permit regular service continue. Morning trains were canceled, afternoon continued, but this arrangement may be upset at any time.

Rice has risen today 30 percent. Dollar exchange continues upward.

Suggest as precautionary measure immediate despatch of naval force of two destroyers to be promptly increased in the event of outbreak of hostilities to the strength indicated in my telegram August 25, noon. Regard as significant General Ho's remark today that the time for heavy fighting had not yet arrived."

Cunningham's telegram repeated to Admiral Washington with my concurrence in his suggestion. Following from American consul, Nanking:

"Mails still continue regularly.

Twenty thousand Kiangsu troops border Chekiang between Ihsing and Kunshan near Soochow. Hostilities almost certain."

Morning press reports to effect Nanking-Shanghai railroad service interrupted and that fighting had commenced between General Chi and General Ho Feng-lin's troops. Not confirmed.

BELL

893.00/5484 : Telegram

The Chargé in China (Bell) to the Secretary of State

PEKING, *August 29, 1924—10 a. m.*
[Received August 29—10 : 20 a. m.]

313. My 312, August 28, 3 p. m. In view of present serious situation British and Japanese Ministers, French Chargé d'Affaires, and I yesterday addressed following note to Minister for Foreign Affairs:

"We, the undersigned representatives of Great Britain, Japan, France and the United States learning of the grave danger of hostilities breaking out between the provincial authorities of Kiangsu and Chekiang feel it our duty to remind the Chinese Government of the terms of the communication addressed by us to you on August 11, 1923 and to repeat and reaffirm in the most solemn manner the declarations contained in that communication regarding the obligations of the Chinese Government in the present crisis, to prevent loss of life and property to members of the foreign community in and around Shanghai."

For text of last year's note see Legation's despatch 1738, August 17, 1923.[2]

BELL

---

[2] *Foreign Relations*, 1923, vol. I, p. 515.

893.00/5487 : Telegram

The Chargé in China (Bell) to the Secretary of State

PEKING, *August 30, 1924—3 p. m.*
[Received August 30—7 : 45 a. m.]

314. My 312, August 28, 3 p. m. Following from American consul general at Shanghai dated August 28, 6 p. m. :

"This morning commissioner of defense notified the superintendent of customs that Chinese naval vessels had left Nanking and Foochow to attack Woosung forts and urged the superintendent to issue notice that shipping should be on guard off Woosung without limiting the area. This might create a virtual blockade of the port of Shanghai. It is anticipated the official notice will be received tomorrow. Since that time superintendent has informed the commissioner of defense that the consular body should properly be notified. In anticipation of such notice the Legation's instructions are requested as to the proper attitude to be taken in conjunction with colleagues.

Admiral Tu, commander in chief of the Chinese Navy, has issued notice through the *North China Daily News* warning shipping not to proceed up river between Woosung and Kiangyin at night.

Request above be transmitted to commander in chief so that he may protect American shipping at Woosung and on the lower Yangtze.

Suggest all telegrams be sent via Great Northern. Understand Chinese mail and telegrams being censored but have no reports of censorship foreign correspondence."

Substance telegraphed Admiral Washington who has sent three destroyers to Shanghai to arrive this morning pursuant to Cunningham's telegram of August 27, 6 p.m.[3]

BELL

893.00/5485 : Telegram

The Chargé in China (Bell) to the Secretary of State

PEKING, *August 30, 1924—4 p.m.*
[Received August 30—2 : 50 p.m.]

315. After a conference this morning regarding situation at Shanghai, British and Japanese Ministers, French Chargé d'Affaires and myself called on Minister for Foreign Affairs and explained to him that we could not regard with equanimity the situation threatening Shanghai by sea. The whole river from the arsenal to Woosung was practically one vast harbor full of ships of every nationality, and the idea of a naval battle in the greatest harbor of the East was unthinkable and, as far as we were concerned, could not be tolerated. Battle between Woosung forts and Nanking navy would practically result in blockade of Shanghai to say nothing of damage to foreign

---

[3] See telegram no. 312, Aug. 28, from the Chargé in China, p. 361.

shipping by misdirected fire and excursion up to [sic] the river of navy to attack arsenal, and Lu's ships would probably result in injury if not destruction of settlements which we could not contemplate. We desired to be absolutely neutral in this matter and did not wish to interfere with China's internal wars but simply could not contemplate such situation as the foregoing. We hoped to receive from Koo a declaration of neutrality in respect of the whole river and its mouth, failing which we proposed to enforce same ourselves and we had the ships and men to do it. Koo did not take these representations amiss and promised to consult Minister of the Navy and give us a reply.

Meanwhile I am telegraphing foregoing to Admiral Washington and consul general at Shanghai so they can concert with British, Japanese and French colleagues.

BELL

893.00/5490 : Telegram

The Chargé in China (Bell) to the Secretary of State

PEKING, September 2, 1924—5 p.m.
[Received September 3—1 a.m.]

318. My 315, August 30, 4 p.m. Following from Cheney [4] from Shanghai:

"September 1, noon. I gather from usual source stage all set here for a fight. Efforts of peacemakers will fail. They have not offered Chi control of Shanghai and he is prepared to fight for it. Lu not sanguine of military success but thinks he will get better terms if he puts up a fight. Expected hostilities will open about September 4th.

On August 28th Wu asked Chi to hold off for one week to e— ble him to complete arrangements for mobilization against Fengtien. Chi has acceded so ball may be expected to open near here about Thursday. Lu has funds to finance his campaign derived from contributions raised by his subordinates and a small dole from Mukden. Chang is giving money cautiously to Lu through third party here.

Littles left last night. I sail Wednesday. Goodbye to all."

2. Above-mentioned source believed to be G. E. Sokolsky who had interview for *North China Daily News* with Marshal Chi at Nanking, August 27th, of which following are pertinent excerpts and of whose credibility military attaché's office thinks [highly?] :

3. "Everybody talks about the unification of China but what are the facts? We have been negotiating for almost 10 years. We are still negotiating. No authority is recognized.

---

[4] Col. Sherwood A. Cheney, military attaché at Peking.

The time comes when there must be action. Kiangsu has always recognized itself as being a part of the Republic of China and loyal to it. General Lu considers Chekiang independent of the Republic of China. The fact that the most important commercial city in China, Shanghai, is a buffer between Kiangsu and Chekiang makes for danger to the whole country. Shanghai is historically, traditionally, and geographically a city of Kiangsu. By a political accident the control of Shanghai has become vested in so-called independent officials of Chekiang. This has led to grave political difficulties as every Chinese and foreigner knows.

According to the peace agreement (of that year) Chekiang should have disarmed rebel troops of Fukien. These rebel troops are now being used to attack Kiangsu. General Lu has broken the peace agreement by these activities.

Anyone who has studied my career will realize I am not impetuous. I would not take this step unless I had the authority to do so and the consent of my colleagues. This effort is designed only to establish what is right, namely, the inclusion politically of Shanghai in Kiangsu, as Shanghai is geographically a part of Kiangsu. My colleagues in the Government and in the neighboring provinces desire that I should take this step, and I have their hearty support and cooperation.

Your newspaper may assure the people of Shanghai that my troops will be orderly. I love peace. I am ready to make peace but China must be unified and if it is necessary to unify China by war then there must be war."

4. I have it from reliable source that Peking Government has raised $3,000,000 within last few days partly from railroads; $1,000,000 given to General Feng Yu-hsiang, disposition of rest unknown.

5. I repeat statement in my 304, August 26, 3 p.m., that impossible to forecast with any degree of certainty what course events will take but in view of Cheney's telegram, other information, and general undercurrent of opinion locally, am inclining more and more to belief that Marshal Chi, Wu, and Peking Government intend to eliminate Lu and return Shanghai before many days and possibly at this time and are setting stage for such eventuality.

6. I also fear that Chang Tso-lin will attack Wu Pei-fu in the rear in which case the whole of China [will] be the melting pot. General Connor and Captain Smith are both in Mukden and I hope to have reliable information from them regarding Chang's intentions in a few days.

BELL

893.00/5489 : Telegram

The Consul General at Shanghai (Cunningham) to the Secretary of State

SHANGHAI, *September 3, 1924—4 p. m.*
[Received September 3—6 : 21 a. m.]

Reliably informed that hostilities broke out at 10 o'clock this morning at Hwangtu 15 miles west of Shanghai between forces of Military Governor Chi and Commissioner of Defense Ho. British, American, Japanese, French, Italian naval contingent in the harbor prepared to land forces to protect foreign settlement if necessary. French consul general has just advised that French naval forces will land at 5 p.m. today in the French concession.

CUNNINGHAM

893.00/5495 : Telegram

The Chargé in China (Bell) to the Secretary of State

PEKING, *September 6, 1924—11 a. m.*
[Received September 6—8 : 28 a. m.]

324. My 315, August 30, 4 p. m.

1. Commander in chief inquires whether you approved position there indicated, as otherwise he considers he should use force on Yangtze only to protect life and American property.

2. Chinese admirals of opposing factions have issued orders restricting traffic on Yangtze for about 80 miles up stream from its mouth and representatives of powers possessing naval vessels in Chinese waters have accordingly decided to inquire of their respective governments whether the latter will approve use of force to prevent application of restrictions.

3. While favoring action indicated in my 315 if it becomes necessary, I feel that proposal in paragraph 2 of this telegram would not be justified.

4. Please reply to both above inquiries.

BELL

893.00/5496 : Telegram

The Chargé in China (Bell) to the Secretary of State

PEKING, *September 6, 1924—noon.*
[Received September 6—8 : 15 a.m.]

325. My 318, September 2, 5 p.m., last paragraph. Naval attaché returned yesterday from Harbin and Mukden, reports after careful inspection he could find no evidence of Marshal Chang Tso-lin intending to move in immediate future. His attitude appeared to be one of watchful waiting.

BELL

893.00/5495 : Telegram

The Secretary of State to the Chargé in China (Bell)

WASHINGTON, *September 6, 1924—3 p.m.*

213. Your 324 September 6 11 a.m.

1. The Department considers that the use of naval forces on the Yangtze should be confined to the protection of American life and property.

2. The Department does not feel that the situation has reached a stage so critical as to justify the use of force in preventing the application of the restrictions on the Yangtze to which you refer, although the right of free navigation on this stream is accorded by treaty.

Your 315 August 30 4 P.M. The naval forces in the Whangpu should be employed as indicated in paragraph 1 above, but the exigencies of the situation seem to demand an appropriate cooperation and that the river should be kept open from Shanghai to the open sea since this stretch of water is to all intents and purposes the harbor of Shanghai. It is assumed that the naval authorities of the powers represented in those waters will use all proper means to that end.

Department desires to be kept fully informed concerning developments and should situation demand more drastic action than that contemplated herein Department would be glad to have the benefit of your recommendations as well as those of Admiral Washington and the Consul-General at Shanghai.

HUGHES

893.00/5498 : Telegram

The Chargé in China (Bell) to the Secretary of State

PEKING, *September 7, 1924—5 p.m.*
[Received September 7—11:50 a.m.]

329. Your 213, September 6, 3 p.m., while clear as to your wishes with regard to use of force on Yangtze only for protection of American life and property, leaves me in some doubt as to your wishes regarding use of force on Whangpoo.

You state in paragraph 3 that force is to be employed on Whangpoo only as in manner indicated above with respect to Yangtze but you at the same time assume that naval authorities of the powers represented in Whangpoo River will use all proper means to keep open Whangpoo from Shanghai to the open sea which may require different and more drastic action.

These instructions appear somewhat contradictory. Most drastic action contemplated so far is, as outlined in my 315, the enforcement of neutrality in respect of whole Whangpoo River and its mouth.

In order to avoid any possible misunderstanding please elucidate Department's position with regard to use of naval force on Whangpoo.

Your telegram and this reply repeated to Admiral Washington, for his information.

BELL

893.00/5500 : Telegram

The Chargé in China (Bell) to the Secretary of State

PEKING, *September 8, 1924—11 a.m.*
[Received September 8—3 : 50 a.m.]

330. My 325, September 6, 12 noon. Following from American consul Mukden:

"September 7, 3 p.m. Marshal Chang Tso-lin called together consuls at Mukden 11 a. m. today and stated as Chihli advance troops are within 10 *li* of Shanhaikwan, mobilization will be immediately ordered in the Three Eastern Provinces. He stated that he does not wish war and will not take offensive but will probably be obliged to fight in self-defense. The rights and safety of foreigners were guaranteed. He is attempting to transmit funds to Shanghai and as the Bank of Chosen apparently refused to remit he took the matter up with the Japanese consul general. The latter stated that Bank of Chosen are [*is*] under the inspectors executives [*sic*] in Japan where there is a gold embargo and made no promise to facilitate shipment. Further information will be submitted later."

BELL

893.00/5499 : Telegram

The Chargé in China (Bell) to the Secretary of State

PEKING, *September 8, 1924—1 p. m.*
[Received September 8—7 : 11 a. m.]

331. My 329, September 7, 5 p.m. Admiral McVay reports from Shanghai that the Chekiang admiral states he will comply with the notification that no firing on the Whangpoo will be permitted and that the Nanking admiral has already informed him that he has no intention of attacking the arsenal.

BELL

893.00/5501 : Telegram

The Chargé in China (Bell) to the Secretary of State

PEKING, *September 8, 1924—3 p.m.*
[Received September 8—2 : 34 p.m.]

332. My 318, September 2, 5 p.m. Following on general situation:

1. Presidential mandate of September 7th quotes telegram to President from Marshal Chi describing rebellious attitude of Gen-

CHINA 369

eral Lu Yung-hsiang as defying Central Government and in company with Ho Feng-lin mobilizing rebel forces for attack on Kiangsu, launching said attack on September 4th to which Kiangsu troops had to offer armed resistance for sake of self-defense and requesting that a punitive order be immediately issued by the President. The mandate then states same request made by Wu Pei-fu; Wang Cheng-pin, Deputy Inspector General of Chihli, Honan and Shantung; Hsiao Yao-han, Inspector General Hupeh and Hunan; Wang Hwai-ching, Inspector General Jehol, Chahar and Suiyuan; and Feng Yu-hsiang, Inspector General the Army. After reviewing deplorable situation caused by continued disorder and floods and pointing out that Kiangsu military authorities had been instructed not to take any rash action, Presidential mandate decrees that Lu Yung-hsiang and Ho Feng-lin are now detailed from respective offices and deprived of all ranks and decorations; Marshal Chi ordered to mobilize troops to suppress rebels and cope with situation at his discretion and to do best to bring war to close as soon as possible and that proper measures should be adopted for protection of all Chinese and foreign life and property.

2. Military situation. Troops of Kiangsu and Chekiang at war on front from Liuho on Yangtze through Hwangtu and Kunshan on Nanking-Shanghai Railway to Suchow on east side of Taihu and at Ihsing on west side of Taihu. Kiangsu being reenforced by small number of inferior troops from Shantung and Honan. Respective strengths of opposing forces estimated at 60,000. Fighting so far only skirmishes and confined to vicinity of Shanghai.

3. Captain Baldwin is being sent by military attaché to Mukden to observe and report situation which according to 330, September 8, 11 a.m., appears to be assuming more threatening aspect.

4. *Far Eastern Times* September 3rd contained an alleged letter to President Tsao from Minister for Foreign Affairs Chang,[5] dated August 30th, sharply critical in tone of Peking administration arraigning Tsao Kun government for lack of thought for people and further impairment of China's present international position if Government goes to war for selfish motives and advising President to stop troops' movements directed against Chekiang and threatening armed intervention unless advice taken. Replying to my telegram regarding authenticity of above letter, consul at Mukden reported on September 4th that commissioner of foreign affairs at Mukden stated that letter similar to one published but without threat of armed intervention was sent to President Tsao by Marshal Chang.

---

[5] Apparently refers to commissioner for foreign affairs in Chang Tso-lin's government at Mukden.

5. Apparently in connection with a recent movement reported from time to time in the press that certain radical Chinese wish to proclaim September 7th as a day of national humiliation since Boxer protocol signed on that date,[6] printed handbills headed "To Foreigners" [were distributed?] yesterday in the Legation Quarter and vicinity north of Chienmen warning foreign diplomats and citizens that Chinese can no longer tolerate further acts of violence and insults by our Governments and threatening our lives if we do not give up predatory treaties which strangle China and protocol of 1901. I do not attach any great importance to this occurrence but send it for what it may be worth as straw in the wind.

In order to save time and relieve Legation in present understaffed condition I have directed consular officers at Shanghai and Nanking to telegraph direct to Department information concerning Kiangsu-Chekiang situation which they might deem essential Department should know, telegraphing only to the Legation other information in that regard which necessary for me to know but not essential for the Department.

BELL

893.00/5502 : Telegram

The Chargé in China (Bell) to the Secretary of State

PEKING, September 8, 1924—5 p.m.
[Received September 8—3 : 39 p.m.]

334. My 315, August 30, 4 p.m. On September 3d, Koo sent a secretary to each of the four Legations in question to make an oral reply to our *démarche* of August 30th. Message vague and unsatisfactory stated Government troops would spare no effort to protect foreign lives and property and assure safety of foreign settlements in Shanghai but omitted any reference to a declaration of neutrality of Whangpoo River and contained a louder [*sic*] reference to our declaration "that our Governments would not if requested intervene in the possible developments of the situation" which of course we never made.

In order to avoid misunderstanding British and Japanese Ministers, French Chargé d'Affaires and myself and Italian Minister, who was absent from Peking on August 30th but who on return joined us in our representations, have today sent memorandum to Minister for Foreign Affairs pointing out that while our Governments had no desire to intervene and did not wish to take sides they could not possibly allow naval engagement to take place in the Whangpoo River or its approaches and that they might have to take steps even possibly of a forcible nature to prevent such hostilities.

---

[6] *Foreign Relations*, 1901, Appendix (Affairs in China), p. 312.

Memorandum took note of assurances that no effort would be spared to protect foreign lives and property and foreign settlements Shanghai but expressed regret that Koo's message contained no reference to neutralization of Whangpoo River.

BELL

893.00/5498 : Telegram

The Secretary of State to the Chargé in China (Bell)

WASHINGTON, *September 8, 1924—5 p.m.*

214. Your 329, September 7, 5 p.m. American forces should be employed for protection of American lives and property. You should, of course, understand that the Executive, unless otherwise authorized by Congress, can use American naval forces only for this purpose. This should be clear, but manifestly there are situations in which suitable protection of American lives and property will require appropriate cooperation. Such a situation is deemed to exist on Whangpu because of the commingling of foreign interests. You were therefore instructed that the exigencies of the situation there seemed to require appropriate cooperation with the naval authorities of the other Powers represented in those waters in keeping that stream open from Shanghai to the open sea. Statements in your 315, August 30, 4 p.m. show importance of this. Department hopes that traffic will be kept moving on the Whangpu without hindrance, and your 331, September 8, 1 p.m. confirms this view.

Preponderant naval forces of Powers on the Whangpu should be able to protect by their cooperation foreign shipping and thus suitably protect American lives and property without actual combat with Chinese forces.

As to Yangtze, it should be said that if restrictions imposed by Chinese should endanger American lives and property the American naval authorities would be expected to take the necessary steps to afford protection. Department assumed from your 324, September 6, 11 a.m., third paragraph, that such a situation had not yet arisen.

HUGHES

893.00/5504 : Telegram

The Consul General at Shanghai (Cunningham) to the Secretary of State

SHANGHAI, *September 9, 1924—4 p.m.*
[Received September 9—10:49 a.m.]

The fighting has continued intermittently since September 3rd on front running roughly from Liuho on Yangtze 33 miles from Shanghai, to Kiating, Hwangtu and Tsingpu. Apparently nearest point about 9 miles from Shanghai. No decisive results so far. Large numbers machine guns and considerable artillery used but practically no airplanes.

Morale both armies excellent. Reports indicate Kiangsu offensive developing on both flanks of this front with Woosung forts on left and Shanghai-Hangchow Railway and Kiangnan Arsenal on right as objective. Chekiang troops reported on the offensive west of Taihu Lake since Sunday. No reliable reports of results. Hundreds of Chekiang wounded being received in Shanghai hospital.

Combined Nanking and Fukien naval forces said to consist of two cruisers, two gunboats, four torpedo boats and two transports anchored off Liuho but so far inactive. Both Chekiang and Kiangsu naval commanders promised not to fire in Whangpoo River.

As precautionary measures only, foreign naval contingents landed at daybreak today and took up stations as did Shanghai Volunteer Corps. Approximate numbers: American 260, British 360, French 500, Japanese 400, Italian 100, Shanghai Volunteer Corps 1,000. Ships in harbor: American 11, British 4, Japanese 2, French 2, Italian 1.

Aside from financial stringency and nervousness of Chinese, conditions in Shanghai normal. Refugees arriving since August 29th at the rate of 6 to 7 thousand daily. Food supply adequate for the present. Necessary arrangements for care are being made. Chairman Municipal Council states he has no fears as to safety of foreign lives and property.

CUNNINGHAM

893.00/5506 : Telegram

The Secretary of State to the Chargé in Japan (Caffery)

WASHINGTON, *September 10, 1924—4 p.m.*

151. Your 226, September 9, 5 p.m.[7] The Department's chief concern in the disturbance in China has been to afford adequate protection to American life and property and to maintain an attitude of strict neutrality. There is no thought of any other course of action and it is assumed that the other principal Powers entertain similar views. There has been no interchange of views with any of the Powers whose interests might be affected by the developments in China. For your information there is quoted below a copy of a telegram sent to Peking on September 8:

[Here follows text of telegram no. 214, printed on page 371.]

HUGHES

---

[7] Not printed.

893.00/5508 : Telegram

The Chargé in Japan (Caffery) to the Secretary of State

[Paraphrase]

TOKYO, *September 10, 1924—5 p.m.*
[Received September 10—1:13 p.m.]

227. Foreign Minister Shidehara in the course of a conversation today told me informally that Japan intended to keep neutral with respect to the present struggle in China. . . . He spoke of reports published in newspapers here alleging that Wu Pei-fu was backed by the United States and Chang Tso-lin by Japan. Both of these reports, he said, were obviously incorrect, and he expressed the hope that they would not gain credence in America. . . . Shidehara also referred to London press despatches printed here to the effect that the British and American Governments were exchanging views on the position to be taken in the present situation. He quickly added that he had not considered such reports to be of much importance.

Shidehara told me as I was leaving that he is disposed to treat me with perfect frankness and would keep me informed of the situation should his Government find it necessary to take action to protect Japanese interests in China.

I have informed Peking.

CAFFERY

893.00/5509 : Telegram

The Chargé in China (Bell) to the Secretary of State

PEKING, *September 11, 1924—3 p. m.*
[Received September 11—9:14 a. m.]

339. My 334, September 8, 5 p. m. Senior consul Shanghai reports defense commissioner on the one side and Nanking admiral on the other have both agreed to the neutralization of the Whangpoo River and to the revocation of the regulations regarding navigation of the lower Yangtze and of the Whangpoo.

This if true is very satisfactory.

BELL

893.00/5508 : Telegram

The Secretary of State to the Chargé in Japan (Caffery)

WASHINGTON, *September 12, 1924—2 p.m.*

154. Your 227, September 10, 5 p. m. You may orally communicate to Baron Shidehara the essential portion of the first paragraph

of the Department's 151, September 10, 4 p.m., down to and including "developments in China."

You may repeat to Peking for its information the above mentioned first paragraph of the Department's 151.

HUGHES

893.00/5518 : Telegram

The Chargé in China (Bell) to the Secretary of State

PEKING, *September 12, 1924—4 p.m.*
[Received September 12—11 : 17 a.m.]

342. Shanghai's September 9, 4 p. m. and my 339, September 11, 3 p.m.

1. American, British, French, Italian, and Japanese senior naval officers present at Shanghai at a meeting September 8th decided that Woosung forts should be "neutralized", that is, that Chekiang garrison should be driven out and that flags of five nations above mentioned should be hoisted over the fort.

2. They referred this question to us through Italian consul general as senior representative at Shanghai of powers having ships of war on China station.

3. Above-referred-to representatives including myself have today telegraphed Italian consul general Shanghai that in view of Ho and Tu's present state of mind, as reported in my 339, we consider that our men-of-war's activities should be limited to protecting the town of Shanghai (foreign settlement understood), the Whangpoo and its mouth, and, if necessary, navigation night and day on the lower Yangtze and at its mouth.

4. We do not agree that foreign detachments should occupy Woosung forts and hoist foreign flags.

BELL

893.00/5520 : Telegram

The Chargé in China (Bell) to the Secretary of State

PEKING, *September 13, 1924—10 a. m.*
[Received September 13—8 : 03 a. m.]

343. My 313 August 29, 10 a. m. Reply received from Foreign Office which states in brief that our memorandum of August 28 has been communicated to Ministries of Navy and War and telegraphed to high military authorities in provinces concerned asking them to give strictest attention thereto; Chinese Government has great regard for safety of lives and property of foreign nationals in vicinity of Shanghai and would be very loath to have them suffer any losses. Sincere and

earnest efforts will be made to utmost of Chinese Government's ability to afford them protection. In order to facilitate protection [it is] requested that warning be issued to foreign nationals that they should on no account involve themselves in any way in present hostilities.

I am sending mail circular to all consuls instructing them to issue warning requested as far as American citizens are concerned.

BELL

893.00/5518 : Telegram

The Secretary of State to the Chargé in China (*Bell*)

WASHINGTON, *September 13, 1924—4 p.m.*

216. Your 342, September 12, 4 p. m. The action taken by you as set forth in paragraphs numbered 3 and 4 has the Department's approval. Apropos of the situation at Shanghai there is quoted below for your confidential information the text of a letter addressed by the Department to the Secretary of the Navy on September 12, 1924, on this subject:

"I have the honor to acknowledge the receipt of a copy of a telegram, dated September 10, 1924,[8] addressed to you by the Commander-in-Chief of the Asiatic Station, concerning conditions incident to the civil war in the vicinity of Shanghai.

In the above mentioned telegram it is noted that the Commander-in-Chief states that two destroyers are en route to Woosung and that they will deliver a letter from the senior naval officers (presumably of the Powers represented in the Shanghai waters) to the two Chinese gunboats, and further that the substance of the letter is that the Nanking navy will not be permitted to enter the Whangpu and that no firing will be allowed in the Whangpu River. A careful reading of the telegram does not disclose that any notice of a similar character was communicated to the Nanking navy and it does not appear that any notice was communicated to the two Chekiang boats that they would not be permitted to remain in the Whangpu (apparently the two Chekiang boats are at Woosung, presumably just inside the mouth of the Whangpu). It appears that the 'Chinese gunboats' referred to are affiliated with the Chekiang forces which are defending Shanghai. A correct interpretation of the telegram therefore would seem to be that the senior naval officers have informed the Chekiang commander that the Nanking navy, which represents the Kiangsu forces that are attacking Shanghai, will not be permitted to enter the Whangpu River.

In view of the above circumstances I fear that the naval authorities of the Powers represented in the Whangpu waters may be subjecting themselves to the charge of favoring one side as against the other in the present factional disturbance, and that the naval authorities, in the absence of any imminent danger or threat to foreign life and prop-

---

[8] Not printed.

erty, were not warranted in forbidding the mere entrance of Chinese naval vessels into the Whangpu as distinguished from any activity which might threaten such life and property."

HUGHES

893.00/5521 : Telegram

The Chargé in China (Bell) to the Secretary of State

PEKING, *September 14, 1924—7 p.m.*
[Received September 14—1:30 p.m.]

Consul Mukden reports by telegraph heavy troop movements from Mukden southward in last three days. I have no information that they have gone further south than Great Wall.

BELL

893.00/5526 : Telegram

The Secretary of State to the Chargé in China (Bell)

WASHINGTON, *September 15, 1924—5 p.m.*

217. Your 343, September 13, 10 A. M. The Department approves your action in circularizing consuls as indicated in last paragraph.

HUGHES

893.00/5530 : Telegram

The Chargé in China (Bell) to the Secretary of State

PEKING, *September 17, 1924—3 p.m.*
[Received September 17—7:25 a.m.]

352. My 347, 2d [paragraph].[9]

1. Following from American consul Mukden:

"September 16, 7 p.m. It is reported on good authority Fengtien forces yesterday disarmed two battalions Chihli troops on Chihli side of border east of Chaoyang."

2. Reports received by military attaché confirm that Fengtien forces are at Chaoyang within Chihli border.

3. Heavy troop movements north from Peking continue.

4. According to best information available Wu Pei-fu arrived in Peking this morning and will probably establish himself at Fengtai junction point of Peking-Mukden and Peking-Hankow Railways some 6 miles out of Peking.

BELL

---

[9] Not printed.

893.00/5532 : Telegram

The Chargé in China (Bell) to the Secretary of State

PEKING, *September 17, 1924—4 p.m.*
[Received September 17—9 : 18 a.m.]

353. Your 216, September 13, 4 p.m. British Minister has today received telegram from British consul general at Shanghai stating that Admiral Anderson, commanding British Yangtze Patrol and senior foreign naval officer present at Shanghai, has now informed the Chekiang gunboats that they must not leave the Whangpoo, has informed the Nanking admiral of this action and has also informed Nanking admiral that he must not enter the Whangpoo.

I trust this will meet the Department's views as to neutrality. To force the Chekiang gunboats to leave Whangpoo River would perhaps cause an engagement with Nanking navy and to allow Nanking naval force to enter Whangpoo could only result in precipitating a naval engagement in that river which we are agreed is to be considered as forming the port of Shanghai and which is the one thing above all others, that in the interest of protecting foreign life and property, we have been striving to prevent, and which I venture to point out we have up to the present been successful in preventing.

Admiral Washington agrees in foregoing.

BELL

893.00/5535 : Telegram

The Chargé in China (Bell) to the Secretary of State

PEKING, *September 17, 1924—5 p.m.*
[Received September 17—12 : 40 p.m.]

354. My 334, September 8, 5 p.m. Koo has replied in a lengthy memorandum reiterating the charge that Chekiang started the fighting, which of course is untrue, taking exception to our statement that we might have to use forcible measures to prevent fighting in Whangpoo River, renewing assurances of desire to safeguard foreign lives and property in Shanghai, expressing desire to restrict as much as possible area of military operations and with this in view making a statement of China's views as to neutralization of "certain areas of Shanghai and Woosung."

Memorandum does not specifically ask foreign representatives to mediate but even if it is so intended we are unanimously of opinion that we should be unable to do so as terms for neutralization of Shanghai which Koo proposes are of such a nature that for us to present them to Chekiang faction would be tantamount to inviting them to give large military advantage to Kiangsu. Terms include dismantling of Woosung forts and closing of arsenal and powder factory all of which are in hands of Chekiang forces, disarming of Chekiang gunboats in Whangpoo River and disarming of Chekiang troops in area to be neutralized in return for which area of 5 miles around Shanghai, 3 miles around Woosung forts and the banks of the Whangpoo are to be neutralized.

Representatives of Italy, Great Britain, Japan and France and I have accordingly replied this afternoon as follows:

"While the five representatives welcome the statement therein contained that it is in line with the policy of the Chinese Government to restrict as much as possible the area of the military operations between the Kiangsu and Chekiang forces, they regret that they are unable to express any opinion on the scheme outlined in the Wai Chiao Pu's memorandum for the neutralization of certain areas of Shanghai and Woosung, as the realization of any such project must obviously be left to the contending parties to settle by agreement among themselves. The five representatives earnestly hope that an arrangement for the neutralization of the area surrounding Shanghai and the Whangpoo River including its mouth at Woosung may be reached but they must again impress upon the Chinese Government that failing such agreement between the combatants they must maintain the declaration made in their memorandum of September 7th that their respective Governments cannot possibly allow a naval engagement to take place in the Whangpoo River and its approaches and that they reserve to themselves the right to take steps even of a forcible nature to prevent such hostilities or any interference with foreign shipping between the port of Shanghai and the open sea."

BELL

893.00/5537 : Telegram

The Chargé in China (Bell) to the Secretary of State

PEKING, September 18, 1924—1 p.m.
[Received September 18—7 : 52 a.m.]

356. Presidential mandate, dated September 17, issued this morning, states that Wu Pei-fu and others have reported various hostile preparations in Manchuria, that the Fengtien troops are advancing along five routes, that it is apparent that Chang Tso-lin is thus taking advantage of the disorder in the Southeast to create a disturbance in China proper and that he must be suppressed by military force. Orders given to all commanders of troops to proceed against him. Protection of Chinese and foreign civilian life and property is ordered.

Other Presidential mandates, also dated September 17th, announce appointment Wu Pei-fu as commander in chief of the forces for the suppression of the rebellion and Wang Cheng-pin, vice commander in chief; Peng Shou-hsin, second army; and Feng Yu-hsiang, third army; Tu Hsi-kwei, commander in chief of the naval forces; and Wen Shu-teh, vice commander in chief. Appointments of many lesser military officials also published.

BELL

893.00/5573 : Telegram

The Chargé in China (Bell) to the Secretary of State

PEKING, *September 26, 1924—11 a. m.*
[Received September 26—9 : 31 a.m.]

364. Chang Tso-lin having bombed Shanhaikwan several times recently by aeroplane although with small success and having, it is reported, also announced intention of bombing Peking, the commandants of the various legation guards memorialized diplomatic body of danger to Legation Quarter from such attacks; as result of which diplomatic body resolved to send memorandum on the subject to the Chinese Government and to Chang. Memorandum sent yesterday summarized as follows:

"Outbreak of hostilities in China makes probable the extensive use of aircraft in conduct of campaign. Though resolved not to interfere in any way in regrettable conflict the heads of legations in Peking deem it necessary to point out that they view with gravest concern use of this weapon against objectives other than military forces in the field, fortified places, or naval units. Bombing of undefended towns is act of wanton destruction and crime against peaceful population. Inaccuracy of bombing such that all buildings in immediate neighborhood of objective are in great danger. In Peking there are not only legations but numerous palaces, temples, and other historical buildings which are monuments of great value in history of mankind. Bombing of towns and villages cannot have military value and can only cause great misery and suffering to inoffensive noncombatants and destruction of priceless monuments. Moreover lives and property of foreign nationals who are nonparticipants and who intend to maintain absolute neutrality would be put in grave and constant danger. For these reasons the heads of legations feel it their duty to make this appeal and while giving expression to this [*their satisfaction*] that intention was made known to afford full protection to lives and property of foreigners they trust that no air attacks will be made endangering the lives of their nationals. However should foreign lives be lost or property destroyed as a result of aeroplane attack on Peking or any treaty port they would feel obliged to hold the authority who ordered the attack strictly responsible therefor."

BELL

893.00/5603 : Telegram

The Chargé in China (Bell) to the Secretary of State

PEKING, *October 9, 1924—4 p.m.*
[Received October 9—4 : 05 p.m.]

381. My 354, September 17, 5 p.m. About September 17th five senior foreign naval officers at Shanghai informed Admiral Tu of Government forces that in order to [insure?] neutrality of Whangpoo they would not permit any vessel of his fleet to enter and simultaneously notified Admiral Lin of Chekiang forces that his vessels might not fire guns in Whangpoo and that if they left the river they could not return. On September 19th I received report from Admiral McVay that Tu had undertaken not to enter Whangpoo provided restrictions against Lin were maintained. Message further stated Lin had previously agreed not to fire guns in the river. Lin's vessels left Whangpoo September 21st as reported in my telegram 362, September 25, 3 p.m.,[10] and went over to the Government forces.

October 1st Tu asked senior naval officers if his ships might enter Whangpoo and was informed not until end of hostilities. Tu thereupon came to Peking. October 6th the Chinese Minister for Foreign Affairs through representative privately informed British Minister and me that in view of changed circumstances and absence of hostile vessels in Whangpoo Admiral Tu desired to be relieved of undertaking described above and wished to enter river and take steps against arsenal and powder factory. Koo considered that moral effect of vessels' presence in rear of Chekiang forces would induce surrender and save much useless bloodshed without fighting by vessels themselves. I consulted with the British Minister and we concurred that passage of Tu's ships up Whangpoo or any other settlements to attack the arsenal would certainly be resisted by Chekiang forces and that this would incur all the dangers to shipping and settlements we originally contemplated at the time of our representation to Koo August 30th. Our respective consular and naval authorities at Shanghai when consulted by telegraph concurred in this view. October 8, 1 p.m., the British Minister and I sent word to the Chinese Minister for Foreign Affairs that we were unable to consent to Lu's [*Tu's*] vessel[s] entering Whangpoo as requested.

BELL

---

[10] Not printed.

893.00/5605 : Telegram

The Chargé in China (Bell) to the Secretary of State

PEKING, *October 11, 1924—4 p.m.*
[Received October 11—6 : 18 a.m.]

383. Marshal Wu Pei-fu left Peking early this morning to direct operations at the northern front. Colonel Barnard and Captain Woodbridge [11] accompanied him as observers at his invitation. British, French and Japanese officers also accompanied Wu in like capacity.

BELL

893.00/5611 : Telegram

The Consul General at Shanghai (Cunningham) to the Secretary of State

SHANGHAI, *October 13, 1924—10 a.m.*
[Received October 13—2 : 43 a.m.]

. . . source of most reliable police information during war states that Generals Lu and Ho have deserted possibly going about 3 a.m. today. Will report later whether confirmation obtained.

CUNNINGHAM

893.00/5612 : Telegram

The Consul General at Shanghai (Cunningham) to the Secretary of State

SHANGHAI, *October 13, 1924—11 a. m.*
[Received October 13—2 : 38 a. m.]

Referring to my telegram today 10 a. m. Practically certain Generals Lu and Ho went aboard *Shanghai Maru* between 4 and 5 this morning. Vessel sailed for Nagasaki at 8 : 30 a. m. Military headquarters at Lunghua completely deserted. Well-founded rumor to the effect that mutineers from the front reached military headquarters about midnight creating great confusion which possibly was the immediate cause of the generals' deserting their loyal troops.

CUNNINGHAM

---

[11] U. S. Army officers attached to the Legation in China.

893.00/5615 : Telegram

The Chargé in China (Bell) to the Secretary of State

PEKING, *October 13, 1924—4 p. m.*
[Received October 13—9 : 51 a. m.]

386. General Connor has just informed me that no trains other than Chinese troop trains having left Tientsin for Shanhaikwan since 9th or arrived from there since 7th, it was decided today at a commandants' meeting, on the urgent representation of the Japanese and French commandants, to send an international train to Shanhaikwan tomorrow to be followed by two per week until more normal traffic restored.

Trains will carry supplies for foreign troops guarding railway beyond Tientsin, will have mixed guards from all foreign forces guarding railway, will take no civilians into war area but will bring in any to Tientsin who desire.

BELL

893.00/5614 : Telegram

The Consul General at Shanghai (Cunningham) to the Secretary of State

SHANGHAI, *October 13, 1924—6 p. m.*
[Received October 13—9 : 40 a. m.]

My telegram of October 13, 10 a. m. confirmed. Probably cause absconding generals due shortage of ammunition, dissension among troops, disloyalty of troops and apparent ultimate defeat by opponents. New commissioner of police for Shanghai and Woosung, Huang Tien-wen, announced to arrive this afternoon to take up duties relinquished by Ho's appointee. Volunteers called out in full strength and naval forces increased as precautionary measure believing that the Chekiang forces likely retreat in disorder seeking shelter in concessions.

CUNNINGHAM

893.00/5617 : Telegram

The Consul General at Shanghai (Cunningham) to the Secretary of State

SHANGHAI, *October 15, 1924—noon.*
[Received October 15—7 : 07 a. m.]

Kiangsu troops consisting of 1,500 Fifth Hupeh Brigade, General Chang Yuen-min commanding, occupied Lunghua Arsenal and yamen without opposition yesterday afternoon. Wen Shih-tsin assumed charge as commissioner for foreign affairs late 14th. Wong

Kuo-pan takes up permanent appointment of commissioner of police Shanghai for Woosung constabulary today. General Sun Chuan-feng is believed to have returned to Hangchow to begin rehabili-tating province. Rumors of disaffection officers Kiangsu forces mini-mized by new Chi officials not regarded serious. Efforts to reorganize Chekiang forces under new leaders will delay restoration of normalcy. Wen and others are confident that Hsü Shu-tseng, known as Little Hsü, who is prominent in these efforts and who has collected a small Chekiang force well armed and is reported this morning to be dig-ging trenches on Markham Road, Chapei, within a hundred yards of concessions cannot offer serious prolonged opposition. Marshal Chi probably arrives today as his personal troops have reached Chenju, 4 miles from Shanghai. Have been reassured by new officials as to protection of Americans for property [sic]. Local conditions regarded quite safe.

CUNNINGHAM

893.00/5669 : Telegram

The Consul General at Shanghai (Cunningham) to the Secretary of State

SHANGHAI, *October 23, 1924—12 a.m.*
[Received October 23—8 : 20 a.m.]

Marshal Chi probably returning Nanking without visiting Shang-hai. Present headquarters Chenju. General Sun Chuan-fang has returned Hangchow. General Bei Bao-shan commander military district corresponding to former commissioner of defense for Shang-hai and Sungkiang. Local conditions improving daily. Shanghai Volunteers demobilized yesterday. Naval landing force is being withdrawn. *Huron* sails tomorrow. Refugees returning to rural districts. Rice only one dollar above pre-war days. Railway serv-ice south of Sungkiang continues interrupted, also to Nanking.

CUNNINGHAM

893.00/5671 : Telegram

The Consul General at Tientsin (Gauss) to the Secretary of State

TIENTSIN, *October 23, 1924—3 p.m.*
[Received October 23—8 : 30 a.m.]

Following message by radio from Chargé d'Affaires at Peking repeated at his request:

"General Feng Yu-hsiang troops are returning to Peking and are now in peaceful occupation of the city. Feng has posted proclama-tion stating he will fight no longer and wishes peace negotiated. All railway, telegraph and telephone connections are cut. Will telegraph again when situation develops further, meanwhile I do not think international train is necessary."

Tientsin situation undisturbed at the present time.

GAUSS

893.00/5673 : Telegram

The Consul General at Tientsin (Gauss) to the Secretary of State

TIENTSIN, *October 24, 1924—1 a.m.*
[Received 5:21 p.m.]

Following by radio from Chargé d'Affaires at Peking:

"Number 402, October 23rd. C. T. Wang has just been to see me, informs me he participated in Feng Yu-hsiang's *coup d'état* as did Huang Fu, Minister of Education, formerly Minister of Foreign Affairs. Wang Ko-ming, Minister of Finance, had been arrested as had General Li of the President's office. President and other Cabinet Ministers were at present under surveillance and would later be sent from Peking after which there will be a government by a committee which would invite Chang Tso-lin, Sun Yat-sen, Tuan Chi-jui and other prominent leaders to a round-table conference with the object of unifying China, adjusting debts and disbanding superfluous troops and forming new government. I told Wang if communications were not restored at once there will be serious trouble with foreign governments and he assured me it would be done as soon as possible. Peking quiet."

GAUSS

893.00/5678 : Telegram

The Chargé in China (Bell) to the Secretary of State

PEKING, *October 24, 1924—11 p.m.*
[Received October 24—11:35 p.m.]

405. My telegram 402, October 23, 2 p. m.[12] Hsu En-yuan, emissary of Tuan Chi-jui, has just conveyed message from latter saying Tuan will come to Peking probably October 26th to be commander in chief of the "National People's Army". Tuan transmitted request for moral support of the American Government for this attempt to rehabilitate Chinese peacefully and disclaimed all pro-Japanese or pro-Anfu leanings.

From well-informed source I learned that this *coup d'état* was formulated and executed by three military leaders, Feng Yu-hsiang commanding 30,000 men, Hu Ching-yi commanding perhaps 20,000 unpaid and unreliable Shensi troops, and Sun Yao commanding about 5,000 men in Peking who admitted Feng's forces yesterday. These leaders and their immediate followers profess to be animated

---

[12] See telegram of Oct. 24, from the consul general at Tientsin, *supra.*

by desire to secure peaceful unification of country and to end selfish militaristic warfare and waste of country's resources.

This afternoon under military coercion the President's bodyguard was disarmed and the President was compelled to issue following mandates: First, deploring war in the northeast and ordering both sides to cease fighting and maintain their respective positions until the Central Government shall devise a settlement. Mandate ends with threat to use force against either side if necessary to secure obedience to it. Countersigned by Premier and entire Cabinet except Huang Fu, Minister of Education, whose failure to sign is not explained. Second mandate addressed posts of commanders and vice commanders of anti-rebel forces and directs military authorities of Chihli Province, Wang Cheng-pin and Peng Shou-hsin, to keep forces in Shanhaikuan region under control. Countersigned by Premier and military. Third mandate deprives Wu Pei-fu of all offices and similarly countersigned. Fourth mandate appoints Wu Pei-fu director general of development of Kokonor. Countersigned by Premier and Minister of Agriculture and Commerce.

Premier W. W. Yen has privately informed me this evening that he knew nothing of the *coup d'état* before it occurred and that he and entire Cabinet have submitted their resignations. Also that two plans are now under discussion, first, involving temporarily government by commission as described in my number 402, of October 23, 2 p. m., and, second, maintaining outward semblance of policy and personnel. He could not predict which policy would prevail. The treaty powers' representatives today addressed note to Koo, Minister for Foreign Affairs, urgently insisting on restoration various means of communication involved in the protocol.[13] I am assured privately from apparently reliable source restoration to normal conditions have place shortly [*sic*]. I understand telegraphic communication already restored. Military restrictions on the streets already greatly relaxed.

I have sent 10 marines to Tungchow as has been done on previous occasions to protect approximately 100 American citizens. Shensi troops there are acting lawlessly but I consider this guard ample.

After consulting with naval and military attaché[s] and commandant of Legation Guard I have sent radio to commander in chief Asiatic Fleet requesting reenforcement be sent 150 marines to Legation Guard.

BELL

---

[13] Final protocol of 1901; *Foreign Relations,* 1901, Appendix (Affairs in China), p. 312.

893.00/5681 : Telegram

The Chargé in China (Bell) to the Secretary of State

PEKING, *October 26, 1924—11 p.m.*
[Received October 27—2:30 p.m.]

410. Wu Pei-fu arrived Tientsin noon today with some of his troops apparently expecting to effect agreement with troops of Chi Hsieh-yuan coming north. I believe Wu has left force to confront Chang Tso-lin at Shanhaikwan and intends trying to reestablish himself in Peking.

BELL

893.00/5686 : Telegram

The Chargé in China (Mayer) to the Secretary of State

PEKING, *October 29, 1924—5 p.m.*
[Received October 29—1:40 p.m.]

416. Legation's 412, October 27, 11 p.m.[14]

1. Peking quiet but decided uneasiness evident in Chinese population. One hundred and twenty-five additional marines arrived October 28, midnight, and the same number on two destroyers en route Peking.

2. It is reported that after some dispute Tuan Chi-jui has been elected commander of the National People's Army replacing Feng Yu-hsiang. This army now composed of the respective forces of Generals Feng and Hu Ching-yi and Sun Yao. I learn that resignation of President Tsao Kun and appointment of new Cabinet are deferred pending elimination of Wu Pei-fu but leaders expect announcement within week. There seems to be considerable difficulty in agreeing upon appointees for various posts, and forecasts are premature. Some jealousy and friction exists in the above triumvirate. Minor officers like directors of railways and commandant *gendarmerie* are being replaced by henchmen of the above. Kuomintang names prominent in discussions. C. T. Wang active and influential under Feng's patronage.

3. Whether Feng or Wu will receive support of different provincial leaders is determining factor in the present situation but continues doubtful. Wu's defeated provincial militarists may support Feng coalition or form new groups among themselves. Chang Tso-lin has announced intention of coming to Peking. Please repeat to War Department.

Number 4 [apparent omission] repeated to Tokyo.

MAYER

---

[14] Not printed.

893.00/5691 : Telegram

The Chargé in China (Mayer) to the Secretary of State

PEKING, *October 31, 1924—10 a.m.*
[Received October 31—2:42 a.m.]

418. American consul Tientsin advises despatch of American naval vessel to Tientsin to afford additional protection American life and property if necessary. Ships of other nationalities now present. I have recommended to commander in chief Asiatic Fleet accordingly.

MAYER

893.00/5701 : Telegram

The Chargé in China (Mayer) to the Secretary of State

PEKING, *November 1, 1924—3 p.m.*
[Received November 1—3:37 p.m.][15]

425. My telegram 417, October 29, 6 p. m.[16]

1. Presidential mandate October 31st, state[s] all former Cabinet Ministers excepting Huang Fu, Minister of Education, have submitted their resignations which are accepted. Huang Fu is appointed concurrently Acting Premier and Minister of Communications. Other new appointments are C. T. Wang, Minister for Foreign Affairs, concurrently Minister of Finance. Although latter's relations with Kuomintang have been strained by the service with Chihli Party, he may still be considered member of Kuomintang and a politician of radical and some say Soviet tendencies. Minister of the Interior is Wang Yung-chiang, now Civil Governor of Fengtien, who is hardly likely to take post. Minister of War is Li Shu-cheng, Kuomintang, not prominent heretofore. Minister of Marine Tu Shi-Kwei, evidently appointed in attempt to secure allegiance to the Navy. Minister of Justice Chang Yao-tseng has had post previously, member of Ch'eng Hsueh Shi [*Hui?*] Party composed of progressive men but not influential. Minister of Agriculture and Commerce Wang Nai-pin has had post previously, member of Fengtien Party. Huang Fu is Kuomintang, formerly Minister for Foreign Affairs. . . .

2. I doubt if this Cabinet possesses element of strength or permanence although C. T. Wang has formulated admirable plans for national improvements in all directions and professes desire for foreign cooperation economic and otherwise. Government departments at present exist in name only, control of Peking being in the hands of the military.

---

[15] Text printed from corrected copy received Nov. 3.
[16] Not printed.

3. C. T. Wang told me October 31, noon, Chang Tso-lin's troops had Lutai near Tangku and that Yangtsun was invested by Feng Yu-hsiang's forces.

4. Hsu En-yuan yesterday stated to Chinese secretary that due to confused situation it was uncertain when Tuan Chi-jui would come to Peking.

5. Attitude of provincial leaders toward Feng Yu-hsiang still generally noncommittal. Military Governor Shangtung has declared he will try to prevent reinforcements reaching Wu Pei-fu from south and is apparently so acting. The public does not feel optimistic in regard to Feng's plan for national conference of heterogeneous political leaders to determine future of the country and the possibility exists that another long period of provincial discord has been initiated.

MAYER

893.00/5703 : Telegram

The Chargé in China (Mayer) to the Secretary of State

PEKING, November 3, 1924—5 p.m.
[Received November 3—2 : 14 p.m.]

427. 1. My telegram number 425, November 1, 3 p.m. Following information from Connor, Tientsin, sent November 2, 11 p.m.:

"Wu's Yangtsun position collapsed. Feng's troops now at Peitang; all precautions taken against entry soldiers into Tientsin. Feng warned to observe protocol."

2. While complete details not received it is now known Chang Tso-lin captured Shanhaikwan and Chinwang-tao October 30th and controls railroad to Peitang. Wu's troops partly disorganized and captured and partly embarked on vessels, destination unknown. Wu appears to be still at Tientsin. Feng headquarters state, although not officially announced, President Tsao Kun yesterday sent resignation to Parliament and Cabinet and that Cabinet will perform duties of the President. See Legation's despatch number 1621, June 20, 1923,[17] enclosure 7 for the similar situation.

3. I likewise learn from Feng headquarters that Tuan Chi-jui and Sun Yat-sen expected to come Peking soon.

4. C. T. Wang has notified me of his assumption of office of Minister of Foreign Affairs November 1st.

MAYER

[17] Not printed.

893.00/5708 : Telegram

The Chargé in China (Mayer) to the Secretary of State

PEKING, *November 5, 1924—1 p.m.*
[Received 3 : 09 p.m.]

429. My 427, November 3, 5 p.m.

Number 1. Under date of November 3rd, Minister for Foreign Affairs officially notified me that President Tsao resigned November 2nd having handed seals to Cabinet with instructions to the latter to perform the duties of the President's office and that on November 2nd, Cabinet announced its assumption of these duties.

Number 2. General Connor telegraphed November 4th, 8 p.m., that Wu left Tangku by commercial vessel November 3, 3 a. m., destination unknown; that Feng's troops and municipal police began disarming Wu's troops November 3rd and continued without disorder. About 12,000 Fengtien troops proceeding to Chünliangcheng, 17 miles from Tientsin to assist in reorganization, Tangku quiet.

Number 3. Yesterday Peck returned my card to Feng and latter stated that previous to *coup d'état* of October 23, he had protested to Wu against lack of preparations for expedition and repeatedly urged President Tsao to reform the Government without effect. Recent action by Feng, Hu and Sun prompted by their duty to the country to secure peace and reunification by conference of leaders. Feng evidenced great desire for American approval and assistance. He placed full responsibility for international and financial affairs on C. T. Wang. He seemed somewhat dispirited and anxious.

Number 4. Jenkins telegraphs Sun leaving Canton November 6th, for Shanghai.

Number 5. International train from Tientsin arrived November 5, 2 a.m., and left November 5, 11 a.m., railway announces hereafter daily train to Tientsin.

Number 6. Repeated to Tokyo.

MAYER

893.00/5707 : Telegram

The Acting Secretary of State to the Chargé in China (Mayer)

WASHINGTON, *November 5, 1924—6 p.m.*

269. Tokyo Embassy telegraphs November 5 [18] that Japanese Consul at Tsingtau advises his Government our Consul there has agreed with Japanese and British colleagues to advise Wu Pei-fu not to land in the event of his arrival there.

---

[18] Telegram not printed.

Please advise Consul immediately that the Department could not approve such intervention in Chinese internal affairs.

Repeat to Tokyo as Department's No. 180.

GREW

893.00/5710 : Telegram

The Chargé in China (Mayer) to the Secretary of State

PEKING, *November 6, 1924—4 p.m.*
[Received November 6—1 : 55 p.m.]

434. 1. Chinese Government troops yesterday compelled Manchu ex-Emperor and entourage to vacate Forbidden City and they removed to Prince Chun's palace, where now residing. Today, by orders of the metropolitan police, as I am informed, the streets are beflagged to celebrate the initiation of "a genuine republic."

2. British, Netherlands and Japanese Ministers called on Minister for Foreign Affairs yesterday afternoon in relation to subject of ex-Emperor's safety, Sir Ronald Macleay having called upon Netherlands Minister and expressed opinion that King George would be solicitous for personal safety of the youth who was formerly Emperor of China and with whose family the British Royal Family had been on terms of friendship; Japanese Minister believes that his own sovereign animated by similar sentiments. At this interview British Minister informed Dr. Wang that if harm should befall ex-Emperor the credit reposed in the Chinese Government by foreign powers would be seriously impaired and referred to "terms of favorable treatment" to be given ex-Emperor and Imperial House as embodied in agreement between Chinese Government and ex-Emperor in 1912. See Legation's despatch number 427, February 13, 1912.[19] Yoshizawa made substantially same remarks, Netherlands Minister saying very little.

3. Minister for Foreign Affairs replied that agreement had been already revised by Yuan Shih-kai in 1916; that it was now intended to effect another revision in consultation with the ex-Emperor. Dr. Wang stated most positively that the Government would take precautions that no harm should befall ex-Emperor either in respect of his own person or private property.

4. Belief by credible persons that above action Bolshevik inspired, working through Kuomintang for purpose finally eliminating monarchical restoration and further inciting anti-imperialist feeling and

---

[19] *Foreign Relations,* 1912, p. 65; the enclosure giving the terms agreed upon with respect to the treatment of the Imperial Family is not printed.

so anti-foreign feeling. I am reliably informed that C. T. Wang
has seen Karakhan [20] daily for past week or two. . . .

5. Repeated to Tokyo.

MAYER

893.00/5724 : Telegram

The Chargé in China (Mayer) to the Secretary of State

PEKING, *November 7, 1924—4 p. m.*
[Received November 7—11 a. m.]

435. 1. Following is the most significant paragraph of the statement given to press by Minister for Foreign Affairs yesterday.

"As Minister for Foreign Affairs I wish to speak frankly. We
shall live up to the letter and spirit of our treaty engagements. In
so doing we wish to remind the friendly powers that China has a
right of her own existence. Any conditions derogatory to her
rights to exist as a free and independent nation must by necessity
be rectified by mutual arrangement as quickly as the exigency of
circumstances requires. It will be my bounden duty to promote
better understanding and to develop greater confidence between
the Chinese people and Government and the peoples and governments of all friendly powers. We are particularly conscious of
our duty in [collaboration?] with all neighboring and friendly
powers to carry out the provisions of the Washington Conference
and thus to ensure durable peace on the Pacific. For the attainment of that end, we the people of China, must first stand on our
own feet. In the name of my fellow countrymen I [fervently?]
invoke the assistance of and cooperation of all friends during the
hour of our need."

2. Preceding portion of statement contained justification of *coup
d'état* of October 23rd and caustic criticism of previous administration of Government.

3. Quoted statement would seem necessarily to imply that Dr.
Wang intends shortly to take up question of treaty revision.

MAYER

893.00/5733 : Telegram

The Chargé in China (Mayer) to the Secretary of State

PEKING, *November 7, 1924—5 p. m.*
[Received November 7—12: 17 p. m.]

436. 1. Your 269, November 5, 6 p. m. received and instructions
carried out.

[20] Soviet Ambassador in China.

2. On November 5, following received from U. S. S. *Pope:*

"Action contemplated by naval forces at Tsingtau if Wu enters harbor. Naval forces consist of Japanese and American. Wang Hun-chung, an Anfu sympathizer, will not allow Wu's troops to land without disarmament. The consular body in which the Japanese and American Navies concur consider only way to protect the foreigners is to prevent landing. To this end should he enter he will be required to anchor in the outer harbor and negotiate with Wang on a Japanese cruiser in the presence of commanding officer U. S. S. *Pope.* Wang stated that he would allow them all provisions and coal they may desire."

3. Upon receipt of which I sent following to American consul Tsingtau:

"November 5, 4 p. m. Wireless message from U. S. S. *Pope* outlines certain plans initiated by consular body for protection of foreigners Tsingtau in connection with possible landing Wu's troops. Having in mind American policy noninterference in Chinese internal affairs I desire you should telegraph at once full particulars and reasons prompting your action."

4. Admiral Washington informed me last night that consular body Chefoo was informed by Chinese authorities that Wu with three Chinese war vessels under Rear Admiral Wen and five transports carrying 10,000 troops en route Chefoo to force landing and that he was withdrawing U. S. S. *Stewart* and U. S. S. *Pillsbury* from Tientsin for service Chefoo.

5. I telegraphed American consul Chefoo as follows:

"November 6, 11 p.m. Following is substance of telegram from Department for instruction American consul Tsingtau repeated for your guidance:

'When Department informed American consul Tsingtau had agreed with Japanese and British colleagues to advise Wu not to land in the event of his arrival at Tsingtau, Department instructed me to advise consul there immediately that Department could not approve such intervention in Chinese internal affairs.' "

Following received from American consul Tsingtau:

"November 7, 3 a.m. Your November 4, 5 p.m. and November 6, 7 p.m., both received tonight. Plans discussed and adopted in conference with American and Japanese naval authorities. There is no foreign settlement at Tsingtau. Foreigners are scattered throughout entire city. Tsingtau is in possession of a force hostile to Wu. Wu's landing force at Tsingtau would mean street fighting under existing circumstances seriously jeopardizing American lives and rendering the naval forces available almost meaningless. Under the circumstances it was decided the only effective measure of insuring protection was to advise Wu not to land in the city and to go as far as firing across bows to prevent it, pending negotiations between the Chinese aboard Japanese cruiser. Naval authorities are being advised of State Department's attitude."

and

"November 7, 11 a.m. [sic] referring to your telegram of November 7, 6 p.m. [sic]. I have notified consuls and naval authorities of the withdrawal of my sanction of the arrangements outlined in my telegram November 7, 3 a.m. Japanese consul general now finds that his Government disapproves arrangement."

MAYER

893.00/5744 : Telegram

The Consul General at Shanghai (Cunningham) to the Secretary of State

SHANGHAI, *November 12, 1924—11 a.m.*
[Received November 12—3:20 a.m.]

Following telegram has been received from Nanking:

"November 11, 5 p.m. Please send following telegram to the Department for me: 'I have seen Marshal Chi today. He and Admiral Tu have sent vessel to meet Wu who is expected to arrive about the 13th for a conference. Chi has sent circular telegram supporting Tuan. Will accept Tuan's leadership but not that of Feng or Chang. Invasion by the last two would be forcibly resisted.

Representatives of the governors of eight provinces now are assembling here to decide upon course of action. Davis.' "

CUNNINGHAM

893.00/5746 : Telegram

The Chargé in China (Mayer) to the Secretary of State

PEKING, *November 11* [*12?*], *1924—4 p. m.*
[Received November 12—2:23 p. m.]

442. Following on general situation:

1. Chang Tso-lin and Feng Yu-hsiang in Tientsin and reported to be conferring with Tuan Chi-jui and others. About 40,000 Fengtien troops in vicinity Tientsin and more antagonistic [sic], who have taken over military control of Tientsin and adjacent railways from Feng's troops. Included in first elements Fengtien troops to arrive Tientsin was battalion of Russians now Machang. Chang believed to be in a position to enforce his will. Chang is stationing his troops beyond Tientsin on Tientsin-Pukow and across Peking-Mukden lines extending his control of railroad to southward. Reported Wu Pei-fu has sailed from Chefoo with three transports with from 5 to 10 thousand troops, destination unknown. Regarding attitude

of provincial leaders see American consul Nanking's telegram November 11, 5 p. m.[21] In announcement of preceding day Hsiao Yaonan indicates support of Wu Pei-fu. Sun Yat-sen has apparently decided to leave for north November 13th. Rail transport situation between Peking, Tientsin, Shanhaikwan still very unsatisfactory, international trains being run between Tientsin-Peking and return every few days. Great activity of Fengtien troop trains at Tientsin, withdrawal of Feng's forces from that point and general disorganization resulting from military control of railways, chiefly failure to restore normal train service. Doubtful if any substantial betterment will take place until after political situation somewhat more settled by anticipated conference at Tientsin since Chang will doubtless wish to keep trains there for possible troop movement. No disturbance Peking-Tientsin or other places. Machang is reported to be principal destination of Fengtien troop train and no Fengtien troops reported north of Yangtsun.

[Paraphrase]

2. Reference my telegrams no. 441 of November 11, noon; [22] no. 438 of November 9, 4 p.m.[22]; no. 435 of November 7, 4 p.m.

3. The present situation causes me much concern. In the present Peking Government the Soviet influence is very strong if not dominant. It is working chiefly through the Kuomintang Party. I do not wish to cause the Department undue alarm, but in my opinion it should be considered as distinctly possible that at any time the foreign powers may have to face a demand for the revision or cancellation of all of the so-called special-privilege treaties which they have with China. I consider Tuan Chi-jui and Chang Tso-lin to be the deciding factors. It is an important question now whether they will join with or oppose the Kuomintang Party which is under Soviet influence or control. Should they join with the Kuomintang I rather think that there will be the probability if not certainty that the Chinese Government will demand treaty revision or cancellation. Even should Tuan Chi-jui and Chang Tso-lin not join with the Kuomintang Party or endorse its policies, the present Peking Government urged on by the Soviets . . . [may] still take precipitate radical action. It is also possible that for a time at least all factions might join on a platform calling for the cancellation or revision of the treaties.

4. It is too early to report more than the possibilities as given above pending more definite information concerning the conferences

---

[21] See telegram of Nov. 12, from the consul general at Shanghai, *supra*.
[22] Not printed.

which Tuan Chi-jui, Feng Yu-hsiang, Chang Tso-lin and others are now holding in Tientsin.

5. It is of course a matter of first importance whether the Japanese will side with or against the Soviets and which of these two, if they oppose each other, will have the controlling influence over Tuan Chi-jui and Chang Tso-lin. This is something which cannot be known at present.

6. This telegram repeated to Tokyo Embassy.

MAYER

893.00/5767 : Telegram

The Consul General at Shanghai (Cunningham) to the Secretary of State

SHANGHAI, *November 13, 1924—3 p.m.*
[Received November 14—7 : 19 a.m.]

Yesterday afternoon one Chinese man-of-war and four Chinese transports heavily loaded with troops arrived Woosung via north channel and were joined by Admiral Fu's flagship, three other men-of-war and a transport. While no confirmation is possible it is believed that Wu Pei-fu is in one of the vessels. Gunboat *Chutai* with Admiral Fu aboard, two cruisers and four transports, proceeded up Yangtze 7 o'clock this morning.

CUNNINGHAM

893.00/5778 : Telegram

The Chargé in China (Mayer) to the Secretary of State

PEKING, *November 18, 1924—4 p.m.*
[Received November 18—2 : 55 p.m.]

448. My November 12, 4 p. m. Following on general situation:

1. Political situation still obscure. Unofficial reports that Chang, Feng and followers have appealed by circular telegram to provinces to support Tuan Chi-jui as "Provisional Chief Executive of the Chinese Republic", a new Chinese term which suggests dictatorship. They apparently await replies before announcing Tuan Chi-jui's assumption of power under this title.

2. Following just received from American consul general Hankow:

"General Wu arrived [garbled groups] this afternoon in advancing [*in advance of?*] his troops numbering 6,000 who will reach here tomorrow. General Hsiao called on Wu today. The Commissioner of Foreign Affairs handed me a pronouncement furnished him by Wu and signed by the high military authorities of the Yangtze-Kiang River and Yellow River provinces announcing the formation of a military government as an emergency measure to uphold the constitution. The agreement contains 10 articles summarized as follows:

(1) A military government for the protection of the constitution is formed; (2) the seat of the government is Wuchang; (3) the military government shall represent China in domestic and foreign affairs; (4) the military government shall be administered by the high commanders of the provincial armies and navies; (5) all state affairs shall be administered by a council presided over by a president and a vice president to be elected by the high commanders from among themselves; (6) high commanders unable to attend the council meeting may appoint representatives; (7) the military government shall consist of five ministries, namely: foreign affairs, finance, home affairs, war and communication; (8) the military government shall be dissolved when the constitution becomes operative again; (9) necessary alterations in the articles may be made by the council; (10) the above articles shall become operative upon the day of promulgation.

The above was signed, sealed and presented to the president on the 17th instant by 20 high military officials of the provinces concerned. The commissioners inform me that Tuan was invited to come to Wuchang to head the military government. Though the commissioner is a strong partisan of Wu, I believe this information is reliable."

3. As yet impossible to estimate effect of the announcement. Tuan Chi-jui has consistently said he would not assume leadership without complete approval of provincial leaders. Therefore this action by Yangtze *tuchuns* may prevent assumption of power by Tuan leaving situation at Tientsin in the air with a choice by Chang between returning to Manchuria or taking control himself at Peking. Reports from well-informed sources have indicated a certain impatience on Chang's part because of Tuan's hesitation in coming to Peking and taking charge of affairs.

4. Under date of November 15th American consul general Tientsin reports conversation with Marshal Chang and one of his close advisers of which following is brief summary of impressions gained by Gauss from conversations: Tuan and Chang dissatisfied with attitude C. T. Wang and Huang Fu and with their Soviet-Japanese exchanges. Their early eliminations from political scene probable. Chang intends more or less to disregard Sun Yat-sen as well as Feng Yu-hsiang. Chang believes there must be a rectification of Yangtze Valley situation by force, if necessary, in order to eliminate Marshal Ch'i, Sun Chuan-fang and Hsiao Yao-nan. Tuan Chi-jui would lend his influence toward peaceful handling of Yangtze situation, avoiding further resort to arms, if possible. Gauss further states Marshal Chang remarked he would come to Peking in few days; that Chang extremely cordial and invited Gauss to accompany him Peking. This Gauss declined with proper expressions of regret, in which decision I, of course, concurred.

5. Sun Yat-sen arrived Shanghai November 17th but not known if and when he will come north. On landing, Sun is reported by American consul general Shanghai to have made following typical statement:

"Understand my arrival causing some agitation. Would like to say to the foreigners Shanghai is China and the Chinese are the hosts, the foreigners guests. We shall have to take drastic measures if this is not realized. The Chinese are determined that the concessions must be returned."

6. Repeated to Tokyo.

MAYER

893.00/5780 : Telegram

The Chargé in China (Mayer) to the Secretary of State

PEKING, *November 20, 1924—4 p.m.*
[Received November 20—9 : 35 a.m.]

451. My 448, November 18, 4 p.m. paragraph 2. Following from American consul general Hankow:

"November 19, 7 p.m. My November 17, 11 p.m. General Wu left yesterday for Chengchow to be followed immediately by his troops who arrived here today.

No steps are being taken to carry out the plan of the proposed military government. Intention to form this government is not definite, the proposal being a temporary emergency measure designed primarily for defensive purposes against the North and also for threatening the North and restoring Chihli Party to power. Wu though anxious to carry out the project may be unable to retain support. Hsiao is opposed to the telegram out of a desire to see Wu leave Hupeh."

Morning press carries the announcement substantially as reported in my 448, November 18, 4 p.m. No information as yet regarding reaction of announcement on Tientsin conferences.

MAYER

893.00/5781 : Telegram

The Chargé in China (Mayer) to the Secretary of State

PEKING, *November 21, 1924—2 p.m.*
[Received November 21—9 : 39 a.m.]

452. My number 448, November 18, 4 p.m.

1. Pursuant to instructions from Minister for Foreign Affairs a secretary from Wai Chiao Pu has just called to inform me that Marshal Tuan Chi-jui is expected to come Peking at least within five days and that upon his arrival here Cabinet will hand over to Marshal Tuan the powers of Premier and President under which Cabinet has been functioning.

2. From my conversation with secretary from Foreign Office and conversation Chinese secretary has just had with apparently well-informed politicians, Marshal Tuan and associates have not yet determined definitely form his anticipated administration will take.

3. In accord with Department's 277, of November 11, 4 p.m.[23] I shall not enter into formal relations with Marshal Tuan or any authorities acting under him should he take charge of affairs at Peking as anticipated, until I receive the Department's instructions in the matter. Should Marshal Tuan cause the question of recognition to be broached I shall be noncommittal.

4. Repeated to Tokyo.

MAYER

893.00/5786 : Telegram

The Consul General at Shanghai (Cunningham) to the Secretary of State

SHANGHAI, *November 22, 1924.*
[Received November 22—1 : 45 p.m.]

Following from Nanking:

"November 22, 11 a.m. Please send following telegram to the Department: 'Marshal Chi embarrassed by Wu's unauthorized use of his name in manifesto proclaiming Yangtze military government, and has repeated circular telegram endorsing Tuan. He will assist Wu defensively but considers aggression impracticable.

Situation delicate and uncertain. Davis.'"

CUNNINGHAM

893.00/5787 : Telegram

The Chargé in China (Mayer) to the Secretary of State

PEKING, *November 24, 1924—7 p.m.*
[Received November 24—11 : 15 a.m.]

455. My 452, November 21, 1 [2] p.m.

1. According to telephone message from Foreign Office Tuan Chi-jui assumed office this morning as "Chief Executive of the Republic of China". Message also stated that official notification of this act would be conveyed to me late tonight or tomorrow.

2. American foreign adviser to Government states Cabinet has not turned over its power to Tuan and that not yet decided whether Cabinet will continue to function, tender its resignation to Tuan or surrender its power to new Cabinet. I shall report further as

---

[23] *Post*, p. 419.

soon as definite information available regarding exact status of Government.

3. Chang Tso-lin arrived Peking today with some thousand troops. Peking is quiet.

4. Repeated to Tokyo.

MAYER

893.00/5796 : Telegram

The Chargé in China (Mayer) to the Secretary of State

PEKING, *November 25, 1924—5 p. m.*
[Received November 25—5 : 27 p. m.]

456. My 455, November 24, 7 p. m.

1. I have received formal note dated November 24th from Minister for Foreign Affairs [C. T. Wang?] as follows:

"I have the honor to state that on November 24th, 1924, I received a mandate from the Chief Executive of the Republic of China Tuan Chi-jui stating as follows:

'On November 24th, 1924, I, Tuan Chi-jui, assumed office as Chief Executive of the Republic of China. At the time of assuming office I formally announced as follows: I, Tuan Chi-jui, although without ability and undeserving assume office as Chief Executive of the Republic of China, I swear that I will endeavor to consolidate the republican government, respect public opinion and strive to bring about reform within the country and raise the nation's standing abroad. I [apparent omission] the foregoing reverently.'

I have the honor Mr. Chargé to transmit the foregoing for your information."

2. Following mandates gazetted November 24th:

"The system of the Provisional Government of the Republic of China is hereby promulgated. Seal of the Chief Executive of the Republic of China.

ARTICLE 1. The Provisional Government of the Republic of China shall have a Chief Executive who shall have supreme control of civil and military affairs and shall be commander in chief of the Army and Navy.

ARTICLE 2. The Chief Executive shall act as the representative of the Republic of China in international affairs.

ARTICLE 3. The Provisional Government shall have Ministers of State to assist the Chief Executive in attending to [apparent omission] of the President state [*sic*]. All mandates of the Provisional Government as well as documents relating to state matters shall be countersigned by the Ministers of State.

ARTICLE 4. The Chief Executive shall empower Ministers of State to control the following Ministries: Foreign Affairs, Interior, Finance, War, Navy, Justice, Education, Commerce and Agriculture and Communications.

ARTICLE 5. The Chief Executive shall summon the Ministers of State to hold Cabinet meetings.

ARTICLE 6. This system of government shall go into effect from the date of promulgation but will be declared null and void when the formal government is established.

The Institution of the Provisional Government of the Republic of China at this time has for its object the reorganization of government on new lines and the initiation of a general change with the cooperation of the people. The task is of great magnitude and questions of every [omission] are awaiting joint solution by all concerned. All former Executive and judicial laws and orders shall continue in effect except insofar as they may be incompatible with the organization of the Provisional Government or may have been canceled by official orders.

The Government has now been established and I, the Chief Executive, have entered upon the performance of my weighty duty to the full extent of my ability. All the multifarious functions of the Government await attention and all civil and military officials in Peking and the provinces shall continue to administer their posts as in the past, lending their united assistance in meeting the difficulties of the times."

Mandate November 24th appoints following Cabinet: Foreign Affairs, Tang Shao-yi; Interior, Kung Hsin-chan; Finance, Li Shih-hao; War, Wu Kuang-hsin; Navy, Lin Chien-chang; Justice, Chang Shih-chao; Education, Wang Chiu-ling; Agriculture and Commerce, Yang Shu-chan; Communications, Yeh Kung-cho.

3. Referring to third paragraph my 452, at meeting of heads of Legations this afternoon senior minister stated Tuan Chi-jui had approached him to ask if foreign representatives would be willing to call upon him in day or two to pay personal respects individually and without ceremony.

4. It was unanimous opinion of chiefs of mission that Tuan Chi-jui is the *de facto* government and for this reason the senior minister was authorized to reply to Tuan Chi-jui that the heads of Legations would call individually on him in day or two to pay him personal respects as head of the provisional *de facto* government, and that the senior minister should make it entirely clear that such action would in no way imply formal *de jure* recognition.

5. I made reservation that, while I personally agreed with proposed procedure, I could not associate myself therewith until I had received instructions to that effect from my Government.

6. It was the sense of the meeting that question of *de jure* recognition was not pending at this time owing to the fact that the present *de facto* authorities in their mandates and in conversation with senior minister stressed the provisional character of the present regime and since the question of *de jure* recognition if and when it arose was a matter for the respective Governments to decide.

7. Tuan Chi-jui is in my opinion and generally so considered I believe the one man in China in whom there is any hope at present of uniting the different factions and leaders in an effort to bring order and stable government out of the present situation. For this reason I believe that the Provisional Government he has set up should be given some measure of support by the foreign powers and that the procedure proposed in today's meeting of heads of Legations as outlined above is well suited to this purpose. It commits us to nothing but a recognition of the fact that there is a *de facto* government under the leadership of Tuan Chi-jui. I strongly recommend that I be instructed immediately by telegraph to associate myself with other heads of Legations and to pay my respects to Tuan as set forth above.

8. It was likewise the sense of today's meeting that the recognition of Tuan Chi-jui as the *de facto* authority would permit the respective Legations to reply in the usual form to the anticipated note from new Minister for Foreign Affairs announcing his assumption of office. He would be merely an officer in the *de facto* government. I shall also adopt this procedure unless otherwise directed by the Department.

MAYER

893.00/5796 : Telegram

The Secretary of State to the Chargé in China (Mayer)

WASHINGTON, November 26, 1924—4 p.m.

295. Your 456, November 25, 5 p.m. You are authorized to associate yourself with the other heads of missions in taking the action outlined in paragraphs 3 and 4 making it entirely clear that your action is in no sense to be interpreted as implying a formal recognition.

The Department concurs in the view generally taken at the meeting of the heads of missions with respect to the provisional character of the present regime and the question of recognition, as reported by you, in paragraph 6.

HUGHES

893.00/5803 : Telegram

The Chargé in China (Mayer) to the Secretary of State

PEKING, November 29, 1924—6 p. m.
[Received November 30—10:10 a.m.]

459. Following on general situation.

1. On November 27th Chang Tso-lin accompanied by the chiefs of his civil and military foreign departments and other officers

called at the Legation in the diplomatic quarter. My conversation with him was of general nature. Incidentally Chang's relations with the Central Government may be considered rectified by mandate issued by the Cabinet November 6th as follows:

"All mandates cashiering and ordering the arrest of officials for political actions as issued from July 29, 1920, to November 2, 1924, are hereby canceled."

2. I returned Chang's call this afternoon and had a long and extremely interesting conversation with him which I will report fully by telegraph tomorrow. The principal burden of his remarks expressed with evident seriousness was the concern with which he viewed Bolshevik activities in China.

3. Referring to the Department's 295, November 26, 4 p.m. The diplomatic representatives yesterday called individually on Tuan. He expressed himself to me optimistically regarding unification and said he had just received a telegram from Wu Pei-fu stating that if those officials who formerly supported Presidents Yuan and Tsao and now announced their support of Tuan were sincere, he, Wu, would likewise support Tuan. I inferred the reference was to Chang Tso-lin concerning whose genuine loyalty to Tuan there seems to be some doubt in Chinese public opinion. Tuan explained his present position as merely a temporary means of bridging over an interval and stated that while not desirous of returning to political life after his withdrawal therefrom in 1920 he had thought it his duty to sacrifice himself in order to unify the country. I took care to make it clear to an officer of the Wai Chiao Pu that my action in calling upon Marshal Tuan was in no sense to be interpreted as implying *de jure* recognition. I was informed that this was well understood. Admiral Tsai Ting-kan informed me most emphatically and in a manner which compels my belief in the sincerity of his statement that Marshal Tuan was much opposed to Soviet activities.

4. I submit following comment on the Cabinet supplementing *China Year Book*: An official of the Foreign Office informed me that it is practically certain Tang Shao-yi will not take up post of Minister for Foreign Affairs and that W. W. Yen is probable next appointee. Following Ministers are of Anfu Party: Finance, Interior, War. Minister of the Navy has been associated with Lu Yung-hsiang and has Anfu affiliations. Appointment of Minister of Education seems designed to please Tang Chi-yao, Military Governor of Yunnan. Minister of Justice is reported to have been closely associated with Tuan lately and to have assisted in drafting his political announcements. Minister of Agriculture represents Kuomintang and Minister of Communications old Communications clique. Latter is privately considered representative of Chang Tso-lin but

Chang denied any desire for representation in the Cabinet. Ministers Interior, War, Justice and Communications have assumed office.

5. Feng Yu-hsiang has for the past few days apparently been trying to resign from the command of his troops and his other official duties. Mandate issued by Tuan November 27th while announcing this desire on Feng's part, urges him in laudatory terms to retain his various posts. Difficult to know whether this is a question of face and whether Tuan and Chang Tso-lin really desire Feng to resign or whether Tuan and Chang are somewhat apprehensive of situation which would be created by resignation and Feng's consequent release from his responsibilities as commander of his troops. . . .

6. Repeated to Tokyo.

MAYER

893.00/5804 : Telegram

The Chargé in China (Mayer) to the Secretary of State

PEKING, *December 1, 1924—4 p.m.*
[Received 10:07 p. m.]

465. My telegram no. 459, November 26, 6 p. m. paragraph 2.

1. During call on Chang on November 29th he spoke without formality with surprising directness and apparently with frankness as well as cordiality and at length regarding Bolshevik activities in China.

2. After exchange of usual greetings Marshal Chang asked me what I thought of the Bolsheviks. I replied that the fact that our Government had not yet recognized the Soviets should adequately answer his question. He then observed that during recent interview with Karakhan latter had indicated a special animosity against United States. Karakhan's remarks were not of a nature Chang considered polite to repeat to me. Karakhan had dwelt mostly on capitalistic imperialism of the United States; that it was seeking to acquire all the wealth of the world and that it was imperatively necessary to accomplish the overthrow of the United States.

[Paraphrase.] Chang then said that in his opinion the most serious menace at present was the "Bolshevik question" and that Soviet activities in China greatly imperiled the lives and property of foreigners in China. He considered most dangerous Sun Yat-sen's close association with the Soviets. Chang said that he would not himself remain in Peking if Sun was coming to Peking to carry out the same program as he had at Canton. Chang expressed the opinion that the diplomatic representatives in Peking of the foreign powers should take some decided stand respecting the question of

Bolshevism. If this were not done he did not know what his own policy would be, but he would take a definite stand if the foreign representatives did. He said that under no circumstances could he associate himself with Sun and his Bolshevik policy. [End paraphrase.]

3. In order to feel Chang out I observed that the problem of dangerous Bolshevik activities in China appeared to me one of Chinese internal administration and to be dealt with by the Chinese Government. Chang replied that he did not consider it such since the danger was an international one and of world-wide extent. I inquired whether Chang thought that there would be any immediate dangerous developments. He expressed belief that coming of Doctor Sun would make question one of immediate urgency; that necessary to wait and see position Tuan would take in the matter but primarily necessary that foreign Ministers should adopt definite policy. American policy of nonintervention in Chinese affairs appreciated but Bolshevik question one with which foreign nations should concern themselves.

4. Chang then discussed Sun Yat-sen's announcements in regard to "unjust treaties" and observed that he thought western nations on considerations of justice would soon modify treaties when proper time came; that however a proper course must be followed in securing revision and inadmissible [*inadvisable?*] to make demand for abrogation "unjust treaties" in sudden manner. Agitation fomented by Doctor Sun was dangerous.

5. Chang spoke in similar vein regarding Bolshevik menace to the Netherlands Minister and I believe likewise to the British Minister and possibly others of the diplomatic body.

6. Although difficult to know reason or reasons why Chang should have spoken so openly, extensively, and hostilely respecting Bolshevik activities in China, following seems a reasonable deduction. As intimated in paragraph 3 of my 442 November 12, 4 p.m.[24] it has been to my mind quite possible that the Bolsheviks through the radical wing of the Kuomintang Party headed by Sun Yat-sen, C. T. Wang, Huang Fu and the like might make demand for immediate revision or cancelation a popular rallying cry; that Chang realizes that he, Tuan and other conservative leaders in China would not be able to oppose such a popular movement and might even have to join with it; that the Soviets through their local followers and sympathizers might thus control Chinese Government isolating Chang in Manchuria and seriously jeopardizing his position there. That Chang desires the foreign powers to take some action which will permit

---

[24] *Ante,* p. 393.

conservative Chinese leaders to work with them and prevent Bolshevik influence from predominating in China. Repeated to Tokyo.

MAYER

893.00/5805 : Telegram

The Chargé in China (Mayer) to the Secretary of State

PEKING, *December 2, 1924—noon.*
[Received December 2—3:33 a.m.]

466. My number 465, December 1, 4 p.m. Chang Tso-lin without warning left Peking December 2, 4 a.m., I am informed, for Tientsin taking headquarters staff and bodyguard. Sun Fo and other Kuomintang leaders in Peking.

MAYER

893.00/5814 : Telegram

The Chargé in China (Mayer) to the Secretary of State

PEKING, *December 3, 1924—3 p.m.*
[Received December 3—1:30 p.m.]

468. My 466, December 2, noon, and 465, December 1, 4 p.m.

1. Chang's sudden departure from Peking has further complicated situation which is very obscure. Numerous rumors, very few facts. Chang has returned to old headquarters at Tientsin. Military attaché reports all Fengtien troops at Peking moving toward Tientsin. Feng Yu-hsiang remains in vicinity of Peking and from all accounts refuses to grant interviews or discuss politics and insists on resigning despite efforts by Government to dissuade him from such action. Ex-Emperor took refuge 29th in Japanese Legation where apparently still remains. I have it from best authority that ex-Emperor originally desired take refuge in British Legation but was dissuaded therefrom. His action a complete surprise.

2. Judging from statements made to me by Chang Tso-lin, as reported my 465, December 1, 4 p.m., and fears entertained rather generally that Feng Yu-hsiang is subject to Kuomintang and Soviet influence as reported in fifth paragraph my 459, November 29, 6 p.m., and persistent statements that Feng Yu-hsiang, Hu Ching-yi and Sun Yao still continue to recruit and have all told about 100,000 men in immediate vicinity of Peking, it seems rather logical to conclude that principal reason for Chang's sudden departure from Peking was his realization that his position here was untenable if not dangerous to his life. He either had to bring to Peking all his troops from the vicinity of Tientsin, judged some 40,000 in number, or retire to vicinity which strategically is far better for him than

Peking. Chang possibly may have suddenly decided to be in Tientsin to meet Sun Yat-sen to see if he could associate himself with Sun. This is not likely.

3. Out of all the welter of rumors and the few facts, straws in the wind, such as Chang Tso-lin's sudden departure, the ex-Emperor's unexpectedly seeking refuge in Diplomatic Quarter, Feng Yu-hsiang's continuing to remain at or near Peking, although having stated he wishes to go abroad, and Sun Yat-sen's imminent arrival, a grave apprehension arises that extreme Kuomintang and Soviet influence may dominate Peking. Except by good fortune and unless the foreign powers are able to devise some defensive action in the circumstances, the chances seem to be that the radical wing of the Kuomintang Party and the Soviets are to have their day in Peking. Tuan Chi-jui's continuance in power seems dependent upon his ability to control allegiance of the various discordant factions. The mere fact, of course, of Chang's withdrawal to Tientsin does not necessarily spell his abandonment of Tuan, since if Chang desires to oppose Sun Yat-sen and the Red element in China he can do so very effectively from Tientsin as a base. However, as I observed, the outlook is far from bright.

4. Feeling, I believe, even more pessimistic than I do in the above regard, the British Minister called upon me yesterday to suggest an informal meeting of the representatives of the Washington Conference powers for the purpose of discussing and exploring into the question of the advisability of recommending to our respective Governments the immediate joint issuance of a statement. This statement would inform the Chinese authorities and people of the continued desire of these powers, as evidenced at Washington Conference, to make [*take?*] up with China, at the very earliest moment that she puts her house in order, the question of treaty revision, and that these powers to this [end?] would support in every proper way any government in China which would show a capacity for undertaking the task of restoring law and order in the country. At the same time the statement should definitely disclose the decision of the powers concerned not to recognize or have truck with any administration which might be set up in Peking by those Peking leaders in China who in the present as in the past have been and are seeking to incite the Chinese people against the friendly attitude [of the] powers.

5. I readily agreed to attend any such informal conference of representatives of Washington Conference powers which is scheduled for morning of 4th. Some such action as suggested by the British Minister might be effective in opposition to extreme nationalist

and Bolshevik trend of events in China, although a double-edged weapon with both good and bad potentialities.

6. After my conversation with Chang Tso-lin, reported in my 465, December 1, 4 p.m., Chinese secretary had a long conversation with General Wang, chief of the Manchurian military foreign affairs department, who appears very close to Chang and who was present both when Chang called on me and my return visit to him. To Peck's inquiry regarding exactly what assistance Chang considered foreign powers could be to the conservative element in China at the present time to help them oppose the Soviets, Wang stated that Marshal Chang had in mind an announcement by the foreign powers of their sympathetic willingness to discuss treaty revision just as soon as a government was established in China capable of giving effect to any international arrangements which would result from such a discussion. Marshal Chang feared that Sun and his Red adherents prompted by Karakhan would raise louder and louder the rallying cry of "down with the unjust treaties" which being a national issue the conservative leaders in China would not be able to oppose. An announcement by the powers as suggested above by Marshal Chang would [,he] believed, cut under this Bolshevik propaganda and enable him and other conservatives to make common cause with the foreign powers against Soviet influence in China. I venture to invite Department's attention to paragraph 6, my 465, December 1, 4 p.m., expressing the possibility that some such idea as there described was in Chang's mind during his conversation with me on November 29th. Repeated to Tokyo.

MAYER

893.00/5804 : Telegram

The Secretary of State to the Chargé in China (Mayer)

[Paraphrase]

WASHINGTON, *December 3, 1924—4 p.m.*

300. Third paragraph of your 465, December 1, 4 p.m. Your observation that the question of dangerous Bolshevist activities in China primarily is one of domestic Chinese administration has my complete approval. I would point out with respect to Marshal Chang's contention that it is world-wide and international, that the American Government cannot concern itself with the matter except in case American interests are directly involved. The serious aspect of propaganda directed from Moscow is, however, fully appreciated by this Government.

HUGHES

893.00/5818 : Telegram

The Chargé in China (Mayer) to the Secretary of State

PEKING, *December 5, 1924—3 p.m.*
[Received December 5—9:15 a. m.]

473. My number 451, November 20, 4 p.m. The following telegram has been received from consul general at Hankow:

"December 4, 5 p.m. Due to the threatened attack by Shensi and Shansi troops on Loyang, Wu fled from there on the evening of the 2nd. Wu's troops refused to support at Chengchow. He conferred with Chang Fu-lai [25] and Li Chi-chen [26] when it was decided that being entirely without troops Wu should continue to Hankow. He is now at Sinyang, Hsiao urges him to retire. Local railway office is informed Yellow River Bridge blown up by the 24th Division to prevent troops under Hu Ching-yi from coming south.

General unrest increasing in Honan besides renewed brigandage due to the withdrawal of troops from bandit-infested areas there are reported. Troop disorders at various points on Peking-Hankow and Lund-Hai Railways and popular feeling against Wu will prevent him from recovering control of troops and recruiting new army".

MAYER

893.00/5840 : Telegram

The Chargé in China (Mayer) to the Secretary of State

PEKING, *December 13, 1924—noon.*
[Received December 13—5:19 a.m.]

480. Mandates issued December 11th dismissed from office Chi Hsieh-yuan, Military Governor of Kiangsu, and appointed Civil Governor Han Acting Director General. Military rules same Province and is under Lu Yung-hsiang, Pacification Commissioner Kiangsu [and] Anhui.

Whether Chi will vacate post or make armed resistance still uncertain.[27] Credibly reported Chang Tso-lin will give Lu Yung-hsiang effective military assistance in removing Chi and securing military control of two Provinces if necessary as Chang is thought to be determined uproot Chihli Party in spite of Tuan's professed policy peaceful unification.

MAYER

---

[25] *Tuchun* of Honan.
[26] Civil Governor of Honan.
[27] The consul general at Shanghai in despatch no. 2837, Dec. 31, 1924, reported that Chi had retired to private life in the International Settlement of Shanghai (file no. 893.00/5960). Chi resumed military activities, Jan. 1925.

893.00/5871 : Telegram

The Minister in China (Schurman) to the Secretary of State

PEKING, *December 22, 1924—3 p. m.*
[Received December 22—7 : 48 a.m.]

500. Legation's 463, December 1, noon.[28] Following sent commander in chief today:

"Legation's November 30, 1 p.m. Referring to our recent conversations I perceive no objection to your withdrawing destroyers from North China waters."

SCHURMAN

MAINTENANCE OF A UNITED FRONT BY THE POWERS IN OPPOSITION TO THE THREATENED SEIZURE OF CUSTOMS AT CANTON BY SUN YAT-SEN [29]

893.51/4580

The British Ambassador (Howard) to the Secretary of State

No. 280　　　　WASHINGTON, *March 26, 1924.*

SIR: With reference to previous correspondence regarding the joint naval demonstration at Canton in consequence of Sun Yat-Sen's threat to seize the Customs at that port, I have the honour to inform you, under instructions from His Majesty's Principal Secretary of State for Foreign Affairs, that His Majesty's Government no longer consider it necessary to maintain the demonstration in question provided that arrangements can be made for its renewal in case of necessity.

In acquainting you with my Government's views on this matter, I am instructed to enquire whether the Government of the United States are in agreement therewith, and in that event I should be most grateful if you would inform me at your earliest convenience whether, in case of necessity, the United States Government would be prepared to co-operate in arranging for a renewal of the naval demonstration referred to above.

A similar enquiry is being addressed to the Governments to which they are accredited by His Majesty's Representatives at Paris, Rome, Tokio and Lisbon.

I have [etc.]　　　　ESME HOWARD

---

[28] Not printed.
[29] For previous correspondence regarding the threatened seizure of customs at Canton, see *Foreign Relations*, 1923, vol. I, pp. 551 ff.

893.51/4580

The Secretary of State to the British Ambassador (Howard)

WASHINGTON, *March 31, 1924.*

EXCELLENCY: I have the honor to acknowledge the receipt of your Note No. 280 of March 26, 1924, stating that the British Government no longer considers it necessary to maintain the naval demonstration in force at Canton in consequence of Sun Yat-sen's threat to seize the Customs at that port, provided that arrangements can be made for its renewal in case of necessity, and inquiring whether this Government is in agreement with this view and would be prepared to cooperate in arranging for a renewal of the naval demonstration in case of necessity.

Although this Government has received no definite recommendation from its Minister in Peking that the demonstration is no longer necessary, it nevertheless understands that there no longer exists any urgent need for the continuance thereof beyond the usual detail of naval forces which it has been customary to maintain at and in the vicinity of Canton.

Without committing itself to any definite engagement such as appears to be suggested in your Note, with respect to any eventual action in regard to the situation at Canton, it is aware of no circumstances which would cause it to alter its previous attitude of cooperation in the event of a similar emergency occurring in the future.

Accept [etc.]   CHARLES E. HUGHES

893.51/4580

The Secretary of State to the British Ambassador (Howard)

WASHINGTON, *April 12, 1924.*

EXCELLENCY: With reference to your note No. 280 of March 26, 1924, concerning the naval demonstration at Canton, and supplementing my reply thereto of March 31, 1924, I have the honor to inform you that the American Minister at Peking, in a telegram, dated April 9, 1924,[30] reports that, although there is still some uncertainty as to what Sun Yat-sen may do, such uncertainty is not greater now than it would be at a future date, and that there is no other reason for continuing the naval demonstration. The Minister further states that both he and his colleagues are of the opinion that no declaration should be made at the time of the withdrawal of the extra vessels, but that the Consuls should make it known in their private conversation that the ships would return if Sun indicates

[30] Not printed.

any intention of carrying out his threat to seize the Customs, or should he attack, or prepare to attack, the Custom House.

Accept [etc.]   CHARLES E. HUGHES

893.51/4604 : Telegram

The Minister in China (Schurman) to the Secretary of State

PEKING, *April 25, 1924—10 a. m.*
[Received April 25—7:11 a. m.]

109. My 99, April 9, 5 p.m.,[31] repeated April 11, 10 a.m., for information to Jenkins, who telegraphs April 24, 4 p.m.:

"As British gunboat will be withdrawn tomorrow and Japanese and French also have withdrawn, Captain Lannon and I have decided American destroyer should proceed to Hongkong there to await further orders. This means discontinuance naval demonstration in accordance with plan outlined in your April 11, 10 a.m."

Commander in chief, Asiatic Fleet, telegraphs:

"Understood that English about to withdraw extra vessel from Canton and that you and American consul and American senior naval officers at Canton consider presence of destroyer no longer necessary. I concur in this opinion and contemplate withdrawing United States ship *Whipple* in the near future. Extra vessel will be available to return to Canton on short notice if necessary."

SCHURMAN

893.51/4699 : Telegram

The Chargé in China (Bell) to the Secretary of State

PEKING, *October 20, 1924—5 p.m.*
[Received 10:35 p.m.]

397. 1. My telegram 394, October 19, 12 a.m. [*noon.*] [31] Following from Jenkins:

"October 19, 1 p.m. Referring to my telegram of October 18, noon. It is rumored persistently Sun will attempt to seize customs tomorrow. No Japanese warship in port at present and neither I nor commander of South China Patrol believe we should consent to cooperate in use of force to prevent seizure unless British, French and Japanese warships are to actually take part.

As this situation will probably be identical with that of last December I assume we should be warranted in opposing seizure by force but I would appreciate instructions in connection with Legation's April 2, 3 p.m., quoting Department's attitude towards question. Please answer as soon as possible.

---

[31] Not printed.

British landing detachment marines Shameen today. If clash with Sun develops, situation with respect to the safety of foreigners will be more serious in my opinion than last December because of local Russian Soviet influence.

French consul just informed me French warships in port will probably not act without definite instructions from the French Minister."

2. The Department's telegram referred to by Jenkins is number 62, March 31, 3 p.m.[33] Since no Japanese vessel is at Canton and since Jenkins emphasizes Soviet influence there I desire the Department's instructions before authorizing participation in another joint action in protection of the Canton customs.

3. Jenkins' recent reports would indicate that the Sun government is completely under domination of Soviet agents. If this is so an initial success at Canton in defying the treaty powers' contention regarding the customs would dangerously assist Soviet agents in their endeavor to incite Chinese to repudiation of all treaties. I assume that seizure of customs at Canton would leave Chang Tso-lin to seize Manchurian customs which he has already threatened (see my telegram 375, October 2, 4 p.m.[33]) Incidentally Manchuria also has become important sphere of Soviet activity. From this standpoint additional weight seems given to the Department's views respecting insuring of Maritime Customs as essential to whole system of treaty rights (see Department's telegram 243 December 5, 1923[34]).

4. There is reason to fear that the apparent efforts of the Soviet Government to achieve the disintegration of China as a national entity are regarded with favor by the Japanese Government at least as concerns Manchuria. I therefore apprehend Japanese reluctance to cooperate again in protection of the Canton customs lest precedent be set requiring Japanese participation later in international support of the Central Government against Chang Tso-lin. Japanese cooperation at Canton therefore seems essential.

5. Although total American portion 1900 indemnity has now been remitted I assume the American Government still asserts former interest in the integrity of the customs based not only on general grounds but also on actual claim to revenues as secondary security for unpaid obligations owed to American citizens.

6. In view of these various considerations and in spite of Jenkins' report of imminent action by Sun I have telegraphed him and the commander in chief of the Asiatic Fleet as follows:

"October 20, 5 p.m. Your telegram October 19, 1 p.m. American vessels should not take forcible measures to prevent seizure customs

---

[33] Not printed.
[34] *Foreign Relations*, 1923, vol. I, p. 562.

until further instructed and unless British, French and Japanese ships cooperate in action. Keep me informed by telegraph regarding all foreign war vessels at or near Canton."

7. I request the Department's early instructions.

BELL

893.51/4699 : Telegram

The Secretary of State to the Chargé in China (Bell)

WASHINGTON, *October 22, 1924—3 p.m.*

243. Your No. 397, October 20, 5 p.m. is being repeated to London and Paris, and reference thereto being made to Tokyo (on the assumption that Tokyo has received a copy) with instructions, without disclosing the text, promptly to discuss the substance thereof with the Foreign Offices concerned with a view to ascertaining, as fully as possible, the views of the respective governments with regard to the maintenance of the integrity of the Canton Customs. The Department's instruction is in part as follows:

"It is the Department's view that the situation at Canton, which again appears to threaten the integrity of the Chinese Customs, is one which does not permit of isolated action but requires, if any action is to be taken, close cooperation on the part of the Powers principally interested. . . . You may state that this Government is prepared to cooperate . . . in the same manner as it did in December, 1923, provided that like cooperation is assured by the British, French, and Japanese Governments."

The Department approves of the telegrams despatched by you to Jenkins and to the Commander in Chief of the Asiatic Fleet as quoted in paragraph 6 of your No. 397, October 20, 1924.

HUGHES

893.51/4704 : Telegram

The Chargé in China (Bell) to the Secretary of State

[Extracts]

PEKING, *October 22, 1924—4 p.m.*
[Received October 22—9 : 55 a.m.]

398. My 397, October 20, 5 p.m. 1. Following from American consul Canton:

"October 21, 3 p.m. Your October 20, 5 p.m. Three British and two French river gunboats now in port, also United States ship *Helena* and *Pampanga.* United States ship *Sacramento* at Hongkong. Understand that Russian cruiser *Vorowsky* still at Whampoa. Japanese consul tells me he will not ask for naval vessel until necessity evident.

Understand that everything essential in customhouse has already been transferred to Shameen and that commissioner could carry on from concession even if Sun seized customs building. Such course might be preferable to forcible measures by the powers."

.   .   .   .

BELL

893.51/4709

The British Ambassador (Howard) to the Secretary of State

No. 1006   WASHINGTON, *October 25, 1924.*

SIR: I have the honour to inform you that His Majesty's Government have learnt that the Canton Government are again threatening to seize the Customs House and to declare Canton a free port.

I am directed by my Government to express the earnest hope that you will authorize the United States Representative at Peking to concert with His Majesty's Representative in arranging for a renewal of the naval demonstration.

I have [etc.]   ESME HOWARD

893.51/4708 : Telegram

The Chargé in Japan (Caffery) to the Secretary of State

TOKYO, *October 25, 1924—7 p.m.*
[Received October 25—1:40 p.m.]

274. Department's telegram 171, October 22, 3 p.m.[35] The Minister for Foreign Affairs informs me that the Japanese Government attaches very much importance to the maintenance of the integrity of the Canton customs; but that the [apparent omission] believes that the consular corps at Canton should address another vigorous protest on the subject of [*to?*] the Canton Government and only in case it becomes apparent that they intend to disregard that protest should the powers take positive measures; that as a last resort the Japanese Government would be inclined to join in a naval demonstration in cooperation with the other interested powers; that however he is inclined to believe that on account of the changed situation at Peking Sun Yat-sen will probably not go ahead with his threat and seize customs. Peking informed.

CAFFERY

[35] Not printed.

893.51/4710 : Telegram

The Chargé in France (Whitehouse) to the Secretary of State

PARIS, *October 26, 1924—11 a.m.*
[Received October 26—11 : 05 a.m.]

463. My 458, October 23, 7 p.m.[36] Léger of the Asiatic Division informed me last evening by order of Laroche [37] that the French attitude regarding the maintenance of the integrity of the Canton customs had in no way been modified. French Government was quite prepared to oppose seizure and considered that the instructions given the French admiral for last December were continuing and would apply automatically at any recurrence of the same situation. Léger was very definite on this question for naval instructions although I had not mentioned either warships or instructions in my conversation with Laroche.

WHITEHOUSE

893.51/4709

The Secretary of State to the British Ambassador (Howard)

WASHINGTON, *November 8, 1924.*

EXCELLENCY : I have the honor to acknowledge the receipt of your Note No. 1006 of October 25, 1924, stating that the British Government has learned that the Canton Government is again threatening to seize the Canton Customs and expressing the hope of the British Government that the American representative in Peking may be authorized to concert with the British representative in arranging for a renewal of the naval demonstration at Canton.

Being likewise informed of the apparent seriousness of the situation at Canton, this Government had already on the 22d instant transmitted a report thereon to its representatives at London, Paris and Tokyo, stating its view that the situation was one which did not permit of isolated action, but required, if any action were to be taken, the close cooperation of the Powers principally interested. The representatives were at the same time instructed to discuss the matter with the respective Foreign Offices concerned and authorized to state that this Government was prepared to cooperate, for the purpose of maintaining the integrity of the Canton Customs, in the same manner as it did in December, 1923.

---

[36] Not printed.
[37] Director of political and commercial affairs, French Foreign Office.

While exchanges of views on this subject were proceeding, this Government was informed by its representative in London that the British Foreign Office had learned that Sun Yat-sen was threatening the seizure only of the "native" Canton Customs and that accordingly the British Minister at Peking and the naval authorities considered there was no need for naval action at the present time.

Accept [etc.]   CHARLES E. HUGHES

893.51/4718

The British Ambassador (Howard) to the Secretary of State

No. 1092   WASHINGTON, *November 12, 1924.*

SIR: I have the honour to acknowledge the receipt of the note which you were so good as to address to me on the 8th instant and in reply to state that His Majesty's Representatives at Paris, Rome, Tokio and Lisbon have been instructed to inform the Governments to which they are accredited that as the Canton Government apparently intend to seize, not the Maritime Customs, but the Native Customs in the area under their control, it is considered that in this case joint naval action would have no value.

I have been instructed by my Government to add that His Majesty's Minister at Peking is of the opinion, which is understood to be shared by the Japanese Government, that the Canton Government will await developments in the civil war in North China before interfering with either the Maritime or the Native Customs, and that therefore naval action is unnecessary at present. This information has also been brought to the notice of the French, Italian, Japanese and Portuguese Governments.

I have [etc.]   ESME HOWARD

RECOGNITION BY THE UNITED STATES AND OTHER POWERS OF THE PROVISIONAL GOVERNMENT AS THE "DE FACTO" GOVERNMENT OF CHINA

893.01/131a : Telegram

The Secretary of State to the Chargé in China (Mayer) [38]

WASHINGTON, *November 6, 1924—6 p.m.*

272. A Secretary of the French Embassy today read to the Division of Far Eastern Affairs a telegram from his Government to the following general effect:—

For 7 or 8 years the interested Powers have been according unconditionally and practically as a matter of routine their recognition

---

[38] See last paragraph for instructions to repeat to Tokyo as no. 183.

of the successive Governments that have followed each other in Peking: these recent Governments have not lived up to their responsibilities or respected the rights of the foreign Powers; it therefore appears to the French Government that the recent *coup d'état* affords occasion for the Powers to withhold recognition to the new Government with a view to forcing it to give satisfactory assurances of its readiness to fulfil its obligations to the Powers. The telegram added that the French Government was approaching in this sense the other Governments principally interested, among them the Belgian Government, which had already assented to the French suggestion.

The Department would welcome your comment upon this suggestion with particular reference to the question of legal authority arising out of the resignation of the President and the assumption of his duties by the Cabinet as reported in your telegram No. 427, November 3, 5 p.m.[39]

Repeat to Tokyo as Department's No. 183.

HUGHES

893.01/132 : Telegram

The Chargé in China (Mayer) to the Secretary of State

PEKING, November 11, 1924—9 a. m.
[Received 9 : 55 a. m.]

439. 1. Your 272, November 6, 6 p. m. At diplomatic body meeting November 5th French in concert Belgian Chargé d'Affaires proposed that, first, all Chiefs of Mission should at their initial call upon new Minister for Foreign Affairs make reserves in respect of new regime, bringing to Dr. Wang's notice that despite solemn promises the recent administrations in China had not kept faith or carried out treaties, agreements, etc.; and that, secondly, the powers concerned should obtain some form of guarantee that China would observe her treaties and agreements before recognizing the new President when elected.

2. Italian Minister concurred but several others dissented especially regarding any making of reserves at first call on Dr. Wang. I stated I would not feel authorized to do so without instructions from my Government and British Minister spoke to same effect. Matter of reserves dropped but agreed that representatives should communicate with respective Governments in regard to advisability of demanding guarantees in the event of election of new President. Several ministers stated that they considered present situation merely as a Cabinet change and not therefore raising the question of recog-

---

[39] *Ante*, p. 388.

nition, etc. This has been exactly my opinion. I have not believed that entering into relations with Dr. Wang amounted to anything more than carrying on with a new Minister for Foreign Affairs. I felt that this demand by French and Belgian Chargés in which Italian Minister concurred was possibly primarily a bid for the diplomatic body's support in gold franc case.[40] I have reason to believe several other ministers of same opinion.

3. The present administration is of course not strictly constitutional since it fails to fulfill the requirements that a new Premier be nominated by President and approved by Parliament. The appointment of an Acting Premier is not authorized by the constitution except when Parliament is adjourned which is not the case now. However, the constitution does clearly provide that when the offices of the President and Vice President are vacant the Cabinet shall perform the duties of Presidential office. It may be borne in mind that there has not been a strictly constitutional government in China for years.

4. If point of view accepted that there is only Cabinet change and constitution observed in the main then question of recognition not now involved and so no opportunity to withhold same with a view to forcing Chinese Government to give satisfactory assurances of readiness to fulfill obligations to powers.

5. However, it may be that events will take a decidedly unconstitutional turn when the French proposition would apply, either through not recognizing a new government or withdrawal of recognition from present Government. I consider either course of very doubtful expediency unless other factors are introduced which might demand a different decision.

6. If it is a fact, as French Chargé d'Affaires stated at diplomatic body meeting, Central Government is only sustained by recognition of the powers, it would seem necessarily to follow that withdrawal of recognition would result in break-up of Government into several separate entities each composed of a group of provinces—a definite disintegration of the Central Government's authority and hence liability each entity would most likely deny obligation for past debts and not afford a very safe or promising prospect for future business or negotiation. . . .

MAYER

---

[40] See section entitled "Concurrence by the United States in the contention by certain powers that the Boxer Indemnity payments should be made in gold currency," pp. 559 ff.

893.01/132 : Telegram

The Secretary of State to the Chargé in China (Mayer)

WASHINGTON, *November 11, 1924—4 p. m.*

277. Your telegram No. 439, November 11, 9 a. m. The Department assumes from your telegram that you and the representatives of the other Powers in Peking have not thus far entered into formal relations with the Chinese authorities now functioning there. In view of the indeterminate situation now existing, the Department desires to avoid any commitment as to the status of the new regime; and while awaiting the evolution of the situation would prefer that the Legation's *de facto* relations with the regime now in control at Peking should be as informal and infrequent as may be compatible with the protection of American interests and the maintenance of good will conducive to that end.

HUGHES

893.01/133 : Telegram

The Chargé in Japan (Caffery) to the Secretary of State

[Extract]

TOKYO, *November 11, 1924—6 p. m.*
[Received November 11—11 a. m.]

291. French Ambassador here informed me that he had handed a note to Shidehara containing suggestions indicated in the Department's 183.[41] Upon reading this communication Shidehara said to him that it was his opinion that due legal forms under the constitution had been carried out in connection with the resignation of the President and the assumption of his duties by the Cabinet and therefore the question of recognition would not necessarily arise; on the other hand he said that of course recognition might be withdrawn by any of the interested powers.

. . . .

CAFFERY

893.01/134

The French Embassy to the Department of State [42]

[Translation [43]]

MEMORANDUM

The French Government is now concerning itself with the gravity of the situation in China. It may be presumed that on account of

---

[41] See footnote 38, p. 416.
[42] Received in the Department Nov. 11, 1924.
[43] File translation revised.

the great division of the parties a rather long time will elapse before there can be established in Peking a central power that would be recognized by the provinces and would be in position and inclination to see of its own motion that the international obligations of China are met. The fact that the latest Chinese Governments have been recognized by the foreign governments imparted some authority to them and the Peking Cabinet was thus placed in position to take advantage of the foreign diplomatic missions accredited to it without, however, caring to entertain the claims of the powers.

The Government of the Republic believes that to maintain longer this diplomatic situation without imposing certain precise conditions, would tend to work injury to all the Governments concerned: the said Governments on the one hand would assume a serious responsibility to their nationals and, on the other hand, would encourage the objectionable inclinations of the Government which is evading its international obligations and would readily sacrifice the rights of foreigners. This might in the future bring about a condition of affairs likely to be attended with grave consequences.

For that reason the French Government believes that it would be to the interest of the Governments concerned to make even now a survey of the situation hereinbefore referred to and agree that they will notify, when the time comes, the next Peking Government that it cannot be recognized by them unless it gives effective assurance that the treaty obligations of China will be carried out.

The French Government would be glad if the American Government would kindly take the suggestion under advisement and, if the suggestion should gain its approval, send appropriate instructions to the Minister of the United States at Peking.

893.01/132 : Telegram

The Acting Secretary of State to the Chargé in China (Mayer)

WASHINGTON, *November 12, 1924—6 p. m.*

279. With further reference to your No. 439, November 11, 9 a. m. On November 8 the French Ambassador confirmed the suggestion of the French Government outlined in the Department's No. 272, November 6, 6 p. m. The following is the substance of my reply:

"The Secretary said that he appreciated the force of the Ambassador's observations; that it was highly desirable that there should be a stable government in China and that the rights which foreigners had should be properly recognized. He called attention to the existing situation. The President had left, attempting to give his authority to a new cabinet. It was difficult to see how this could be called a government entitled to recognition; it was an anomalous condition. However, the future was uncertain. It did not seem to the Secretary wise to lay down a program to cover eventualities which could not now be defined. He had no difference so far as the principle suggested by the Ambassador was concerned, for, of course, when a government was recognized it was either explicit or implicit that international obligations should be performed. A government seeking recognition would be supposed to be willing to give assurances to that effect. The question was whether there was a solid basis for confidence that such assurances would be made good. In China we had a peculiar situation because of the extreme difficulty in establishing a strong central government. It was necessary to encourage a hopeful effort in that direction and on the other hand to have it clearly understood that the rights of other powers could not be trifled with. It seemed to the Secretary necessary to await developments."

The Italian Ambassador on the same date stated that his Government, before replying to the French note, would like to know the views of the American Government on the French suggestion. The reply made to him was of the same tenor as that to the French Ambassador.

Repeat the above to Tokyo as No. 190, November 12, 6 p. m.; together with the Department's No. 277, November 11, 4 p.m., as No. 189, November 12, 5 p.m.; and your No. 439, November 11, 9 a.m.

GREW

893.01/135 : Telegram

The Chargé in China (Mayer) to the Secretary of State

PEKING, *November 13, 1924—6 p.m.*
[Received November 13—1 : 23 p.m.]

445. Your 277, November 11, 4 p. m.

1. Dr. Wang's note informing me of his assumption of duties as Minister for Foreign Affairs replied to in usual course employed when new Foreign Minister appointed. British, Japanese, French, Belgian, Italian and Netherlands Legations acted likewise as I understand did the other Legations.

2. I returned Dr. Wang's call but have refrained from calling at Foreign Office on regular diplomatic day and have sent my card to Acting Premier in return for his. I understand other chiefs of mission acted similarly. Diplomatic body generally considered situation merely as a Cabinet change, an opinion which I shared as expressed in my telegram aforementioned.[44]

3. However, at the diplomatic body meeting of November 10th it was decided that we would not attend Acting Premier's afternoon reception this week (all had been invited) in order to show Huang Fu, C. T. Wang, and those now in authority that although we had

---

[44] See telegram no. 439, Nov. 11, from the Chargé in China, p. 417.

not made any formal reserves yet we had not accepted Cabinet change without a mental reservation of waiting to see how the situation would develop [before?] according it our entire approval. We have apparently achieved our purpose, since day following most of diplomatic body were visited by emissaries from the Foreign Office who informed us on Huang Fu's behalf that he had issued the invitation to afternoon reception in his private capacity. I referred Foreign Office secretary who called on me to senior minister who had informally conveyed our position to the Wai Chiao Pu. I assured secretary that no personal affront was intended the Acting Premier and that the United States had no feeling of special affinity or antipathy to any political faction in China, being entirely neutral. The reception, I understand, has been canceled.

4. I have only visited the Minister for Foreign Affairs the one time and intended to have as little to do with the present administration as possible compatible with the protection of our interests. I note Department's instructions in the above regard and will carry them out.

MAYER

893.01/137 : Telegram

The Chargé in Japan (Caffery) to the Secretary of State

TOKYO, *November 15, 1924—1 p.m.*
[Received November 15—1 p.m.]

294. My telegram number 293, November 4 [*14*], 7 [*8*] p. m.[45] Minister for Foreign Affairs handed to French Ambassador this morning the following *aide-mémoire:*

"The Japanese entirely share with the French Government the opinion that a new government which may be established in China is entitled to recognition by foreign powers only when it is capable of fulfilling China's international engagement[s]. The Japanese Government further realize the importance of obtaining from a new government in China satisfactory assurance respecting such international obligations in case it becomes opportune to consider the question of recognition to be extended to include government.

Instructions will be given to the Japanese Minister at Peking to cooperate with his colleagues of the principal powers interested in China in examining at an opportune moment all questions relating to recognition subject to the approval of their respective governments."

.   .   .   .

Peking informed.

CAFFERY

___

[45] Not printed.

893.01/139 : Telegram

The Ambassador in Great Britain (Kellogg) to the Secretary of State

[Extract]

LONDON, *November 18, 1924—5 p.m.*
[Received November 18—3 : 04 p.m.]

479. Department's 413, November 12, 6 p. m.[46] Department's November 12, 6 p. m., to Peking was read to Foreign Office today which stated that the reply of the British Government to the French representations made here was in substance identical with the reply of Secretary Hughes. Foreign Office added you may sum up our position in the words, "We agree with the diplomatic body in Peking in a wait and see attitude."

. . . .

KELLOGG

893.01/141b : Telegram

The Secretary of State to the Ambassador in Great Britain (Kellogg) [47]

[Paraphrase]

WASHINGTON, *November 24, 1924—6 p.m.*

434. 1. At an early occasion you may tell the Foreign Minister that I appreciate his expression of a particular desire to cooperate with the United States regarding Chinese affairs. In that connection inform him of my views on the present Chinese crisis as set forth in the Department's memorandum to the French Embassy.[48] The substance of this memorandum will be cabled to you through the Paris Embassy.

2. You may further explain my views by saying that the fundamental necessities of the situation in my judgment are as follows:

(*a*) No foreign intervention on the side of any faction or group in the present civil conflict;

(*b*) All appropriate encouragement and countenance to any governing body which may emerge independently with a reasonable likelihood of stability;

(*c*) The exercise upon such a new regime of what influence may be practicable with the object of assuring that it will more faithfully observe the treaty obligations which more and more the recent Chinese administrations have been seeking to evade.

---

[46] Not printed.
[47] See last paragraph for instructions to repeat to Embassy in France, as Department's no. 412.
[48] *Infra.*

3. With respect to points (*a*) and (*b*), it is my belief that the Chinese Government is now passing through a phase which is abnormal and temporary. I hope that a more substantial regime will soon be established. I think it is vital until then that the powers do not interfere, actually or apparently, with the working out of the internal forces of China, either by assisting any group or by efforts for mediation which would tend to give an appearance of stability before the situation has actually reached an equilibrium. However, as soon as a central governing body giving a reasonable hope of permanent authority shall have been produced, I think it would be the part of wisdom for the powers to formally recognize it and encourage it with the hope of helping it as far as may be possible to reestablish unity of political control throughout China.

4. With respect to point (*c*), the growing disposition of the Chinese to evade their treaty responsibilities causes me deep concern— in recent reports from our Legation in China there is the intimation of the possibility that this tendency may soon become manifest in more active opposition to the special rights now held by foreigners. When Minister Schurman was here recently for consultation he confirmed the apprehension that there is the likelihood that in the relatively near future the Chinese will demand that what they call the "unequal treaties" shall be revised, insisting upon control of their tariff, freedom to tax foreigners, and the abolition of extraterritoriality. If such a policy were enunciated it would without doubt bring forth a degree of enthusiasm and popular approval such as no recent Chinese regime has been able to win. Should the powers unite in opposition to such a policy, it seems likely that the Chinese would be able to render of no worth foreign treaty rights by mere passive resistance if not by the use of more aggressive means such as a boycott.

5. Of course the proposal that the powers withhold recognition until a new Chinese administration has given assurances that it will carry out its treaty obligations, is intended to meet this situation. However, even though such foreign pressure might indeed be the means of causing the Chinese officials to yield upon any particular case in controversy, I am unable to make myself believe that it would bring about any general or permanent improvement in the attitude of the Chinese toward the treaty rights of foreigners. I fear on the contrary that if such pressure were used it would result either in a deadlock between the powers and the Chinese regime seeking recognition, or else cause that regime to lose support and therefore weaken its chances of becoming established as the actual government of the country in proportion to the degree to which it agreed to the conditions demanded by the powers. In either case

the particular tangible advantages that might be secured would be obtained at too great a price.

6. It is my firm conviction that, without resorting to force such as for present purposes is out of the question, the peril to foreign interests in China cannot be met by merely exercising pressure without regard to the temper which underlies the Chinese attitude on this subject. Unquestionably the Chinese have a strong feeling that the powers have not played fairly with them with respect to the Washington Conference treaties, and this feeling has influenced their temper with regard to foreign rights. It may be admitted that this feeling is without justification because in any case the political chaos in China would have frustrated our desire for the realization of the concrete plans which the Conference accepted. It is a psychological fact, nevertheless, that it is generally believed by the Chinese that the failure to go ahead with the extraterritoriality conference and the customs conference justifies them in disregarding their own responsibilities. However unjustifiable this feeling may be, it is too firmly fixed and widespread to be left out of consideration as a factor in the situation. I think it is essential therefore that the powers should prove their integrity by showing that they are willing, as soon as circumstances allow, to take up the promised consideration of matters which the Chinese consider fundamental. The decision as regards the extraterritoriality conference rests entirely with the foreign offices of the powers concerned.

7. As I understand the situation, France is withholding action both upon the extraterritoriality conference and upon the acceptance of the two Washington Conference treaties regarding China, and the consequent holding of the conference on customs, in accordance with a definite policy of taking no action favorable to the Chinese until France receives satisfaction with respect to the payment in gold of its share of the Boxer Indemnity. The fact that France has apparently a good case at least prima facie in the matter makes the situation harder to handle. In fact there is some reason to think that if it could be done without "loss of face" in view of the strong national sentiment aroused on this subject in China, the Chinese would now gladly yield. The reference of the issue to the World Court might bring about a settlement practicable for the Chinese. It is, however, understood that France is so sure of its position that it is inclined to consider only a direct settlement with China.

8. Apparently this attitude on the part of France not only delays a possible satisfactory settlement of this case but it directly strengthens and makes more bitter a tendency increasingly endangering all foreign rights in China by preventing any progress in making effective the decisions concerning China taken at the Wash-

ington Conference. The French, therefore, have in their hands the only key to the situation. I hope that the British Foreign Minister may understand the situation as I see it and may be disposed to cooperate with me, if opportunity is presented, to endeavor to influence the Government of France to take action in such a way as to resolve the present deadlock.

9. It is understood that the French Ambassador at London, who until a short while ago was Minister at Peking, is fully informed on the gold franc question. You might take occasion to discuss the matter with him, saying that the American Government is apprehensive that unless the existing deadlock is broken a settlement will be unduly delayed, and that it hopes that some method by which a settlement could be assisted by other governments might be disclosed by a frank and informal discussion of the subject. The British Foreign Minister may of course be informed of this.

10. I have given you the above full explanation of my views so that you will be in a position to discuss the matter with the Foreign Minister confidentially and informally. Considering that there might be possible misunderstandings in other quarters I do not wish you to put these views into any memorandum or note.

11. Please repeat for information to Embassy in France as Department's no. 412.

HUGHES

893.01/134

The Department of State to the French Embassy

MEMORANDUM

The Department of State has carefully considered the memorandum left with it on November 11, 1924, in which were set forth the views of the French Government on the subject of the situation now existing in China, as previously explained by the French Ambassador in a conversation with the Secretary of State on November 8.

The Government of the United States fully shares the concern of the French Government as to the gravity of the situation of China, and would therefore be disposed to associate itself with other treaty Powers in adopting an attitude of reserve until there shall have developed a regime warranting a hope of its stability and giving satisfactory evidence of its intention to carry out in good faith the obligations which China has assumed towards those Powers.

But while recognizing the fact that the Chinese Government has of late manifested an increasing tendency to ignore the rights of the foreign Powers, this Government cannot blind itself to the fact that this tendency has found an excuse and an encouragement in the minds of the Chinese by reason of the fact that they conceive the foreign Powers to have abandoned the policy of cooperation and mutual accommodation embodied in the decisions with respect to Chinese affairs adopted by the Washington Conference on the Limitation of Armament. Not only do they observe the fact that the two treaties, with respect to Principles and Policies concerning China, and with respect to the Chinese Customs Tariff, remain unratified, with the result that certain concrete advantages provided by the Conference in favor of China remain unrealized; but they are able to point out that the Resolution regarding Extraterritoriality in China—although an agreement ostensibly binding without any necessity for ratifications or other formalities—has not yet resulted in any action by the signatory Powers with a view to the promised inquiry into the present practice of extraterritoriality and into the laws and the judicial system and the methods of judicial administration in China.

While by no means disposed to extenuate any tendency of the Chinese Government to repudiate or evade its international responsibilities, the American Government feels that it would be ignoring the realities of the situation to overlook the effect produced upon the minds of the Chinese by their conviction that the Powers have on their part failed to give effect to measures adopted by them for the purpose of furthering the aspirations of the Chinese people for the development of their political life. The Powers are thus prejudiced and weakened in their insistence that China should observe their treaty rights in full, unless and until those rights may be modified by mutual consent; and in the opinion of the American Government there is grave danger of the inculcation of a spirit of distrust which might even more seriously attenuate the sense of responsibility of the Chinese with respect to their obligations.

It is therefore the opinion of the Government of the United States that, in order to deal with the grave situation to which the French Embassy's memorandum refers, it is essential that the Powers should make evident their own good faith and their intention to afford China the opportunity to obtain relief from what her people regard as oppressive restrictions upon their national freedom of action, to the extent that its Government may prove itself willing and able to exercise the normal functions of a Government in its treatment of those foreign interests for which the treaty restrictions were designed to afford a protection not yet available from the Chinese governing authorities.

To that end, the Government of the United States considers it indispensable that the interested Powers, in the course of making clear their view that any new regime could expect to enjoy their confidence and cooperation only upon the condition that it gives satisfactory evidence of a willingness to observe existing treaty rights, should be prepared to offer reciprocal assurances of their own intentions towards China, and should in particular be in a position to promise that they will at the earliest practicable date undertake the investigation for which provision is made by the Washington Conference Resolution on Extraterritoriality. While making this suggestion with regard to the particular matter of the Conference on Extraterritoriality, the American Government takes occasion to express its earnest hope that means may be found by which the Government of France may be enabled to contribute towards the amelioration of the present difficult situation in China by according the ratifications which would bring into force the two treaties concerning China concluded at Washington on February 6, 1922.

WASHINGTON, *November 25, 1924.*

893.01/143 : Telegram

The Ambassador in Great Britain (Kellogg) to the Secretary of State

LONDON, *December 1, 1924—6 p. m.*
[Received December 1—4: 32 p. m.]

502. Department's 434, November 24, 6 p. m., was informally brought to Mr. Chamberlain's [49] attention through the Foreign Office and Waterlow [50] advises today as follows: Mr. Chamberlain very much appreciates the Secretary's frank statement of his views on the Chinese situation with which he is in absolute accord and has instructed the Foreign Office to continue informal discussions of views and information with the Embassy.

Foreign Office states it will in the near future take occasion to express to the French similar views to those in the last paragraph of Department's 439 of November 26, 3 p. m.[51] British Minister in Peking has already urged upon Tuan an early compromise with French toward gold payments of Boxer Indemnity.

KELLOGG

---

[49] J. Austen Chamberlain, British Secretary of State for Foreign Affairs.
[50] Sydney P. Waterlow, Counsellor in the British Foreign Office.
[51] Not printed; it transmitted text of memorandum of Nov. 25 to the French Embassy, *supra.*

893.00/5816 : Telegram

The Ambassador in Japan (Bancroft) to the Secretary of State

Tokyo, *December 4, 1924—noon.*
[Received 3 : 11 p. m.]

314. Shidehara handed me today following statement on Japan's attitude in China situation which he said had already been prepared at the request of the British Ambassador here:

"It is believed to be generally conceded that no useful purpose can be served by any intervention in the domestic affairs of China. With a long historical background and amidst the surroundings peculiar to the country the Chinese people must be left free to order their own national life in their own way. Such plans as have often been discussed in unofficial quarters aiming at an international control of certain branches of Chinese administration would, in the opinion of the Japanese Government, prove disastrous to the independent existence of China and productive of international complications.

At this time the foreign powers cannot with fairness be called upon to suffer any infringement upon their legitimate rights and interests in China. They are entitled to expect from any government which may be established at Peking both the ability and the readiness to fulfill all the conventional obligations of China and in particular to afford due protection to the persons and property of their nationals. Such aims can hardly be realized however unless the military leaders now maintaining themselves quasi independently in various provinces be brought effectively under the direction the Central Government, at least in matters involving the rights and interests of foreign nations.

It is now known that on November 24th General Tuan Chi-jui provisionally assumed the functions of the Chief Executive of the Chinese Republic in response to the call of a fair majority of the practically autonomous province[s] in China and with the approval of the then existing Government under Mr. Huang Fu. On the same day he announced the formation of a new Cabinet composed of men who have long figured prominently in various factions and provinces. It appears that all these arrangements are intended to be only provisional and that a more lasting regime is reserved for discussion and settlement at a national assembly shortly to be convoked.

The Japanese are not directly concerned in the question who will assume the reins of government in China or what form of political institution the proposed national assembly will adopt. Their chief preoccupation[s] have been in the question whether or not China will soon be provided with a sufficiently strong government to maintain law and order within her borders and to discharge her international obligations.

But it is evident that whatever government may be established in China cannot possibly endure if it fails to find a way out of its pressing financial difficulties. Without funds to meet the expenditure it will be impossible for any government at Peking to organize an effective administration and to carry out the disbandment of troops and other measures of readjustment now urgently needed. Nor in the opinion of the Japanese Government can the destitution of China's public treasury be remedied without the cooperation of foreign powers. In order to secure stabilization of China it will be necessary for the powers when they [*the time?*] becomes opportune to take up the question of financial assistance to be rendered to the Chinese Government. Such assistance is to be extended only upon full communication and understanding among the powers and in case it takes the form of a loan it should be undertaken in accordance with the principles that govern the existing consortium.

In all cases the fullest opportunity should be afforded to the Chinese people to work out a practical system of government and to restore peace and unity in the country. It is reported that the Provisional Government just inaugurated at Peking and its supporters are now seriously striving to attain these objects. The powers should watch their efforts with sympathy, toleration and hope".

Peking informed.

BANCROFT

___

893.01/143 : Telegram

The Secretary of State to the Chargé in Japan (Caffery)

WASHINGTON, December 4, 1924—2 p. m.

199. Your 308, December 1, 11 a. m.,[52] and 311, December 3, 5 p. m.[52]

1. You are authorized to communicate orally and informally to the Minister for Foreign Affairs the substance of the memorandum to the French Government[53] contained in the telegram repeated to you by Peking as the Department's number 195.[52]

2. In your informal discussions with the Minister for Foreign Affairs concerning the situation in China, you will be guided in general by the views contained in the telegram repeated to you by Peking as the Department's number 194,[54] and you may intimate to him that the American Ambassador at London has been authorized to discuss the matter in a similar manner with the Foreign Office.

3. In connection with the telegram referred to in paragraph 2, the following telegram from London is repeated for your information:

[Here follows telegram no. 502, December 1, 6 p. m., printed on page 428.]

4. Repeat to Peking as Department's number 301.

HUGHES

___

[52] Not printed.
[53] Memorandum of Nov. 25, p. 426.
[54] Not printed; this telegram quoted text of telegram no. 434, Nov. 24, to the Ambassador in Great Britain, p. 423.

893.01/144 : Telegram

The Chargé in China (Mayer) to the Secretary of State

PEKING, *December 4, 1924—3 p. m.*
[Received 6 : 09 p. m.]

472. 1. My 468, December 3, 3 p. m.,[55] especially paragraphs 5 and 6. Informal meeting this morning of British, Japanese, French, Italian, Belgian, Netherlands representatives and myself decided to recommend our Governments to authorize us at earliest possible moment to despatch following note to Chinese Government and to give same widest publicity.

"The representatives at Peking of the United States of America, Belgium, Great Britain, France, Italy, Japan, the Netherlands and Portugal declare in the names of their Governments that, taking note of the communication addressed to them on November 24th by the Wai Chiao Pu announcing the assumption of office by the Provisional Chief Executive and of the mandates issued by the new Chief Executive on the same date, they will lend their full support to the Provisional Government in Peking under the present Provisional Chief Executive and that they have entered into *de facto* relations with the same on the understanding that this Provisional Government has been constituted with the concurrence of the nation for the purpose of taking charge of the affairs of the Chinese Republic pending the establishment of a formal government representing all the provinces and parties in the Republic and on the understanding that it is the intention of the Provisional Government and of any formal government that may hereafter be established to respect all treaties, conventions, and other engagements entered into by the former Manchu and Republican governments and all rights, privileges, and immunities enjoyed by foreigners in China by virtue of such international engagements until such time as these international engagements shall be modified by mutual consent of the contracting parties. They further declare that on the above understanding their Governments are willing and anxious to proceed as soon as possible with the carrying out of the measures contemplated in the Washington treaties and resolutions."

2. I make this recommendation for following reasons: First, I have believed for some time that we should combat Bolshevik attack in China in particular reference to so-called "unjust treaties" by an announcement that we were ready and willing to discuss treaty revision at earliest moment practicable. Second, I have considered that we have been and are severely handicapped by inability to initiate action under Washington Conference agreements and resolutions owing to French attitude. I believe that if nothing more eventuates from the effort to have the powers concerned agree upon

---

[55] *Ante*, p. 405.

proposed statement, such effort will at least bring pressure upon French Government toward ratification of Washington treaties. I deem this is in line with Department's attitude and desire as expressed in its 294, November 26, 3 [*2*] p. m.,[56] and 293, November 25, 6 p. m.[57] Third, a statement similar to above may be of great assistance to conservative element in China. As couched I do not believe it can do harm. Should Sun in cooperation with Feng overthrow Tuan administration after proposed statement is made we would at least be on record as continuing to entertain toward a government in China, to whom we could at least accord *de facto* recognition, the same policy of cooperation and mutual accommodation as embodied in the decisions with respect to Chinese affairs adopted by Washington Conference. We would have a base from which to project further efforts to defend ourselves against Bolshevik propaganda. If and when Tuan or some other conservative government would replace Sun regime we would be in the greatly [*sic*] superior position than if proposed statement had not been made.

3. Both British Minister and myself after careful consideration believed it wise not to include any direct statement to the effect that powers concerned would not recognize or have truck with any administration which might be set up in Peking by political leaders hostile to us. This would be two-edged weapon. Point impliedly covered in proposed statement.

4. I would have preferred to have strengthened statement by definitely stating in so many words that the powers concerned would take up with a formally established Chinese Government the subject of treaty revision at the earliest moment practicable, thus turning this phase against those who now using it to our disadvantage. Statement as adopted this morning's meeting by implication puts us on record as desirous to this effect.

5. Both British Minister and myself fearful that further strengthening our proposed statement might prevent French and Italian Governments from associating themselves therewith, the chances being that these two Governments would even oppose statement as now drafted.

6. Japanese Minister stated he had reason to believe Feng and Sun Yat-sen contemplate another *coup* in the very near future. Impossible to know Feng's attitude as Tuan may be simply playing him off against foreigners demanding immediate treaty revision or cancellation. It would be difficult for us to issue proposed statement which Sun could then make to appear as result of his threats.

[56] Not printed; this telegram quoted text of memorandum of Nov. 25 to the French Embassy, p. 426.
[57] Not printed; this telegram quoted text of telegram no. 434, Nov. 24, to the Ambassador in Great Britain, p. 423.

7. For above reasons I most earnestly recommend that if Department approves proposed statement I be instructed to this end at very earliest possible moment.

8. I venture to add that I consider the making of a statement similar to that proposed of so great importance at this time that I would favor its being made to present Chinese Government even if only by Great Britain and the United States; with Japan, the Netherlands and Belgium if possible. If necessary, however, I believe Japanese Government would be willing to join in such a statement even if all powers concerned would [not?] agree thereto. Possibly more danger of playing into Japanese hands by proposed statement is less than that of ill-advised agitation for treaty revision in my opinion. Of the two it goes without saying I greatly prefer to assist the Japanese. I would much appreciate simultaneous instructions on this point should the Department approve proposed statement in principle. British Minister of same opinion and is requesting similar instructions.

9. Repeated to Tokyo with request to hand copy to Minister Schurman.[57a]

MAYER

893.01/165

The Netherland Minister (De Graeff) to the Secretary of State

The Netherland Minister presents his compliments to the Honorable, the Secretary of State, and has the honor to inform him that the Minister of Foreign Affairs at The Hague has learned from Her Royal Majesty's Minister at Peking that the diplomatic representatives there of the nine Powers signatory to the Treaty of Washington being afraid for another *coup d'état* with the purpose of establishing a soviet government in China are of the opinion that it would be serviceable to lend their moral support to the actual provisional Government of China by declaring that their respective Governments for that reason desire to carry out the measures stipulated in the said treaty and in the resolutions which with regard to China have been agreed upon at the time of the Washington Conference.

Jonkheer van Karnebeek has instructed me to point out to the Secretary of State that the Royal Government at no time has opposed against the carrying out of the said measures but that it seems to him that at the present time a declaration as has been planned will be considered as a proof of weakness and not only will not lead to any desirable result but will be even hurtful to the preparations of the Powers.

[57a] Jacob Gould Schurman, Minister to China, temporarily absent from his post.

The Minister of Foreign Affairs at The Hague being very anxious to learn the opinion of the American Government in this matter, Jonkheer de Graeff would highly appreciate if Mr. Hughes would be kind enough to give him the desired information at his earliest convenience.

WASHINGTON, *December 5, 1924.*

893.01/144 : Telegram

The Secretary of State to the Chargé in China (Mayer)

WASHINGTON, *December 5, 1924—2 p. m.*

302. Your 472, December 4, 3 p. m.

The Department approves proposed statement and you may sign if all your colleagues named in the statement also sign.

Your paragraph 8.

You will of course notify the Department immediately, with a view to its taking up the question with the appropriate Governments, in the event that any of the representatives of Powers signatory to the Washington Conference Treaties fail to receive authorization to join in the statement.

HUGHES

893.01/165

The Secretary of State to the Netherland Minister (De Graeff)

The Secretary of State presents his compliments to the Netherlands Minister and has the honor to acknowledge the receipt of his memorandum of December 5, 1924, concerning the political situation in China.

The Government of the United States fully realizes the gravity of the situation in China and is disposed to associate itself with other treaty Powers in adopting an attitude of reserve until there shall have developed a régime warranting a hope of its stability and giving satisfactory evidence of its intention to carry out in good faith the obligations which China has assumed towards those Powers.

But while recognizing the fact that the Chinese Government has of late manifested an increasing tendency to ignore the rights of the foreign Powers, this Government cannot blind itself to the fact that this tendency has found an excuse and an encouragement in the minds of the Chinese by reason of the fact that they conceive the foreign Powers to have abandoned the policy of cooperation and mutual accommodation embodied in the decisions with respect to Chinese affairs adopted by the Washington Conference on the Limitation of Armament. Not only do they observe the fact that the two treaties, with respect to Principles and Policies concerning China, and with respect to the Chinese Customs Tariff, remain unratified, with the result that certain concrete advantages provided by the Conference in favor of China remain unrealized; but they are able to point out that the Resolution regarding Extraterritoriality in China—although an agreement ostensibly binding without any necessity for ratifications or other formalities—has not yet resulted in any action by the signatory Powers with a view to the promised inquiry into the present practice of extraterritoriality and into the laws and the judicial system and the methods of judicial administration in China.

While by no means disposed to extenuate any tendency of the Chinese Government to repudiate or evade its international responsibilities, the American Government feels that it would be ignoring the realities of the situation to overlook the effect produced upon the minds of the Chinese by their conviction that the Powers have on their part failed to give effect to measures adopted by them for the purpose of furthering the aspirations of the Chinese people for the development of their political life. The Powers are thus prejudiced and weakened in their insistence that China should observe their treaty rights in full, unless and until those rights may be modified by mutual consent; and in the opinion of the American Government there is grave danger of the inculcation of a spirit of distrust which might even more seriously attenuate the sense of responsibility of the Chinese with respect to their obligations.

It is therefore the opinion of the Government of the United States that, in order to deal with the grave situation to which the Netherlands Minister's memorandum refers, it is essential that the Powers should make evident their own good faith and their intention to afford China the opportunity to obtain relief from what her people regard as oppressive restrictions upon their national freedom of action, to the extent that its Government may prove itself willing and able to exercise the normal functions of a Government in its treatment of those foreign interests for which the treaty restrictions were designed to afford a protection not yet available from the Chinese governing authorities.

To that end, the Government of the United States considers it indispensable that the interested Powers, in the course of making clear their view that any régime could expect to enjoy their confidence and cooperation only upon the condition that it gives satisfactory evidence of a willingness to observe existing treaty rights, should be prepared to offer reciprocal assurances of their own intentions towards China, and should in particular be in a position to promise that they will, as soon as possible, proceed with the carrying out of the measures contemplated in the Washington Conference treaties and resolutions. With a view to contributing something towards the amelioration of the present difficult situation in China the representatives at Peking of the United States, Belgium, Great Britain, France, Italy, Japan, The Netherlands and Portugal have proposed to despatch to the present Government at Peking the following note:

[Here follows text of proposed note reported in telegram no. 472, December 4, from the Chargé in China, printed on page 431.]

The Secretary of State ventures to hope that The Netherlands Government will instruct its representative at Peking to join his colleagues in signing the proposed note.

WASHINGTON, *December 6, 1924.*

893.01/147 : Telegram

The Chargé in China (Mayer) to the Secretary of State

PEKING, *December 6, 1924—5 p. m.*
[Received December 6—2 : 11 p. m.]

474. Your 302, December 5, 2 p. m., second paragraph, and last sentence paragraph 8 my 472, December 4, 3 p. m.

1. British Minister has likewise received authority to sign proposed statement. His Government has informed him that they are urging French Government to join in proposed action. He is further authorized to sign even without French concurrence if I agree.

2. While I consider far preferable that all Powers concerned should join in proposed action, I respectfully request authority to sign without French concurrence if representative here not instructed to sign by the time Department's reply to this telegram received.

3. Effectiveness of the proposed action would be greatly impaired if not destroyed, it is submitted, should statement not be transmitted to Chinese Government and published prior to any hostile declaration by Dr. Sun Yat-sen advocating immediate cancelation or revision of so-called "unjust treaties". See last sentence paragraph 6 my 472 mentioned above.

MAYER

893.01/144 : Telegram

The Secretary of State to the Chargé in China (*Mayer*)

WASHINGTON, *December 6, 1924—6 p. m.*

303. The draft note quoted in your 472, December 4, 3 p. m., and the Department's reply to that telegram,[58] have been repeated through Paris to Brussels, The Hague, Rome and Lisbon with instructions to take occasion to discuss, informally and orally, with the Minister for Foreign Affairs of the countries concerned the situation in China, using as the basis of such discussion the above-mentioned telegrams and the memorandum to the French Embassy[59] quoted in the Department's 294, November 26, 2 p.m., to you[60] and paragraphs 2 to 10 of the Department's 293, November 25, p. m.,[60] quoting the telegram to London.[61] The Department has also expressed the hope that the several Governments approached would promptly instruct their representatives at Peking to sign the note quoted in your No. 472.

HUGHES

893.01/147a : Telegram

The Secretary of State to the Ambassador in France (*Herrick*)

WASHINGTON, *December 6, 1924—7 p. m.*

440. Assuming that you have sent to Brussels, The Hague, Lisbon and Rome the memorandum addressed to the French Embassy here on November 25, quoted in the Department's No. 419 of November 26, 3 p.m.,[62] you will now supplement that memorandum by repeating to the Missions above mentioned paragraphs 2 to 10 of the Department's No. 412 which was repeated to you from London,[63] and request the Missions concerned to take occasion to discuss, informally and orally, the situation in China with the Ministers for Foreign Affairs of the countries concerned, and in so doing to be guided in general by the views contained in the memorandum to the French Government and the telegram to London above mentioned. The draft note to the Chinese Government[64] and the Department's reply to the telegram from Peking[58] containing it are being repeated to

---

[58] No. 302, Dec. 5, p. 434.
[59] Memorandum of Nov. 25, p. 426.
[60] Not printed.
[61] *Ante*, p. 423.
[62] Telegram not printed.
[63] See footnote 47, p. 423.
[64] See telegram no. 472, Dec. 4, from the Chargé in China, p. 431.

you in the Department's No. 439,[65] and should also be repeated to Brussels, The Hague, Rome and Lisbon for their further information and guidance in the discussions above mentioned. It is hoped that the Powers concerned will authorize their respective representatives at Peking to join with their colleagues in signing the proposed note.

HUGHES

893.01/166

The Netherland Minister (De Graeff) to the Secretary of State

WASHINGTON, *December 8, 1924.*

SIR: I beg to acknowledge the receipt of your note of the sixth instant and to offer you my most sincere thanks for your early and circumstantial reply to my memorandum of the 5th instant concerning the political situation in China.

It gives me great pleasure to inform you that I received yesterday a cablegram from the Foreign Minister at The Hague to whom I had transmitted by cable your views on the question as explained to me verbally Friday last, stating that he has authorized the Netherland Minister at Peking to join his colleagues in signing the note quoted in your letter.

Please accept [etc.]   DE GRAEFF

893.01/147 : Telegram

The Secretary of State to the Chargé in China (Mayer)

[Paraphrase]

WASHINGTON, *December 9, 1924—11 a.m.*

307. Your 474, December 6, 5 p.m.

In case British and Japanese representatives are both authorized to take like action, Department authorizes you to join with them and representatives of any other powers which signed the Washington Conference treaties who may be able to do so, in sending to the Chinese Government the proposed joint statement. This action may be taken at your discretion any time after December 11, noon, or before that, should the French representative indicate that his Government had decided not to join in sending the statement. Repeat as Department's no. 205 to Embassy at Tokyo.

HUGHES

---

[65] Telegram not printed.

893.01/149 : Telegram

The Chargé in China (Mayer) to the Secretary of State

PEKING, *December 9, 1924—5 p.m.*
[Received December 9—1:25 p.m.]

478. Department's 302, December 5, 2 p.m.

1. With certain minor changes as set forth below, proposed statement signed this noon by representatives of the United States, Belgium, Great Britain, France, Italy, Japan and the Netherlands. It will be delivered this afternoon by senior Minister to Vice Minister for Foreign Affairs and be given to press tomorrow, Wednesday noon.

2. Following are amendments:

(*a*) "And Portugal" omitted as British Minister not yet authorized by Portugal to sign. Its adherence will be later communicated to Wai Chiao Pu.

(*b*) "And duly fulfill" inserted between "respect" and "all treaties, conventions and other engagements, et cetera" in first sentence.

(*c*) "Which according to international usage can only" substituted for "until such time as these international engagements shall" toward end of first sentence.

(*d*) "Practicable" substituted for "possible" middle of last sentence.

3. Following brief explanation of amendments. In accord with instructions from home government, French representative sought to have statement inserted in last sentence of draft to effect that failure to carry out Washington Conference agreements not through fault of powers concerned. I strongly opposed this. To my mind very inadvisable to insert such controversial observation. Less said the better concerning failure execution Washington Conference agreements. I stood alone at first but finally, after much discussion, British Minister joined me. Latter suggested amendment (*a*) and I amendment (*d*) which together satisfied French Chargé.

4. Japanese Government had authorized its representative to sign draft with omission of "until such time as these international engagements shall be modified by the mutual consent of the contracting parties" at end of first sentence. Japanese argument in favor of this omission was that clause might incite Chinese Government to bring up treaty revision at once. British Minister and self opposed elimination of this clause. I regretted omission since I felt it advantageous to have mild intimation in our state-

ment to effect that question of treaty revision not entirely remote from minds of powers concerned. Amendment (c) agreed to in view of great importance of immediate despatch and publication of statement and in view of delay which would ensue from re-submission of matter to Japanese Government. Clause substituted merely a truism.

5. I did my best to maintain statement as originally drafted and rather deplore the whittling away of some of its strength by amend-ments as made. However time element first importance and as all other representatives seemed satisfied I assented and signed.

MAYER

893.01/158

The French Ambassador (Jusserand) to the Secretary of State

[Translation [66]]

WASHINGTON, *December 10, 1924.*

MR. SECRETARY OF STATE: In a memorandum of November 25 last, the Department of State was pleased to inform this Embassy that the Government of the United States was inclined to take towards China an attitude of reserve until there should be constituted a regime holding out prospects of stability and showing in a positive manner its intention to fulfill in good faith the obligations taken by China towards the powers.

In addition, the memorandum mentioned the regret felt by the American Government that certain powers, France among them, had not yet ratified the treaties concerning China signed at the close of the Washington Conference, and especially that the said powers have not given attention to the putting into effect of the resolution adopted with regard to extraterritoriality. In the opin-ion of the Government of the United States the delay in ratifying those instruments was not of a nature to encourage China to carry out her obligations.

My Government, which I did not fail to keep advised of the Ameri-can Government's viewpoint, has just instructed me to inform Your Excellency that it repeatedly gave official notice to the Chinese Gov-ernment that it would not be in a position to lay before the French Parliament, for its approval, the two treaties concerning China signed in Washington or to join in carrying out the resolution rela-tive to extraterritoriality as long as China should not discharge her

---

[66] File translation revised.

obligations to France with respect to the resumption of the service of the Boxer Indemnity in gold. The justice of the French claim appears both from the general provisions of the protocol of 1901,[67] which has been likewise invoked by Belgium, Spain, and Italy, and also the special provisions of the Franco-Chinese agreement of 1922, relative to the application of the French share of the indemnity under consideration.

In this connection I wish to take the liberty of reminding Your Excellency that the Government of the United States was pleased to recognize that my Government's attitude was justified and that it has for two years officially associated itself with the collective action of the signatories of the protocol of 1901 to remind China that one of the most important provisions of that international instrument must be respected.

In the opinion of my Government the fact that the payment in gold of the Boxer Indemnity is one of the foremost obligations of the Chinese Government should not be overlooked; and it believes that to grant to China the benefit of the treaties of Washington as long as she continues to evade the treaties validly concluded with the powers, would be an injustice to these powers and would lead China into a path full of dangers to herself. That opinion, moreover, seems to be shared by the majority of the powers signatory to the Washington agreements, since their representatives in Peking believe that the present situation of China does not permit of assembling the Commission on Extraterritoriality.

The very sincere wish of the Government of the Republic is that the new Chinese Cabinet will gain sufficient authority and form a sufficiently accurate idea of its own interests to cast into oblivion the bad faith of the governments that have succeeded each other for the last two years in Peking. It has, therefore, just instructed me to remind Your Excellency that in its opinion the result could be better achieved if the Government of the United States would bring its influence to bear upon the Chinese Government, and give it to understand that the removal of the last obstacle which still stands in the way of the putting into effect of the treaties of Washington depends upon its good will and that the best way to bring to its country the benefits of the advantages flowing from the said treaties would be to meet the engagements heretofore signed by China.

Be pleased [etc.]   JUSSERAND

---

[67] *Foreign Relations*, 1901, Appendix (Affairs in China), p. 312.

893.01/149 : Telegram

The Secretary of State to the Chargé in China (Mayer)

WASHINGTON, *December 10, 1924—4 p. m.*

309. Your telegram No. 478, December 9, 5 p. m.

I am much gratified by this result, and approve your action with regard to modifications of draft which seem entirely satisfactory.

Repeat the above to Tokyo as the Department's number 207, together with your 478, December 9, 5 p. m.

HUGHES

893.01/177

The Minister in China (Schurman) to the Secretary of State

No. 2696   PEKING, *January 5, 1925.*

[Received February 3.]

SIR: I have the honor to refer to Mr. Mayer's telegrams Nos. 472 and 478 of December 4, 3 p. m., and December 9, 5 p. m., relative to the note addressed to the Chinese Government on December 9th by the representatives of the United States, Belgium, Great Britain, France, Italy, Japan, and The Netherlands, in which it was declared in the names of their Governments that they would lend their full support to the Provisional Government in Peking under the present Provisional Chief Executive, upon certain understandings.

My telegram No. 501 of December 24, 3 p. m.,[74] contained a summary of the Wai Chiao Pu's reply of December 23rd. I now have the honor to transmit herewith enclosed, for the Department's information, a copy of a translation of the last mentioned note.

I have [etc.]   JACOB GOULD SCHURMAN

[Enclosure—Translation]

The Chinese Acting Minister for Foreign Affairs (Shen Jui-lin) to the American Minister (Schurman)

In acknowledging the receipt of the joint Communication of the Heads of Missions at Peking of the United States of America, Belgium, Great Britain, France, Italy, Japan and The Netherlands under date of December 9, 1924, which has been acceded to by Portugal in a Note dated December 18th, 1924, from the British Minister on behalf of the Portuguese Government, the Chinese Government desire to express their gratification at the declaration made by them in the names of their Governments, that they will lend their full support to the Provisional Government in Peking under the present Chief Executive which, they are correct in understanding, has been

---

[74] Not printed.

constituted with the concurrence of the Nation and will lead to the establishment of a formal Government truly representative of the Republic. The Chinese Government desire to assure them that the Chinese Government will continue to respect, as they have always respected, all the Treaties, Conventions, and other engagements duly entered into by China, and even in exceptional cases where a divergence of interpretation has arisen the Chinese Government have always endeavored to seek an equitable solution with the Power or Powers concerned in accordance with international usage.

The Chinese Government are gratified to be apprised that the Governments signatory to the Washington Treaties are willing and anxious to proceed as soon as practicable with the carrying out of the measures contemplated in the Washington Treaties and Resolutions. These measures, which are purposely restricted to those which were immediately practicable, were unconditionally agreed upon to be forthwith carried out. The Chinese Government regret the delay which has unexpectedly occurred and sincerely hope that, with the assurance of friendly assistance now given by the Governments concerned, these measures could soon be put into execution, in accordance with the intentions and agreements of the Washington Conference. They wish to add, furthermore, that in view of the desire of the Chinese Government to consolidate the friendship between China and the friendly Powers on a permanent and sound basis, they hope that the Powers concerned will also at an early date give sympathetic consideration to the other well-known national aspirations of the Chinese people, submitted in recent years to different international conferences by the Chinese Government, so that their relations may be further improved to their mutual benefit.

PEKING, *December 23, 1924.*

NEGOTIATIONS LEADING TO THE OCCUPATION OF THE RUSSIAN LEGATION AT PEKING BY THE NEWLY ACCREDITED SOVIET AMBASSADOR TO CHINA

706.6193/23 : Telegram

The Minister in China (Schurman) to the Secretary of State

[Extract]

PEKING, *June 11, 1924—11 a. m.*
[Received 3 : 05 p. m.]

170. 1. Following note from Koo, dated June 9, has been received by Netherlands Minister, acting dean of diplomatic corps:

"With reference to the premises of the former Russian Legation in Peking, Your Excellency will recall that according to the note of Monsieur Pastor, the former *doyen* of the diplomatic corps, received by this Ministry October 4, 1920, the members of the diplomatic corps had agreed to entrust at first temporarily the said premises to the custody of Prince Koudacheff. According to *doyen's* note of January 11, 1921, the premises in question were entrusted, in view of Prince Koudacheff's departure from Peking, to the custody of His Excellency Monsieur Oudendijk as representative of the diplomatic corps until the arrival [at] Peking of a representative of a recognized Russian government. These notes were duly acknowledged by this Ministry.

As the Chinese Government has recognized the Soviet Government upon the conclusion of the Sino-Russian agreements and restored its normal diplomatic and consular relations with the latter, all the premises of the former Russian Legation as well as articles appurtenant thereto should of course be returned to the representative of the Soviet Government to China, in accordance with the original arrangement. I have the honor therefore to request that Your Excellency will be so kind as to bring this matter to the attention of the interested resident ministers at Peking and to favor me with a reply at your convenience."

[Paraphrase]

2. Koo's note leaves out of consideration the statement in the dean's note of October 3, 1920, to the effect that the Russian Legation would be taken in charge by the representatives of the protocol powers until Russian representation recognized by the powers should be again established. See enclosure in despatch no. 317 of October 14, 1920, from this legation.[74a]

3. An informal meeting of the representatives of the protocol powers yesterday considered the Chinese note. Several days previously this meeting had been called to discuss Russian problems affecting these representatives.

4. The meeting decided unanimously that the Dutch Minister should reply on behalf of the protocol powers to Koo.[75] The reply should state that if and when a duly accredited diplomatic representative of Russia wished to gain possession of the Russian Legation he should apply to the Dutch Minister who represented the group.

. . . . . .

SCHURMAN

706.6193/2 : Telegram

The Minister in China (Schurman) to the Secretary of State

[Paraphrase]

PEKING, *June 30, 1924—11 a.m.*
[Received 3 : 40 p.m.]

209. On June 27 the Chinese Minister for Foreign Affairs answered the note of June 11 from the Dutch Minister regarding the transfer

---

[74a] Not printed.
[75] The note of the Dutch Minister, dated June 11, 1924, is not printed.

of the premises of the Russian Legation to the Government of the Soviet Union. An informal conference of the representatives of the protocol powers will consider the reply tomorrow. The crucial points of the Chinese note follow: [76]

"1. In reply I have the honor to observe that the assumption by the foreign representatives of the signatories of the protocol of 1901 of the responsibility of guarding the buildings and premises of the former Russian Legation in Peking was an act undertaken by the said representatives without the consent of the Chinese Government, although it was occasioned by the recognition [termination] of the then Russian diplomatic representative [representation] in Peking decreed by a Presidential mandate of the Republic under the date of September 23rd, 1920.

2. How long such custody on the part of the said diplomatic representatives should last is a question which in its origin does not fall within the discretion of the said representatives but must rather depend upon the decision of China to decree [restore] such relations with the new Russian Government.

3. Your Excellency's suggestion to consider the question of handing over the former Russian Legation only on a request addressed to the foreign representatives by a Russian representative duly accredited to the Chinese Government appears to overlook the special interest of the Chinese Government to see the premises of the former Russian Legation promptly handed back to an authorized representative of the Russian Government. It will be recalled that the Diplomatic Quarter, though under the control of the foreign legations by the protocol of 1901, remains part of Chinese territory and that the premises of the Russian Legation, though situated in the said quarter, are themselves not subject to the control of the representatives of other powers. Indeed they cannot be subject to such control, as they are the property of a foreign power with which China has reestablished diplomatic relations and which is anxious to take possession of the Legation through its authorized representative for use as its Legation. In asking for the delivery of the said premises to an authorized representative of the Soviet Government, the Chinese Government sought only to extend to a foreign government that act of friendly assistance which international courtesy expected of China to do in order to facilitate the establishment of [a] diplomatic representative [representation] which it has agreed to receive. They feel the more concerned because, as I may add for your information, it is their desire to discharge an obligation which they have undertaken vis-à-vis the Soviet Government in the Sino-Russian agreement of May 31, 1924.

4. They are further inclined to the view that the conventional status of the Diplomatic Quarter should not make it difficult for the foreign representatives to comply with the request of the Chinese Government, since they have not asked to take control themselves of the said premises but have requested only to have them delivered to an authorized representative of the Soviet Government.

5. I hope the more sincerely that Your Excellency will see your way to arrange for compliance with this request, as any other course

---

[76] Text of Chinese note not paraphrased.

of action in the present case would not only embarrass the Chinese Government in their desire to extend every courtesy and facility prescribed by international usage to the representatives of foreign government[s] maintaining amicable relations with China, but would also appear to prejudice the right of foreign powers to establish their Legations on Chinese territory free from any condition other than the consent of the Chinese Government."

SCHURMAN

706.6193/2 : Telegram

The Acting Secretary of State to the Minister in China (Schurman)

WASHINGTON, July 9, 1924—4 p. m.

145. Your 209, June 30, 11 a. m. Department's telegram No. 144, July 9, 3 p, m.,[77] will have indicated to you the Department's feeling that the property of the former Russian Legation should be turned over to the Russian representative upon his request for possession.

The Department however approves the stand taken by the Diplomatic Body in refusing to transfer the property at the request of the Chinese authorities. In view of the abnormal situation arising out of the fact that the Legation Quarter has been set aside by the Boxer Protocol for the joint use and control of the Legations in such manner as to insure its defensibility, the Chinese Government can claim no voice in the disposition of the property beyond determining who is to be recognized as the representative of Russia in China. The Chinese Foreign Office may be informed accordingly.

GREW

706.6193/3 : Telegram

The Minister in China (Schurman) to the Secretary of State

PEKING, July 12, 1924—3 p.m.
[Received 8 : 45 p.m.]

230. 1. My number 209, June 30, 11 a. m. Following is synopsis of salient features of considerately and moderately phrased note sent today by dean to Chinese Government replying to its note of June 27.[78]

2. Representatives of powers signatory to protocol of 1901 affirm their fixed desire not to concern themselves with relations between Chinese and foreign governments but must clearly indicate that agreements between Chinese and Soviet Governments must not

---

[77] Not printed.
[78] See telegram no. 209, June 30, from the Minister in China, p. 444.

weaken or infringe upon undertakings entered into with them individually or collectively by Chinese Government.

3. Special regime of Diplomatic Quarter and international servitudes laid upon Chinese Government and upon representatives of foreign powers resident within the quarter are discussed. Freedom of action of Chinese Government and signatory powers restricted by above, and action can be taken only within the limits imposed thereby and the detailed arrangements which have arisen within past 24 years.

4. This complicated situation which compelled request from the powers in 1920 to assume responsibility for safeguarding real property of Russian Government now obliges them not to hand back this property except to representative of Russian Government by whom they may be preliminarily assured of maintenance of arrangements constituting conventional statute of diplomatic quarter. This should be simple of attainment. These *pourparlers* not within province of Chinese Government but instrumentality of Minister for Foreign Affairs will gladly be sought in initiating them.

5. The eight Ministers must be notified of name of diplomatic representative officially accredited to Chinese Government by Russian Government, and Minister for Foreign Affairs is requested to ask this representative to put himself directly in touch with them to discuss and determine the matter.

6. This note was drafted at meeting of eight Ministers July 1st but despatch delayed because of absence from Peking of some of them.

7. Department's 145, July 9, 4 p. m. It is important to bear in mind that neither Karakhan nor anyone else has yet presented credentials to President of China as Ambassador or Minister since Karakhan's credentials were for the special purpose of concluding an agreement.

8. Foreign powers recognize they cannot permanently exclude duly accredited Russian representative from Russian Legation which was Russian Government property long before Legation Quarter was created but feel they are entitled in the interest of good neighborhood and order that the Russian representative when accredited to China shall undertake to abide by the rules and regulations for the Government upkeep and defense of the quarter as the German Minister did when he took back the German Legation in 1921.

For the Minister:

BELL

706.6193/5 : Telegram

The Minister in China (Schurman) to the Secretary of State

PEKING, *July 25, 1924—noon.*
[Received 10:30 p. m.]

258. Your 144, July 9, 3 p. m.,[79] penultimate paragraph, your 145, July 9, 4 p. m., and my 230, July 12, 3 p. m., especially paragraph 5.

1. In compliance with note of July 12th from the Netherlands Minister,[80] who has gone to Japan on a visit, Chinese Minister for Foreign Affairs yesterday invited me as senior representative of protocol powers present in Peking to his residence to meet Karakhan. He there informed me that Karakhan had been appointed Ambassador to China by the Soviet Government and introduced me to Karakhan as dean. After drinking tea together, the Minister for Foreign Affairs excused himself from attendance and I held a conversation of over two hours with Karakhan regarding transfer of Russian Legation to him.

2. Karakhan remarked that he could not understand on what ground the protocol powers prescribed conditions which they asked him to accept before turning over to him premises of the Russian Legation. I replied that Legation Quarter had been granted to the signatory powers for their joint use and control and as [it] was understood that Russia had renounced her interest under the protocol, my colleagues desired an assurance that he would accept the arrangements of the conventional regime to which they continued to adhere with particular reference to defense, taxation, municipal regulations. He categorically and emphatically [stated] that the Soviet Government had not abandoned their rights and interests under the protocol and that their status was still that of a cosignatory. In response to my inquiry he admitted that they contemplated such abandonment in the future, and I pointed out that the position of my colleagues was intended for that contingency whenever it might occur. He declared that the other signatories of the protocol had no right to lay down conditions for him and that he would not accept them either now or at any other time.

3. I went on to say that my colleagues were, in view of his published utterances, apprehensive as to his attitude with respect to their rights and prerogatives under the protocol. He admitted that he had expressed disapproval of the protocol provisions but assured me that he desired on entering the quarter to maintain good neigh-

[79] Not printed; it quoted telegrams exchanged with the Ambassador in Great Britain; paragraph referred to is also the penultimate paragraph of telegram no. 189, July 7, to the Ambassador in Great Britain, p. 466.
[80] For synopsis of note to the Chinese Government, see telegram from the Minister in China, printed *supra.*

borly relations and observe municipal regulations. He added that if his Government should renounce its rights under the protocol they would notify the other powers in accordance with international usage. He also made and reiterated the statement that his Government would not bring any Red troops into the Legation Quarter.

4. I inquired whether I might communicate to my colleagues the statements he had just made. He consented on the express understanding however that they were not to be regarded as the fulfillment of preliminary conditions laid down by others but the voluntary expression of his own sentiments. He agreed to send me a written record of these observations. He will also make a formal demand of the powers for the transfer of the Legation premises.

5. Karakhan will never assent to conditions to get back the property. On the other hand most if not all of my colleagues insist on some stipulations. My hope is that Karakhan's voluntary statement, unless he minimizes it in the note he is to send me, can be used to satisfy my colleagues. It is on this I base my hope of an early settlement of the difficulty.

6. I had a conference this morning with my British colleague who has just returned to Peking for a few days and informed him of my instructions on the subject and reported to him fully my conversation with Karakhan. He expressed much gratification at the prospect of a settlement. No other minister of the protocol powers is in Peking.

7. As soon as I receive Karakhan's written statement I will call a meeting of the representatives of the protocol powers.

SCHURMAN

706.6193/5 : Telegram

The Acting Secretary of State to the Minister in China (*Schurman*)

WASHINGTON, *July 29, 1924—6 p. m.*

175. Your telegram No. 258, July 25, noon, presents a very gratifying prospect of settlement which the Department would consider satisfactory. In the light of the Department's views (as expressed in its telegram No. 144, July 9, 3 p. m.[81]) that the Protocol Powers would not be warranted in denying or conditioning the transfer of the Russian Legation property to a recognized Soviet representative, this Government would not feel justified in authorizing you to associate yourself with any effort to stipulate conditions precedent to the transfer to Karakhan. The necessities of the case would appear to be satisfactorily met by his communicating as a voluntary expression of his intentions a written statement of the assurances offered in

---

[81] Not printed.

conversation with you, provided that such assurances are (as your telegram leads the Department to hope) sufficiently definite to cover questions of defence, taxation and municipal regulations of the Legation Quarter, not only under present circumstances but also in the event that the Soviet regime abandons Russian rights and interests under the Boxer Protocol as it contemplates doing.

GREW

706.6193/7 : Telegram

The Minister in China (Schurman) to the Secretary of State

PEKING, *August 1, 1924—4 p. m.*
[Received August 1—1:45 p. m.]

270. 1. Your number 175, July 29, 6 p. m.; my 258, July 25, noon.

2. The diplomatic representatives of the eight protocol powers met here today and I presented to them Karakhan's formal note requesting that the Russian Legation property and keys be handed over to him, as well as his unsigned typewritten report of the substance of his conversation with me . . .

. . . .

3. Nothing was said by Karakhan about the defense of the Diplomatic Quarter.

The meeting lasted nearly three hours and the subject was considered from every point of view. The result was embodied in the draft of a reply to be made by me as dean to Karakhan which the diplomatic representatives were first to telegraph to their Governments for approval. That draft is as follows:

"I have the honor to inform you that I have this day laid the communication you addressed to me as dean on July 26, 1924, before my colleagues, the diplomatic representatives of the powers signatory to the protocol of 1901, and also informed them that in the conversation of July 24 to which you refer you informed me that the Soviet Government considered itself actually to be a cosignatory of the aforesaid protocol.

In view of this circumstance and the consequence thereof, namely, that the Soviet Government enjoys all the rights and is impressed with all the obligations of that protocol and of the protocol of 1904 [82] and all subsequent arrangements which bound all the cosignatories to the maintenance of the conventional status of the Diplomatic Quarter, the diplomatic representatives of the signatory powers have consented to hand over to Your Excellency the Russian Legation and the keys thereof and have appointed the Chargé d'Affaires of the Netherlands Legation, Mr. Roell, to represent them in this business.

---

[82] For text of protocol of 1904, see MacMurray, *Treaties and Agreements with and concerning China*, vol. I, p. 315.

As to the intimation given me by Your Excellency in the conversation above referred to that the Soviet might in the future renounce its interest in the protocol of 1901 which I also reported to my colleagues, I am requested to say that the representatives of the other powers signatory of the 1901 and 1904 protocols must reserve full liberty of action for their Governments in respect to the effect of such renunciation upon the rights, privileges and mutual obligations which accrue to and devolve upon all the signatories of these collective agreements.

If Your Excellency will acquaint me with the name of the person you may delegate to take over the Russian Legation and the keys, I will communicate the information to Mr. Roell."

4. I think it is the expectation of all the diplomatic representatives that this draft perhaps with minor changes will be approved by their Governments. If the respective Governments cabled their replies next week the matter could be settled before I left Peking for America.

SCHURMAN

706.6193/7 : Telegram

The Acting Secretary of State to the Minister in China (Schurman)

WASHINGTON, *August 6, 1924—2 p. m.*

183. Your 270, August 1, 4 p. m. While the Department approves the note in principle, with the amendment suggested below, and you may so inform your colleagues, it would, in view of the fact that this Government has not recognized the Soviet regime, prefer that it should be signed by some other representative of the Protocol Powers. Would it not therefore be practicable for the note, *mutatis mutandis*, to be signed after your departure from Peking by some other diplomatic representative of the Protocol Powers, preferably the ranking diplomatic representative of a power which has recognized the Soviet regime, and to be then despatched to Karakhan. The Department is not informed of the exact date of your departure from Peking but it assumes that you will be leaving within a day or two in order that you may spend a few days in Shanghai before sailing.

You will readily appreciate that your action in signing a formal note of this character addressed to the duly accredited Soviet Russian representative, even though you do so in your capacity as dean of the Protocol Powers, and not as the American Minister, might be construed as an act of recognition and that those who would benefit from such an erroneous impression would make no effort to discourage it. It is essential to avoid any such contingency. As a further precaution, the Department suggests that the following paragraph be added to the note and trusts that the representatives of the Protocol Powers will acquiesce:

"It is, of course, understood that nothing in this note shall be construed as constituting recognition of the regime known as the Union of Soviet Socialist Republics by any Protocol Power which has not recognized that regime."

GREW

706.6193/8 : Telegram

The Minister in China (Schurman) to the Secretary of State

PEKING, *August 9, 1924—11 a. m.*
[Received August 9—5:02 a. m.]

277. Your 183, August 6, 2 p. m. Holland, Belgium, France, and Japan have approved the note as it stands. Objections are not anticipated from England and Italy which have recognized the Soviet regime, nor from Spain which generally follows others. Therefore, while sharing the Department's feeling as to the need of special precaution I respectfully recommend that the Legation be authorized to omit the presentation to the representatives of the protocol powers of the Department's suggestion in the last paragraph of the above-mentioned telegram, provided the question of such reservation is not raised by any representative of the other five powers who have not recognized the Soviet regime. The suggestion would involve delay and presumably another reference to the home governments. I deem it desirable from every point of view that the matter of the transfer of the Russian Legation be disposed of as soon as practicable.

At conference of diplomatic representatives of protocol powers August 1st I stated I was leaving Peking morning 13th and asked what should be done in case note to Karakhan had not been sent before that date. It was agreed that the note *mutatis mutandis* should be sent by the Italian Minister who in absence of French Minister on leave follows me in order of seniority. This arrangement accords completely with the views expressed by the Department. And it will make my observance of the Department's instructions seem merely a natural outcome of the events themselves. It is scarcely necessary to say that even if in the three days remaining before I leave Peking I should be notified of the replies of England, Italy, and Spain I will take no further action in the matter.

SCHURMAN

706.6193/8 : Telegram

The Acting Secretary of State to the Minister in China (Schurman)

WASHINGTON, *August 11, 1924—3 p. m.*

191. Your 277, August 9, 11 a. m.

You are authorized to omit the suggested reservation contained in the Department's 183, August 6, 2 p.m., provided the question of such a reservation is not raised by any representative of the other powers concerned who have, or who have not, recognized the Soviet regime. If you have reason to believe, however, that the suggested reservation would be accepted by your interested colleagues without the delay incident to a reference to their respective governments the Department considers that it would still be advisable to propose the reservation. If this is not deemed expedient you will endeavor to have the note amended so as to include the following paragraph:

"I am to add on behalf of my American colleague, that his action in acquiescing in the understanding embodied in this note in no wise constitutes or implies recognition on the part of the Government of the United States of the regime known as the Union of Socialist Soviet Republics."

In view of the fact that the note to Karakhan will be signed by the Italian Minister instead of by yourself as Dean, and that certain changes in the text must necessarily be made in consequence thereof, it is suggested that such changes, in so far as they refer to your conversation of July 24 with Karakhan and to the note received by you from him, should avoid, as far as possible, the use of your name or title of American Minister, merely making reference to such negotiations and correspondence taking place between Karakhan and the "Dean of the Protocol Powers".

GREW

_____

706.6193/9 : Telegram

The Chargé in China (Bell) to the Secretary of State

PEKING, *August 18, 1924—3 p. m.*
[Received August 18—11:35 a. m.]

292. Your 191, August 10 [*11*], 3 p. m.

1. Italy, Spain, and Great Britain having also agreed to draft note, it was today decided at a meeting of representatives of protocol powers to despatch it in original form with such verbal changes [as] were made necessary by Dr. Schurman's departure and signature of note by Japanese Minister (not Italian Minister as previously reported).

2. Alterations suggested in your 191, paragraph three, were also made.

3. I sounded colleagues on, suggestion made in your 183, August 6, 2 p. m.; found them all opposed and therefore dropped it.

4. With regard to suggestion in your 191, paragraph 2, it [apparent omission] that other representatives were unwilling to accept it without telegraphing to their governments to inquire whether the latter also wished similar reservation made on their behalf. Other representatives felt also that as far as they were concerned such reservation was of doubtful value. I therefore agreed in order to avoid delay and meet Department's wishes, [apparent omission] this statement in separate note referring to the other note and send them both to Karakhan at the same time. Notes will be delivered to Karakhan this afternoon and copies given to the press and to the Chinese Foreign Office for information.

5. Persistent reports which I cannot yet confirm are reaching me from reliable sources that prior to Karakhan's conference with Schurman he had exchanged notes with Koo definitely giving up Russia's extraterritorial rights, which of course would mean that Russia could no longer consider herself a protocol power.

BELL

706.6193/12 : Telegram

The Chargé in China (Bell) to the Secretary of State

PEKING, *August 20, 1924—4 p. m.*
[Received 10:55 p. m.]

296. My 292, August 18, 3 p. m., paragraph 4. Two notes were presented by Japanese Minister to Karakhan, August 18. This morning's newspapers contain text of note which Karakhan is reported to have sent yesterday to Japanese Minister.

"Mr. Minister: I have the honor to inform Your Excellency that I do not consider possible to accept the note under date of August 18, 1924, which you presented me at the request of the American Minister.

I really regret very much that you could not decline this American commission at a time when Japan is herself engaged in negotiations whose very object is to restore normal relations between the Government of the Union of Soviet Socialist Republics and the Government of Japan. I hope however that if and when the Union of Soviet Socialist Republics recognizes the Government of Japan while Japan recognizes Government of the Union, this will not be interpreted in the sense that the Government of the Union will have recognized the bourgeois capitalist[ic] regime of Japan, nor will [it] be taken to mean the recognition by Japan of the socialistic regime of the dictatorship of the proletariat. I may likewise express the hope that you have no doubt as to the fact that the negotiations we are carrying on with you at present are being conducted not between two regimes but between the Government[s] of the Union of Soviet Socialist Republics and of Japan. This understanding may make it easier for Your Excellency as it seems to me to explain to your American colleague the limits of courtesy beyond [which] his fear might lead him.

It should also be added for the information of Your Excellency's American colleague and for that matter of your other colleagues who may have not had time yet, like the American Minister, to formulate their anxiety that there does not exist in international law and practice a method of restoration of diplomatic prerogative [*relations*] between two governments by way of returning to one of them a legation belonging to the latter government and situated in the capital of a third power by the other of those two governments which, but accidentally and without the consent of the real owner, has in its [hands] the keys from the buildings of such a legation.

Herewith I beg to return the above-mentioned note of August 18, 1924.

I avail myself of this opportunity to renew to you, Mr. Minister, the assurance of my highest consideration. Signed L. Karakhan."

The Bolshevik Rosta News Agency has also issued the following statement.

"In a conversation he had with a representative of the Soviet Embassy the correspondent of the Rosta News Agency had the following statement made to him.

The note which was returned to Mr. Yoshizawa by Mr. Karakhan was written by the former at the request of the American Minister. Mr. Karakhan has no doubt that if Mr. Yoshizawa, who is now engaged in negotiations with the Government of the Union, had the right to refuse he would have declined to undertake the ungrateful task of representing American interests before [*in regard to*] the Soviet Government. The idiosyncrasy of the American diplomacy has up till now been forcing and still forces it today to act foolishly and [incorrectly] *vis-à-vis* the Government of the Union. In this respect American diplomacy differs widely from the American people which is endowed with common sense, favorably distinguishing them even from other nations. As for American diplomacy it is so afraid and has such a hatred of the Soviet Union that in an official document presented to the Soviet representative it cannot refrain from discourteous formula[e].

It would be an ungrateful task to teach good manners and politeness to the representatives of the present American Government, it being, however, not so much a question of politeness or courtesy as one of bitter hatred which some of the elements now ruling in America feel towards the Soviet Government. No wonder that in China the American diplomacy is particularly sensitive with regard to the Soviet Union, for it is here in China that America has more strongly and acutely than other powers felt the blow which was dealt to her policy by the sincere and straightforward policy of the Soviet Government. Indeed the hypocrisy and Christian bigotry in which the Americans enveloped their policy in China have now been fully exposed in the eyes of the Chinese people. Much lustre has been taken off from good words about the respect for and the rights of the Chinese people since the Lincheng note, the threatening speeches of the American Minister at Harbin and the appearance and arbitrary actions of American warships in Chinese home waters.

Of course the Americans who have made Mr. Yoshizawa write the note which was returned today could be told: You do not wish to recognize the regime existing in the Soviet Union? Well you know that at any future time the Soviet Government does not at all intend compelling you to do it. And they could also be told that the American people will force them to recognize the Government of the Union without any reservations. Then the present rulers of America could also be told that the day relations will be restored between America and the Union it will not in any way mean that the Government of the Union will have to recognize the regime which presently [at present] holds sway in America—if of course this regime will still be existing at the time. The regime of violence in China, the infringement of the sovereignty of the Chinese people; the regime of the troops of the Philippines; the regime of the most unashamed interference with the affairs of the American Republics; the regime which has made of a negro a dog whom anyone may [with impunity] kill; the regime lastly which but quite recently has revealed itself in an unutterably monstrous form of corruption, decay, pillaging of state property—in which all take part whether senators, ministers or judges; a regime under which the President has had to use many an effort and much time to find an honest judge to investigate the oil scandal, for every judge on whom his choice fell happened himself to be involved in the scandal and the robbing of state property.

It is to be hoped at least that the American Minister does not mean to say that the powers which recognize the Washington Government have also recognized all the above-enumerated brilliant aspects of the American regime. And we certainly hope that when we are going to resume relations with the American Government the latter is not going to insist upon the recognition of this regime on our part too. We have no doubt as to the fact that the best part of the American people, that is its huge majority, are against the policy of the present American Government with regard to the Soviet Union; nor do we have any doubts that today's rulers of America know that their days are numbered and that those who will come after [in] their place will—whoever they may be—either by compulsion or their own free will, correct the mistake[s] made with regard to the Soviet Union and would, we [express the hope,] not only in regard to the Soviet Union but [also] to other peoples and in particular the Chinese nation."

I have just received call from Japanese Minister who incidentally ceased to be dean last night on return to Peking of British Minister. He is deeply offended at tone and substance of Karakhan's note, particularly reference to Government of Japan being in the midst of negotiations with Karakhan regarding resumption of relations between two countries; feels this is an uncalled-for affront to him and has telegraphed home for instructions as to whether he should return note to Karakhan. If he does so, as he has ceased to be dean, it will have to be as Japanese Minister and not as dean. If he decides to refer the matter to British Minister it will be extremely awkward for the latter whose only wish is to prevent friction with Bolshevik representative . . .

I consider that I have discharged my duty to our Government in causing our Government's views to be conveyed to Karakhan which they unquestionably have been and I do not intend to take any further part if I can possibly avoid it in the imbroglio which has arisen . . .

.   .   .   .

BELL

706.6193/13 : Telegram

The Chargé in China (Bell) to the Secretary of State

PEKING, *August 25, 1924—10 a. m.*
[Received August 25—4 : 47 a. m.]

303. My 296, August 20, 4 p. m. There have been no developments of importance since the foregoing was sent.

Neither Japanese nor British Minister has returned Karakhan's note of August 19 while Karakhan has not replied to note of August 18 offering to return Legation nor has he asked for keys. It is reported that he is dissatisfied with reservations in third paragraph of latter note and has telegraphed Moscow for instructions.

Russo-Japanese negotiations have made no advance and merely [*nearly?*] broke down last week on the question of Saghalien.

BELL

706.6193/15 : Telegram

The Chargé in China (Bell) to the Secretary of State

PEKING, *August 26, 1924—5 p. m.*
[Received August 26—9 : 27 a. m.]

305. My 303, August 25, 10 a. m. Japanese Minister informs me that under instructions from Tokyo he is negotiating with Karakhan for the withdrawal of the latter's note of August 19th and the substitution of another the same date which will be regarded as the original and which will omit the statements objectionable to the Japanese Government. Note will, however, undoubtedly return Japanese Minister's note of August 18th containing our reservation and will probably hold the same or other offensive language concerning our Government as did the original.

If this takes place I think I should ask Japanese Minister not to address me formally sending me copy of such a communication, as I do not think I should receive such a note at the hands of the representative of any government with which we maintain diplomatic relations. Otherwise I think it best to let the matter drop, as Karakhan's note will be addressed to Japanese Minister and not to me.

Please instruct.

BELL

706.6193/16 : Telegram

The Chargé in China (Bell) to the Secretary of State

PEKING, August 26, 1924—6 p. m.
[Received August 26—1 : 07 p. m.]

306. My 303, August 25, 10 a. m.

1. British representative as senior protocol representative has received note dated yesterday from Karakhan which, after acknowledging receipt of note of August 18th offering to return Russian Legation (but without alluding to reasons given therein for doing so) and after naming representatives to take over Legation, continues:

2. "At the same time I beg to inform Your Excellency that I consider that this handing over is being effected in view of the fact that the Union of Soviet Socialist Republics is the owner of the buildings of the former Russian Legation. As regards the other considerations laid down in the note of His Excellency the Japanese Minister, under date of 18th instant, I feel it is my duty to state that I cannot fully endorse all the said considerations but that inasmuch as a coordination of viewpoints preliminary to the handing over of the Embassy would be in contradiction with the position of the Soviet Government which I had the opportunity to expound exhaustively in my conversation with the American Minister, Mr. Schurman, on July 24 of this year, I may however express my firm belief that the existing differences will not prevent to establish a *modus vivendi* between the Soviet Embassy and the Legations situated in the Diplomatic Quarter."

3. British Minister in circulating foregoing expresses opinion that this may be considered satisfactory acknowledgment of our note and thinks reservations in third paragraph of our note sufficiently safeguard liberty of action of the other signatories of the 1901 protocol in the event of its subsequent cancelation by the Soviets or of renunciation of their interests therein and also in the event of its being found impossible to establish the *modus vivendi* mentioned in Karakhan's reply.

4. I do not consider it a satisfactory reply as it appears to repudiate the conditions of the return as set forth in prefaced paragraph of protocol representative's note of August 18th; and I fear that on publication of Karakhan's note, which is to take place after he receives our final reply, it will appear that he has through the medium of the American Minister hoaxed the diplomatic body with regard to his position as a protocol representative.

5. However, it is probably the best we can hope for and, having regard to Department's views as expressed in your telegram 144, July 9, 3 p. m.,[83] I assume you will desire me to accept Karakhan's note of August [25] as satisfactory and to assent to his taking over Russian Legation.

BELL

706.6193/16 : Telegram

The Secretary of State to the Chargé in China (*Bell*)

WASHINGTON, *August 28, 1924—10 a. m.*

204. Your 306, August 26, 6 p. m. While the note creates some doubt as to Karakhan's attitude towards the arrangements set forth in the note of August 18, the Department considers that the *modus vivendi* mentioned by him may afford the means of arriving at a more definite understanding, and since it appears from your telegram that it is the best that might well be hoped for from Karakhan at the present moment you are advised that the Department perceives no objection to the note as the basis of concluding such a *modus vivendi*.

Department believes it unwise to engage in further negotiations on the subject and that it is best to concur in opinion expressed by British Minister as stated in paragraph 3 your 306.

HUGHES

706.6193/15 : Telegram

The Secretary of State to the Chargé in China (*Bell*)

WASHINGTON, *August 28, 1924—11 a. m.*

205. Your 305, August 26, 5 p. m. Since the Japanese Minister, in transmitting the American declaration to Karakhan, was acting in his capacity as Dean of the Protocol Powers, and not as Japanese Minister, Department doubts the advisability of your formally requesting or pressing him not to transmit to you a copy of Karakhan's

---

[83] Not printed.

note of August 19 if he desires to do so. While the Department hopes that Yoshizawa will not transmit a copy of the note to you in its present form, it nevertheless feels that if he should do so you would have no other recourse than to receive it. Should the note be formally transmitted to you either by Yoshizawa or by the British Minister as Dean, is the Department correct in assuming that copies will also be sent to other representatives of the Protocol Powers?

While the Department trusts that the tone of the note, which was obviously designed for propaganda purposes, may yet be modified in such a way as to remove its offensiveness, it is anxious not to add to Yoshizawa's discomfiture or to embarrass the British Minister should this particular phase of the matter be intrusted to him as Dean.

If note is transmitted to you simply file it as unworthy of further notice.

HUGHES

706.6193/17 : Telegram

The Chargé in China (Bell) to the Secretary of State

PEKING, *August 31, 1924—1 p. m.*
[Received August 31—10 : 50 a. m.]

316. Your 205. Negotiations looking to withdrawal by Karakhan of his note to Yoshizawa of August 19th having [failed?], Yoshizawa has addressed Karakhan following note of which he has given me a copy. Note is dated August 20th, and I understand it was only sent within last 48 hours.

"I have the honor to acknowledge the receipt of your note of the 19th instant wherewith Your Excellency sent back the note which I addressed you on the day [*sic*] at the request of the American Chargé d'Affaires.

I regret to find your note under acknowledgment contains terms which apparently are not calculated to conduce to the promotion of international good understanding. It however seems neither necessary nor useful to enter into discussion on these points. I only desire to point out that my communication of August 18th embodying the remarks of the American Chargé d'Affaires was no more than in fulfillment of what I conceived and still conceive to be my obligation and duty as senior representative of the protocol powers and that it was in no way to be construed as containing any insinuation against your Government or institutions.

In these circumstances I feel constrained to decline to receive back the note in question which as stated before was addressed to Your Excellency in my capacity of senior representative of the protocol powers at the specific request of the American Chargé d'Affaires."

BELL

706.6193/19 : Telegram

The Chargé in China (Bell) to the Secretary of State

PEKING, *September 3, 1924—5 p.m.*
[Received September 3—3 : 12 p.m.]

321. [My] 316, August 3 [*31*], 1 p.m. Karakhan has sent Yoshizawa following note August 30th:

"I have the honor to acknowledge that on the 29th instant Your Excellency handed me your note with the note of August 18th embodying the statement of the American Government, and which I have already received once before, opposed [*apposed?*] to it.

I take note with satisfaction of the statement made by Your Excellency to the effect that it was only your obligation and duty as senior representative [of] eight protocol powers, as to which moreover I never had any doubts, [that made] Your Excellency undertake the task of conveying to me such a statement of the American Government.

However, I feel constrained to state that I cannot accept the explanation of Your Excellency to the effect that the note in question 'was in no way to be construed as containing any insignia [*insinuation*] against my Government or institution,' and that I still hold my view that the form of the statement made by Your Excellency's American colleague is neither proper nor courteous for relations between two governments.

I may be allowed together with Your Excellency to express the hope that the American Government will make no further attempts at presenting me with a communication which I cannot accept and which, as I already had the honor to remark, [is not] supported by international law and practice.

Herewith I beg to enclose the note of August 18, 1924, which Your Excellency sent me a second time on the 29th instant."

Yoshizawa, after consulting Netherlands Minister who has returned to Peking and resumed duties as dean of the diplomatic corps, sent the following reply to Karakhan yesterday:

"In acknowledging the receipt of your note of the 30th August I have the honor to inform Your Excellency that your note under acknowledgment together with its enclosure has been transmitted to [His Excellency] the Netherlands Minister, the senior representative of the protocol ministers."

On learning today of this last exchange of notes I told the Japanese Minister I considered he had done all that could be asked as a colleague and as senior protocol minister and I begged that as far as I was concerned he would now let the matter drop as I thought nothing was to be gained by his continuing this controversy with Karakhan. He agreed and will take no further action.

BELL

706.6193/20 : Telegram

The Chargé in China (Bell) to the Secretary of State

PEKING, *September 8, 1924—4 p.m.*
[Received September 8—12 : 43 p.m.]

333. My 320, September 3, 4 p.m.[84] Karakhan informed Italian Minister that omission in his note of August 26th [*25th*] and [*of*] reference to Russia's being a protocol power was inadvertence and offered for [*to*] write a supplementary note to be dated August 26th tacitly confirming his statement to Dr. Schurman of July 24th, namely, "that the Government of the [Union] of Soviet Socialist Republics considers itself as a circulatory signatory [*as a cosignatory*] power to the final protocol of 1901."

At the meeting on 5th all representatives were willing to answer this with a simple acknowledgment except French Chargé d'Affaires who submitted long draft reply restating our position that no future renunciation by Soviets of their rights under the protocol could affect ours. Italian Minister submitted this to Karakhan who was willing to accept it with slight modifications. At the meeting today French Chargé d'Affaires said he would have to telegraph Paris for permission to accept modifications, so matter will drag on for several days longer.

BELL

706.6193/21 : Telegram

The Chargé in China (Bell) to the Secretary of State

PEKING, *September 12, 1924—2 p. m.*
[Received September 12—10 : 47 a. m.]

340. My 333, September 8, 4 p. m. French Minister agreed. We have accepted Karakhan's note of August 26th, sent him our acknowledgment, and he entered into possession of former Russian Legation noon today. He will not occupy it for two or three weeks as it needs cleaning.

BELL

---

[84] Not printed.

EFFORTS TO OBTAIN UNANIMITY AMONG THE POWERS REGARDING
THE PROPOSAL TO RAISE THE DIPLOMATIC RANK OF THEIR
REPRESENTATIVES IN CHINA

124.93/56a : Telegram

*The Secretary of State to the Ambassador in Great Britain
(Kellogg)* [85]

[Paraphrase]

WASHINGTON, *June 14, 1924—5 p. m.*

163. 1. I have been informed today by the Chinese Minister that
his Government has instructed him to inquire regarding the intentions of the American Government concerning the raising of its
Peking Legation to the rank of an Embassy, considering the probability of such action being taken by other principal powers. Minister
Sze added his private conjecture that this inquiry is based on the
expectation that the Soviet Union, which recently has resumed diplomatic relations with the Chinese Government, will appoint an
Ambassador.

2. Please make a discreet effort to learn from the Foreign Office of
the Government to which you are accredited its intentions in this
matter.

3. The following is for your guidance and information. On April
19, 1921, the Department was informed by the British Embassy [86]
that the British Ambassador to Japan had obtained an assurance
from the Japanese Government that it would take no action of that
nature without consulting with the British Government. The British
Embassy asked that the American Government give a statement of
its intentions. On May 11, 1921, the Department answered [86] that it
did not feel that it was warranted in giving any promise as to the attitude which might be taken by the President should Congress indicate
a desire to raise the rank of our Legation in China but that the Executive did not intend to take or to recommend such action.

4. Repeat this telegram to Embassy in Paris as our no. 184. Indicate that the third paragraph is only for confidential information.

HUGHES

---

[85] See last paragraph for instructions to repeat to Paris as Department's no.
184. The same telegram sent to the Chargé in Japan as no. 97, for his information, as a basis for discreet inquiry at the Foreign Office, and with instructions
to repeat to Peking as Department's no. 124 for information.
[86] Memorandum not printed.

124.93/56 : Telegram

The Chargé in Japan (Caffery) to the Secretary of State

[Paraphrase]

TOKYO, *June 17, 1924—8 p. m.*
[Received June 17—3 : 41 p. m.]

155.   Your 97, June 14, 5 p. m.[88]   I discreetly inquired of Shidehara yesterday during an informal conversation whether he had received any information from Peking with respect to the possibility that any of the principal powers would change the Legations in China to Embassies.

In reply Shidehara said that he had not received any information on the subject from the Japanese Legation and that for this reason he had not given any thought to the matter.   Shidehara added that from the standpoint of his Government there would be, in any event, obvious difficulties involved, as, in the first place, the question would have to be presented to the Diet, and, secondly, next year's budget had been voted already.   He told me, however, that he would look into the matter and that if any change in the status of the Legation was contemplated by his Government, he would inform me.

CAFFERY

124.93/58 : Telegram

The Ambassador in France (Herrick) to the Secretary of State

[Extract—Paraphrase]

PARIS, *June 19, 1924—3 p. m.*
[Received June 19—2 p. m.]

308.   Your telegram no. 184 of June 14.[88]   I was informed yesterday at the Foreign Office by the Chief of the Asiatic Bureau that the French Government would definitely be opposed to changing its Legation in China to an Embassy. . . .

HERRICK

124.93/59 : Telegram

The Ambassador in Great Britain (Kellogg) to the Secretary of State

LONDON, *July 2, 1924—11 a. m.*
[Received July 2—8 : 03 a. m.]

229.   Since sending 221, June 18, 5 p. m.,[89] the Foreign Office informs me that it has been formally approached by the Chinese Chargé

[88] See footnote 85, p. 463.
[89] Not printed.

d'Affaires in the matter of raising the Legation at Peking to the rank of an Embassy and that it would be glad to deal with this question harmoniously with the views of the United States. I am now in receipt of an informal note from Waterlow [90] enclosing a draft of a communication which the Foreign Office proposes to send to the Chinese Chargé d'Affaires but stating that he prefers not to send it without first communicating its actual terms to me. He asks that it be cabled to Washington with the object of obtaining your views as soon as possible. Waterlow further states that he proposes to instruct the British representatives at Paris, Rome and Tokyo to inform the Governments to which they are accredited of the British Government's views and to urge them to reply on the lines of the draft which reads as follows:

"Chinese Chargé d'Affaires. Sir: With reference to the communication which you made at this Department on the 18th ultimo, I have the honor to inform you that His Majesty's Government see no reason why the appointment at Peking of a diplomatic representative of the Soviet Union with the rank of Ambassador which is understood to be impending should be made the occasion of their considering any proposal to change the status of belligerents [sic] either of His Majesty's representative at Peking or of the representative of the Chinese Government in London."

Please instruct. Copy to European Information Center.

KELLOGG

124.93/59 : Telegram

The Secretary of State to the Ambassador in Great Britain
(Kellogg)

WASHINGTON, *July 7, 1924—2 p. m.*

188. Your telegram No. 229, July 2, 11 a. m. You may express to the Foreign Office my appreciation of its action in consulting with us as to the position to be taken in reference to the suggested raising to ambassadorial grade of the Legations at Peking, and say that I share the views of the British Government and propose to communicate to the Chinese Chargé d'Affaires, in the same informal way in which the Minister presented the question to me, my feeling that there is no occasion for any alteration in the status of diplomatic representation between the United States and China.

Repeat to Paris for information as Department's 219.

HUGHES

---

[90] Sydney P. Waterlow, Counsellor in the British Foreign Office.

124.93/59 : Telegram

The Secretary of State to the Ambassador in Great Britain
(Kellogg)[91]

WASHINGTON, *July 7, 1924—3 p. m.*

189. In further reference to your No. 229, July 2, 11 a. m. In connection with your communication to the Foreign Office as to my concurrence in its views on the question of raising the rank of the Legations at Peking it seems desirable that you should take occasion to discuss very frankly with the appropriate officer the situation created by China's receiving an Ambassador from the Soviets.

Your telegram No. 221, June 18, 5 p. m.,[92] reported a tentative opinion of the Foreign Office that it might be possible by agreement among the principal Powers to ignore the Soviet Ambassador as ex-officio Dean of the Diplomatic Body. It seems doubtful whether, in view of his appointment by a Government recognized by China itself and by several of the principal Powers concerned, his status as the ranking member of the Diplomatic Body could be disputed or ignored.

The Diplomatic Body in Peking has of course built up for itself a wholly unique character in the nature of a continuing Conference of the Treaty Powers, representing their collective rights and interests, and exercising the functions of an organized cooperation for the purposes of those foreign rights and interests which the Powers have heretofore shared.

It is understood that by its recent Treaty arrangements with China the Soviet régime has renounced such rights and concessions as the Powers have heretofore enjoyed in common; and that its representatives have moreover openly avowed their antagonism towards the whole system of foreign rights established in favor of the Treaty Powers. If this be the case, a representative of the Soviet, whether as Dean or otherwise, could not be expected to cooperate with his colleagues for those purposes for which the Diplomatic Body exists. On the other hand, his exclusion from that body would appear inevitably to force him into the position of encouraging and cooperating with the Chinese Government in opposition to what would be termed the "pretensions" of the Treaty Powers—an alternative which would be particularly dangerous to the just rights of the Powers at this time when the disintegration of governmental authority in China has already resulted in so greatly impairing the sense of obligation and of responsibility.

[91] See last paragraph for instructions to repeat to Paris as Department's no. 220.
[92] Not printed.

It would seem that the inevitable recognition of a Soviet Ambassador as a member of the Diplomatic Body must tend to paralyse the activity of that organization as an instrumentality for the expression of the collective interests of the Powers, and it is to be anticipated that the Diplomatic Body, in so far as concerns its present peculiar character and functions, will fall into desuetude. It will be unfortunate to lose the benefit of the system of cooperation embodied in that organization; but at a time when cooperation among the Powers is more than ever necessary, it is to be hoped that this loss will be compensated by a cooperation suited to the exigency among the particular nations interested in such cases as from time to time may arise.

A related question concerns the transfer to the Soviet Ambassador of the property of the Russian Legation in the Legation Quarter. It would seem an untenable position for the other Legations which have had this property in custody to claim a right to deny or to condition its transfer, upon his demand, to the person recognized by China as the duly accredited diplomatic representative of Russia. On this point, however, I should be happy to learn the views of the British Government, particularly in reference to the possibility that the occupation of the Russian Legation by the representatives of the Soviet might have the result of impairing the defensibility of the Legation Quarter for which provision is made by the Boxer Protocol.[93]

You will of course bear in mind that this Government, while not itself considering it advisable or feasible to enter into diplomatic relations with the Soviet régime, desires to stand aloof from any question of the relationships of other Governments with the Soviets.

Repeat to Paris for information as Department's 220.

HUGHES

124.93/66a

Memorandum by the Under Secretary of State (Grew) of a Conversation with the Chinese Chargé (Yung Kwai)

[WASHINGTON,] *July 10, 1924.*

I asked Mr. Yung Kwai to call and with reference to the Minister's talk with the Secretary on June 14, in which the Minister informally inquired whether this government would be willing to raise its representation at Peking to the rank of an Embassy, I told the Chargé, informally, that this government did not feel that there was occasion for any alteration in the status of our diplomatic representation in Peking.

J. C. G[REW]

[93] *Foreign Relations,* 1901, Appendix (Affairs in China), p. 312.

124.93/64 : Telegram

The Chargé in Japan (Caffery) to the Secretary of State

TOKYO, *July 11, 1924—9 p. m.*
[Received July 11—8 : 50 p. m.]

184. My telegram no. 155, June 17, 8 p. m. Baron Shidehara handed me the following written statement this afternoon:

"The Japanese Government attaching great importance to their relations with China have the intention of agreement by [*to?*] the exchange of Ambassadors between Japan and China. Having regard, however, to practical considerations, more particularly in relation to budget, they are not yet in a position finally to determine the date for effecting such exchange.

Should other powers interested in China be disposed to agree to the course indicated the Japanese Government propose that the powers so disposed will jointly inform the Chinese Government of that decision in principle, with necessary reserves respecting the date for the actual exchange of Ambassadors.

It is hoped that such date will be fixed by the powers upon previous communication with one another and that the powers may find it possible to raise simultaneously their respective Legations at Peking to Embassies. So far as the Japanese Government are concerned it is their present intention to proceed to the establishment of an Embassy at Peking on or about April 1st, 1925, provided that the necessary requirements under Japanese laws be completed in that time".

Baron Shidehara stated British, French, Italian Governments also being informed but their [*this?*] information not being transmitted to China until reply of four other interested Governments to this communication received here.

He added that Japanese Government felt that there was strong sentiment in the Diet calling for this gesture on the part of Japan.

Peking informed.

CAFFERY

124.93/63 : Telegram

The Ambassador in Great Britain (Kellogg) to the Secretary of State

LONDON, *July 12, 1924—12 p. m.* [*noon.*]
[Received July 12—8 : 50 a. m.]

248. I am informed by a note from the Foreign Office that the Government has replied to the Chinese Government in accordance with the proposed communication as contained in my 229, July 2, 11 a. m.

The note to me adds:

"His Majesty's Government regard it as a matter of the utmost importance in the interest of international solidarity in China that the powers should act in concert and I trust therefore that Your

Excellency's Government will concur in the view of His Majesty's Government in this matter and that they will reply to the suggestion of the Chinese Government in a similar sense.

I am addressing a similar communication to the Japanese, French and Italian Ambassadors at once."

Copy to European Information Center.

KELLOGG

124.93/64 : Telegram

The Acting Secretary of State to the Chargé in Japan (Caffery)[94]

WASHINGTON, *July 12, 1924—3 p. m.*

121. Your telegram No. 184, July 11, 9 p. m. You may advise Baron Shidehara that this Government has indicated to China that it sees no occasion for any change in the status of its diplomatic representation to China. You may add that, if the decision of the Japanese Government to appoint an Ambassador is still open to reconsideration, this Government would venture to hope that the question be examined from the viewpoint of the interests of international solidarity in China.

Repeat to Peking as Department's 152 for information.

GREW

124.93/68 : Telegram

The Chargé in Japan (Caffery) to the Secretary of State

[Extract]

TOKYO, *July 16, 1924—6 p. m.*
[Received July 16—2:05 p. m.]

186. Department's telegram no. 121, July 12, 3 p. m.. Yesterday afternoon I communicated orally the Department's message to Baron Shidehara and he was plainly much concerned over it. He stated that Japan had not the least desire "to steal a march on the other powers" but that on the contrary she was only desirous of acting in harmony with them in this matter; that it seemed that the other powers had acted without waiting to hear Japan's opinion on the subject; that he understood that the British reply, of the same tenor as ours, had been sent to Peking on the 11th instant. He asked me if I knew when our reply had been sent and I said that I did not, whereupon he remarked that if not considered indiscreet he would be interested in knowing. He then proceeded at length to recount the reasons why the Japanese Government felt it should raise the

---

[94] See last paragraph for instructions to repeat to Peking as Department's no. 152.

rank of its mission at Peking: that public opinion calls for it; that there had already been various interpellations in that connection in the Diet and there had been a good deal of criticism in the House of Peers against the Government for not acting sooner; that the vernacular press had been calling upon the Cabinet to demonstrate in some concrete way their friendship for China; that he could not now say to the Diet that the Government was unable to act, as the other great powers did not wish it; he emphasized the point that the Japanese Government had as yet made no reply to the Chinese Government in spite of the latter's reiterated representations and had no intention of acting before receiving the replies of powers to his communication of Friday last. He asked me repeatedly, "Will Americans' interests be injured if Japan pilots move? How would your Government construe it?"

I replied that I had no information as to the official attitude of the Department of State other than that in the Department's telegram of July 12th; however that I personally believed any action of any power at Peking tending to break up the international solidarity there was to be deplored; that I believed that isolated action in this case on the part of the Japanese would tend in that direction.

During the past few weeks the British and French Ambassadors here both have had several conversations with Baron Shidehara on this subject and I understand that yesterday the British Ambassador took occasion to make some remarks to him in that connection similar to my own mentioned above.

. . . .

CAFFERY

124.93/68 : Telegram

The Acting Secretary of State to the Chargé in Japan (Caffery)

WASHINGTON, *July 18, 1924—6 p. m.*

126. Your telegram No. 186, July 16, 6 p. m. The Department has felt somewhat disturbed by the apparent feeling on the part of Baron Shidehara that this Government has ignored his views in the matter of raising the status of Legations in China. There was certainly no such intention, however, and I cannot but feel that that impression on his part and the somewhat difficult situation out of which it arises result from causes over which this Government had no control.

From the time when it was first suggested, over a month ago, this Government has considered that the Chinese proposal was particularly inopportune at a time when the authority of the Peking Government and its ability to live up to its responsibilities to foreign interests have so far diminished. Before rejecting the Chinese proposal, however, the Department took occasion to ascertain whether the Governments of Japan, France and Great Britain entertained contrary views. The inquiries then made indicated that France and Great Britain were actively opposed to the project, and that Japan (as reported in your telegram No. 155, June 17, 8 p.m.) had no predilection for the Chinese proposal (which would in fact involve practical difficulties), although the Foreign Office was prepared to advise you in the event of any alteration in what appeared to be a negative attitude on its part. The Department therefore had no anticipation of the proposal communicated to you on July 11 (your telegram No. 184, July 11, 9 p. m.), and had in the meanwhile felt that it was acting with due consideration for the views of other interested Powers when, on July 10, it had advised the Chinese Chargé d'Affaires, in the same informal manner in which the proposal had been suggested four weeks earlier by the Chinese Minister, that it saw no occasion for any change in the status of its diplomatic representation in China.

It is very much to be regretted if the Department's refusal of the Chinese proposal occurred so shortly before the Japanese Government's suggestion of a contrary course of action as to give rise to a question of the possibility of our having acted in disregard of Japan's suggestion.

You may explain the matter fully and frankly to Baron Shidehara.

GREW

124.93/72 : Telegram

The Minister in China (Schurman) to the Secretary of State

PEKING, *July 22, 1924—noon.*
[Received July 22—7 : 47 a. m.]

253. Your 152, July 12, 10 [*3?*] p. m.[95] In a long and intimate talk at his house with Koo yesterday he told me that Japanese Government regarded favorably the idea of raising Peking Legation to Embassy and that Italian Government had replied they would give the matter careful consideration. . . .

In reply to my inquiry Koo stated that Karakhan had been appointed Ambassador and would be received by the President in a few days.

SCHURMAN

---

[95] See footnote 94, p. 469.

124.93/73 : Telegram

The Chargé in Japan (Caffery) to the Secretary of State

Tokyo, *July 22, 1924—5 p. m.*
[Received July 22—8 : 30 a. m.]

192. Department's 126, July 18, 6 p.m. This morning I explained the situation to Baron Shidehara who said that he appreciated the Department's attitude. He asked me if I thought that the powers who had already notified China of their decision in the premises would be disposed to say further to the Chinese authorities that they did not believe that the question of raising the rank of the diplomatic missions at Peking should be taken up so long as the present unsatisfactory conditions prevailing in China continued, and he asked me if I would transmit his informal suggestion to the Department. I replied that I could not answer his question but was disposed to transmit his question.

He said that the Chinese Chargé d'Affaires here had told him that the Chinese Government was very much disappointed with the reply of the other powers and was pressing him for the Japanese answer which had not yet been given. He said that he would now send him a written reply which would refer to the opening paragraph of the original Chinese memorandum which had called attention to the recent decision for an exchange of Ambassadors between China and Soviet Russia; in this connection he would state that Japan could not allow her action in the premises to be influenced by that of Russia, that the Japanese Government was still studying the matter and would let China have a reply in due course.

However I am still of the opinion that the Japanese Government for reasons hitherto given has not yet changed its decision to send an Ambassador to China some time next year.

Caffery

—

124.93/76a : Telegram

The Acting Secretary of State to the Chargé in Japan (Caffery)

Washington, *July 26, 1924—4 p. m.*

130. Embassy at London is being instructed [96] to discuss with Foreign Office your telegrams 186, July 16, 6 p. m., 192, July 22, 5 p. m., and 200, July 26, 10 a. m.,[97] and Department's 126, July 18, 6 p. m., and inquire whether Shidehara's suggestion of July 22 has also been conveyed to the British Government, and if so what is its disposition

---

[96] Telegram no. 236, July 26, 1 p. m., to the Ambassador in Great Britain not printed.
[97] Telegram no. 200 from the Chargé in Japan not printed.

thereto. London has further been informed that the Department would not be averse from acting concurrently with the British, French and Japanese Governments in communicating to the Chinese Foreign Office an unreadiness to make the proposed change in the missions at Peking while disunion and disorder prevail in China and while the rights of foreign nationals continue to be so inadequately safeguarded as at present.

The Department assumes that your Embassy and Peking Legation are making full exchange of reports in this matter.

Repeat to Peking as No. 172.

GREW

124.93/91

Memorandum by the Acting Chief of the Division of Far Eastern Affairs, Department of State (Lockhart)

[WASHINGTON,] July 31, 1924.

Mr. Butler Wright telephoned me today stating that Signor Rosso of the Italian Embassy had today informed him that the Embassy had received information from Rome to the effect that the Italian Government had decided not to raise its Legation at Peking to the rank of an Embassy, and that the decision had been arrived at for reasons of economy. Mr. Wright suggested that this information be made of record in order that it might be considered in connection with the general question of raising the American Legation at Peking to an Embassy.

F. P. L[OCKHART]

124.93/79 : Telegram

The Ambassador in Great Britain (Kellogg) to the Secretary of State

[Paraphrase]

LONDON, August 1, 1924—3 p. m.
[Received August 1—2:01 p. m.]

302. I have had a conversation at the Foreign Office based on Department's telegram 236 of July 28 [*26*] [98] with the result that I am informed that the Foreign Office is telegraphing the British Ambassador in Japan to suggest to the Japanese Government that it would be well for the great powers to inform the Chinese Government that while there is disorder and disunion in China and while adequate protection is not given to the rights of foreign

---

[98] Not printed; see telegram no. 130, July 26, to the Chargé in Japan, p. 472.

nationals they are not willing to change the rank of their missions in China. The Foreign Office is authorizing the British Ambassador in Japan to say that instructions will be sent to the British Minister in China to act with the Japanese Minister there if the Japanese will instruct their Minister in this sense. It is the hope of the Foreign Office that similar action at Tokyo will be taken by the Department of State.

Copy of this telegram has been sent to European Information Center.

KELLOGG

124.93/82 : Telegram

The Acting Secretary of State to the Chargé in Japan (Caffery)[99]

WASHINGTON, *August 6, 1924—1 p. m.*

135. Your telegrams 203, August 4, 8 p. m. and 204, August 4, 11 p. m.[1]

If you have not already done so on the basis of the Department's telegram 130 July 26, 4 p.m. you may orally inform Shidehara that the Department would not be adverse from acting concurrently with the British, French and Japanese Governments in communicating to the Chinese Foreign Office an unreadiness to make the proposed change in the missions at Peking while disunion and disorder prevail in China and while the rights of foreign nationals continue to be so inadequately safeguarded as at present. Nevertheless if you are convinced, after talking with Shidehara, that he will not reconsider his unwillingness to accept the foregoing formula definitely suggested to him by the British Ambassador, the Department is disposed not to press further consideration of that specific suggestion, and you may so advise your British colleague. You may also say to him that you are informing Baron Shidehara that this Government is prepared, however, to instruct its representative at Peking to inform the Chinese Government in the sense informally suggested by Baron Shidehara as reported in your telegram 192, July 22, 5 p.m., in the event of the Japanese Government taking like action.

The Department appreciates the somewhat difficult situation in which Baron Shidehara apparently finds himself, and it would wish to adjust itself to his convenience, but the British, French and Italian Governments, as well as this Government, having definitely

---

[99] See last paragraph for instructions to repeat to Peking as no. 182. Telegram, except for last paragraph, repeated to the Ambassador in Great Britain (no. 264), for his information and that of the British Government, with instructions to repeat to Paris as Department's no. 256.

[1] Neither printed.

decided not to raise the status of their missions at Peking, the Department is strongly of the opinion that there should be unity of action in this matter and that the Japanese Minister for Foreign Affairs, if he is not disposed to follow the suggestion of the British Ambassador, might now desire to proceed on the basis which he suggested to you on July 22 as described in your 192 of that date.

The French Chargé d'Affaires has inquired whether this Government would be disposed to instruct you to consult with your French and British colleagues with a view to making representations to the Japanese Government urging further postponement of the sending of a Japanese Ambassador to Peking. You may join in such consultation if proposed by your French colleague, submitting to the Department any conclusions or recommendations that may be proposed. The French Chargé d'Affaires is being informed to that effect.

The Italian Government, as you have already been informed through Peking, will not change the status of its representation at Peking for reasons of economy.

Repeat to Peking as Department's No. 182.

GREW

124.93/89 : Telegram

The Acting Secretary of State to the Ambassador in Great Britain (Kellogg)

WASHINGTON, *August 12, 1924—4 p.m.*

293. Your 323, August 7, 5 p.m.[2] and the Department's 264, August 6, 5 p.m.[3]

The following telegram (No. 207 August 9, 4 p.m.) has been received from Tokyo:

"This morning I discussed informally with Baron Shidehara along lines indicated in the Department's telegram 135 August 6, 1 p.m. the matter of the status of diplomatic mission at Peking and he told me that after full consideration the Japanese Government had decided that instead of making a communication to the Chinese Government as had been suggested to postpone making a definite reply to the Chinese proposal until the beginning of next year 1925; that in the meantime he would let his note to the Chinese Chargé d'Affaires of July 25th stand (see my telegram 200 July 26, 11 [10] a.m.[4]) ; that if the Chinese brought up the matter again he will send reply that the matter was still under consideration; that during the month of December next he would probably propose to the powers

---

[2] Not printed.
[3] See footnote 99, p. 474.
[4] Not printed; see second paragraph of telegram no. 192, July 22, from the Chargé in Japan, p. 472.

involved a reconsideration of the question; that however for domestic reasons it is necessary for the Japanese Government to include in the budget estimate for the fiscal year beginning April 1st 1925 an item for an Embassy at Peking although this would not necessarily mean that the government had decided to change the status of the mission.

My opinion is that Baron Shidehara means during December next to suggest to the powers that the status of their diplomatic missions at Peking be raised to that of Embassies and that in case the powers decline the Japanese Government intends nevertheless next spring to raise the status of their mission."

The telegram above quoted seems to indicate that the Japanese Government is unwilling to accept the proposal contained in your 302, August 1, 3 p.m. In view of the determination of the Japanese Government to postpone action on the matter until December, the Department doubts whether a formal note as suggested in your 323 August 7, 5 p.m. would be the means of causing the Japanese Government to reconsider its decision. It now seems apparent that the Japanese Government not only declines to accept the formula which was orally suggested by the British Ambassador at Tokyo and by the American Chargé d'Affaires, but it appears also to have definitely receded from its original suggestion that the Chinese Government be notified in the sense informally suggested by Baron Shidehara as reported in Tokyo's telegram 192, July 22, 5 p.m., which was repeated to you in the Department's 236 July 26, 1 p.m.[5] It would seem to be useless to urge the Japanese Government to change its decision in this matter and the Department therefore desires to suggest to the British Government that it would seem to be both inexpedient and futile to despatch the formal note as suggested in your 323, August 7, 5 p.m.

If the British Government has in mind good reasons to the contrary the Department will be glad to consider the matter further. It desires, however, to stress the point that the action of the Japanese Government seems to close the matter for the time being at least. Tokyo's 200 July 26, 11 [*10*] A. M. was repeated to you in Department's 237 July 26, 2 p. m.[6]

You may bring the foregoing orally to the attention of the Foreign Office.

Repeat to Paris as Department's No. 265.

GREW

---

[5] Telegram no. 192, *ante*, p. 472; telegram no. 236 not printed.
[6] Neither printed.

124.93/97

The British Embassy to the Department of State

AIDE MEMOIRE

His Majesty's Government have had under careful consideration the question of taking some action in regard to the decision of the Japanese Government to raise their Legation at Peking to the status of an Embassy.

It appears to His Majesty's Government that some attempt is now being made by the various conflicting groups in China to arrive at some form of cooperation which may emerge into an effective Government and His Majesty's Government feel that any action which might discourage such efforts would be unfortunate. Inasmuch, however, as the present Provisional Government in China includes a strong element favourable to Japan, it is thought that the present moment is unfavourable for asking the Japanese Government to cancel their decision regarding a Japanese Embassy at Peking. On the other hand, it is thought that if the situation in China does in fact show definite improvement the Powers might, in due time and acting in concert, use the proposal to raise the status of their Missions in China to Embassies as an inducement to persuade the Chinese Government to press on with the re-organization of the Administration and to afford effective protection to foreign interests in China. To take such joint action might more easily enable the Powers to exercise their influence in China for the general benefit in the future. For these reasons His Majesty's Government would welcome the postponement of the actual execution of the decision of the Japanese Government to raise their Legation at Peking to an Embassy.

In making this suggestion His Majesty's Government are not in any way binding themselves to appoint an Ambassador at Peking under any circumstances, but their idea is that it would be unfortunate not to take advantage of any means of joint influence such as the execution of the above suggestion would offer.

If the United States Government agree and will send instructions to the United States Ambassador at Tokio to approach the Japanese Government unofficially in the above sense, with a view to the postponement of the execution of their decision in this matter, His Majesty's Government will be happy to instruct their Representative at Tokio to support the action of his United States Colleague.

[WASHINGTON,] *December 3, 1924.*

The Department of State to the British Embassy

AIDE-MÉMOIRE

With reference to the Aide-Mémoire which was left with the Secretary of State on December 3, 1924, stating that the British Government would welcome the postponement of the actual execution of the decision of the Japanese Government to raise its Legation at Peking to the status of an Embassy, and suggesting that, if the situation in China shows a definite improvement, the Powers might, in due time and acting in concert, use the proposal to raise the status of their Missions in China to Embassies as an inducement to the Chinese Government to press on with the reorganization of the Administration and to afford effective protection to foreign interests, the British Embassy is informed that the Department of State at once caused inquiry to be made by the American Ambassador in Tokyo concerning the present status of this matter. He has now informed the Department that, although the Japanese Government, for domestic reasons, found it necessary to include in the budget for the fiscal year beginning April 1, 1925, an item for an Embassy at Peking, this does not necessarily mean that the Government has decided to change the status of the Mission; and that, although there has been considerable speculation on the subject, both in the vernacular press and among the public in general, the Foreign Office has as yet made no public declaration in the premises. The Ambassador is of the opinion that the action thus far taken may be construed to indicate not a present intention on the part of the Japanese Government to raise the status of its Mission in Peking, but a desire to be in a position to make such a change during the next Japanese fiscal year in case it should then deem it expedient to do so.

In view of the present indeterminate status of the matter, and of the unlikelihood of the Japanese Government proceeding further in it without consultation with the governments of the other Powers principally interested, it would appear that the present moment is somewhat premature to approach the Japanese Government in regard to it. Should the British Government, however, in the light of the situation as known to it, feel that there is occasion for urgency in dealing with the question, the Department of State would be glad to give further consideration to the matter upon being so informed.

[WASHINGTON,] *December 17, 1924.*

RESERVATIONS BY THE UNITED STATES AND OTHER POWERS REGARDING DISPOSAL TO BE MADE OF THE CHINESE EASTERN RAILWAY UNDER THE SINO-SOVIET AGREEMENT[1]

861.01/745 : Telegram

The Minister in China (Schurman) to the Secretary of State

[Paraphrase]

PEKING, *February 28, 1924—noon.*
[Received February 28—8:55 a.m.]

66. Karakhan seriously intended to go to Canton but the trip was suddenly canceled, probably because the Chinese Government used its influence against his going. The two parties have since been conducting negotiations with more hope. The Chinese wanted settlement of outstanding questions to precede recognition, while Karakhan demanded just the opposite. They are proceeding now on the basis of a new formula, which is that the establishment of principles for the settlement of their national differences shall come first, then China shall recognize the Soviet Union, and after that the difficulties between the two countries will be actually adjusted.

The problem of the Chinese Eastern Railway is the one fundamental obstacle. China wishes to gain ownership by purchase before the date fixed in the original agreement. The Chinese are prepared to accept in the meantime cooperative management on a 50-50 plan. The Soviet Union is holding out for Russian rights in accordance with the provisions of the agreement.

Karakhan and the Japanese Minister here are also holding conversations.

SCHURMAN

861.01/760 : Telegram

The Minister in China (Schurman) to the Secretary of State

[Paraphrase]

PEKING, *March 11 [12?], 1924—11 a. m.*
[Received March 12—3:20 p. m.]

76. My telegram February 28, noon. C. T. Wang, Director of the Commission on Sino-Russian Affairs, presented to the Cabinet on March 8 a long report regarding his negotiations with Karakhan.

---

[1] For previous correspondence concerning the Chinese Eastern Railway, see *Foreign Relations*, 1923, vol. I, pp. 758 ff.

This report has been discussed since by the Cabinet in long sessions. I had an intimate after-dinner talk with Yen on March 10 and a similar conversation with Koo on March 11. I have also talked with others who are close to Karakhan. The following is the situation:

1. China has been affected to a marked degree by British recognition of the Soviet Union.

2. Public opinion, so far as it exists in China, has not been hostile at any time to recognition. Forty-seven professors in the National University of Peking quite recently petitioned the Cabinet in favor of immediate recognition. This has stimulated and encouraged the Cabinet members to go ahead with recognition, for this is a country where scholars always have exerted a great influence on the Government and continue to do so, though to a lessened degree.

3. The Chinese do not want to be among the last to recognize the Soviet Union and specifically they do not want to be behind the Japanese.

4. Karakhan has been exceedingly conciliatory according to all the information I have received.

5. The Cabinet approved in substance Wang's report which is now before the President. The Cabinet will probably consider it again this week.

6. The present agreement is preliminary and only lays down the general lines for the final settlement. After recognition detailed agreements are to be signed.

7. Apparently agreement has been reached on the following points: reestablishment of full diplomatic relations between China and Russia; formal cancellation by Russia of extraterritoriality; abrogation of old treaties; return of Boxer Indemnity; Russian [recognition] that Mongolia is part of China; withdrawal of all Russian influence from Mongolia, determination of frontiers; drafting of new commercial agreement; drafting of new rules for the navigation of the Sungari and Amur Rivers.

8. The chief difficulty has always been the Chinese Eastern Railway. Apparently, however, the general lines of a settlement have been agreed upon. Russia declares that the title to the Chinese Eastern belongs to China and gives up all claims to sovereignty in the Railway Zone. The Chinese may take over the Chinese Eastern by paying for it earlier than the time fixed in the 1896 agreement, which was to be 40 years from that date. Russia is to share equally in the management in the meantime. Probably this will be accomplished by Russia's merely replacing the Russo-Asiatic Bank in its relation to the railway.

9. The purchase price for the Chinese Eastern is to be fixed later. Russia wants China to pay the original cost. Yen told me that Ka-

rakhan put this at 1,100,000,000 gold rubles. This figure includes the cost of building the South Manchuria Railway, said to be 400,000,000 rubles. This would make 700,000,000 rubles for the Chinese Eastern alone. Yen thought that the railway could be reproduced today for not more than half that amount.

10. Karakhan probably foresees that it will be a generation or more before the Chinese treasury bills to be given in payment for the Chinese Eastern are redeemed and is willing to trust to influence and time for [Russia?] to gain dominant control in effect through China's [*Russia's?*] 50-percent share in the management, or it may be that the Soviet Union already cherishes an alliance or entente with China. I do not see in any case how Russia can get along without the Chinese Eastern for transporting troops, etc.

11. It may be predicted that China will soon recognize the Soviet Union unless some difficulty arises not anticipated at present by either side. . . .

SCHURMAN

861.01/761 : Telegram

The Minister in China (Schurman) to the Secretary of State

PEKING, March 13, 1924—6 p. m.
[Received March 13—4 : 20 p. m.]

78. My 76, March 12, 11 a. m.

1. French Minister warned Minister for Foreign Affairs afternoon 12th against endangering French rights and interests of Russo-Asiatic Bank in respect of Chinese Eastern Railway by recognition of Soviet Russia for which, as he added, the liability might prove embarrassing to Chinese finances.

2. I am reliably informed that Japanese are opposing recognition not only in Peking but especially in Mukden. If the Peking and Moscow governments get together, the position of Chang Tso-lin who now practically controls the Chinese Eastern Railway would be seriously [apparent omission].

3. Raindre of Russo-Asiatic Bank, who was already much depressed by his Harbin experiences and especially by the discovery that Ostroumoff had given in [*sic*] his adherence to Soviet Russia and who is now greatly disturbed by the prospect of the elimination of the bank through Chinese recognition of Russia, intimated to me today that the French Minister would come to me with the draft of a joint note to the Chinese Government for the protection of the bank which Raindre hoped I would be able to sign along with Japanese Minister, though in view of British recognition of Russia it was not believed our British colleague could also join. I read in reply Washington

resolution on the Chinese Eastern Railway [9] and expressed the opinion that it did not warrant me in taking such a step and that I should have to consult my Government. I also had in mind Department's instruction number 520, December 18th, 1923,[10] which of course I did not allude to. Raindre argued that he was only asking our assistance for the protection of "foreign stockholders, bondholders and creditors of the Chinese Eastern Railway Company" as contemplated by the Washington resolution.

4. Please telegraph instructions as soon as possible.

SCHURMAN

861.01/764 : Telegram

The Minister in China (Schurman) to the Secretary of State

PEKING, *March 17, 1924—1 p. m.*
[Received March 17—7 : 40 a. m.]

81. My 76, March 12, 11 a. m., and 78, March 13, 6 p. m. Cabinet has not yet adopted Karakhan–Wang agreement. Cabinet intimates in [apparent omission] that the hitch is over Mongolia but political and personal rivalries in the Government probably more potent. From best available Soviet sources it is learned Karakhan has placed time limit on negotiations which is to expire March 19th. Koo confirms this confidentially to the extent of saying there was a time limit.

SCHURMAN

861.01/765 : Telegram

The Minister in China (Schurman) to the Secretary of State

PEKING, *March 21, 1924—11 a. m.*
[Received March 21—10 a. m.]

87. My 76, March 12, 11 a. m.; 78, March 13, 6 p. m.; and 81, March 17, 1 p. m.

1. Koo told me 19th immediately after expiration of Karakhan's time limit that latter had wrong idea in regard to finality of agreements between him and Wang, since these had to be approved by the Government before ratification. Cabinet was considering them when Karakhan fixed time limit. This has made situation more difficult. But as Karakhan had declared his object was to establish friendly relations with China, Koo could not see that any other way than diplomacy was open to him.

2. Chinese Government's self-respect compelled them to ignore Karakhan's time limit. Whether Karakhan imagined he could rush

---

[9] *Foreign Relations*, 1922, vol. I, p. 297.
[10] Not printed.

Chinese diplomacy or foresaw some eventual advantage in breaking off negotiations, is not clear. He professed to believe that Wang fully represented Chinese Government and claimed that it disavowed his official signature. Koo now explains that Wang has no such authority—Wang himself maintains silence. Doubtless Wang was ambitious to play the leading part in bringing about recognition of Russia.

3. Koo asked Karakhan night[s] of 19th and 20th to withdraw time limit and continue negotiations. Karakhan declined to do so or to transmit such request to his Government.

4. This morning's papers publish long letter from Karakhan to Wang, dated 19th, justifying both of them and indicting the Chinese Government especially for its subserviency to the imperialistic powers (who hold it in servitude) in regard to everything affecting Soviet Russia. Letter says:

5. "Chinese Government was informed exactly of the course of negotiations including all the details and the Chinese delegate was acting with the full approval of his Government. However, suddenly, on the eve of the signing on March 12th an event took place which turned upside down all the work done theretofore; on the 12th instant France presented to the Chinese Government a warning and threatening note. This is the undeniable cause of the situation created. There are some other powers that have also conveyed a warning to China, but they did not do it in such an open way as France which of all the powers of the world is the one most hostile to us. . . . Agreement gives full satisfaction to the national and state interests of China in a measure which will never be filled voluntarily towards China by any other power. Chinese Government would certainly be most happy and thankful to any third power which would accord but a tenth part of the respect for China's sovereignty [rights] and the national demands of the Chinese people embodied in the agreements signed on March 14th. . . . It suffices to point out our abandonment of the right of consular jurisdiction, of special rights and privileges relative to concessions, of the Boxer Indemnity. In vain did China strive at Versailles and Washington to get free of the humiliating fetters bound [with these] privileges. China got a promise at Washington that commission would be created to discuss the question of extraterritorial rights. However, until today this commission has not been created yet, for France is against it. . . . At Washington it was promised to China that the customs tariffs would be raised, but up to the present time this pledge has not been redeemed and yet in the agreements of March 14 we refuse to force upon China commercial and customs agreements and we establish in this matter the principle of equality and reciprocity. . . . With regard to the Chinese Eastern Railway, we have given more to the Chinese Government than it could in fairness demand. The Chinese Government is satisfied with our fairness and yet it passes over in silence its attainments in this matter."

6. In concluding, letter declares Russian Government will not renew discussions and will not hold itself bound by the conditions contained in the agreements signed on March 14, and will reserve full liberty of action with regard to future agreements with China, and "wishes to warn that henceforth the Chinese Government can resume negotiations only after it will have unconditionally and without any agreements established official normal relations with the Government of the Union of Soviet Socialist Republics."

SCHURMAN

861.01/766 : Telegram

The Minister in China (Schurman) to the Secretary of State

PEKING, March 21, 1924—1 p. m.
[Received March 21—7 : 40 a. m.]

88. My 87, March 21, 11 a. m. My 76, March 12, 11 a. m., last sentence. The following Presidential mandate dated March 20 has just been received:

"Sino-Russian negotiations are very important. Since Dr. C. T. Wang has been in charge, although his ideas and those of the Russian representative have been gradually coming closer and closer, the conditions of the agreement have not yet been completely settled. It is necessary to charge the Ministry of Foreign Affairs with responsibility for taking over this matter and carrying on discussions as rapidly as possible with the Russian representative in order that the responsibility be not divided."

SCHURMAN

861.01/770 : Telegram

The Minister in China (Schurman) to the Secretary of State

PEKING, March 24, 1924—noon.
[Received March 24—9 : 30 a.m.]

91. My 78, March 13, 6 p.m. Rosta published text of the main agreement signed by Karakhan and Wang which provides in respect to Chinese Eastern Railway the following:

1. Railway is a purely commercial enterprise and with the exception of matters pertaining to its business operations "all other matters affecting the rights of the national and the local governments of the Republic of China . . . shall be administered by the Chinese authorities."

2. Russia "agrees to the redemption by the Chinese Government with Chinese capital of the Chinese Eastern Railway."

3. Russia "agrees to be responsible for the entire claims of the shareholders, bondholders and creditors [of] the Chinese Eastern Railway incurred prior to the revolution of March 9, 1917."

4. Russia and China mutually agree that the future of the Chinese Eastern Railway shall be determined by them "to the exclusion [of] any third party or parties."

5. Russia and China "agree to draw up an arrangement for the provisional management of the Chinese Eastern Railway."

6. Until the final settlement the rights of the two Governments arising out of the contract of 1896 "which do not conflict with the present agreement and with the agreement for the provisional management of the said railway and which do not prejudice China's right of sovereignty, shall be maintained."

According to circular telegram sent out by Cabinet only the following three matters remain in dispute, namely, China's demand for cancellation treaties between Soviet and Outer Mongolia in which latter is considered as independent country, China's demand for immediate withdrawal of Russian troops from Mongolia, Chinese refusal to grant Russian demand that Russian properties such as churches and immovable property should be handed over to the Russian Government.

SCHURMAN

861.01/799

The French Embassy to the Department of State [11]

[Translation [12]]

By its charter, approved by the Russian Government in 1910, the Russo-Asiatic Bank derives its legal status of successor to the Russo-Chinese Bank.

By the provisions of paragraph one of this charter the Russo-Chinese Bank with which the Banque du Nord combines assumes the new name Russo-Asiatic Bank, the whole of the assets and liabilities of the Russo-Chinese Bank and of the Banque du Nord being considered as transferred to the Russo-Asiatic Bank from the date of the publication of the said charter in the bulletin of laws.

The American Government acknowledged the Russo-Asiatic Bank to possess the status of stockholder of the Chinese Eastern Railway by joining in July and August, 1923, in the action taken by the British, Japanese, and French Governments for the protection of the land department of the railway from threatened seizure by the Chinese authorities of Manchuria.

It was in the capacity of representative of the stockholders of the railway that the general manager of the Russo-Asiatic Bank induced the consuls at Harbin to place their seals on the title deeds of the

---

[11] Handed to the Chief of the Division of Far Eastern Affairs by the Counselor of the French Embassy Apr. 2, 1924.

[12] File translation revised.

company. In the joint note sent on August 11 to the Chinese Government by the Ministers of the United States, Great Britain, Japan, and France,[13] the same capacity is officially acknowledged as being vested in the general manager of the Russo-Asiatic Bank.

The question at this juncture is not to oppose the conclusion of a Sino-Russian agreement but to bring the Chinese Government, which is responsible to the third parties for the legal status arising from the concession and operation contracts of the Chinese Eastern Railway, to refuse to deal in this matter with the Soviet Government without having made a formal reservation of the rights of the foreign stockholders and creditors of the railway company.

Resolution No. XIII at Washington [14] has for its very object the protection of those rights.

861.01/799 : Telegram

The Secretary of State to the Minister in China (Schurman)

WASHINGTON, April 26, 1924—6 p. m.

81. Your telegram 78, March 13, 6 p. m. The French Ambassador at Washington presented April 2 an informal note to the Department stating that the object of the French warning to China was not to oppose the conclusion of a Sino-Russian agreement but to induce the Chinese Government "to refuse to deal with [in] this matter with the Soviet Government without having made a formal reservation of the rights of foreign stockholders and creditors of the Railway Company. Resolution No. XIII of the Washington Conference has for its very object the protection of these rights."

Resolution XIII clearly imposes upon China the responsibility for "performance or non-performance of the obligations towards the stockholders, bondholders and creditors of the Chinese Eastern Railway Company which the Powers deem to result from the contracts under which the railroad was built," et cetera.

The Department considers that while that Resolution must be upheld, this Government cannot intervene on that basis expressly in behalf of the reorganized Russo-Asiatic Bank unless and until its legal identity with the original Russo-Asiatic Bank shall have been established.

In order to avoid the possibility of any misunderstanding on the part of the Chinese, you should not join with the representatives of France or other countries in protests against China's recent negotiations with Russia; but you may send to the Chinese Foreign Office a separate note recalling that China's responsibility as trustee under

[13] See telegram no. 284, Aug. 12, 1923, from the Minister in China, *Foreign Relations*, 1923, vol. I, p. 779.
[14] *Ibid.*, 1922, vol. I, p. 298; also quoted in American Minister's note no. 810, May 3, 1924, to the Chinese Minister for Foreign Affairs, *post*, p. 487.

the terms of Washington Conference Resolution XIII (quoting the Resolution) is an obligation that is not to be ignored or unilaterally invalidated by China in the course of any negotiations with other parties regarding the railway. This note should avoid mentioning the Russo-Asiatic Bank, and should make it clear to the Chinese that the United States Government stands for the protection of all interests including Russian and is not endeavoring to prevent the conclusion of a Sino-Russian agreement.

Your telegram No. 70, March 3, 1 p. m.[15] In reply to inquiries from Dr. Wang and others you may state that this Government upholds Washington Conference Resolution XIII and could not approve a change of any kind in the *status quo* (whether initiated by China, Russia or any other nationality or by the old or new Russo-Asiatic Bank) unless the rights of all creditors and other parties in interest were adequately protected.

HUGHES

861.01/825

The Minister in China (Schurman) to the Secretary of State

No. 2242

PEKING, *May 5, 1924.*
[Received June 10.]

SIR: I have the honor to transmit herewith enclosed a copy of a note which I addressed to the Minister for Foreign Affairs on the 3rd instant regarding the Chinese Eastern Railway pursuant to the instructions contained in your telegram No. 81 of April 26th, 6 P. M.

I have sent copies of this note to the British, French and Japanese Ministers for their information.

I have [etc.]

JACOB GOULD SCHURMAN

[Enclosure]

The American Minister (Schurman) to the Chinese Minister for Foreign Affairs (Wellington Koo)

No. 810

PEKING, *May 3, 1924.*

YOUR EXCELLENCY: With regard to the negotiations which I understand are taking place between the Government of the Republic of China and the Soviet Government, I am directed by my Government to recall to Your Excellency's attention the Thirteenth Resolution adopted by the Conference on the Limitation of Armament at Washington at its Sixth Plenary Session, February 4, 1922, which reads as follows:

"The powers other than China, in agreeing to the Resolution regarding the Chinese Eastern Railway, reserve the right to insist hereafter upon the responsibility of China for performance or non-per-

---

[15] Not printed.

formance of the obligations towards the foreign stockholders, bondholders and creditors of the Chinese Eastern Railway Company
which the Powers deem to result from the contracts under which
the Railroad was built and the action of China thereunder and the
obligations which they deem to be in the nature of a trust resulting
from the exercise of power by the Chinese Government over the
possession and administration of the Railroad."

and to remind Your Excellency's Government that China's responsibility as Trustee for the Chinese Eastern Railway is an obligation
that is not to be ignored or unilaterally invalidated by China in the
course of any negotiations with other parties regarding the Railway.
The Government of the United States of America stands for the
protection of all interests in the Railway, including Russian, and
could not approve a change of any kind in the *status quo* by whom-
soever initiated unless the rights of all creditors and other parties
in interest were adequately protected.

I take the opportunity afforded by the communication of the foregoing declaration and reminder to repeat to Your Excellency, what
Your Excellency already knows from my earlier oral assurances,
that the Government of the United States has no desire to prevent
the conclusion of a Sino-Russian Agreement. The object of my Government is to prevent future embarrassments, specially for Your
Excellency's Government, by calling timely attention to the rights
and interests as well as to the obligations which China is bound
respectively to safeguard and to fulfill in performance of the duties
she has undertaken in respect of the Chinese Eastern Railway, as set
forth in the Resolution quoted above.

I avail myself [etc.]   JACOB GOULD SCHURMAN

861.01/799

The Department of State to the French Embassy

Careful consideration has been given to the note handed to the
Chief of the Division of Far Eastern Affairs by the Counselor of
the French Embassy, on April 2, 1924, on the subject of the Chinese
Eastern Railway and the status of the Russo-Asiatic Bank.

It is the understanding of the United States Government that the
institution known as the Russo-Asiatic Bank, as established by the
amalgamation of the Russo-Chinese Bank and the Banque du Nord
in 1910, was reorganized about 1919. The circumstances attending
its reorganization and the legality of its present status in Russian
law are not within the cognizance of this Government.

The fact that the United States Government, in the protection of
the common interests of the Powers which had assumed responsibilities in connection with the Chinese Eastern Railway, joined in a

protest against the aggressive measures of the Chinese authorities in connection with the Land Department of the Railway, does not constitute a recognition on the part of this Government of the legal status of the Russo-Asiatic Bank, although the bank may have benefited by that protest.

The United States Government agrees with the French Government as to the object of Resolution No. XIII of the Washington Conference, and has accordingly, on April 26, 1924, instructed its Minister at Peking to present to the Chinese Government a note pointing out its inability to accept any settlement of the Chinese Eastern Railway question which does not afford adequate protection to foreign creditors and all other interested parties, as contemplated by Resolution No. XIII. In the absence of any showing as to the legal identity of the reorganized Russo-Asiatic Bank with the original bank of the same name, the Government of the United States has not felt that it would be warranted in taking any action expressly on behalf of the Russo-Asiatic Bank.

WASHINGTON, *May 6, 1924.*

861.01/801 : Telegram

The Minister in China (Schurman) to the Secretary of State

PEKING, *May 14, 1924—5 p. m.*
[Received May 14—12 : 06 p. m.]

128. Your 81, April 26, 6 p. m.

1. Note in accordance with your instructions delivered to Ministry of Foreign Affairs May 3rd, copy enclosed in despatch no. 2242, May 5, in today's pouch. French Minister addressed note of similar tenor May 7th. British Minister states he intends to communicate orally with Koo and to say that British Government indorses view expressed in my note. Japanese Minister, to whom I also communicated copy of my note, has given no indications of what action if any he intends taking.

2. Purport of my note and French Minister's having duly leaked out of Foreign Office and appeared in local press, Karakhan, Bolshevik representative, has issued statement appearing today in Chinese and English language papers of which following is summary:

3. Chinese Government denies interference with Russo-Chinese relations but Karakhan has brought forth evidence of French interference, and America has now come into the open on the same side. Chinese Eastern Railway question relates only to China and Russia, and if other powers intervene, it is only to hamper understanding

between Russia and China. French and American protests mean they will not allow Russo-Chinese Agreement without their participation. Powers refer to Washington Conference resolutions as if they had acquiesced in rights thereby, although resolutions were adopted without the master Soviet Russia. Present case usual imperialistic action by France, America and possibly other powers who believe world is theirs. Soviet has taught all great powers not to meddle with Russian affairs and now hopes to teach them not to interfere with Russo-Chinese affairs. Difficulty is that China is weak, cannot defend national dignity and sovereignty and takes more stock in French and American threats than friendship with Soviet. France and America are very strict about Washington resolutions when it is question of hostility toward Chinese interests but resolutions forgotten when same would benefit China. During several years France and America have failed to carry out decisions regarding extraterritoriality or customs tariff in disregard of China's requests and in manner humiliating to China. If powers ever begin this work, it will only be to dupe China. Soviet alone could voluntarily renounce treaties imposed by force on [China].

SCHURMAN

861.01/802 : Telegram

The Chargé in China (Bell) to the Secretary of State

PEKING, *May 15, 1924—noon.*
[Received May 15—9 : 44 a. m.]

129. My 128, May 14, 5 p. m.

1. Yesterday Marshall, United Press correspondent here, received following telegram his agency via London office:

2. "Washington State Department, replying questions, admits intervened recent Russo-Chinese negotiations warning China recognition Soviet might [have] unpleasant consequences. Intervention due desire protect claims 6 to 8 million dollars American share reorganization Chinese Eastern Railway during Siberian expedition 1918."

3. Subsequent to leakage of information that our note of May 3d had been sent and prior to receipt of the above telegram, I had shown Marshall our note for his guidance. Nevertheless, on receipt of above message he distributed latter to Chinese and foreign press without saying anything to me.

4. First sentence of message above quoted is misleading or contrary to fact in two particulars and places Legation and the Chinese Government in an embarrassing position.

5. Chinese Government has all along insisted contrary to Bolshevik allegations that interruption of negotiations 6 weeks ago was not due to intervention of any foreign powers; while Legation has categorically denied similar allegations that American Minister endeavored to interrupt negotiations. Negotiations were suspended or dormant on May 3d when our note was sent but above message makes it appear that we actively attempted to arrest their progress. Moreover, the statement that we had warned China that recognition of Soviet might have unpleasant consequence is contrary to terms of note which was based on Department's telegram 81, April 26, 6 p. m., and contained phrase, "Government of the United States has no desire to prevent the conclusion of a Sino-Russian Agreement."

6. Legation and Foreign Office endeavoring to mitigate effect of first sentence of message, but I fear that Karakhan and Chinese opponents of Government will make capital of it.

7. Assuming that sentence in question is a misrepresentation of Department's remarks, I request authority so to state publicly and also in my discretion, if Chinese Foreign Office agrees, to publish note, text of which I shall telegraph you if desired.

8. Further, I venture to suggest that the United Press be approached in regard to their handling of news. They are the only American agency selling a news service in China and the fact that they are able to do so is entirely due to the Department's attitude in refusing to permit distribution gratis of radio news service from Cavite which if done would drive their service out of China. That our Government in these circumstances should be made to suffer by their errors or carelessness, is intolerable.

For the Minister:
BELL

861.01/802 : Telegram

The Acting Secretary of State to the Chargé in China (Bell)

WASHINGTON, *May 15, 1924—6 p. m.*

95. Your telegram No. 129, May 15, noon, paragraph 7. You may make public the text of Legation's note, together with a statement referring to reports in local press (without naming the United Press) which allege that this Government had intervened in the negotiations, and stating the facts that the Department of State has given out no comment whatsoever with regard to the negotiations and that that note embodies the whole relationship of this Government to the matter in question.

The matter will be taken up with the United Press as regards the action of its correspondents both here and in Peking.

GREW

861.77/3467 : Telegram

The Minister in China (Schurman) to the Secretary of State

PEKING, *June 4, 1924—3 p. m.*
[Received June 4—8:35 a. m.]

156. Italian Minister reminds me that he had formerly joined in note to the Chinese Government regarding its responsibility for the Chinese Eastern Railway under the terms of the Washington Conference resolution [16] but says that in view of the recognition of Soviet Russia by China he does not know what stand he should now take and desires to be informed of the policy and attitude of the American Government. I should greatly appreciate a statement for my own guidance also.

SCHURMAN

861.77/3467 : Telegram

The Secretary of State to the Minister in China (Schurman)

WASHINGTON, *June 12, 1924—2 p. m.*

121. Your 156, June 4, 3 p. m. It appears probable that no essential change in respect to Chinese Eastern Railway will occur until after the forthcoming Sino-Russian Conference.

The attitude of this Government remains unchanged from that expressed in Department's telegram No. 81 of April 26, 6 p. m. Pending the outcome of the proposed Conference the Department believes that no further action is advisable on your part unless changes in the situation of the Chinese Eastern should necessitate further representations. Do you concur in this opinion?

Forward texts of all Sino-Russian Agreements as soon as obtained and keep Department informed of the negotiations at the Conference, especially those regarding the Railway.

You may inform Italian Minister this Government's position remains unchanged pending results of the proposed Conference.

HUGHES

---

[16] See telegram no. 253, Oct. 27, 1922, to the Minister in China, *Foreign Relations*, 1922, vol. I, p. 925; also telegram no. 229, Nov. 17, 1922, from the Chargé in Italy, *ibid.*, p. 929.

861.77/3473 : Telegram

The Minister in China (Schurman) to the Secretary of State

PEKING, *June 13, 1924—5 p. m.*
[Received June 13—8 : 45 a. m.]

175. My 128, May 14, 5 p. m. Japanese Minister informs me he addressed following communication to Chinese Government and also to Karakhan on June 7th:

"The Japanese Government declares that the rights and interests of Japan and her nationals in regard to the Chinese Eastern Railway shall not in any way be affected by the agreement recently concluded between the Governments of Soviet Russia and the Republic of China or by any arrangements that may hereafter be made between them in virtue of that agreement concerning the said railway."

SCHURMAN

861.77/3481 : Telegram

The Minister in China (Schurman) to the Secretary of State

PEKING, *June 13, 1924—7 p. m.*
[Received June 13—12 : 55 p. m.]

176. Your 121, June 12, 2 p. m. I received almost simultaneously the following telegram from the consul at Harbin:

"June 12, 3 p.m. The Japanese consul general and the French, American and British consuls have agreed that they, acting on their own initiative, should jointly remove, in case no objection to this course is made by one of their respective Legations (Governments), their respective seals placed on July 31, 1923, on two cabinets containing the more valuable documents of the land department of the Chinese Eastern Railway,[17] if and when the present higher Russian officers of the board of directors and/or of the administration of the railway are actually replaced by Russian appointees of the Soviet Government, replaced until local circumstances demand, in the judgment of the consular officers concerned, that such action be taken. To remove the seals at present would probably cause uneasiness and misunderstanding at Harbin.

Has the Legation any objection to this plan of action?"

I will defer reply to Harbin until I have consulted my interested colleagues.

---

[17] See telegram of July 31, 1923, from the consul at Harbin, *Foreign Relations,* 1923, vol. I, p. 778.

Apparently consuls at Harbin wish to anticipate removal of seals by the new Soviet regime. I fear, however, that if removal is deferred until new regime is established their action may then be construed as tacit recognition of the new agreements and consider that it would be preferable to effect removal at an earlier date if suitable pretext can be found. French Minister shares this view.

British Minister does not appear to attach great importance to the issue and seems indifferent to the possible interpretation referred to above. I infer he has in mind British recognition of the Soviet Government. He, however, reserves expression of opinion until consultation between four Ministers which will take place June 16th.

I am of the opinion that no action other than above indicated called for at present.

SCHURMAN

861.77/3483 : Telegram

The Minister in China (Schurman) to the Secretary of State

PEKING, June 17, 1924—4 p. m.
[Received June 17—10:15 a. m.]

184. My despatch 2242, May 5; my telegrams number 128, May 14, 5 p. m. and 175, June 13, 5 p. m. I have today received a note from Chinese Minister for Foreign Affairs dated June 16, which in translation reads as follows:

"I have the honor to acknowledge the receipt of Your Excellency's note of May 3rd, 1924, in which Your Excellency referring to the 13th resolution adopted by the Washington Conference concerning the Chinese Eastern Railway requesting [*requested?*] that China take note of its responsibility as trustee thereunder. You also stated that the rights of all creditors should be adequately protected.

The history and agreements relating to the Chinese Eastern Railway all show that it consists of the two countries of China and Russia. Prior to the conclusion of the Sino-Russian Agreement the pronouncement of the Washington Conference referred to China's responsibility during the time of its trusteeship. Now Sino-Russian relations have been established and the state of affairs is entirely different from what it was formerly. In future the two Governments of China and Russia will deal with the question of the Chinese Eastern Railway in which only the two countries of Russia and China are concerned. This is a right which properly rests in the two Governments of China and Russia.

As regards the temporary arrangement made between China and Russia concerning the Chinese Eastern Railway, this, it may also be stated, is not prejudicial to the rights of the various powers. The Chinese Government considers that there is no need for excessive anxiety in reference to the points raised by the American Government.

I have the honor, Mr. Minister, to transmit the foregoing reply and trust that you will appreciate the position."

I understand similar replies have been sent to French and Japanese Ministers.

SCHURMAN

861.77/3482 : Telegram

The Minister in China (Schurman) to the Secretary of State

PEKING, *June 17, 1924—5 p. m.*
[Received June 17—8 : 15 a. m.]

185. My 176, June 13, 7 p. m. At conference of interested colleagues today it was decided to approve proposal of consuls at Harbin with the understanding that should future developments appear to make it desirable we would order them to remove seals at once.

SCHURMAN

761.93/494

The Minister in China (Schurman) to the Secretary of State

No. 2324   PEKING, *June 18, 1924.*
[Received July 15.]

SIR: Referring to my telegram No. 186 of June 17, 7 p.m., 1924,[18] and to previous correspondence regarding the Sino-Russian Agreements, Declarations, and exchange of notes, signed May 31, 1924, I have the honor to transmit herewith three copies of the pamphlet issued yesterday by the Ministry of Foreign Affairs containing the above documents.[19]

.   .   .   .

I have [etc.]

(For the Minister)
EDWARD BELL

[Enclosure]

Sino-Russian Agreements, Signed at Peking, May 31, 1924

AGREEMENT ON GENERAL PRINCIPLES FOR THE SETTLEMENT OF THE QUESTIONS BETWEEN THE REPUBLIC OF CHINA AND THE UNION OF SOVIET SOCIALIST REPUBLICS

The Republic of China and the Union of Soviet Socialist Republics, desiring to re-establish normal relations with each other, have agreed to conclude an agreement on general principles for the settlement of

---

[18] Not printed.
[19] *Agreements between the Republic of China and the Union of Soviet Socialist Republics and Annexes.* The declarations and exchange of notes printed in this pamphlet are not reproduced here. They are included in the agreements printed in the League of Nations Treaty Series, vol. xxxvII, pp. 176 ff.

the questions between the two countries, and have to that end named as their Plenipotentiaries, that is to say:

His Excellency the President of the Republic of China:

Vi Kyuin Wellington Koo

The Government of the Union of Soviet Socialist Republics:

Lev Mikhailovitch Karakhan

Who, having communicated to each other their respective full powers, found to be in good and due form, have agreed upon the following Articles:

ARTICLE I. Immediately upon the signing of the present Agreement, the normal diplomatic and consular relations between the two Contracting Parties shall be re-established.

The Government of the Republic of China agrees to take the necessary steps to transfer to the Government of the Union of Soviet Socialist Republics the Legation and Consular buildings formerly belonging to the Tsarist Government.

ARTICLE II. The Governments of the two Contracting Parties agree to hold, within one month after the signing of the present Agreement, a Conference which shall conclude and carry out detailed arrangements relative to the questions in accordance with the principles as provided in the following Articles.

Such detailed arrangements shall be completed as soon as possible and, in any case, not later than six months from the date of the opening of the Conference as provided in the preceding paragraph.

ARTICLE III. The Governments of the two Contracting Parties agree to annul at the Conference as provided in the preceding Article, all Conventions, Treaties, Agreements, Protocols, Contracts, etcetera, concluded between the Government of China and the Tsarist Government and to replace them with new treaties, agreements, etcetera, on the basis of equality, reciprocity and justice, as well as the spirit of the Declarations of the Soviet Government of the years of 1919 and 1920.

ARTICLE IV. The Government of the Union of Soviet Socialist Republics, in accordance with its policy and Declarations of 1919 and 1920, declares that all Treaties, Agreements, etcetera, concluded between the former Tsarist Government and any third party or parties affecting the sovereign rights or interests of China, are null and void.

The Governments of both Contracting Parties declare that in future neither Government will conclude any treaties or agreements which prejudice the sovereign rights or interests of either Contracting Party.

ARTICLE V. The Government of the Union of Soviet Socialist Republics recognizes that Outer Mongolia is an integral part of the Republic of China and respects China's sovereignty therein.

The Government of the Union of Soviet Socialist Republics declares that as soon as the questions for the withdrawal of all the troops of the Union of Soviet Socialist Republics from Outer Mongolia—namely, as to the time-limit of the withdrawal of such troops and the measures to be adopted in the interests of the safety of the frontiers—are agreed upon at the Conference as provided in Article II of the present Agreement, it will effect the complete withdrawal of all the troops of the Union of Soviet Socialist Republics from Outer Mongolia.

ARTICLE VI. The Governments of the two Contracting Parties mutually pledge themselves not to permit, within their respective territories the existence and/or activities of any organisations or groups whose aim is to struggle by acts of violence against the Governments of either Contracting Party.

The Governments of the two Contracting Parties further pledge themselves not to engage in propaganda directed against the political and social systems of either Contracting Party.

ARTICLE VII. The Governments of the two contracting Parties agree to redemarcate their national boundaries at the Conference as provided in Article II of the present Agreement, and pending such redemarcation, to maintain the present boundaries.

ARTICLE VIII. The Governments of the two Contracting Parties agree to regulate at the aforementioned Conference the questions relating to the navigation of rivers, lakes and other bodies of water which are common to their respective frontiers, on the basis of equality and reciprocity.

ARTICLE IX. The Governments of the two Contracting Parties agree to settle at the aforementioned Conference the question of the Chinese Eastern Railway in conformity with the principles as hereinafter provided:

(1) The Governments of the two Contracting Parties declare that the Chinese Eastern Railway is a purely commercial enterprise.

The Governments of the two Contracting Parties mutually declare that with the exception of matters pertaining to the business operations which are under the direct control of the Chinese Eastern Railway, all other matters affecting the rights of the National and the Local Governments of the Republic of China—such as judicial matters, matters relating to civil administration, military administration, police, municipal government, taxation, and landed property (with the exception of lands required by the said Railway)—shall be administered by the Chinese Authorities.

(2) The Government of the Union of Soviet Socialist Republics agrees to the redemption by the Government of the Republic of China, with Chinese capital, of the Chinese Eastern Railway, as

well as all appurtenant properties, and to the transfer to China of all shares and bonds of the said Railway.

(3) The Governments of the two Contracting Parties shall settle at the Conference as provided in Article II of the present Agreement, the amount and conditions governing the redemption as well as the procedure for the transfer of the Chinese Eastern Railway.

(4) The Government of the Union of Soviet Socialist Republics agrees to be responsible for the entire claims of the shareholders, bondholders and creditors of the Chinese Eastern Railway incurred prior to the Revolution of March 9th 1917.

(5) The Governments of the two Contracting Parties mutually agree that the future of the Chinese Eastern Railway shall be determined by the Republic of China and the Union of Soviet Socialist Republics, to the exclusion of any third party or parties.

(6) The Governments of the two Contracting Parties agree to draw up an arrangement for the provisional management of the Chinese Eastern Railway pending the settlement of the questions as provided under Section (3) of the present Article.

(7) Until the various questions relating to the Chinese Eastern Railway are settled at the Conference as provided in Article II of the present Agreement, the rights of the two Governments arising out of the Contract of $\frac{\text{August 27th}}{\text{September 8th, 1936,}}$ for the Construction and Operation of the Chinese Eastern Railway, which do not conflict with the present Agreement and the Agreement for the Provisional Management of the said Railway and which do not prejudice China's rights of sovereignty, shall be maintained.

ARTICLE X. The Government of the Union of Soviet Socialist Republics agrees to renounce the special rights and privileges relating to all Concessions in any part of China acquired by the Tsarist Government under various Conventions, Treaties, Agreements, etcetera.

ARTICLE XI. The Government of the Union of Soviet Socialist Republics agrees to renounce the Russian portion of the Boxer Indemnity.

ARTICLE XII. The Government of the Union of Soviet Socialist Republics agrees to relinquish the rights of extraterritoriality and consular jurisdiction.

ARTICLE XIII. The Governments of the two Contracting Parties agree to draw up simultaneously with the conclusion of a Commercial Treaty at the Conference as provided in Article II of the present Agreement, a Customs Tariff for the two Contracting Parties in accordance with the principles of equality and reciprocity.

ARTICLE XIV. The Governments of the two Contracting Parties

agree to discuss at the aforementioned Conference the questions relating to the claims for the compensation of losses.

ARTICLE XV. The present Agreement shall come into effect from the date of signature.

In witness whereof, the respective plenipotentiaries have signed the present Agreement in duplicate in the English language and have affixed thereto their seals.

Done at the City of Peking this Thirty-First Day of the Fifth Month of the Thirteenth Year of the Republic of China, which is, the Thirty-First Day of May One Thousand Nine Hundred and Twenty-Four.

[SEAL] V. K. WELLINGTON KOO
[SEAL] L. M. KARAKHAN

AGREEMENT FOR THE PROVISIONAL MANAGEMENT OF THE CHINESE EASTERN RAILWAY

The Republic of China and the Union of Soviet Socialist Republics mutually recognizing that, inasmuch as the Chinese Eastern Railway was built with capital furnished by the Russian Government and constructed entirely within Chinese territory, the said Railway is a purely commercial enterprise and that, excepting for matters appertaining to its own business operations, all other matters which affect the rights of the Chinese National and Local Governments shall be administered by the Chinese Authorities, have agreed to conclude an Agreement for the Provisional Management of the Railway with a view to carrying on jointly the management of the said Railway until its final settlement at the Conference as provided in Article II of the Agreement on General Principles for the Settlement of the Questions between the Republic of China and the Union of the Soviet Socialist Republics of May 31, 1924, and have to that end named as their Plenipotentiaries, that is to say:

His Excellency the President of the Republic of China:
Vi Kyuin Wellington Koo
The Government of the Union of Soviet Socialist Republics:
Lev Mikhailovitch Karakhan

Who, having communicated to each other their respective full powers, found to be in good and due form, have agreed upon the following Articles:

ARTICLE I. The Railway shall establish, for discussion and decision of all matters relative to the Chinese Eastern Railway, a Board of Directors to be composed of ten persons, of whom five shall be appointed by the Government of the Republic of China and five by the Government of the Union of Soviet Socialist Republics.

The Government of the Republic of China shall appoint one of the Chinese Directors as President of the Board of Directors, who shall also be the Director-General.

The Government of the Union of Soviet Socialist Republics shall appoint one of the Russian Directors as Vice-President of the Board of Directors, who shall also be the Assistant Director-General.

Seven persons shall constitute a quorum, and all decisions of the Board of Directors shall have the consent of not less than six persons before they can be carried out.

The Director-General and Assistant Director-General shall jointly manage the affairs of the Board of Directors and they shall both sign all the documents of the Board.

In the absence of either the Director-General or the Assistant Director-General, their respective Governments may appoint another Director to officiate as the Director-General or the Assistant Director-General (in the case of the Director-General, by one of the Chinese Directors, and in that of the Assistant Director-General, by one of the Russian Directors).

Article II. The Railway shall establish a Board of Auditors to be composed of five persons, namely two Chinese Auditors, who shall be appointed by the Government of the Republic of China and 3 Russian Auditors who shall be appointed by the Government of the Union of Soviet Socialist Republics.

The Chairman of the Board of Auditors shall be elected from among the Chinese Auditors.

Article III. The Railway shall have a Manager, who shall be a national of the Union of Soviet Socialist Republics, and two Assistant Managers, one to be a national of the Republic of China and the other to be a national of the Union of Soviet Socialist Republics.

The said officers shall be appointed by the Board of Directors and such appointments shall be confirmed by their respective Governments.

The rights and duties of the Manager and the Assistant Managers shall be defined by the Board of Directors.

Article IV. The Chiefs and Assistant Chiefs of the various Departments of the Railway shall be appointed by the Board of Directors.

If the Chief of Department is a national of the Republic of China, the Assistant Chief of Department shall be a national of the Union of Soviet Socialist Republics, and if the Chief of Department is a national of the Union of Soviet Socialist Republics, the Assistant Chief of Department shall be a national of the Republic of China.

Article V. The employment of persons in the various departments of the Railway shall be in accordance with the principle of equal representation between the nationals of the Republic of China and those of the Union of Soviet Socialist Republics.

ARTICLE VI. With the exception of the estimates and budgets, as provided in article VII of the present Agreement, all other matters on which the Board of Directors cannot reach an agreement shall be referred for settlement to the Governments of the Contracting Parties.

ARTICLE VII. The Board of Directors shall present the estimates and budgets of the Railway to a joint meeting of the Board of Directors and the Board of Auditors for consideration and approval.

ARTICLE VIII. All the net profits of the Railway shall be held by the Board of Directors and shall not be used pending a final settlement of the question of the present Railway.

ARTICLE IX. The Board of Directors shall revise as soon as possible the statutes of the Chinese Eastern Railway Company, approved on December 4, 1896, by the Tsarist Government, in accordance with the present Agreement and the Agreement on General Principles for the Settlement of the Questions between the Republic of China and the Union of Soviet Socialist Republics of May 31, 1924, and in any case, not later than six months from the date of the constitution of the Board of Directors.

Pending their revision, the aforesaid statutes, insofar as they do not conflict with the present Agreement on General Principles for the Settlement of the Questions between the Republic of China and the Union of Soviet Socialist Republics, and do not prejudice the rights of sovereignty of the Republic of China, shall continue to be observed.

ARTICLE X. The present Agreement shall cease to have effect as soon as the question of the Chinese Eastern Railway is finally settled at the Conference as provided in Article II of the Agreement on General Principles for the Settlement of the Questions between the Republic of China and the Union of Soviet Socialist Republics of May 31, 1924.

ARTICLE XI. The present Agreement shall come into effect from the date of signature.

In witness whereof, the respective Plenipotentiaries have signed the present Agreement in duplicate in the English language and have affixed thereto their seals.

Done at the City of Peking this Thirty-First Day of the Fifth Month of the Thirteenth Year of the Republic of China, which is, the Thirty-First Day of May One Thousand Nine Hundred and Twenty-Four.

[SEAL]   V. K. WELLINGTON KOO
[SEAL]   L. M. KARAKHAN

861.77/3494 : Telegram

The Minister in China (Schurman) to the Secretary of State

PEKING, *June 24, 1924—3 p. m.*
[Received June 24—8 : 55 a. m.]

199. My 175, June 13, 5 p. m. and 184, June 17, 4 p. m. Japanese Chargé d'Affaires has communicated to me following English translation of note which he has addressed to Chinese Minister for Foreign Affairs in reply to latter's note of June 16.

"I have the honor to acknowledge the receipt of your note of the 16th instant in which Your Excellency states in reply to the Japanese Minister's note of June 7th that inasmuch as the agreement between China and Russia in regard to the Chinese Eastern Railway deals only with problems that concern the two parties alone and which it is indisputably within their rights to settle between them, the Chinese Government cannot recognize the reservation made by the Japanese Government in this matter.

The substance of your note having been communicated to my Government, I am instructed further to state to Your Excellency that although the reservation concerning the Japanese rights and interests in regard to the Chinese Eastern Railway is a matter of course hardly calling for a specific declaration on their part, the Japanese Government deem it none the less advisable to invite the attention of the Chinese Government to that phase of the matter in order to avoid the possibility of any unnecessary difficulty arising in future in this connection."

SCHURMAN

861.77/3496 : Telegram

The Minister in China (Schurman) to the Secretary of State

PEKING, *June 26, 1924—4 p. m.*
[Received 5 p. m.]

204. Press today publishes an interview with Karakhan regarding Chinese Eastern Railway of which following is summary :

"Reports from Washington show American Government is dissatisfied with China's last note regarding railway. Hughes has evidently decided to punish China by opposing preliminary conference and has advised France not to ratify Washington treaties. At same stroke he wishes to chastise Soviet Government and has decided not to recognize it because of its evil influence on China. Soviet undisturbed well knowing there is not a single honest and reasonable American who understands interests of his country who supports short-sighted Russian policy of Hughes. Soviet has outlived many governments and will certainly without injury to itself outlive present rulers of America.

No countries but China and Soviet have anything to do with Chinese Eastern Railway and all other powers must know that we will not allow them to interfere with our own business. I do not care even to know to what extent their references are correct with regard to the Washington resolutions. The latter are nonexistent in our eyes and they evidently do not exist either for the powers which have signed them. At any rate as far as China is concerned things do not go further than promises and blackmailing nor does anyone seem to have any intention of carrying out these decisions. Indignation felt in Washington at China's action unworthy of notice. Hughes believes China owes him so much that she must accept with gratitude anything American Government may choose to give her. Hopes people will realize China no longer submissive and obedient to acts of violence at the hands of imperialism. The Chinese people well able itself see who are its enemies and who its friends. Work of imperialistic agents in China who have perfect disregard for Chinese people is itself best schooling for right understanding of China's interests and it does not need to be supplemented by influence from Moscow."

Schurman

861.01/841

The Chinese Legation to the Department of State

Aide Memoire

Recent press reports from Washington seem to indicate that there exists an impression which does not fully reflect the true meaning and purport of the reply [20] to the American note of May 3, 1924,[21] relative to the question of the Chinese Eastern Railway. The position of the Chinese Government as defined in the said reply, however, is a simple one. The agreements recently concluded between China and Soviet Russia dealt with certain general principles for the settlement of questions outstanding between China and Soviet Russia including among the principal ones that of the Chinese Eastern Railway, and do not, as indeed they are not intended to, prejudice any claims which other Powers may wish to prefer against the Railway on account of money advanced to it by them or their nationals at one time or another. Such claims remain unaffected by the Sino-Russian agreements. Under the agreement of October 2, 1920, signed with the Russo-Asiatic Bank,[22] the holder and owner of the entire stocks and shares of the Railway, which provided among other things that the said agreement should terminate whenever the Chinese Government had come to an agreement with a Government of Russia recognized by China, etc., the Chinese Government in addition to its rights and interests in the Railway as the territorial sovereign and as a co-partner of the commercial undertaking has been acting also as trustee on behalf of Russia in so far as her rights and

---

[20] See telegram no. 184, June 17, from the Minister in China, p. 494.
[21] Ante, p. 487.
[22] Foreign Relations, 1920, vol. I, p. 713.

obligations concerning the Railway were concerned. In making the arrangement about them embodied in the recent Sino-Russian agreements the Chinese Government therefore based its action on the agreement of 1920, which itself was based upon the original agreement of 1896, concluded with the Russian Government. The fact that some of the Powers having claims against the Railway have not yet entered into normal relations with Soviet Russia and therefore are not in a position to prefer those claims directly, in so far as Russia the principal beneficiary of the Railway is concerned, cannot affect the existence or nature of such claims. It is not contemplated by the Chinese Government in their recent agreements with the Union of the Soviet Socialist Republic that any legitimate claims of the other Powers or of their nationals should be jeopardized. On the contrary, they will continue to be disposed to take steps with a view to the protection of those claims if circumstances should be such as to make friendly interposition on the part of the Chinese Government desirable as well as useful.

WASHINGTON, *June 30, 1924.*

861.01/841

The Department of State to the Chinese Legation

AIDE-MÉMOIRE

The Department of State has been glad to receive the Aide-Memoire under date of June 30 in which the Chinese Legation communicated certain views of its Government, in supplement to the note which the Minister for Foreign Affairs of China had addressed on June 16 to the American Minister at Peking in reply to the latter's note of May 3, making reservation of this Government's rights in reference to the Chinese Eastern Railway. This fuller and more friendly exposition of the views of the Chinese Government appears to reveal a confusion which this Government had not anticipated could exist in view of its well known attitude and activities with respect to the Railway. The interest felt by this Government in the Railway has been such as was prompted by a realization that the legal and economic status of that line of communication must have a direct and important bearing upon the administrative integrity of China and upon the principle of the equality of opportunity in China; and the steps taken by this Government in that regard—in refusing recognition to the political and administrative powers asserted by the Railway; in taking an initiative in constituting the Inter-Allied Technical Board (in which the Chinese Government participated) to maintain and operate the

Railway during the war; and in supporting the Chinese claim, at the Washington Conference, to have the Chinese Government recognized as trustee for those interested in the Railway—were motivated by the policies above indicated, and taken with what appeared to be the full and sympathetic approval of the Chinese Government.

These steps are not and have not been made the basis of any claim by the Government of the United States to any right of control or other interest merely in its own behalf. This Government does, however, possess and assert a direct right as a creditor of the Chinese Eastern Railway Company for a principal amount of $4,177,-820.06, which it advanced to the Inter-Allied Technical Board for the purpose of saving the Railway from breakdown and deterioration at a time when its operations were of necessity conducted at a loss. That debt from the Railway Company to the American Government was among the obligations which the Chinese Government, in assuming the responsibilities of the trusteeship recognized by the Conference upon the understanding set forth in Resolution No. XIII, undertook to preserve and safeguard. The Government of the United States does not consider that the Chinese Government, in devolving that trusteeship upon another party, without consultation with others in interest and without any reservation of their rights, can have divested itself of the responsibilities incidental to that trust.

The American Government has therefore felt it necessary, in order to safeguard its position in any eventual adjustment of the affairs of the Chinese Eastern Railway, to renew the reservation made in the American Minister's note of May 3 last to the Minister for Foreign Affairs.

WASHINGTON, *July 11, 1924.*

861.01/841 : Telegram

The Secretary of State to the Minister in China (Schurman)

[Extract]

WASHINGTON, *July 11, 1924—9 p. m.*

151. Supplementing Department's telegram No. 141, July 3, 5 p.m.[23]

In reply to his note communicated in your telegram No. 184, June 17, 4 p.m., you will please address the Minister for Foreign Affairs as follows:

"Having referred to my Government your note of June 16, I am now instructed to advise you that the Government of the United

---

[23] Not printed.

States renews the reservation of rights made in its behalf by the Legation's note of May 3, with respect to the responsibility of the Chinese Government, as trustee for the Chinese Eastern Railway, as regards the obligations towards that railway's foreign bondholders, stockholders and creditors, of which the American Government is one."

HUGHES

861.77/3483 : Telegram

The Acting Secretary of State to the Minister in China (Schurman)

WASHINGTON, *July 15, 1924—6 p. m.*

156. Your 176, June 13, 7 p. m. and 185, June 17, 5 p. m. In concert with your colleagues whose Consuls at Harbin participated in sealing the archives of the Chinese Eastern Railway you should agree upon an early date when the Consuls will remove the seals. It is suggested that at the time when the seals are removed, which should be as soon as possible, the Legations make public announcement to the general effect the [*that?*] while maintaining such reservations as they have had occasion to make concerning the recent Sino-Russian agreement regarding the Chinese Eastern Railway as affecting their respective claims upon the Railway Company, the interested Powers consider that the conclusion of that agreement has resulted in a situation which no longer calls for such measures as were taken by the Consuls at Harbin for the protection of the archives of the Company.

GREW

861.77/3521 : Telegram

The Minister in China (Schurman) to the Secretary of State

PEKING, *July 22, 1924—1 p. m.*
[Received July 22—7 : 52 a. m.]

254. Your 156, July 15, 7 [*6*] p.m. At a meeting of representatives of British, French, Japanese and American Legations July 18 it was decided to send following telegrams *mutatis mutandis* to four consuls at Harbin subject to approval of Japanese Government which has now been obtained. Telegrams are accordingly being sent today.

"July 22, 1 p. m. Referring to my telegram June 17. If you and your British, French and Japanese colleagues perceive no reason to the contrary, you, in concert with your colleagues, should at once remove your seals from cabinets containing documents of land department of the Chinese Eastern Railway."

SCHURMAN

861.77/3542a : Telegram

The Acting Secretary of State to the Minister in China (Schurman)

WASHINGTON, *July 26, 1924—3 p. m.*

170. Department's telegram No. 151, July 11, 9 p. m. French Chargé d'Affaires informs the Department the British Government has suggested that French Minister in Peking should arrange for a conference of the representatives of Powers participating in Washington Conference Resolution No. XIII with a view to examining and recommending to their Governments what steps may be practicable for the purpose of protecting foreign rights in the Chinese Eastern Railway. French Chargé added his Government would be glad if you could be authorized to take part in such a discussion.

The Department has not hitherto understood that the British Government had concerned itself in this matter, and feels doubtful whether the proposed discussions can be expected to lead to any further result than has already been arrived at in the informal conversations which would appear to have taken place already among the Legations more particularly interested.

You may however take part in the proposed discussions, basing your attitude upon the views communicated to you in the Department's telegram of July 11, 9 p. m., and submitting to the Department any proposals arising out of the discussions.

GREW

861.77/3541 : Telegram

The Minister in China (Schurman) to the Secretary of State

PEKING, *July 30, 1924—7 p. m.*
[Received July 30—10 : 53 a. m.]

268. Your 156, July 15, 7 a. m. [*6 p. m.*] Following telegram was sent today to consul Harbin:

"July 30, 6 p. m. My July 22, 1 p. m. Four Ministers today agreed on following telegram to Harbin consuls.

'While the Ministers accept the conclusion of the consuls that the present time is not opportune for the removal of the seals, they desire to impress the consuls with their conviction that the seals should be removed at the earliest practicable date. As to this date they would desire to be advised by the consuls'.

For your knowledge and guidance I would say that I am very desirous of the early removal of the seals which is the instruction of the Department."

SCHURMAN

861.77/3543 : Telegram

The Minister in China (Schurman) to the Secretary of State

PEKING, *July 31, 1924—4 p. m.*
[Received July 31—4 p. m.]

266. Your telegram 170, July 26, 3 p.m.

1. At a conference here today of the diplomatic representatives of the United States, Great Britain, Japan and France, my French colleague stated that his Government had consulted the other three Governments on the unsatisfactory position taken by the Chinese Government in reply to our notes on the Chinese Eastern Railway question and that the British Government had suggested referring the matter to their Ministers in Peking in order that they might "devise effective measures" for dealing with the matter, and his Government had instructed him accordingly. He expressed the opinion from which there was no dissent that a joint note to the Chinese Government would be the most effective measure that could be adopted under the circumstances and submitted a draft which after being amended was agreed to for submission to our Governments as follows:

"The representatives of the United States, Great Britain, Japan and France, acting under instructions from their Governments, have the honor to recall to His Excellency the Minister for Foreign Affairs the solidarity which exists between China and the powers signatories of the Washington Conference with regard to the principles which constitute the basis of the policy adopted by the conference.

They desire especially to refer to the two resolutions of the Washington Conference concerning the Chinese Eastern Railway and to emphasize the obligations which those resolutions impose upon the Chinese Government. In addition they wish to call the special attention of His Excellency to the serious consequences which would ensue from change in the economic and legal status of the railway should such a change impair the administrative integrity of China and the principle of equal opportunity.

In view of the signature of the Sino-Russian Agreement of May 31st the representatives of the four Powers would be glad to receive satisfactory assurances on the above-mentioned points for communication to their Governments."

3 [*sic*]. My British colleague said he had thus far sent nothing in writing on this subject to the Chinese Government.

4. My Japanese colleague said that in view of his instructions he believed his Government would not unite in a joint note. The position of his Government in Manchuria was a little different from

ours as their note of June 7th [24] indicated. To join in sending this proposed note might prejudice their own.

5. Please instruct.

SCHURMAN

861.77/3543 : Telegram

The Acting Secretary of State to the Minister in China (Schurman)

WASHINGTON, *August 7, 1924—7 p. m.*

184. Your 266, July 31, 4 p.m. The Department does not feel that the draft joint note is calculated to improve the status of our position *vis-à-vis* the Chinese Government with respect to the Chinese Eastern Railway as that position now exists as the result of the Legation's note of May 3 [25] and the Chinese Government's reply of June 16.[26] Should, however, the British, Japanese, and French representatives all be authorized to join in the proposed note, the Department would not feel disposed to object to your taking the same action, notwithstanding the note would seem to be quite unnecessary and would perhaps afford the Chinese Government a further opportunity to give expression to the unreasonable attitude manifested in its note of June 16. In the event of unanimous agreement to despatch the note the Department, to obviate any implication of a threat, suggests as a substitute for "serious consequences" the words "confused situation" or "unfortunate results."

GREW

761.93/533 : Telegram

The Chargé in China (Bell) to the Secretary of State

PEKING, *September 27, 1924—noon.*
[Received September 27—8:25 a. m.]

368. My 361, September 25, noon.[27] Rosta's agency in this morning's press confirms negotiations between Soviet Government and Chang Tso-lin, stating that the understanding arrived at is almost a textual repetition of Koo–Karakhan agreement for provisional management of the Chinese Eastern Railway, of May 31st. There are other reports, however, that secret clauses are attached and Foreign Office on September 25th lodged protest with Soviet Embassy, Peking, against reported Chang Tso-lin–Soviet agreement calling

[24] See telegram no. 175, June 13, from the Minister in China, p. 493.
[25] *Ante,* p. 487.
[26] See telegram no. 184, June 17, from the Minister in China, p. 494.
[27] Not printed.

the attention of the Russian Ambassador to Chang Tso-lin's being in open rebellion against the Central Government and declaring if the report is true that it will not recognize such an agreement.

American consul Harbin reports as follows:

"At present detailed report difficult to obtain but it would appear that it was agreed that railway concession be reduced from 80 to 60 years. Local situation being carefully watched.

Strongly rumored at Harbin that under Mukden agreement Russian members of the board of directors and general manager of the railway will soon be replaced by Soviet appointees and that Chinese members of the board remain changed slightly so that Pao Kuei-ching becomes President".

BELL

867.77/3654 : Telegram

The Consul at Harbin (Hanson) to the Secretary of State

HARBIN, September 29, 1924—5 p. m.
[Received September 29—10 : 25 a. m.]

American, British, French and Japanese consular seals removed from cabinets in the land department Chinese Eastern Railway this afternoon on the initiative of the four consuls. Informed the Embassy.

HANSON

861.77/3660 : Telegram

The Consul at Harbin (Hanson) to the Secretary of State

HARBIN, October 3, 1924—6 p. m.
[Received 8 : 50 p. m.]

General Manager Ostroumoff arrested and imprisoned by Chinese police; charges unknown. Informed the Legation and Mukden.

HANSON

761.93/537 : Telegram

The Chargé in China (Bell) to the Secretary of State

PEKING, October 4, 1924—5 p. m.
[Received October 4—12 : 55 p. m.]

377. My telegram number 368, of September 27, noon. Chinese text Manchurian-Soviet Agreement received from Hanson. Preamble indicates contracting parties are "the government of the Three Eastern Provinces of the Chinese Republic" and Soviet Government. Article 1 in 15 sections concerns Chinese Eastern and incorporates without important change except in identity of contracting parties article 9, sections 4, 5 and 7 of the agreement on general principles

and articles 1 to 9 of the railway agreement signed Peking, May 31st. Section 2, however, provides free reversion of railway to China at end of 60 instead of 80 years and that when mutually agreed further shortening may be discussed. Soviet agrees that after signature present agreement China shall be entitled to redeem the railway with Chinese capital at actual just value mutually determined. Section 15 provides that portions of the agreement relating to the railway shall become void after redemption of [or] free return indicated. Article 2 amplifies article 8 agreement general principles and provides that details shall be arranged by a conference of representatives of the contracting parties within two months, with special attention to safeguarding for China and Soviet, respectively, transportation of passengers and freight on lower Amur to the sea and on Sungari to Harbin. Articles 3, 4 and 5 are substantially the same as articles 7, 13 and 6, respectively, of general principles agreement substituting Manchurian for Chinese Government. Article 6 provides that all joint commissions named in the agreement shall begin operations within one month and conclude within six months unless otherwise stipulated. Article 7 states agreement operative when signed and of three texts, Russian, Chinese and English, latter authoritative in case of [dispute].

BELL

861.77/3668 : Telegram

The Consul at Harbin (Hanson) to the Secretary of State

HARBIN, *October 8, 1924—10 a.m.*
[Received October 9—6:40 a.m.]

Since the Bolsheviks took over Chinese Eastern Railway, conservative Russians in the railway zone have been terror stricken. On October 3rd General Manager Ostroumoff, Chief of the Land Department Gondatti, and Chief of the Economic Bureau Mikhailoff were arrested by Chinese police, acting under orders from Mukden, without charges being preferred, placed in solitary confinement, treated like desperate criminals and not permitted to consult with the counsel or to see their wives. Arrests were made before they were able legally to transfer their offices to their Soviet successors. On October 6th Kirin provincial authorities prohibited departure of Russians from Harbin. On October 7th a merchant, Gavriloff, and the chief bookkeeper of the railway were arrested without charges made and placed in prison. As the first three mentioned worked with and under Inter-Allied Technical Board, as the first two were given American, British, French and Japanese diplomatic support and encouragement in their efforts to resist Chinese encroachments in the land department question, and as I suspect that certain Chinese authorities with Bolshevik approval are attempting to persecute them for attempting to preserve the interests of the railway in accordance with the resolutions of the Washington Conference, it is my opinion that the matter of these outrageous arrests and the conduct of these railway officials while in charge of railway administration should be investigated immediately by an international commission, if possible. If not possible, then foreign consular officers should be present at the trials of the accused.

This matter is urgent as Ostroumoff who has long been in ill health and suffering from a severe strain may become seriously if not fatally ill in the Chinese prison. It is suggested that pressure be brought upon Chang Tso-lin to have the prisoners moved to Mukden because it is feared they may at any moment be handed over by the local authorities, willing or unwilling, to the Bolshevists for transportation to and punishment in Siberia.

The Department might suggest to the Associated Press or other news agency that it detail to Harbin a special correspondent in order to report regarding Bolshevik activities in North Manchuria and on the Chinese Eastern Railway, arrests of foreigners by Chinese military and police and trials of foreigners by Chinese courts. Such reports would enlighten the American public in regard to communism and the necessity of retaining extraterritorial rights in China.

Informed the Legation.

HANSON

861.77/3669 : Telegram

The Chargé in China (Bell) to the Secretary of State

PEKING, *October 10, 1924—4 p.m.*
[Received October 10—10: 14 a.m.]

382. 1. Referring to telegrams to the Department from Hanson, Harbin. Consular body asked diplomatic body to take some action in respect of situation at Harbin created by arrest of Ostroumoff, Gondatti, Mikhailoff and others, consular body stating local foreigners seriously alarmed and fearing extension of arbitrary acts for the treaty-power nationals.

2. Diplomatic body meeting today decided they could take no action as such in matter of arrest of Ostroumoff and others, Harbin consular body being so informed by telegraph.

3. Japanese, British and French representatives here have all informally interceded with Chang on behalf of arrested men on ground of humanity and justice asking that they be admitted to bail or brought to speedy trial but with no success thus far. I have telegraphed American consul Mukden to associate him[self] in these informal representations. Hanson informed.

BELL

861.77/3669 : Telegram

The Acting Secretary of State to the Chargé in China (Bell)

WASHINGTON, *October 13, 1924—3 p. m.*

237. Your 382, October 10, 4 p.m. The Department does not perceive that any further action in this matter would be warranted, and considers it unlikely that such action would produce any good result. Advise Consuls at Mukden and Harbin.

GREW

861.77/3753 : Telegram

The Chargé in China (Mayer) to the Secretary of State

PEKING, *December 9, 1924—3 p. m.*
[Received December 9—8 : 50 a. m.]

476. American consul Harbin's recent telegram to Department [29] to effect that Ostroumoff and others turned over to Chinese procurator general who can keep prisoners in solitary confinement for four months prior to discharge or trial, and Department's 237, October 13, 3 p.m. After careful consideration, in view of this new factor in situation, I consented to join with French, British and Japanese colleagues in addressing informal communication to Marshal Chang Tso-lin expressing hope on grounds of humanity that he would bring the prisoners to speedy trial, if trial is to take place, and to permit Ostroumoff to reside at his house in Harbin while awaiting trial in view of the fact that latter's health appears menaced.

MAYER

PROPOSAL BY THE CHINESE GOVERNMENT TO CONVENE A PRELIMINARY CUSTOMS CONFERENCE, AND THE REJECTION OF THE PROPOSAL BY THE POWERS

500.A 4e 1/51 : Telegram

The Minister in China (Schurman) to the Secretary of State

PEKING, *March 13, 1924—4 p. m.*
[Received 7 : 08 p. m.]

77. I have received from the Minister for Foreign Affairs a note dated March 10th [29] relative to special conference to be held Washington nine-power treaty [30] which rehearses proposals of

---

[29] Not printed.
[30] *Foreign Relations, 1922*, vol. I, p. 282.

Chinese delegates at Washington and action taken; points out that because of the fact that all signatory powers have not yet given approval, special conference has not been called and stresses difficulty of Chinese Government in reorganizing its finances and inability to pay internal and foreign obligations which they had hoped to do from surtax. Since conference cannot yet be called Chinese Government hopes that a preliminary conference may first be held to make preparations for future formal conference. Preliminary conference to decide tentative agenda for formal conference and investigate and decide questions to be presented to it. Representatives of signatory powers could exchange views and do in advance the work which would be referr[ed] to committees of future special conference. Hope is expressed that in putting surtax into operation condition of China's finance will be improved and that both internal and foreign debts can be reorganized.

I imagine this move is the result of reports to Chinese Government of Yen's commission for the readjustment of finances, see my 319 September 21, 10 a. m. 1923,[31] and that its object is to obtain some specific promise from the foreign powers at the preliminary conference relative to imposition of surtax.

Other ministers have received identic notes and we shall hold meeting next week to consider proposal.

SCHURMAN

500.A 4e 1/51 : Telegram

The Secretary of State to the Minister in China (Schurman)

WASHINGTON, *March 18, 1924—5 p. m.*

55. Your No. 77 March 13, 4 p. m. and Evans' telegram to Buforcom March 15.[32] Pending the receipt of further instructions, you should not take such a part in conference with your colleagues as to indicate or commit in any way the position of this Government with respect to the proposal for a preliminary conference.

HUGHES

500.A 4e 1/52 : Telegram

The Minister in China (Schurman) to the Secretary of State

PEKING, *March 18, 1924—5 p. m.*
[Received March 18—3 : 53 p. m.]

83. My 77, March 13, 4 p. m.

1. Following is a translation of the French text of an identic telegram to their Governments adopted at a conference today by the

---

[31] *Ibid.*, 1923, vol. I, p. 548.
[32] Telegram from Mr. Arthur H. Evans, assistant commercial attaché at Peking, to the Bureau of Foreign and Domestic Commerce; not printed.

representatives of the signatory powers of the treaties of Washington Conference and of the powers which adhered to those treaties.

2. "The representatives of the powers signatory to the treaties of Washington consider that their Governments might in reply to the Chinese note of March 10, 1924, authorize them to examine with the Chinese Government the financial situation of China and the future "destinations" (purposes) of the surtax of two and a half percent but they should be instructed to demand that the Chinese Government communicate to them in advance the measures contemplated by it for the abolition of likin and the interim provisions to be applied prior to the time of such abolition."

3. There were objections to the proposed preliminary conference and to the name which seemed too formal. All agreed that the proposal was inspired by the need of money and contemplated preeminently to determine the purposes to which the surtax revenue should be devoted. Representatives were of the opinion this question should not be considered without (1) examination of Chinese finances, and (2) receipt of Chinese plan for abolition of likin, etc.

4. While favoring the program suggested, I consider it my duty to point out to the Department that if it is carried out and the representatives cannot agree among themselves as to the purposes for which the surtax revenue is to be used that might hereafter be urged as an argument against the holding of the special conference itself.

SCHURMAN

500.A 4e 1/53 : Telegram

The Minister in China (Schurman) to the Secretary of State

PEKING, *March 19, 1924—10 a. m.*
[Received March 19—6 : 21 a. m.]

84. My 83, March 18, 5 p. m. Please add the following as paragraph 5 :

Though the diplomatic representatives felt that the Chinese Government should be reminded of its obligations in respect of the abolition of likin, they are all convinced that whatever plan the Government may present for that purpose no practical results will follow as the Government is powerless to assert its will in the provinces.

SCHURMAN

500.A 4e 1/54 : Telegram

The Minister in China (Schurman) to the Secretary of State

PEKING, *March 20, 1924—10 a. m.*
[Received March 20—7 : 38 a. m.]

86. Your 55, March 18, 5 p. m. You will since have received my 83, March 18, 5 p. m., and 84, March 19, at 10 a. m., which show that

neither I nor any of my colleagues have committed our Governments in any way or indicated what their position might be with respect to Koo's proposal for a preliminary conference.

I had received visits from representatives of the Government as well as from Acting Governor Chang, Bank of China, urging me to support the proposal and recommend it to my colleagues, and I listened to them all, asked questions, and remained absolutely noncommittal. Privately, I considered Koo's proposal impossible of acceptance but thought it might possibly be used to bring about a financial show-down. . . .

.   .   .   .

SCHURMAN

500.A 4e 1/53 : Telegram

The Secretary of State to the Minister in China (Schurman)

WASHINGTON, *March 22, 1924—4 p. m.*

60. The Department is informing London of the substance of your Nos. 77 March 13, 4 p. m. and 83 March 18, 5 p. m.

Commenting upon the identic telegram, the Department states in substance that

1. This recommendation while not approving of the proposed preliminary conference, apparently favors a preliminary discussion of matters which are essentially for determination by the Conference. Such a discussion could not, therefore, in the opinion of this Government be distinguished from the proposal made by the Chinese Government for a preliminary conference.

2. This Government might find difficulty, from the administrative standpoint, in arranging for its suitable representation in a preliminary conference ancillary to the Special Conference for which definite authority exists and for which appropriations have been made.

3. Inasmuch as the foreign delegates to such a preliminary conference would presumably be without plenipotentiary powers it is believed that they might find themselves at a tactical disadvantage in that they would be unable to carry on effective negotiations, impose any conditions, or give any assurances; and their activities would therefore of necessity be limited to expressions of views and formulation of preparatory plans which might possibly serve to prejudice and embarrass the work of the Special Conference itself.

4. In view of the widespread disregard of treaty rights by Chinese officials in the provinces, even in those professing allegiance to the Peking Government, as instanced by the Kiangsu cigarette tax; and in view of the growing attitude of irresponsibility on the part of the Peking Government itself as evidenced by the imposition of dis-

criminatory railway rates, and by numerous instances of failure to accord prompt satisfaction in cases of outrages upon foreigners, this Government questions whether it is not now inopportune and even dangerous to assume a responsive attitude toward requests from the Peking Government which are not based upon any definite right.

5. In furtherance of the cooperation with the British Government in this matter which was initiated by Mr. Wellesley's conferences with the Department a year or so ago,[33] it is desired that the Embassy consult informally with the British Foreign Office and explain this Government's views as above outlined, and inquire concerning the attitude of the British Government toward the proposed preliminary conference.

HUGHES

500.A 4e 1/56 : Telegram

The Secretary of State to the Minister in China (Schurman)

WASHINGTON, March 31, 1924—4 p. m.

63. With reference to the Department's 60 of March 22, 4 p. m., the Department has been informed that the British Prime Minister, while not yet prepared to make a definite decision with regard to the proposed Preliminary Conference, is inclined to agree completely in principle with the views of this Government, and that he is consulting Macleay[34] in order to give him an opportunity to express his views before the British Government definitely commits itself.

The Counselor of the Japanese Embassy in an informal conversation with the Chief of the Division of Far Eastern Affairs has indicated that his Government, while not yet decided, is disposed to an unfavorable view of the Chinese proposal for reasons substantially the same as those of this Government.

HUGHES

500.A 4e 1/62 : Telegram

The Secretary of State to the Minister in China (Schurman)

WASHINGTON, April 24, 1924—4 p. m.

80. With reference to the Department's 63, March 31, 4 P. M., the Department has received the following telegram from London:

"At a conference at the Foreign Office I was informed that the British Government is entirely in agreement with the views expressed by the Department. If the Department will inform the Foreign Office through me the instructions it proposes to send to the

---

[33] Mr. Victor Wellesley, head of the Far Eastern Department, British Foreign Office, conferred with officials in the Department of State in January 1923.

[34] Sir J. W. R. Macleay, British Minister in China.

American Minister at Peking in accordance with those views, the Foreign Office is prepared to instruct the British Minister to join with his American colleague. The Foreign Office believes, however, that it would be impolitic to give a flat refusal to the Chinese Government's request for a preliminary conference; that it might be wise to state while refusing the request that the treaty powers are thoroughly alive to the importance of the situation and intend to consult together concerning the best means of giving practical effect to the Washington agreements having regard to present conditions in China. The Foreign Minister suggests that the form of the note be left to the Diplomatic Body at Peking *ad referendum*."

The Department is replying to London [36] that it is telegraphing you to consider as definite instructions the views in Department's telegram to you No. 60 March 22, 4 P. M., and that the text of the telegram from London above quoted is being transmitted to you with the statement that the Department concurs in the opinion of the British Foreign Office that it would be impolitic to state the refusal of the Chinese Government's request too flatly.

HUGHES

500.A 4e 1/63 : Telegram

The Secretary of State to the Minister in China (Schurman)

WASHINGTON, May 1, 1924—5 p. m.

84. With reference to the Department's 80, April 24, 4 p. m., the Embassy at London has reported [36] that the Foreign Office has telegraphed the British Minister at Peking that he is to regard as definite instructions the views shared by the American and British Governments as to the reply that should be returned to the Chinese request for a preliminary conference, and to act with you in this connection.

HUGHES

500.A 4e 1/65 : Telegram

The Minister in China (Schurman) to the Secretary of State

PEKING, May 7, 1924—5 p. m.
[Received May 7—1:09 p. m.]

123. Your 84, May 1, 5 p. m.

1. I have conferred with British Minister who has prepared the following draft reply to Minister for Foreign Affairs.

2. "The representatives of the powers signatories of the treaty concluded at Washington on February 6, 1922, relative to the Chinese customs tariff and of the powers which have subsequently adhered thereto duly referred to their respective Governments the suggestion

---

[36] Telegram not printed.

contained in the Wai Chiao Pu's identic notes of the 10th March,[37] that in view of the delay which had occurred in holding the special tariff conference a preliminary conference should be arranged for the purpose of preparing the ground for the formal conference.

The aforesaid representatives have been instructed by their respective Governments to inform the Chinese Government in reply that they are unable to accept this suggestion because in the opinion of their Governments, the foreign representatives at the proposed preliminary conference would be debarred from carrying on effective negotiations and the task of the preliminary conference would be limited to the formulation of views and plans which might prejudice the work of the special tariff conference when it is held.

In making this communication the above-mentioned representatives are authorized to state that the powers concerned are thoroughly alive to the importance of the situation and intend to consult together as to the best means for giving practical effect to the Washington agreements, having regard to present conditions in China."

3. I consider foregoing satisfactory if Department approves of consultations contemplated in last paragraph and participation therein by all the powers mentioned in the first paragraph. It is based on instruction by telegraph to British Minister for which see your 80, April 24, 4 p. m., and these instructions vary somewhat from your 60, March 22, 4 p. m., especially in its fourth heading.

4. Please telegraph whether draft is satisfactory and if not what alterations you wish made.

5. Above draft contemplates collective note from foreign representatives in accordance with instructions received by Macleay but we anticipate difficulty in securing assent of representatives of certain powers to the last paragraph of the draft. In such event I assume Department wishes me to address an individual reply in accordance with your views to the Minister for Foreign Affairs which would be natural course as Chinese notes of March 10 were addressed to each foreign minister individually.

SCHURMAN

500.A 4e 1/65 : Telegram

The Secretary of State to the Minister in China (Schurman)

WASHINGTON, *May 9, 1924—3 p. m.*

91. Your 123 May 7, 5 p. m. It is suggested that the objections anticipated by you and your British colleague to the last paragraph of the draft note may be obviated by substituting therefor the following:

"In making this communication, I am authorized to state that the Powers concerned appreciate the importance of the situation and

---

[37] Not printed; see telegram no. 77, Mar. 13, from the Minister in China, p. 513.

will continue, having regard to present conditions in China, to give consideration to the question of bringing into effect the provisions of the Washington Treaty."

In view of the fact that the Chinese Government addressed separate notes, it is believed preferable that the replies should likewise be made separately, though so far as possible in identic language.

HUGHES

500.A 4e 1/69 : Telegram

The Minister in China (Schurman) to the Secretary of State

PEKING, *June 6, 1924—2 p. m.*
[Received June 6—9 : 15 a. m.]

163. Your 91, May 9, 3 p. m.

1. Action has hitherto been delayed by failure of British Minister to receive his Government's assent to proposed collective note submitted to you in my 123, May 7, 5 p. m. Macleay has now received approval of first two paragraphs but British Government desire to omit entirely third paragraph which was originally drafted in accordance with their instructions. This affords an interesting indication of development of the views of the MacDonald government regarding China. At meeting [of] the diplomatic body to consider matter June 3rd it became apparent that a collective note would not be possible, as French, Belgian and Italian representatives had already informed Wai Chiao Pu orally that their Governments would agree to no conference of any description until gold franc question settled, while Japanese Minister stated his Government would be willing to consider holding preliminary conference after France had ratified Nine-Power Treaty and before deposit of ratifications in Washington as they did not want to discourage the Chinese Government.

3 [*sic*]. In the circumstances it was decided to address individual notes and I have today written Chinese Foreign Office as follows on the basis of first two paragraphs of draft submitted May 7, 5 p. m. :

"I duly referred to my Government the suggestion contained in your note of March 10, 1924, that in view of the delay which has occurred in holding the special tariff conference a preliminary conference should be arranged for the purpose of preparing the ground for the formal conference.

Under instructions from the Secretary of State at Washington I have now the honor to inform Your Excellency that my Government is unable to comply with this suggestion because in their opinion the foreign representatives at the proposed preliminary conference would not be in a position to carry on effective negotiations and the task of the preparatory conference would be limited [to] the formation [*formulation*] of views and plans which might prejudice the work of the special tariff conference when it is held."

4. British Minister sending similar note. I shall forward texts of all notes when copies received.[38]

SCHURMAN

FURTHER POSTPONEMENT OF THE MEETING OF THE COMMISSION ON EXTRATERRITORIALITY IN CHINA [39]

793.003 C 73/116 : Telegram

The Minister in China (Schurman) to the Secretary of State

PEKING, *February 16, 1924—1 p. m.*
[Received February 16—9 : 37 a. m.]

60. My telegram no. 400, December 14, 5 [*3*] p. m.[40] The Chinese Minister for Foreign Affairs at interview February 13 again expressed a desire to know nature of the reply received from each government. He expressed gratitude for past good offices of the United States and requested their continuance. The following unofficial record of his remarks left with me by a secretary of the Foreign Office on February 15, 3 p. m., is correct:

"The Minister of Foreign Affairs requested Dr. Schurman to telegraph to Mr. Hughes requesting his good offices to prevail on the signatory powers for the despatch of the Commission of Inquiry of Extraterritorial Jurisdiction to come to China in November next. In making this request, the Minister suggested the following reasons:

1. One of the main objects of the Washington Conference was to promote better international cooperation. The United States being the convener of the conference, China naturally looks upon it as the intermediary through whom to arrange for the execution of the treaties and agreements made at Washington in her interest. If there should be any, there ought to be a frank exchange of views. It was, therefore, hoped that the State Department would not hesitate to inform China fully as regards the real situation concerning the visit of the Commission this November. If China knew which powers were not able to agree to the suggested extension of one year, she could explain her point of view in regard to it.

2. China has been hoping that the signatory powers who attended the Washington Conference would carry out the covenants made at Washington as early as possible.

3. The nonfulfillment of the covenants in the present case may be seized as a precedent by other powers who may not be anxious to carry out the terms of the other treaties and agreements.

4. Since there was a special resolution providing that the powers are free to accept or reject all or any portion of the recommendations of the Commission, it does not seem necessary for the powers to take

---

[38] Notes not printed; in despatch no. 2348, June 26, the Minister transmitted copies of notes sent to the Chinese Minister for Foreign Affairs by the American, Belgian, British, French, Italian, and Japanese Ministers.
[39] Continued from *Foreign Relations*, 1923, vol. I, pp. 620–631.
[40] *Foreign Relations*, 1923, vol. I, p. 630.

a collective attitude and share the responsibility for delaying the visit of the Commission.

5. The early despatch of the Commission will further demonstrate the importance of the Washington Conference to the Chinese people and stimulate the interest and encourage them to get together to solve their political problems."

In reply to Dr. Koo's question regarding the attitude of each of the individual governments, I replied that I was not fully informed on these conditions.

The danger of further delay in the visit of the Commission affects. Dr. Koo very strongly, the more so [as] he was one of China's delegates to the Washington Conference.

SCHURMAN

793.003 C 73/120

The Chinese Legation to the Department of State

MEMORANDUM

With reference to the time for the meeting of the Extraterritoriality Commission provided for in Resolution V adopted on December 10, 1921, by the Washington Conference on the Limitation of Armament,[41] the American Government suggested in November, 1923, to the Powers participating in or adhering to the Resolution that November 1, 1924, should be the date fixed for the convening of the Commission.

The result of the inquiry on the part of the American Government brought out the fact that unanimity with respect to this date could not be obtained, and the Chinese Government was accordingly informed to this effect in the Department's note of January 18, 1924.[42]

Ever since the adjournment of the Washington Conference in February, 1922, the Chinese Government has spared no efforts to obtain all available data bearing upon extraterritoriality in China in preparation for the meeting of the Commission. The Chinese Government, therefore, earnestly requests that the American Government approach again all the participating or adhering Powers concerned in regard to the matter and use its powerful influence to secure their unanimous consent for the convening of the Commission on a definite date.

---

[41] *Foreign Relations*, 1922, vol. I, p. 289.
[42] Not printed.

This request of the Chinese Government has been presented to the American Government through the American Minister at Peking.

In connection with this subject the Chinese Government has been informed by the French Minister at Peking that the French Government informed the American Ambassador in Paris to the effect that the consent of the French Government to take part in the Extraterritoriality Commission would be dependent upon the settlement of the question now pending between China and France regarding the payments of the French share of the Boxer indemnity. Now the Boxer indemnity question has no bearing whatever upon matters that concern the Extraterritoriality Commission, and will no doubt be adjusted in due time to the satisfaction of both Governments.

The Chinese Minister begs leave to point out that the position taken by the French Government does not seem to be compatible with the spirit of the Resolution as expressed in the concluding clause thereof.

WASHINGTON, *March 27, 1924.*

793.003C73/120

The Secretary of State to the Chinese Minister (*Sze*)

WASHINGTON, *April 10, 1924.*

SIR: I have the honor to refer to your memorandum of March 27, 1924, in which you convey the request of the Chinese Government that this Government should approach the Powers participating in, or adhering to, Resolution V of the Washington Conference regarding extraterritoriality in China with a view to obtaining their unanimous consent to the convening of the Commission on a definite date.

After careful consideration of your request, this Government is convinced that the present moment is not an opportune one to make the representations in question. It accordingly suggests that the Chinese Government may wish to reconsider its request and postpone the proposed action for the time being. Let me, however, assure you that this Government will not, in any case, fail to urge the fixing of a definite date for the convening of the Commission as soon as it may appear that such action would be likely to bring about a favorable result.

Accept [etc.] CHARLES E. HUGHES

CONSENT BY THE UNITED STATES TO JOIN OTHER POWERS IN NEGOTIATIONS TO RESTORE THE SHANGHAI MIXED COURT TO THE CHINESE

893.053Sh/23 : Telegram

The Minister in China (Schurman) to the Secretary of State

PEKING, *March 11, 1924—10 a. m.*
[Received March 12—2:41 a. m.]

75. My despatch no. 1572 of May 30, 1923.[43]　On January 26 the Chinese Foreign Office addressed a note to the dean [43] pressing for a reply to its note of October 26, 1922,[43] asking for the rendition of the Mixed Court at Shanghai.

Further consideration of the rendition was postponed in 1923 because of the impending meeting of the Extraterritoriality Commission.　My colleagues and I now feel that owing to the uncertainty of the date of the Commission no strong reason remains for further postponing resumption of rendition negotiations on the basis of the draft agreement of 1915,[43] as subsequently modified by the Foreign Office note of October 26, 1922, and consular body report.[44]　I favor such resumption not only in order to remedy disadvantageous results of present isolated status of the court and similar reasons but also to offset possible impressions of obstructiveness of the powers arising from lack of progress in Washington Conference program.

Proposed note from dean to the Chinese Foreign Office after indicating readiness to negotiate on the above basis requires guarantees from the Chinese Government as follows: 1. That provision will be made for meeting court expenses. 2. That all Mixed Court decisions will be recognized and given effect where necessary by all Chinese courts throughout Republic. 3. That the local authorities at Shanghai will execute terms of rendition arrived at.

The note further states that the diplomatic body would be glad to receive in addition to guarantees an assurance from the Chinese Government that it is prepared to enter into early negotiations for satisfactory settlement of other questions also outstanding, as for instance: (1) settlement extension; (2) port improvements; (3) Chinese representation on Municipal Council; (4) foreign representation in municipal councils of the adjoining Chinese areas.　I opposed making this a condition precedent to rendition negotiations as was generally favored by my colleagues, and the formula finally adopted

---

[43] Not printed.
[44] Report not printed. The consular body at Shanghai had assumed control of the Mixed Court in 1911, during the revolution of that year, and had continued to exercise control.

and expressed in the preceding sentence appears to me consistent with the Department's views relative to separate settlement of the rendition question.

Many considerations appear to render my concurrence in this note highly advisable. I request the Department's instructions by telegraph.

SCHURMAN

893.053 Sh/23 : Telegram

The Secretary of State to the Minister in China (Schurman)

[Paraphrase]

WASHINGTON, *March 18, 1924—6 p. m.*

56. Legation's telegram 75 of March 11, 10 a.m. The actual conditions in China seem to give confirmation to the position which was taken generally by the diplomatic corps as indicated by the comments on circular 69 forwarded with Legation's despatch 1572 of May 30, 1923,[45] that the Government at Peking does not have sufficient control in the vicinity of Shanghai to make it possible for it to offer satisfactory guarantees that it will fulfill any agreements which might result from negotiations for the rendition of the Mixed Court and possibly other matters affecting port of Shanghai. This opinion appears to be given support especially by the passage of an act for a cigarette tax by the Provincial Assembly of Kiangsu and its imposition, imminent if not actual, in spite of your protests.[46] Moreover, the widespread disregard which provincial authorities show for treaty rights and the lack of any evidence of a real desire on their part to correct this situation causes the Department to question the advisability of taking action which many elements among the Chinese might interpret as resulting from weakness or as indicating, or being preliminary to, a surrender of extraterritorial rights in the near future. As the reasons given by your colleagues last year for not entering into negotiations seem more cogent now than then, the Department is at a loss to understand their present willingness to do so.

Furthermore, the Department is not ready to admit that the date for the meeting of the Commission on Extraterritoriality is so indefinite as to bar the hope that that body may make a survey of the status of the Mixed Court.

The Department would like to receive your comments regarding the views presented above before it authorizes you to concur in the

---

[45] Not printed.
[46] For protests against internal taxes, see *Foreign Relations, 1923*, vol. I, p. 579.

proposed note of the dean of the diplomatic corps. More complete information is desired with respect to the considerations which seem to make it advisable to concur in the proposed note.

HUGHES

893.053 Sh/24 : Telegram

The Minister in China (Schurman) to the Secretary of State

PEKING, *March 22, 1924—11 a. m.*
[Received March 22—10 : 34 a. m.]

89. Your 56, March 18, 6 p. m.

1. It is true that Chinese Government does not today exercise effective control at Shanghai but its powerlessness does not vitally affect Mixed Court which functions in the International Settlement and through the municipal police.

2. The present proposal is merely to resume negotiations interrupted by the Great War and does not necessarily imply rendition which would depend upon the obtaining of satisfactory guarantees. Such negotiations might also afford the opportunity for consideration of the violation of treaties like the cigarette taxes.

3. Rendition of court and surrender of extraterritoriality are not associated in the public mind and former would not therefore be taken as indicative of latter.

4. Court belongs to Chinese. We foreigners found it a derelict in 1911 and took possession of it. Chinese have never been reconciled to the seizure and the court's decisions are not recognized anywhere in China. If we returned the court the regard shown for China's rights would strengthen not weaken us in the assertion of our own treaty rights.

5. If it were certain that the Extraterritoriality Commission would meet this year I should be willing to renew the observation I made on circular number 69 in April 1923 [47] but the outlook for the meeting seems too dubious.

6. [Paraphrase.] Objections offered by members of the diplomatic corps in 1923 circular 69 appear to indicate greater concern for other interests than for the Mixed Court. This was especially true with respect to the British Minister. I had a conversation with him yesterday in which he admitted that political conditions had not improved, but said that, despite these conditions, longer experience as a Minister had strengthened his feeling of the importance of the rendition of the court. I also gathered that he had come to realize the unquestionable fact that, until this basic cause of Chinese resentment is removed, it will not be possible to secure any public improvement

---

[47] Not printed.

in Shanghai, which is dependent upon Chinese concurrence. [End paraphrase.]

7. The American consul general at Shanghai in despatch just mailed to the Department [48] strongly urges resumption rendition negotiations at earliest practicable moment. Among urgent reasons he advances are desirability of securing effect in other Chinese courts for the Mixed Court decisions and processes and hope that through rendition appeal court may be organized, lack of which is universally regretted and condemned. He also refers to the continual Chinese agitation for return of court especially in the matter of purely Chinese civil cases, which agitation negotiations will serve to appease.

8. [Paraphrase.] It would put the United States in an embarrassing and false position in China should our Government oppose negotiations for rendition of the Mixed Court. A policy of conciliation toward China has been adopted by Japan and, more recently, by Great Britain. As an example, note the way the British Minister has reversed himself in this matter. The Soviet Union also is now courting China and is casting odium upon the Chinese policy of other powers. To put ourselves in the position of leadership in a program with respect to the Mixed Court which would be denounced by many foreigners, as well as by the Chinese, as perpetuating an injustice to China, would be fatal to our policy and interests in this country. I am all the more earnest in urging a policy which I consider wise and just, as, in negotiations with the Minister for Foreign Affairs and other officials, as well as in public addresses, I have firmly insisted that China observe all our rights, especially the treaty rights which guarantee to our citizens their lives, liberty, and property. [End paraphrase.]

SCHURMAN

893.053 Sh/24 : Telegram

The Secretary of State to the Minister in China (Schurman)

WASHINGTON, *April 5, 1924—3 p. m.*

69. Your 89, March 22, 11 a. m. The Department regrets that the proposal to resume negotiations for the rendition of the Mixed Court seems to demand consideration at the present time by the Diplomatic Body and not to permit such further postponement as would enable a thorough survey of the Court's status to be made by the Extraterritoriality Commission, since such a survey would appear to form an important part of the work of that Commission. The Department,

---

[48] Not printed.

however, recognizes the force of your argument that this Government could not well take an isolated position in opposing the rendition of the Court even for a temporary period; and, in view of your statement that this matter would not be associated in the public mind with the surrender of extraterritoriality, you are authorized to join with your colleagues in negotiations looking toward rendition as outlined in your 75, March 11, 10 a.m., subject to the understanding that such negotiations are to be strictly limited to the question of the rendition of the Court, and that this Government is not prepared to make rendition conditional upon obtaining from the Chinese Government any benefits or concessions upon extraneous subjects such as the extension of the International Settlement or the development of the Shanghai Harbor even if such subjects appear to have a certain relation to the rendition of the Court in connection with a general adjustment of present Sino-foreign problems at Shanghai.

HUGHES

893.053Sh/27 : Telegram

The Secretary of State to the Minister in China (Schurman)

WASHINGTON, *May 23, 1924—3 p. m.*

108. Your despatch No. 2207 April 14.[49] The Chinese Minister under instructions from the Ministry of Foreign Affairs has informally inquired concerning the attitude of this Government with respect to making the resumption of negotiations for the return of the Mixed Court conditional upon the discussion of other extraneous questions at Shanghai as inferred from the Dean's note of April 10,[49] and has stated that Koo [50] is disposed to consider that the proposal for Settlement extension is in contravention of Article I of the Nine Power Treaty Relating to Principles and Policies concerning China.[51] The Minister was informed that, without passing on the merits of this contention, the Department desired to adhere to the position which it had consistently taken that the question of the Mixed Court should be kept free from extraneous matters, and had so instructed the Legation.

In order to dispel the misunderstanding which has arisen, it is suggested that you should, in such manner as seems most suitable, inform the Chinese Government of the position of this Government as stated in the Department's 69, March 22, 11 A. M. [*April 5, 3 p. m.*], at the same time informing your colleagues of your action.

HUGHES

---

[49] Not printed.
[50] V. K. Wellington Koo, Chinese Minister for Foreign Affairs.
[51] *Foreign Relations*, 1922, vol. I, p. 276.

893.053Sh/29 : Telegram

The Minister in China (Schurman) to the Secretary of State

Peking, *May 30, 1924—1 p. m.*

[Received 3 p. m.]

145. Your telegram number 108 of May 23, 3 p.m. On May 7th the Chinese Minister for Foreign Affairs questioned me regarding the dean's note of April 10th [52] and I assured him in the clearest terms that the note did not make the settlement of any extraneous questions a condition to the rendition of the Mixed Court and that if such had been the intention the draft would not have received unanimous approval. Dr. Koo stated that he had observed that the note was drawn up in this sense.

On May 28th I asked Koo why incident to above conversation he had telegraphed the Chinese Minister in the sense you indicate. He replied that his telegram was sent before our conversation and that my assurances had so far allayed his fears that he had materially modified his contemplated reply to the dean sent May 9th. This reply expressed the opinion of the Chinese Government that after the rendition of [sic] the three guarantees enumerated in the dean's note could be agreed to and indicated the Government's willingness to prepare for negotiations on the other subjects with a view to attaining a satisfactory result at an early date, provided such matters will contribute to Chinese and foreign welfare and can be put into practice without difficulty. I placed on May 14 on the circular transmitting this reply a notation again stating that the American Government desired forthcoming negotiations to be strictly limited to the rendition of the Court [53] and was "not prepared to make rendition conditional upon obtaining from the Chinese Government any benefits or concessions upon extraneous subjects."

I also concurred in the dean's opinion that the three guarantees enumerated in the dean's note of April 10 be given before rendition takes place. I explained the matter to the Chinese Chamber of Commerce in Shanghai and am confident that the Chinese Government and public thoroughly understand that the question of rendition will be decided on its own merits solely.

Schurman

---

[52] Not printed.

[53] Prolonged negotiations between the diplomatic corps and the Chinese Foreign Office and between the consular representatives at Shanghai and the Kiangsu provincial officials resulted in the signing of an agreement Dec. 31, 1926, for the rendition of the Shanghai Mixed Court.

FAILURE OF EFFORTS TO SECURE FROM THE INTERESTED POWERS A GENERAL ACCEPTANCE OF THE ARMS EMBARGO RESOLUTION PROPOSED AT THE WASHINGTON CONFERENCE [54]

893.113/745

The Chargé in Portugal (Carroll) to the Secretary of State

No. 896   LISBON, *September 15, 1924.*
                                              [Received October 6.]

SIR: Referring to my despatch No. 893, of August 27th, last,[55] and to previous correspondence concerning the attitude of the Portuguese Government in regard to the proposal for the modification of the terms of the existing embargo on the shipment of arms and munitions of war to China, I have the honor to transmit herewith copies in the original and in translation of a note from the Portuguese Foreign Office, dated September 12, 1924,[55] and received today, stating that the Portuguese Government approves the terms of the embargo and of the interpretative note of the diplomatic body in Peking,[56] and that it has instructed its representative in that capital to make known his readiness to accord the formal assent of his Government upon obtaining unanimity of action by the interested powers.

I have [etc.]   J. W. CARROLL

893.113/755

The British Ambassador (Howard) to the Secretary of State

No. 997   WASHINGTON, *October 24, 1924.*

SIR: I have the honour to inform you that the attention of His Majesty's Government has been called to the fact that military aircraft and machine guns were recently conveyed to Dairen by the French Mail steamer *Chantilly*, and are understood to have now been delivered at their destination. According to a report on the subject which appeared in the London *Times* on October 17th last this vessel, although a mail steamer, was actually diverted from her course for this purpose.

In the opinion of His Majesty's Government a grave breach of the whole spirit of the embargo agreement has thus been committed and the repetition of such incidents would exercise a most detrimental effect upon the adoption and enforcement of the Washington–Peking

---

[54] For previous correspondence regarding efforts by British and American Governments to secure acceptance of the arms embargo resolution, see *Foreign Relations, 1923,* vol. I, pp. 606 ff.
[55] Not printed.
[56] See telegram no. 405, Oct. 4, 1922, from the Minister in China, *Foreign Relations, 1922,* vol. I, p. 742.

resolution. In these circumstances, I have the honour to request that you will be so good as to bring the matter to the urgent attention of the competent United States authorities, and to enquire whether the United States Government would be prepared to instruct their Representative at Paris to associate himself with his British Colleague in addressing strong representations on the subject to the French Government.

I may add that according to the information at the disposal of His Majesty's Government, the Japanese Government have taken steps to prevent the delivery of anticipated further consignments via Dairen, and regret that the necessary precautions to this end were not taken at an earlier date.

I have [etc.]

(For the Ambassador)
H. G. CHILTON

893.113/757

The British Ambassador (Howard) to the Secretary of State

No. 1014   WASHINGTON, *October 29, 1924.*

SIR: I have the honour to refer to the note which you were so good as to address to Mr. Chilton on October 17th, 1923,[57] and to previous correspondence regarding the embargo upon the export of arms and munitions of war to China, and to inform you, by direction of Mr. Secretary MacDonald, that His Majesty's Government feel that the time is now ripe for the definite adoption by the signatory powers of the revised Arms Embargo resolution proposed at the Washington Conference, and of certain portions of the interpretative note. As you are aware, this resolution provides for the prohibition of the export of arms or munitions of war, whether complete or in parts, to China, while the interpretative note appended thereto further provides for the prohibition of the export of aircraft other than commercial aircraft, together with machinery and materials destined exclusively for the manufacture of arms or the equipment of arsenals. You will further be aware that the only Powers of importance who have not yet accepted the whole resolution in principle are now the Netherlands, Norway and Sweden.

Mr. Secretary MacDonald has lately been in consultation with the competent departments of His Majesty's Government in regard to the action which it would be necessary to take to enforce the Washington resolution above-mentioned, and in the circumstances, I have been instructed to furnish you with the following explanation of the position of my Government in the matter. By means of

---

[57] *Foreign Relations*, 1923, vol. I, p. 613.

an Order in Council dated December 13th, 1921, copies of which are enclosed herein for facility of reference,[58] the export of the arms and munitions of war enumerated therein is already prohibited to all destinations except under licence from the Board of Trade, who will continue to refuse to issue licences for the export of such goods to China. As regards the export of aircraft and parts thereof as mentioned in the interpretative note, I would state that although there is at present no restriction upon the export of aeroplanes from the United Kingdom, His Majesty's Government are prepared to take the necessary steps to obtain the addition of the words "aircraft and component parts thereof" to the Order in Council referred to above. In order, however, that the export of aircraft to countries other than China may suffer no interference, His Majesty's Government propose to issue through the Board of Trade a general licence permitting aircraft to be exported freely to countries other than China.

As regards machinery and materials destined for warlike purposes, also referred to in the interpretative note, His Majesty's Government do not consider it possible to prohibit the export of "machinery destined exclusively for the manufacture of arms or the equipment of arsenals," as in the opinion of my Government this would not only be impossible to administer but also it is very doubtful whether they have the power to prohibit the exportation of such machinery, in view of the provisions of Section 8 of the Customs and Inland Revenue Act, 1879, as amended by Section 17 of the Finance Act, 1921. His Majesty's Government desire me to point out, however, that materials so destined are already very largely covered by the list of articles specifically prohibited to be exported by the Order in Council of December 13th, 1921.

In so far as my Government are concerned, therefore, the situation is that they are now in a position practically to enforce the Washington resolution and a considerable portion of the interpretative note. Consequently, now that sufficient unanimity has been reached among the signatories of the Embargo Agreement, I have been instructed to enquire whether the United States Government, assuming that they are prepared, if they have not done so already, to adopt equivalent administrative measures themselves, would be disposed to make formal proposals to the various governments concerned for the adoption, from January 1st, 1925, of the Washington resolution and of at least so much of the interpretative note as His Majesty's Government are able to enforce. In this connection, I would add that my Government, although, as has been explained above, unable to enforce the portion of the interpretative note re-

---

[58] Not printed.

lating to machinery destined exclusively for the manufacture of arms or the equipment of arsenals, will nevertheless continue to discourage transactions coming under this heading, on the understanding that the other governments concerned do likewise. The Governments of His Majesty's Dominions overseas and the Government of India are prepared to take corresponding action. In conclusion I would state that if the other governments concerned express their willingness to adopt the resolution and to take steps to enforce it, the necessary additions will be made to the Order in Council of 1921.

I request that I may be favoured at an early date with an expression of the views of the United States Government upon the matters dealt with in this note.

I have [etc.] ESME HOWARD

893.113/755

The Secretary of State to the British Ambassador (Howard)

WASHINGTON, *November 11, 1924.*

EXCELLENCY: I have the honor to acknowledge the receipt of your Note, No. 997 of October 24, 1924, in which you state that the attention of the British Government has been called to the fact that military aircraft and machine guns were recently conveyed to Dairen by the French Mail steamer *Chantilly*, and inquire whether this Government would be prepared to instruct its representative at Paris to associate himself with his British Colleague in addressing strong representations on the subject to the French Government.

This Government shares the view of the British Government that, if the report appearing in the London *Times* of October 17 last is based on fact, a serious contravention of the Arms Embargo Agreement has occurred. Similar press reports have reached this Government, but they have not as yet been officially confirmed. The American Chargé d'Affaires ad interim in Paris is, nevertheless, being instructed to discuss the matter with his British Colleague.

Accept [etc.] CHARLES E. HUGHES

893.113/769 : Telegram

The Chargé in France (Whitehouse) to the Secretary of State

[Extract—Paraphrase]

PARIS, *November 14, 1924—4 p. m.*

[Received 10:15 p. m.[59]]

502. . . . It seems evident that with the present definition for commercial aircraft the French have not broken the letter of the

---

[59] Telegram in 3 sections.

law and for that reason no purpose would be served by further representations. Phipps, the British Minister, concurs with this opinion. It would take too much time to secure the adoption of a different definition of commercial aircraft. I told Phipps that the only solution I could see to serve the purpose would be for all the interested powers to adopt an agreement embargoing the shipment of airplanes of any kind to China until political conditions there cleared up.

I told Phipps that the above was merely my own suggestion and I did not at all know whether you would be inclined to accept it. Phipps seemed to think that the British Government would be willing to adopt such a proposal should you make it.

Although I have not sounded the French, I think they might agree if the suggestion is practicable and if it is clearly understood that it is a temporary measure. Another possible way to meet the situation would be to point out to the French Government that the purchases are obviously made for military reasons, as commercial aviation does not exist in China, and to ask them therefore to get their manufacturers to postpone delivery.

WHITEHOUSE

893.113/776

The Chargé in Denmark (Harriman) to the Secretary of State

No. 796   COPENHAGEN, *November 17, 1924.*
[Received December 3.]

SIR: In reply to the Department's Instruction No. 226, of August 13th last,[60] in which reference is made to an Instruction dated October 17, 1923,[61] requesting this Legation to communicate to the Danish Foreign Office the views of the United States Government with respect to the proposed modification of the terms of the existing embargo on the shipment of arms and munitions of war to China, and to express the hope of the Government of the United States that the Danish Government would approve the terms of the modified embargo, I have the honor to enclose, herewith, copy and translation of a Note from the Royal Danish Foreign Office, dated November 6, 1924, setting forth the views of the Danish Government in regard to this matter.

I have [etc.]   OLIVER B. HARRIMAN

---

[60] Not printed.
[61] See *Foreign Relations*, 1923, vol. I, p. 614, footnote 45.

[Enclosure—Translation 62]

*The Danish Minister for Foreign Affairs (Moltke) to the American
Chargé (Harriman)*

COPENHAGEN, *November 6, 1924.*

MR. CHARGÉ D'AFFAIRES: By a note dated November 5, 1923, you
were good enough to submit to the Royal Government an interpretation of the draft resolution in regard to the prohibition of the importation of arms and munitions into China, presented at the
Washington Conference, and discussed at a meeting of the Chiefs
of Mission at Peking on October 3, 1922. At the same time you
informed my predecessor that your Government intended to advise
its Minister at Peking that it would be ready to adhere formally
to the resolution, as well as to the interpretation, on the condition
that there should be substantial unanimity on the subject between
the powers represented at Peking.

In making this communication you expressed the hope that the
Danish Government might find it possible to instruct its representative at Peking in a similar sense.

By a note of September 10th last, Mr. Prince 63 subsequently advised my Government that the United States Government would appreciate being informed without delay as to the point of view of the
Royal Government with regard to this question.

After having had recourse to the competent authorities, I have
the honor to inform you as follows:

The Royal Government shares warmly the general desire to see
normal conditions reestablished in China. For that same reason
it adhered in due course without hesitation to the agreement of
1919, within the limits permitted by legislation.

The Danish Government considers it of great importance that the
arrangement eventually adopted on the subject in question shall
obtain the approval of all the powers whose adherence would have
real importance for its efficacy.

The Royal Government has subjected the draft resolution discussed at the Washington Conference to a thorough examination,
and, as far as it is concerned, would see with much pleasure a sufficiently general support of the resolution in order to attain the
object sought.

The interpretation of the draft discussed at the meeting of the
Chiefs of Mission at Peking on October 3, 1922, does not conform
to the Danish laws now in force. However, the reports of the

---

62 File translation revised.
63 John D. Prince, Minister in Denmark.

King's Minister at Peking have given the Royal Government the impression that some doubt has arisen as to the results of that meeting, inasmuch as there is some uncertainty as to whether the interpretation in question can be adopted to an extent necessary to insure its efficacy. The Ministry for Foreign Affairs has again requested information from the Royal Legation at Peking on that point.

The Royal Government would, however, be disposed—on the condition that all the other powers interested adopt an analogous position—to adhere, in conformity with the recommendation voted by the Chiefs of Mission at Peking on February 9, 1923, to the resolution proposed at the Washington Conference without interpretation, with the reservation, however, that airplanes be excluded insofar as the regulations in force governing the prohibition of exportation in Denmark are concerned.

Please accept [etc.]   C. MOLTKE

893.113/772

The British Ambassador (Howard) to the Secretary of State

No. 1127   WASHINGTON, *November 20, 1924.*

SIR: I have the honour to refer to your note of the 11th instant, in which you were so good as to inform me that the United States Chargé d'Affaires ad interim in Paris had been instructed to discuss with his British colleague the question of the alleged breach of the Arms Embargo Agreement by the French mail steamer *Chantilly.* I now understand from His Majesty's Government that the United States Chargé d'Affaires in Paris is suggesting to you that, for the purpose of arresting the export of a large number of aircraft recently ordered in France, a gentleman's agreement should be negotiated between the United States Government, the French Government and His Majesty's Government, prohibiting absolutely the export of all aircraft to China during the present revolutionary disturbances in that country.

His Majesty's Government have instructed me to inform you that they welcome this proposal and would be prepared to co-operate with the United States Government in the event of their deciding to approach the French Government to this end. His Majesty's Government feel that it might be desirable to include other governments in such an agreement, for example, the Japanese and Italian Governments.

I should be grateful if you would inform me in due course of the views of the United States Government in this matter and as to the inclusion of other governments in such an agreement.

I have [etc.]   ESME HOWARD

893.113/780

The Chargé in the Netherlands (Sussdorff) to the Secretary of State

No. 367   THE HAGUE, *November 20, 1924.*
                                    [Received December 8.]
SIR: With reference to the Department's unnumbered Instruction of October 17, 1923,[64] and to the Legation's despatch No. 340, of September 15, 1924,[65] I have the honor to inform the Department that I have just received a Note from the Netherlands Minister for Foreign Affairs in which he outlines the views of his Government with respect to the proposed modification of the terms of the existing embargo on the shipment of arms and munitions of war to China. A copy and translation of the Foreign Minister's communication is enclosed herewith.

I have [etc.]   LOUIS SUSSDORFF, Jr.

[Enclosure—Translation [66]]

The Netherland Minister for Foreign Affairs (Karnebeek) to the American Chargé (Sussdorff)

THE HAGUE, *November 18, 1924.*
MR. CHARGÉ D'AFFAIRES: In his note no. 87, of November 2, 1923, His Excellency Mr. Tobin,[67] was good enough to bring to my attention the desire of the American Government that the Government of the Queen should approve the amended draft resolution concerning the embargo on the shipment of arms and munitions of war to China (draft presented to the Washington Conference), with a subsequent interpretative note adopted by the diplomatic corps at Peking on October 3, 1922.

In reply, I have the honor to inform you that, as the Netherlands Delegation to the Washington Conference has already pointed out, the legislation of the Netherlands relating to trade in arms and munitions does not permit an embargo on exports to other countries of the articles mentioned in the interpretative note of the diplomatic corps at Peking which is referred to above. Moreover, Her Majesty's Government wonders whether it is opportune at the present moment to extend the scope of the draft resolution of Washington, inasmuch as, according to information in the possession of the Royal Government, this draft, even in its most limited original form, has not yet been adopted by all the interested States. And one is justified in wondering whether the anticipated action is desirable at the present

---

[64] See *Foreign Relations*, 1923, vol. I, p. 614, footnote 45.
[65] Not printed.
[66] File translation revised.
[67] Richard M. Tobin, Minister in the Netherlands.

moment when, it seems, important shipments of arms and munitions of all kinds continue to be forwarded to China from all sides. On the other hand, the Government of the Queen is in principle disposed to cooperate as far as possible towards any project which would offer serious international guarantees of success.

Please accept [etc.]   KARNEBEEK

893.113/793

The Chargé in Sweden (Gittings) to the Secretary of State

[Extract]

No. 319   STOCKHOLM, *December 1, 1924.*
[Received December 17.]

SIR: With reference to this Legation's despatch No. 272 of September 10, 1924,[68] and previous correspondence concerning the proposed modification of the terms of the existing embargo on the shipment of arms and munitions of war to China (as set forth in the Department's unnumbered instruction of October 17, 1923 [69]), I have the honor to transmit, as enclosures, in the original French text and in translation, the reply of the Royal Swedish Ministry for Foreign Affairs, dated November 26, 1924.

.   .   .   .

I have [etc.]   JOHN STERETT GITTINGS, Jr.

[Enclosure—Translation [70]]

The Swedish Minister for Foreign Affairs (Undén) to the American Chargé (Gittings)

STOCKHOLM, *November 26, 1924.*

MR. CHARGÉ D'AFFAIRES: In a letter of November 6, 1923,[68] Mr. Cord Meyer, then Chargé d'Affaires ad interim of the United States, was good enough to inform the Minister for Foreign Affairs that the Government of the United States had notified its Peking representative of its acceptance of the resolutions discussed by the diplomatic corps in Peking in a meeting held on October 3, 1922, concerning the embargo on the export of arms and munitions destined for China. These recommendations were based, according to the letter in question, on the adhesion of the powers represented in Peking to the amended project of the resolution on this subject presented on January 31, 1922, to the Washington Conference, and to a more ex-

---

[68] Not printed.
[69] See *Foreign Relations*, 1923, vol. I, p. 614, footnote 45.
[70] File translation revised.

tensive interpretative formula of this project of which the letter contained the text.

At the same time Mr. Cord Meyer expressed the hope of his Government that the Swedish Government would find itself in a position to give to its representative in Peking instructions in the same sense.

The question having been subjected to a thorough study, I find myself to-day able to communicate to you the following:

The Swedish Government is fully convinced of the extreme importance of the reestablishment in China of a normal situation, and is willing to believe that measures having for their object the effective prevention of the importation of arms and munitions into that country cannot fail to contribute to that end. It will therefore not refuse, on condition that all the interested powers do likewise, to adhere in equal degree to the aforementioned project of resolution, presented to the Washington Conference. It is also disposed, subject, to the same condition, to join in the recommendation adopted on February 9, 1923,[71] by the Chiefs of Mission at Peking, which has for its object extending the projected resolution aforementioned to cover aircraft other than commercial aircraft.

As to the far greater extension of the prohibition of export set forth in the meeting of October 3, 1922, this would not be in accordance with the dispositions of Swedish law and so the Swedish Government does not find itself in a position to acquiesce therein. It would, moreover, feel itself less warranted in doing so in view of the fact that the reports concerning the deliberations of Washington and Peking and information received from still other sources scarcely permit a full reliance on a general adhesion to such an extension by the powers concerned.

The Swedish Government, at this juncture, permits itself to call your attention to the fact that an additional conference, summoned for the purpose of studying the question, is about to meet in Geneva next year. And it wonders, inasmuch as the prohibition of export of arms and munitions to China does not seem on the whole to have had the desired efficacy up to the present, whether it would not be better to submit the question in hand for study by that conference.

Pray accept [etc.] ÖSTEN UNDEN

893.113/784

The British Ambassador (Howard) to the Secretary of State

No. 1205 WASHINGTON, *December 10, 1924.*

SIR: I have the honour to refer to my note No. 1127 of the 20th ultimo in which I informed you that His Majesty's Government

---

[71] See telegram no. 46, Feb. 9, from the Minister in China, *Foreign Relations,* 1923, vol. I, p. 606.

would be prepared to co-operate with the United States Government in the event of their deciding to adopt the proposal submitted to them by the United States Chargé d'Affaires in Paris suggesting that for the purpose of arresting the export of a large number of aircraft recently ordered in France, a gentleman's agreement should be negotiated between the United States Government, the French Government and His Majesty's Government, prohibiting absolutely the export of all aircraft to China during the present revolutionary disturbances in that country.

His Majesty's Government now inform me that they are desirous of ascertaining at an early date whether the United States Government are disposed to adopt the proposal in question, and in the affirmative event, I am instructed to enquire whether the United States Government would be prepared to consider the possibility of giving greater efficacy to the suggested agreement by including in it other aircraft-producing Powers, irrespective as to whether or no such Powers are already parties to the existing agreement enforcing the embargo upon the export of arms to China.

I have [etc.]

(For the Ambassador)
H. G. CHILTON

893.113/784

The Secretary of State to the British Ambassador (Howard)

WASHINGTON, *December 20, 1924.*

EXCELLENCY: With reference to your notes No. 1127 of November 20, 1924, and No. 1205 of December 10, 1924, in which you refer to a suggestion made by the American Chargé d'Affaires at Paris that an informal understanding should be negotiated between the American, British, and French Governments prohibiting absolutely the export of any kind of aircraft to China during the present revolutionary disturbances in that country, and stating that the British Government would welcome such a proposal and would be prepared to cooperate with this Government in the event of its deciding to approach the French Government to this end, I have the honor to inform you that this Government would be happy to inquire of the French Government whether it would be receptive to a proposal to the effect that the interested Powers agree to restrain their citizens and subjects from exporting any kind of aircraft to China in so far as their respective laws and regulations will permit.

This Government appreciates that the qualified character of the proposal as herein set forth may fall short of the absolute degree of prohibition which the British Government appears to have in mind. For its own part, however, this Government would, under existing legislation, find it difficult to obligate itself in the matter without reservation concerning the legal limitations of its competence with regard to the export of aircraft. In this connection, there is enclosed herewith a copy of the Joint Resolution of January 31, 1922,[73] and of the Presidential Proclamation of March 4, 1922,[74] issued pursuant thereto, under the provisions of which this Government is restraining its citizens from the export of arms and munitions of war to China. As a matter of actual practice, however, I may state that, for a period of over two years, this Government has discouraged (with entire success, as it understands) the exportation of any kind of aircraft to China, since it appears that, at the present time, there is no such thing as commercial aviation in China and that shipments of this character almost invariably are found to fall into the hands of militarists and to be used by them for military purposes.

The suggestion of the American Chargé d'Affaires at Paris, to which you refer, related to an agreement regarding aircraft by all the interested Powers rather than merely by the three Powers named in your notes. In the opinion of this Government, the participation of France in such an agreement is of particular importance; and, should the French Government indicate a willingness to accede to such a proposal, this Government would be glad to join with the British and French Governments in giving immediate effect to an agreement of the nature above indicated and to cooperate in afterward extending its scope so as to include as many as possible of the other Powers whose adherence might be deemed desirable.

I shall be glad if you will inform me of the attitude of the British Government toward such a proposal, and whether it will be disposed to instruct its representative at Paris to cooperate in sounding the French Government with regard thereto.

Accept [etc.] CHARLES E. HUGHES

893.113/787

The Secretary of State to the British Ambassador (Howard)

WASHINGTON, *December 24, 1924.*

EXCELLENCY: With reference to your note No. 1014 of October 29, 1924, concerning the China Arms Embargo Agreement in which you state that the British Government feels that the time is now ripe for

---

[73] See telegram no. 157, June 2, 1922, to the Ambassador in Great Britain, *Foreign Relations*, 1922, vol. I, p. 729.
[74] *Ibid.*, p. 726.

the definite adoption by the signatory Powers of the revised Arms Embargo resolution proposed at the Washington Conference, and of certain portions of the interpretative note recommended by the Diplomatic Body at Peking, I have the honor to inform you that this Government, in its desire to strengthen in every way the effectiveness of the embargo, has given most careful consideration to the suggestion made in your note that it should undertake to make formal proposals to the various governments concerned with a view to the adoption, from January 1, 1925, of the revised Washington Resolution and of at least so much of the interpretative note as the British Government is able to enforce.

With regard to the question of "substantial unanimity" in the adoption of the revised formula, on which this Government originally predicated its readiness to proceed in the matter, it appears that the governments of Norway, The Netherlands, and Brazil have not as yet signified their willingness to adopt the formula in question, and that the Government of Sweden is prepared to do so only in the event that all the other interested Powers adopt the formula and in equal degree with Sweden. It appears, moreover, that although the Danish Government is prepared to adopt the language of the revised Washington Resolution, it is not prepared to adopt the interpretative note, and desires to make the reservation that airplanes be excluded from the scope of the embargo in so far as concerns the regulations governing the prohibition of exportation in Denmark. In this connection, there is quoted the final paragraph of a note on the subject, dated November 17 [6], 1924, from the Danish Ministry of Foreign Affairs to the American Chargé d'Affaires at Copenhagen: [75]

"Le Gouvernement Royal serait cependant disposé—sous condition que tous les autres États interessés adoptent un procédé analogue—à adhérer, en conformité de la recommandation votée par les chefs de mission réunis à Pékin le 9 février 1923, à la résolution présentée à la Conférence de Washington sans interprétation, sous la réserve toutefois que les aéronefs ne sont pas compris par les règles concernant la prohibition d'exportation en vigueur en Danemark."

It is the understanding of this Government that the new formula is to be adopted in substitution for the Agreement of May, 1919;[76] for it would seem impracticable for the Powers to apply two varying formulae simultaneously. If the new formula were, therefore, to be

---

[75] For English text of note, see p. 535.
[76] See *Foreign Relations*, 1919, vol. I, pp. 667ff.

adopted at the present time, we should lose the adherence to the embargo of the Netherlands and Brazilian Governments, which are signatory to the Agreement of May, 1919; and we should have, on the part of Denmark, only a qualified adherence of substantially the same character as the 1919 Agreement.

With reference, moreover, to the question of the adoption of the new formula in its entirety, the British Government, as explained in your note under reference, finds itself unable to enforce the portion of the interpretative note relating to machinery destined exclusively for the manufacture of arms or the equipment of arsenals, although it is stated that transactions of this character will continue to be discouraged on the understanding that the other governments concerned do likewise. The situation confronting the British Government in this particular is similar to that in which this Government would find itself with respect to its strict legal authority to prohibit the export of materials and machinery destined exclusively for the manufacture of arms and the equipment of arsenals; although, as a matter of actual practice, this Government has, with a very fair degree of success, discouraged the shipment to China of exports of this character on the part of its nationals. It would seem, however, that, before definitely binding themselves to the new formula, it would be necessary for both the American and British Governments to qualify the acceptance on their part of a very considerable portion of the interpretative note.

From a survey of the actual working of the Agreement of May, 1919, it is the view of this Government that the precise formula in use has been of less importance than the intent and spirit of the various governments concerned in carrying out the Agreement entered into at that time. In spite of the infractions of the embargo which have occurred from time to time, this Government is of the opinion that the embargo has attained a measurable success, and it desires in every way to strengthen its effectiveness. In view, however, of the difficulties apparently to be met at the present time in substituting the revised Washington formula (with the interpretative note) for the Agreement of May, 1919, this Government questions whether any practical benefits would be derived from an attempt to do so until a more complete unanimity can be had among the interested Powers. I need hardly say that I regret that no greater success has thus far attended the efforts which have been made to procure substantial unanimity in this matter.

Accept [etc.]   CHARLES E. HUGHES

DECISION BY THE CONSORTIUM COUNCIL TO CONTINUE UNMODIFIED THE CONSORTIUM AGREEMENT OF OCTOBER 15, 1920, AFTER ITS EXPIRATION ON OCTOBER 15, 1925 [77]

893.51/4628

The American Group to the Secretary of State

NEW YORK, *June 12, 1924.*

[Received June 14.]

SIR: We hand you herewith copy of a memorandum prepared by one of the representatives of the British Group in Peking, in association with the Chairman of the British & Chinese Corporation, Ltd., together with copy of letter of May 23rd from Sir Charles Addis to Mr. C. F. Whigham. This memorandum is submitted to us by the British Group for consideration in advance of a meeting of the Consortium Council arranged to be held in London on July 14th, which will be attended by Mr. Lamont, Chairman of the American Group. We would appreciate very much any expression of opinion the Department may care to make on this memorandum, as of assistance to the American Group in discussing it at the proposed meeting.

We also enclose for the information of the Department a very brief suggestion from our Group of matters to be placed upon the agenda of the meeting.[78] If the Department has any suggestions in connection with any of these topics, they will be gratefully received.

Respectfully,

J. P. MORGAN & CO.
For the American Group

[Enclosure]

The Chairman of the British Group (Addis) to Mr. C. F. Whigham, Representative in London of the American Group

LONDON, *May 23, 1924.*

MY DEAR WHIGHAM: I understand that Mr. Lamont is expected here sometime in July and, if it would suit his convenience, I should propose to convene a meeting of the Consortium Council at this office for Monday, July 28.

As soon as we have agreed the date of the meeting with Lamont I should advise the other groups and invite them to give me as early notice as possible of any items they desire to place on the agenda.

---

[77] For text of the agreement, see *Foreign Relations,* 1920, vol. I, p. 576.
[78] Proposed agenda not printed.

I may take this opportunity of reminding you that the Consortium Agreement, which was for a period of five years, will expire in October, 1925. It may be expedient, therefore, at our meeting to consider in advance what step, if any, should be taken to provide for its renewal. It might take the form, for instance, of a resolution for its renewal without any limit of time, subject to the right of any Group to withdraw on giving six or twelve months' notice.

I have taken advantage of the return from China of Major Nathan, C. M. G., who has recently been appointed Chairman of the British and Chinese Corporation, and of the presence of Mayers, to ask them to formulate what in their view constitutes the chief difficulties in the way of industrial progress in China. I enclose an advance copy of the memorandum which they have prepared.

With the permission of my colleagues on the Council I should propose to ask these gentlemen to be present at our meeting in July for the purpose of answering any questions which the Council may wish to put to them. Their proposals, which, it will be noted, involve the elimination of Residuary Participation, are intended to secure greater individual freedom of action on the part of the Peking Representatives of the Consortium.

I reserve the expression of any opinion on the merits of the proposals until their authors have had an opportunity of explaining them to the Council.

As soon as the date of the meeting is fixed I propose to communicate a copy of the Memorandum to each of the other Groups who will, no doubt, wish to discuss this very important matter with their respective Governments.

Yours sincerely,

C. S. ADDIS

[Subenclosure]

Memorandum by Mr. S. F. Mayers, of the British Group in Peking, and Mr. W. S. Nathan, Chairman of the British and Chinese Corporation, Ltd.

LONDON, *May 12, 1924.*

LACK OF PROGRESS IN RAILWAY CONSTRUCTION

1. It is now two years since the Consortium recorded the view that there was no reason why the development of railways should wait on the solution of China's administrative problems.

2. During these two years the increase of disorder in China and the continued reluctance of the Government to seek assistance from the Consortium have rendered progress impossible.

3. We suggest that the time has arrived to bring to a test the question as to how far assistance from the Consortium, as at present constituted, is practicable.

CHINESE RELUCTANCE TO NEGOTIATE WITH THE CONSORTIUM

4. In the sphere of general debt consolidation the Chinese objections to dealing with the Consortium are apparently less pronounced than in the sphere of railway development. In the opinion of our representatives on the spot, the prospects of assistance from the Consortium being ultimately found practicable for financial or administrative loans are better than the prospects of making a Consortium loan for railway purposes.

5. The reason they assign for this is that the Chinese have less fear of losing their liberty of action by concluding a financial loan with an international combination such as the Consortium than they have of seeking from such a combination the funds needed for railway purposes. In the case of a financial loan the Chinese feel that once the security has been allocated and the arrangements made for its supervision by the Customs or Salt Revenue departments, there will be no marked increase in foreign control of their affairs. On the other hand, in the case of railway loans, they foresee serious administrative difficulties in entrusting to the nominees of a quadruple international body the increased foreign control of their railways which they know is inevitable if they are to regain the confidence of foreign investors.

DISSOLUTION OF THE CONSORTIUM UNDESIRABLE

6. The disordered condition of China, with the consequent lack of security, renders it difficult to see any advantage, at the present time, in considering either the dissolution of the Consortium or the separation of industrial or railway loans from the scope of its intended activities. If such loans were now thrown open to international competition, it is at least doubtful whether railway development would be accelerated. In any case, before such considerations are taken into account, it appears advisable to examine the possibility of making some progress by means of an understanding which would permit of greater liberty of action on the part of the individual Groups.

POSSIBILITY OF DEVELOPING EXISTING BRITISH-FINANCED RAILWAYS

7. The various existing railways, for example those in which the British Group is especially interested, viz. the Peking-Mukden, Tientsin-Pukow, Shanghai-Nanking, Shanghai-Hangchow-Ningpo and Canton-Kowloon lines, could each profitably employ a consider-

able amount of new capital; but the Ministry of Communications will not entertain any suggestion of a Consortium loan for these railways, and the Consortium Agreement precludes any proposal for public issues for these lines without participation being offered to the other groups. In these circumstances it would conduce to progress if the British Group were at liberty to arrange for the finance required by these existing railways without the obligation of offering participation to the other groups.

POSSIBILITY OF DEVELOPING OTHER EXISTING OR NEW RAILWAYS

8. As regards other existing railways, the Peking-Hankow and Peking Suiyuan lines are in urgent need of new capital for the payment of debts and for further development. We believe that an offer of a loan for the rehabilitation of these two railways would be welcomed by the Ministry of Communications, if means can be found to present such an offer in a manner acceptable to Chinese public opinion. We therefore suggest that, so soon as any one of the groups has decided on its ability to make such an offer, it should inform the other groups of its intention and proceed with negotiations individually.

9. Similarly, in the case of loans for the construction of new railways any group which is in a position to make proposals to the Ministry of Communications for the issue of a loan should be at liberty to do so individually, after informing the other groups of its intention.

10. In both of these cases it would be understood that upon signature of an agreement the group concerned would be bound to offer a share to any other group desirous of actual participation but without obligation to offer residuary participation.

PROPOSALS FOR GREATER INDIVIDUAL LIBERTY OF ACTION

11. In order to put the foregoing into concrete form, we suggest the adoption by the Consortium of a resolution on the following lines:—

With a view to giving effect to the opinion expressed in Article 12 of the Report of the Consortium Council dated May 1922, that the development of railways in China should not wait upon the solution of China's administrative problems it is resolved that:—

(a) With regard to existing railways in respect to which any group holds mortgage rights or rights in respect of further finance, such group shall be free to conclude agreements for the further finance of such railways by public issue without offering participation to other groups.

(*b*) With regard to other existing railways, new railways or industrial enterprises, any group which is in a position and desires to make a public issue shall be free, after informing the other groups, to negotiate and conclude agreements for such railways or enterprises either individually or with any other group or groups who are also in a position and desire to take their share of the public issue for the same purpose.

(*c*) It shall be understood that no negotiations for any one of the railways for which an agreement has been pooled by an individual group shall be initiated without the consent in writing of that group.

ALTERNATIVE PROPOSAL FOR INTER-GOVERNMENT NEGOTIATIONS

12. If, on the other hand, it is felt by all the groups that the principle of equal participation must be strictly maintained, it appears to us advisable to ask the four Governments to ascertain, either through their Ministers in Peking, or by sending a special mission to China, by what means and under what conditions the Chinese Government can be induced to agree to a Consortium loan for railways on the lines of equal participation contemplated by the Agreement. In the absence of an understanding between the Chinese Government on the one side and the Consortium Powers on the other, it appears to us improbable that the Consortium Agreement as it stands can be made operative for railway loans.

W. S. NATHAN
S. F. MAYERS

893.51/4628

The Secretary of State to the American Group

WASHINGTON, *June 26, 1924.*

SIRS: I have received the letter of June 12, 1924, with which you enclosed a copy of a memorandum prepared by Mr. S. F. Mayers, of the British Group in Peking, in association with Mr. W. S. Nathan, Chairman of the British and Chinese Corporation, Ltd., containing certain proposals in modification of the Consortium Agreement of October 15, 1920; also a copy of a letter dated May 23, 1924, relating to these proposals from Sir Charles Addis to Mr. C. F. Whigham.

In view of the fact that the existing Consortium Agreement will expire in October, 1925, the question has arisen of the advisability of continuing that Agreement and of the possible necessity of making arrangements in the near future to that end. I approve of the continued application to the field of Chinese finance of the principles which that Agreement embodies, namely, that loans made to

China should be based upon sound investments, and that this result should be assured by a mutual undertaking among the principal national financial groups to abstain from reckless competition. While it is no doubt true that the results of the past few years have been purely negative, and that it is of course impossible to appraise the value of such results, I nevertheless venture the opinion that, but for the existence of the Consortium during this period, the financial situation of the Chinese Government would present an even more difficult problem than it now does. I therefore see no occasion for dissatisfaction with the policy which has been followed, and I should welcome the making of arrangements to continue that policy substantially unmodified.

With regard to the proposals contained in the memorandum prepared by Mr. Mayers and Mr. Nathan, I am frankly disposed to concur in the criticism made by Mr. Anderson in his telegram to Mr. Lamont of June 14 (a copy of which was enclosed with Mr. Simpson's letter to Mr. MacMurray of June 16),[79] that these proposals "seem almost tantamount to abandoning Consortium principles entirely", at least in so far as concerns loans for industrial purposes. I am apprehensive that the adoption of the phraseology of Clause 11 of the memorandum would be likely to lead to misunderstandings among the several national groups of the Consortium, such as might tend to disrupt their unity of action and lead to a reversion to the former régime of nationalistic competition which it was the fundamental purpose of the Consortium to obviate.

It is possibly premature to make more detailed comment upon these proposals until Mr. Mayers and Mr. Nathan shall have had an opportunity to elaborate them at the meeting of the Consortium Council on July 14 next. If it is then felt that there is sufficient ground for their belief that the Chinese Government would be more readily inclined to negotiate with individual groups, it would seem that the modifications to the proposals, as outlined by Mr. Anderson in his telegram above mentioned, might afford a means of facilitating dealing with the Chinese Government and at the same time conserving the essential basis of principle animating the Consortium Agreement, in the event that it should still appear desirable, in spite of the progressive disintegration of the Chinese Government, that the development of railways should proceed without awaiting a solution of China's administrative problems.

---

[79] Not printed; the telegram referred to was sent from Paris by Mr. A. M. Anderson of the staff of the American group to Mr. Thomas W. Lamont, representative of the American group. Mr. Malcolm D. Simpson was secretary for the American group and Mr. John Van A. MacMurray was Chief of the Division of Far Eastern Affairs of the Department of State.

I have read with much interest the proposed agenda which you have submitted for the meeting of the Consortium Council in London on July 14, 1924.

I am [etc.]   CHARLES E. HUGHES

893.51/4668

The American Group to the Secretary of State

NEW YORK, *July 29, 1924.*
[Received July 30.]

SIR: We enclose, for the information and files of the Department, printed text of Minutes of the Meeting of the Consortium Council held in London on July 14th. . . .

Respectfully,

J. P. MORGAN & Co.
For the American Group

[Enclosure—Extracts]

Minutes of a Meeting of the Consortium Council Held July 14, 1924, in the Office of the Hongkong & Shanghai Banking Corporation, London

CONSORTIUM AGREEMENT. It was resolved [*It was agreed to rec-ommend*][80] that the Consortium Agreement of October 15, 1920, remain in force on and after October 15, 1925, subject to the right of any party thereto on or after October 15, 1924, to give twelve months' previous notice in writing addressed to the other parties thereto withdrawing from such Agreement, and on the expiration of such notice such party shall forthwith be released from all obligations incurred by him by reason or arising out of such Agreement, and shall cease to participate in any future rights, privileges and obligations thereunder.

.   .   .   .

RAILWAY DEVELOPMENT. At the invitation of the Council Major W. S. Nathan, C. M. G., and Mr. S. F. Mayers attended in person in support of their Joint Memorandum containing proposals for greater elasticity in the working of Railway loans.

It was decided to leave the Memorandum for further consideration in order to enable the writers to discuss further the proposed resolu-

---

[80] Corrected on the basis of a letter, dated Aug. 7, 1924, from the American group (file no. 893.51/4674).

tions therein contained with the object of meeting the views of the Delegates.

. . . .

CHINESE GROUP. Referring to the original declaration of the Consortium, made upon its meeting at New York, October 15, 1920, expressing its desire to receive co-operation from a Chinese Banking Group, it is the sense of the Council that the Peking Representatives of the Consortium be requested to consider again measures for undertaking at some appropriate moment conversations with Chinese Bankers in order to discuss possible means looking to the formation of a Representative Chinese Banking Group organised to co-operate with the Consortium.

The meeting then adjourned.

C. S. ADDIS
R. TH. DE LA CHAUME
THOMAS W. LAMONT
K. YANO

JOINT RESOLUTION OF CONGRESS AUTHORIZING THE PRESIDENT AT HIS DISCRETION TO REMIT TO CHINA FURTHER PAYMENTS ON THE BOXER INDEMNITY [81]

493.11/960a : Telegram

The Secretary of State to the Minister in China (Schurman)

WASHINGTON, *January 18, 1924—3 p. m.*

18. With reference to the Department's instruction No. 261 of August 1, 1921,[82] a joint resolution was introduced in the Senate on December 6, 1923, in language identical with that of the resolution introduced in 1921, authorizing the President in his discretion to remit the balance of the Boxer Indemnity, such remission to begin as from October 1, 1917, and to be at such times and in such manner as the President shall deem just. The Department, in view of the actual situation and present tendencies in China, desires your opinion as to what is likely to be the effect produced by the passage of this resolution both upon the minds of Chinese and Americans residing in China; also as to its bearing, beneficial or adverse, upon American interests in that country.

HUGHES

[81] For previous correspondence regarding the Boxer indemnity, see *Foreign Relations*, 1923, vol. I, pp. 592 ff.
[82] Not printed.

493.11/961 : Telegram

The Minister in China (Schurman) to the Secretary of State

PEKING, *January 21, 1924—2 p. m.*
[Received January 22—3 : 48 p. m.]

40. Your 18, January 18, 3 p. m.

1. As regards the policy of remitting to China the remainder of Boxer Indemnity permit me to say at once that I have been and am strongly in favor of it. This also the sentiment of overwhelming majority of Americans in China. In view of all the past American legislation and of utterances official and unofficial the Chinese also expect it though the Chinese Government has refrained from any allusion to the subject.

2. A practical difficulty at the present time is that there is no agency to receive the funds representing the Chinese people as a whole for whose benefit remission would be made here. From one-third to one-half of the provinces are independent of Peking Government. People of these provinces would have just ground for complaint if the benefits of the returned funds were monopolized by the rival if larger group of provinces which accept the Peking Government.

3. Another practical difficulty is that Peking Government is in desperate financial straits. It cannot collect taxes, yet military governors of the provinces and the other military commanders insist that it shall make them appropriations for their forces which are practically personal armies. Politicians too get public funds for their own purposes. If in these circumstances the remainder of the indemnity funds were liberated for the uncontrolled use of the Peking Government at the present time they would quickly disappear through these military and political channels greatly to the injury of the Chinese people. Both Chinese and Americans would however oppose an unconditional grant of the balance of the Boxer Indemnity funds to the Peking Government.

4. The time is inopportune for the enactment of the proposed legislation. Not only does the Chinese Government persist in its refusal to pay loans and debts to American citizens, not only were American ships engaged in lawful traffic last season on the Yangtze fired on, but today American treaty rights in regard to trade and commerce are violated in several provinces and 6 American missionaries within the last 60 days have been attacked or carried off or murdered by bandits or soldiers. Against these enormities the American Government has protested. The display at this juncture of the generosity and friendship towards China contemplated in the joint resolution introduced in the Senate December 6, 1923, could

not fail seriously to weaken the force of these protests both with the Chinese Government and the Chinese public opinion.

5. If the passage of the joint resolution involves the relinquishment by the United States of the position it has maintained in relation to the Chinese Maritime Customs since the indemnity was imposed upon China in 1901, I should consider this result under existing conditions in China gravely detrimental to Chinese interests. China must soon face the great issues of unification, stabilization of government, financial rehabilitation, disbandment of troops, etc., and she will need the help of America. Until these questions are disposed of America should not either in her own interest or in the interest of China part with any of the leverage she now enjoys in common with other nations. In comparison with the British, French and Japanese our diplomatic position has already been impaired by our nonparticipation in the control of the salt revenues. To turn over to these nations the power and influence we now share with them in connection with the customs revenues would be a fatal mistake.

6. There is an inherent difficulty in combining with an unconditional act of grace like the remission of the remainder of the indemnity some stipulation or at least understanding with regard to the uses to which the funds shall be put. Though it was overcome in 1908 it would be much more difficult to overcome today in a divided China with an impotent government and a racially self-conscious people. Yet the great majority of Americans in China and practically all thoughtful Chinese insist on this feature as an essential part of the program for the remission of the remainder of the indemnity. This is therefore an additional consideration in favor of delay.

7. In connection with this subject I have the honor to refer to my despatch number 1793 dated August 29, 1923.[83]

8. Warmly as I support the policy of remitting the indemnity I am of the opinion for the reasons set forth that the best interests both of the United States and of China demand that for the present the matter should be left *in statu quo* and that American guardianship of the funds should continue unimpaired.

SCHURMAN

493.11/961

The Secretary of State to the Minister in China (Schurman)

No. 638   WASHINGTON, *April 22, 1924.*

SIR: With reference to the Legation's telegram No. 40 of January 21, 2 p. m., concerning the proposed remission of the Boxer Indem-

---

[83] Not printed.

nity, there is enclosed herewith, for the information of the Legation, a copy of the "Hearings before the Committee on Foreign Affairs, House of Representatives, on H. J. Res. 201",[84] which provides for the remission of the balance of the Indemnity.

Your views with respect to the advisability of such action at the present time received most careful consideration. The legislative aspect of the situation, however, was such as seemed to present the immediate alternatives of supporting the Resolution at the present time, and opposing its passage—a course which appeared likely to defeat entirely the policy of remission. While fully appreciating the force of your views as to the danger of misconstruction which might be placed by the Chinese upon such action by this Government at the present time, I therefore deemed it preferable to give my support to the Resolution, and instructed the Chief of the Far Eastern Division to appear before the House Committee for this purpose.

　I am [etc.]　　　　　　　　　　　　　　　CHARLES E. HUGHES

493.11/997

The Secretary of State to the Chinese Minister (Sze)

WASHINGTON, *June 14, 1924.*

SIR: I have the honor to enclose herewith a copy of an act of Congress, approved May 21, 1924, whereby the President is authorized, in his discretion, to remit to China the balance of the Boxer Indemnity, such remission to begin as from October 1, 1917, and to be at such times and in such manner as the President shall deem just, the intent of the Congress, as stated in the preamble to the Act, being further to develop the educational and other cultural activities of China.

　Accept [etc.]　　　　　　　　　　　　　　CHARLES E. HUGHES

[Enclosure]

Joint Resolution of Congress, Approved May 21, 1924, Providing for the Remission of Further Payments of the Annual Installments of the Chinese Indemnity

WHEREAS by authority of a joint resolution of Congress approved May 25, 1908,[85] the President of the United States was authorized to remit unto China the sum of $11,961,121.76 of the Boxer indemnity fund accredited to the United States, which sum the President on December 28, 1908, duly remitted and which, at the request of China, was specified to be used for educational purposes; and

---

[84] 68th Cong., 1st sess.; not printed.
[85] *Foreign Relations*, 1908, p. 65.

WHEREAS it is deemed proper as a further act of friendship to remit the balance of said indemnity fund amounting to $6,137,552.90 in order further to develop the educational and other cultural activities of China: Now therefore be it

Resolved by the Senate and House of Representatives of the United States of America in Congress assembled, That the President is hereby authorized, in his discretion, to remit to China as an act of friendship any or all further payments of the annual installments of the Chinese indemnity due under the bond received from China pursuant to the protocol of September 7, 1901,[86] as modified by Executive order on the 28th day of December, 1908,[87] pursuant to the authority of the joint resolution of Congress approved May 25, 1908, for indemnity against losses and expenses incurred by reason of the so-called Boxer disturbances in China during the year 1900, such remission to begin as from October 1, 1917, and to be at such times and in such manner as the President shall deem just.

493.11/1014

The Chinese Minister (Sze) to the Secretary of State

WASHINGTON, *June 14, 1924.*

SIR: I have the honor to acknowledge the receipt of your note of June 14th, 1924, in which you are good enough to convey to me the welcome information that the President has approved the Joint Resolution passed by the American Congress to provide for the remission of further payments of the annual installments of the Chinese indemnity. I hasten to express to you the thanks of the Government and people of China for this signal proof of American friendship for China. The Chinese Nation will ever hold this generous action on the part of the United States in grateful remembrance.

The first remission by the American Government in 1908 enabled the Chinese Government to devote the annual payments of the indemnity thus set free to educational purposes. The results of the experiment have convinced the Chinese Government of the wisdom of the step taken in this direction. It is the purpose of the Chinese Government to continue the policy with the further payments remitted by the present act of the American Government with such modifications as experience and the demands of the times may dictate. As the demand for scientific education has in recent years been increasingly urgent in China my Government now proposes to devote the funds thus made available by the generosity of the

---

[86] *Ibid.,* 1901, Appendix (Affairs in China), p. 312.
[87] *Ibid.,* 1908, p. 72.

American Government to educational and cultural purposes, paying especial attention to scientific requirements. Moreover, it is the intention of my Government to intrust the administration of the funds to a Board which shall be composed of Chinese and American citizens as members, and also to avail itself of the services of experts in working out the details along the lines indicated. Upon the formulation of some definite plan I shall take pleasure in laying it before you for your consideration.

Accept [etc.]   SAO-KE ALFRED SZE

493.11/1015

The Chinese Minister (Sze) to the Secretary of State

WASHINGTON, *June 14, 1924.*

SIR: I have the honor to inform you that I have received a cable message addressed by the President of the Republic of China to the President of the United States of America,[88] the text of which is enclosed herewith.

I shall be greatly obliged if you will be so kind as to transmit the message to its high destination.

Accept [etc.]   SAO-KE ALFRED SZE

[Enclosure—Telegram]

The President of China (Tsao Kun) to President Coolidge [89]

MR. PRESIDENT: I consider it a privilege to bespeak, on behalf of my fellow citizens, to Your Excellency and the people of the United States our sincere appreciation of the generosity shown in the remission of their portion of the 1901 indemnity. The remission of a part of this indemnity in 1908 contributed much to the special friendliness toward the people of the United States, which had developed in the hearts of the Chinese people ever since the beginning of intercourse between our two peoples. The present action will still further increase the friendliness, and Your Excellency's Government have thus placed the people of China under an endless debt of gratitude to the people of the United States.

TSAO KUN

---

[88] On the same day the Chinese Minister transmitted a similar expression of appreciation from the Chinese Minister for Foreign Affairs to the Secretary of State (file no. 493.11/1016).

[89] Acknowledgment of this message was transmitted in telegram no. 134, June 28, 1924, to the Minister in China (file no. 493.11/1045a).

493.11/1103a

The Secretary of State to President Coolidge

WASHINGTON, *December 15, 1924.*

MY DEAR MR. PRESIDENT: I have the honor to invite your attention at this time to the matter of the exercise of your authority in remitting to China the balance of the Boxer Indemnity. This remission is to be in accordance with the provisions of the Joint Resolution of May 21, 1924, (a copy of which is enclosed),[90] at such times and in such manner as you shall deem just.

The steps heretofore taken are these: On June 14 the Department transmitted to the Chinese Minister in Washington a copy of the Joint Resolution. Mr. Sze then stated that his Government intended to intrust the administration of the funds to a Board which should be composed of Chinese and American citizens, to avail itself of the services of experts in working out the details of this arrangement, and, upon the formulation of a definite plan, to lay it before the Department for its consideration. In pursuance of this plan, Doctor Paul Monroe, Director of the Teachers College of Columbia University, proceeded to Peking last August at the instance of the Chinese Government, and held conferences with Chinese officials and educators. As a result of conclusions thereby reached, a Presidential Mandate was issued on September 17, creating the "China Foundation for the Promotion of Education and Culture," and appointing nine Chinese and five American citizens members of the Foundation and trustees of the funds to be realized from the successive remissions of the balance of the Indemnity. It is my understanding that, by this action, the Chinese Government definitely divorced itself from any future control or supervision over the funds of the Indemnity, surrendering the authority, which it would otherwise normally exercise, to the Foundation, which, under the terms of its constitution is a self-perpetuating body.

While not undertaking to give formal approval to the measures which the Chinese Government has thus far adopted, the Department has made known to the Minister of Foreign Affairs that it perceived no objection to the personnel of the Board of Trustees. Before, however, venturing to recommend to you affirmative action on this matter, it has seemed to me highly desirable, and perhaps essential, that this Government should receive some reasonably definite statement as to the general purposes to which the Foundation contemplates devoting the Indemnity funds. While appreciating that the determination of the specific uses of the funds within its control will perhaps form the most important function of the Board of

---

[90] *Ante,* p. 554.

Trustees, and not desiring inappropriately to circumscribe its latitude of action, I have felt that this Government might subject itself to criticism, were it not to require some such statement as I have indicated, in order that there may be an assurance that the funds will actually be expended in conformity with the intent of the Congress. With a view to providing a satisfactory formula, there has been informally suggested to me the following Resolution:

"That the Board of Trustees of the China Foundation for the promotion of Education and Culture resolves that the released Boxer Indemnity funds shall be used for the promotion of scientific study, for the application of modern science to the specific needs of China, and for the training of individuals and the conduct of experiment, either individual or group, for the application of modern science to the specific conditions of China."

The language of this resolution appears to me quite satisfactory, but before proceeding further with respect to this question I should like to have your views. Should the course suggested meet with your approval, I shall be glad to take such further action as will, within the near future, I hope, enable the Department formally to submit to you its recommendations.

There are certain other facts in our relations with China, which, although not directly connected with the question of the remission of the Indemnity, nevertheless seem to me to deserve consideration simultaneously. There have been within the last few years numerous instances in China of assaults and depredations by Chinese bandits and soldiers upon the persons and property of American citizens. In a majority of these cases, the Department has had reason to hold that the outrages, as well as the failure to take steps properly to punish those guilty of them, were due to the negligence of the Chinese Government; and, as a result, numerous claims for damages have been presented to that Government, a large portion of which remain unsatisfied.

I also regret to be obliged to bring to your attention the further fact that, in order to tide over financial emergencies in the last few years in connection with the maintenance of Chinese students in this country, representatives of the Chinese Government in Washington have borrowed from local banks amounts aggregating approximately $180,000, which sums, although long overdue, have not as yet been repaid. These banks have sought to have a sufficient sum to cover these obligations retained from any funds that may be remitted to China. The Department has, however, taken the position that these loans, from a strictly legal point of view, are on the same basis as any other financial obligation of the Chinese Government to American citizens, and that it could not recommend the action desired by the banks without, at the same time, discriminating against numerous American creditors of the Chinese Government, the total of whose overdue obligations far exceeds the amount involved in the remission of the Indemnity.

In both of the above classes of claims against the Chinese Government, I am, however, of the opinion that not only a legal, but a particular moral, obligation rests upon the Chinese Government to pay those American citizens whose interests are suffering by reason of a failure to liquidate their just claims. At the moment this Government is demonstrating its friendship for China by the return of the Indemnity, it would seem peculiarly fitting for the Government of that country to make an endeavor to satisfy these claims.

I therefore propose, if it meets with your approval to make these views known to the Chinese Government in such manner as may seem most appropriate for the purpose of bringing those now in authority in that country to a realization of the peculiar obligation resting upon the Chinese Government promptly to meet its commitments to American citizens of the character which I have described.

Faithfully yours,

CHARLES E. HUGHES

CONCURRENCE BY THE UNITED STATES IN THE CONTENTION BY CERTAIN POWERS THAT THE BOXER INDEMNITY PAYMENTS SHOULD BE MADE IN GOLD CURRENCY[91]

493.11/962 : Telegram

The Minister in China (Schurman) to the Secretary of State

PEKING, *January 25, 1924—4 p. m.*
[Received January 26—1 : 10 a. m.]

44. 1. Protocol circular of January 18th submitted proposed draft of note from dean of the diplomatic corps, acting in behalf of all the powers signatory to the protocol of 1901,[92] to Minister of Foreign Affairs, concerning execution by Chinese Government of Sino-Belgian understanding of February 15 [5?], 1918, respecting Boxer Indemnity payments referred to in my telegram no. 15, January 10, 11 a. m. [*noon?*].[93] After rehearsing the negotiation of the undertaking and that up to now no payments have been made, or funds set aside to cover such payments, the draft note contains a concluding paragraph as follows:

"The representatives of the powers above mentioned (protocol powers) are of opinion that under these circumstances the obliga-

---

[91] Continued from *Foreign Relations*, 1923, vol. I, pp. 592–605.
[92] *Foreign Relations*, 1901, Appendix (Affairs in China), p 312.
[93] Not found in Department files.

tions arising from the final payments of 1901 with regard to the indemnity have not entirely been met and consequently they wish me to request Your Excellency to be good enough to instruct the Inspector General of Customs that, as the payments due to the Belgian Government for the refunding of the suspended indemnity installments have—together with the other indemnity payments and the services of the loans concluded previous to 1900—priority before all other payments out of the customs funds, he should make the necessary arrangements accordingly."

2. I indorsed observation on circular to effect that this arrangement did not appear to have been communicated to the American Government and since United States was not signatory to the Allied Powers' joint memorandum of that year relative to method of effecting individual arrangements for the payment of the suspended portion of the indemnity, I desired to hear from my Government before taking action in the matter.

3. In requesting telegraphic instructions whether I should participate in supporting the Belgian Government in this matter, I venture to direct the Department's attention to the fact that it would appear from the joint memorandum of 1918 [94] referred to in my observation that each of the powers signatory, namely, Belgium, France, Great Britain, Italy, Japan, Portugal and Russia, are at liberty to effect individual arrangements with the Chinese Government as to the method by which the suspended portion of the indemnity shall be paid. Therefore, if we now assist the Belgian Government in securing execution of its preferential treatment arrangement with the Chinese authorities, a precedent will be established for our acting similarly in the event of any other of the afore-mentioned of having made or making such individual arrangements with the Chinese Government possibly in terms especially advantageous to the respective powers. Likewise, it is to be observed that thus far we have made no arrangement ourselves with the Chinese Government regarding the payment of the suspended portion of the indemnity. While the desirability of perfect unanimity among the protocol powers in all that relates to the execution of that instrument is evident, I venture to suggest that disadvantages may arise from our associating ourselves with the other signatories in invoking the protocol to support an arrangement like the present one. I am not convinced that the obligation of China to pay the suspended Belgian indemnity at a particular time and in a particular manner is an obligation of the same order

---

[94] For correction of date, see Minister's no. 51, Feb. 2, p. 561.

as the obligations arising from the final protocol of 1901 with regard to the indemnity generally.

4. I am informed by the Belgian Minister that he has addressed a formal note to the Chinese Government requesting the payment in question to which no reply has been received and I also have it on good authority that the Inspector General of Customs states that he has no money with which to liquidate the Sino-Belgian undertaking.

SCHURMAN

493.11/962 : Telegram

The Secretary of State to the Minister in China (Schurman)

WASHINGTON, *January 31, 1924—4 p. m.*

30. Your No. 44, January 25, 4 p. m. Since this Government appears not to have been privy to, or cognizant of, the Allied joint memorandum of 1918, the Department considers that you should not associate yourself with any representations based upon separate arrangements made thereunder by other Protocol Powers either individually or as a group.

In view of the fact that this Government has not been apprised of any such arrangements, the Department furthermore questions the advisability of the Legation lending its further cooperation in any representations in connection with Indemnity payments until it shall have been informed in detail of those arrangements.

HUGHES

493.11/967 : Telegram

The Minister in China (Schurman) to the Secretary of State

PEKING, *February 2, 1924—noon.*
[Received February 2—6 : 35 a. m.]

51. Your 30, January 31, 4 p. m. I now find Allied joint memorandum was presented to the Chinese Government in 1917, not 1918. Preliminary draft was submitted to the American Minister for his approval but the files of the Legation contain no indications of the nature of his comment nor of any report to the Department. Subject to Department's approval, I shall decline to participate in the joint support of the Belgian arrangement on the ground that United States was not signatory to 1917 memorandum nor apprised of 1918 Belgian arrangement.

SCHURMAN

493.11/968 : Telegram

The Minister in China (Schurman) to the Secretary of State

Peking, *February 3, 1924—2 p. m.*
[Received 4:21 p. m.]

52. Your January 31, 4 p. m. I trust the second paragraph does not preclude my signing the diplomatic body's reply to Koo's note of December 26 [96] in which Koo constructs his entire argument on the assumption that the word "gold" in the protocol and agreement connotes not so much metal of such a fineness but the currency of a country having a gold standard. It will be seen that Koo's position involves the interpretation of a collective treaty to which the United States is signatory. An effective reply has been drafted and will be submitted for approval to full diplomatic body at meeting tomorrow morning.

[Paraphrase.] At a dinner February 1 which Koo gave for Mrs. Roosevelt I was informed by Yen that the Government wished for a reply as soon as possible from the diplomatic body. The Government would then place before Parliament both the Chinese note of December 26 and the reply of the diplomatic body and with both sides presented leave Parliament to act. Yen expected that the Cabinet and Parliament would ask that the issue be arbitrated. It would be possible, he said, for China and the powers which participated in the Washington Conference, as soon as that disposition of this vexing problem is accepted by the other side, to make arrangements immediately for holding the special conference on surtaxes. [End paraphrase.]

It is very desirable that the gold franc question be speedily settled. It has got entirely beyond the control of the politicians who first raised it. The Chinese press and people, as well as Parliament, have come to espouse the antigold side as a great national issue. The Government know that in the end they must pay in gold and they really desire that the diplomatic body should make a strong reply to Koo's note so that it will be obvious to everybody that no settlement is possible except by arbitration.

If at this critical juncture the American Minister refused to sign the diplomatic body's reply, a new situation would be created and further delay become unavoidable.

Please telegraph instructions.

Schurman

---

[96] *Foreign Relations*, 1923, vol. I, p. 600.

493.11/968 : Telegram

The Secretary of State to the Minister in China (Schurman)

WASHINGTON, *February 5, 1924—3 p. m.*

32. Your telegrams 51 February 2, 12 M, 52 February 3, 2 p. m. The Department approves your declining to participate in support of the Belgian arrangement in view of this Government's having had no cognizance of it, and, as indicated in its telegram No. 30 January 31, 4 p. m. leaves to your discretion the matter of joining in further representations in connection with Indemnity payments. The Department has no objection to your signing the proposed note of the Diplomatic body to Koo, if such action recommends itself to you. It is assumed that the note insists upon payment in gold or its equivalent.

HUGHES

493.11/977 : Telegram

The Minister in China (Schurman) to the Secretary of State

PEKING, *February 28, 1924—11 a. m.*
[Received February 28—2 : 30 a. m.]

65. In informal conversation 27th, Minister for Foreign Affairs remarked that if gold franc case were arbitrated it might be referred to Hague or League Court or to distinguished individual. The objection to Hague was the time consumed before final decision; as to League Court, he wondered if United States would have any objection. He took for granted that as the arbitration would concern the interpretation of a treaty to which the United States was one of the signatories the United States would be one of the parties to the arbitration. I was noncommittal on these points and have the honor to ask for instructions for my guidance should the matter come up again.

SCHURMAN

493.11/984

The Minister in China (Schurman) to the Secretary of State

No. 2108   PEKING, *February 29, 1924.*
[Received March 31.]

SIR: Referring to my despatch No. 1999 of January 2, 1924,[97] and pertinent correspondence relative to the payment in gold of the Indemnity of 1901 by the Chinese Government, I have the honor to transmit herewith for the Department's information copy of an

---

[97] *Foreign Relations, 1923,* vol. I, p. 600.

English translation made by the Legation of a note transmitted to the Chinese Government on February 11, 1924, by the Dean of the Diplomatic Body on behalf of the Governments of the Netherlands, Belgium, The United States, France, Italy, Great Britain and Japan in reply to separate notes on this subject addressed by the Wai Chiao Pu to the Ministers of the aforementioned Powers on December 26, 1924 [*1923*].[98]

I have been informed by an American adviser to the Chinese Government, in respect of the Chinese Government's note of December 26, that the arguments advanced therein by Dr. Koo were with a view to a possible future submission of the entire matter to some form of arbitration.

I have [etc.]   JACOB GOULD SCHURMAN

[Enclosure—Translation]

The Dean of the Diplomatic Corps at Peking (*Oudendijk*) to the Chinese Minister for Foreign Affairs (*Wellington Koo*)

[PEKING, *February 11, 1924.*]

MONSIEUR LE MINISTRE: The eight undersigned Ministers of the Netherlands, Belgium, The United States, France, Italy, Great Britain and Japan have taken cognizance of the note which Your Excellency addressed to them separately on December 26th last in reply to their collective notes of February 24 [99] and November 5 [*3*], 1923,[1] regarding the payment in gold of the Indemnity stipulated for by Article 6 of the Final Protocol of September 7, 1901. The eight Ministers conclude from the above-mentioned note that the Chinese Government claims a right to pay the arrears of the Indemnity of 1901 at the rate of what it calls the current exchange of each one of the currencies inscribed upon the national bonds belonging to each of the Signatory Powers.

The Chinese Government bases its claim on the definition which it gives to the words "in gold" in the sentence of the letters of July 2, 1905,[2] cited by the eight Ministers' notes of February 24 and November 5 [*3*], 1923: "For each Haikwan Tael due to each one of the Powers China must pay 'in gold' the sum indicated in Article 6 of the Final Protocol as the equivalent of a tael".

According to the Chinese Government's contention, the words "in gold" have been used in this sentence to distinguish the gold standard monetary systems of the Signatory Powers from the silver standard

---

[98] *Foreign Relations*, 1923, vol. I, p. 600.
[99] See telegram no. 65, Feb. 23, 1923, from the Minister in China, *ibid.*, p. 593.
[1] *Ibid.*, p. 595.
[2] *Ibid.*, 1905, p. 156.

monetary system to which belongs the Haikwan Tael, the currency in which the total of the Indemnity has been expressed.

The Chinese Government bases its claim in equal measure on the manner of payment of the Indemnity which, according to it, was definitively fixed by Section 3 of the letters of July 2, 1905; this method of payment (telegraphic transfer) appearing to it as solely devoted to the exchange of national currencies customarily used in the international exchanges.

The eight Ministers ought not to conceal from Your Excellency that study of your note has not altered the opinion expressed in their notes of February 24 and November 5 [*3*], 1923. The sentence taken from the letters of July 2, 1905, seemed to them and still seems to them to be perfectly clear. It means that for each Haikwan Tael due to each of the Powers China must pay in gold the sum which is indicated in Article VI. of the Final Protocol as the equivalent of a tael, comformably to the respective weights and legal standards of each one of the eight gold currencies mentioned in the said Article VI.; in other words, insofar as the franc is concerned, for each Haikwan Tael owed to Belgium or to Spain or to France or to Italy, China must pay 3.75 francs in gold or 3.75 x 0 gr. 290322 of fine gold.

In support of its definition of the words "in gold", the Chinese note does not present any argument except the assertion that the known reports of the discussions between the Signatory Powers leading up to the Final Protocol were favorable to the Chinese Government's contention. The eight Ministers are in a position to state that the reports of these discussions show the unanimous desire of the Signatory Powers to give to the words "in gold" the sense which they have set forth in the preceding paragraph. That is confirmed, moreover, by the documents pertaining to this matter. It suffices to call to mind the principal ones.

China having accepted the principle of the Indemnity on October 20, 1900, the Powers concerned themselves on the one hand in making separate estimations of the sums to which each one was entitled under this count and on the other hand in fixing the total sum which could be paid by China without hampering the progress of its Government and the development of the country. This last sum was fixed, on May 7, 1901, at 450,000,000 Taels by a letter from the Dean of the Diplomatic Body to the Chinese Plenipotentiaries. It was less than the total amount of the individual indemnities of the Powers which it was finally necessary to reduce. To bring about these reductions, to subsequently settle their respective portions of the total indemnity and finally to assure the just division of the arrears of the total indemnity in the proportions to be agreed upon among themselves, the Signatory Powers adopted gold as the basis of their calculations and the payments to be received. They decided and China agreed that the indemnity although expressed in Haikwan Taels was an indemnity "in gold" and that the rate in gold of the Haikwan Tael should be fixed on a definite day. This decision was transmitted to the Chinese Plenipotentiaries on July 30, 1901, in the following terms: "The sum of 450,000,000 Haikwan Taels payable 'in gold' at the rate of exchange of April 1, 1901, at 4% interest, represents the grand total of the indemnity demanded by the Powers.["]

The rates of exchange of the Haikwan Tael on April 1, 1901, were inserted in Article 6 of the Final Protocol whose text it is fitting to quote below in order to cause to stand out clearly how the Powers and China insisted at that time on the importance of a payment "in gold".

"Article 6. By an Imperial Edict dated the 22nd [*29th*] of May, 1901, His Majesty the Emperor of China agreed to pay the Powers an indemnity of 450,000,000 Haikwan Taels.

(*a*) These 450,000,000 constitute a debt in gold based on the rate of exchange of the Haikwan Tael in relation to the gold currency of each country in the manner set forth hereinafter.

One Haikwan Tael	= Marks	3,055
	= Austro-Hungarian Crown	3,595
	= Gold dollar	0,742
	= Francs	3,750
	= Pound Sterling	0.3.0
	= Yen	1,407
	= Netherlands Florin	1,796
	= Gold rouble (17,424 dolias fine)	1,412

This sum in gold shall bear interest . . .

Capital and interest shall be payable in gold or at the rates of exchange corresponding to the dates at which the different payments fall due."

In the above-mentioned text, the Powers were careful to define the meaning which they intended to give, and which China agreed to give, to the words "in gold":

1) The United States of America which has just adopted the gold standard specified that the rate of exchange of 0,742 referred to the "gold dollar".

Russia took the same precaution with regard to the gold rouble in adding the legal weight of fine gold of this currency.

2) The currencies of Belgium, France and Italy have always been quoted at different rates in the international exchanges. On April 1, 1901, Belgian and French francs were quoted at 3.75 a Tael and were at rates almost alike and equivalent to par in gold; the Italian lire was valued at about 3.85 and the Spanish peseta at 5 to a Tael. But,

even if the exchange currencies of these four states differ, their gold coinage is legally of the same weight and the same denomination, and it was to represent this weight of 0,290322 of fine gold to a franc that Belgium, Spain, France and Italy all adopted the same rate of exchange of 3.75 to a Tael.

3) Finally all the Signatory Powers as well as China in using the words "rate of the Haikwan Tael to the gold currency of each currency [*country?*]", excluded from the measures aimed at by Article 6 every evaluation of the Haikwan Tael in relation to the currencies of each country other than their gold currency. They have the right to refuse payment of a Tael in their silver currency, their fiduciary money, their exchange currencies, etc. . . . .

The measures which the interested Powers took in the Final Protocol were confirmed by China in the text of the letters exchanged on July 2, 1905, as well as in the wording of the bonds delivered to each of the Powers and in the coupons attached to these bonds because Payment "in gold" was the procedure which they adopted in order to assure the distribution of the total Indemnity in the proportions agreed upon by them. To return to the definition of the words "in gold" in the sentence given above from the letters of July 2, 1905, it is clearly the gold value in conformity to the weight and legal standard of each of the currencies specified in Article 6, (*a*) and at the rates of exchange indicated in the same Article as the equivalent of a Tael which China must pay to each Power for each Tael of the Indemnity of 1901 which she owes.

The eight Ministers have desired to show on what foundations the definition which was given by their governments and accepted in 1901 and 1905 by the Chinese Government for the payment in gold of the Indemnity of 1901 rested. In answering the first contention of the note of December 26, 1923, regarding the meaning of the words "in gold" they have, in so doing, refuted the second which, as the Chinese note itself admits, refers solely to the manner of execution of the obligations subscribed to by the Chinese Government in 1901. The character and the total amount of the debt owed by virtue of an obligation cannot depend upon the means adopted for the settlement of this debt.

After having recalled this principle of law which is certainly recognized by the Chinese Government, the eight Ministers consider it their duty to take up the principal points of the portion of the notes of December 26, 1923, which concern the exchange of letters of July 2, 1905. The arrangement resulting from this exchange confirmed and carried out Article 6 of the Final Protocol which it had completed. Such as it is, it answers perfectly to their present needs and the Signatory Powers have never thought of modifying it.

In recalling the circumstances which preceded and brought about the exchange of letters of 1905, the note of December 26, 1923, makes it evident that at that time the Chinese Government endeavored to secure payment of the arrears of the Indemnity of 1901 in silver and that it was obliged to recognize its obligation to pay "in gold". This fact furnishes a new argument in favor of the ruling "in gold" as it has been set forth above. This is worth noting in passing.

It would be possible to dispute the correctness of this statement of the Chinese note to which the preceding paragraph refers. But the eight Ministers limit themselves in this instance to the repairing of one omission in the said recital and of noting that the arrangement of 1905 had for aim and object the solution of the problem presented by the changing of silver, the currency of China the debtor, into gold.

China, having no gold, has had to buy and still has to buy with the silver she possesses, that is to say, with Taels, the gold necessary for the service of the Indemnity of 1901. The method of this transaction not having been settled by the Protocol of 1901, occasioned the subsequent rise of discussions and difficulties ended by the exchange of letters of July 2, 1905.

By the terms of Section 3 of these letters China was entitled to bring about the payment to the Powers of the Indemnity of 1901 by one of three systems: "either in silver according to the price of silver on the London market, or in gold bills, or in telegraphic transfers." The machinery of the two last systems, gold drafts and telegraphic transfers, differ only in the more or less rapid means of transmission of the document of exchange from one place to another with a resulting difference corresponding to the rates of exchange.

In the two cases, China, the debtor, buys with silver Taels instruments of exchange representing the amount of gold which she owes to her creditor. These purchases, insofar as the service of the Indemnity of 1901 is concerned, are generally made of the banking agents of the Signatory Powers at Shanghai. The arrangement of 1905 has at the same time and quite justly reserved to China the right "to obtain drafts and telegraphic transfers to the best of her interests in any locality and in any bank as cheaply as possible, or by award."

The three methods of payment enumerated in Section 3 of the letters of July 2, 1905, lend themselves perfectly to payment "in gold" as it has been defined above by the eight Ministers. The note of December 26 last has confused the quotations of the international exchanges by telegraphic transfer with the telegraphic transfer itself. Telegraphic transfer, in effect, is applied as well to a gold currency as to a silver currency, to a paper currency or an exchange currency.

When, on December 30, 1922, the Chinese Government attempted to resume the service of the Indemnity of 1901, in the matter indicated by its note of December 26 [1923?], her representative presented himself, according to established custom, to the Shanghai agents of the interested Governments to negotiate the purchase of telegraphic transfers in francs. The disagreement which ensued was solely about the rates of exchange of the Tael quoted by the two parties. If the representative of the Chinese Government had accepted the rate of the gold franc quoted by the agents of the interested Governments, these agents would have effected the required telegraphic transfers.

The Chinese Government, moreover, cannot be ignorant of the possibility of carrying on transactions in gold francs, since it must pay its share of the expenses of the League of Nations in gold francs and since it has accepted the gold franc as the currency of the Universal Postal Union and of its postal conventions with several countries.

The eight Ministers, accordingly, support the conclusions drawn in their notes of February 4 [24] and November 5 [3], 1923, and in definitely affirming that for each Haikwan Tael due to each of the Powers under the heading of the Indemnity of 1901, China must pay in gold the sum which is indicated in Article 6 of the Final Protocol as the equivalent of a Tael conformably to the respective weights and legal standards of each of the gold currencies enumerated in the said Article 6.

The explanations which the eight Ministers have given above authorize them to state that they require only the complete and unmodified execution of the conventions drawn up in 1901 between China and the Signatory Powers with regard to the Indemnity of 1901. They insist upon this complete execution in order to cause to be respected the right of each one of the interested Powers to receive the proportion of a total Indemnity determined among themselves, whose service and guarantees have been placed under their common control.

[File copy not signed]

493.11/977 : Telegram

The Secretary of State to the Minister in China (Schurman)

[Paraphrase]

WASHINGTON, *March 1, 1924—3 p. m.*

46. Your February 28, 11 a. m. The American Government does not have any such direct interest in the controversy regarding the

payment of the indemnity in gold francs as would lead it to offer any suggestion as to means whereby the dispute might be settled. If occasion requires, you may inform Minister for Foreign Affairs to this effect.

You are confidentially informed that should the issue be referred to the World Court while the relation of the United States to it continues as at present, the Senate not having acted on the proposal that this country accept the Court, the American Government would probably not desire to make use of its right to appear in such a case regarding the interpretation of the protocol of 1901.

HUGHES

[For further information regarding the attitude of the French Government on the gold franc controversy, see note from the French Ambassador, December 10, 1924, printed on page 440.]

CONTINUED SUPPORT BY THE UNITED STATES TO THE FEDERAL TELEGRAPH COMPANY IN EFFORTS TO OBTAIN EXECUTION OF ITS CONTRACT WITH THE CHINESE GOVERNMENT [3]

893.74/416 : Telegram

The Minister in China (Schurman) to the Secretary of State

[Paraphrase]

PEKING, January 4, 1924—5 p. m.
[Received January 4—9 : 53 a. m.]

5. My telegram 433 of December 31.[4] Yesterday W. W. Yen [5] called at the Legation, apparently at the instance of the Foreign Office, and quite unofficially asked whether some compromise measure could not be suggested by the Legation which would induce the Japanese to abandon their strong diplomatic pressure in opposition to the Federal Telegraph Company's contracts and in favor of the Mitsui Company. His suggestion was that some joint operation of the Mitsui Peking station might be arranged. It would be appreciated by the Chinese authorities if some method of relief could be devised by the American Government, as they feel that they have

---

[3] Continued from *Foreign Relations*, 1923, vol. I, pp. 783–826. For texts of agreements between the Federal Telegraph Company and the Chinese Government, see *List of Contracts of American Nationals with the Chinese Government*, etc., annex VIII (Washington, Government Printing Office, 1925).

[4] *Foreign Relations*, 1923, vol. I, p. 825.

[5] Prominent Chinese political leader, appointed Minister of Agriculture and Commerce on Jan. 12.

been loyally supporting American rights in spite of the great difficulties they have been called upon to face.

. . . .

For the Minister:

BELL

893.74/425 : Telegram

The Acting Secretary of State to the Minister in China (Schurman)

[Paraphrase]

WASHINGTON, *January 24, 1924—3 p. m.*

25. With reference to your telegram 5 of January 4, Schwerin [6] informs Department that he would be very glad if a solution could be found which would end the continued agitation to which the Chinese are subjected because of the Federal contract. He does not believe, however, that the Federal Telegraph Company can take over the Mitsui station at Peking to relieve the Japanese of a bad bargain. He says that should his company try to unite with the Japanese, the latter would insist upon sharing in the activities of all the company's stations. He also says that this would nullify all the efforts of his company to give the American and Chinese people the right of communication with each other without interference from any other country.

Schwerin says he cannot go back to China before March.

PHILLIPS

893.74/434

The British Chargé (Chilton) to the Secretary of State

No. 87   WASHINGTON, *January 29, 1924.*

SIR: I have the honour to refer to the note which you were so good as to address to me on November 24th last,[7] on the subject of radio and cable communications in China, and to inform you that, after giving the contents thereof the most careful consideration, His Majesty's Government have come to the conclusion that the refusal of the Japanese Government to accept the recommendations signed by their expert at Washington [8] has placed His Majesty's Government under the necessity of maintaining the existing rights of the cable companies pending the conclusion of an agreement based on those recommendations.

---

[6] R. P. Schwerin, president of the Federal Telegraph Co. of Delaware.
[7] *Foreign Relations*, 1923, vol. I, p. 823.
[8] *Ibid.*, 1922, vol. I, p. 840.

In coming to this decision His Majesty's Government have been influenced by the fact that there is no difference of opinion between the United States Government and His Majesty's Government, who both consider the recommendations to represent a practicable adjustment of the interests of the four Powers concerned and who both still hope that they may furnish a basis of a satisfactory understanding. The only point seriously at issue is between the United States and Japan in regard to Section 2 of the experts' memorandum, and my Government greatly regret that they are unable to allow this divergence of view to operate to the disadvantage of the cable companies, whose existing agreements provide that until December 31st, 1930, no other party will be allowed without their consent "to establish telegraphic connections which might create competition with, or injure the interests of, the existing lines".[9]

In these circumstances, His Majesty's Ambassador at Tokio has been instructed to inform the Imperial Japanese Government that, while His Majesty's Government would have been glad if the views of the United States and Japanese Governments could have been harmonised in respect of Section 2, they are in agreement with the United States Government in considering the experts' recommendations as providing a reasonable compromise which it is hoped will still furnish a basis for a satisfactory understanding, but that His Majesty's Government cannot allow this divergence of views between the United States and the Japanese Governments to operate to the prejudice of the existing contractual interests of the cable companies.

In bringing to your notice the sense of the instructions sent to Sir C. Eliot I have been directed to assure you that the action of His Majesty's Government in China has been taken in no spirit of hostility to the United States interests concerned, but as the only course available in the circumstances to protect the existing rights of the Eastern Extension Telegraph Company.

I have [etc.]   H. G. CHILTON

———————

893.74/434

The Secretary of State to the British Chargé (Chilton)

WASHINGTON, *February 16, 1924.*

SIR: I beg to acknowledge the receipt of the note (No. 87) under date of January 29 last, in which you advised me of the conclusion of the British Government that the refusal of the Japanese Govern-

———————

[9] See telegram no. 17, Feb. 17, 1921, from the Minister in Denmark, *Foreign Relations*, 1921, vol. I, p. 414.

ment to accept the recommendations formulated at Washington on February 4, 1922, by the radio experts of the American, British, French and Japanese Governments, had placed the British Government under the necessity of maintaining the existing rights of the cable companies pending the conclusions of an agreement based on those recommendations.

While frankly disappointed by what appears to be the abrupt abandonment by the British Government of the position which it had urged this and the other interested Governments to adopt, I am happy to note the assurance that this action of the British Government has been taken in no spirit of hostility to the American interests concerned, and trust that I may construe this assurance to mean that the British Government has no intention of renewing direct or indirect pressure upon the Chinese Government to prevent the carrying out of the contracts between that Government and the Federal Telegraph Company with regard to the establishment of radio stations in China.

Accept [etc.]   CHARLES E. HUGHES

893.74/454a : Telegram

The Secretary of State to the Minister in China (Schurman)

WASHINGTON, *April 3, 1924—4 p. m.*

67. The Department has been requested by Mr. Schwerin to assure the Chinese Government that there will be no evasion on the part of the Federal Telegraph Company of Delaware in the fulfillment of its part of the contract between that Company and the Chinese Government. The Radio Corporation of America, so far as concerns its part in relation to the contract, also desires that the Chinese Government shall be assured that the Corporation has a very vital interest in seeing the terms of the contract carried out by both parties at the earliest practicable date, and states that it is greatly interested in doing everything it can to expedite the erection of the stations in China.

While the Department, for its part, is not in a position to give any guarantees on behalf of this Government, you are authorized on behalf of the Companies above mentioned to give to the Chinese Government the assurance as requested by them. In so doing you will make it plain to the Chinese Government that the Department assumes no responsibility in connection with the matter and is merely conveying the assurance at the request of the companies concerned.

HUGHES

893.74/458

*The President of the Radio Corporation of America (J. G. Harbord)
to the Secretary of State*

New York, *April 18, 1924.*
[Received April 23, 1924.]

My Dear Mr. Secretary: I have the honor to invite your attention
to the following resolution adopted by the Board of Directors of the
Radio Corporation of America at a meeting held this date:

"Whereas, it has been brought to the attention of the Board of
Directors of the Radio Corporation of America, that Rudolph
Spreckels, a director and the principal stockholder of the Federal
Telegraph Company of California, by communication dated April
8th, 1924, to the Directors of the Federal Telegraph Company of
California did state:

'After careful consideration, I am convinced that the language used in the
Chinese contracts is deceptive in that they create a partnership, but do not
disclose the fact that the Chinese Government is to actually provide the entire
sum necessary to complete the project.
'I cannot believe that the State Department at Washington has been correctly
informed of the true situation in connection with these contracts.
'The contracts were negotiated by Mr. R. P. Schwerin as President of the
Federal Telegraph Co. (California), but said contracts have been assumed by
the Federal Telegraph Co. of Delaware in which company the Federal Telegraph
Co. (California) holds a thirty per cent stock interest.
'I acquired my stock holdings in the Federal Telegraph Co. (California)
after the contracts were consummated, but I cannot permit this company to
become further involved in a transaction of this character without protest.
'It is quite clear to me that the present attitude of the Chinese Government
toward the contracts concern the Federal Telegraph Co. of Delaware alone, but
I am unwilling that any officer of the Federal Telegraph Co. (California) shall
be involved in negotiations with the Chinese Government in connection with
these contracts, or in the execution of the contracts. In other words, it is no
longer satisfactory for this company and the Federal Telegraph Co. of Delaware
to have the same individual as the executive head.
          Yours very truly,
                                        (Signed)   R. Spreckels'

and

Whereas, at a meeting of the Board of Directors of the Federal
Telegraph Company of California on April 15th, 1924, R. P.
Schwerin was removed as President of that corporation and all
powers of attorney theretofore given by that corporation to him as
President or General Manager or otherwise to act for or on behalf
of that corporation were revoked, and

Whereas, notwithstanding the fact that the Board of Directors
of the Radio Corporation of America understand and believe that
the State Department at Washington has been correctly informed
of the true situation in connection with these contracts and has
always understood the precise scope and meaning thereof, and

Whereas, Radio Corporation of America does not believe that any
advantage has been taken of the ignorance or lack of understanding
of the Chinese Government in the negotiation of these contracts, and

Whereas, Radio Corporation of America did cause to be organized
the Federal Telegraph Company of Delaware, for the purpose of
taking over said Chinese concessions from the Federal Telegraph
Company of California and the financing and construction of the

Chinese stations, in which Federal Telegraph Company of Delaware the Radio Corporation of America owns seventy per cent of the capital stock.

Nevertheless, the Radio Corporation of America being unwilling to proceed with the carrying out of these contracts, if it be true that the Chinese Government has acted under misapprehension or lack of knowledge and if the said Chinese Government shall so assert,

Resolved that the Radio Corporation of America is willing and tenders itself ready to join with the Federal Telegraph Company of California in cancelling all contracts relating to the said concessions or to the carrying out thereof, and

Further Resolved, that the President be and he hereby is authorized and instructed to take steps to ascertain whether the State Department has been correctly informed of the true situation in connection with these contracts and whether the Chinese Government makes any claim or complaint as to having signed these contracts under misapprehension of fact or lack of knowledge."

The Radio Corporation of America entered upon this Chino-Federal enterprise on direct assurance from Mr. R. P. Schwerin that it had the hearty approval of both the American State Department and the Chinese Government. Copies of all the contracts were long since furnished to the State Department. That it has understood and has had no question of their integrity has been shown by its continued and efficient support of them to this day. The signatures of the proper officials of the Chinese Government to the contracts have been witnessed by proper American Legation officials in Peking. Our information is that Dr. Sun, the Chinese Vice Minister of Communications, is a graduate of Cornell University, knowing English well, and that he repeatedly discussed these contracts with Mr. Bell, Mr. Peck, Mr. Julean Arnold of the American Legation and Mr. Schwerin and Mr. Moss. These gentlemen with Minister Schurman had numerous discussions with Dr. Koo, Wu Yu Lin, the Minister of Communications, and the Prime Minister Chan Tze Ti'In[sic]. Of the integrity of the contracts we have had no doubt.

Mr. Rudolph Spreckels, of San Francisco, very recently and suddenly purchased a control in the Federal Telegraph Company of California, and now charges that our State Department has not been correctly informed of the true situation in connection with these contracts and that the Chinese Government signed them under deception. I am instructed by the Board of Directors of the Radio Corporation of America to ask assurance of the State Department on these two points, in order that we may know whether it is proper for us to proceed in this enterprise from the standpoint of morality and business integrity.

Very respectfully,

J. G. HARBORD

893.74/458

The Secretary of State to the President of the Radio Corporation of America (J. G. Harbord)

WASHINGTON, *April 26, 1924.*

SIR: I have received the letter of April 18, 1924, in which you quote a resolution adopted on that date by the Board of Directors of your corporation, with reference to a letter understood to have been addressed on April 8 to the Directors of the Federal Telegraph Company of California by Mr. Rudolph Spreckels, a Director of that company, in which (referring to the contracts originally concluded on January 8, 1921, and September 19, 1921, between the Federal Telegraph Company of California and the Chinese Government, and thereafter assigned to the Federal Telegraph Company of Delaware by arrangement with the Radio Corporation and in accordance with a further agreement with the Chinese Government under date of July 13, 1923) he states that

"After careful consideration, I am convinced that the language used in the Chinese contracts is deceptive in that they create a partnership, but do not disclose the fact that the Chinese Government is to actually provide the entire sum necessary to complete the project.

"I cannot believe that the State Department at Washington has been correctly informed of the true situation in connection with these contracts."

I have noted that the resolution of your Board of Directors further sets forth that, while your corporation believes that the contracts with the Chinese Government were not concluded without the full understanding of the Chinese Government and of this Department, it is nevertheless unwilling to proceed with the carrying out of these contracts if it be true that the Chinese Government has acted under misapprehension or lack of knowledge and if that Government so asserts; that your corporation would in that case be willing and ready to join with the Federal Telegraph Company of California in cancelling all the contracts in question; and that you are therefore instructed to take steps to ascertain whether the Department of State has been correctly informed of the true situation in regard to these contracts and whether the Chinese Government makes any claim or complaint of having signed these contracts under misapprehension of fact or lack of knowledge.

In reply I am happy to inform you, for the reassurance of your Board of Directors, that I know of no basis whatsoever for the assumptions stated in the letter quoted in the resolution.

As you are no doubt aware, the several contracts between the Federal Telegraph Company of California and the Chinese Government in regard to this matter were all negotiated with the cognizance of the Department of State and in consultation with the American Legation at Peking, were witnessed by officials of that Legation, and were in each case communicated immediately to this Department, which considered the project to be of primary importance to American interests in China as a test of the practical application of the principle of the open door or equality of opportunity in such enterprises in China and as a means of establishing a direct and wholly independent Chinese-American circuit between the two countries.

It is understood that the American interests concerned are to construct the proposed wireless stations for the Chinese Government at a cost to that Government of approximately $13,000,000, $6,500,000 of which is to be paid in bonds and the balance to be paid in cash over a period of ten years from the time of completing the last station; and that during the period to elapse until the cash payments are completed, the contractors are to participate with the Chinese Government, under an arrangement analogous to a partnership, in the operation of the stations. The project thus contemplated has not been the subject of any complaint by the Chinese Government to the Department of State, and I have no reason to believe that that Government misapprehends the arrangement or considers that the contracts establishing it were concluded under any misunderstanding or in ignorance of their scope and meaning.

I am [etc.] CHARLES E. HUGHES

893.74/465

The British Ambassador (Howard) to the Secretary of State

No. 434 WASHINGTON, *May 15, 1924.*

SIR: In the note which you were so good as to address to Mr. Chilton on February 16th last, on the subject of radio and cable communications in China, you stated that, while frankly disappointed by what appeared to be the abrupt abandonment by the British Government of the position which it had urged the United States and other interested Governments to adopt, you were happy to note the assurance that this action of the British Government had been taken in no spirit of hostility to the American interests concerned.

Under instructions from His Majesty's Principal Secretary of State for Foreign Affairs, I now have the honour to inform you, in order that there may be no misunderstanding of the attitude of my Government, that His Majesty's Government have not abandoned their position in this matter. His Majesty's Government continue in agreement with the United States Government in considering that the Washington recommendations provide a reasonable compromise and, like the United States Government, they still hope that those recommendations will furnish a basis for a satisfactory settlement of this complicated question. Since, however, the carrying out of the recommendations has been obstructed by a difference of view which concerns the United States and Japan, His Majesty's Government also feel that they are justified in drawing the attention of both the United States and the Japanese Governments to the fact that the cable companies have rights, which, in the absence of a general agreement based on the recommendations, cannot be ignored.

In this connection, I am instructed to add that it is of course always open to the United States wireless interests to come to a reasonable arrangement with the cable companies.

I have [etc.]   ESME HOWARD

893.74/479

The Secretary of State to the President of the Radio Corporation of America (J. G. Harbord)

WASHINGTON, *August 21, 1924.*

SIR: The Department has received your letter of June 3 [*30*], 1924,[10] with which you transmitted copies of correspondence which you exchanged with Mr. Rudolph Spreckels, Chairman of the Board of Directors of the Federal Telegraph Company of California.

The following statement made in Mr. Brown's [11] memorandum dated June 28, 1924, a copy of which accompanied your letter of June 30 to Mr. Spreckels, is noted:

". . . I therefore submit that the Delaware Company is clearly entitled to charges and reimbursement above production cost as above set forth. This subject has been thoroughly discussed with the Washington authorities, without their voicing objections. . . ."

If, as appears to be intended, this mention of "the Washington authorities" has reference to the Department of State, I feel it is due alike to this Department and to your corporation to obviate the possibility of any such misunderstanding as might arise out of the use of the language quoted from Mr. Brown's memorandum. The Department desires to state, therefore, that while the scope and effect of the contracts between the Federal Telegraph Company of California and the Chinese Government were the subject of discussion

[10] Not printed.
[11] Mr. William Brown, general attorney for the Radio Corporation of America.

on the occasion of several of Mr. Schwerin's visits to the Department and although, in its letter to you of April 29 [26], 1924, the Department stated in a general way what its understanding of the obligations of the two contracting parties was, it should be stated that the Department has not considered the relations of the Radio Corporation of America, the Federal Telegraph Company of California and the Federal Telegraph Company of Delaware with each other or the respective rights of those companies, nor has the Department considered the question whether the contracts between the Federal Telegraph Company of California and the Chinese Government include the terms and conditions which are usually contained in such contracts or whether they contemplate the payment of reasonable or excessive compensation for the services to be rendered and the material to be furnished by the Company. This is a question which, of course, the contracting parties should consider and decide for themselves.

In iteration and confirmation of what has already been orally communicated to Mr. Schwerin by representatives of this Department it should be stated that it is not within the province of the Department to negotiate contracts between foreign governments and American interests, and that the Department's activities in relation to the contracts between the Federal Telegraph Company of California and the Chinese Government have been calculated to obtain a practical application of the principle of the open door in China and to assist the American interests concerned in their negotiations with the Chinese Government to the end that a circuit of communication might be established which would prove advantageous to the relations between the United States and China.

I am [etc.]

> For the Secretary of State:
> LELAND HARRISON
> *Assistant Secretary*

893.74/499 : Telegram

The Chargé in China (Mayer) to the Secretary of State

PEKING, *November 29, 1924—11 a. m.*
[Received November 29—6:43 a. m.]

457. Legation's despatch 2514, September 23 [20], 1924.[12] Yeh Kung-ch'o who signed original Federal radio contract has assumed office as Minister of Communications and Chiang Tsun-wei [*Chiang Tsun-i?*], former Director General of Telegraphs, is also to be re-

---

[12] Not printed.

appointed to that post. I am led to believe they will shortly reopen negotiations with a view to executing this contract and I respectfully suggest Department ascertain at once whether American parties prepared to proceed and how negotiations are to be conducted. If Federal Company has not abandoned plan I consider it most desirable that representative with full powers should come to Peking immediately.

.   .   .   .

MAYER

893.74/499 : Telegram

The Secretary of State to the Chargé in China (Mayer)

WASHINGTON, *December 9, 1924—4 p. m.*

308. The pertinent portion of your 457, November 29, 11 a. m., was communicated to the Radio Corporation which now has the matter under consideration with officers of the Federal Telegraph Company. The Federal Company does not contemplate abandoning the project and it seems probable that an agent will proceed to China in the near future to conduct negotiations. The Department will advise you as soon as the Company formulates definite plans.

HUGHES

EXPLANATIONS OF POLICY BY THE DEPARTMENT OF STATE RESPECTING QUESTIONS OF TREATY RIGHTS RAISED BY AMERICANS IN CHINA

693.11171/66

Report of the Annual Meeting of the Associated American Chambers of Commerce of China, at Shanghai, October 16 and 17, 1923 [13]

AMERICAN RELATIONS WITH CHINA

"America has a definite and well-established policy toward China, based upon the open-door policy of John Hay and the principles of the Nine-Power Treaty adopted at the Washington Conference,[14] but the trouble with America's relations with China at the present time is due principally to the lack of a definite program." This statement by a prominent American observer of conditions in China summarizes pretty well the general feeling of the American resi-

[13] Transmitted by the consul general at Shanghai with despatch no. 2026, Jan. 14, 1924. The Associated American Chambers of Commerce of China consisted of representatives of American Chambers of Commerce at Shanghai, Hankow, Tientsin, Peking, and Harbin.
[14] *Foreign Relations,* 1922, vol. I, p. 271.

dents of China, whether they are interested in commercial enterprises or missionary-educational work.

The resolutions adopted at the annual meeting of the Associated American Chambers of Commerce in China held on October 16, and 17, 1923, in the city of Shanghai do not attempt to outline an American program suitable for coping with the serious situation which has developed in China in recent years. The resolutions do, however, represent the feelings or reactions of the American commercial communities in China in respect to certain matters which we believe should receive the serious attention of our people at home, both in government service and outside.

The lack of a definite program on the part of the American Government in respect to China which has been very much in evidence since the close of the Washington Conference, has been nothing short of disastrous to American interests in this country. The uncertainty has prevented the extension of business generally and in the case of firms with branches in the interior of China it has caused withdrawals and losses or depreciation of investment which has been most serious.

Practically the same thing applies to American missionary and educational endeavor in the interior of the country. Obviously a country harassed by unrestrained banditry and uncontrolled soldiery offers little opportunity for the efficient conduct of missionary educational work. The American people have probably invested in China an amount of money in missionary-education work which far exceeds the amount which has been invested in business and it obviously is the affair of the American Government to adopt measures for protecting these enterprises as well as the enterprises of business men.

It is our hope that these resolutions will be of service to American Governmental officials, chambers of commerce and other bodies in the United States which are interested in China and in a continuance of American effort in this part of the world, as well as a further cementing of the relations of the American and Chinese peoples.

Inasmuch as America took the lead in calling the Washington Conference and in directing its discussions, it is to be expected that this leadership on the part of the United States is to be maintained, otherwise the prestige which accrued to America as a result of the Washington meeting is likely to be lost.

[RESOLUTIONS]

ILLEGAL TAXATION

Various treaties between China and the foreign powers have put a limitation upon the taxation of imported goods, without regard to their nature. Any taxation levied in excess of those provided for in these treaties is therefore a violation of the said treaties. The first exception to this principle appears in the Washington Agreement in the provision that has been made for the levying of a tax on luxuries. It therefore applies that any violation of treaties by the illegal taxation of any article of commerce jeopardises the principle established by treaty and would further establish a precedent which might be extended to all importations.

Under the treaties, when goods are imported into China they may be shipped from treaty ports to the interior under transit pass, the payment for which exempts goods from all other taxation. This however, has been a point in dispute between the Chinese Government and foreign powers, the Chinese claiming that when goods reach their destination they are subject to additional taxes. This position has been strongly contested by the various Legations and the maintenance of the spirit of the treaties has been insisted upon although the Government in Peking does not successfully exercise its authority over all the provinces.

Under the provisions of the treaties providing for the use of the transit pass the shipper is given the option of either using the transit pass or shipping his goods to the interior without a transit pass, paying instead the local taxes. When the tax is paid by the use of the transit pass the funds are put into the regular Customs revenues which are hypothecated for certain purposes. Taxes paid in this form do not directly reach the provincial Governments or any other branch of the Central Government than the Customs. Certain provinces, however, have fixed the local taxes at such rates as would induce shippers to forward their goods without transit passes thus benefiting the particular locality. The effect of the treaties has therefore been to make the cost of the transit pass the limit of taxation on any article of commerce shipped into the interior. The treaties also provide that trade in the treaty ports be free from taxation so that the only taxes a merchant has to consider are those levied upon his goods when they leave the treaty port. But in spite of treaty obligations and special agreements arrived at between the Chinese Government and several Legations, various provinces have illegally imposed further taxes on certain commodities not only in the interior districts but even in treaty ports. The action of these provinces has been strongly protested by the British and American Legations both to the Peking Government and thru the consulates to the provincial authorities. The Peking authorities have admitted the illegality of the action on the part of the provinces but declare themselves helpless to enforce the rights and obligations created by the treaties and agreements made thru the Legations. But as these violations of the rights of foreign merchants established a precedent which may be followed and extended by military leaders in all sections of the country in order to secure funds for the maintenance of their armies: therefore, in view of the action taken at the Washington Conference wherein it is provided that a Special Conference is to be held in China for the purpose of revising China's customs revenues by the addition of a 2½ percent surtax on ordinary commercial goods and a 5 percent surtax on luxuries, the Associated American Chambers of Commerce of China recommend that the American Delegation to the Special Conference in association with the other delegations from the various nations give serious consideration to this matter of illegal taxation before agreeing to China's request for further increases in the customs tariff.

DISORDER IN CHINA

In view of the long series of outrages in China culminating in the so-called Lincheng Incident of May 5, 1923, which constitute a menace to the lives and property of American citizens and other foreign nationals residing in the country, the Diplomatic Body consisting of official representatives of sixteen nations on August 10, 1923, addressed a formal note of protest to the Chinese Government.[15] This note demanded that the foreign passengers be reimbursed for property losses, for loss of time and injuries sustained and also demanded the punishment of Chinese officials responsible and that proper means be taken at once by the Chinese Government for the protection of travelers and transportation of merchandise on the Chinese Government Railways.

The Ministry of Foreign Affairs of the Chinese Government in reply to this note stated among other things that

"The safety of foreigners has always been the subject of very deep solicitude on the part of the Chinese Government," and said further "That through the series of measures recently adopted the lives, property and interests of foreigners in China will enjoy added security."[16]

Since this reply of the Chinese Government was written there have been additional bandit and military outrages, one of which in Szechuan province resulted in the murder of two missionaries, and others in Honan and Hupeh provinces resulting in the murder of a Catholic priest, the kidnapping of two women missionaries and the destruction of considerable missionary property. In addition to these incidents there has been frequent firing upon peaceful American cargo and passenger boats on the Upper Yangtsze and in the case of a ship belonging to another foreign nation interested in this trade the vessel was raided by soldiers, several members of

---

[15] *Foreign Relations*, 1923, vol. I, p. 682.
[16] For text of note of Minister of Foreign Affairs, see *ibid.*, p. 696.

the crew killed, the chief officers carried into captivity and the cargo destroyed. Lists of these outrages affecting the lives and property interests of American and other foreigners and the Chinese people as well have been compiled by the Associated American Chambers of Commerce of China and are on file at the American Legation in Peking.

These outrages are a direct consequence of the condition of military anarchy which has developed in China since the country became a republic in 1911 which matter received the attention of the Washington Conference on February 1, 1922, when a resolution was adopted[17] expressing the earnest hope that immediate and effective steps would be taken by China to reduce the military forces and expenditures. This resolution received the signature of the Chinese Delegates as well as those of the delegates representing other nations at the Conference.

In spite of the foregoing action of the Washington Conference and the continued protests of foreign governments, the recruiting of troops into the various Chinese armies has steadily continued until the number of soldiers under arms in the country at the present time, according to the 1923 edition of the *China Year Book*, amounts to 1,335,835 [*1,332,835*] men, the largest standing army in the world.

The inability of the Chinese Government to keep this army paid and under control is the chief cause of unsettled conditions existing in the country. As the authority of the Central Government has broken down through conspiracy and civil war, the army has broken up into provincial units under the control of Military Governors or *Tuchuns*. Sections of the army, unable to obtain pay, constantly rebel and become bandits. The bandit gangs in turn terrorize the country, pillaging villages, burning property or menacing the lives of foreigners until they become strong enough to force their way back into some provincial army.

This situation of military anarchy which has developed in China constitutes a menace not only to the peace of the Far East, but to the entire world. It is a matter of special and vital interest on the part of the United States on account of our well known policies and trade relations with this part of the world, and especially because of our position of leadership in the calling and deliberations of the Washington Conference.

The Associated American Chambers of Commerce of China has always been of the opinion that nothing short of a definite stand on the part of the Powers would be sufficient to bring China's military dictators to a realization of the obligations of China as a sovereign and independent country among the nations of the world.

---

[17] See Resolution x, *Foreign Relations*, 1922, vol. I, p. 295.

Until such time as the nations which participated in the Washington Conference are prepared to adopt a definite policy in respect to China, it is vital that the United States take steps to secure to American citizens their just treaty rights in China.

To this end we feel that at the present time the maximum of protection in China for our interests can only be obtained by increasing our military and naval forces to the strength we are entitled to under treaty rights. This involves the bringing of our military and marine forces stationed in Peking and Tientsin under the Boxer protocol of 1901 [18] up to their full strength, and additions to the China section of the Pacific Fleet and the Yangtsze Patrol Squadron.

Both the State and Navy Departments at Washington in correspondence with the American Legation at Peking dated August 6 and 21, 1923, have signified the necessity for immediately increasing our naval force on the Yangtsze River and other navigable streams of China.[19] It is understood that the Navy Department has put in its estimates for the Budget to be presented to the next session of Congress, a request for the immediate construction of six river patrol boats of special construction for service on the Upper Yangtsze. It has been recommended that these boats be built on the Asiatic station in order to expedite their being put into service and for economy in the cost of construction. The Associated American Chambers of Commerce of China desire to go on record as being heartily in favor of these recommendations and urges that Congress give immediate and serious consideration to the proposals.

NEED FOR AMERICAN OWNED CONSULAR PROPERTY IN CHINA

The United States Government maintains consular officials in nineteen different treaty ports in China and with the exception of Shanghai and Amoy has never acquired property for the housing of the consul or office space for the transaction of the official business of the United States.

In the cases of Shanghai and Amoy where the consular property is owned, the property consists of antiquated residence buildings in a dilapidated condition which have been converted to office use. The condition of these buildings is such that frequent repairs are necessary to keep them in a habitable condition. In all of the other points in China, the American Government follows the shortsighted policy of renting property usually from native landlords and in very few cases is the property suitable for the purpose desired. In Tientsin

---

[18] *Foreign Relations*, 1901, Appendix (Affairs in China), p. 312.
[19] Department's instruction of Aug. 21, 1923, to the Minister in China, not printed; it transmitted a letter from the Acting Secretary of the Navy dated Aug. 6, 1923, and the Department's reply dated Aug. 20, 1923, *Foreign Relations*, 1923, vol. I, pp. 746–747.

a few years ago, the American Consul was forced to vacate his premises at short notice because the property was desired for other purposes by a Japanese landlord. In the city of Antung, the house occupied by the American Consul in 1923 collapsed during a heavy rain storm and had it not been for the hospitality offered by the Commissioner of the Chinese Customs, the official representative of the United States Government would have had no place to go. At one station in South China the house occupied by the American Consul is located on ground so poorly located as to be frequently flooded at high tide. In Hankow the foreign concession where the American Consulate is located has become so congested that it is questionable whether the present lease can be renewed on any terms.

The examples above, which are typical of the situation, point to the necessity of the United States Government acquiring its own consular property in China. The present rented property in use at most of the ports is inadequate from the standpoint of efficient conduct of the business of the United States which has grown proportionately with the rapid increase of American interests in this part of the world. America's share in the direct foreign trade of China has increased from 6½ per cent in 1910 to 16.3 per cent in 1922. The amount of money expended for rentals would pay for suitable consular property in a few years and when the rapid increase in property values at all of the Chinese ports is considered, there can be no question of the benefit of property ownership from the standpoint of investment.

In addition to the foregoing obvious reasons for the ownership of its own consular property on the part of the United States Government, there is the additional element of prestige which would accrue to America through the ownership of suitable structures for the residences and office requirements of the American consuls. It is difficult for the average Chinese, whose principal knowledge of the United States comes from his acquaintance with the American consul and his surroundings, to understand why America which plays such an important part in the affairs of the Far East, should be so negligent in respect to the housing of its official representatives.

The Associated American Chambers of Commerce of China recommend that a Government architect be sent to China to make a report and recommendation on the possibility of obtaining suitable land and the construction of buildings at the principal Chinese ports and cities where American consular officials are maintained.

IMPROVEMENT OF DIPLOMATIC AND CONSULAR SERVICES

There has been before Congress for several years a measure known as the "Rogers Bill" which is intended to improve the consular and diplomatic services of the United States through combining the two services into a unified foreign service.

According to the terms of the Rogers Bill provision is made for increases in salaries, travelling expenses, retirement and for promotions in accordance with the abilities of the individual.

In view of the fact that the question of improvements in the United States Consular and Diplomatic Services in China have been a frequent source of consideration on the part of this body as well as other American organizations in China the Associated American Chambers of Commerce of China desire to go on record as being in favor of and fully endorsing the Rogers Bill and expresses the hope it may be speedily enacted into law by Congress.

AMERICAN POLICY TOWARD CHINA

The Washington Conference which met in Washington on November 12, 1921, while called principally for the purpose of discussing the limitation of naval armament devoted most of its time to a consideration of the problem of China. At the close of the Conference a number of treaties and resolutions were adopted calculated to improve not only the international status of China but also provide a basis for an improvement of the internal situation.

In spite of the hopes of the leading statesmen of the world as expressed in the treaties and resolutions of the Washington Conference in respect to China, conditions in this country have deteriorated rather than improved and up to the present the leaders of China have shown an absolute disregard of the obligations of China as a sovereign power among the nations of the world.

Owing to the failure of the unanimous ratification of the various treaties and resolutions adopted at the Washington Conference the United States has made no move toward bringing into effect the Washington Conference decisions. In view of the serious situation which has developed in China as a result of the continued serious internal disorder the practical effect has been to damage the prestige of the United States which nation took the lead in the call and deliberations of the Washington Conference. Unless all Governments concerned ratify the Washington Conference treaties without further delay the Associated American Chambers of Commerce of China recommend that the United States Government take up this question with the Governments prepared to adopt a united policy in respect to the protection of their nationals and the general improvement of conditions in this country.

Inasmuch as America took the lead in calling the Washington Conference and in directing its discussions it is to be expected that this leadership on the part of the United States is to be maintained, otherwise the prestige which accrued to America as a result of the Washington Meeting is likely to be lost.

EXTRATERRITORIALITY

In accordance with the terms of a resolution adopted at the Washington Conference [21] an international commission of jurists was to visit China within six months after the adjournment of the Conference to report upon the status of extraterritoriality and to make recommendations for improvements.

On May 6, 1922,[22] the Chinese Minister to the United States requested the State Department to postpone the visit of the Commission for a year owing to the desperate political situation existing in China. In view of the fact that the year's postponement requested by the Chinese Minister has now expired and conditions in China have deteriorated rather than improved it is the opinion of the Associated American Chambers of Commerce of China that any consideration of a revision of the system of extraterritoriality now existing in China should be indefinitely postponed.

TONNAGE DUES IN CHINESE PORTS

The tonnage dues which China is permitted to charge foreign vessels are based upon treaties between China and other nations beginning with the Tientsin treaty between China and Great Britain signed in 1858. These dues amount to 4 mace (equivalent to 30 cents U. S. currency) per net registered ton on vessels of over 150 tons and 1. mace (equivalent to 8 cents U. S. currency) per net registered ton on vessels of 150 tons and under. The dues are levied in a lump sum upon any foreign ship that touches at a Chinese port, and cover a period of four months. These dues are higher than those charged by any other country and were adopted originally more than a half century ago because of the fact that few foreign ships touched Chinese ports and the high dues were necessary to provide funds for the construction and maintenance of light houses, etc. Since these high rates work a handicap upon American shipping not engaged in the coastwise trade of China, the Associated American Chambers of Commerce of China recommend that steps be taken by the United States Government to revise these regulations which have been in effect without change for 64 years.

The Associated American Chambers of Commerce of China recommend that all foreign vessels be granted the privilege of paying tonnage dues at the rate of 4 mace (equivalent to 30 cents U. S.

[21] *Foreign Relations*, 1922, vol. I, p. 290.
[22] According to Department files, this request was made on Apr. 13, 1922; see *ibid.*, p. 822.

currency) per net registered ton and good for a period of 4 months
or the privilege of paying tonnage dues at a fair rate per net registered ton per call.

SPECIAL TARIFF CONFERENCE

In accordance with the terms of a treaty adopted at the Washington Conference on February 6, 1922,[23] a special conference of the
powers is to be held in China to prepare the way for the speedy abolition of likin with a view to levying surtaxes provided for in the
treaty, the surtax to be levied at the uniform rate of 2½ per cent
ad valorem provided that in case of certain articles of luxury which
in the opinion of the special conference can bear a greater increase
without unduly impeding trade the total surtax may be increased to
but may not exceed 5 percent ad valorem.

Although two years have elapsed since the close of the Washington
Conference the special Tariff Conference has not been called owing
to the non-ratification of the various treaties and resolutions by all
of the Powers concerned. In case the various Governments finally
ratify the treaties and the special Conference is called, the Associated
American Chambers of Commerce of China desire to go on record that
any increases granted to China under the Washington Conference
treaty be predicated upon the condition that all defaulted foreign
obligations be secured out of the increased monies resulting from
the revised tariff regulations; it being understood that obligations
incurred by the operating departments of the Chinese Government
for materials supplied take precedence over all bonded indebtedness.

EXCHANGE OF NEWS BETWEEN UNITED STATES AND CHINA

Among the resolutions adopted by this body at its last annual meeting was one urging the importance of a fuller exchange and distribution of American news in this part of the world. Since the passage
of this resolution the Federal Telegraph Corporation of San Francisco in association with the Radio Corporation of America has
made a contract with the Chinese Government whereby a number of
high powered American radio stations are to be constructed in China,
the chief one being at Shanghai with feeder stations in the interior.

Owing to protests by other foreign interests the work of the American companies in the construction of these radio stations has been
seriously retarded. The Chamber heartily approves of the policy
of Secretary of State Hughes in upholding American rights in connection with the Federal Telegraph Company's contract [24] and hopes
that his vigorous policy in this connection will be continued.

---

[23] *Foreign Relations*, 1922, vol. I, p. 282.
[24] See *ante*, pp. 570 ff.

It is the belief of the Associated American Chambers of Commerce of China that the erection here of a high powered radio station will be of tremendous service in placing China in direct communication with the United States for the exchange not only of news but of commercial messages as well at reasonable rates.

YANGTZE PATROL FORCE

In view of the serious political situation existing along the Yangtze River which constitutes a menace to the lives and property of American citizens engaged in business and missionary activities, the Associated American Chambers of Commerce of China desire to incorporate as a part of this report a pamphlet entitled "For the Protection of American Lives and Property in China," [25] which was published on October 1st, 1923 and circulated to members of Congress and other officials of the United States Government and to Chambers of Commerce in the United States.

For years the American Chambers of Commerce in China have protested against the frequent changes in American officials assigned to posts in China. The Associated American Chambers of Commerce of China desire to repeat this protest and especially emphasize the importance of retaining experienced men in control of the Yangtze Patrol. In the past the policy of the United States has been to send naval officers to this post and as soon as they became familiar with conditions and have made connections with Chinese officials transfer them to other posts. This has had an unfortunate effect upon American prestige and has militated against the development of a definite and continuing American policy on the Yangtze. It is therefore recommended that experienced men be retained in this work as well as in other lines of American Governmental activity in this part of the world.

REPRESENTATION AT WASHINGTON

The Associated American Chambers of Commerce of China realize that more suitable action may be obtained on matters pertaining to China and the Far East, affecting American business and interests generally, if the Associated Chambers were directly represented at Washington. It is therefore recommended that arrangements be made at once to appoint a resident representative of the Associated American Chambers of Commerce of China at Washington who shall be empowered to give publicity to all matters which may be referred to him from time to time, to enlist the aid of the Chamber of Commerce of the United States of America, Government officials and de-

---

[25] Not printed.

partments and commercial and other organizations interested in the various subjects referred to him for attention.

PAYMENT OF CLAIMS AGAINST THE CHINESE GOVERNMENT

As a result of the disorder which has existed in China for many years American interests have suffered greatly by the loss or destruction of property resulting from bandit outrages, uncontrolled soldiery and internal fighting.

Claims covering these losses have been on file at the various consulates and the Legation in Peking for years with no settlement being made by the Chinese Government.

The Associated American Chambers of Commerce of China recommend that these claims be brought forward by the American authorities at the special conference and that the American Delegation be instructed to insist upon payment of these claims before agreement is given to the revision of the Customs Tariff.

PUBLICITY CAMPAIGN IN AMERICA

Owing to the fact that foreign trade occupies such a small portion of the interest or activities of the American people generally, it is always difficult to induce the American Government to adopt constructive and continuing policies in foreign affairs and especially in respect to American interests in this part of the world. The lack of familiarity on the part of many of the officials at Washington in respect to the protection of the lives and property of its own citizens not to mention the larger diplomatic and strategic interests of America in the Far East has made it necessary for American citizens both individually and through their organizations to frequently conduct publicity campaigns in the United States. Such publicity campaigns in the past, although largely unorganized, have nevertheless been of considerable benefit in concentrating the attention of the American people and through them of the government upon particular problems affecting the interests of Americans in this part of the world.

In view of the serious situation now existing in China which constitute[s] a menace to the lives and interests of American citizens residing in the Chinese Republic, it is recommended that the Associated American Chambers of Commerce of China give this subject special attention and that a special committee be appointed to work out in cooperation with other American organizations, a definite publicity campaign calculated to bring to the attention of the American people, members of Congress and other officials of our government the necessity of a definite policy in respect to the present situation of China.

THE BOXER INDEMNITY

In view of the fact that Congress has not yet taken action in respect to the disposition of the unexpended balance of the American share of the Boxer Indemnity amounting to approximately fifteen million gold dollars, it was decided that it would not be in accordance with traditional American policy toward China for the United States Government to withhold payment of this money on account of the present default on the part of the Chinese Government of American loans or obligations for materials purchased by the Chinese Government Railways and other departments.

In view of the great number of proposals which have been placed before this body covering possible uses for this money it was decided that the Associated American Chambers of Commerce of China should take no action on this subject at the present time.

The Associated American Chambers of Commerce of China are of the opinion however that any expenditure for educational or other purposes in China should be closely supervised by an American committee composed of representatives of the United States diplomatic or consular services and of the American business and missionary organizations in China.

AMERICAN INCOME TAX

American Chambers of Commerce in London, Paris, Mexico City, Buenos Aires, Manila and elsewhere representing American commercial interests engaged in foreign trade have for many years agitated against the injustice of the United States Government enforcing its domestic income tax regulations upon Americans residing abroad who derive their income from non-American sources.

The American Chamber of Commerce (Shanghai) after an agitation lasting over several years was able to obtain the passage by Congress of a measure known as the China Trade Act [26] which exempts American companies registered under the Act from the operation of the domestic income and excess profits taxes but was unable to obtain an exemption of American citizens generally from the domestic personal income taxes.

The provision in the Revenue Bill passed by Congress in 1921 intended to exempt Americans residing in the Far East including the Philippine Islands, and China was stricken from the bill when it went to conference before final passage.

There are approximately 240,000 foreigners residing in China of which number about 9,000 are Americans. Americans are the only foreigners who are required by their home Government to pay in-

---

[26] Of 1922; 42 Stat. 849.

come taxes upon income derived from activities in this part of the world and entirely outside of the United States.

The handicap which this places upon the American citizen in his competition with the British, Japanese, French, Germans and other foreigners interested in foreign trade in this part of the world is self-evident. Governor-General Leonard Wood of the Philippine Islands has well stated the case in letters and cables to the Secretary of War and to the President of the United States dated September 7 and 8, 1923. In these communications Governor-General Wood said:

"Filipinos and foreign residents of the Philippine Islands, business competitors of Americans, are exempt from Federal income tax paying only local taxes which are very much lower. Resulting discrimination against Americans on an outpost of our foreign commerce is grossly unjust. —— British subjects abroad have never been subjected to British taxation on income derived from sources outside of Great Britain. By the Finance Act of 1920 Great Britain has even gone to the extent of refunding to overseas British subjects taxes heretofore levied on income derived solely from British sources. Relief on the part of Congress would greatly facilitate the general efforts to build up our foreign trade now seriously interfered with by subjecting it here and elsewhere abroad to the handicap of heavier income taxes than those paid by foreign competitors. . . . I feel very strongly that the least the home Government can do is to give a considerate hearing to the American business men of this community in order that all the facts may be before you before definite action is taken."

The situation affecting Americans interested in business and other activities in China is exactly the same as the situation outlined by Governor-General Wood in the Philippines. All foreigners residing in China are subject to certain municipal and other taxes in the communities wherein they live but it is only the Americans residing in China who are subjected by their home Government to all of the domestic taxes of the United States even though the incomes are derived from sources entirely outside of the United States.

In view of the above factors the Associated American Chambers of Commerce of China desire to approve of the action of other American Chambers of Commerce in various parts of the world, and especially the action of the American Chamber of Commerce of the Philippine Islands, as well as the action of the Chamber of Commerce of the United States of America to the effect that Congress in framing the next Revenue Bill may exempt Americans residing overseas and deriving their income from non-American sources from the operation of our domestic income tax law.

UNPAID ACCOUNTS FOR MATERIALS SUPPLIED TO THE CHINESE GOVERNMENT RAILWAYS AND OTHER SERVICES

With regard to the obligations of the Chinese Government Railways the United States Government has adopted the position that obligations for materials supplied to the Chinese Government Railways "constitute a part of the operating expenses of the railways, and as such should be met before any charges on the surplus revenues are provided for, or before, in fact, it can be said that any surplus exists" or in other words, "that such obligations for equipment become a part of the operating expenses of the railways and as such form a prior lien on the actual earnings of the railways before any surplus can be said to exist," which position was transmitted to the Chinese Government by the American Minister in his notes No. 168, May 18, 1922,[27] and No. 219, July 7 [8], 1922.[27]

On September 27, 1923, the American Minister, in his note No. 627,[27] addressed to the Minister for Foreign Affairs, called attention to the fact that although almost a year had elapsed no reply had been received, covering the principle outlined above to the effect that "obligations for the payment of equipment become a part of the operating expenses of the railways and as such form a prior lien on the actual earnings of the railways before any surplus can be said to exist for the payment of bonded indebtedness." To this note an answer has been received which entirely ignores the point at issue.

In view of this continued disregard of the rights of American creditors of the Chinese Government, the Associated American Chambers of Commerce of China urge that the State Department instruct the American Minister to bring more pressure on the Chinese Government and that he insist that immediate arrangements be made to meet the obligations incurred by the Chinese Government Railways for materials supplied.

693.11171/66

The Secretary of State to the Minister in China (Schurman)

No. 600   WASHINGTON, *March 15, 1924.*

SIR: The Department has received from the Consul General at Shanghai a pamphlet entitled "Report of the Annual Meeting of the Associated American Chambers of Commerce of China, Shanghai, October 16 and 17, 1923", a copy of which has doubtless been transmitted to the Legation. Much of this report is devoted to criticisms

---

[27] Not printed.

of the conduct of the foreign relations of this Government with respect to China, which suggest to the Department the desirability of making, for the information and guidance of the Legation, such observations as appear pertinent to the criticisms made by the Chambers of Commerce.

The statement will be noted, in the introduction to the Report, that

"the lack of a definite program on the part of the American Government in respect to China . . ."[28] has been nothing short of disastrous to American interests in this country".

The introduction also contains the statement that

"the resolutions adopted . . . do not attempt to outline an American program suitable for coping with the serious situation which has developed in recent years."

While, therefore, complaining of the "lack of a definite program", the Chambers do not offer any suggestion as to measures which the Department might consider with a view to improving the very serious situation which unquestionably exists with respect to the adequate protection of the rights of all foreigners in China. The business men who have adopted the sixteen resolutions contained in this report presumably represent the leadership of American business in China. They are doubtless well informed with respect to conditions in that country. Although they may not have in general as full a knowledge of the political conditions, of which they complain, as diplomatic and consular officials have, they nevertheless come in even closer contact, in some respects, with the resulting practical conditions, than do government officials. They have a first-hand access to many sources of information which the Government's representatives lack; and the information obtained by Government officials comes in large part from the business firms represented by these Chambers of Commerce.

It may furthermore be remarked that the problems to be solved in connection with the maintenance of our treaty rights in the protection of persons and property are not, in general, of a technical character. The problems, and the practical remedies to be applied, if such may be found, are such as may appropriately be made the subject of discussion and recommendation by any group of intelligent persons having an accurate knowledge of the existing conditions. The question of the adequate protection of American interests in China is one in which these business men may be presumed to have a vital interest; for the failure to receive an adequate degree of protection means the serious impairment, if not the ultimate de-

---

[28] Omissions here and in the excerpts that follow are indicated on the original instruction.

struction, of the business interests which they have built up. The Department, accordingly, notes with surprise that (with such few exceptions as will be noted later) these resolutions are phrased in the most general language and contain almost nothing which is of assistance to the Department either by way of concrete proposals or by way of suggestions from which it might be possible to evolve some practical method of dealing with the situation.

By way of example, your attention is invited to the recommendation with respect to illegal taxation (page 5 [29]) that

". . . the American Delegation to the Special Conference . . . give serious consideration to this matter of illegal taxation before agreeing to China's request for further increases in the Customs tariff."

On the subject of disorders in China, the Chambers are of the opinion (page 8) that

"nothing short of a definite stand on the part of the Powers would be sufficient to bring China's military dictators to a realization of the obligations of China . . . Until such time as the nations . . . are prepared to adopt a definite policy in respect to China, it is vital that the United States take steps to secure to American citizens their just treaty rights in China."

In the section entitled "American Policy in China", it is stated (pages 13–14) that

"Unless all governments concerned ratify the Washington Conference treaties without further delay, the Associated American Chambers of Commerce of China recommend that the United States Government take up this question with the governments prepared to adopt a united policy in respect to the protection of their nationals and the general improvement of conditions in this country."

Under the heading of "Publicity Campaign in America", reference is made to the "necessity of a definite policy in respect to the situation in China" (page 22). The Report closes with the recommendation, relating to the unpaid accounts due from the Chinese Government for materials supplied by American firms (page 27), that

"The State Department instruct the American Minister to bring more pressure to bear on the Chinese Government and that he insist that immediate arrangements be made to meet the obligations incurred by the Chinese Government."

The phrases underlined above indicate the vagueness of the resolutions forming this report; and I cannot but acknowledge my regret that, in matters so vital to their interests, the Chambers have not found it possible to make, for my consideration, more definite and

---

[29] Refers to the page number of the original pamphlet.

more helpful suggestions as to measures that might prove practical to adopt for the better safeguarding of American interests in China.

This sense of disappointment is deepened by a consideration of the one or two concrete suggestions which the Chambers have offered. On page 8 occurs the statement:

". . . we feel that at the present time the maximum of protection in China for our interests can only be obtained by increasing our military and naval forces to the strength we are entitled under treaty rights. This involves the bringing of our military and marine forces stationed in Peking and Tientsin under the Boxer Protocol of 1901 up to their full strength, and additions to the China section of the Pacific fleet, and the Yangtze Patrol Squadron."

To the best of the information and judgment of both this Department and the War Department, the contingents now stationed at Peking and Tientsin are sufficient in point of numbers for the purposes of their detail; and, in the absence of any special emergency, there would appear to be no special advantage to be derived by adding to the number of Marines at Peking or by transferring from Manila to Tientsin another battalion of the 15th Infantry. As to the latter of these alternatives, it should be understood that such a disposition of troops is considered by the War Department not to be feasible, in view of the requirements to be met elsewhere with the limited available military establishment which the Congress has determined in accordance with the manifest desire of the people of this country. Quite apart from the administrative impracticability of this proposal, however, it seems plain that the presence of these few hundred soldiers would have no effect whatsoever upon the general protection of the persons and property of American citizens scattered throughout China, and would afford no remedy for the widespread conditions of which the Chambers complain.

It is not clear what is the interest in the Chamber's recommendation that "additions to the China section of the Pacific fleet" should be made. The cruising ships of the Asiatic fleet, including a large number of destroyers, have been readily available at Chinese seaports; and this Government recently assembled at Canton a larger number of vessels for a naval demonstration than did any other foreign Power. On this point, it would appear that the Chambers are in error as to the facts, and that there is no paucity of naval units of this character for the purpose of such conditions as exist at present. The recommendation with respect to an increase in the force of the Yangtze Patrol is, on the other hand, most pertinent; and as you are aware, the Department has for a long time been endeavoring, in cooperation with the Navy Department, to obtain legislative authority for the construction of new ships for this purpose. You were informed in the Department's instruction No. 578, of February 20, 1924,[30] that the Navy Department has, with the sanction of the Director of the Budget, introduced appropriate legislation into Congress for the construction of six high-powered light-draft gunboats for service on Chinese rivers.

In view of the serious actualities which confront Americans in China, both business men and missionaries, the Department does not regard it as surprising that they should feel strongly upon the subject of obtaining adequate protection, and should feel some anxiety lest the Government should prove indifferent to their interests. And it is no doubt but natural that, in their concern for those interests, they should fail to realize that the state of domestic opinion in this country would not permit the despatch of any further considerable military forces to China unless in the event of some impending catastrophe such as the Boxer movement of 1900. The extent of possible protection is, and must remain, substantially that which may be obtained by Diplomatic means and by the presence, actual or potential, of our naval forces in Chinese waters. Under these circumstances, I regard it as unfortunate that the American Chambers of Commerce should so far fail to appreciate the essential nature of the situation and the limits of action permissible to this Government as to give publicity to the resolutions contained in this report. Such publication serves but to emphasize the very precarious condition in which the whole system of foreign treaty rights in China now, unfortunately, finds itself in consequence of the great changes which are taking place in China which it is not within the power of the interested foreign nations to control or to restrain in any effective degree. It is my opinion that it would better serve the ends of American business and other interests in China not to invite public attention to this regrettable but unavoidable state of affairs, but, carefully and quietly, to give thought to the devising of practical means by which the problems involved may be met. I would heartily welcome the considered expressions of American residents in China upon this subject.

Deploring the evident existence of a feeling of dissatisfaction and misunderstanding among American business men in China as to the attitude of the Department toward the protection of their interests, I hope that, in the exercise of a sound discretion, you may find occasions to acquaint representative business men and others with the facts of the situation in such a way as will lead them to bring a less impetuous judgment to bear upon the question of dealing with those common American interests, with the protection of which this Department is charged. It is particularly suggested that you might find it possible to impress upon the more responsible and influential members of the American community the futility and the danger of

---

[30] Not printed.

the reiteration of threats of intervention, which, when for any reason not carried out, tend inevitably to lead the Chinese to the conviction that the remonstrances of the foreign Powers may safely be ignored.

The unfortunate state of domestic politics now existing in China, approaching a condition of political chaos, has likewise, and even to a greater degree, affected adversely the interests of foreign missionaries. The very great extent of American enterprise in this direction, constituting, both in the number of persons engaged and in the amount of capital invested, a larger element of American activity than is found in trade, adds materially to the problem of affording protection to our nationals in China. The right of residence in the interior, of which this group of our citizens has taken full advantage, has resulted in a diffusion of American missionaries throughout even the most remote and isolated parts of the country. This movement, over which the Government cannot exercise any degree of positive control, and which it would only reluctantly use its influence to restrict, has, in the growing disorder now so general, greatly complicated the problem of protection. In this particular, it is not possible to separate the interests of the trader from those of the missionary; and an act of violence to a member of either group reacts equally unfavorably upon the safety and well-being of both. It is felt that this has possibly not been wholly appreciated by the Chambers of Commerce, although the recent report of the formation in Shanghai of a joint committee, composed of both traders and missionaries, for the study of matters affecting their common interests, would indicate a quickening perception in this respect.

It may be remarked, furthermore, that the missionaries, as a group, have reacted to the present adverse situation in a somewhat different manner than have the business interests. With the exception of the Lincheng outrage, cases of actual violence to American persons and property have occurred chiefly to the missionaries. In so far as the Department is informed, however, missionaries have refrained from public resolutions of the kind passed by the American Chambers of Commerce, and have sought rather to keep their Boards at home informed of the very dangerous trend of Chinese affairs and to bring to the attention of the Department through various agencies, the difficulties of their situation and the very real need of such protection as the Government is able to extend. This attitude has suggested to the Department the desirability of obtaining a measure of direct cooperation with these interests in matters relating to the direction of their policies in China, in so far as such policies have a bearing on the problem of protection; and it has been felt that a frank exchange of views with representatives of the various Boards, in confidence, would be of service to this end. For this purpose I authorized the Chief of the Far Eastern Division to meet in New York, on February 21, with representatives of the Foreign Missions Conference of North America. In the course of this conference he made it clear that the Department had no intention of dictating to them or even of advising them, but desired only to give them an exposition of the present situation in China from the viewpoint of the Department, in order that they might be in a position to understand the problems of protection involved, and make their own decisions accordingly. He quite unreservedly explained the impossibility of controlling the situation by a display of force, or by such diplomatic methods as a proposal to withdraw recognition from the Peking Government; and he pointed out that this Government would in all probability find it increasingly difficult to give adequate protection to our missionary and other interests in the interior of China, and that it is possible only to rely upon our moral position, and to deal with each individual case as it arises. Under such circumstances, the mission Boards would have to take into consideration, in formulating the policies of their respective organizations, the very considerable limitations upon our ability to afford protection, especially in isolated stations, against the dangers likely to result from the revulsion of Chinese feeling against the special privileges enjoyed by foreigners and from the greatly lowered prestige of our western civilization in the eyes of the Chinese. The response of those present seemed to indicate an understanding of the limitations imposed by the changed situation in China, and the consequences involved therein.

It may be of interest to the Legation to note that there was a report from one of the representatives present of a strong and growing movement among the missionaries in China against any reliance upon such special privileges as extraterritorial rights, or upon any form of force, since it was not thought consistent with missionary ideals to ask indemnities for depredations, or even to expect to be forcibly rescued or ransomed in case of capture by brigands. To such an attitude, Mr. MacMurray made it clear that the Department is unreservedly opposed: in the interest of all our residents in China, and in the interest of China itself, it is felt to be necessary to hold the Chinese Government to as rigorous fulfillment as we may of the obligations due to foreigners. He pointed out that it is untimely to yield our rights in the face of an effort on the part of the Chinese to break them down, and that the interests of all Americans would be jeopardized by making any such renunciations so long as China does not in good faith and effectively live up to existing obligations.

The Department is hopeful that the discussion of these matters will prove of value in assuring sympathetic cooperation between the missionary interests and the various agencies of the Government charged with the protection of American interests in China.

I should also be glad to receive from you such comments on the matters herein discussed as may suggest themselves to you.

I am [etc.]   CHARLES E. HUGHES

393.116/310

The Foreign Secretary of the American Board of Commissioners for Foreign Missions (James L. Barton) to the Chief of the Division of Far Eastern Affairs, Department of State (MacMurray)

BOSTON, *March 18, 1924.*
[Received March 19.]

DEAR MR. MACMURRAY: Bearing directly upon the subject of the conference you were so kind as to give us the honor of having with you in New York two weeks ago on the subject of China and the relation of American missionaries to the present situation, I would like to submit to you a question which is evidently coming to the front in China, perhaps more rapidly than some of us are aware.

It is evident that a spirit of opposition to the extra-territorial conditions and of government protection for American missionaries is rising in some parts of China. There has just come into my hands a statement in terms as follows:

"Without attempting to enter into the general question of extra-territorial rights but having regard to the fact that we are here as messengers of the Gospel of peace and that our task is to establish peace by leading men and women one by one into that new life in Christ which takes away the occasion for all wars, we express our earnest desire that no form of military pressure may be exerted to protect us or our property, that in the event of our capture by lawless persons or our death at their hands no money be paid for our release, no punitive expedition be sent out and no indemnity exacted. We take this stand believing that the way to maintain righteousness and peace is through suffering without retaliation and through bringing the spirit of personal good will to bear on all persons under all circumstances. So we understand the teaching and example of Jesus Christ our Lord and it is to the extension of His Kingdom that our lives are dedicated. In signing this statement we wish it to be clear that we have no authority to speak for our missions or churches, and sign simply in our individual capacity."

This statement originated in China, but I have no information as to how many if any signatures were secured thereto. I would like to ask therefore if you can make a ruling upon some points which seem to bear upon this entire question.

1. The extra-territorial rights in China are rights by treaty as I understand. Has an American the right and privilege of vacating rights thus secured?

2. Should a missionary, in accordance with the above statement, decline to accept those rights as they relate to his person and property? Would that position endanger the life and property of other American missionaries, and if other American missionaries, then other Americans engaged in other pursuits in China?

3. If a missionary, contrary to the treaty, should be arrested and imprisoned and should refuse to make an appeal to his consul or the representatives of his government in China for protection, would the consul or representatives of the government, for that reason, refuse to insist that the Chinese Government should observe the treaties existing between the United States and China quite irrespective of the wishes of the party more directly affected? In a word, has an American the right in any country, and would that right be recognized by the U. S. government, to vacate his rights which belong to him as an American citizen by treaty, thus excusing the government in his case from insisting that treaties shall be observed? That is, can an American in China in some respects be an American citizen and in other respects not, so far as the claiming of his rights as a citizen are concerned?

I am preparing an article bearing upon some of these subjects for the general instruction of mission boards represented in the Committee of Reference and Counsel, and I would very much appreciate a ruling if you could give me one upon the question involved in this communication for use with these boards and with the missionaries concerned.

I have [etc.]　　　　　　　　　　　　　　　JAMES L. BARTON

393.116/310

The Secretary of State to the Foreign Secretary of the American Board of Commissioners for Foreign Missions (James L. Barton)

WASHINGTON, *April 1, 1924.*

SIR: The Department has received your letter of March 18, 1924, stating that there exists among American missionaries in China a growing spirit of opposition to the extraterritorial conditions and to government protection of missionaries thereunder, and making certain inquiries with regard to the right of American citizens to waive such privileges, if they so desire. In general, I may state that American citizens are not entitled to waive rights of the character to which you refer. The treaties concluded between China and the United States are contracts between the two governments. They expressly provide that American citizens in China shall enjoy, with respect to their person and property, the protection of the local authorities of government, and that they shall be exempt from the processes of Chinese law. The observance of these provisions of the treaties this Government has a right to insist upon, and doubtless would insist upon, irrespective of the wishes of particular individuals who may be influenced by religious or other beliefs. It has been repeatedly held that a citizen cannot by his independent act control the right of his government to intervene or afford protection in an appropriate case. In this connection, you may be interested to refer to Moore's *International Law Digest*, Vol. VI, p. 293.

With reference to the exercise of extraterritorial rights, Congress has, furthermore, enacted legislation extending to American citizens in China the laws of the United States. No American citizen in China, so long as he remains such, can waive the application to his person or property of such laws by the claim of a preference to be subject to the laws of China.

I think you will agree with me that the surrender of such rights by a portion of the American community in China, even if by a very small number of individuals, would seriously impair the whole system of the treaties as designed for the protection of all classes of American citizens in that country. It is hoped, therefore, that, in the article which you are preparing for the general instruction of mission boards, you may be in a position to make clear the attitude of the Department with respect to this subject.

I am [etc.]

For the Secretary of State:
J. V. A. MacMurray,
Chief, Division of Far Eastern Affairs

393.116/311

The Foreign Secretary of the American Board of Commissioners for Foreign Missions (James L. Barton) to the Chief of the Division of Far Eastern Affairs, Department of State (MacMurray)

Boston, *April 3, 1924.*
[Received April 5.]

Dear Mr. MacMurray: I am grateful indeed for yours of April 1st in reply to my inquiry of the 18th March on the subject of American missionaries surrendering extra-territorial rights in China. The position which you have taken is one that I have always taken in correspondence and in discussion, namely, that no American can be half American and half not American.

When I was in Turkey many years ago I wished to set the college press in action which had been closed and sealed by the Turkish government. I was informed that if I would forego my rights as an American citizen under the capitulations in so far as my relations to the press were concerned, they would allow me to open the press. This would have made me subject to all the Turkish laws and courts in so far as I was related to the press as its responsible head. I reported the situation to Washington and received back very speedily from Secretary Blaine a statement that, as an American citizen, I had the full right to abrogate my citizenship and become a citizen of Turkey or any other country, but that the Department could not recognize my right to be in some respects an American citizen and in other respects not. In a word, I could not be part American citizen and part citizen of some other country. I am not quoting his words, but the principle is the same as that which you enunciate it seems to me.

I understand from your closing words that I am at liberty to quote from your communication to the mission boards of the United States having missionary work in China and also in substance in the article to which I referred.

I want to thank you for the clear answer to a question which has a very important bearing, I believe, on mission work in China, and I think it is unanswerable. With much appreciation [etc.]

JAMES L. BARTON

PROTEST BY THE UNITED STATES AGAINST PARDON AND RESTORATION TO COMMAND OF THE CHINESE GENERAL HELD RESPONSIBLE FOR THE MURDER OF AN AMERICAN MISSIONARY [31]

393.1123 Reimert, William A. : Telegram

The Minister in China (Schurman) to the Secretary of State

PEKING, *January 4, 1924—11 a. m.*
[Received January 4—9 : 12 a. m.]

3. Legation's despatch no. 350, January 30, 1922.[32] Presidential order of December 27, 1923, authorizes cancellation of the mandate ordering trial and punishment of Chang Ching-yao. This is believed to be a political move to please Chang Tso-lin,[33] Chang Ching-yao being his personal friend. I was not consulted either before or after the granting of the pardon. American prestige is closely involved and we shall undoubtedly be severely criticized if we do not enter emphatic protest.

I do not think it would be possible to secure withdrawal of the pardon; but I request authority to lodge a very strong protest against it as a violation of the assurance given in the third paragraph the Chinese Foreign Office note of October 7, 1920, see despatch number 272,[32] same date, adding that such procedure is a discourtesy

---

[31] For documents relating to the murder of Rev. William A. Reimert by troops under command of Gen. Chang Ching-yao, see *Foreign Relations*, 1920, vol. I, pp. 435, 462, 806, 810–814.

[32] Not printed.

[33] Military ruler of Manchuria.

to my Government and also is an act that cannot but affect most seriously the confidence my Government can in the future place in the official utterances of the Government of China.

I think the substance of the protest should be made public and I propose to inform the diplomatic body of the circumstances.

For the Minister:

BELL

393.1123 Reimert, William A.: Telegram

The Secretary of State to the Minister in China (Schurman)

WASHINGTON, *January 14, 1924—4 p. m.*

14. Your No. 3 January 4, 11 a. m. You are directed to lodge with the Chinese Government a protest against the issuance of the Presidential Mandate of December 27, 1923, authorizing the cancellation of the mandate for the arrest and trial of Chang Ching-yao which is regarded as a breach of faith on the part of the Chinese Government and a specific violation of its undertaking in this particular as stated in the note addressed by the Minister for Foreign Affairs to the Legation, dated October 7, 1923.[34] In your discretion, you may add that this action cannot but affect most seriously the confidence of this Government in the future in the official utterances of the Government of China. You are authorized to make public the terms or substance of the protest.

HUGHES

393.1123 Reimert, William A.: Telegram

The Minister in China (Schurman) to the Secretary of State

PEKING, *January 24, 1924—9 a. m.*

[Received January 24—5 a. m.]

43. Your 14, January 14, 4 p. m. On January 18 I addressed note to the Chinese Minister for Foreign Affairs in the sense indicated. January 23rd at an interview I intimated to him that, in the absence of some satisfactory measure by the Chinese Government, I should feel obliged to publish substance of my note.

Minister for Foreign Affairs replied that apparently the nature of the mandate pardoning Chang had been misconstrued since in it Chang had been named with others in a general amnesty to political offenders as customarily granted on the accession of a new Executive. Not having particular reference to Reimert case, it could not be regarded as a breach of faith with the American Government.

---

[34] Not printed.

I replied that the fact remained that the Chinese Government had promised that the charge against Chang in condition [*connection*] Reimert murder would be included with the other charges for investigation, and the present mandate absolved Chang from trial.

Referring to the alleged political character of the pardon, I inquired whether the Chinese Government intended that Chang should still be tried in connection with Reimert charge. Dr. Koo replied that my note had been referred to Ministry of War and he wished to defer expressing himself definitely until he had received a reply. I consented to refrain from publicity or other measure until I heard further from him.

SCHURMAN

393.1123 Reimert, William A. : Telegram

The Chargé in China (Bell) to the Secretary of State

PEKING, *October 16, 1924—3 p. m.*
[Received October 16—10 a. m.]

390. My 43, January 24, 9 a. m. Further correspondence and interviews between American merchants [*Minister?*] and Chinese Minister for Foreign Affairs failed to result in cancellation of the pardon and on October 11th Chang was appointed by Presidential mandate one of the vice commanders of the rear guard army. On learning of this yesterday I immediately lodged strong oral protest with Koo who states that he had never heard of the mandate, denied that Chinese Government had any intention of disregarding views of the American Government and attributed issue of mandate to inadvertence incident to extraordinary pressure on Government departments. He seemed presumably very grateful and promised take up matter at once with Prime Minister. Meanwhile I shall address Koo strong note in line with your 14, January 14, 4 p. m.

BELL

393.1123 Reimert, William A.

The Chargé in China (Mayer) to the Secretary of State

No. 2624   PEKING, *November 22, 1924.*
[Received December 30.]

SIR: Referring to my despatch No. 2575 of October 31, 1924,[35] regarding the negotiations concerning the trial and punishment of General Chang Ching-yao for the death of an American missionary,

---

[35] Not printed.

Mr. William A. Reimert, I have the honor to transmit herewith enclosed a translation of the reply made by the Minister for Foreign Affairs [36] to the note which Mr. Bell addressed to him on October 22, 1924,[36] in which he protested against the appointment of Chang Ching-yao to a position of high rank in one of the military units of the Chinese army. The Minister for Foreign Affairs in his reply states that on October 24, 1924, a Presidential Mandate was issued cancelling the appointment of Chang Ching-yao to the position of Vice Commander of Reinforcements. The mandate referred to is doubtless that abolishing the posts of Commander-in-Chief and Vice Commanders for the Suppression of Rebellion, as no mandate has been issued specifically cancelling the appointment of Chang Ching-yao. A translation of the mandate of October 24th was transmitted to the Department with my despatch No. 2583 of November 5, 1924.[36]

I have [etc.] FERDINAND MAYER

---

[36] Not printed.

COLOMBIA

BOUNDARY DISPUTE WITH PANAMA

(See pages 287 ff.)

BOUNDARY DISPUTE WITH PERU

(See pages 293 ff.)

CUBA

PASSAGE OF AN AMNESTY BILL BY THE CUBAN CONGRESS

837.00/2513

The Ambassador in Cuba (Crowder) to the Secretary of State

No. 730   HABANA, *June 2, 1924.*

[Received June 7.]

SIR: I have the honor to refer the Department to previous reports from me at the time when I was Special Representative of the President regarding an Amnesty Bill which has been before the Cuban Congress for over three years.

I had addressed President Zayas on the subject on June 16, November 10, and December 9, 1921,[1] and on February 6, 1923, I quoted to the President a passage contained in a telegram dated November 4, 1922, from the Cuban Chargé d'Affaires in Washington to his Government (see my Special Mission despatch No. C–S–258, February 3, 1923 [2]) in connection with the Loan Statute, to the following effect:

"That this Government (i. e. of the United States) when granting said authorization, wished to express its great worry regarding two matters, that is: First, the Amnesty recently voted by the Cuban Senate, and, secondly, the possibility of changes being attempted in the present Cabinet, and from the phrases and tone used by the Sub-Secretary, I deduct that this Government would be greatly displeased and alarmed by the realization of any of these two propositions."

When this Amnesty Bill was again actively being considered by the House of Representatives, I once more addressed the President, on April 22, 1924, and reminded him of my letter of February 6, 1923, and of the above quotation.

The Cuban House of Representatives on April 22, 1924, rejected the Senate amendments to the original Amnesty Bill of 1921, and appointed a committee of five of its members to confer with a similar committee of the Senate and to report on the Bill. Upon being reported by this joint committee, the Senate passed it on May 26,

---

[1] Notes of June 16 and Nov. 10 not found in Department files. Note of Dec. 9 not printed; see telegram no. 149, Dec. 10, 1921, from Crowder, *Foreign Relations*, 1921, vol. I, p. 768. For excerpts from these three notes, see letter of June 2, 1924, from President Zayas to the Ambassador, *post*, p. 611.

[2] *Foreign Relations*, 1923, vol. I, p. 838.

1924, and at midnight it was, with unseemly haste, passed by the House. The votes were 13 to 4 in the Senate, and 62 to 18 in the House.

As I deemed it of importance that the President, before acting upon this bill, should have before him the views of this Embassy, I wrote a further letter to President Zayas under date of May 30, 1924, in which I reviewed the original bill as revised by the Congress in order that the comments of the Embassy might be responsive to the bill awaiting the President's action. A copy of this letter is transmitted herewith for the information of the Department.[3]

The President has not as yet signed the bill but according to newspaper forecasts he is likely to do so.[4] Even though he should veto it, the significant majority with which it passed both Houses would probably ensure its being passed over his veto.

I have [etc.]   E. H. Crowder

837.00/2514

The Ambassador in Cuba (*Crowder*) *to the Secretary of State*

No. 735   Habana, *June 6, 1924.*
                                                    [Received June 11.]

Sir: I have the honor to refer to my despatch No. 730 of June 2, 1924, transmitting copy of my communication to President Zayas *in re* the then pending Amnesty Bill, and to enclose herewith of [a] copy of his reply thereto.

It is pertinent to note the fact that he expresses the opinion that not more than thirty individuals will be released from the prisons in pursuance of this amnesty. I hope that this estimate may be correct, but in case this Amnesty Bill is like that of sixteen other amnesties which have preceded it in the history of the Republic of Cuba, we shall never have any report of the execution it has received.

The main application of the Amnesty Bill which the President signed will be to pending indictments in which, as yet, no sentence has been adjudged and which will now be dismissed; and to the still larger number of cases in which, for one reason or another, no indictment has ever been found. The Department will recall the Whereas Clauses of the original Amnesty Bill, setting forth the justification therefor. One of these clauses reads as follows:

"It is therefore a fact that no one can deny or ignore that during a period of more than fifteen years it has been the custom in this country to favor a multitude of persons with imaginary positions

---

[3] Not printed.
[4] The Ambassador informed the Department on June 5 that President Zayas signed the amnesty bill that day.

and *collectorias*, which were made to appear in the name of non-existent persons, which practice has prevailed in absolutely all of the branches of the administration, and that absolutely all social classes have taken advantage of this situation. The influence of the personages was measured by the number of these favors which he was able to distribute."

All cases of the character described in this quotation are covered by the amnesty and, in addition, those that are pointed out in the clipping from the *Havana Post* of June 6th hereto attached marked Enclosure "B".⁵

I have [etc.]   E. H. CROWDER

[Enclosure—Translation ⁶]

President Zayas to the American Ambassador (*Crowder*)

HABANA, *June 2, 1924.*

MY DEAR MR. AMBASSADOR: I take pleasure in acknowledging the receipt of your kind communication of May 30th last, relative to the Project of Amnesty Law, now pending my sanction.

In truth, I remember that when steps were being taken to obtain a Foreign Loan to take up the Floating Debt of the Cuban State, the Honorable Secretary of State of the United States, upon notifying our Chargé d'Affaires of the assent of his Government to said transaction, in accordance with the provisions of the Permanent Treaty, indicated that that Government was confident that the Secretaries of the Cabinet would not be removed, nor the Amnesty Law, which was already projected, approved. Naturally, I accept these friendly recommendations thankful to their good purposes, and I complied with them, although considering them as inspired by the circumstances of the moment in which they were made, and not as permanently maintained.

I also remember the communications from Your Excellency of June 16th, November 10th and December 9th, 1921. These communications contain remarks on the Amnesty Law, likewise circumstantial, and with reference to a determined and special situation. In fact, it is so demonstrated by the following phrases contained in your communication of June 16th: "it seems to extend amnesty as to most of the grave crimes, which are likely to be disclosed by the Superior Liquidating Commission." (This objection is now out of place, because the Law pending excludes said cases from the Amnesty, in paragraph 3 of Section (*a*) of Article I.) "I know of no measure that would strike more directly and effectively at the financial credit

⁵ Not printed.
⁶ Spanish text not in Department files.

of Cuba, at a time when every effort is being made to restore public confidence." (The words underlined refer to a moment which has already passed.) "No amnesty bill will be passed at the present session of Congress."

In the communication of November 10th, Your Excellency said: "It would be very unfortunate if any Amnesty legislation were passed by the Cuban Congress pending the loan negotiations. This is an inopportune time to agitate the question of amnesty."

Your communication of December 9th, more lengthy than the two previous ones, was for the purpose of suggesting your points of view in connection with the amnesty then pending, "in order that they may be the cause of revision by such persons whose services I might request, and whose knowledge in the matter and in the application of the Law might be better than your own." It is precisely the line of conduct which I have followed, because I consider your friendly advice as proper, and, after obtaining a delay of nearly three years, I have succeeded in reducing in an extraordinary manner the extension of the benefits of the amnesty.

It will suffice, to demonstrate this, that on December 9, 1921, when Your Excellency examined Article I of the Project of Law pending, listed up to 29 crimes or faults as included in the amnesty; and in the present Law, after my efforts with the Members of the Mixed Committee of Congress, they have been reduced to 17, and of these cases, there are two which have not given rise to sentences.

Article II of the former Project has been left out entirely.

Article I of the Law pending, in Section (b), does not seem to me to deserve the commentaries which Your Excellency makes, because it unquestionably presents a wide range to doubt of the justice or equity of a sentence of condemnation, the fact that three Magistrates, out of seven which formed the Court, may have given a vote of absolution.

As to the inclusion in the amnesty of such cases in which the offender alleged the complete circumstances of legitimate defence, but it is declared that the manner in which the facts were initiated or occurred, was not known or not proved, that is to say, the circumstances result incomplete, I must remind you that in Article 59 of the Electoral Code so much consideration was given to this circumstance, that, when they concur in the crimes of homicide, greater and lesser injuries, these are exempted from constituting penal antecedents, for the effects of said Code.

Within the opinion which peoples of saxon origin have of oath, and the respect which they have for it, Your Excellency is right in criticising Section (a) of Article II of the Law pending. I wish oath deserved the same respect among us, but unfortunately this is not so, in general, and it is for this reason that Congress includes such crime in the Amnesty, together with that of duel, to which importance is not given also, and to simple infractions and disciplinary corrections. It is precisely because I am convinced of the little efficacy of oath, that I have been trying to induce Congressmen that when Article 102 of the Electoral Code is modified, they may demand some proof in writing to effect any inscription of electors.

Section (b) of Article II concedes amnesty to public officials and employees. It is the second time, during the existence of the Republic that this has been done. The first time I was the promotor in the Senate, in the year 19)2 [*sic*], of an amnesty which included all American citizens and their co-offenders who had committed crimes during the Intervention, and the principal object pursued was to grant amnesty to the high officials of the Post-Office Department, General Rathbone, Mr. Neely and Mr. Reeve.

I wish to state that the Project of Law which I saw before approving the present, conceded the benefits of amnesty to the public officials and employees without limiting it to the crimes or misdemeanors committed in the exercise of their duties, or because of them; and, at my suggestion, that limitation was introduced, for the Constitution does not permit pardon in such circumstances.

Section (c) of said Article II has for its actual object the amnesty for members of the same Congress which has voted it, and from the point of view of principles, Dr. Dolz was right in attacking this extreme of the Law: but the same Senator, in a letter, which I have before me, directed to Mr. Wifredo Fernandez, says: "I have combatted that law with my word and my vote: But, once it is approved by Congress, it represents the will of the latter, which I revere, and which in my judgment, should also weigh in the consideration of the President of the Republic."

The two paragraphs of Article III seem to Your Excellency to be drawn up to cover certain cases of individuals, and not a general situation. It is probable that that is so, but they are without importance, for it is not an attempt to pardon crimes, but to annul penal antecedents only for political crimes, committed previous to the year 1915; for the crime of infidelity in the custody of prisoners, of the same epoch, and for those crimes whose penalty was accomplished, or pardoned (it does not include those who have not fulfilled the penalty involved), if in the sentence there were absolutory votes, which implies doubts as to the culpability.

I think that Your Excellency wrongly interprets the provision of Article VI of the pending Law, in thinking that it may infringe on the Constitution, in Article XIII. To reject such an idea, it is sufficient to consider that it does not annul nor alter any civil liability originating from the criminal actions for which amnesty is granted. Rather, the former Laws of Amnesty, in obliging the parties interested to discuss before the Courts of civil jurisdiction that liability, injured them, for they had to resort to proceedings that were costly, complicated and delayed.

By the prevailing Law of Civil Procedure, in every criminal case, the Fiscal exercises, in addition to penal action, the civil action, for the restoration of the things, reparation of damages, and indemnification for injuries, and on issuing the sentence, the Court should decide all questions referring to the civil liability. The new Law leaves in the charge of the Criminal Court, the obligation which it had to fix the amount of the indemnification, which has always been fixed by analogy with former cases, but in treating of injuries, as these require proofs, and admit of discussion, the Law follows the rule established in Article 116 of the Law of Civil Procedure, even though there had been no sentence, for, if it had been issued and were final, they would comply with that point.

It is true that the electoral crimes, because of the importance of the penalty imposed, are included in the Amnesty but there will be very few cases pending. As for the extinction of penal antecedents, for the effects of the Electoral Code, paragraph four of Article 59 of said Code prevents the consideration of this amnesty, which in no way influences in the application of the Electoral Code.

I do not believe that the American citizens can feel aggrieved at a Law of Amnesty which is constitutionally issued by Congress, and which obligates them in accordance with Article X of the Constitution; but, of course, the diplomatic way is a perfectly legal channel through which to treat of any concrete case.

I have detained, for three years, the definite passing of the Law of Amnesty, and I have succeeded in so reducing the cases which it includes, that, according to calculations made, there will not be more than thirty individuals who will come out of the Prison. I must not systematically and for a longer time oppose the manifest and persistent will of the Legislative Power, which, I am sure, would reject the veto, for I have in my possession a communication supporting and requesting the passing of the Law, signed by 18 Senators and 80 Representatives. With the same purpose, of supporting and soliciting said approbation, I was visited by a goodly number of journalists, who represented the majority of the newspapers of this city.

Very truly yours,

ALFREDO ZAYAS

CZECHOSLOVAKIA

EXCHANGE OF NOTES BETWEEN THE UNITED STATES AND CZECHO-SLOVAKIA PROLONGING THE CUSTOMS AGREEMENT OF OCTOBER 29, 1923 [1]

611.60 f 31/21

The Chargé in Czechoslovakia (Pearson) to the Secretary of State

No. 746   PRAGUE, *December 9, 1924.*

[Received January 6, 1925.]

SIR: Referring to the Department's instruction No. 212 of October 13, 1924 [2] directing the Legation to take steps with a view to renewing indefinitely the commercial agreement concluded October 29, 1923, between the United States and this country,[3] and to the Legation's telegram No. 48, December 5, 4 p. m.,[2] stating that it had been renewed "until the conclusion of a definitive treaty of commerce", I have the honor to transmit herewith a translation and copies of the Foreign Office Note on this subject, as well as copies of my own. In this connection I venture to observe that the interested Czecho-slovak authorities objected to renewing the treaty "indefinitely" on the ground that the use of this word might seem to imply unwilling-ness on the part of the United States to conclude, eventually, a defini-tive treaty of commerce; and that in view of the Department's de-sire to renew the existing agreement for an indefinite period and of its wish to negotiate a comprehensive commercial treaty with this country, it seemed more desirable to prolong the agreement at once, for what is in effect an indefinite period, than, through in-sistence upon the use of the word "indefinitely", to incur the risk, which the prospective absence of the competent Foreign Office of-ficials appreciably increased, that the actual agreement expire before renewal with consequent injury to American interests.

I have [etc.]   FREDERICK F. A. PEARSON

---

[1] For correspondence concerning the agreement of 1923, see *Foreign Relations,* 1923, vol. I, pp. 866 ff.
[2] Not printed.
[3] *Foreign Relations,* 1923, vol. I, pp. 873–875.

[Enclosure 1]

The American Chargé (Pearson) to the Czechoslovak Minister for Foreign Affairs (Beneš)

No. 628   PRAGUE, *December 5, 1924.*

Mr. MINISTER: I have the honor to acknowledge the receipt of Your Excellency's note of this day, by which you were good enough to inform me that your Government desires to prolong the commercial arrangement between Czechoslovakia and the United States concluded on October 29, 1923, and which not having been denounced before that date was to remain effective until December 31, 1924.

The Government of the United States being animated by the same intentions is in entire agreement with the proposition of the Czechoslovak Government.

Under these circumstances I have the honor to inform Your Excellency that my Government considers the agreement in question prolonged as from the exchange of the present notes until the conclusion of a definitive treaty of commerce, under the reservation, however, that each of the High Contracting Parties be empowered to denounce this agreement on condition that it give thirty days advance notice of such denunciation.

Accept [etc.]   FREDERICK F. A. PEARSON

[Enclosure 2—Translation]

The Czechoslovak Minister for Foreign Affairs (Beneš) to the American Chargé (Pearson)

No. 198.805/24   PRAGUE, *December 5, 1924.*

MONSIEUR LE CHARGÉ D'AFFAIRES: I have the honor to acknowledge the receipt of your note of this day, by which you were good enough to inform me that your Government desires to prolong the commercial arrangement between the United States and Czechoslovakia, concluded on October 29, 1923, and, which not having been denounced before that date was to remain effective until December 31, 1924.

The Government of Czechoslovakia being animated by the same intentions is in entire agreement with the proposition of the United States Government.

Under these circumstances I have the honor to inform you, Monsieur le Chargé d'Affaires, that my Government considers the agreement in question prolonged as from the exchange of the present notes until the conclusion of a definitive treaty of commerce, under the reservation, however, that each of the High Contracting Parties can denounce this agreement on condition that it gives thirty days advance notice of such denunciation.

I avail myself [etc.]   DR. EDUARD BENEŠ

611.60 f 31/21 : Telegram

The Acting Secretary of State to the Minister in Czechoslovakia (Einstein)

WASHINGTON, *January 12, 1925—2 p. m.*

1. Your 35, September 3, 4 p. m.[4] Your despatch No. 746, December 9. Does exchange of notes of December 5 require legislative and presidential approval and publication? Department wishes to publish in Treaty Series as soon as all Czechoslovak formalities are completed. Your omission of "indefinitely" approved.

GREW

611.60 f 31/22 : Telegram

The Minister in Czechoslovakia (Einstein) to the Secretary of State

PRAGUE, *January 13, 1925—5 p. m.*
[Received January 13—3 : 30 p. m.]

1. Your telegram number 1, January 12, 6 [2] p. m. Presidential and legislative approval to complete formalities and this must await reassembling of Parliament but the agreement has already been published in December 31st issue of *Official Record* and under a special law designed to meet legislative delay became effective January 1st.

EINSTEIN

_____

[4] Not printed.

DOMINICAN REPUBLIC

THE ELECTION OF HORACIO VASQUEZ TO THE PRESIDENCY AND THE EVACUATION OF THE FORCES OF THE UNITED STATES [1]

839.00/2782 : Telegram

The Commissioner in the Dominican Republic (Welles) to the Secretary of State

SANTO DOMINGO, *January 5, 1924—11 a. m.*
[Received January 7—2:35 a. m.]

2. As the result of repeated suggestions on my part General Vasquez and Señor Peynado, the two Presidential candidates, published yesterday official statements in which each declared that, should he be elected President of the Republic in the coming elections, he would maintain the Policia Nacional Dominicana upon the same basis as that which now exists; that it would be kept free from politics; that no appointments would be made except in accordance with the present regulations of the force; and that no promotions would be [made] except by merit. Finally, that the strict impartiality of the Policia Nacional would be considered an essential safeguard of the Republic.

These declarations which I consider of great importance provide a definite guarantee that public order will be maintained after the Occupation is terminated by a well-drilled nonpolitical force. Both candidates have declared confidentially to me that they will request the United States Government to continue American officers here as instructors of the Policia Nacional after the evacuation takes place.

WELLES

839.00/2786 : Telegram

The Commissioner in the Dominican Republic (Welles) to the Secretary of State

SANTO DOMINGO, *January 17, 1924—3 p. m.*
[Received January 18—5:11 p. m.]

4. Since an active propaganda has been initiated by certain elements in both parties in different sections of the Republic to the

---

[1] For previous correspondence concerning the holding of elections in fulfillment of the plan of evacuation, see *Foreign Relations*, 1923, vol. I, pp. 892 ff.

effect that the Government of the United States is supporting the candidacy of one or the other of the two Presidential candidates, I request your authorization to issue a brief statement comprising the following points: That the candidacies of General Vasquez and of Señor Peynado are equally agreeable to the Government of the United States; that the election of either would in its opinion constitute a guarantee that the coming government of the Republic would devote itself to safeguarding the maintenance of constitutional government in the Dominican Republic, to the continuance of peace and order and to the commercial and economic development of the nation; and finally that the sole interest of the United States in the coming elections is that the Dominican people have the opportunity to indicate with the utmost freedom their choice between the two candidates for the Presidency and that the candidate declared elected be installed as Constitutional President as soon thereafter as the terms of the Plan of Evacuation may permit.[2]

WELLES

839.00/2793 : Telegram

The Commissioner in the Dominican Republic (Welles) to the Secretary of State

SANTO DOMINGO, *February 4, 1924—10 a. m.*
[Received February 5—9 : 35 p. m.]

6. Señor Peynado advised me last night that he had definitely determined to resign as candidate the Presidency of the Coalition Party. He will so advise the national convention of his party today. He stated that the reason for his decision was the fact that he had spent all of his personal fortune in campaign expenditures, that he could obtain no further funds, and that his supporters would spend no additional sums in view of the certainty of the defeat of his party in the coming elections.

It is impossible for the Coalition to select any other candidate for the Presidency who can keep together the various political elements of which the party is composed. An attempt which will be at least in part successful is therefore being made by the executive committee of the Coalition to reach an agreement with the leaders of the Alliance Party by means of which the Coalition will be granted representation in the Senate and Congress and among the provincial officials in return for Coalition support of General Vasquez and Señor Velasquez

---

[2] The Commissioner was informed on Jan. 21 that the statement was authorized. For text of plan as amended and signed Sept. 18, 1922, see *Foreign Relations*, 1922, vol. II, p. 54.

as sole national candidates for the Presidency and Vice Presidency respectively.

Should this agreement be reached with the accord of the majority of the members of the Coalition executive committee it will result in the Senate and Congress being composed of the best elements in both parties. It will provide assurance that the coming constitutional government will always have majority support in the national legislature being in carrying out [*sic*] of the Government's policies and it will guarantee the successful execution of the Plan of Evacuation with the additional certainty that factional disputes will be obviated in this Republic for some years. An apparent disadvantage lies in the fact that if only one list of candidates is presented to the voters in the coming elections the number of voters will be comparatively small and the charge will be made by the critics of the United States Government that the coming constitutional government does not represent the majority of the Dominican people and that consequently the ratification of the treaty of evacuation stipulated in the plan will have been obtained by a minority vote. This charge can be easily disproved by reference to the registration figures for the elections which indicate 150,000 voters desiring to vote for candidates pledged to carry out the Plan of Evacuation and by reference to the fact that the opponents of the plan although they have had ample opportunity to do so have never brought forward candidates pledged to combat the carrying out of the Plan of Evacuation.

I am [confident?] should this agreement be satisfactorily carried out that the ablest men in the country will be disposed to enter the Cabinet, the Senate and the House making it possible for the majority of the old school politicians who are responsible for the disastrous history of this country to be permanently eliminated from participation in public affairs. With the written commitment which I have obtained from General Vasquez and Señor Velasquez regarding the Policia Nacional Dominicana referred to in my telegram of January 5, 11 a.m., with their like written commitment to maintain the civil service law in all branches of the Executive department and to obtain the adoption of a constitutional amendment providing for life tenure of office during good behavior, I have reason to believe that the Government of the United States can be reasonably confident that a period of peace and progressive government is assured for this Republic.

WELLES

839.00/2796 : Telegram

The Commissioner in the Dominican Republic (Welles) to the Secretary of State

SANTO DOMINGO, *February 9, 1924—10 a. m.*
[Received February 10—11 p. m.]

9. My telegram of February 4, 10 a. m. Señor Peynado's friends have persuaded him for the time being from insisting upon the immediate acceptance of his resignation as candidate for the national assembly of the Coalition Party, the knowledge of his resignation is, however, general and defections from the party's ranks are widespread. Señor Enrique Jimenez, president of the former Liberal Party, of the members of which the coalition is largely composed, has resigned from the Coalition Party and all of his friends will follow him. Whether or not an agreement is reached between the leaders of the coalition and the candidates of the alliance, the Alliance Party will now undoubtedly receive the support of majority of the better elements in the Coalition Party as stated in my telegram above referred to.

Señor Peynado and Señor Brache yesterday requested me to exert my influence to force General Vasquez to resign his candidacy in order that a national candidate satisfactory to both parties might be elected. I advised them that I would not. I called to their attention article 1 of the Plan of Evacuation which constitutes the agreement on the part of the United States to enable the Dominican people to elect freely their future constitutional government, and stated that since General Vasquez was the legally nominated candidate of one of the parties, I should assure myself that he was given equal rights with the candidate of any other party to prove by means of the national election whether or not his candidacy had the support of the majority of the voters. In reply to a further inquiry in accordance with [my?] position before my departure for Washington, I stated that the mere fact that one of the two parties did not vote in the elections would not be considered proof that the party which did go to the polls did not represent the will of the people, nor that the candidates which might be so elected were not elected in accordance with the Constitution. Finally in response to a plea that the date of the elections be once more postponed in order that Señor Peynado's friends might be given an opportunity to obtain additional funds for the campaign, I stated that the date of the elections had been set with the consent of both parties, and that the elections without change positively take place on that day.

Every attempt will now be made by certain elements in the coalition to obstruct the electoral procedure and to protest against the result of the elections, should the Alliance Party be the only party to go to the polls. After conversation with all the leaders of the former party, however, I am convinced that the saner element will cooperate with a government headed by General Vasquez, should Señor Peynado persist in his resignation, and that only a few for purely political ends will insist upon obstruction.

WELLES

839.00/2797 : Telegram

The Commissioner in the Dominican Republic (Welles) to the Secretary of State

SANTO DOMINGO, *February 13, 1924—4 p. m.*
[Received February 15—1 : 44 a. m.]

10. My telegram of February 4, 10 a.m., and February 9, 10 a.m. Upon ascertaining that neither the threatened abstention of the Coalition [candidate?] from the elections nor his threatened withdrawal as a candidate would bring about a further postponement of the elections nor cause the Alliance Party to consent to enter into a political deal, Señor Peynado on February 11 definitely advised the national assembly of his party that he would continue as Presidential candidate. The chances of success for the Coalition Party in the national elections appear exceedingly small and it seems to be the endeavor of the leaders of the party at present to concentrate their efforts upon the few provinces where they have an opportunity of winning the elections. Obstructive methods are already being employed by the Coalition Party with a view to retarding the electoral procedure, but I do not consider that these tactics can meet with success.

WELLES

839.00/2800 : Telegram

The Commissioner in the Dominican Republic (Welles) to the Secretary of State

SANTO DOMINGO, *February 26, 1924—4 p. m.*
[Received February 27—11 : 53 p. m.]

15. The legal period for the completion by the municipal electoral boards of the permanent electoral registers in their respective communes expired at midnight February 24. The boards of the three largest communes—Santo Domingo, Santiago and La Vega—have each failed to include some hundreds of citizens who had registered before the legal period for the completion of the lists had terminated. This failure was largely due to the obstructive methods pursued

by the representatives of the Coalition Party on the electoral boards in question.

The Coalition Party yesterday advised the Commission that it protest[s] against the legality of the election to be held in those communes as well as in others on the ground that qualified voters will be deprived of their legal privileges as well as on the ground that the electoral boards had resorted to illegal methods in the formation of electoral registers. This protest was made notwithstanding the fact that the electoral law makes specific provision for the inclusion or exclusion of qualified voters in the electoral registers after the lists are terminated by means of petitions addressed during the five days subsequent to the municipal boards, which petitions may also be carried on appeal to the Central Electoral Board. The Coalition Party through its representative on the Commission demanded that the requirement in the electoral law that citizens in order to vote must be included in the permanent electoral register, be abolished. It demanded that all inhabitants in the Republic be permitted to vote on election day, the only control maintained to be the presence of political observers in polling booths or without. After prolonged discussion lasting over 18 hours the members of the Commission unanimously adopted my counter-proposal that in order to obviate the difficulties presented, an extension of two days be granted the municipal boards above referred to in which to complete the electoral register; and that a similar extension be granted for the purpose of demanding the inclusion or exclusion of voters in those communes after the registers were completed. The adoption of the proposal of the Coalition Party would necessarily have implied complete abandonment of the basic principle upon which the entire electoral procedure under the present law is built up.

The promulgation today by the President of a decree embodying the modification adopted by the Commission has rendered it impossible for any elections to be annulled on the ground that the electoral registers were not completed within the legal time limit.

WELLES

839.00/2809 : Telegram

The Commissioner in the Dominican Republic (Welles) to the Secretary of State

SANTO DOMINGO, *March 17, 1924—11 a. m.*
[Received March 19—8 : 15 a. m.]

17. The national election took place March 15th without disturbance of any kind. Every precaution had been taken by the

national police to prevent disorder but not a single arrest had to be made in the entire Republic for breach of peace. In all the provinces I visited the voting took place with entire order and apparent cordiality between the members of the opposing parties. As an indication of this the candidate for the Presidency of the Coalition Party and the candidate for the Vice Presidency of the Alliance Party went together to vote in the same precinct board.

The returns received from the municipal electoral boards indicate that General Vasquez and the candidates of the Alliance Party have swept the country. It appears that the Alliance Party will have 11 out of 12 members of the Senate and 25 out of 31 members of the House of Deputies. That party has likewise apparently elected 90 percent of the municipal governments.

While the Coalition Party will undoubtedly protest against the electoral returns in certain communes, it is my belief that these protests will be resolved shortly by the Central Electoral Board and that the final results of the elections will be officially announced by that body before March 25th.

WELLES

839.00/2814 : Telegram

The Commissioner in the Dominican Republic (Welles) to the Secretary of State

SANTO DOMINGO, *March 25, 1924—9 a. m.*
[Received March 26—12:45 a. m.]

23. I have just been advised that the Navy Department is relieving General Lee, present Military Governor, and that General Cole will arrive here to replace him before April 15th. General Lee has been Military Governor since the installation of the Provisional Government and has done most effective work in maintaining cordial relations between the Provisional Government and the Military Government. From present indications I believe that the newly elected Constitutional Government will be installed by July 1st. Under these circumstances it appears to me that the appointment of a new Military Governor at this time may be misinterpreted and also that the appointment of a new Military Governor unfamiliar with local conditions is prejudicial to the satisfactory completion of the carrying out of the Plan of Evacuation. I hope the Department may feel disposed to request Navy Department not to make any change in the Military Government during the short period that remains before evacuation takes place.

WELLES

033.3911/orig. : Telegram

The Commissioner in the Dominican Republic (Welles) to the Secretary of State

SANTO DOMINGO, *March 27, 1924—3 p. m.*
[Received March 28—12: 42 a. m.]

25. In view of the precedents created by the visits to the United States of the Presidents-elect of several Latin American Republics which produced in general such excellent results, will you authorize me to inform the President-elect of this Republic that should he visit United States for reasons of health as he now purposes for a short stay prior to his inauguration, he will be invited to come to Washington for a few days as the guest of the United States Government.

I believe that the opportunity so afforded him of conferring with the President and yourself, of learning your views and of thus establishing a personal relationship would prove exceedingly beneficial in the carrying out of our future policy here. I also believe that the honor so paid the newly elected Chief Executive of the Republic will be highly appreciated by the Dominican people.

WELLES

033.3911/orig. : Telegram

The Secretary of State to the Commissioner in the Dominican Republic (Welles)

WASHINGTON, *April 1, 1924—5 p. m.*

10. Your 25, March 27, 3 p.m. Since no provision therefor exists it is not the practice of the Federal Government to invite Chiefs of States or Presidents-elect to visit the United States as the guests of the Government; but you may say to the President-elect that should he desire to come to the United States and to visit Washington, the President will be most happy to receive him.

See confidential circular February 28, 1903,[3] to diplomatic officers, in Legation's files.

HUGHES

---

[3] Not printed; in it diplomatic officers were informed that neither American law nor usages provided for inviting foreign sovereigns and chiefs of state to visit the United States.

839.00/2814 : Telegram

The Secretary of State to the Commissioner in the Dominican
Republic (Welles)

WASHINGTON, *April 7, 1924—3 p. m.*

13. Your 23, March 25, 9 a. m. Department informed by Secretary of the Navy that he has decided to keep General Lee in his office as Military Governor until after July 1, and has therefore directed that the order for his relief in April be revoked.

HUGHES

839.00/2833 : Telegram

The Commissioner in the Dominican Republic (Welles) to the
Secretary of State

SANTO DOMINGO, *May 16, 1924—4 p. m.*
[Received May 17—4 : 42 a. m.]

30. Since my return [4] I have held various conferences with the Provisional President, the President-elect, the members of the Commission and the presidents of the Senate and House of Deputies. The constitutional reforms submitted to the Senate by the Provisional President will be approved by the Senate in the form presented to-morrow. They will be finally approved by the House of Deputies not later than May 21st. These reforms were agreed upon prior to my departure and are entirely satisfactory.

The President-elect advised me yesterday that the Cabinet appointments tentatively agreed upon with me April 11th will be definitely made. They are as follows: Enrique Jimenez, Minister of Foreign Affairs; Angel Morales, Minister of the Interior and Police; Juan B. Vicini Burgos, Minister of the Treasury; Andres Pastoriza, Minister of Fomento and Communication; Rafael Espaillat, Minister of Agriculture and Immigration. The positions of Minister of Justice and Public Instruction and Minister of Sanitation are to be filled by followers of Señor Velasquez. These have not yet been definitely determined. I cannot speak too highly of the quality of the men above mentioned selected by General Vasquez to form his Cabinet. Politics have been completely disregarded and he has selected the men of the greatest ability in the country whose capacity and integrity are recognized by all.

It is the intention of General Vasquez to go to the United States nominally for a vacation in the beginning of June. He will be accompanied by Señor Ariza whom he has selected as Dominican Min-

---

[4] From Honduras, to which country, on Apr. 8, the Commissioner had been instructed to proceed ; see vol. II, p. 300.

ister at Washington and Señor Alfredo Ricart president of the Ayuntamiento of Santo Domingo. I have heartily encouraged this decision in order that he may in this manner obtain the opportunity of conversing with yourself and the President regarding the future policy of his Government as well as its relations with the Government of the United States. It is in particular the desire of General Vasquez to reach an agreement with the Department of State looking towards the refunding of the foreign debt of the Republic through the flotation of a loan in the United States. The satisfactory carrying out of this operation which of course by reason of the convention 1907 [5] requires the consent of the Government of the United States would make it possible for the Dominican Government to obtain the use of a larger portion of the customs revenues for current expenses and at the same time obtain additional funds to be used in the carrying out of the complete program of public works. This operation in my opinion is essential if the Republic is really to progress. Futhermore it is the desire of General Vasquez to discuss the possibility of negotiating a new commercial treaty with the United States.

In this connection I desire to refer to my telegram of March 27, 3 p. m., and to the Department's reply thereto of April 1, 5 p. m. I appreciate of course that under ordinary circumstances it is not desirable for the Government of the United States to invite the Presidents-elect of Latin American Republics to visit the United States before they assume office. The approaching evacuation of this Republic by the American Forces of [Occupation?] after eight years of Military Government and the installation of a Constitutional Government in the Dominican Republic friendly disposed to American interests create an exceptional case. Even if the Department does not desire to invite General Vasquez to be the guest of the nation during his brief stay in Washington, I trust that in view of these special circumstances the attempt will be made to accord him an official reception and to facilitate the accomplishment of the objective which he is seeking.

The situation here is in general entirely satisfactory. My information leads us to believe that the program of evacuation will be carried through speedily and without delay. I consider that it would be highly desirable for me to be in Washington during the time of General Vasquez's visit there and for this reason I request your permission to return to Washington without delay. I am also exceedingly desirous of laying before you certain considerations of the utmost importance regarding conditions in Central America. I believe the situation in certain of the Central American countries

---

[5] *Foreign Relations*, 1907, pt. I, p. 307.

to be exceedingly precarious and I desire to have the opportunity
of suggesting important changes in our policy.   In addition for personal reasons it is necessary for me to return to the United States
without delay.   In view of these considerations I hope that you will
authorize me to return to Washington during the week.[6]

WELLES

839.00/2835 : Telegram

*The Minister in the Dominican Republic (Russell) to the Secretary
of State*

SANTO DOMINGO, *May 25, 1924—noon.*
[Received May 26—10:15 a. m.]

16. The Government has named the following plenipotentiaries for
the negotiation of the treaty provided for in the Plan of Evacuation: Horacio Vasquez, President-elect; Federico Velásquez, Vice
President-elect; and Francisco J. Peynado.

RUSSELL

839.00/2852

*The Commissioner in the Dominican Republic (Welles), Temporarily
in the United States, to the Secretary of State*

WASHINGTON, *June 4, 1924.*

DEAR MR. SECRETARY: In accordance with Article 7 of the Plan of
Evacuation, the Provisional President of the Dominican Republic has
appointed General Vasquez, President-elect, as one of the three plenipotentiaries of the Dominican Government to sign the Treaty of
Ratification.   This treaty, of course, was actually negotiated in August, 1922, and the form agreed upon is published textually in the
Plan of Evacuation.   All that is required, therefore, in order to
carry out the provisions of Article 7, is the sending of the necessary
authorization to the American Minister in Santo Domingo to sign
the Treaty on behalf of the Government of the United States.

In a telegram dated June 3rd, copy of which I attach herewith,[7]
the American Minister states that General Vasquez does not feel that
he can leave Santo Domingo in order to visit the United States until
this treaty has been signed.   I beg to request, therefore, that the necessary instructions be sent to the American Minister without delay
in order that the treaty may be signed in the course of the coming

---

[6] The authorization requested was granted.   Mr. Welles did not return to
the Dominican Republic, and resigned as Commissioner July 13, 1925.
[7] Not printed.

week, since General Vasquez would have to leave Santo Domingo by June 15th in order to reach Washington for the week of June 23rd.

WELLES

839.00/2836a

The Secretary of State to the Secretary of the Navy (Wilbur)

WASHINGTON, *June 4, 1924.*

SIR: The final provisions of the Plan for the Evacuation of the Dominican Republic by the American Forces of Occupation are now being carried out. It is probable that all the remaining steps will have been taken before the end of the present month and that the Constitutional President of the Republic will be inaugurated upon some day between July 1st and July 10th. Since the Plan of Evacuation provides that as soon as the Constitutional President has taken office and has signed the Convention and the legislation stipulated in the Plan of Evacuation, the Military Forces of the United States will at once evacuate the territory of the Dominican Republic, I have the honor to request that the necessary instructions be sent to the Military Governor to take all the steps necessary to make possible the immediate evacuation of the Republic after the inauguration of the Constitutional President. I am informed by the American Commissioner in the Dominican Republic that he is advised by the Military Governor that no instructions have been received by him relative to the evacuation of the Forces of Occupation. The Military Governor has stated that some time will be required to make the necessary arrangements, and in view of the fact that the inauguration of the Constitutional President of the Dominican Republic will take place approximately a month from the present date, I have the honor to request that the Military Governor be instructed to expedite the arrangements for evacuation.

I have [etc.]   CHARLES E. HUGHES

033.3911/2a : Telegram

The Secretary of State to the Minister in the Dominican Republic (Russell)

WASHINGTON, *June 4, 1924—noon.*

12. Please transmit the following confidential message to General Vasquez from Mr. Welles:

"In accordance with our conversation the night prior to my departure from Santo Domingo, I trust that it will be possible for you and the members of the party which you have selected to visit Washington during the present month. I have ascertained that the most desirable time for your visit would be during the week commencing June 23rd. As you know, I attribute the greatest importance to the opportunity which your visit here will afford for the reaching of an agreement in principle regarding the various matters which we have discussed. I shall be grateful if you will advise me, by cable through the American Legation, as soon as you have determined the date of your departure and the steamer upon which you are sailing in order that I may make appropriate arrangements. Please accept my most cordial greetings."

HUGHES

839.00/2836 : Telegram

The Secretary of State to the Minister in the Dominican Republic (Russell)

WASHINGTON, June 7, 1924—6 p. m.

16. Your June 3, 6 p. m.[8] The President has executed the full powers authorizing you to conclude and sign the Convention of Ratification as contained in the Agreement of Evacuation of June 30, 1922, in the form published on September 23, 1922.

The full powers read as follows:

[Here follows text of full powers.]

The full powers have been exhibited today to the Dominican Minister in Washington who has found them to be in due and proper form. He is so informing his Government. You are therefore authorized to meet the plenipotentiaries appointed by the Dominican Government and with them to conclude and sign this Convention. You are instructed to observe the alternate in signing and to verify carefully the English text and the Spanish translation.

Full powers are being forwarded by mail.

HUGHES

839.00/2841

The Minister in the Dominican Republic (Russell) to the Secretary of State

No. 1009   SANTO DOMINGO, *June 12, 1924.*

[Received June 20.]

SIR: I have the honor to transmit herewith, in English and Spanish, the Convention of Ratification provided for in the Plan of Evacuation agreed upon on June 30, 1922. This Convention was signed today, and I am sending it by General Vasquez who is leaving for Washington tomorrow. Copies of the Convention will be forwarded by next mail.

I have [etc.]   WILLIAM W. RUSSELL

---

[8] Not printed; see the Commissioner's letter of June 4, p. 628.

Treaty Series No. 729

Convention between the United States of America and the Dominican Republic, Signed at Santo Domingo, June 12, 1924 [9]

WHEREAS, in the month of May, 1916, the territory of the Dominican Republic was occupied by the forces of the United States of America, during which occupation there was established, in substitution of the Dominican Government, a Military Government which issued governmental regulations under the name of Executive Orders and Resolutions and Administrative Regulations, and also celebrated several contracts by virtue of said Executive Orders or by virtue of some existing laws of the Republic;

WHEREAS, the Dominican Republic has always maintained its right to self-government, the disoccupation of its territory and the integrity of its sovereignty and independence; and the Government of the United States has declared that, on occupying the territory of the Dominican Republic, it never had, nor has at present, the purpose of attacking the sovereignty and independence of the Dominican Nation; and these rights and declarations gave rise to a Plan or *Modus Operandi* of Evacuation signed on June 30, 1922, by Monseñor A. Nouel, General Horacio Vasquez, Don Federico Velasquez y H., Don Elías Brache, hijo, and Don Francisco J. Peynado, and the Department of State, represented by the Honorable William W. Russell, Envoy Extraordinary and Minister Plenipotentiary of the United States in the Dominican Republic, and the Honorable Sumner Welles, Commissioner of the President of the United States, which met with the approval of the Dominican people, and which approval was confirmed at the elections that took place on March 15, of the present year;

WHEREAS, although the Dominican Republic has never delegated authority to any foreign power to legislate for it, still, it understands that the internal interests of the Republic require the validation or ratification of several of the Executive Orders and Resolutions, published in the Official Gazette, as well as the Administrative Regulations and Contracts of the Military Government celebrated by virtue of said Orders or of any Law of the Republic; and, on its part, the United States considers that it is also to its interest that said acts be validated or ratified; for these reasons one of the stipulations in the above-mentioned Plan of Evacuation provides for the celebration of a Treaty or Convention of Ratification or Validation of said Orders, Resolutions, Regulations and Contracts;

[9] In English and Spanish; Spanish text not printed. Ratification advised by the Senate, Jan. 21, 1925; ratified by the President, June 1, 1925; ratified by the Dominican Republic, June 30, 1925; ratifications exchanged at Santo Domingo, Dec. 4, 1925; proclaimed by the President, Dec. 8, 1925.

THEREFORE, the United States of America and the Dominican Republic, desirous of celebrating the above-mentioned Treaty or Convention, have named for this purpose their Plenipotentiaries as follows:

The President of the United States, William W. Russell, Envoy Extraordinary and Minister Plenipotentiary of the United States in Santo Domingo, and,

The Provisional President of the Dominican Republic, Don Horacio Vasquez, Don Federico Velasquez y H., and Don Francisco J. Peynado,

who, after having exchanged their full powers, and after having found them in due and proper form, have agreed upon the following:

I. The Dominican Government hereby recognizes the validity of all the Executive Orders and Resolutions, promulgated by the Military Government and published in the Official Gazette, which may have levied taxes, authorized expenditures, or established rights on behalf of third persons, and the administrative regulations issued, and contracts which may have been entered into, in accordance with those Orders or with any law of the Republic. Those Executive Orders and Resolutions, Administrative Regulations and Contracts are those listed below:

EXECUTIVE ORDERS

2	75
8	79
9	81—85 inclusive
14	88
17	89
19	91
23	92
27	94
28	95
31	97
34—38 inclusive	104
43	106
44	108
46	110—112 inclusive
48	114
52	116
53	118
55	119
58	121
60	126
61	128—130 inclusive
64	133—136 inclusive
65	139
68	142
69	143
71	145

146
148—151 inclusive
153—163 inclusive
166
168
169
171
173
174
176—178 inclusive
183
185—187 inclusive
190—195 inclusive
197—203 inclusive
205—212 inclusive
214
215
218
220
223—225 inclusive
229—231 inclusive
233—243 inclusive
245—250 inclusive
252
254—260 inclusive
262—266 inclusive
269—277 inclusive
280—282 inclusive
285—298 inclusive
300—302 inclusive
304—307 inclusive
311
312
314—318 inclusive
320—322 inclusive
324—326 inclusive
328—336 inclusive
338—367 inclusive
369—375 inclusive
377—391 inclusive
393
395
396
398
400
402—413 inclusive
415—433 inclusive
435—443 inclusive
445
447
449
451
454—461 inclusive
463—489 inclusive

491—498 inclusive
500
502
504—506 inclusive
509
510
513—517 inclusive
519—526 inclusive
530
532—547 inclusive
549
550
552—556 inclusive
558—563 inclusive
566
569
570
574—577 inclusive
579—590 inclusive
593
594
596
597
599—610 inclusive
612—615 inclusive
617—629 inclusive
634—643 inclusive
645
647—651 inclusive
653—656 inclusive
658
660—668 inclusive
670—685 inclusive
687
689
690
692—697 inclusive
699
701—703 inclusive
706—710 inclusive
712—719 inclusive
721
723—733 inclusive
735—738 inclusive
741—748 inclusive
750
752—759 inclusive
761—764 inclusive
766
768—775 inclusive
777—779 inclusive
782
783
784

785	793
786	794
787	795
789	796
790	799
791	800
792	

RESOLUTIONS

FOMENTO AND COMMUNICATIONS

Resolution—Official Gazette No. 2790—Barahona Company.
"   "   "   "   2821—Sante Fe Plantation Sugar Co.
"   "   "   "   2845—Central Romana.
"   "   "   "   2849—Central Romana.
"   "   "   "   2850—Santa Fe Plantation Sugar Co.
"   "   "   "   2861—Central Boca Chica Co.
"   "   "   "   2862—Installation of a telephone line.
"   "   "   "   2911—Installation of a telephone line.
"   "   "   "   2911—Santa Fe Plantation Sugar Co.
"   "   "   "   2929—Ingenio Cristobal Colon.
"   "   "   "   2967—Cancellation.
"   "   "   "   2993—Cía. Anónima de Explotaciones Industriales.
"   "   "   "   2993—San Cristobal Mining Co.
"   "   "   "   3008—Bentz Hnos.
"   "   "   "   3015—Bentz Hnos.
"   "   "   "   3036—Barahona Company.
"   "   "   "   3037—Julio V. Abreu.
"   "   "   "   3076—Central Romana.
"   "   "   "   3076—Barahona Company.
"   "   "   "   3093—Luis del Monte.
"   "   "   "   3093—Jose Mota Ranché.
"   "   "   "   3106—Central Romana.
"   "   "   "   3106—Central Romana.
"   "   "   "   3106—Castillo Hnos.
"   "   "   "   3106—Barahona Company.
"   "   "   "   3106—Barahona Company.
"   "   "   "   3121—Cónsuelo Sugar Co.
"   "   "   "   3126—Sres. Noboa Hnos.
"   "   "   "   3129—Barahona Company.
"   "   "   "   3129—Consuelo Sugar Co.
"   "   "   "   3159—Barahona Company.
"   "   "   "   3159—Central Romana.
"   "   "   "   3160—Barahona Company.
"   "   "   "   3162—Pardo y Ely Dorsey.

Registered 1, 2 and 3

Resolution—Official Gazette No. 3162—J. Amando Bermudez.
"   "   "   "   3196—Lorenzo Gautier Olives.
"   "   "   "   3203—Barahona Company.
"   "   "   "   3235—Barahona Company.
"   "   "   "   3242—Central Romana.
"   "   "   "   3243—Manuel Bermudez.
"   "   "   "   3274—Cía. Anonima de Inversiones Inmobiliarias.
"   "   "   "   3243—Cía. Anónima de Inversiones Inmobiliarias.
"   "   "   "   3354—Barahona Company.
"   "   "   "   3313—Ingenio Santa Fe de San Pedro de Macoris.
"   "   "   "   2786—Central Romana.
"   "   "   "   2787—L. E. Alvarez.
"   "   "   "   3358—Barahona Company.

AGRICULTURE AND IMMIGRATION

Resolution No. 61—Official Gazette No. 2838—Declaración de Zonas Agrícolas en la Provincia de Barahona.
"   " 64—Official Gazette Nos. 2853 and 2854—Declaración de Zonas Agrícolas en la Provincia de Barahona.
"   " 66—Official Gazette No. 3003—Declaración de Zonas Agrícolas en la Provincia de Barahona.
"   " 86—Official Gazette No. 3089—Luis Holguer. Todos los permisos de inmigración y ordenes de deportación expedidos por esta Secretaría.
"   " 88—Official Gazette No. 3133—Declaración de Zonas Agrícolas en Barahona.
"   " 89—Official Gazette No. 3145—Declaración de Zonas Agrícolas en la Provincia de Barahona.
"   " 91—Official Gazette No. 3167—Declaración de Zonas Agrícolas en la Provincia de Santo Domingo.
"   " 92—Official Gazette No. 3180—Industrial Alcohol Cía.
"   " 93—Official Gazette No. 3180—Declaración de Zonas Agrícolas en la Provincia de Santo Domingo.
"   " 94—Official Gazette No. 3197—Declaración de Zonas Agrícolas en la Provincia de Santo Domingo.
"   " 95—Official Gazette No. 3219—Declaración de Zonas Agrícolas en la Provincia de Monte Cristi.
"   " 96—Official Gazette No. 3242—Alvaro Fernández.
"   " 97— "   "   " 3243—Rectificación Limites Mencionados en Resolución No. 94 referente a Baní.
"   " 98—Official Gazette No. 3301—Cancelando Resolución No. 97.
"   " 99—Official Gazette No. 3332—Asociación de Regantes.

Water titles issued by the Secretariat of State for Agriculture by virtue of Executive Order No. 318, to the following:

Domingo Rodriguez— Agua del Río San Juan, Azua.
Jesús M. Vargas— " " " el Caño de Boña, Neiba, Barahona.
Alberto Perdomo— " " " Plaza Cacique.
Santiago J. Rodriguez— " " " Macasía, Matas de Farfán.
J. Julio Coiscou— " " " Birán, Barahona.
Asociación La Altagracia—Agua del Río El Manguito, Neiba.
Arbaje Hnos— Agua del Río Macasía, Matas de Farfán.
A. Santiago— " " " " " " "
Manuel de Pérez— " " " Camana, Neiba.
Sociedad de Irrigación Los Tres—Agua del Río San Juan, San Juan, Azua.
Joaquín Gracia—Agua del Río Yaque del Sur, Barahona.
Sociedad de Irrigación Amantes de las Agricultura—Agua del Río San Juan, San Juan, Azua.
Ismael Mateo—Agua del Río de Jacahueque, Matas de Farfán.
Inomina Palmer—Agua del Río Jacahueque, Matas de Farfán.
Sociedad de Irrigación La Unión—Agua del Río San Juan, San Juan, Azua.
Sociedad de Irrigación La Unión—Agua del Río Macasía, Matas de Farfán.
Sociedad de Irrigación La Competencia—Agua del Río María Chiquita, Neiba.
Francisco Tomillo—Agua del Río San Juan, San Juan, Azua.
Sociedad de Irrigación El Porvenir—Rio Las Marías, Neiba.
" " " El Esfuerzo—Agua del Rio Bani.
" " " El Progresso— " " " "
" " " La Voluntad— " " " "
" " " La Legalidad— " " " "
" " " El Adelanto— " " " "
Wenceslao Ramirez—Agua del Río Mijo, San Juan, Azua.

Resolution No. 74—Official Gazette No. 3355—Luis L. Bogaert.

All letters of naturalization and permits to establish residence granted for the purpose of naturalization, in accordance with Article 11 of the Constitution.

All permits issued to establish legal residence in the Republic in accordance with Article 14 of the Civil Code.

[INTERIOR AND POLICE]

Resolution regarding the sale of the Cruiser *Independencia*, under date of February 20, 1918, and the tugboat *Aguila*, under date of June 6, 1918. (Not yet published.)

Resolution—Official Gazette No. 3203, approving the increase in the tariff tax of the municipal aqueduct (Puerto Plata).

All the resolutions passed by the Ayuntamientos and approved by the Military Government.

SANITATION AND CHARITY

Sanitary Code published in the Official Gazette No. 3181, December 29, 1920.

TREASURY

Circular E–105, December 8, 1919.

INTERNATIONAL CONVENTIONS ENTERED INTO DURING THE PERIOD OF THE MILITARY GOVERNMENT

FOMENTO AND COMMUNICATIONS

Spanish-American Postal Convention of Madrid of November 2, 1920. Resolution No. 7, of March 12, 1921.
Universal Postal Convention of Madrid of November 30, 1920. Resolution No. 21 of December 31, 1921.
Universal Parcel Post Convention of Madrid of November 30, 1920. Resolution No. 32 of December 31, 1921.
Dominican-Spanish Postal Convention of November 17, 1921. Resolution No. 13 of April 29, 1922.
Pan-American Convention of Buenos Aires dated September 15, 1921. Resolution No. 25 of July 26, 1922.

Resolution approving the Postal Convention between the Dominican Republic and the United States of America, under date of May 19, 1917.

ADMINISTRATIVE REGULATIONS

FOMENTO AND COMMUNICATIONS

Departmental Order—Official Gazette No. 2801—Department of Fomento Order No. 1.

"	"	—No. 6—Official Gazette No.				2841.
"	"	" 8—	"	"	"	2852.
"	"	" 10—	"	"	"	2856.
"	"	" 12—	"	"	"	2861.
"	"	" 11—	"	"	"	2862.
"	"	" 14—	"	"	"	2863.
"	"	" 15—	"	"	"	2868 B.
"	"	" 16—	"	"	"	2923.
"	"	" 19—	"	"	"	2933.
"	"	" 21—	"	"	"	2960.
"	"	" 22—	"	"	"	2988.
"	"	" 23—	"	"	"	2998.
"	"	" 24—	"	"	"	3026.
"	"	" 25—	"	"	"	3035.
"	"	" 27—	"	"	"	3124.
"	"	" 28—	"	"	"	3159.
"	"	" 29—	"	"	"	3192.

AGRICULTURE AND IMMIGRATION

Departmental Order No.	2—Official Gazette No.	2992.
"	"	"	5—	"	"	"	3084.
"	"	"	13—	"	"	"	3124.
"	"	"	20—	"	"	"	3128.
"	"	"	21—	"	"	"	3128.
"	"	"	27—	"	"	"	3152.
"	"	"	31—	"	"	"	3355.
"	"	"	36—	"	"	"	3153.
"	"	"	38—	"	"	"	3159.
"	"	"	57—	"	"	"	3203.
"	"	"	60—	"	"	"	3211.
"	"	"	85—	"	"	"	3291.
"	"	"	89—	"	"	"	3328.
"	"	"	92—	"	"	"	3346.

INTERIOR AND POLICE

Departmental Order No. 13 granting authorization to the Junta de Caridad "Padre Billini" in order that it might contract a loan of $15,000. (Not yet published.)

JUSTICE AND PUBLIC INSTRUCTION

Departmental Order No. 1 of 1921, under date of February 19 of the same year. (Division of "comunero" lands.)

All the Departmental orders of the Department of Justice and Public Instruction relative to public instruction, with the exception of Orders Nos. 5, 9 and 16 of 1917; No. 97 of 1918; and Special Order No. 1 of 1919, until the installation of the Provisional Government.

CONTRACTS

TREASURY

Contracts entered into between the Military Government and the persons listed below for the rental of urban properties of the Republic:

Contract No. 58 with A. Humberto Aybar, under date of March 7, 1918. (one lot)

Contract with Selidonia Petitón Vda. Parisién, under date of December 12, 1918. (one lot)

Contract with Elías José, under date of December 4, 1918. (one lot)

Contract with Justiniano Acosta, under date of December 6, 1918. (one lot)

Contract with Donato Pérez, under date of December 2, 1918. (one lot)

Contract with Anita Buenrostro, under date of December 4, 1918. (one lot)

Contract with Urbano Acosta, under date of December 2, 1918. (one lot)

Contract with Celestino Fontana, under date of December 20, 1918. (one lot)

Contract with Ulises Cuello, under date of May 26, 1919. (one lot)

Contract with Alejandro Deño, under date of May 26, 1919. (one lot)

Contract No. 59 with Agustín Hernández, under date of July 21, 1919. (one house)

Contract No. 60 with R. O. Galvan, under date of October 31, 1919. (one lot)

Contract No. 61 with Pablo Gobaira, under date of November 11, 1919. (one lot)

Contract No. 62 with Abelardo José Romano, under date of November 11, 1919. (one lot)

Contract No. 63 with Jorge Bazil, under date of November 11, 1919. (one lot)

Contract with Earle T. Fiddler for the extraction of sand and other products.

Contract No. 1 with Francisco J. Peynado, under date of December 14, 1917; Rental of house No. 33 de la Calle José Reyes.

Contract No. 2 with Felix Gonzalez, under date of January 1, 1918: Transfer service in the Port of Macoris.

Contract with Francisco J. Peynado, No. 4, under date of April 12, 1918: Rental of house No. 46 de la Calle Mercedes.

Contract No. 5 with Alej. Penso, under date of December 17, 1918: Rental of house No. 15 Calle Beler and the upper floors of house No. 13/36 de la Calle Beler, corner of Comercio, both in Santiago.

Contract No. 6 with J. L. Manning, under date of July 12, 1919: (Designating International Banking Corporation as depositary of Government funds)

Contract No. 8 with the La Fé Lodge, under date of September 29, 1919: Rescinding a rental contract covering the building known by the name of "Logia La Fé".

Contract No. 9 with Ig. Cat. Apostólica Romana, under date of September 25, 1919: Establishing an agreement pending the determination of ownership of the buildings annexed to the Iglesia de Regina.

Contract No. 26 with Suc. Juan Nieves Reyes, under date of June 4, 1920: Transfer of rights to a tract of land in Nigua.

Contract No. 27 with Agapito, Lorenzo and Mercedes Ant. Reyes, under date of June 27, 1920: Purchase of land in Nigua for the National Leper Colony of Nigua.

Contract No. 29 with Alberto Ascensio, under date of October 1, 1920: Rental of a piece of land located in Santiago in Bella Vista which measures 96 tareas. (The Government is the renter.)

Contract No. 30 with Junta Fábrica Iglesia del Rosario in Moca, under date of September 30, 1920: Payment of $32,315.52 in order that the Board might relieve the Government of all responsibility occasioned by Executive Order No. 420 and its amendments.

Contract No. 31 with Junta Fábrica Iglesia Salcedo, under date of October 5, 1920: Payment of $26,400.00 in order to relieve the Government of all claims by reason of Executive Order No. 420.

Contract No. 32 with Melendez y Godoy, under date of March 14, 1921: Payment of $85,891.00 in order that the Government might be relieved of all claims by reason of Executive Order No. 513.

Contract No. 35 with R. M. Lepervanche, under date of March 16, 1921: Printing stamps.

Contract No. 34 with R. M. Lepervanche, under date of February 11, 1922: Printing stamps.

Contract with Divanna-Grisolia & Compañia, under date of November 18, 1920: Purchase and sale of Tobacco.

Contract with Grace & Co., under date of November 18, 1920: Purchase and sale of Tobacco in Europe.

Contract with Grace & Co., under date of September 29, 1919: Purchasing Agency.

Contract with Frank L. Mitchell, under date of September 19, 1921: Construction of a pump and installation of piping for pumping salt water.

Contract with Frank L. Mitchell, under date of March 16, 1921: Construction of a railroad bridge.

Contract with Gaetan Bucher y Nicolas Cortina, under date of March 4, 1921: Construction of warehouses.

Contract with Frank L. Mitchell, under date of March 16, 1921: Construction of a wharf.

Contract with G. H. Lippitt, under date of September 3, 1920: Installation of a pipe line for molasses.

Contract with Lee, Higginson & Co., under date of April 4, 1922: Loan of $6,700,000.

Contract with the Compañia de Mieles Dominicana C. por A., under date of March 25, 1922: Extension of the concessions and for a pipe line for molasses.

FOMENTO AND COMMUNICATIONS

All the contracts existing between the Department of Fomento and Communications and other persons for the rental of buildings for postoffices in force on the date of the installation of the Provisional Government.

Marck Engineering & Contracting Co.—Contract dated August 23, 1921, for "Construction Barahona Market".

Chief of Surveyors:—(Land Survey) Four contracts which have been made for the advance of funds as follows:

(a) Central Romana, Inc., June 29, 1921.
(b) Barahona and allied companies: December 31, 1921.
(c) Ingenio Santa Fé—March 3, 1922.
(d) Ingenio Santa Fé, May 16, 1920.

INTERIOR AND POLICE

Contract between the Military Government and the Commune of Azua for a loan of $20,000.00 (viente mil pesos) at a rate of interest of 5%, under date of December 31, 1919.

Contract between the Commune of Azua and the International Banking Corporation for a loan of $15,000.00 (quince mil pesos), under date of December 31, 1919.

Cancellation, under date of June 8, 1920, of the loan of $15,000.00 (quince mil pesos) with the International Banking Corporation mentioned above.

Loan of the Military Government to the Commune of Azua of $15,000.00 (quince mil pesos) at a rate of interest of 5%, under date of June 8, 1920.

Contract between the Commune of Barahona and the Military Government for a loan of $25,000.00 (veinticinco mil pesos) at a rate of interest of 5%, under date of April 8, 1920.

Contract between the Commune of Villa Mella and the Military Government for a loan of $14,650.00 (catorce mil seis cientos cincuenta pesos (at a rate of interest of 5% under date of May 25, 1920.

The Dominican Government likewise agrees that those Executive Orders, those resolutions, those administrative regulations, and those contracts shall remain in full force and effect unless and until they are abrogated by those bodies which, in accordance with the Dominican Constitution, can legislate. But, this ratification, in so far as concerns those of the above mentioned Executive Orders, resolutions, administrative regulations, and contracts, which have been modified or abrogated by other Executive Orders, resolutions, or administrative regulations of the Military Government, only refers to the legal effects which they created while they were in force.

The Dominican Government further agrees that neither the subsequent abrogation of those Executive Orders, resolutions, administrative regulations, or contracts, or any other law, Executive Order, or other official act of the Dominican Government, shall affect the validity or security of rights acquired in accordance with those orders, those resolutions, those administrative regulations and those contracts of the Military Government; the controversies which may arise related with those rights acquired will be determined solely by the Dominican Courts, subject, however, in accordance with the generally accepted rules and principles of international law, to the right of diplomatic intervention if those Courts should be responsible for cases of notorious injustice or denial of justice. The determination of such cases in which the interests of the United States and the Dominican Republic only are concerned shall, should the two Governments disagree, be by arbitration. In the carrying out of this agreement, in each individual case, the High Contracting Parties, once the necessity of arbitration is determined, shall conclude a special agreement defining clearly the scope of the dispute, the scope of the powers of the arbitrators, and the periods to be fixed for the formation of the arbitral tribunal and the several stages of the procedure. It is understood that on the part of the United States, such special agreements will be made by the President of the United States, by and with the advice and consent of the Senate thereto, and on the part of the Dominican Republic shall be subject to the procedure required by the Constitution and laws thereof.

II. The Dominican Government, in accordance with the provisions of Article I, specifically recognizes the bond issue of 1918 and the twenty-year five and one-half percent Customs Administration Sinking Fund Gold Bond Issue authorized in 1922, as legal, binding, and irrevocable obligations of the Republic, and pledges its full faith and credit to the maintenance of the service of those bond issues. With reference to the stipulation contained in Article 10 of the Executive Order No. 735, in accordance with which the loan of five and one-half percent authorized in 1922 was issued, which provides:—

"That the present customs tariff will not be changed during the life of this loan without previous agreement between the Dominican Government and the Government of the United States;"

the two Governments concerned agree in interpreting this stipulation in the sense that, in accordance with article 3 of the Convention of 1907, a previous agreement between the Dominican Government and the United States shall be necessary to modify the import duties of the Dominican Republic, it being an indispensable condition for the modification of such duties that the Dominican Executive demonstrate and that the President of the United States recognize that, on the basis of exportations and importations to the like amount and the like character during the two years preceding that in which it is desired to make such modification, the total net customs receipts would at such altered rates of duties have been, for each of such two years, in excess of the sum of $2,000,000 United States gold.

III. The Dominican Government and the Government of the United States agree that the Convention signed on February 8, 1907, between the United States and the Dominican Republic, shall remain in force so long as any bonds of the issues of 1918 and 1922 shall remain unpaid, and that the duties of the General Receiver of Dominican Customs appointed in accordance with that Convention shall be extended to include the application of the revenues pledged for the service of those bond issues in accordance with the terms of the Executive Orders and of the contracts under which the bonds were issued.

IV. This arrangement shall take effect after its approval by the Senate of the United States and the Congress of the Dominican Republic.

DONE in four originals, two in the English language, and two in the Spanish, and the representatives of the High Contracting Powers signing them in the City of Santo Domingo, this twelfth day of June, nineteen hundred and twenty-four.

[SEAL]	WILLIAM W. RUSSELL
[SEAL]	HORACIO VASQUEZ
[SEAL]	FED^co VELÁSQUEZ Y H.
[SEAL]	FRAN^c J. PEYNADO

839.00/2844 : Telegram

The Minister in the Dominican Republic (Russell) to the Secretary of State

SANTO DOMINGO, *July 3, 1924—5 p. m.*
[Received July 4—2 : 35 p. m.]

30. Electoral College has elected Horatio Vasquez and Doctor Velasquez President and Vice President respectively. Proclamation will be issued July 4th and the inauguration will be set for July 12.

RUSSELL

839.00/2861 : Telegram

The Minister in the Dominican Republic (Russell) to the Secretary of State

SANTO DOMINGO, *September 18, 1924—5 p. m.*
[Received September 19—9 : 30 a. m.]

55. Provisions of the Plan of the Evacuation have been completed and all of the Forces of Occupation have left the country.

RUSSELL

APPROVAL BY THE UNITED STATES OF THE ISSUE OF $2,500,000 OF TWO-YEAR NOTES BY THE DOMINICAN REPUBLIC

839.51/2386

The Minister in the Dominican Republic (Russell) to the Secretary of State

No. 909   SANTO DOMINGO, *November 24, 1923.*
[Received December 17.]

SIR: I have the honor to enclose herewith a translation of a note to me from the Foreign Office [10] requesting the approval of the Government of the United States for the issuance of bonds to the nominal amount of two million dollars of the balance of the total not issued but authorized by Executive Order No. 735 of the Military Government.[11]

There is also enclosed a statement [10] showing the application of the funds derived from the bond issue of $6,700,000.00 in accordance with the provisions of said Executive Order No. 735.

I have [etc.]   WILLIAM W. RUSSELL

[10] Not printed.
[11] *Foreign Relations*, 1922, vol. II, p. 85.

839.51/2388 : Telegram

The Minister in the Dominican Republic (Russell) to the Secretary of State

SANTO DOMINGO, *January 7, 1924—noon.*
[Received January 8—3 : 40 p. m.]

1. Provisional Government has prepared decree similar to Executive Order 735 by which [$]6,700,000 bonds were issued out of total authorized issue of [$]10,000,000. New decree contemplates issue of [$]2,000,000 of the remainder in accordance with plan forwarded in my despatch number 909 of November 24. Government requests me to ascertain if the Department agrees to this new issue in order to have everything in readiness to comply with obligations of contract with Santo Domingo Water, Light and Power Company.[12]

RUSSELL

839.51/2388 : Telegram

The Secretary of State to the Commissioner in the Dominican Republic (Welles)

WASHINGTON, *January 12, 1924—6 p. m.*

1. With reference to telegram number 1, January 7, noon, from American Minister, Santo Domingo, the Department desires your views regarding the possible effect of bond issue on political situation in view of approaching elections. This of course does not refer to obligations of Power Company contract. Reply by cable.

HUGHES

839.51/2389 : Telegram

The Commissioner in the Dominican Republic (Welles) to the Secretary of State

SANTO DOMINGO, *January 17, 1924—11 a. m.*
[Received January 18—1 : 27 a. m.]

3. Your January 12, 6 p. m. I do not consider that the bond issue for which authorization is requested by the Provisional Government can have any prejudicial effect upon the political situation. The proceeds of the issue, except for the amount required by fulfillment of the Light and Power Company's contract (should that contract be carried out), are destined for the completion of the Government's road construction program, of which the entire Republic is now enthusiastically in favor. Should the bond issue not be authorized, the construction of the projected highways—essential to the

---

[12] See *post,* pp. 670 ff.

development of the country—cannot be continued and a strong reaction in public opinion would undoubtedly result.

The Dominican people in general are so heartily in favor of road construction by the Government that the *nacionalista* elements will not be able to oppose any governmental measure necessary to continue this work. I therefore recommend that the Department's authorization to the bond issue be granted.

WELLES

839.51/2400

The Secretary of State to the Commissioner in the Dominican Republic (Welles)[13]

No. 550   WASHINGTON, *February 27, 1924.*

SIR: The Department is in receipt of a letter dated February 4, 1924, addressed to the Secretary of State by the Secretary of the Navy, in which Mr. Denby calls Mr. Hughes's attention to the alleged excessive expenditures of the Provisional Government of the Dominican Republic, which have reduced the surplus of $814,934.03 existing on October 1, 1922, to a deficit on September 30, 1923, of $294,943.57. It is also stated that the Military Governor, in his report for the year ending September 30, 1923, estimates that the deficit on December 31, 1923, will be $660,000. The Secretary of the Navy concludes that "with definite signs of an approaching financial crisis in the Dominican Republic it would appear highly desirable to consider and develop some plan to meet the situation". A copy of Mr. Denby's letter is enclosed herewith.[14]

From information at the disposal of the Department it would appear that the year 1922 began with a deficit of about a million dollars, and that the surplus of $814,934.03 of October 1, 1922, was occasioned by the sale of bonds, amounting in nominal value to $6,700,000, of the 5½ per cent loan of 1922. In other words, the surplus of October 1, 1922, was apparently not produced either by a large income from taxation or other sources, or by a policy of economy on the part of the Military Government. The Department understands, furthermore, that a large part of the expense incurred by the Provisional Government is due to extensive road building and the training of the Dominican National Police, both of which measures have been strongly advocated by the military authorities. It is also reported that the sales of government-owned tobacco, to

---

[13] This instruction was misdirected to the Legation and was numbered accordingly; Mr. Welles did not receive it before his reply to the Department's subsequent instruction, no. 5, March 21, *infra*. (File no. 839.51/2411.)
[14] Not printed.

which reference is made in Mr. Denby's communication, did not yield as much revenue as had been anticipated when the budget of 1923 was compiled.

Before making a definite reply to the letter of the Secretary of the Navy, the Department would be glad to receive such comments as you may desire to make concerning the statements contained therein.

I am [etc.]   CHARLES E. HUGHES

839.51A/orig.

The Secretary of State to the Commissioner in the Dominican Republic (Welles)

No. 5   WASHINGTON, *March 21, 1924.*

SIR: With reference to the Department's instruction No. 550, dated February 17 [*27*], regarding the financial situation in the Dominican Republic, there is transmitted herewith for your information and comment a copy of a letter dated March 8, 1924,[15] from the former Secretary of the Navy inviting the Department's attention to the increasingly critical condition of the Republic's finances. Mr. Denby also states that "an American financial adviser in the Dominican Government, with authority established by mutual assent of the two countries, somewhat along the lines of the arrangement in Haiti, is imperatively needed."

The Department desires an expression of your opinion by cable, whether you consider the situation so serious as to make it advisable for the Department to authorize you to discuss this matter informally with the Provisional President in order to ascertain his views in the premises, and more especially whether he would make the suggestion to the Commission that the Provisional Government ask the United States to designate a suitable person as Financial Adviser. It is, of course, considered essential by the Department that the initiative in this matter should come from the Dominicans themselves, that any decision on this point should be arrived at by the Provisional Government of its own judgment and that the Commission should be committed to such a decision, so that there would be reasonable assurance that, later on, there would be no serious opposition to such a course either among the political leaders or the people in general. The Department considers it especially important that no unfounded suspicion should arise in the minds of the Dominican people that an attempt is being made to prolong the control of this Government over the Republic beyond the time of evacuation, other than that provided in the Treaty of 1907.[16]

---

[15] Not printed.
[16] *Foreign Relations*, 1907, pt. I, p. 307.

The Department's desire in this matter is merely to render such assistance as it properly can to the Dominican Government and people in order that they may solve, in a satisfactory manner, their financial and other problems.

I am [etc.]   CHARLES E. HUGHES

839.51A/1 : Telegram

The Commissioner in the Dominican Republic (Welles) to the Secretary of State

SANTO DOMINGO, *March 29, 1924—9 a. m.*
[Received April 1—2: 33 a. m.]

26. Department's instruction no. 5 of March 21st. Department's instruction of February 17th [*27th*], numbered 550, was not received by me.

The Military Governor's report for the quarter ending December 31, 1923, to which Mr. Denby's letter of March 8 to the Secretary of State refers, is evidently due to his failure to comprehend the financial statements issued quarterly by the Treasury Department of the Dominican Government owing to their complicated and somewhat misleading form.

The facts relating to the governmental receipts and governmental expenditures for the year 1923 are as follows: The total receipts for that period were $5,980,000; the total actual expenditures for that period were $6,136,000, leaving an apparent deficit of $156,000. This apparent deficit was, however, offset by a special reserve fund of $800,000, so that at the end of 1923 the Dominican Government had on deposit a supposed $664,000 instead of having incurred the deficit of $987,825 reported by the Military Governor. Against the cash surplus mentioned there may, however, be deducted bills outstanding but not presented totaling approximately $200,000, so that the Government at the beginning of the year 1924 had a clear balance to its credit of about $450,000.

The deficit estimated by the Military Governor consists of appropriations authorized but not expended under the budgets of 1921–22 and '23. Not only have these sums not been expended for reasons of economy, but under Dominican law appropriations authorized but not expended lapse in the second fiscal year after authorization. Such appropriations authorized in 1921 or 1922 can, therefore, in no sense be termed liabilities.

The figure for total expenditures in 1923 includes the cost of continuing the public works program amounting to $1,200,000. The President determined to meet this cost from ordinary government revenues rather than from the special reserve fund of $800,000 remaining from the loan of 1922 and destined for public works above mentioned, for the reason that the latter fund was drawing 6 percent interest while ordinary government deposits draw but 3 percent. It is likewise to be noted that this total of expenditures includes extraordinary electoral expenses of $200,000.

The statement of the Military Governor to the effect that from now on the Dominican Government will incur a monthly deficit of $100,000 [omission?] will be by the month of May when the remainder of the reserve fund of $800,000 for public works, which has been drawn upon since January 1st, will be exhausted. This estimated monthly deficit corresponds to the amount expended monthly on the continuation of the public works program. It is, however, the President's hope that a speedy settlement of the controversy with the Santo Domingo Water, Light and Power Company will make possible the issuance in the month of April of the authorized $2,000,000 of bonds of the 1922 loan as the result of which the public works expenditures would no longer be a charge upon the general governmental revenues but would naturally be met from the proceeds of this loan.

The statement of the Military Governor regarding the inability of the Provisional Government to meet necessary educational expenses is incident [incorrect?]. The Government is expending over $35,000 monthly on the public instruction chapter of the budget. All schools provided for by law are functioning for the first time since the Military Government closed the majority of the schools for lack of funds in 1921. Every possible economy has been effected. The salaries of the Government employees outside of the Policia Nacional [Dominicana] have been reduced by 33 percent and all unnecessary employees have been discharged. The Government has likewise increased revenues by imposing special license taxes on motor vehicles and by increasing the wharfage taxes. It is, however, unable to accomplish more because of the restrictions occasioned by the contracts entered into by the Military Government for the issuance of the 1918 and 1922 loans which permit the Government to receive only 15 percent of all customs receipts in excess of 3,000,000 and because internal revenue taxes on national products are now as high as the industries can stand. The decision of the Department that the imposition of internal revenue taxes on imported articles constitutes a modification of the tariff infringing the terms of the convention of 1907,[17] makes it impossible for the Government to increase its revenues by establishment of a luxury or excise tax. In view of the difficulties which it has encountered, I believe that the financial administration of the Provisional Government has been eminently successful and the actual

---

[17] See *Foreign Relations*, 1911, pp. 139 ff.

financial situation of the Government demonstrates that there is no basis for the concern shown by the Military Government.

With reference to the opinion of Mr. Denby that an "American financial adviser in the Dominican Republic is imperatively needed," I am strongly of the belief that the suggestion by the United States Government, even made informally, would tend to destroy the beneficial effects of the Department's policy here. It was because of President Henríquez's refusal to accede to our instructions on this point that his resignation and the resignations of the members of his Cabinet were forced in 1916, resignations which brought about the establishment of a Military Government.[18] I feel certain that the President especially would refuse to assume the office to which he has been elected rather than accept it under such conditions. Furthermore, were it possible to induce the Dominican Government on its own apparent initiative to request the appointment of an American financial adviser, such an appointment would destroy public confidence in the good faith of the Government of the United States since it would undoubtedly be believed that it had not been sincere in stating to the Dominican people when the Plan of Evacuation was adopted that it desired no control over this Republic other than that provided in the convention of 1907. In conclusion it is my belief that such an appointment is neither necessary nor desirable.

WELLES

839.51/2423a : Telegram

The Acting Secretary of State to the Commissioner in the Dominican Republic (Welles)

WASHINGTON, *May 15, 1924—6 p. m.*

15. For your information and such use as you in your discretion may deem advisable, Department informed Mr. [W.] McCormick Blair, the member of Lee, Higginson and Company, who is especially conversant with and interested in Dominican affairs, is leaving for Europe at the end of May. It would probably be advantageous, therefore, to the Dominican Government that the flotation of the $2,000,000 installment of the unissued portion of the 1922 loan be submitted to the consideration of this firm before his departure.

You will remember that under the provisions of the loan contract and agreement between Lee, Higginson and Company and the Dominican Republic, acting through the Military Government of Santo Domingo, covering the purchase by that firm of $6,700,000 of the $10,000,000 loan of 1922,[19] it is provided that "Lee, Higginson

[18] See *Foreign Relations*, 1916, pp. 220 ff.
[19] Not printed.

and Company shall have the first opportunity to purchase any bonds of this issue that may hereafter be authorized and offered".

GREW

839.51/2425 : Telegram

The Commissioner in the Dominican Republic (Welles) to the Secretary of State

SANTO DOMINGO, *May 17, 1924—9 a. m.*
[Received May 19—9 : 14 p. m.]

31. Department's 15, May 14 [*15*], 10 [*6*] p. m. During my absence from Santo Domingo, [and] due to the serious illness of the Provisional President or for some other reason, the settlement of the Water, Light and Power Company case with which the issuance of the $2,000,000 of bonds is connected was not pressed. It was always my desire to have both of these matters handled by the Provisional Government prior to the installation of the National Congress. The Congress is now in session and should the Provisional President attempt to take the necessary action at the present time, although he is entitled to do so by the terms of the Plan of Evacuation, a break would at once occur between the Provisional Government and the Congress which it is essential to avoid. General Vasquez is entirely in accord with the settlement of the Water, Light and Power Company case on the basis proposed by the Director of Public Works and the issuance of the $2,000,000 of bonds immediately after the installation of the Constitutional Government. Both of these questions I believe could be agreed upon in advance of the installation of the Constitutional Government during the course of General Vasquez' intended visit to Washington. Should it be possible for Mr. McCormick Blair to postpone his departure until after the arrival in Washington of General Vasquez I believe it to be highly desirable.

WELLES

839.51/2437a : Telegram

The Secretary of State to the Minister in the Dominican Republic (Russell)

WASHINGTON, *July 11, 1924—3 p. m.*

28. Please convey the following message to General Vasquez from Welles:

"I am truly hopeful that it may be possible for you to obtain the necessary authorization by Congress before July 17th, to conclude the negotiations for the short time loan on the terms approved by you. I also trust that Mr. Ariza's appointment [20] may be confirmed before the same date and authorization be extended to him to act on behalf of his Government. I am fearful that any considerable delay might cause changes in the offer made because of the shifting condition of the market."

HUGHES

839.51/2438 : Telegram

The Minister in the Dominican Republic (Russell) to the Secretary of State

SANTO DOMINGO, *July 16, 1924—noon.*
[Received 11:05 a. m.]

41. Your 28, July 11, 3 p. m. Nominations of Ariza and Alvarez [21] confirmed by the Senate yesterday and Dominican Government complying with the formalities of the occasion desire to know whether Ariza is *persona grata.* Matter of short-time loan of two and one half millions [22] was presented to Congress and referred to Finance Committee of the Senate.

RUSSELL

839.51/2447

The Dominican Chargé (Ariza) to the Secretary of State

[Translation]

WASHINGTON, *August 8, 1924.*

MR. SECRETARY OF STATE: The Government of the Dominican Republic has decided to make a short term loan in the sum of $2,500,-000,[23] secured by $3,300,000 of the Dominican 5½ percent loan of 1922 bonds which have not been used.

This money was deemed to be necessary to continue the public works for the development of the natural resources of the country and to meet urgent needs of the Government. The Dominican Government has already approved the loan and negotiations are on foot with Messrs. Lee, Higginson and Company, who appear to be inclined to supply the funds; but before carrying on the negotiations I should like to know whether this loan would also meet with the approval of the Government of the United States.

I avail myself [etc.] J. C. ARIZA

[20] José del Carmen Ariza, Dominican Chargé and Appointed Minister, July 22; he became Minister, Sept. 2.
[21] Frederico C. Alvarez, Secretary of the Dominican Legation.
[22] The same loan that had previously been proposed for $2,000,000.
[23] Authorized July 25, 1924 (*Gaceta Oficial* No. 3562); authorization amended by resolution of the Dominican Congress on Sept. 4, 1924 (*Gaceta Oficial* No. 3574).

839.51/2447

The Secretary of State to the Dominican Chargé (*Ariza*)

WASHINGTON, *August 15, 1924.*

SIR: The receipt is acknowledged of your note dated August 8, 1924, in which you inform me of the decision of your Government to contract a short term loan to the amount of $2,500,000, to be secured by $3,300,000 of the Dominican 5½ per cent bonds of 1922 which have not been issued.

You state that this sum is considered necessary for the continuance of the construction of public works, for the development of the natural resources of the Dominican Republic, and to meet the urgent requirements of your Government.

You add that the Dominican Congress has already approved the loan referred to and that negotiations have been entered into with Messrs. Lee, Higginson and Company, who are disposed to supply the funds in question, but that before proceeding further with these negotiations you desire to be informed whether this loan would meet with the approval of the Government of the United States.

In reply, I desire to state that in order that the Department may have before it all pertinent information which might be of assistance to it in its consideration of the question which you have presented, I should appreciate it if you would be so good as to inform the Department of the details of the proposed contract for the loan under discussion.

Accept [etc.]

For the Secretary of State:
JOSEPH C. GREW

839.51/2451

The Dominican Chargé (*Ariza*) *to the Secretary of State*

[Translation]

WASHINGTON, *August 16, 1924.*

MR. SECRETARY OF STATE: Supplementing my communication of August 8, 1924, I have to inform Your Excellency that the $2,500,000 loan now being negotiated with Messrs. Lee, Higginson and Company, is to be for two years with an option for the Dominican Government to redeem the bonds of that loan in whole or in part six months after the issue.

I forward herewith to Your Excellency a copy of the draft of contract submitted by Messrs. Lee, Higginson and Company.[24]

---

[24] Not printed; for text of the signed contract, see p. 657.

Before closing the negotiations I should like to know whether the President of the United States would give his consent to this loan in accordance with the provision in the Convention of 1907, and would agree to let the bonds given as security ($3,300,000, 5½%, 1922) enjoy the following securities granted by the Executive Order No. 735 of March 28, 1922, to the bonds issued in that year for the face value of $6,700,000, namely

1. The Receiver General of the Dominican Customs appointed in accordance with the Convention of 1907, will effect, while the said Convention is in force, the payments that may be necessary for the service of the bonds issued as security ($3,300,000, 5½%, 1922) derived from the revenues belonging to the Dominican Government;

2. That after the expiration of the Convention of 1907 the said Customhouse receipts will be collected and applied by an official appointed by the President of the United States in the same manner as was appointed the present Receiver General of the Dominican Customs;

3. After the expiration of the Convention of 1907 the $10,000,000 of bonds authorized in March 1922, or any part thereof that may still be outstanding, will constitute a first lien on the said customs revenues subject to the necessary expenses of collection, until all the bonds shall have been entirely paid for. (Executive Order No. 735, Article 8.)

I hope that there will be no objection to having the security above mentioned inserted in the bonds.

I avail myself [etc.] J. C. ARIZA

839.51/2461

Lee, Higginson & Company to the Secretary of State

BOSTON, *September 9, 1924.*
[Received September 10.]

DEAR MR. SECRETARY: We have submitted an offer to the Dominican Republic to sell for its account $2,500,000. 5½% Two-year notes to be secured by $3,300,000. 5½% bonds, being the remainder of the $10,000,000 Loan authorized by the Military Government of Santo Domingo March 1922 and approved by you. The proposed Contract, the Trust Indenture, a draft of the Two-year Note and a draft of the Bonds securing such Notes were sent for examination to Dr. Dana G. Munro [25] September 8th. We would appreciate it if you will write us stating that the assurances set forth in the Note and Bond concerning the cooperation of the United States Government

---

[25] Assistant Chief of the Division of Latin American Affairs; letter to Mr. Munro not printed.

in the future collection of the Customs revenues and their application can be made with your consent?

Very truly yours,

LEE, HIGGINSON & CO.

839.51/2451

The Secretary of State to the Dominican Minister (Ariza)

WASHINGTON, *September 25, 1924.*

SIR: I have the honor to acknowledge the receipt of your note of
August 16, 1924, in which you convey additional information with
regard to the projected issue of short term notes to the amount of
$2,500,000. I understand that these notes are to be issued in accord-
ance with a contract similar to the draft transmitted by you with
your note of September 5, 1924,[26] and that the proceeds of the sale of
the notes are to be used mainly for road construction and port
improvements.

You state that you desire to know before concluding the contract
with Lee, Higginson and Company whether this Government will
consent to the proposed loan, in accordance with the Convention of
1907, and whether it will agree that certain assurances be extended in
connection with the five and one-half per cent bonds of 1922 to the
amount of $3,300,000 which would be pledged as collateral for the
loan. You state that the assurances which you outline are similar to
those extended in connection with the bonds issued in 1922 to the
amount of $6,700,000 by Executive Order No. 735, dated March 28,
1922.

In reply I have the honor to inform you that the Government of
the United States agrees to the issuance by the Dominican Government of the proposed $2,500,000 two year notes. The Government of
the United States further agrees that the Dominican Government
may issue and pledge as security for these two year notes $3,300,000
of the five and one-half per cent bonds authorized in 1922, being
the remainder of the issue of $10,000,000 authorized in that year. It
is understood that these bonds are to be in form similar to the $6,700,-
000 of this issue now outstanding, with such appropriate changes
as are made necessary by the difference in the amount of the bonds
and the establishment of the Constitutional Government in the
Dominican Republic. This note may be regarded as conveying the
agreement of the United States Government to the issues specified
above, as required in Article III of the Convention of 1907 between
the Government of the United States and the Government of the
Dominican Republic.

---

[26] Not printed. For signed text of the contract, see p. 657.

The Government of the United States will interpose no objection should the Government of the Dominican Republic desire to extend the following assurances in connection with the five and one-half per cent bonds of 1922 to the amount of $3,300,000, which are to be pledged as collateral for the two year notes:

1. That the Receiver General of Customs of the Dominican Republic, appointed under the Convention of 1907, shall during the life of that Convention make from the customs revenues accruing to the Dominican Government such payments as may be necessary for the service of the bonds pledged as collateral to secure the short term notes now to be issued.

2. That, if the Convention of 1907 should expire before the bonds of 1922 are paid in full, the customs revenues shall continue to be collected and applied by an official appointed by the President of the United States in the same form as the present Receiver General of Customs of the Dominican Republic, so long as any of the bonds authorized in 1922 remain outstanding.

3. That, after the expiration of the Convention of 1907, the bonds authorized in 1922 to the amount of $10,000,000, or any portion of these bonds which remain unpaid, shall enjoy a first lien on the customs revenues subject to the necessary expenses of collection until these bonds have been paid in full.

Accept [etc.]   CHARLES E. HUGHES

839.51/2461

The Secretary of State to Lee, Higginson & Company

WASHINGTON, *September 25, 1924.*

SIRS: I beg to acknowledge the receipt of your letter of September 9 with reference to your offer to the Dominican Republic to sell for its account $2,500,000 5½% two-year notes to be secured by $3,300,-000 of 5½% bonds, the balance of the $10,000,000 loan authorized in March 1922 by the Military Government of Santo Domingo and approved by the Department. You request to be advised in writing whether certain statements you desire to insert in these notes and bonds concerning the cooperation of the Government of the United States in the future collection of the customs revenues of the Dominican Republic and their application can be made with the consent of this Government.

In reply I beg to inform you that this Department perceives no objection to printing on each of the bonds in question a statement similar to that proposed. The statement which is contained in a draft of the bond transmitted on September 8, by Mr. C. R. Clapp [27]

---

[27] Legal counsel for Lee, Higginson & Co.; Mr. Clapp's letter not printed.

of the firm of Ropes, Gray, Boyden & Perkins, should be slightly modified to read as follows:

"The Department of State of the United States, as required by Article III of the treaty between the United States and the Dominican Republic, has consented to the issuance by the Dominican Republic of this Second Series of $3,300,000, completing the total bond issue of $10,000,000 authorized in 1922.

"The Government of the United States, through the State Department, has consented that the General Receiver of Dominican Customs, appointed under the Convention of 1907, shall, during the life of that Convention, make such payments as are necessary for the service of this new Loan, from the revenues accruing to the Dominican Government, and has further consented to the giving of assurances by the Dominican Republic—

"1. That after the expiration of said Convention of 1907, the Customs revenues pledged for the service of this Loan shall be collected and applied by an official appointed by the President of the United States in the same manner as the present General Receiver of Customs;

"2. That after the expiration of said Convention of 1907, this Loan now authorized, together with and equally with the bonds of the same issue of 1922, amounting to $6,700,000 previously issued, shall have a first lien upon such Customs revenues, after the payment of the necessary expenses of collection, until all the bonds thereof are paid in full."

Furthermore, this Department perceived no objection to the printing of a statement on each of the two-year notes to the effect that the notes are "issued with the consent of the Government of the United States of America, as required by Article III of the treaty between the United States and the Dominican Republic." It will be understood by you, however, that while the fact of this consent may appropriately appear, this letter is not to be published in any circular or statement to be issued in connection with these securities.

With reference to your letter of September 10, 1924,[28] to Mr. Munro, I may add that this Department, in a note to the Dominican Minister, has expressed its consent that these bonds should be in form similar to the $6,700,000 of this issue now outstanding with such appropriate changes as are made necessary by the difference in the amount of the bonds and the establishment of a Constitutional Government in the Dominican Republic, and has stated that the note may be regarded as conveying the consent of the United States Government to these issues of bonds and notes as required by Article III of the Convention of 1907 between the Government of the United States and the Government of the Dominican Republic.

[28] Not printed.

This Department also stated that the Government of the United States will interpose no objection to the giving of assurances by the Dominican Government similar to those contained in the proposed draft of the bonds.

I am [etc.]   CHARLES E. HUGHES

839.51/2482

Lee, Higginson & Company to the Department of State

NEW YORK, *October 30, 1924.*
[Received October 31.]

SIRS: At Mr. Greene's [29] request, we take pleasure in enclosing copy of a contract with the Dominican Republic dated September 25, 1924, regarding the issue of $2,500,000 Dominican Republic Two-Year 5½% Collateral Trust Gold Notes.

Very truly yours,

LEE, HIGGINSON & CO.

[Enclosure]

Loan Contract and Agreement of Fiscal Agency between the Dominican Republic and Lee, Higginson & Company

1. Lee, Higginson & Company agree to offer and sell for the account of the Dominican Republic its notes to the aggregate principal amount of $2,500,000. at par and interest that has accrued thereon to the date of sale. These notes are to be secured by $3,300,000. par value of the Dominican Republic 5½% bonds of 1922 in denominations of $1000 and $500 pieces, being part of the loan then authorized and as yet unissued. Said $3,300,000. bonds shall be in the same form as the $6,700,000. bonds of 1922 now outstanding, but with such appropriate changes as are made necessary by the difference in the amount of the issue of the bonds, and by the evacuation of the Military Government and the establishing of the permanent government of the Dominican Republic; they shall bear similar statements as to the consent of the Government of the United States to the issue of these bonds and the collection and application of the Customs revenues of the Dominican Republic on which they are a lien; they shall be duly authorized by the Congress of the Dominican Republic and signed by the official or officials designated by law for that purpose; they shall be countersigned and certified in the same manner as the bonds of the Loan of 1922 now outstanding.

[29] Jerome D. Greene, a partner in the firm of Lee, Higginson & Co.

Lee, Higginson & Company shall hold said pledged bonds as Trustees for the noteholders under an Indenture containing appropriate provisions for that purpose.

During the term of said notes Lee, Higginson & Company shall retain from the monthly deposits to be made with them by the Dominican Republic for the payment of interest on the pledged bonds in accordance with the provisions thereof, the following sums: From the first of such deposits which shall be made on or before October 20, 1924, two-twelfths ($\frac{2}{12}$) of the annual interest charge on said notes, and from each of such subsequent monthly deposits one twelfth ($\frac{1}{12}$) of the annual interest charge on said notes which at the time may be outstanding. The sums so retained shall be applied in payment of interest on said notes and if said notes are not in default the excess of each monthly deposit over the amount so retained shall be placed at the disposal of the Dominican Republic.

2. Said notes are to be duly authorized by the Congress of the Dominican Republic, to be signed by the official or officials designated by law for that purpose. They are to be substantially in the form hereto annexed and marked Exhibit A.[30] They are to bear the seal of the Department of Finance and Commerce of the Dominican Republic, and are to be signed for the purpose of identification only by Lee, Higginson & Company as Fiscal Agents for the service of this Loan and as Trustees. They are also to be certified by Farmers' Loan & Trust Company of New York, Registrar.

3. The notes are to be dated September 1, 1924, and to be payable September 1, 1926. At the option of the Dominican Republic they may be called for redemption as a whole or in part on March 1, 1925, or on any interest day thereafter upon reasonable notice and in accordance with suitable provisions to be set forth in the Trust Indenture at a premium of one-half of one per cent. They are to be in coupon form, in denominations of $1000 and $500 each, in such proportions as Lee, Higginson & Company may designate.

4. They are to bear interest at the rate of five and one-half ($5\frac{1}{2}$) per cent. per annum and are to be paid principal and interest in gold coin of the United States of the present standard of weight and fineness at the offices of Lee, Higginson & Company in Boston, New York and Chicago, at the option of the holders. They shall be exempt from any taxes or impositions now or hereafter to be established or levied by or within the Dominican Republic against the notes or the income arising therefrom or the holders thereof.

5. Interest is to be payable semi-annually on the first days of March and September.

---

[30] Not printed.

6. The notes, bonds and legal instruments connected therewith are to be in form appropriate to carry out the above provisions, and they and the governmental authority therefor are to be satisfactory to counsel of Lee, Higginson & Company. The Dominican Republic agrees to make provision for the payment of these notes, principal and interest, in accordance with their terms, and to have on deposit with Lee, Higginson & Company funds sufficient for the payment of each instalment of interest and of the principal amount at least eleven days before such payment is due.

7. A temporary note or notes and a temporary bond in form satisfactory to counsel for Lee, Higginson & Company, without coupons may be issued in anticipation of the definitive notes and bonds and to be exchanged therefor.

8. Lee, Higginson & Company may associate with themselves in the disposal of these notes, such banks, banking firms, and other agencies as they may in their discretion deem desirable. They may issue their own interim receipts to purchasers of the notes.

9. All expenses in connection with the printing, engraving, and executing of said notes and of said pledged bonds, and all expenses including legal expenses incidental to their preparation shall be paid forthwith as they accrue by the Dominican Republic, but Lee, Higginson & Company and their associates shall bear all expenses in connection with the advertising and sale of said notes.

10. Lee, Higginson & Company are hereby appointed by the Dominican Republic Fiscal Agents for the service of the Loan, and accept said appointment.

11. The Dominican Republic states that its formal intention is to use the proceeds of these notes in connection with its public highways and public works.

12. The proceeds from the sale of these notes by Lee, Higginson & Company, as set forth in paragraph 1. of this contract, shall be credited on the books of Lee, Higginson & Company to the account of the Dominican Republic as of the dates of the sales thereof, less the compensation to be allowed said firm as hereinafter set forth; and until the proceeds of the sale are withdrawn by the Dominican Republic, interest is to be allowed at the same rate as similar balances on deposit with them are receiving at the time.

13. Lee, Higginson & Company shall hold all such deposits at the disposal of the Dominican Republic and subject to its draft or cheque.

14. Lee, Higginson & Company agree that if they have not effected the sale of said notes within ten (10) days after the temporary note duly executed has been delivered to them and the temporary bond and Indenture of Trust duly executed have been delivered to them as

trustees, that they will at once purchase all of said notes then remaining unsold at par and accrued interest.

15. Lee, Higginson & Company shall receive as compensation for their services in arranging this Loan and selling said notes a commission of 1½% on the entire issue of $2,500,000.

16. Lee, Higginson & Company shall receive for the authentication and countersignature of receipts and definitive notes and the pledged bonds the sum of twenty-five cents each.

17. Lee, Higginson & Company shall receive one-fourth of one per cent. of the amounts paid out for interest on these notes and one-twentieth of one per cent. on principal. They shall be reimbursed for all expenses incurred in connection with the call and redemption of said notes.

18. All coupons and notes paid shall be cancelled by Lee, Higginson & Company by perforation and then delivered to the Auditor of the Dominican Republic for further cancellation.

19. Lee, Higginson & Company shall allow the Dominican Republic interest on deposits held for the payment of interest and for redemption requirements at a rate of two per cent. less than the rediscount rate of the Federal Reserve Bank of New York, with a minimum of two per cent. and a maximum of four and one-half per cent. while such sums are on deposit with Lee, Higginson & Company.

20. In acting under this agreement, Lee, Higginson & Company may, subject to the provisions of these notes, not [act] in accordance with the written order of the Secretario de Estado de Hacienda y Comercio of the Dominican Republic, and the drafts, cheques or orders of the said Secretario de Estado de Hacienda y Comercio shall be full protection to them for action in accordance therewith.

21. All accounts connected with the service of the Loan shall be kept by Lee, Higginson & Company, either in their office in the City of Boston or in their office in the City of New York, and a statement of such accounts shall be rendered by them to the Auditor of the Dominican Republic within a reasonable time after the maturity of the issue. Unless objection to this statement of account shall be made by said Auditor to them within ninety days, particularly specifying the ground or grounds of such objection or objections, said statement of account shall be deemed to be correct and conclusive between the parties. The Dominican Republic shall have the right at any time to examine and audit the books and accounts of Lee, Higginson & Company in connection with their note as such Fiscal Agents and Trustees.

22. In case any of the notes of this issue shall at any time become mutilated, lost, or destroyed, the Dominican Republic may issue new notes of like amount, tenor and date, and bearing the same serial numbers, and Lee, Higginson & Company, at the request of the De-

partment of Finance and Commerce of the Dominican Republic shall authenticate the same for delivery in exchange for, and upon cancellation of the notes so mutilated, or in lieu of the note so lost or destroyed, but, in case of lost or destroyed notes, only upon receipt by the Dominican Republic and Lee, Higginson & Company of evidence satisfactory to them that such notes were lost or destroyed and upon receipt also of indemnity satisfactory to them in their discretion.

23. All notices, demands or requests from Lee, Higginson & Company to the Dominican Republic in connection with this agreement or the notes shall be sufficiently given if mailed in a securely enclosed postpaid envelope addressed to the Secretario de Estado de Hacienda y Comercio of the Dominican Republic, Santo Domingo City, Dominican Republic, or if given by cable so addressed. All notices, demands or requests from the Dominican Republic to Lee, Higginson & Company may similarly be given addressed to them at 43 Exchange Place, New York, N. Y.

24. This employment of Lee, Higginson & Company as Fiscal Agents is irrevocable, except for good and sufficient cause, but they may resign at any time as such Agents by giving notice of such resignation to the Dominican Republic in the manner provided above, and by publishing such notice at least twice a week for six successive weeks in two daily newspapers published and of general circulation in the City of New York. Such resignation shall take effect upon the expiration of such publication. The appointment of a successor to the Fiscal Agents shall be by mutual agreement between the Dominican Republic and the Fiscal Agents who may be retiring.

25. The provisions of this agreement shall be applicable to said firm of Lee, Higginson & Company as the same now is or may be hereafter constituted. It is agreed between the parties that upon the death or withdrawal of any partner or partners of Lee, Higginson & Company, the remaining partners, with such persons, if any, who have or may become partners of said firm, shall have all the rights and duties and be subject to the obligations conferred or imposed upon said firm by these presents.

26. This agreement for the sale of said notes is conditional upon receipt by Lee, Higginson & Company of assurance satisfactory to their counsel as to the procedure in the issue and execution of said notes and said bonds as security therefor, and upon delivery to said firm of the temporary note or notes herein mentioned, duly executed, and upon delivery of the temporary bond or bonds and Indenture of Trust to Lee, Higginson & Company as Trustees, duly executed on or before September 26th, 1924.

27. It is intended that this note issue be refunded by bonds authorized by a new Convention now under discussion.

28. The provisions of the contract between Lee, Higginson & Company and the Dominican Republic of April 4, 1922, shall apply to the pledged bonds so far as applicable under the changed circumstances of their issue and under the changed conditions of the Dominican Government.

IN WITNESS WHEREOF the Dominican Republic has caused this Contract to be signed and the seal of its Legation in the United States of America to be affixed by Jose del Carmen Ariza, its Envoy Extraordinary and Minister Plenipotentiary, and said Lee, Higginson & Company by Jerome D. Greene, a partner, have hereunto affixed their firm name and seal this Twentyfifth day of September, 1924.

DOMINICAN REPUBLIC
By J. C. ARIZA
E. E. and Minister Plenipotentiary

LEE, HIGGINSON & CO.,
By JEROME D. GREENE

CONVENTION BETWEEN THE UNITED STATES AND THE DOMINICAN REPUBLIC, SIGNED ON DECEMBER 27, 1924, TO REPLACE THE CONVENTION OF FEBRUARY 8, 1907 [31]

Treaty Series No. 726

Convention between the United States of America and the Dominican Republic, Signed at Washington, December 27, 1924 [32]

WHEREAS a convention between the United States of America and the Dominican Republic providing for the assistance of the United States in the collection and application of the customs revenues of the Dominican Republic, was concluded and signed by their respective Plenipotentiaries at the City of Santo Domingo, on the eighth day of February, one thousand nine hundred and seven, and

WHEREAS that convention was entered into to enable the Dominican Government to carry out a plan of settlement for the adjustment of debts and claims against the Government; and

WHEREAS, in accordance with that plan of settlement, the Dominican Republic issued in 1908, bonds to the amount of $20,000,000, bearing 5 per cent interest, payable in 50 years and redeemable after 10

[31] For text of the 1907 convention, see *Foreign Relations,* 1907, pt. 1, p. 307.
[32] In English and Spanish; Spanish text not printed. Ratification advised by the Senate, Jan. 21, 1925; ratified by the President, Jan. 26, 1925; ratified by the Dominican Republic, Aug. 17. 1925; ratifications exchanged at Washington, Oct. 24, 1925; proclaimed by the President, Oct. 26, 1925.

years at 102-½, and requiring payment of at least 1 per cent per annum for amortization; and

WHEREAS additional obligations have been incurred by the Dominican Government in the form of the issuance, in 1918, of bonds to the amount of $5,000,000, bearing 5 per cent interest, payable in 20 years, and redeemable at par on each interest date as the amount of amortization fund available on such interest dates will permit, and requiring payment of at least 5 per cent per annum for amortization; and in the form of the issuance of bonds, in 1922, to the amount of $10,000,000, bearing 5-½ per cent interest, payable in 20 years, and redeemable after 8 years at 101. and requiring payment after such period of at least $563,916.67 per annum for amortization; and

WHEREAS certain of the terms of the contracts under which these bonds have been issued have proven by experience unduly onerous to the Dominican Republic and have compelled it to devote a larger portion of the customs revenues to provide the interest and sinking fund charges pledged to the service of such bonds than is deemed advisable or necessary; and

WHEREAS it is the desire of the Dominican Government and appears to be to the best interest of the Dominican Republic to issue bonds to a total amount of $25,000,000, in order to provide for the refunding on terms more advantageous to the Republic of its obligations represented by the bonds of the three issues above mentioned still outstanding and for a balance remaining after such operation is concluded to be devoted to permanent public improvements and to other projects designed to further the economic and industrial development of the country; and

WHEREAS the whole of this plan is conditioned and dependent upon the assistance of the United States in the collection of customs revenues of the Dominican Republic and the application thereof so far as necessary to the interest upon and the amortization and redemption of said bonds, and the Dominican Republic has requested the United States to give and the United States is willing to give such assistance:

The United States of America, represented by Charles Evans Hughes, Secretary of State of the United States of America; and the Dominican Republic, represented by Señor José del Carmen Ariza, Envoy Extraordinary and Minister Plenipotentiary of the Dominican Republic in Washington, have agreed:

ARTICLE I

That the President of the United States shall appoint, a General Receiver of Dominican Customs, who, with such Assistant Receivers and other employees of the Receivership as shall be appointed by the President of the United States in his discretion, shall collect all the customs duties accruing at the several customs houses of the Dominican Republic until the payment or retirement of any and all bonds issued by the Dominican Government in accordance with the plan and under the limitations as to terms and amounts hereinbefore recited; and said General Receiver shall apply the sums so collected, as follows:

First, to paying the expenses of the receivership; second, to the payment of interest upon all bonds outstanding; third, to the payment of the annual sums provided for amortization of said bonds including interest upon all bonds held in sinking fund; fourth, to the purchase and cancellation or the retirement and cancellation pursuant to the terms thereof of any of said bonds as may be directed by the Dominican Government; fifth, the remainder to be paid to the Dominican Government.

The method of distributing the current collections of revenue in order to accomplish the application thereof as hereinbefore provided shall be as follows:

The expenses of the receivership shall be paid by the Receiver as they arise. The allowances to the General Receiver and his assistants for the expenses of collecting the revenues shall not exceed five per cent unless by agreement between the two Governments.

On the first day of each calendar month shall be paid over by the Receiver to the Fiscal Agent of the loan a sum equal to one twelfth of the annual interest of all the bonds issued and of the annual sums provided for amortization of said bonds and the remaining collection of the last preceding month shall be paid over to the Dominican Government, or applied to the sinking fund for the purchase or redemption of bonds or for other purposes as the Dominican Government shall direct.

Provided, that in case the customs revenues collected by the General Receiver shall in any year exceed the sum of $4,000,000, 10 per cent of the surplus above such sum of $4,000,000 shall be applied to the sinking fund for the redemption of bonds.

Article II

The Dominican Government will provide by law for the payment of all customs duties to the General Receiver and his assistants, and will give to them all needful aid and assistance and full protection to the extent of its powers. The Government of the United States will give to the General Receiver and his assistants such protection as it may find to be requisite for the performance of their duties.

ARTICLE III

Until the Dominican Republic has paid the whole amount of the bonds of the debt, its public debt shall not be increased except by previous agreement between the Dominican Government and the United States.

ARTICLE IV

The Dominican Government agrees that the import duties will at no time be modified to such an extent that, on the basis of exportations and importations to the like amount and the like character during the two years preceding that in which it is desired to make such modification, the total net customs receipts would not at such altered rates have amounted for each of such two years to at least 1-½ times the amount necessary to provide for the interest and sinking fund charges upon its public debt.

ARTICLE V

The accounts of the General Receiver shall be rendered monthly to the Ministry of Finance and Commerce of the Dominican Republic and to the State Department of the United States and shall be subject to examination and verification by the appropriate officers of the Dominican and the United States Governments.

ARTICLE VI

The determination of any controversy which may arise between the Contracting Parties in the carrying out of the provisions of this Convention shall, should the two Governments be unable to come to an agreement through diplomatic channels, be by arbitration. In the carrying out of this agreement in each individual case, the Contracting Parties, once the necessity of arbitration is determined, shall conclude a special agreement defining clearly the scope of the dispute, the scope of the powers of the arbitrators, and the periods to be fixed for the formation of the arbitral tribunal and the several stages of the procedure. The special agreement providing for arbitration shall, in all cases, be signed within a period of three months from the date upon which either one of the Contracting Parties shall notify the other Contracting Party of its desire to resort to arbitration. It is understood that on the part of the United States, such special agreements will be made by the President of the United States by and with the advice and consent of the Senate thereto, and on the part of the Dominican Republic, shall be subject to the procedure required by the Constitution and laws thereof.

Article VII

This agreement shall take effect after its approval by the Contracting Parties in accordance with their respective Constitutional methods. Upon the exchange of ratifications of this convention, which shall take place at Washington as soon as possible, the Convention between the United States of America and the Dominican Republic providing for the assistance of the United States in the collection and application of the customs revenues, concluded and signed at the City of Santo Domingo on the 8th day of February, 1907, shall be deemed to be abrogated.

Done in duplicate in the English and Spanish languages at the City of Washington this 27th day of December, nineteen hundred and twenty-four.

Charles Evans Hughes [seal]

J. C. Ariza [seal]

EXCHANGE OF NOTES BETWEEN THE UNITED STATES AND THE DOMINICAN REPUBLIC ACCORDING MUTUAL UNCONDITIONAL MOST-FAVORED-NATION TREATMENT IN CUSTOMS MATTERS

611.3931/8a

The Secretary of State to President Coolidge

Washington, *June 20, 1924.*

My Dear Mr. President: It appears that the approaching visit to Washington of the President-elect of the Dominican Republic will offer a most favorable opportunity to discuss with him and with the members of his party various questions of importance affecting the relations between the United States and the Dominican Republic. Among these questions is the proposed revision of the Dominican customs tariff, which will presumably be undertaken immediately after the new Constitutional Government of the Dominican Republic is installed. Under the terms of the Convention between the United States and the Dominican Republic of 1907,[33] the consent of the President of the United States is required before any modification of its customs tariff can be made by the Dominican Government.

The principal export of the Dominican Republic is sugar. Owing to the fact that Porto Rico is able to import sugar into the United States free of all duty and that Cuba is enabled to import sugar into the United States with a preferential rate of 20%, Dominican sugar is unable to compete in the United States market with the sugar pro-

---

[33] *Foreign Relations,* 1907, pt. 1, p. 307.

duced in either of those two Islands, and consequently, all sugar exported from the Dominican Republic is sold either in Europe or in Canada. Because of this situation, it is possible that the Dominican Government, when it undertakes the revision of its customs tariff, will determine that it is to its best advantage to grant preferential rates to Great Britain or to certain European Nations. To preclude the possibility, should this be undertaken, of American exporters finding themselves in a disadvantageous position in the Dominican Republic, it has occurred to me that it might be desirable to undertake with the new Dominican Government an exchange of notes similar to the notes which this Government has recently exchanged with the Governments of Brazil[34] and Czecho-Slovakia,[35] and which are now being negotiated with Nicaragua[36] and with Poland. The effect of this exchange of notes would constitute an agreement between the two Governments pending the arrival of a convenient time for the conclusion of a comprehensive commercial treaty, by which each country will maintain for the commerce of the other a basis of equality with the commerce of every foreign country, an exception will of course be made in the case of the United States to allow for the preferential rates granted by the United States to Cuba.

Should this suggestion meet with your approval, I will endeavor to reach an agreement in principle in this matter with the President-elect of the Dominican Republic in order that the suggested notes may be exchanged as soon as possible after his inauguration as Constitutional President of the Republic.

Faithfully yours,

CHARLES E. HUGHES

611.3931/14a

The Secretary of State to the Dominican Minister (Ariza)

WASHINGTON, *September 25, 1924.*

SIR: I have the honor to make the following statement of my understanding of the agreement reached through recent conversations held at Washington by representatives of the Government of the United States and the Government of the Dominican Republic with reference to the treatment which the United States shall accord to the commerce of the Dominican Republic and which the Dominican Republic shall accord to the commerce of the United States.

These conversations have disclosed a mutual understanding between the two Governments which is that, in respect to import,

[34] *Foreign Relations*, 1923, vol. I, pp. 453 ff.
[35] *Ibid.*, pp. 866 ff.
[36] Vol. II, pp. 510 ff.

export and other duties and charges affecting commerce, as well as in respect to transit, warehousing and other facilities, the United States will accord to the Dominican Republic and the Dominican Republic will accord to the United States, its territories and possessions, unconditional most-favored-nation treatment.

It is understood that

No higher or other duties shall be imposed on the importation into or disposition in the United States, its territories or possessions, of any articles the produce or manufacture of the Dominican Republic than are or shall be payable on like articles the produce or manufacture of any foreign country;

No higher or other duties shall be imposed on the importation into or disposition in the Dominican Republic of any articles the produce or manufacture of the United States, its territories or possessions than are or shall be payable on like articles the produce or manufacture of any foreign country;

Similarly, no higher or other duties shall be imposed in the United States, its territories or possessions, or in the Dominican Republic on the exportation of any articles to the other, or to any territory or possession of the other, than are payable on the exportation of like articles to any foreign country;

Every concession with respect to any duty or charge affecting commerce now accorded or that may hereafter be accorded by the United States or by the Dominican Republic, by law, proclamation, decree or commercial treaty or agreement, to the products of any third country will become immediately applicable without request and without compensation to the commerce of the Dominican Republic and of the United States, its territories and possessions, respectively:

Provided that this understanding does not relate to

(1) The treatment which the United States accords or may hereafter accord to the commerce of Cuba or any of the territories or possessions of the United States or the Panama Canal Zone, or to the treatment which is or may hereafter be accorded to the commerce of the United States with any of its territories or possessions or to the commerce of its territories or possessions with one another;

(2) Prohibitions or restrictions of a sanitary character or designed to protect human, animal or plant life or regulations for the enforcement of police or revenue laws.

The present arrangement shall become operative on the day of signature and, unless sooner terminated by mutual agreement, shall continue in force until thirty days after notice of its termination shall have been given by either party; but should either party be prevented by future action of its legislature from carrying out the terms of this arrangement, the obligations thereof shall thereupon lapse.

I shall be glad to have your confirmation of the accord thus reached.

Accept [etc.] CHARLES E. HUGHES

611.3931/14

The Dominican Minister (Ariza) to the Secretary of State

[Translation]

WASHINGTON, *September 25, 1924.*

MR. SECRETARY OF STATE: I have the honor to acknowledge receipt of the note dated this day in which your Excellency sums up the agreement reached in the conferences recently held in this city between the Government of the United States and the Government of the Dominican Republic concerning the treatment which the United States will grant to the commerce of the Dominican Republic and which the Dominican Republic will grant to the commerce of the United States.

Those conferences disclosed a mutual understanding between the two Governments which is that with regard to importation, exportation and other duties and dues to which commerce is subject as also with regard to the transit, storage, and other facilities, the United States, its territories or possessions will grant to the Dominican Republic, and the Dominican Republic will grant to the United States, its territories or possessions, unconditional most favored nation treatment.

It is understood that there shall not be imposed duties of importation or of disposal in the United States, its territories or possessions on articles that are the products of the soil or of the industry of the Dominican Republic higher or other than those that are, or may be payable on said articles when they proceed from the soil or the industry of any other foreign country and, in the same manner, there shall not be levied duties of importation or disposal in the Dominican Republic on articles that are the products of the soil or of the industry of the United States, its territories or possessions higher or other than those which are or may be payable on said articles when they proceed from the soil or the industry of any other foreign country whatsoever.

In the same sense there shall not be imposed in the United States, its territories or possessions, nor in the Dominican Republic on articles exported from one country to the other or to any territory or possession of the other, export duties higher or other than those that are or may be assessed when the said articles are exported to any other foreign country whatsoever.

Any concession granted or that may be hereafter granted by the United States, or by the Dominican Republic by means of a law, decree, resolution, or agreement on the products of any other country with respect to the duties or dues that affect commerce, will as of right extend without request or compensation of any kind to the commerce of the Dominican Republic and that of the United States, its territories and possessions respectively.

Provided, however, that this understanding does not refer:

1. To the treatment that the United States now accords or may hereafter accord to the commerce of Cuba or any of the territories or possessions of the United States or the Panama Canal Zone or to the treatment that is granted or may be granted to the commerce between the United States and any of its territories or possessions or to the commerce of its territories and possessions with one another.

2. To the prohibitions or restrictions of a sanitary character or for the protection of human beings, animals or plants, or the regulations for the enforcement of the revenue or police laws.

It is understood that this agreement will go into effect immediately upon the date of its signature and unless terminated before, by common accord, will continue in force until thirty days shall have elapsed after the notice given by one party to the other of its intention to terminate the agreement; but in case either one of the two parties should be unable to fulfill the terms of this agreement by reason of future action of its legislature the obligations which it imposes will be without effect.

I have the honor to inform your Excellency that I have received instructions from my Government to confirm this agreement and to send to Your Excellency this note in reply to yours.

I avail myself [etc.]   J. C. ARIZA

PURCHASE OF THE PROPERTIES OF THE SANTO DOMINGO WATER, LIGHT AND POWER COMPANY BY THE DOMINICAN GOVERNMENT [37]

839.6463/136 : Telegram

The Secretary of State to the Minister in the Dominican Republic (Russell)

WASHINGTON, *January 26, 1924—6 p. m.*

1. Your 3, January 17, 11 A. M.[38] Department considers proposed bond issue should cover provision for issuance of bonds to Santo Domingo Water, Light and Power Company pursuant to obligations

---

[37] For previous correspondence concerning the properties of the Santo Domingo Water, Light and Power Co., see *Foreign Relations*, 1923, vol. I, pp. 918 ff.
[38] Not printed.

of Dominican Government under contract dated June 15, 1923,[39] and is advised by A. F. Hunt, Jr., company's representative, that pursuant to his letter sent June 14, 1923, to Dominican Secretary of the Interior, at the latter's request, he will recommend to his principals that they furnish sum required for rehabilitation of properties as determined by expert provided in contract, provided Dominican Government shall put in escrow in hands of its fiscal agent under proposed bond issue $951,000 par value of the bonds, with instructions that they be delivered to the order of the Liberty Trust Company of Boston, Massachusetts, simultaneously with the delivery to said fiscal agent by Dwight P. Robinson and Company of certificate contemplated by Article 5th of contract.

Ascertain and telegraph promptly intentions of Dominican Government.

HUGHES

839.6463/137 : Telegram

The Minister in the Dominican Republic (Russell) to the Secretary of State

SANTO DOMINGO, *January 28, 1924—5 p. m.*
[Received January 29—6 : 54 p. m.]

5. Your telegram no. 3[*1*], January 26, 6 p. m. Government's position is that Mr. Hunt had always insisted that amount necessary to place plant in working condition could never exceed $50,000 and that article 4 of the contract stipulated $60,000 but that Mr. Hunt in a letter to the Minister of the Interior agreed to induce Government [*company?*] to advance for this purpose an amount not to exceed $75,000 so that Government never had the least [expectation?] that repairs would cost any such sum as reported by expert but that the entire amount for settlement in bonds including estimated value of plant would be in the neighborhood of $500,000 and this was what municipalities had in mind.

RUSSELL

839.6463/138 : Telegram

The Minister in the Dominican Republic (Russell) to the Secretary of State

SANTO DOMINGO, *February 1, 1924—noon.*
[Received February 2—9 : 48 a. m.]

6. In the matter of the Santo Domingo Water, Light and Power Company, further interview with the President, and he states that

---

[39] Not printed.

he does not think that the two million loan should be subordinated to the matter of bonds for delivery to Light and Power Company. As it appears the former is not authorized, all public works will have to be shut down next month. He states that he is also disposed to arrange with Light and Power Company and provide for reasonable settlement in some other way.

RUSSELL

839.6463/139 : Telegram

The Secretary of State to the Minister in the Dominican Republic
(Russell)

WASHINGTON, *February 6, 1924—1 p. m.*

2. Your 5, January 28, 5 p. m., and 6, February 1, noon.

Hunt has shown Department copy letter mentioned your January 28, 5 p. m., and this does not appear to contain any limitation upon amount which he agreed to recommend to his principals should be advanced for repairs.

In view Dominican Government's apparent disinclination to carry out its obligations under contract of June 15, 1923, Department is disposed to recommend to Santo Domingo Company to accept $450,-000 gold, or its equivalent in Dominican bonds at 90% of their par value in full payment of properties described in contract, which shall thereupon be transferred to the order of the Dominican Government in their present condition.

Department desires to be promptly advised whether Dominican Government will agree to settlement on this basis which will afford that Government opportunity to make its own repairs on plant and apparently render it unnecessary in order to place it in operative condition to expend full amount set forth in expert's report for repairs and improvements.

HUGHES

839.6463/141 : Telegram

The Minister in the Dominican Republic (Russell) to the Secretary
of State

SANTO DOMINGO, *February 8, 1924—4 p. m.*
[Received 11 p. m.]

8. Interview with the President today in regard to Santo Domingo Water, Light and Power Company. He states that he will immediately commence careful study of the report of the expert with the assistance of the former Minister of the Interior who signed the contract of last June with a view to reaching an equitable solution

of the matter in the interest of the company and the municipalities. He said that he could not definitely state what he would do in regard to issuing bonds for the value of the property for $450,000 until he had time to go over the matter carefully but that he will give an answer as soon as possible. The President stated that as the expert had given a basis for the present value of the property the question as to how much the municipalities could afford to spend for putting the plant in working condition would have to be considered. He stated that he thought the report of the expert was greatly in excess of what was needed for furnishing water and light. Commander Warfield, U. S. Navy, reported that repairs could be made for $35,000.

RUSSELL

839.6463/142 : Telegram

The Commissioner in the Dominican Republic (Welles) to the Secretary of State

SANTO DOMINGO, *February 8, 1924—4 p. m.*
[Received February 11—1:31 a. m.]

8. For Francis White:[40] Referring to the Department's telegram to American Legation dated February 6, 1 p. m., I desire to bring following consideration to your attention:

I cannot concur in the expression used in instruction under reference, namely, "apparent disinclination of Dominican Government to carry out its obligations," under contract entered into with Santo Domingo Water, Light and Power Company. The contract of the Government with that company provided that the latter agreed to sell to the former the properties specified at a price to be fixed by an expert to be selected by common accord; the latter likewise agreed to advance to the former a sum not to exceed $60,000 and receive in return therefor Government bonds to pay for whatever repairs said expert might determine were necessary to place properties in proper condition. The expert in his report values the properties at $533,000 and fixes the necessary expenditure for repairs at $324,000. Under the terms of the contract the Government did not obligate itself to issue bonds the proceeds of which would be destined to repay the company for necessary repairs to an amount greater than $60,000 and its present disinclination or rather inability to purchase the properties on the basis set by the expert cannot in any sense be termed unwillingness to carry out the terms of the contract. Hunt, in his statement to the Government in May, 1923, declared

[40] Chief of the Division of Latin American Affairs.

specifically that necessary repairs could be carried out for a sum less than $60,000, and while in a letter to the Secretary of the Interior subsequent to the signing of the contract, he implied that his company would be willing to advance a sum somewhat larger than $60,000 for repairs, should it be necessary, neither he nor the Government had in mind an excess of more than a few thousand dollars.

The President, as the Department has been informed, I understand, by the American Minister, is most favorably disposed to the most speedy settlement possible of this controversy but he, of course, cannot, in view of the financial situation of the Government, accept a settlement on a basis never foreseen by either party and a settlement to which his Government is in no wise obligated. If the company desires the matter adjusted, it should send Hunt to Santo Domingo immediately to negotiate directly with the Government.

In addition please refer to my telegram of January 17, 11 a. m.[41] The desired authorization should be granted immediately and should not be made in any sense contingent on a settlement of the controversy with the Santo Domingo Water, Light and Power Company. Unless the authorization is granted at once, all public works will cease next April with disastrous results not only with regard to the economic condition of the Republic, but to the whole question of our policy here.

WELLES

839.6463/142 : Telegram

The Secretary of State to the Commissioner in the Dominican Republic (Welles)

WASHINGTON, *February 18, 1924—3 p. m.*

4. Your 8, February 8, 4 p. m. The contract between the Santo Domingo Water, Light and Power Company and the Dominican authorities provided that the property specified would be sold at a price to be fixed by an expert to be selected by common accord. In fact, however, the Department understands the expert was picked by the Dominican Government and the Company acceded to the choice. The Government wished the Company to advance the cash necessary for the repairs for whatever sum that might be, taking bonds at 90 therefor. As Hunt did not have authority to bind his principals for an indefinite sum he was only willing to pledge himself in the contract to make repairs up to $60,000 although he states the Government repeatedly requested him not to fix a limit. However, in order to meet the wishes of the Dominican Government as far as possible he signed a letter to the Secretary of the Interior

---

[41] *Ante*, p. 644.

before the conclusion of the contract by which he agreed, should the expert fix the expenditure necessary for repairs at an amount greater than $60,000. to recommend to his principals that they advance the money for this purpose. The expert picked by the Government reported the value of the property in its present condition at $533,012. and fixed the expenditures necessary for the repairs at $323,420. Upon receipt of this information Mr. Hunt, in accordance with his promise to the Secretary of the Interior, recommended to his principals that they advance the money necessary for these repairs. The latter agreed to do so and requested that $951,000. in bonds (equivalent at 90 to $856,432. in cash) of the projected loan issue be held in escrow for the Company to be turned over to it at such time as the expert should state that the necessary repairs had been satisfactorily completed. The Company and Hunt have scrupulously lived up to their agreement. The Government apparently has endeavored to find a technicality in the $60,000. provision for not living up to the agreement. The Government is doubtless surprised that an impartial expert should find the property as valuable as it is but this does not appear to furnish grounds not to carry out its obligations under the contract.

However, in view of the apparent feeling of the Government that the estimate for repairs is too high, the Department stated in its telegram to the Legation of February 6, 1 p. m., that it would be disposed to recommend to the Company to accept $450,000. gold or its equivalent in Dominican bonds at 90 per cent of their par value in full payment of properties described in contract which shall thereupon be transferred to the order of the Dominican Government in their present condition. This was practically the same settlement that the Department had suggested in its telegram No. 7 to the Legation at Santo Domingo of March 8, 1923, 3 p. m.,[42] before the property had been appraised and when the bonds were quoted at approximately 85. If the Dominican Government should wish to settle on this basis it would receive the property at $83,000. gold less than its appraised value and telegram No. 8, February 8, 4 p. m., from this Minister would indicate that the President is giving this matter careful consideration.

However, the Department, in view of your telegram and without awaiting the President's reply, has recommended to the Company that it accept the proposition contained in the penultimate paragraph of the Department's telegram No. 2, February 6, 1 p. m., to the Legation. The Company has therefore made an offer either "(1) to furnish the sum required to pay the cost of rehabilitation of the properties described in the contract of June 15, 1923, as determined

---

[42] *Foreign Relations*, 1923, vol. i, p. 918.

by the experts therein named, provided the Dominican Government shall put in escrow in the hands of its Fiscal Agent under its proposed bond issue $951,000. par value of the bonds agreed to be issued with instructions that the same be delivered to the order of the Liberty Trust Company of Boston, Massachusetts, simultaneously with the delivery to said Fiscal Agent by Dwight P. Robinson and Company, Incorporated, of the certificate provided to be given by said last named company under the terms of Article 5th of said contract; or (2) accept $450,000. gold, or its equivalent in Dominican 5½ per cent bonds at 90 per cent of their par value, in full payment of the properties described in said contract of June 15, 1923, which shall thereupon be transferred to the order of the Dominican Government in their present condition." Mr. Hunt states that the "above offer is made without prejudice to the rights of my principals under the record of this case as filed in the State Department."

In view of all the circumstances of this case, the difficulties experienced by the Company in coming to an agreement with the municipalities and with the Government, the fact that Mr. Hunt has already made three trips to Santo Domingo and has negotiated a contract for the settlement of the matter, the Department is not disposed to ask Mr. Hunt to go again to Santo Domingo to try to make another contract. In view of the attitude which the Government has apparently taken on the contract of June 15, 1923, there would appear to be no assurance that a new contract, if made, would be carried out. The Department feels that the two alternative propositions made by the Company offer the basis for a fair and equitable settlement and when it is advised that one of these propositions is accepted it will then be in a position to inform the Legation regarding the proposed bond issue. The Department hopes that you will use your influence to have one of these propositions accepted by the Dominican Government.

HUGHES

839.6463/145 : Telegram

The Commissioner in the Dominican Republic (Welles) to the Secretary of State

SANTO DOMINGO, *February 23, 1924—11 a. m.*
[Received February 26—5 : 29 a. m.]

14. I received yesterday the Department's telegram of February 18, 3 p. m. In view of the fact that the more recent developments in this case may not have been brought to [your?] knowledge and because of my belief that a basic question is involved affecting the excellent results of the policy towards this Republic which you have estab-

lished, I venture to communicate to you the following considerations with the earnest hope that the instructions referred to may be modified.

The relation of the facts in this case contained in the Department's telegram under reference is incomplete and in part inaccurate. The following is an outline of the more important points:

As a result of constant difficulties extending over a term of years between the Santo Domingo Water, Light and Power Company and the municipalities of Santiago and Puerto Plata, to which municipalities the company was supplying electric light and water under a concession extended by the two municipal governments, the company decided in 1921 to abandon the operation of its properties. Upon ascertaining that the municipalities refused to purchase the properties upon terms acceptable to it the company endeavored to induce the American Military Government to purchase the properties on behalf of the municipalities. This the Military Government refused to do on the ground that the national Dominican Government had no interest in the question which in its opinion was a matter which solely concerned the two municipalities. Early in 1923 as a result of popular agitation in Santiago the people of which city had been without electric light or running water for over a year, caused by a shutting down of the company's plants, the municipalities of Santiago brought suit to obtain a forced sale of the company's properties on the ground that the company had violated the terms of its concession.

In order to avoid the serious problems which the continuance of this suit might entail and in order to obtain a settlement of the dispute which would prove satisfactory to the American interests involved, I had, upon my return to Santo Domingo in April, 1923, several interviews with the Provisional President and stated to him that while I realized the dispute was one with which the National Government was not directly concerned, nevertheless, the continuance of it would prove detrimental to Dominican credit in the United States and would tend to promote ill feeling on the part of the Dominican people against American interests at a time when it was our common object to remove all causes of friction. The President took that point of view of the situation and adopted my suggestion that the National Government agree to lend the municipalities sufficient money to purchase the properties of the company, the National Government assuring itself that the interest and sinking fund charges on its loan to the municipalities would be paid by taking over the collection of a portion of the municipal revenues of the two cities concerned. It was upon this basis—a basis which the Military Government had refused to consider—that Mr. Hunt, representative of the American interests, negotiated the contract of June 15, 1923, mentioned in the Department's telegram under reference.

This contract provides that the Government will pay the company in Dominican Government bonds the equivalent of whatever price might be fixed as the value of properties specified by an expert selected by common accord.

Article 4 of said contract reads as follows:

"The expert will make a detailed study of the properties and of every part of them, determining their actual condition and price and specifying the cost which the repairs and improvements to assure good and regular operation may require *in toto* as well as in detail, it being understood that the costs of such repairs and improvements shall not exceed $60,000 American money."

The amount of $60,000 was set because Mr. Hunt stated to me several times and stated in my presence to the Minister of the Interior, that the properties were in such good condition that the necessary repairs could be accomplished for less than that sum. His statements were confirmed by the fact that an American engineer under the Military Government the preceding year had estimated the cost of repairs at $45,000. To be certain, however, that an appraisal of repairs by the expert a few thousand dollars in excess of the limit set in the contract would not endanger the execution of the contract, Mr. Hunt, in accordance with the Government's request, stated in a letter to the Minister of the Interior, that should the cost of repairs be fixed at a sum somewhat in excess of $60,000, he would recommend to his principals that the necessary sum be advanced by them. The expert set the value of the properties in their present condition at $533,012 and fixed the cost of necessary repairs at $323,424. The value of the properties is $133,012 in excess of the price at which the company was willing to sell to the municipalities.

2. After some delay the Government, however, would be willing to buy at this price since this is the price set by the expert in accordance with the contract were it possible to place the municipalities [*properties*] in good condition for a sum within or near the limit set in the same contract. It is not, however, willing to buy the plant at the price fixed by the expert when the cost of repairs fixed by the same expert is $263,424 above the limit set in the contract.

In view of these facts the final sentence of the first paragraph of the Department's telegram referred to appears to me misleading since the Government is entirely willing to carry out its obligations to purchase the plant at the sum fixed by the expert but is not willing to spend over six times the amount for repairs when [*which*] it expressed its willingness to pay in the contract, which amount as fixed in the contract it was informed by the representative of the company would be ample to pay for all necessary repairs.

It is, therefore, my feeling that an attempt on our part to force the Dominican Government to accept either one of the propositions contained in the Department's cable referred to would constitute material injustice; as regards the first proposition for the reasons above expressed; as regards the second because it would constitute an effort on the part of our Government to force the Dominican Government to purchase properties at a price $50,000 higher than that at which the company was willing to sell two years ago when the properties have depreciated during those two years and when the Government would have to spend $300,000 on repairs before the properties could be profitably operated.

The question of policy is, however, the following: When the Provisional Government took over from the Military Government it was with the understanding that the public works program of roads construction inaugurated in 1922 would be carried on. The funds for carrying out of this program were obtained by the 1922 loan of $10,000,000 authorized by the Department of which only $6,700,000 of bonds were actually issued, it being the understanding that the Department would agree to the issuance of the remainder whenever the public works program demanded. With this understanding the Provisional President framed his budget for 1924. He has repeatedly endeavored since last October to obtain the Department's consent to the issuance of a portion of the remainder of the bonds of the authorized loan, without success. The situation is now such that if authorization is not granted at once the whole program must cease, when the present slight improvement in the economic situation here is due entirely to the opening up of these roads and when such cessation also means the throwing out of work of thousands of laborers at a time when the unemployment situation is peculiarly acute.

I am, however, informed by the Department's telegram under reference that when the Department is advised that one of the propositions presented by the Santo Domingo Water, Light and Power Company is accepted by the Dominican Government, it will then be in a position to reach a decision regarding the proposed bond issue. In other words, the Department's apparent intention is to force the Dominican Government to accept one of two propositions each of which appears unfair or else resign itself to do without funds upon the obtaining of which the present tenuous prosperity of the country actually depends. I cannot help but feel that a policy of this nature in former years has been directly responsible for the suspicion and ill will toward the United States which exists in so many of the smaller Latin American countries. And I cannot in particular reconcile the adoption of the policy outlined in the Department's telegram referred to with our announced intention of assisting the Dominican people in every way possible to establish a stable government and to increase the prosperity of the Republic.

It is because of my strong belief in the unwisdom of the policy to be adopted according to the Department's telegraphic instructions that I have ventured to express my views at such length as well as to recommend most earnestly that the Department grant immediately the necessary authorization for the issuance of that portion of the remainder of the 1922 loan requested by the Dominican Government.

The Santo Domingo Water, Light and Power Company will find the Provisional President disposed to meet it more than half way as he has been disposed since the original negotiations were initiated in reaching an agreement which is equitable to both parties and in overcoming the difficulties which the expert's report has presented.

WELLES

839.6463/149a : Telegram

The Secretary of State to the Minister in the Dominican Republic (Russell)

WASHINGTON, *March 5, 1924—6 p. m.*

4. Your No. 1, January 1 [7], 12 noon.[43]

You will please inform the Dominican Government that this Government authorizes the issuance of a further issue of $2,000,000 par value of bonds remaining out of the total issue of $10,000,000 authorized in 1922 provided that $951,000. par value bonds thereof shall be held in escrow by the Fiscal Agent of the Dominican Government pending an agreement between the Government and the Power Company. In this connection consult with Mr. Welles to whom detailed instructions are being sent today.

HUGHES

839.6463/145 : Telegram

The Secretary of State to the Commissioner in the Dominican Republic (Welles)

WASHINGTON, *March 5, 1924—7 p. m.*

6. Your 14, February 23, 11 a. m.

The Department desires to aid so far as it properly can in promoting a settlement of the difficulty between the Dominican Government and the Santo Domingo Water, Light and Power Company which will be fair and just to both sides and acceptable to both. The Department furthermore is particularly interested in the carrying out of the public works program and in aiding the Dominican Government in all proper ways in the rehabilitation of the country.

---

[43] *Ante,* p. 644.

Three methods of settling the Power Company's controversy suggest themselves:

1. The Company and the Government could agree to abide by the findings of the expert. As you are aware the Company is willing to do so. It appears that the Government however found the cost of repairs too high and as they were vastly in excess of the $60,000 mentioned in the contract it does not wish to do so.

2. In view of the Government's feeling regarding proposition No. 1 the Company offered to accept $450,000 gold, or its equivalent in Dominican 5½ per cent bonds at 90 per cent of their par value, in full payment of the properties which would thereupon be transferred to the order of the Dominican Government in their present condition. The Company takes the position that although it was willing to sell this property in 1921 for $400,000, the sum of $450,-000 should not now be regarded as excessive, as the Company has incurred considerable losses and expenses in the last three years, such as interest on its investment, the fee of over $10,000 to Dwight P. Robinson and Company, attorney's fees, and the cost of the maintenance of the property, the latter amounting to from $12,000 to $15,000 annually. In considering this position of the Company the Department cannot disregard the fact that the expert selected by the Dominican Government has valued the properties in their present condition at $533,012. If the matter were to be adjusted on the basis of taking the properties over as they are without reference to repairs, it would be difficult for the Department, in the face of the expert's report, to insist that the Company should take less than $450,000 which is $83,000 under the valuation.

This proposal, however, would mean that the Government would perhaps have to make new contracts for the reconditioning of the plant and they may prefer an arrangement by which the plants would be put in operating condition by the issuance of Dominican bonds to cover the cost thereof and thus acquire possession of the plants in working order in one transaction. The Department would therefore be willing to approve the following settlement should it meet with the Dominican Government's approval. The Department is advised that this would be acceptable to the Company.

3. The Government to buy the plant at the value fixed by the expert, namely $533,012. The Government would then designate the repairs it desires made (the Department presumes that the expert's valuation was based on putting the plant in an absolutely perfect condition whereas it may be possible to put it in working condition for very much less and that this is what the Dominican Government desires). The repairs would then be made by the Power Company at cost under the supervision of the Dwight P. Robinson Company, the latter to certify to the cost of the repairs and that they have been

properly carried out. The Company would be given sufficient bonds at par value to amount to $533,012 at 90 per cent, and a sufficient number of bonds at par value to cover the cost of repairs at 90 per cent would be held in escrow by the Fiscal Agent until he is advised by the Robinson Company that the repairs have been made whereupon he will immediately turn over bonds to the Power Company to the amount certified by the Robinson Company. While the Company would prefer to receive immediately the bonds covering the present value of the property the Department understands that it would be willing, should the Government prefer, to have the bonds for that amount also held in escrow by the Fiscal Agent until the repairs are made.

It is furthermore possible that the Dominican Government may have still another proposal to make and the Department understands that the Company would be glad, in that case, to have the Government make their proposal as soon as possible whereupon the Company will give it careful consideration.

Your statements in paragraphs eleven and twelve imply that the Department is attempting to force the Dominican Government to accept one of the Power Company's proposals by not authorizing the loan. This is not the Department's policy. The Department is constantly solicitous that all matters should be dealt with on the fairest possible basis and with due consideration of the exigencies of the Dominican Government. You are referred to the note from the Minister of Foreign Affairs to Minister Russell dated November 23, 1923 [44] (enclosed in the latter's despatch No. 909 of November 24 [45]) in paragraph 4 of which it is stated that

"it is estimated that it will be necessary to issue bonds for the nominal amount of $2,000,000 of the balance of the total not issued but authorized under Executive Order No. 735 in order to continue the program of public works; to meet the obligations assumed by the Government in the contract celebrated between the Municipalities of Santiago and Puerto Plata and the Water and Light Company of these cities; and for other purposes."

This was the first request received by the Department for authorization to issue the loan and shows that the Dominican Government itself considered that the two questions of the bond issue and the settlement of the Power Company's contract could not be wholly disassociated. The point is that if the Company is to be paid in bonds there certainly must be bonds to make the payments, and a reservation should be made sufficient for this purpose. The Department could not agree to any other course without depriving the Company of its fair opportunity to be reimbursed in the manner desired by

---

[44] Not printed.
[45] *Ante,* p. 643.

the Dominican Government. The Department is entirely willing to authorize, and is instructing the Minister immediately to authorize the issuance of a further loan of $2,000,000 on the understanding that $951,000 par value bonds thereof shall be held in escrow by the Fiscal Agent of the Dominican Government pending an agreement between the Government and the Company. This amount is suggested merely because it is the maximum and is the amount of the valuation plus the repairs as fixed by the expert, but of course this amount will be subject to reduction to meet the terms of any new agreement that is made.

The Department feels that the above arrangement offers a fair basis for an adjustment of the difficulty, giving the Government wide latitude of choice as to the method to be followed out in acquiring the property, protecting the interest of the Company and permitting the Government to carry on its other needed public works. The Department hopes that the Government will be prepared to accept one of the above proposals or to make immediately a reasonable counter proposal.

HUGHES

839.6463/152 : Telegram

The Commissioner in the Dominican Republic (Welles) to the Secretary of State

SANTO DOMINGO, *March 21, 1924—9 a. m.*
[Received 9:25 a. m.]

19. Department's March 5, 7 p. m. I have had several conferences with the President and have impressed upon him that the suggestions offered by the Department for the settlement of the power company's controversy afforded the Dominican Government fair and practical opportunities of settling the difficulty presented by the expert's report. While the President appreciates the friendly attitude of the Department as evidenced by your instructions to me he is unwilling to issue the $2,000,000 of bonds under the conditions contained in the Department's authorization. He apparently feels, notwithstanding my arguments to the contrary, that acceptance by him of the conditions imposed by the Department would constitute a public admission by his Government of the fact that the Government of the United States had no confidence in the willingness of the Provisional Government to meet its just obligations.

He is, however, exceedingly anxious to reach a definite agreement with the company immediately in order that issue of the $2,000,000 of bonds may be made subsequent to the conclusion of such agreement. He is considering making a proposition to the company on the basis of method number 2 suggested in your instructions to me. To this end he has instructed the Director of Public Works who is already thoroughly familiar with the condition of the properties to make a report to him estimating the cost of placing the properties in working condition. The Director of Public Works has confidentially informed me that he believes that this can be done satisfactorily for an amount between $60,000 and $75,000. Once the President has received this report it is my belief that he will make the company an offer for the properties in their present condition and thereafter instruct the Department of Public Works to undertake the necessary repairs in order to place the properties in operating condition, using Public Works funds for the cost of such repairs. The President is therefore inclined to the belief that the properties should be purchased by the National Government for its own account.

I am making every effort to have the Government make proposition to the company at the earliest possible moment. The report of the Director of Public Works will be forwarded by March 31st, and I trust that the Government will be in a position to make the desired counterproposal within a week after the reception of the report.

WELLES

839.6463/168 : Telegram

The Minister in the Dominican Republic (Russell) to the Secretary of State

SANTO DOMINGO, *September 26, 1924—5 p. m.*
[Received 6 : 55 p. m.]

56. Congress has authorized the purchase by the Government of the plants of the Santo Domingo Water, Light and Power Company for $400,000; $100,000 cash and the remainder in two years. I have stated to the President that if Government's offer were made there was no doubt but that it would be accepted by the company and I hope this [*there*] will be no hitch in the matter. Minister of Fomento has been very active in Government's settlement and has fulfilled all of his promises to me.

RUSSELL

839.6463/168 : Telegram

The Secretary of State to the Minister in the Dominican Republic (Russell)

WASHINGTON, *September 29, 1924—5 p. m.*

37. Your 56, September 26, 5 p. m.

Department informed by Hunt and Dominican Minister that on September 25, they signed the contract of sale of the Santo Domingo

Water, Light & Power Company's properties to the Dominican Government. The terms of this contract are in accordance with statement in your telegram.

HUGHES

839.6463/169

The Secretary of State to the Dominican Minister (Ariza)

WASHINGTON, *October 1, 1924.*

SIR: I have the honor to acknowledge the receipt of your note dated September 25, 1924,[46] in which you inform me that you had on that date signed on behalf of the Dominican Republic a contract already executed by the Compañia Anónima Dominicana de Agua y Luz y Fuerza Motriz and the Liberty Trust Company of Boston, Massachusetts, under which the property described in this contract is transferred to the Dominican Republic. The Department acknowledges the receipt of a copy of this document duly certified by you.

Inasmuch as this contract of sale necessitates an increase in the public debt of the Dominican Republic to the extent of $300,000, to be represented by twelve notes of $25,000 each bearing 5½% interest, dated September 1, 1924, and payable to the order of the Liberty Trust Company on September 1, 1926, you request, on behalf of your Government, that the Government of the United States give such consent to this increase in its debt as may be required by Article III of the Convention of 1907, between the United States and the Dominican Republic.[47] It is noted that Mr. Hunt, in a postscript to your note under acknowledgment, makes the same request on behalf of the Compañia Anónima Dominicana de Agua y Luz y Fuerza Motriz and the Liberty Trust Company of Boston.

In reply, I have the honor to inform you that the Government of the United States consents to the issuance by the Dominican Government of the proposed two-year notes to the amount of $300,000 in the amount and upon the terms described in the contract to which reference has already been made. This consent is given in accordance with the provisions of Article III of the Convention of 1907 between the Dominican Republic and the United States.

Accept [etc.]   CHARLES E. HUGHES

---

[46] Not printed.
[47] *Foreign Relations,* 1907, pt. 1, p. 307.

REJECTION OF CLAIM BY A BRITISH SUBJECT AGAINST THE UNITED STATES FOR INJURIES AT THE HANDS OF DOMINICAN BANDITS [48]

439.41 St 3/16

The British Ambassador (Howard) to the Secretary of State

No. 290   WASHINGTON, *April 1, 1924.*

SIR: Under instructions from His Majesty's Principal Secretary of State for Foreign Affairs, I have the honour to transmit to you herewith a memorial [49] drawn up by Messrs. Ballantine, Haddow and McLay of 39 Bath Street, Glasgow, as the legal representatives of Mr. D. McPhail, a British subject until recently a sugar planter in Santo Domingo. This document sets forth the circumstances which attended the brutal attack made upon Mr. McPhail by Dominican bandits on the night of September 27th/28th, 1921, in the course of which he received such serious injuries that besides being compelled forthwith to resign from his position as agricultural manager of the "Angelina" estate, Mr. McPhail has been unable since to perform any serious work.

Inasmuch as at the time of the outrage referred to above, all foreigners in Santo Domingo were under the protection of the Armed Forces of the United States then in occupation of that Republic, Mr. McPhail feels entitled to seek compensation for his injuries and severe financial losses from the United States Government and in that connection presents a claim for twenty-five thousand dollars.

I should be grateful to be informed in due course that this case is receiving careful consideration at the hands of the appropriate authorities.

I have [etc.]   ESME HOWARD

439.41 St 3/18

The Secretary of State to the British Chargé (Brooks)

WASHINGTON, *July 7, 1924.*

SIR: Referring to your note No. 290 of April 1, 1924, with which you enclosed a memorial of claim prepared by the legal representatives of Mr. D. McPhail setting forth that he claims indemnity from the Government of the United States on account of personal injuries and financial losses suffered by him in the Dominican Republic arising from an attack made upon him by bandits September 27, 1921, I have the honor to recall to your attention that this matter

[48] For previous correspondence concerning this claim, see *Foreign Relations,* 1922, vol. II, pp. 95 ff.
[49] Not printed.

has previously formed the subject of correspondence between the Department and your Embassy, and, as stated in the Department's note of July 5, 1922,[50] this Government considers that Mr. McPhail's claim, if any, is against the Government of the Dominican Republic, and cognizable by the courts of that country, and in such correspondence as the Department conducted relative to the case it acted merely as the medium of transmission, and at the express request of your Embassy, in acquainting the Embassy with the views of the Dominican Foreign Office with regard to the claim.

As further stated in the Department's note of July 5, 1922, the Dominican Foreign Office advised the American Legation at Santo Domingo that Mr. McPhail should submit his claim to the Procurador Fiscal of the Judicial District of San Pedro de Macoris.

Your Embassy replied August 16, 1922,[51] that Mr. McPhail had been advised to apply to the authority mentioned, but that your Government reserved the right to press the claim through diplomatic channels if there should be a denial of justice in the courts.

It does not appear from the memorial of Mr. McPhail that he acted upon the advice of your Embassy to resort to his remedies in the Dominican courts, and it is inferable from statements contained in the memorial that he failed to take this step. Therefore, it would seem that Mr. McPhail is not at this time in a position to assert his claim diplomatically since he has not complied with the generally accepted principle that the legal remedies in the country against which a claim is made should be exhausted before diplomatic intervention is resorted to.

The foregoing statements have been based upon the possibility that Mr. McPhail may have a just claim against the Dominican Republic. So far as concerns his assertion of a claim against the Government of the United States, I beg to refer you to the position consistently taken by the Department in the previous correspondence with your Embassy regarding this case that Mr. McPhail's claim, if any, is against the Dominican Republic.

With respect to the merits of the claim, and as bearing upon statements contained in Mr. McPhail's memorial, the following observations may be made:

Mr. McPhail seems to imply that bandit activities in the Dominican Republic did not exist prior to the time when American troops entered the Republic, or in 1916. On this point it may be observed that in a letter addressed to the Department October 3, 1921,[52] by Mr. F. A. Vicini, President of the company which owned the plantation upon which Mr. McPhail was employed at the time he suffered

---

[50] *Foreign Relations*, 1922, vol. II, p. 97.
[51] *Ibid.*, p. 98.
[52] Not printed.

the injuries in question, Mr. Vicini referred to the bandits who committed the outrage, and said: "Bands of this nature are called in Santo Domingo 'gavilleros', and they operated in the country long before the American occupation and were usually formed during revolutionary times."

As you are aware the British subject Thomas J. Steele was kidnapped by bandits on the occasion when Mr. McPhail was injured, and in a report on this matter from the American Legation at Santo Domingo dated October 9, 1921,[53] the Legation said: "The Marines had been quite active around the neighborhood of the sugar estate of which Mr. Steele is manager for several weeks, and the very night he was taken they caught up with the band that had him but were unaware of this fact. In the encounter that followed, several of the bandits were wounded, but all escaped." Referring to the leader of the band which committed the outrage in question, the Legation said: "From the time of the death of 'Vicentico', Nateras has been the acknowledged leader of the bandits in the East. For some time he has been, apparently, quiet." The Legation added: "It is a very difficult matter to deal with this present condition of bandit revolution. Every sugar estate has amongst its own employees emissaries of the bandits, who are working peacefully during the day and in connection with the bandits at night. The bandits are bold and with absolutely no respect for life."

The Navy Department advised this Department November 21, 1921,[53] that during the month following the attack upon Mr. McPhail 223 bandits were captured by the United States military forces in the Dominican Republic, of whom, at the date of the letter, 105 had already been tried, convicted and sentenced by Provost Court.

In your Embassy's note of December 21, 1921,[54] the Embassy submitted statements by Messrs. Steele and McPhail of the incident in question, and in Mr. Steele's statement he referred to the "successful efforts of the United States troops" as against the bandits, and stated that because of the information he had given the troops it would be necessary for him to leave the country, and therefore requested the British Government to support his claim for $120,000 against the Dominican Government. However, in neither of the statements is it alleged that the troops of the United States failed to afford proper protection to the plantation on which Messrs. Steele and McPhail were employed, or to the officers or employees of that plantation.

As you were advised in the Department's note of May 10, 1924,[53] the claim of Mr. McPhail was referred to the appropriate author-

---

[53] Not printed.
[54] *Foreign Relations, 1922*, vol. II, p. 95.

ity of this Government. That authority has now replied at length to the statements contained in the memorial, and I beg to set forth below a synopsis of certain portions of that reply:

The forces of the United States did not proceed to the Dominican Republic in 1915, and it was only on May 15, 1916, that they were landed in the Republic.

Mr. McPhail's veiled assertion that banditry did not exist in the Dominican Republic before the military government was constituted is not only unfounded but preposterous. Ample evidence exists in the possession of authorities of the United States to demonstrate that banditry was rife in the Dominican Republic prior to the constitution of the military government, and that sugar estates and planters were victims of depredations by bandits. Indeed, it may be stated that the lawless acts of bandits and the inability of the Republic to suppress them was one of the main causes for the landing of naval forces of the United States. Banditry in the Dominican Republic was closely associated with the political and revolutionary movements, which perpetually disturbed the Republic, and it was customary for each new government to grant amnesty to bandits upon the conclusion of a revolution, thus, not only preventing the suppression of brigandage but countenancing its existence.

Mr. McPhail's statement that the Dominican Government afforded protection to planters in the Republic is hardly conceivable in the light of Dominican history, since between 1899 and 1916 parts of the Republic were in almost constant revolution, and thirteen different Presidents functioned during this time, who, with but one exception, were inaugurated and deposed by revolutionists. It is unreasonable to believe that a country so affected by political and revolutionary strife could guarantee protection to planters, and if such protection were enjoyed it was not afforded by the Dominican Government but attained by the employment of other means. In this relation it may be said that a communication in the possession of authorities of the United States from a manager of one of the large sugar estates concedes that during the various revolutionary movements the Dominican Government was unable to afford any relief to the property and that protection was afforded through the efforts of a notorious bandit chief. It is common knowledge that when the American forces entered the Republic a large number of bandit leaders were carrying on operations.

Mr. McPhail's statements that less, rather than more, protection was afforded after the advent of the United States forces, and that the estate by which he was employed was deprived of any protection from such forces, are misleading and erroneous. United States marines were frequently stationed on sugar estates between the years

1917 and 1921, and the properties of the sugar estates were constantly patrolled by the American forces, which action constituted a greater protection to the estates than would have been afforded by the posting of fixed guards within the enclosures of the sugar mill premises. However, the American forces could not, of course, devote their entire energies to the protection of sugar estates, and extended their efforts to protect the people of the Republic as a whole, and to this end were obliged to adopt offensive measures for the suppression of bandits, the primary necessity of which was to maintain fresh troops in the field of operation to pursue bandits unceasingly.

The rugged and inaccessible character of the country was a great obstacle to military operations and largely rendered it difficult to keep in constant touch with the bandit groups, and this was especially the case in the Provinces of Seibo and Macoris, the territory of which constituted a principal field of bandit operations and comprised within its borders the rich sugar cane belt and other sources of wealth which were tempting to the bandits.

The military government was not delinquent in affording reasonable protection, and did not fail in taking adequate measures to suppress banditry. From January 10, 1917, to February 25, 1919, the First Battalion, Third Regiment, continuously occupied the Provinces of Macoris and Seibo and constantly maintained patrols in the field. The record of this Battalion for the period mentioned shows that its detachments covered thousands of miles of territory and captured large quantities of firearms, had over a hundred contacts with the bandit groups, and inflicted losses on them estimated at 350 killed and wounded.

February 26, 1919, the First Battalion was relieved by the Fifteenth Regiment, consisting of approximately 800 officers and men, which was assigned to garrison the Provinces of Macoris and Seibo, and devoted its entire attention to the suppression of banditry and restoration of peace and order within these two Provinces. During 1919, 1920 and 1921 it conducted over 600 patrols resulting in about 270 bandit contacts, and losses to the bandits estimated at 600 killed and wounded. The Regiment maintained from 10 to 14 permanent outposts within these Provinces, and continuously sent patrols and detachments from these outposts, keeping the entire territory under close surveillance.

The forces of the United States in the Dominican Republic never received repeated requests from the sugar estates for more protection. Such requests as were received were given every consideration possible under the circumstances, and every resource at the disposal of the military government was fully utilized to destroy banditry.

The Guardia Nacional was organized April 17, 1917, and was a variable quantity fluctuating with the amount of available national funds, but was not fully established as a definite fixed force until October 20, 1922.

After the abduction of Mr. Steele every means at the disposal of the military government was set in operation to effect his immediate release, and the pressure exerted against the bandits became so strong that they were compelled to release Mr. Steele September 30, 1921, or two and one-half days after his abduction.

Banditry in the Eastern district was completely suppressed in May 1922, practically seven months after the abduction of Mr. Steele, and as a result of the persistent and continuous operations of the Marine forces of the United States. Since that time the Dominican Republic has enjoyed a state of tranquillity never before realized, and which is reflected in the improvement of conditions in general.

Accept [etc.] CHARLES E. HUGHES

ECUADOR

RESUMPTION OF INTEREST PAYMENTS BY ECUADOR ON THE BONDS OF THE GUAYAQUIL AND QUITO RAILWAY COMPANY [1]

422.11 G 93/1310

The Secretary of State to the Minister in Ecuador (*Bading*)

No. 377   WASHINGTON, *June 13, 1924.*

SIR: There is transmitted to you herewith a copy of a letter dated April 17, 1924, from the Guayaquil and Quito Railway Company,[2] stating that the Government of Ecuador has failed to live up to its contractual obligations and that the bondholders of the Railway request their government to use its good offices in protecting them in their rights to the full amount of the customs pledged to them.

You are instructed to submit a full report on the matter, setting forth particularly the disposition that is being made of the revenues pledged to the bondholders, and the Department would be glad to have your views as to the desirability of making appropriate representation at this time.

I am [etc.]

For the Secretary of State:
LELAND HARRISON

422.11 G 93/1321

The Minister in Ecuador (*Bading*) *to the Secretary of State*

No. 373   QUITO, *August 15, 1924.*
[Received September 8.]

SIR: With reference to the Department's instructions No. 377 of June 13, 1924 and No. 385 of July 17, 1924,[3] requesting me to submit a report on the matter of the failure of Ecuador to live up to its contractual obligations to the bondholders of the Guayaquil and Quito Railway Co., in the matter of payment of interest on the outstanding indebtedness and the Department's request for my personal views as to the desirability of making appropriate representations

---

[1] For previous correspondence concerning the railway bonds, see *Foreign Relations*, 1923, vol. I, pp. 931 ff.
[2] Not printed.
[3] Latter not printed.

to the Ecuadorian Government at this time, I have the honor to report that I have given this question serious thought and have arrived at the following conclusion:

There is of course no question as to the fact of the Government of Ecuador failing to live up to her obligations, and as to the amount of interest and sinking fund due on the outstanding bonded indebtedness, figures of which are quoted in Mr. T. H. Powers Farr's letters to the Department under date of April 17, 1924 and June 30, 1924; [4] nor is there any question as to the fact that the Ecuadorian Government pledged the income from the customs in guaranteeing the payment of the interest on these bonds. However, the fact also remains that on numerous occasions in the past representations in the matter have been made to the Ecuadorian Government through this Legation, without obtaining any results whatsoever.

Mr. Powers Farr states in his letter of April 17th that "the ability of the Ecuadorian Government to pay this obligation is indicated by the recent contract entered into with the Ethelburga Syndicate for a new loan in which the Ecuadorian Government agrees to pay twice the amount of interest and sinking fund called for by the outstanding Guayaquil and Quito Railway bonds". As the Department is aware, this Ethelburga Syndicate loan contract has not as yet materialized, and from all information obtainable on the present status of these loan negotiations it will in all probability never be realized. The contract itself embodied terms which to any well informed person indicated that they would not be carried out.

Mr. Powers Farr further states that "the bondholders have waited patiently for Ecuador to meet this obligation in the expectation that steps would be taken to reorganize the financial structure of the country" and bases his request that the United States Government use its good offices in protecting the rights of the bondholders to the full amount of the customs pledged to them on the statement that there is no immediate prospect of relief from this source: (reorganization of the financial structure).

The Ecuadorian Government has in the past and is at the present time utilizing the revenue obtained from the *aduana* (customs) and from other sources for general governmental purposes, including, of course, the item of the upkeep and maintenance of the army, which in the past year has consumed 40% of the total revenue obtained by it, and the total revenue thus obtained is not sufficient to meet those expenditures, much less any obligations assumed as to foreign indebtedness. Realizing the situation, the Government of Ecuador has finally engaged the services of a financial expert in the

---

[4] Neither printed.

FOREIGN RELATIONS, 1924, VOLUME I

person of John S. Hord, who, however, arrived here at a time when Congress was in session and who therefore did not have sufficient time to make a detailed and careful study of the finances of the country with a view to presenting a program of reform to the Congress then in session. However, since his arrival Mr. Hord has devoted his time to investigation and study, as I have had the honor to inform the Department from time to time, and is now prepared to present to the Congress which has just opened its session a complete program for the financial reorganization of the various governmental departments, as well as a balanced budget, which it is hoped Congress will endorse and adopt, and Mr. Hord informs me that this budget provides for the taking care of Ecuador's external obligations.

Under the circumstances it would seem to me ill-timed to make representations to the Ecuadorian Government on a matter which it cannot possibly meet unless Mr. Hord's program is carried out, and by making such representations at the present time it might possibly handicap Mr. Hord in carrying out his plans.

I have talked over the situation with Mr. Harman, president of the Guayaquil and Quito Railway Company, who is now here, as well as with Mr. Hord, Financial Advisor to the Ecuadorian Government, both of whom agree with me that by making representations to the Government at this time nothing can be gained and much may be lost.

Mr. Hord feels optimistic as to the attitude towards his program which Congress may adopt, and as he has the assurance of President elect Córdova, who takes office September 1st, that he is in full agreement with the plans so far prepared, it would seem to me that it might be a more opportune time to call the Ecuadorian Government's attention to its delinquency in connection with these bonds in case Congress should adopt an attitude antagonistic to the proposed reforms, (which we do not now expect) in which case strong representations, in my opinion, would be indicated and opportune, and I would request the Department to give me such instructions as would enable me to use my discretion as to the time such representations might be made, and in case it becomes necessary to make these representations it is requested that I be permitted to present them in a strong and forceful manner.

With the hope that the Department will concur with my view of the situation at the present time,

I have [etc.] G. A. BADING

422.11 G 93/1321

The Secretary of State to the Minister in Ecuador (Bading)

No. 396   WASHINGTON, *September 26, 1924.*

SIR: The receipt is acknowledged of your despatch No. 373 dated August 15, 1924, with reference to the advisability of making representations to the Ecuadoran Government for its failure to live up to its contractual obligations to the bondholders of the Guayaquil and Quito Railway.

It is noted that you have discussed the situation with Mr. Harman, president of the Railway Company, and that you are both of the opinion that nothing can be gained and much may be lost by making representations to the Ecuadoran Government at this time. You request instructions authorizing you to make representations should it become advisable to do so later.

In reply you are informed that the Department agrees with you that the present is not a desirable time to make the representations in question. However, it does not appear necessary to instruct you in advance. If a situation arises which calls for action on the matter, you should report the facts at once to the Department by cable together with your recommendations.

I am [etc.]

For the Secretary of State:
JOSEPH C. GREW

422.11 G 93/1326

The Minister in Ecuador (Bading) to the Secretary of State

No. 394   QUITO, *September 29, 1924.*
[Received October 16.]

SIR: With reference to my despatch No. 373, of August 15, 1924, in which I outlined to the Department my reasons for not believing it an opportune time for calling the Ecuadorian Government's attention to her obligations as to the interest and sinking fund due on the outstanding bonded indebtedness in connection with the Guayaquil and Quito Railway Co., as requested by Mr. T. H. Powers Farr in the letters addressed to the Department on April 17, 1924, and June 30, 1924, and in which despatch I also requested the Department to give me instructions enabling me to use my discretion as to the time representations might be made, I have the honor to report that while Mr. Hord, the Financial Expert, had informed me that the budget bill contained provisions for the taking care of Ecuador's external obligations, it seems that all reference to the first mortgage bonds of the Guayaquil and Quito Railway Co., and any provisions for the future payment of interest and sinking fund on such bonds were eliminated from the budget by the Permanent Legislative Commission, just prior to the introduction of this budget bill in Congress.

Lord Hervey, the British Minister, who had come to Quito at the time of the inauguration of the President and presented his credentials as British Minister to Ecuador, just prior to his leaving for Peru had an interview with the Minister of Hacienda on this subject and had been informed by that official that the Government of Ecuador found itself unable to make any provision whatsoever for the payment of any interest and sinking fund on the outstanding bonded indebtedness of the Guayaquil and Quito Railway Company, but that the Permanent Legislative Commission had decided that if the financial condition of the country permitted there would be an endeavor made next year to find ways and means of beginning payments on the many years' overdue interest in connection with these bonds.

. . . .

When, therefore, an editorial appeared in *El Comercio*, calling attention to the fact that any budget which did not take into consideration the country's external indebtedness was not a budget based on sound principles, I thought the moment opportune to discuss this entire question with the Minister of Hacienda and for that purpose secured an interview with him.

I informed the Minister of Hacienda that it was not my purpose at this time to protest to the Ecuadorian Government against the continued ignoring of its obligations guaranteed by the customs receipts, but that my only purpose was to discuss with him the effect such neglect of obligations on its part had exercised on Ecuador's credit and further informed him that my conference with him on this subject was sought merely in order to enable me to correctly inform my Government as to what were the intentions of the Government of Ecuador towards satisfying the increasing clamor and demand on the part of the bondholders for satisfaction; informing him at the same time that I had had instructions from the Department of State to bring this matter to the attention of the Ecuadorian Government, that I had, however, exercised my discretion in withholding action on these instructions, because I had understood that the budget bill would contain provisions for meeting the guaranteed obligations of the Ecuadorian Government in connection with these bonds, but that my attention had been called by the editorial in *El Comercio* to the action of the Permanent Legislative Commission, which had unquestionably acted in harmony with the ideas of the Minister of Hacienda, in eliminating from the budget all reference to these obligations, and I asked him for a frank expression of his opinion as to how the situation was to be met, and what information might be given the bondholders.

The Minister of Hacienda gave me what was presumably the same answer he had given to Lord Hervey, that the Permanent Legislative Commission had decided that the financial situation at the present time did not permit the payment of any of these external obligations at this time but it was thought some sort of provision could be made next year.

I thereupon requested the Minister of Finance to permit me to discuss the entire situation with him in a sincere and frank manner and to permit me to express to him the opinion I had formed after living in Ecuador for two years and a half, and after having given careful study to the entire subject of Ecuador's credit and economic situation. The Minister not only gave me permission but invited me openly and frankly to discuss the situation with him.

I proceeded to outline to him that Ecuador's failure to take definite action in connection with her external bonded indebtedness and her failure definitely to settle the Agriculturists' Association–Mercantile Bank matter had been the principal underlying factors in destroying Ecuador's credit abroad and had been in the past as it would be in the future the reason for Ecuador's failure to secure a loan.

I pointed out that Ecuador invariably had failed to live up to her guarantees in the matter of the bonded indebtedness and had failed to live up to her promises in the Mercantile Bank matter; that it was expected of Ecuador that the new administration, with its intended program of fiscal reform under the guidance of the financial expert employed, find means to carry out some action which would at least in part restore confidence in her good intentions by satisfying to the best of her ability at this time the just demands of these external creditors; that I had personally had confidence that such action would be taken until Congress, which up to this time had apparently completely ignored the recommendations contained in President Córdova's inaugural address as well as the recommendations made by Mr. Hord, the financial expert, has passed a bill which not only called for an increase in the per diem allowance for each Senator and Congressman but had also in addition to that passed a bill materially increasing the pay to the army, the latter increase totaling not less than one million five hundred thousand sucres per annum; that under such circumstances it would be exceedingly difficult to persuade the bondholders that the financial situation of the country and Government was such that it could not at least in part satisfy demands not only based on justice but secured by the absolute guarantee of the Government of Ecuador as such an attitude would imply bad faith and the effect would be disastrous.

I pointed out to him that my personal experience extending over a period of a considerable number of years of budget making for a city of more than five hundred thousand population had taught me that the only proper course to pursue, and the only course which would restore confidence in the promises of the Ecuadorian Government and thereby have the tendency to improve her credit situation was to cut to the bone all unnecessary expenses, such as increase in pay of the army, which at the present time is better equipped and in every respect on a far greater basis of efficiency than ever before, and it certainly was no time to provide an increase in the per diem pay of the members of Congress who were expected to have the welfare and good name of their country at heart.

I informed him that under the circumstances I hesitated to inform my Government of the actual state of affairs unless he, as Minister of Finance assured me that the course adopted so far by the Permanent Legislative Commission and by Congress met with his approval, and that if he, on the other hand agreed with me I would withhold a report which necessarily would come to the knowledge of the external creditors until it had been demonstrated one way or the other what would be the attitude of the Government and the final action; that there was now on deposit in the banks in Guayaquil a sufficient amount of money to enable the Government to make a part payment on the back interest due on these bonds and that this money had been accumulated for that purpose but withheld by action of President Tamayo merely because of the exchange situation.

The Minister was greatly impressed and rather depressed with the manner in which I presented the entire situation to him. He informed [me] that I was correct, that Congress had made a mistake and that he would immediately call a meeting of the Permanent Legislative Commission for the purpose of trying to induce them to reverse their action and would also discuss the matter with the President with a view to getting his support.

Late in the afternoon, I was called by phone and informed that the Legislative Commission had delegated Mr. Hord, the Financial Adviser, and Mr. Dobbie, the General Manager of the Guayaquil and Quito Railway Co., who had been called in by the Permanent Legislative Commission to give his opinion in the matter, to call upon me to discuss ways and means by which the situation might be remedied and the bondholders satisfied. In due course of time these two gentlemen appeared at the Legation both of them informing me that I had made a profound impression on the Minister of Finance who had outlined my position to the Permanent Legislative Commission, informing that body at the same time that he was exceedingly grateful to me for the courteous, although emphatic manner, in which I had expressed myself and that he felt convinced that I had the welfare of his country at heart in the position I had taken.

Mr. Dobbie informed me that if it met with my approval, the Permanent Legislative Commission had decided to provide, by decree, for the payment to the bondholders of one coupon either immediately or on the regular interest day in January and follow that up by the payment of a second coupon six months later, Mr. Hord having assured them that with the money now available additional sums could be deposited to secure these two payments and that he felt confident that he could make the necessary arrangements to secure by monthly deposits in the banks a sufficient sum of money to insure regular payments thereafter, providing however, at this time there would be no demand made for the payment of additional amounts for sinking fund purposes. Mr. Dobbie communicated by telegram with Mr. Archer Harman, President of the Guayaquil and Quito Railway Company, who is now at Huigra, and secured his consent to this arrangement with also a statement by Mr. Harman that sinking fund requirements might be deferred until all back interest payments had been met. In accordance with the agreement arrived at between myself, Mr. Archer Harman and Mr. Dobbie, the Permanent Legislative Commission was notified that we expected the first coupon payment to be made on January 2nd, the regular interest paying date.

. . . I am inclined to feel confident that the action I have taken in connection with this matter was opportune and may, in all probability, result in a settlement of this old source of irritation and complaint. It is, of course, understood that the above arrangement, if carried out, will meet with the entire satisfaction of the bondholders and induce them to withhold further complaint against the Government of Ecuador.

When the necessary decrees providing for this payment have actually been issued, I will inform the Department by cable.

I hope that the Department will approve of my attitude and action taken in the above matter.

I have [etc.]   G. A. BADING

422.11 G 93/1326

The Secretary of State to the Minister in Ecuador (*Bading*)

No. 402   WASHINGTON, *November 6, 1924.*

SIR: The receipt is acknowledged of your despatch No. 394 dated September 29, 1924, concerning your conversation with the Minister of Hacienda with a view to bringing about payments on the Guayaquil and Quito Railway bonds.

The Department approves of your action and desires to commend you for the energy and effectiveness with which you have handled this matter.

I am [etc.]

For the Secretary of State:

JOSEPH C. GREW

422.11 G 93/1336

The Minister in Ecuador (*Bading*) *to the Secretary of State*

No. 449   QUITO, *December 30, 1924.*

[Received January 21, 1925.]

SIR: With reference to my despatch No. 440 of December 13, 1924,[6] in which I reported to the Department the Ecuadorian Government's and Mr. Dobbie's efforts to secure the consent of the Bondholders Association of the Guayaquil and Quito Railway Company to utilize the funds on deposit in the British Bank of Spanish America for the purpose of paying one of the long overdue coupons of the 5% bonds, I have the honor to report that I was notified today that the Minister of Hacienda had cabled to Glynn Mills Curry & Co., of London, $222,988.03 with instructions to apply from that amount about $107,000. for payment of interest and sinking fund on the prior lien bonds, which amount falls due on January 2nd. He also has cabled the above mentioned firm that the balance, amounting to $115,988.03 plus $8,000. (balance on deposit in London) is to be utilized for the payment of a coupon of the 5% bonds. As this payment requires a sum of approximately $270,000. the Minister of Hacienda has instructed the Banco Comercial y Agricola, in which there is also a certain amount of Government funds on deposit, to retire from this deposit a sum amounting to $105,000. to be cabled to London, which leaves a balance of approximately $40,000. which the Government treasurer in Guayaquil has been instructed to forward to London. Glynn Mills Curry & Co., have been assured by cable that the entire amount will be in their possession within a day or two.

Thus it seems that the vigorous representations which I made to the Minister of Hacienda, as reported in despatch No. 394 of September 24 [*29*], 1924 have borne fruit, and it is to be hoped that the Ecuadorian Government will continue in the future to retire the coupons of these 5% bonds, the last one of which was paid in 1913.

As the Department will note, in report No. 14 of December 26, 1924,[6] the Ecuadorian Government through the Ministry of Hacienda

---

[6] Not printed.

is endeavoring to ascertain why the Guayaquil and Quito Railway Co. has not lived up to its agreement to pay a minimum of 500,000 sucres annually as its share for the interest and amortization payments on the prior lien bonds. As the information which I have received bears out the fact that nothing whatsoever has been contributed by the Guayaquil and Quito Railway Company, it will be noted that this is the first time that the Ecuadorian Government has carried the entire burden alone in addition to the payment of the long overdue 5% coupon, for which it deserves credit.

I have [etc.]
G. A. BADING

CLAIM OF THE MERCANTILE BANK OF THE AMERICAS AGAINST ECUADOR FOR THE DEBT OF THE CACAO GROWERS ASSOCIATION[7]

822.61334/130 : Telegram

The Secretary of State to the Minister in Ecuador (Bading)

WASHINGTON, *August 30, 1924—1 p. m.*

14. Department is informed by representative of Mercantile Bank of the Americas that an article in the Budget Bill recently presented to the Ecuadoran Senate, authorizes the executive to liquidate the Association of Agriculturists. The representative of the Bank states that this is contrary to promises made by the President of Ecuador. If the facts are as stated and you deem it advisable you are authorized to bring the matter to the attention of the President, pointing out the injustice of such a measure to the Bank. Report briefly by cable.

HUGHES

822.61334/132 : Telegram

The Secretary of State to the Minister in Ecuador (Bading)

WASHINGTON, *September 16, 1924—12 noon.*

16. Disregard Department's 14, August 30, 1 p. m. Information of Mercantile Bank of the Americas mentioned therein was based on a mutilated telegram from its representative in Ecuador which was misconstrued by both the Bank and the Department. The Bank now informs the Department that the following article, dangerous to its interests, is proposed in the budget bill recently presented to the Ecuadorean Congress:

"In any event, the subvention of sucres 2,000,000 for year 1925 (amount estimated tax will produce 1925) is the final amount which the State will deliver to the Association and from December 31, 1925,

---

[7] For previous correspondence concerning the debts of the association, see *Foreign Relations*, 1923, vol. I, pp. 940 ff.

all obligation of the State ceases in conformity with law of 1921 in respect to the Association as well as to its creditors if such exist."

If the facts are as stated and you deem it advisable, you are authorized to bring the matter to the attention of the President, pointing out the injustice of the measure to the Bank.

You may also refer to former President Tamayo's letter of February 5, 1922, to Minister Hartman,[8] a copy of which was enclosed in your Legation's despatch No. 787 dated February 9, 1922.[9]

If you see no objection you may mention to the President that the Bank wishes to suggest the convenience of passage by the Senate of last year's bill, which provides for liquidation of the Association and extension of the two sucres tax until debts are paid, as this appears to the Bank to be the only way the promises of the former Executive can be complied with, and that bank believes, if situation remains in *status quo ante*, debts of the Association will not be paid and the credit of Ecuador in exterior will be thereby impaired. Report briefly by cable.

HUGHES

822.61334/135 : Telegram

The Minister in Ecuador (Bading) to the Secretary of State

QUITO, *September 22, 1924—4 p. m.*
[Received 9 : 15 a. m.]

14. Department's telegram 16, September 16, noon. I have received direct assurance from the President that the Mercantile Bank matter will be arranged satisfactorily. The President favors last year's bill providing for liquidation of the Association and continuation of tax, and is opposed to budget article providing for denial of obligation of the state after December 31st, 1925.

BADING

822.61334/135 : Telegram

The Secretary of State to the Minister in Ecuador (Bading)

[Paraphrase]

WASHINGTON, *October 1, 1924—4 p. m.*

17. Your 14, September 22, 4 p.m. Department now advised by Mercantile Bank that Mr. Stabler[10] has cabled that he has been informed that the President, despite assurances given you, has definitely instructed his advisors not to have bill passed as he fears

---

[8] Not printed.
[9] *Foreign Relations*, 1921, vol. I, p. 902.
[10] Jordan Herbert Stabler, representing the Mercantile Bank.

to assume responsibility of obligating the Government. Foregoing is solely for your information.

You will see President at once and remind him of the assurance mentioned in your telegram; you will say that the Department confidently expects he will not delay in having matter arranged satisfactorily. Telegraph brief report on situation and the result of your interview.

HUGHES

822.61334/139 : Telegram

The Minister in Ecuador (Bading) to the Secretary of State

QUITO, *October 7, 1924—3 p. m.*
[Received October 8—9:30 a. m.]

15. Department's telegram number 17, October 1, 4 p. m. Have had interview with the President, and his answer submitted in writing absolutely ignores promises; merely quotes law of 1921 and states he favors strict compliance therewith.

Recommend immediate instructions by telegraph calling for the fulfillment of promises without evasion.

BADING

822.61334/139 : Telegram

The Acting Secretary of State to the Minister in Ecuador (Bading)

WASHINGTON, *October 14, 1924—5 p. m.*

18. Your 15, October 7, 3 p. m. You should discuss this matter again earnestly with the President at the earliest opportunity, stating that the Department relies on the assurances given by ex-President Tamayo, who in his letter of February 5, 1922, to Minister Hartman [11] declared that if in 1925 the credit of the Mercantile Bank of the Americas has not been extinguished the tax will be extended until its cancellation.

You should impress upon the President the importance which the Department attaches to the matter and reiterate that the Department relies on his assurances mentioned in your 14, September 22, 4 p. m. and that the Department therefore confidently expects that he will use his influence to have a law passed extending the tax until the debt is paid.

You may also point out the decidedly adverse effect upon the credit of Ecuador, should it fail to provide for the payment of its debts, as was recognized by President Tamayo in his letter above referred to.

GREW

---

[11] Not printed.

822.61334/146a : Telegram

The Secretary of State to the Minister in Ecuador (*Bading*)

WASHINGTON, *November 26, 1924—6 p. m.*

19. Department has been informed that the Association of Agriculturists has made full payment on its debts to local banks and holders of "vales". Endeavor to confirm and cable the facts to the Department as soon as possible.

Department has also been informed that Article 4 of the Law of Centralization of Revenues provides that the fiscal officials collect all revenues which are not directly provided for in the budget. Cable promptly exact text of Article 4 of this law, or any portion thereof which relates to this matter. Send complete copy of the law by mail.

HUGHES

822.61334/149

The Minister in Ecuador (*Bading*) *to the Secretary of State*

No. 433   QUITO, *November 29, 1924.*
[Received December 29.]

SIR: With reference to the Department's cable No. 19, of November 26th, 6 P.M., concerning the matter of the indebtedness of the Asociación de Agricultores del Ecuador to the Mercantile Bank of the Americas, the partial answer to which was cabled in my telegram No. 18 of November 29th, 3 P.M.,[12] I have the honor to report that immediately upon receipt of the Department's cable we secured the copy of the law of *centralisacion de las rentas* and subjected it to a careful study which convinced me that the law does not in any way apply to the law of October 15, 1921, by which was established the tax of three sucres per quintel on cacao for the benefit of the Asociación de Agricultores del Ecuador.

I called Mr. Hord, the financial adviser of the Ecuadorian Government, into conference, and he concurred with me in this opinion.

In order to ascertain the opinion of the Ecuadorian Government on this question, the matter was referred to Sr. Albornoz, the Minister of Hacienda, and both he and his Undersecretary, Mr. Rivas, expressed the opinion that in view of the fact that the Asociación is a "private institution" the law of centralization is not applicable, and this is further borne out by the fact that the funds derived from this three sucre tax never have been for the benefit of the Ecuadorian Government and that the tax always has been collected by

---

[12] Not printed.

the treasurer of the Asociación and never by officials of the Government.

Furthermore, we have ascertained that the three sucre tax is being collected and deposited for the benefit of the Asociación as heretofore.

The budget finally adopted by the Government, in spite of the protests of Mr. Hord, does not contain any provision whatever in regard to the amount to be collected by this three sucre tax nor as to its disposal.

Copy and translation of the law of centralization are hereto attached.[13]

With regard to the first paragraph of the Department's cable above mentioned, I may state that we are now making an investigation as to whether the Asociación has made full payment of its debts to local banks and holders of "vales" and a report will be made by telegraph, doubtless some time before this despatch reaches the Department.

I have [etc.]   G. A. BADING

822.61334/148 : Telegram

The Minister in Ecuador (Bading) to the Secretary of State

QUITO, *December 2, 1924—11 a. m.*
[Received December 3—9:10 a. m.]

19. Department's telegram November 26, 6 p. m. From sources believed to be reliable it is learned that all debts to local banks and *vale* holders have been paid except one *vale* in litigation.

BADING

822.61334/149a : Telegram

The Secretary of State to the Minister in Ecuador (Bading)

WASHINGTON, *December 18, 1924—3 p. m.*

21. You will please deliver the following note to the Ecuadorean Government:

"I have the honor to inform you that I am instructed by my Government to state that it has given very careful consideration to the question of the debt of the Association of Agriculturists of Ecuador to the Mercantile Bank of the Americas and desires to make known to the Ecuadorean Government its position as follows:

His Excellency President Cordova assured the American Minister that this matter could be arranged satisfactorily and expressed his concurrence with a bill introduced into the Ecuadorean Congress in

---

[13] Not printed.

1923 providing for the continuation of the export tax on cacao until the liquidation of this indebtedness.   The Government of the United States confidently expects the President to comply with the promises mentioned by urging passage of the necessary legislation in the next session, either ordinary or extraordinary, of the Ecuadorean Congress.   In this connection it is pertinent to point out that the President of Ecuador on February 5, 1922 formally promised the American Minister in Quito:

1. That if in 1925 the debt to the Mercantile Bank of the Americas shall not have been extinguished the export tax on cacao will be extended until its cancellation;
2. That the Association will apply to the debt of the Mercantile Bank, in addition to 22 per cent of the tax, any other balance left after carrying out its operations according to the Decree creating said tax;
3. That if the Government obtains a foreign loan it will immediately pay half of the debt due to the above mentioned Bank.

The Government of the United States has learned with profound surprise that not only has the 22 per cent of the tax aforementioned not been devoted to the cancellation of the Mercantile Bank debt but that there has been actual discrimination against the Bank in favor of Ecuadorean nationals as evidenced by the payment by the Agricultural Association of all its debts to the banks in Guayaquil and to all the holders of "vales" with the exception of one "vale" now in litigation.   The United States Government consequently expects that the 22 per cent of the tax allocated to the Mercantile Bank which has been withheld up to now will immediately be paid to the Bank and that the full 66 per cent of the tax allocated for the payment of the debts of the Association will, now that the other debts have been paid with the exception indicated, be paid to the Mercantile Bank in the future or else that the Government of Ecuador will oblige the Association to deposit in a bank acceptable to both parties all the funds now on hand and regularly in the future those to be collected, to be held in escrow until a settlement of the accounts has been reached.   In furtherance of this proposal the Government of the United States must express its expectation that there will be immediate compliance with the provisions of the law of 1921 and the appointment of a comptroller or interventor for the Association to assure that the latter will make a just settlement of its debts to the American creditors.

The Government of the United States is constrained to consider the Government of Ecuador responsible for the discrimination mentioned in the preceding paragraph as, according to the aforementioned Ecuadorean law of 1921, the Government of Ecuador appears obligated to control the activities of the Association and moreover it is understood that the President of Ecuador assigned, as stated above, a certain portion of the proceeds of the tax which should be paid to the Mercantile Bank at the same time that another portion of the proceeds of the tax was allocated to the remaining creditors.

The Government of the United States furthermore confidently expects that the export tax on cacao will be continued after its expiration December 31, 1925, until the debt is fully satisfied as was promised by the President of Ecuador in the note above referred to.

The question of the debt of the Association of Agriculturists to the Mercantile Bank of the Americas has been pending for a number of years without any efficacious action on the part of the Ecuadorean Government and the Government of the United States feels that it must now ask for a prompt settlement and desires to be informed without delay of the steps contemplated by the Ecuadorean Government to bring the matter to a satisfactory conclusion."

A copy of the above note has been handed to the Ecuadorean Minister in Washington and he has been informed that this Government is wholly dissatisfied with the attitude and action of the Ecuadorean authorities in the premises and that this Government feels that a settlement of the matter cannot well be prolonged and it expects to be advised without delay of the intentions of the Ecuadorean Government in the premises.

HUGHES

BOUNDARY DISPUTE WITH PERU

(See pages 304 ff.)

EGYPT

REFUSAL BY THE UNITED STATES TO ASSENT TO THE COLLECTION OF THE GAFFIR TAX FROM AMERICAN NATIONALS

883.512/14

The Minister in Egypt (Howell) to the Secretary of State

No. 415   CAIRO, *November 3, 1923.*

[Received November 23.]

SIR: I have the honor to call the Department's attention to the subject of taxation as applied to Egypt, same known as Gaffir Tax, a police provision respecting which there has recently arisen, by reason of suspension of Martial Law, not a little agitation. While Egypt was under Martial Law in 1915 (and only recently abolished) a proclamation was issued by British authority as follows: "All persons in Egypt wherever resident and of whatever nationality who are, or shall be assessed by the local authorities for the payment of Gaffir cess in accordance with the rule and practice heretofore followed, are hereby required regularly and punctually to pay such cess during the period of the war."

Investigation develops the fact that this Gaffir cess was claimed from and paid by foreign residents before the war, and that the proclamation was issued merely as a military order to facilitate the collection of a particular and recognizable tax, ear-marked to contribute to the public security.

.   .   .   .

I have [etc.]   J. MORTON HOWELL

[Enclosure—Translation]

NOTE ON THE GAFFIR TAX [1]

[CAIRO, *September 1923.*]

The Gaffir Tax was established by a Decree of November 10, 1884, as a police regulation for the security of rural property, and as a true complement of the land tax. Article 49 of this Decree pro-

---

[1] This note was sent by the Egyptian Ministry of Finance to the British Consulate at Cairo with a view to its subsequent communication to the consuls of the other powers.

vides in intent that "collectors of taxes are also charged with the collection of the Gaffir Tax and that the Sarrafs of the villages shall inform the authorities of the names of persons who refuse to pay their quota, in order that they may be treated as those who are in arrears with their taxes."

Subsequently the Gaffir Tax was extended to cities by a Decree of February 17, 1896, which, at the same time established "joint and separate liability between proprietors and tenants of each house for the payment of his quota as a contribution to the Gaffir Tax."

In taking this position the Egyptian Government has kept within the limits which were imposed upon it by international agreements concerning real property of foreigners. Article 2 of the Ottoman Law of the 7th of Safar, 1284, specifies in intent that "foreign proprietors of landed property, city or rural, are likened to Ottoman subjects in all that concerns their real property, and that this assimilation is for legal effect:

"1st. It binds them to conform to all laws, and to all police or municipal regulations which govern at the present time, or will govern in the future, the possession, transmission, legal conveyance of property to another, and the mortgaging of landed property.

"2nd. To pay all charges and taxes, under whatever denomination they are levied, or shall hereafter be levied, on city or rural property."

Now it is manifest that all this taxation applies as well to the owner as to the tenant of city or rural property, and that, therefore, it is perfectly right that the Government address the tenants as well as the proprietors for payment.

To insure the collection of this tax, the Egyptian Government orders the seizure and administrative sale against the tax-payer. But these methods of procedure are necessarily slow, and in order to avoid all difficulty or delay during the war, the General Commander-in-Chief of the forces of His Britannic Majesty in Egypt, responsible for order and security, thought it necessary to support by proclamation these means of coercion respecting tax-payers. Under these conditions the said proclamations were not able to be considered as having established the Gaffir Tax since it already existed and was perfectly legal, but simply as having been used as a mode of additional coercion, for its collection. Consequently the abolishment of Martial Law would not have any effect upon the legality of the tax which continues to be due from all the inhabitants of the territory.

883.512/14

The Secretary of State to the Minister in Egypt (Howell)

No. 141   WASHINGTON, *January 23, 1924.*

SIR: The Department has received your despatch No. 415 dated November 3, 1923, with reference to the "Gaffir Tax" which the Egyptian Government appears to be desirous of collecting from foreigners in Egypt. . . .

While under the Real Estate Protocol of 1874 between the United States and the Ottoman Empire,[1a] American citizens may be required to pay taxes levied upon real property, owned by them, under the reserve of the immunities attached to their persons and their movable goods according to the Treaties (Article II), it does not appear that the tax here in question is properly to be considered a real property tax. On the contrary it is understood to be in addition to such tax, and is assessed against the occupants of property without regard to the ownership thereof.

This Government has not given its consent to the collection of taxes of this kind from American citizens, and it does not appear that the tax has been assented to by other Capitulatory Powers, or that it can be justified under the real estate protocol of 1874. In so far as regards American citizens it is not perceived that the law can have any application. . . .

It has not been the practice of this Government to withhold assent to the collection of taxes from its nationals and *ressortissants* in countries where it enjoys capitulatory privileges when such assent is requested and it is shown that the taxes are intended for the benefit of the community as a whole, and are reasonable in amount and apply alike to all nationals. The assent of this Government does not appear to have been requested in this case nor has there been any showing that the tax and the method of assessment are reasonable, or that it is imposed for the benefit of the community at large. Under these circumstances and in view of the fact that other capitulatory powers in Egypt have not given their assent to the collection of the tax from their nationals, the Department cannot admit the application of it to American nationals.

Should occasion arise you may inform the Egyptian Government of this Government's views on the subject.

The Department will be pleased to receive for possible future use a copy of the law.

I am [etc.]

For the Secretary of State:
LELAND HARRISON

[1a] Malloy, *Treaties*, 1776–1909, vol. II, p. 1344.

883.512/17

The Egyptian Minister for Foreign Affairs (Boutros) to the American Minister (Howell)[2]

[Translation]

No. 48.2/1 (2572)

Circular CAIRO, *March 20, 1924.*

MR. MINISTER: Permit me to remind you that the Gaffir Tax was established by a Decree of November 10, 1884, and that the Egyptian Government has always considered this tax as applicable to foreign citizens, as it constitutes a police law for the security of land owners, and as a complement of the land tax to which foreigners are subject.

However, certain Consular Authorities have raised objections against this interpretation and the question had not been definitely settled when by the Proclamation of September 23, 1915, of the British Military Authorities, the payment of the Gaffir Tax was declared obligatory for all persons residing in Egypt of whatever nationality they might be.

Now the effect of the Proclamation of September 23, 1915, having ended, the question is in the same state it formerly was, that is to say, that it gives occasion for a divergence of views between the Egyptian authorities and the Representatives of Foreign Countries, and under these conditions it becomes necessary to avoid all controversy on this subject in the future.

I should state that the Gaffir Service is of a general utility character, since its aim is essentially to guarantee the security of real estate for the benefit of all the inhabitants of the country without distinction, and, moreover, that it can only function efficiently if sufficient resources are obtained by the participation of all persons who profit by it. It would then be quite unjust that one category of beneficiaries be able to avoid their duty of paying the tax above mentioned, and the Egyptian Government is right in expecting that Capitulatory citizens continue to pay this tax as they have already done for many years.

Consequently I have the honor to transmit herewith the text of a Decree rendered February 16th, last,[3] on the subject of the payment of Gaffir Tax throughout the whole territory of Egypt, and I have recourse to your kind intervention with your Government to the end that it kindly give its assent to the provisions of this Decree in respect of American citizens, from the date above mentioned.

[2] Transmitted by the Minister in Egypt as an enclosure to his despatch no. 470, Mar. 21; received Apr. 9.
[3] Not printed.

In the hope that the American Government will appreciate the reason for this service and the justice which prompts the present request of the Egyptian Government, and thanking you in advance for your co-operation in this respect, I seize this occasion to renew to you, Mr. Minister, the assurance of my high consideration.

WACYF BOUTROS GHALI

883.512/18

The Secretary of State to the Minister in Egypt (Howell)

No. 156   WASHINGTON, *May 5, 1924.*

SIR: The Department acknowledges the receipt of your despatch No. 470 of March 21, 1924, together with its enclosures,[4] and of your despatch of April 1, 1924,[5] with reference to the Gaffir Tax of February 16, 1924 and to the request on the part of the Egyptian Government that this Government consent to the collection of this tax from American nationals in Egypt.

If the other Powers enjoying capitulatory rights in Egypt consent to the collection of this tax from their nationals in the cities of Cairo, Alexandria, Port Said, Ismalia and Suez, you may inform the Egyptian Government that this Government has no objection to the collection of the Gaffir Tax from its nationals resident in the cities above mentioned.

Until some system of collecting the Gaffir Tax outside of the cities above mentioned is devised so as thoroughly to safeguard the tax payers from unreasonable assessment, this Government cannot admit the application of the Gaffir Tax to American citizens resident outside of these cities.

The Department will be pleased to have you keep it informed of the progress made towards devising a method of collection of the Gaffir Tax, outside the cities referred to above, so as to avoid the present difficulties.

I am [etc.]

For the Secretary of State:
LELAND HARRISON

883.512/19

The Chargé in Egypt (Johnson) to the Secretary of State

No. 499   CAIRO, *June 13, 1924.*
[Received June 30.]

SIR: I have the honor to acknowledge the receipt of the Department's instruction No. 156, May 5, 1924, with reference to the

---

[4] Despatch not printed; for one enclosure, see *supra.*
[5] Not printed.

collection from foreigners enjoying capitulatory rights of the Gaffir Tax under the decree of Feb. 16, 1924, and to the request on the part of the Egyptian Government that the American Government consent to the collection of this tax from American nationals in Egypt.

Just prior to the receipt of the Department's instruction, under reply, a further inquiry was received from the Ministry for Foreign Affairs with regard to the views of the Government of the United States. A copy and translation of the note of inquiry referred to is enclosed.[6]

The Department states that if the other Powers enjoying capitulatory rights in Egypt consent to the collection of this tax from their nationals in the cities of Cairo, Alexandria, Port Said, Ismalia and Suez, the Legation may inform the Egyptian Government that this Government has no objection to the collection of the Gaffir Tax from its nationals resident in the cities above mentioned. I accordingly made inquiry and ascertained that, pending the establishment of an equable system of collecting the Gaffir Tax outside of the cities mentioned, the British Government, for one, have withheld their consent to the collection of the tax, even in the cities. As long as one important Power has thus made its consent conditional upon the devising of the system referred to, it was obvious under the instruction that the Department would not desire the Legation to give as yet the formal consent of the United States to the collection of this tax, even in the cities mentioned. I am very reliably informed that all the other Powers have adopted the same attitude. The British High Commissioner very kindly furnished me with a copy of the formal reply of his Government, a copy and translation of which I transmit herewith.[6] I also enclose a copy of the Legation's *Note Verbale* of today adopting the same attitude.

I have [etc.] STEWART JOHNSON

[Enclosure]

The American Legation to the Egyptian Ministry for Foreign Affairs

No. 168

The Legation of the United States of America presents its compliments to the Royal Egyptian Ministry for Foreign Affairs, and has the honor to acknowledge receipt of the latter's *Note Verbale* No. 48.2/1 (2796), dated May 26, 1924,[6] referring to its circular letter of March 20, 1924, concerning the application of the decree of

---

[6] Not printed.

Feb. 16th last, relative to the recovery of the Gaffir Tax from for-eigners resident in Egypt, and requesting the reply of the Govern-ment of the United States on this subject.

The Legation has now received the views of the Government of the United States which are to the effect that in principle it has no ob-jection to the collection of the Gaffir Tax from its nationals resident in the cities of Cairo, Alexandria, Port Said, Ismalia and Suez. However, until some system of collecting the Gaffir Tax outside of the cities above mentioned is devised so as thoroughly to safeguard the tax payers from unreasonable assessment, the American Govern-ment cannot admit the application of the Gaffir Tax to American citizens resident outside of the cities.

The Department of State would be pleased to have the Legation keep it informed of the progress made towards devising a method of collection of the Gaffir Tax outside of the cities referred to above, in order to avoid present difficulties, before pronouncing itself defi-nitely upon the question of the application to its nationals, whether resident within or outside of the cities mentioned, of the provisions of the decree of February 16th last. The Legation will appreciate in-formation from time to time, with regard to progress made in the direction indicated, in order that it may transmit it to the Depart-ment of State.

CAIRO, *June 13, 1924.*

EFFORTS BY THE UNITED STATES TO PROTECT THE INTERESTS OF AMERICAN ARCHEOLOGISTS IN EGYPT

883.927/5

The President of the Metropolitan Museum of Art (De Forest) to the Secretary of State

NEW YORK, *January 15, 1923.*
[Received January 20.]

SIR: In behalf of the Metropolitan Museum of Art I transmit to you the following resolutions unanimously adopted by our Board of Trustees today, and trust that in so far as it properly comes within your powers you will seek to obtain, in behalf of the Metropolitan Museum of Art and the other art museums of the country, the desired action.

WHEREAS: The Trustees of the Metropolitan Museum of Art have received formal notification from the Service des Antiquités of the Egyptian Government that at the end of the season of 1922–23 the said Government intends to modify article 11 of the Law No. 14 of 1912 relating to the division of antiquities unearthed in Egypt by foreign excavators. The purpose of this modification, as set forth in the communication of the Service, is to revoke the provision under which the Metropolitan Museum of Art, in common with all other organizations excavating in Egypt, has for many years been entitled to and has received one half of the objects found in its excavations, and to give the said Service full power to retain everything thus found that it may desire for its own collections, without any obligatory division whatever, this new arrangement to become operative for the season of 1923–24, and

WHEREAS: The Trustees of the Metropolitan Museum of Art would not be justified in using its funds for work in Egypt under conditions of such uncertainty as regards results of direct benefit to the Museum, be it

RESOLVED: That the Director of the Museum be and hereby is instructed to see that the work of its Expedition in Egypt is brought to an end as soon after the new ruling of the Service des Antiquités goes into effect as can be done consistently with the interests of the Museum.

RESOLVED: That a copy of these preambles and resolutions, with the seal of the Museum affixed, be forwarded to the Director-General of the Service des Antiquités through Mr. Lythgoe.

Yours respectfully,

ROBERT W. DE FOREST

883.927/5

The Secretary of State to the Minister in Egypt (Howell)

WASHINGTON, *January 29, 1923.*

SIR: There is enclosed herewith for your information copies of letters dated January 15 from the Metropolitan Museum of Art and from the American Federation of Arts [9] with regard to the modification of the provisions of Egyptian law relating to the division of antiquities unearthed in Egypt by foreign excavators. You will note that The Metropolitan Museum of Art and The American Federation of Arts have reached the conclusion that, if the proposed changes are put into effect and foreign excavators deprived of the right to share in the results of their excavations, the trust funds of the interested American societies could no longer be applied to excavation work in Egypt and that all such work on the part of American institutions or individuals would necessarily be brought to an end. A copy of the Department's reply to these communications is enclosed herewith.[10]

It is desired that you consult with your British, French and Italian colleagues in order to ascertain what steps, if any, they may contemplate on behalf of their nationals. If you deem it appropriate you may act with your colleagues, who, in the opinion of the Department, may be equally interested, in presenting this matter in an appro-

---

[9] Latter not printed.
[10] Not printed.

priate and tactful manner to the Egyptian Government. You may indicate that you presume it is not the desire of that government to take action which would eliminate American enterprise from a share in the excavation work in Egypt as such a step would not appear to be in the interest of either American or Egyptian nationals and that you hope some arrangement may be made for a satisfactory adjustment of the question.

In case you should ascertain that no representations are contemplated by either the British, French, or Italian Governments or that special arrangements may have been reached by these governments to protect the interests of their nationals, you should refer the matter to the Department by telegraph before making representations to the Egyptian Government.

You will note that this matter is also being brought to the attention of the American Embassies at London, Paris, and Rome.

I am [etc.]

For the Secretary of State:
WILLIAM PHILLIPS

883.927/17

The Minister in Egypt (Howell) to the Secretary of State

No. 284   CAIRO, *March 5, 1923.*
[Received March 28.]

SIR: I have the honor to advise that in an interview with Lord Allenby [11] held this morning at the Residency touching the proposed Egyptian law, with regard to the modification of same which affects the Division of Antiquities un-earthed in Egypt by foreign excavators, his Lordship stated after a brief review of the measure or law now in vogue: that the law giving to foreign excavators substantially one-half of the antiquities un-earthed would expire with the season of 1923, and that it was true that there was a proposition made, as he understood it, from the Director of Antiquities in Egypt, M. Lacau, to modify this law so that all antiquities unearthed in Egypt would remain the property of the Egyptian Government and that under this provision it would be wholly optional with the Egyptian Government as to whether or not any such findings would be turned over to foreign excavators. His Lordship further said that many protests had been filed with him by societies in the British Empire interested in these antiquities, against this proposed law. That he had also received like protests from various societies in the same category from the United States; that there was no question but what this proposition by M. Lacau was supported by the late Egyptian Minis-

<hr>

[11] British High Commissioner for Egypt.

try, but as indicated, this was only a proposed law, that the Ministry, which had indicated its desire to support the proposition of M. Lacau was a thing of the past, and that he had a letter (and at the same time read the letter to me) from Soliman Pasha, the Undersecretary of Public Works of Egypt, to the effect that no law touching this matter would be promulgated until after a very careful consideration of the protests of the various governments interested, had been very carefully considered.

It may be stated in this connection that Lord Allenby fully shares the opinion expressed by the Metropolitan Museum of Art, and the American Federation of Art, with respect to this proposed law, and has already filed a protest against this step which would not appear to be in the interest of either English, American, French or Egyptian nationals.

Following the interview with Lord Allenby, the French Minister called at the American Legation and substantially said: that he would speak to the head of the Antiquities, M. Lacau, as to his opinion of this matter, that he personally was opposed to the passage of this proposed law; that he would also telegraph his Government if the projected measure should become more probable and he would write his Government in any case, touching the matter. He said that probably the French Government would agree with his personal opinion which was that of the English and American Governments, and that any such proposed law would prevent their national excavators continuing their work here. He thought his Government would take the same view as the English and American Governments against such a provision.

It is not believed the Italian Government is interested at this time. The Italian Minister is out of the country and the Chargé d'Affaires is in Alexandria. I have this day written a protest to the Egyptian Government against this proposed law, a copy of which is herewith enclosed.[12]

I have [etc.] J. MORTON HOWELL

883.927/18 : Telegram

The Minister in Egypt (Howell) to the Secretary of State

CAIRO, *March 29, 1923—5 p. m.*
[Received March 29—2 : 51 p. m.]

9. Officially informed that antiquities law now prevailing will continue season of 1923–24 permitting our museums to continue their work.

HOWELL

---

[12] Not printed.

883.927/30a : Telegram

The Secretary of State to the Minister in Egypt (Howell)

[Paraphrase]

WASHINGTON, *February 23, 1924—4 p. m.*

10. Legation's March 29, 1923, 5 p.m., and previous correspondence. The question of a further extension of its right to excavate and to keep half of the antiquities discovered has recently been taken up with the Department by the Metropolitan Museum of Art. The Department desires telegraphic report as to whether the Egyptian Government has recently arrived at any decision in this matter affecting the rights held by American archeological institutions under article 12 of the Egyptian law of 1912.

The difficulties respecting the tomb of Tutankhamen reported between Howard Carter [13] and the Egyptian Government lead the Department to believe that this may not be the best time to make representations in behalf of American institutions. Pending further instructions, therefore, you should not make formal representations. A telegraphic report on the situation is desired, however, to enable the Department to take the most timely and effective action in behalf of American institutions of learning which are interested in archeological enterprise in Egypt.

HUGHES

883.927/31 : Telegram

The Minister in Egypt (Howell) to the Secretary of State

CAIRO, *February 25, 1924—5 p. m.*
[Received February 25—3 : 55 p. m.]

19. Yours of February 23, 4 p.m. Egyptian Government has not reached a decision affecting the right of American archaeological institutions under article 12, law 14,1912, and believed cannot do so under decision reached by it March 1923.

My number 9, March 24 [*29*], 5 p.m. [Paraphrase.] M. Lacau, the Director of Antiquities, failed in his alleged attempt since this decision was reached to have the American excavators sign an agreement. Representatives of American interests informed M. Lacau that they wanted a decision which would extend the old law through 1924. The present is not an opportune time to make representations on behalf of American institutions. See my despatch no. 459 of February 22 [*23*] [14] regarding question of rights between Egyptian

---

[13] Director of expedition excavating tomb of Tutankhamen under concession granted to Lord Carnarvon and later renewed to Lady Carnarvon.
[14] Not printed.

Government and Carter which come up for trial in Mixed Court February 26. [End paraphrase.]

HOWELL

883.927/40

The Director of the Metropolitan Museum of Art (Robinson) to the Secretary of State

NEW YORK, *May 20, 1924.*
[Received May 21.]

MY DEAR MR. SECRETARY: In conformity with my agreement to keep your Department closely in touch with the progress of events concerning the endeavors of this Museum to prevent a change in the antiquity laws of Egypt which would affect the rights we have hitherto enjoyed, especially that entitling us to one half of the portable antiquities discovered in our excavations, I beg to inform you of the following developments which have occurred since my return from Washington on May 15.

On May 17 a cablegram was received at this Museum from Mr. Ambrose Lansing, a member of our expedition who still remains in Egypt, which decoded reads as follows:

Old antiquities law will not be changed, but permits will include Lacau's proposed basis of division which will be interpreted liberally, the Egyptian Government not desiring cessation of work. Howell's sailing delayed.

As you will observe, in spite of the statement that the law will not be changed, the words which I have underscored do constitute a very important change, and one which affects most seriously the conditions under which we should be allowed to work. Indeed it embodies the very project which M. Lacau has been trying to enforce for the last two years, and which we have been doing our utmost to prevent. It will bring about a situation in which this Museum cannot continue its work of excavation in Egypt, as it gives us no rights or assurances whatever on the point at issue. Consequently, at a meeting of our Board of Trustees yesterday afternoon the following vote was unanimously passed:

RESOLVED: That the Director be instructed to forward the following cablegram to Mr. Lansing:

Yours received. Inform Dr. Howell that Trustees positively decline to resume excavations under conditions proposed or under any permit which threatens or infringes upon the eminently fair and equitable arrangement under which Metmusart has hitherto excavated.

This vote was transmitted to Mr. Lansing by cable immediately after the meeting.

In sending you this information, and in behalf of the Trustees of the Museum, I beg to express the hope that we may continue to count upon the sympathy of the State Department in our position, and the continuance of the support which has been so very helpful to us in the past towards maintaining the rights and privileges which we, in common with all other foreign excavators in Egypt, have enjoyed for many years past. The situation appears to be critical and to call for immediate action.

Very respectfully yours

EDWARD ROBINSON

883.927/45

The Minister in Egypt (Howell) to the Secretary of State

No. 495   CAIRO, *May 27, 1924.*
                                               [Received June 17.]

SIR: Supplementing my number 38 of May 27th, 6 p.m.,[15] I have the honor to herewith enclose a copy of the full text of the decision rendered in regard to the Antiquities Law. I am at the same time enclosing a copy of my *Aide-Memoire* on this question, dated April 22, 1924.[16]

I may state that on April 26th, I saw the Minister of Public Works who controls for the time being this matter, and made a strenuous effort to have this question remain exactly as it was during the year 1922–1923, but I was unable to do so. It will be seen, however, that no reference is made to the Lacau proposition, that is to say, leaving the decision wholly in the hands of Lacau to say whether or not there shall be a division of any of the articles found.

I shall be glad to discuss this question further with the Department and with the Metropolitan Museum when I am in the States.

I have [etc.]   J. MORTON HOWELL

[Enclosure 1]

The American Legation to the Egyptian Ministry for Foreign Affairs

                                               CAIRO, *April 22, 1924.*

AIDE-MEMOIRE

The American Minister in a conversation with His Excellency the Royal Egyptian Minister for Foreign Affairs this morning, briefly outlined the situation as he understood it, with regard to the proposed change in the Antiquities Law (adopted 1912).

---

[15] Not printed.
[16] This enclosure was inadvertently omitted from the despatch, but was forwarded with despatch no. 513, July 31 (file no. 883.927/48).

The American Minister observed that this measure was proposed and its passage was insisted upon by M. Lacau, Director of Antiquities, one year ago and that those engaged in the work of excavation, holding concessions from the Egyptian Government representing various museums in other countries, had found the proposed law so out of keeping or conformity with the provisions which had hitherto obtained (in the Law of 1912), and at the same time prejudicial to the interests of these various museums, as to positively preclude the possibility of further work being carried on by these museums if this contemplated change was made effective.

It was held by them, and especially by the Metropolitan Museum of New York, that the work carried on by them, was wholly dependent upon voluntary subscriptions by individuals interested in archaeology and in the securement of these institutions of objects of historical interest discovered in the excavations being made here.

It was pointed out by the Minister that as he understood it, these various museums had not and would not, be technical in the division of articles found as the result of excavations; that only such articles as were, perhaps, found to be duplicates of those already possessed by the Royal Egyptian Government would be available for foreign museums; and such other objects as might be agreed upon within keeping of the Law on the fifty-fifty percent basis.

The Minister further called attention to the fact that during the course of a conversation with His Excellency the Minister of Public Works, Morcos Hanna Pasha, on or about March 25, 1924, he alluded to this proposed change in the Law of 1912, and observed that the various museums of the United States had the impression, probably derived from the agitation as to this proposed change in the law, together with the feeling which had gone forth in America regarding the Carter controversy, that work of these various museums in America was at an end. The Minister referred to a newspaper clipping of April 1, 1924, which showed that already one of the large museums in Pennsylvania, had decided to withdraw all forces from Egypt engaged in this line of work.

It was further pointed out, that as noted above, this proposed measure whereby it was left entirely optional with the Egyptian Government as to whether any articles found by those engaged in excavation work in Egypt would be subject to division, would positively put a stop to all work by other museums in America, and especially was this true of the Metropolitan Museum of New York.

His Excellency, the Minister of Public Works in his reply stated substantially, that: the Egyptian Government appreciated the work which had been done by Americans in this country and when the proper time arrived this matter referred to would be adjusted to the satisfaction of the American people and American museums. Later on, however, the Minister in question observed: "that all modification of the laws, depends upon Parliament."

The American Minister, wishes finally to observe, with respect to this question, in speaking particularly of the Metropolitan Museum of New York, that its budget is made up for the year's work, for work of this kind in Egypt, about May 15th, and it is most solicitous with respect as to what it may depend upon for the coming year; indeed, it is incumbent upon it to know upon what it may depend, if work this coming year and in future years be continued.

[Enclosure 2—Translation]

The Egyptian Ministry for Foreign Affairs to the American Legation

No. 53/7/1 (2563)   CAIRO, *May 27, 1924.*
                        NOTE

By an *aide memoire,* dated April 22nd, last, the American Legation informed this Ministry of the fears of American Museums and especially those of the Metropolitan Museum of New York concerning the matter of the modifications which the Egyptian Government proposes to make in the Law of 1912 concerning antiquities.

The competent Department, which the Ministry for Foreign Affairs has not failed to address on this subject, has just advised that it cannot abandon the plan of modifying the law in question in so far as it concerns the division of antiquities found. However, it adds that it is not accurate that the Egyptian Government does not wish to give any of the objects found. It desires only not to be bound by the word "half" at the time of the division, so as to establish easily and in conformity with general scientific interests, complete and logical series of documents representing the continuity of Egyptian civilisation. This duty fulfilled regarding science, the Egyptian Government will be pleased to give foreign museums objects of equal importance which will be sufficiently representative in their collections. It desires in that way to thank and to encourage the excavators and to facilitate the study of ancient Egypt in foreign university centers.

This change may, in fact, momentarily embarrass some scientific institutions from a financial point of view, but this embarrassment should not permit the sacrifice of scientific interests.

Besides, it should not be a matter of surprise, the Egyptian Government having informed all those interested by a circular letter

dated October 10, 1922, No. 27/2/1, of which a copy is hereto attached,[17] pointing out that the system of division by halves would
be applied for the last time during the season of 1922–1923.

In bringing the foregoing to the attention of the American Legation, the Ministry for Foreign Affairs seizes this occasion to renew
to it the assurance of its high consideration.

---

[17] Not printed.

FINLAND

EXTRADITION TREATY BETWEEN THE UNITED STATES AND FINLAND, SIGNED AUGUST 1, 1924

Treaty Series No. 710

Treaty between the United States of America and Finland, Signed at Helsingfors, August 1, 1924 [1]

The United States of America and Finland desiring to promote the cause of justice, have resolved to conclude a treaty for the extradition of fugitives from justice between the two countries and have appointed for that purpose the following Plenipotentiaries:

The President of the United States of America, Charles L. Kagey, Envoy Extraordinary and Minister Plenipotentiary of the United States of America to Finland, and

the President of the Republic of Finland, Hj. J. Procopé, Minister of Foreign Affairs of Finland.

Who, after having communicated to each other their respective full powers, found to be in good and due form, have agreed upon and concluded the following articles:

ARTICLE I

It is agreed that the Government of the United States and the Government of Finland shall, upon requisition duly made as herein provided, deliver up to justice any person, who may be charged with, or may have been convicted of, any of the crimes specified in Article II of the present Treaty committed within the jurisdiction of one of the High Contracting Parties, and who shall seek an asylum or shall be found within the territories of the other; provided that such surrender shall take place only upon such evidence of criminality, as according to the laws of the place where the fugitive or person so charged shall be found, would justify his apprehension and commitment for trial if the crime or offence had been there committed.

---

[1] Ratification advised by the Senate, Feb. 16, 1925; ratified by the President, Feb. 19, 1925; ratified by Finland, Mar. 21, 1925; ratifications exchanged at Helsingfors, Mar. 23, 1925; proclaimed by the President, Mar. 24, 1925.

ARTICLE II

Persons shall be delivered up according to the provisions of the present Treaty, who shall have been charged with or convicted of any of the following crimes:

1. Murder, comprehending the crimes designated by the terms parricide, assassination, manslaughter when voluntary, poisoning or infanticide.

2. The attempt to commit murder.

3. Rape, abortion, and the carnal knowledge of a girl under the age of twelve years.

4. Abduction or detention of women or girls for immoral purposes.

5. Bigamy.

6. Arson.

7. Wilful and unlawful destruction or obstruction of railroads, which endangers human life.

8. Crimes committed at sea:

(a) Piracy, as commonly known and defined by the law of nations, or by statute;

(b) Wrongfully sinking or destroying a vessel at sea or attempting to do so;

(c) Mutiny or conspiracy by two or more members of the crew or other persons on board of a vessel on the high seas, for the purpose of rebelling against the authority of the Captain or Commander of such vessel, or by fraud or violence taking possession of such vessel;

(d) Assault on board ship upon the high seas with intent to do actual bodily harm.

9. Burglary, robbery with violence, and larceny when the amount stolen exceeds two hundred dollars or Finnish equivalent.

10. Forgery or the utterance of forged papers and including the forgery or falsification of the official acts of the Government or public authority, including Courts of Justice, or the uttering or fraudulent use of any of the same.

11. The fabrication of counterfeit money, whether coin or paper, counterfeit titles or coupons of public debt, created by National, State, Provincial, Territorial, Local or Municipal Governments, bank notes or other instruments of public credit, counterfeit seals, stamps, dies and marks of State or public administrations, and the utterance, circulation or fraudulent use of the above mentioned objects.

12. Embezzlement committed within the jurisdiction of one or the other party by public officers or depositaries, and embezzlement by any person or persons hired, salaried or employed, to the detriment

of their employers or principals, where, in either case, the amount embezzled exceeds two hundred dollars or Finnish equivalent.

13. Kidnapping of minors or adults, defined to be the abduction or detention of a person or persons, in order to exact money from them, their families or any other person or persons, or for any other unlawful end.

14. Obtaining money, valuable securities or other property by false pretences or receiving any money, valuable securities or other property knowing the same to have been unlawfully obtained through theft, robbery or extortion, where the amount of money or the value of the property so obtained or received exceeds two hundred dollars or Finnish equivalent.

15. Perjury or subornation of perjury.

16. Crimes and offences against the laws of both countries for the suppression of slavery and slave trading.

17. Extradition shall also take place for participation in any of the crimes before mentioned as an accessory before the fact; provided such participation be punishable by the laws of both the High Contracting Parties.

Article III

The provisions of the present Treaty shall not import a claim of extradition for any crime or offence of a political character, nor for acts connected with such crimes or offences; and no person surrendered by or to either of the High Contracting Parties in virtue of this Treaty shall be tried or punished for a political crime or offence. When the offence charged comprises the act either of murder or assassination or of poisoning, either consummated or attempted, the fact that the offence was committed or attempted against the life of the Head of a foreign State or against the life of any member of his family, shall not be deemed sufficient to sustain that such crime or offence was of a political character; or was an act connected with crimes or offences of a political character.

Article IV

No person shall be tried for any crime or offence other than that for which he was surrendered.

Article V

A fugitive criminal shall not be surrendered under the provisions hereof, when, from lapse of time or other lawful cause, according to the laws of the place within the jurisdiction of which the crime was committed, the criminal is exempt from prosecution or punishment for the offence for which the surrender is asked.

Article VI

If a fugitive criminal whose surrender may be claimed pursuant to the stipulations hereof, be actually under prosecution, out on bail or in custody, for a crime or offence committed in the country where he has sought asylum, or shall have been convicted thereof, his extradition may be deferred until such proceedings be determined, and until he shall have been set at liberty in due course of law.

Article VII

If a fugitive criminal claimed by one of the parties hereto, shall be also claimed by one or more powers pursuant to treaty provisions, on account of crimes committed within their jurisdiction, such criminal shall be delivered to that State whose demand is first received.

Article VIII

Under the stipulations of this Treaty, neither of the High Contracting Parties shall be bound to deliver up its own citizens.

Article IX

The expense of arrest, detention, examination and transportation of the accused shall be paid by the Government which has preferred the demand for extradition.

Article X

Everything found in the possession of the fugitive criminal at the time of his arrest, whether being the proceeds of the crime or offence, or which may be material as evidence in making proof of the crime, shall so far as practicable, according to the laws of either of the High Contracting Parties, be delivered up with his person at the time of surrender. Nevertheless, the rights of a third party with regard to the articles referred to, shall be duly respected.

Article XI

The stipulations of the present Treaty shall be applicable to all territory wherever situated, belonging to either of the High Contracting Parties or in the occupancy and under the control of either of them, during such occupancy or control.

Requisitions for the surrender of fugitives from justice shall be made by the respective diplomatic agents of the High Contracting Parties. In the event of the absence of such agents from the country or its seat of Government, or where extradition is sought from territory included in the preceding paragraphs, other than the

United States or Finland, requisitions may be made by superior consular officers. It shall be competent for such diplomatic or superior consular officers to ask and obtain a mandate or preliminary warrant of arrest for the person whose surrender is sought, whereupon the judges and magistrates of the two Governments shall respectively have power and authority, upon complaint made under oath, to issue a warrant for the apprehension of the person charged, in order that he or she may be brought before such judge or magistrate, that the evidence of criminality may be heard and considered and if, on such hearing, the evidence be deemed sufficient to sustain the charge, it shall be the duty of the examining judge or magistrate to certify it to the proper executive authority, that a warrant may issue for the surrender of the fugitive.

In case of urgency, the application for arrest and detention may be addressed directly to the competent magistrate in conformity to the statutes in force.

The person provisionally arrested shall be released, unless within two months from the date of arrest in Finland, or from the date of commitment in the United States, the formal requisition for surrender with the documentary proofs hereinafter prescribed be made as aforesaid by the diplomatic agent of the demanding Government, or, in his absence, by a consular officer thereof.

If the fugitive criminal shall have been convicted of the crime for which his surrender is asked, a copy of the sentence of the court before which such conviction took place, duly authenticated, shall be produced. If, however, the fugitive is merely charged with crime, a duly authenticated copy of the warrant of arrest in the country where the crime was committed, and of the depositions upon which such warrant may have been issued, shall be produced, with such other evidence or proof as may be deemed competent in the case.

ARTICLE XII

In every case of a request made by either of the High Contracting Parties for the arrest, detention or extradition of fugitive criminals, the appropriate legal officers of the country where the proceedings of extradition are had, shall assist the officers of the Government demanding the extradition before the respective judges and magistrates, by every legal means within their power; and no claim whatever for compensation for any of the services so rendered shall be made against the Government demanding the extradition; provided, however, that any officer or officers of the surrendering Government so giving assistance, who shall, in the usual course of their duty, receive no salary or compensation other than specific fees for services performed, shall be entitled to receive from the Government demanding the extradition the customary fees for the acts or services performed by them, in the same manner and to the same amount as though such acts or services had been performed in ordinary criminal proceedings under the laws of the country of which they are officers.

Article XIII

The present Treaty shall be ratified by the High Contracting Parties in accordance with their respective constitutional methods and shall take effect on the date of the exchange of ratifications which shall take place at Helsingfors as soon as possible.

Article XIV

The present Treaty shall remain in force for a period of ten years, and in case neither of the High Contracting Parties shall have given notice one year before the expiration of that period of its intention to terminate the Treaty, it shall continue in force until the expiration of one year from the date on which such notice of termination shall be given by either of the High Contracting Parties.

In witness whereof the above-named Plenipotentiaries have signed the present Treaty and have hereunto affixed their seals.

Done in duplicate at Helsingfors this 1st day of August nineteen hundred and twenty-four.

[SEAL]   CHARLES L. KAGEY

[SEAL]   HJ. J. PROCOPÉ

FRANCE

CONVENTION BETWEEN THE UNITED STATES AND FRANCE REGARDING RIGHTS IN SYRIA AND THE LEBANON, SIGNED APRIL 4, 1924[1]

890d.01/171 : Telegram

The Ambassador in France (Herrick) to the Secretary of State

[Paraphrase]

Paris, *January 4, 1924—noon.*
[Received January 4—9 : 22 a. m.]

3. The French Foreign Office does not want to insert in mandate convention mention of our extradition treaty of 1909 [2] . . . The Foreign Office states that we are fully protected by article 7 of the mandate [3] . . .

Study is being made of the question of consular conventions. I do not expect there will be any opposition unless there is some special privilege granted in our consular convention of 1853 [4] which the French might have to extend to everyone else if it was mentioned in our convention. I was questioned by Fromageot [5] about our convention regarding Palestine and replied that I was uninformed. Fromageot is going to confer with Hurst [6] who is coming Sunday for the Claims Commission. I anticipate that I will be informed afterwards that the French are ready to sign our convention.

Do you accept French view on extradition? To me it appears reasonable.

HERRICK

---

[1] For previous correspondence concerning negotiations to ensure treaty rights of United States in Syria and the Lebanon, see *Foreign Relations*, 1923, vol. II, pp. 1 ff.
[2] Malloy, *Treaties*, 1910–1923, vol. III, p. 2580.
[3] Quoted in the convention between the United States and France, *post*, p. 742.
[4] Malloy, *Treaties*, 1776–1909, vol. I, p. 528.
[5] Legal Adviser in the French Foreign Office.
[6] Legal Adviser in the British Foreign Office.

890d.01/171 : Telegram

The Secretary of State to the Ambassador in France (Herrick)

[Paraphrase]

WASHINGTON, *January 12, 1924—3 p. m.*

13. Your telegram 3 of January 4. . . . The question is not one of making a new extradition treaty with France but of extending the present treaty as provided by article 7 of the mandate. The Department understands that under article II of the proposed convention and under article 7 of the mandate it would be the duty of France to extradite to the United States from Syria. It is doubtful, however, whether there would be a reciprocal obligation for the United States to extradite to Syria. Under the laws of the United States this Government would not have the power to extradite in the absence of such an obligation. (*See* Moore, J. B.: *Digest of International Law*, vol. IV, pp. 246–253.) A special provision extending the extradition treaty to Syria should be included in the convention in order to meet this objection. This was proposed in our telegram 466, December 17.[7]

The Department believes that the insertion in the convention of a provision for reciprocal extradition, as indicated in the new article VII proposed in our telegram 466, would be in the interest of France, but it is ready to proceed to the signing of the convention with the reference to extradition omitted if the Foreign Office prefers that procedure after you have orally presented these considerations.

You may inform the Foreign Office that a further communication regarding the Palestine convention has been received from the British Government and that the Department plans to take up negotiations with that Government for an early conclusion of a convention regarding Palestine similar to the one concerning Syria. The Department in 1922 made the same proposals, *mutatis mutandis*, as you doubtless know, regarding Syria and Palestine.

HUGHES

890d.01/173 : Telegram

The Ambassador in France (Herrick) to the Secretary of State

[Paraphrase]

PARIS, *January 16, 1924—noon.*
[Received 3 : 55 p.m.]

20. Department's 13, January 12, 3 p.m. It is the contention of the Foreign Office that by the terms of the Syrian mandate any

[7] *Foreign Relations*, 1923, vol. II, p. 6.

provisions in our convention relative to Syria must be applied to the benefit of all other countries. . . . Your attitude is thoroughly understood by the French and they appreciate your notifying them that unless our extradition treaty is mentioned in the convention its benefits will only be unilateral. The French, however, believe that the advantage of not having to give such privileges . . . greatly outweighs this disadvantage, and for this reason they do not wish to have our extradition treaty mentioned.

The only point in our consular convention which raises any difficulty is the right of either Government to appoint consuls to any place that it sees fit. The French fear that . . . might take advantage of this to appoint consuls in all the little frontier towns, where they might foment trouble. It is therefore proposed by the Foreign Office that the convention remain as at present but that in an official note the French will agree that all the advantages mentioned in your telegram 466 of December 17 [8] will be granted to the United States. The note would mention the rights derived under our consular convention and particular mention would be made of our right to appoint consuls at any place we wish.

Fromageot and Bargeton [9] have talked the whole matter over with me and should the suggestion of a covering note from the Foreign Office for any reason not be acceptable to you I am sure they will be glad to adopt any other plan which you might prefer which would meet their objections . . .

HERRICK

890d.01/173 : Telegram

The Secretary of State to the Ambassador in France (*Herrick*)

[Paraphrase]

WASHINGTON, *January 21, 1924—3 p.m.*

26. Your telegram 20 of January 16, noon.

(1) On understanding outlined in your telegram Department is willing to proceed to signing of convention regarding mandate for Syria and Lebanon. We understand the proposal to be as follows: The French will write a note confirming the understanding outlined in our telegram 466 of December 17, 1923, [8] regarding most-favored-nation treatment and agreeing to grant to the United States the other advantages in Syria and Lebanon mentioned in that telegram with particular respect to consular rights and extradition.

(2) In order to eliminate unnecessary correspondence, as substantial agreement has now been reached, it would facilitate matters if

---

[8] *Foreign Relations*, 1923, vol. II, p. 6.
[9] Assistant Chief of the Asiatic Division, French Foreign Office.

the French would submit to you tentatively in draft form the communication mentioned above for you to telegraph to the Department. In this way the Department could ascertain whether the points which it desires to safeguard are covered satisfactorily.

(3) The Department will promptly send you full powers to sign if the communication from the Foreign Office is satisfactory.

HUGHES

890d.01/185

The Ambassador in France (Herrick) to the Secretary of State

No. 3908   PARIS, *February 1, 1924.*
[Received February 14.]

SIR: With reference to your telegraphic Instruction No. 26, January 12 [*21*], 4 [*3*] p.m., Paragraph 2, I have the honor to transmit herewith copy and translation in triplicate of the draft note which is to be written by the Minister for Foreign Affairs on the occasion of the signing of the Franco-American Convention relative to Syria and the Lebanon.

This note was sent to me by the Foreign Office with the statement that they only desire to meet your wishes and are prepared to conclude matters as soon as you have either signified your approval or indicated any modifications in the text of the note which you may desire.

I have [etc.]   MYRON T. HERRICK

[Enclosure—Translation]

Draft of Note To Be Sent by the French Minister for Foreign Affairs (Poincaré) to the American Ambassador (Herrick)

MR. AMBASSADOR: By your letter of December 18th last,[10] Your Excellency was good enough to make known the points which your Government would like to have defined in view of the conclusion of the convention relative to the Mandate of France in Syria and the Lebanon.

The Federal Government would like to receive the assurance that its nationals, as well as itself, will benefit in these countries by the most favorable treatment resulting not only from the Agreement recently concluded between France and Italy, but by all other agreements or conventions which may be concluded between the French Government and other governments concerning Syria and the Lebanon. The French Government willingly gives this assurance to the Government of the United States of America.

[10] See Department's telegram no. 466, December 17, 1923, to the Ambassador in France, *Foreign Relations*, 1923, vol. II, p. 6.

In the second place, the Federal Government desires that it should be agreed that the extradition treaties concluded between the United States and France should be applicable to the Syrian and Lebanon territories. I have the honor to point out to Your Excellency that Article 7 of the Mandate provides that: "while awaiting the conclusion of special extradition conventions, the extradition treaties in force between foreign Powers and the Mandatory shall be applied in the territories of Syria and the Lebanon". On this account, the extradition treaties between the United States and France are already applicable and would only cease to be so if the Federal Government should desire to have substituted therefor a convention applying especially to the mandated countries.

Lastly, the Federal Government expresses the desire that the Consular Convention in force between the United States and France may also be applicable in Syria and the Lebanon and especially those of its provisions which refer to the immunities and privileges of consuls. The French Government would very willingly introduce a clause on this subject into the draft convention to be concluded with the United States of America if, on account of the peculiar regime of the mandated countries, the insertion of this clause in a convention might not cause reactions, as regards a still undetermined number of other states, whose bearing it is difficult to foresee. Therefore, the French Government thinks it preferable to give in the present letter to the Federal Government the assurance that it will see no objection to the establishment, in any part of Syria and the Lebanon where the Federal Government might deem it useful, of consuls, vice-consuls and consular agents of the United States who will enjoy the treatment accorded by international custom. It also gives the assurance that as far as the privileges and immunities attached to their duties are concerned, the consuls and vice-consuls of the United States will benefit by all the provisions of the Franco-American Convention of 1853, it being understood that the said consuls and vice-consuls shall be citizens of the United States.

The French Government having agreed, at the request of the Federal Government, not to maintain in favor of consuls of both countries the right stipulated in the Convention of 1853 to request the arrest in the United States and in France of deserters from war and merchant ships, it is understood, on the other hand, that this right will not be exercised by the consuls of France with regard to Syrian and Lebanon sailors in the United States.

I would be much obliged if Your Excellency would be good enough to inform me if these assurances give satisfaction to the Federal Government and allow it to proceed to the signature of the draft convention drawn up on July 13, 1922, with the sole changes in drafting proposed by Your Excellency and recalled in the enclosure herewith.[11]

Please accept, Mr. Ambassador, the assurances of my very high consideration.

890d.01/185 : Telegram

The Secretary of State to the Ambassador in France (Herrick)

WASHINGTON, *February 28, 1924—3 p. m.*

64. Your written despatch 3908, February 1, regarding Syrian Mandate.

(1) Paragraph 5 of French draft note refers to agreement of French Government "not to maintain in favor of consuls of both countries the rights stipulated in the Convention of 1853 to request the arrest in the United States and in France of deserters from war and merchant ships, etc., etc." The United States considers that Articles 8 and 9 of the Consular Convention of 1853 with France, which deal with this matter, were abrogated on July 1, 1916, by notice given in pursuance of the La Follette Act of March 14 [4], 1915.[12] In this connection it is noted that in the previous sentence of the draft note (i. e. last sentence, paragraph four) the French Foreign Office gives assurances that so far as the privileges and immunities attached to their duties are concerned the consuls and vice consuls of the United States will benefit by "all the provisions of the Franco-American Convention of 1853". The statement in the French note might be taken to imply that Articles 8 and 9 are not abrogated but that there is an understanding not to exercise the rights conferred thereby. In order not to bring into question the position of the United States that Articles 8 and 9 of the Convention are abrogated, it is desired that the statement last quoted should be amended to read "all the existing provisions of the Franco-American Consular Convention of 1853".

(2) For the reasons hereafter set forth, Paragraph five of the French draft note should be omitted. The reference in that paragraph to rights not to be exercised by consuls of France with regard to Syrian and Lebanon sailors in the United States carries the inference that the application of the Consular Convention of 1853 would be reciprocal, i. e., apply to nationals of Syria and the Lebanon in the United States as well as to American nationals in the mandate territory. This is not the correct view. The same principles apply to the Consular Convention as in the case of the Extradition Treaty. (See Department's telegram 13, January 12, 3 p.m.) In the case

---

[11] Enclosure not printed. For the draft convention drawn up in 1922, see *Foreign Relations*, 1922, vol. II, p. 131.
[12] 38 Stat. 1164.

of the Consular Convention it is even clearer that its provisions cannot be made applicable to nationals of Syria and the Lebanon in the United States, since there is no provision in the Mandate extending the application of Consular Conventions between France and other countries such as is found in Article 7 of the Mandate with respect to extradition conventions. The extension of treaty rights enjoyed by French nationals under the Consular Convention to nationals of Syria and the Lebanon in the United States could only be effected by Treaty. An appropriate Article in the proposed Convention was accordingly suggested by this Government. If France, for reasons which she deems satisfactory, does not desire to have such an Article incorporated in the Convention, the Department will not press the matter, since the French Government states that it is prepared to extend to the United States and its nationals in Syria the benefits of the provisions of the Extradition Treaty and the Consular Convention. It is believed, however, in order that the record may be entirely clear, that the Department's view in this matter should be communicated in writing to the French Government along the following lines, with appropriate reference to your previous written and oral representations.

(3) "In previous communications and conversations (here make appropriate reference by date) I have had the honor to bring to Your Excellency's attention the desire of my Government that the existing provisions of the Extradition Treaty of 1909 and Consular Convention of 1853 between the United States and France should be reciprocally extended to the United States and to Syria and the Lebanon by an appropriate provision to this effect in the proposed Convention with regard to the Mandate. It is my understanding that for reasons which have already been explained it is not the desire of your Government to include such a provision but that the French Government is prepared to assure to the United States and to American nationals in the mandated territory the rights and privileges provided under the Treaty and Convention respectively.

I am instructed by my Government to express its appreciation of the assurances of the French Government in this respect and to state that on the basis of this understanding, and of the assurances which you have embodied in your communication of November 2, 1923,[13] and of this date (here insert date of French draft note as finally communicated) is prepared to proceed to the signature of the Convention.

In order, however, that there may be no misunderstanding with regard to the position of nationals of Syria and the Lebanon in the United States, my Government desires me to state that the provisions of the Consular Convention of 1853 would not be applicable with respect to such nationals in the absence of a treaty provision specifically providing for such application, and that, furthermore, the Government of the United States could not assure the applica-

---

[13] *Foreign Relations*, 1923, vol. II, p. 4.

tion to such nationals in the United States of the provisions of the Extradition Treaty of 1909, in the absence of a treaty provision so providing. At the same time, I take pleasure in informing you that upon the conclusion and ratification of the Mandate Convention my Government will raise no objection to the assumption by the diplomatic and consular officers of France of the protection of the interests of the nationals of Syria and the Lebanon in the United States."

(4) You may show above note to the French Foreign Office in draft form and in case the latter is prepared to omit paragraph five of their draft note and to make the slight amendments suggested in paragraph one of this telegram and in the paragraph next below numbered (5) and thoroughly appreciates the position of this Government with regard to the non-reciprocal character of the Consular and Extradition Treaties, the Department is prepared to proceed to the immediate signature of the Mandate Convention as enclosed with your written despatch 3645 November 7, 1923 [14] with the slight modifications indicated in enclosure to your 3908, February 1, 1924.[15] The French note enclosed with your 3908 together with Department's draft communication quoted above should be exchanged at the time of and just prior to the signature of the Convention.

(5) In view of fact that the French note of November 2, 1923 [14] enclosed with your 3645, November 7, contains important assurances which supplement the draft note enclosed with your 3908, Department desires that latter French note should refer to the former. Such reference could appropriately be inserted in the concluding paragraph of draft note, after "these assurances" and before "give satisfaction", as follows: "as well as the assurances contained in the communication of November 2, 1923".

(6) Telegraph promptly whether agreement can be reached on this basis and full powers will be immediately sent you for signature.

HUGHES

890d.01/190 : Telegram

The Ambassador in France (Herrick) to the Secretary of State

[Paraphrase]

PARIS, *March 7, 1924—noon.*
[Received March 7—9:37 a. m.]

105. Department's telegram 64 of February 28. All changes which you propose in draft note are accepted by the Foreign Office which much appreciates the attitude of the American Government with

---

[14] *Foreign Relations*, 1923, vol. II, p. 4.
[15] Enclosure not printed.

respect to the nonreciprocal character of the extradition and consular treaties. However, the Foreign Office would like to eliminate the reference to conversations in the first line of your draft note. These conversations were between Bargeton and Whitehouse [17] and everything in them is already expressed in the notes or the convention. In the opinion of the Foreign Office, while it would be harmless at the time to refer to oral conversations it might bring up the impression at a late date that some agreement was made not included in the written documents.

HERRICK

890d.01/190 : Telegram

The Secretary of State to the Ambassador in France (Herrick)

[Extract]

WASHINGTON, *March 14, 1924—4 p. m.*

85. Your 105, March 7, noon.

Department concurs in omission of reference to "conversations" in first line of draft note contained in Department's 64, February 28, 3 p.m. You may proceed to immediate signature of convention in English and in French and to exchange of communications as heretofore outlined. President has issued full power reading as follows:

.   .   .   .

HUGHES

890d.01/198

The French President of the Council (Poincaré) to the American Ambassador (Herrick) [18]

[Translation]

PARIS, *April 4, 1924.*

MR. AMBASSADOR: By your letter of December 18th, last,[19] Your Excellency was good enough to make known the points which your Government would like to have defined in view of the conclusion of the convention relative to the Mandate of France in Syria and the Lebanon.

The Federal Government would like to receive the assurance that its nationals, as well as itself, will benefit in these countries by the most favorable treatment resulting not only from the Agreement recently concluded between France and Italy, but by all other agree-

---

[17] Counselor of the Embassy at Paris.
[18] Transmitted by the Ambassador in France as an enclosure to his despatch no. 4084, Apr. 10; received Apr. 22.
[19] See Department's telegram no. 466, Dec. 17, 1923, to the Ambassador in France, *Foreign Relations,* 1923, vol. II, p. 6.

ments or conventions which may be concluded between the French Government and other governments concerning Syria and the Lebanon. The French Government willingly gives this assurance to the Government of the United States of America.

In the second place, the Federal Government desires that it should be agreed that the extradition treaties concluded between the United States and France should be applicable to the Syrian and Lebanon territories. I have the honor to point out to Your Excellency that Article 7 of the Mandate provides that: "while awaiting the conclusion of special extradition conventions, the extradition treaties in force between foreign Powers and the Mandatory shall be applied in the territories of Syria and the Lebanon". On this account, the extradition treaties between the United States and France are already applicable and would only cease to be so if the Federal Government should desire to have substituted therefor a convention applying especially to the mandated countries.

Lastly, the Federal Government expresses the desire that the Consular Convention in force between the United States and France may also be applicable in Syria and the Lebanon and especially those of its provisions which refer to the immunities and privileges of consuls. The French Government would very willingly introduce a clause on this subject into the draft convention to be concluded with the United States of America if, on account of the peculiar regime of the mandated countries, the insertion of this clause in a convention might not cause reactions, as regards a still undetermined number of other states, whose bearing it is difficult to foresee. Therefore, the French Government thinks it preferable to give in the present letter to the Federal Government the assurance that it will see no objection to the establishment, in any part of Syria and the Lebanon where the Federal Government might deem it useful, of consuls, vice-consuls and consular agents of the United States who will enjoy the treatment accorded by international custom. It also gives the assurance that as far as the privileges and immunities attached to their duties are concerned, the consuls and vice-consuls of the United States will benefit by all the existing provisions of the Franco-American Convention of 1853, it being understood that the said consuls and vice-consuls shall be citizens of the United States.

I would be much obliged if Your Excellency would be good enough to inform me if these assurances, as well as those contained in my communication of November 2, 1923,[20] give satisfaction to the Federal Government and allow it to proceed to the signature of the draft convention drawn up on July 13, 1922, with the sole changes in wording proposed by Your Excellency and which have just been made therein.

Please accept [etc.] R. Poincaré

---

[20] *Foreign Relations*, 1923, vol. II, p. 4.

890d.01/198

The American Ambassador (Herrick) to the French President of the Council (Poincaré) [21]

No. 2675   PARIS, *April 4, 1924.*

MONSIEUR LE PRÉSIDENT DU CONSEIL: In previous communications dated October 24th [22] and December 18th, 1923,[23] I have had the honor to bring to Your Excellency's attention the desire of my Government that the existing provisions of the Extradition Treaty of 1909 and the Consular Convention of 1853 between the United States and France should be reciprocally extended to the United States and to Syria and the Lebanon by an appropriate provision to this effect in the proposed convention. With regard to the Mandate, it is my understanding that, for reasons which have already been explained, it is not the desire of your Government to include such a proposal, but that the French Government is prepared to assure to the United States and to American nationals in the mandated territory the rights and privileges provided under the Treaty and Convention respectively.

I am instructed by my Government to express its appreciation of the assurances of the French Government in this respect and to state that, on the basis of this understanding and of the assurances which you have embodied in your communication of November 2, 1923,[24] and of April 4, 1924, it is prepared to proceed to the signature of the convention.

In order, however, that there may be no misunderstanding with regard to the position of nationals of Syria and the Lebanon in the United States, my Government desires me to state that the provisions of the Consular Convention of 1853 would not be applicable with respect to such nationals in the absence of a treaty provision specifically providing for such application, and that, furthermore, the Government of the United States could not assure the application to such nationals in the United States of the provisions of the Extradition Treaty of 1909 in the absence of a treaty provision so providing. At the same time I take pleasure in informing you that, upon the conclusion and ratification of the mandate convention, my Government will raise no objection to the assumption by the diplomatic and consular officers of France of the protection of the interests of the nationals of Syria and the Lebanon in the United States.

I have [etc.]   MYRON T. HERRICK

---

[21] Transmitted by the Ambassador in France as an enclosure to his despatch no. 4084, Apr. 10; received Apr. 22.

[22] See Department's telegram no. 391, Oct. 23, 1923, to the Ambassador in France, *Foreign Relations,* 1923, vol. II, p. 2.

[23] See Department's telegram no. 466, Dec. 17, 1923, to the Ambassador in France, *ibid.,* p. 6.

[24] *Ibid.,* p. 4.

Treaty Series No. 695

Convention between the United States of America and France, Signed at Paris, April 4, 1924 [25]

THE PRESIDENT OF THE UNITED STATES OF AMERICA AND THE PRESIDENT OF THE FRENCH REPUBLIC,

Whereas by the Treaty of Peace concluded with the Allied Powers, Turkey renounces all her rights and titles over Syria and the Lebanon, and,

Whereas Article 22 of the Covenant of the League of Nations in the Treaty of Versailles provides that in the case of certain territories which as a consequence of the late war ceased to be under the sovereignty of the states which formerly governed them, mandates should be issued and that the terms of the mandate should be explicitly defined in each case by the Council of the League, and,

Whereas the Principal Allied Powers have agreed to entrust the mandate for Syria and the Lebanon to France, and,

Whereas the terms of the said mandate have been defined by the Council of the League of Nations as follows:

ARTICLE 1.—The Mandatory shall frame, within a period of three years from the coming into force of this mandate, an organic law for Syria and the Lebanon.

This organic law shall be framed in agreement with the native authorities and shall take into account the rights, interests, and wishes of all the population inhabiting the said territory. The Mandatory shall further enact measures to facilitate the progressive development of Syria and the Lebanon as independent States. Pending the coming into effect of the organic law, the government of Syria and the Lebanon shall be conducted in accordance with the spirit of this mandate.

The Mandatory shall, as far as circumstances permit, encourage local autonomy.

ARTICLE 2.—The Mandatory may maintain its troops in the said territory for its defence. It shall further be empowered, until the entry into force of the organic law and the re-establishment of public security, to organise such local militia as may be necessary for the defence of the territory, and to employ this militia for defence and also for the maintenance of order. These local forces may only be recruited from the inhabitants of the said territory.

The said militia shall thereafter be under the local authorities, subject to the authority and the control which the Mandatory shall retain over these forces. It shall not be used for purposes other than those above specified save with the consent of the Mandatory.

Nothing shall preclude Syria and the Lebanon from contributing to the cost of the maintenance of the forces of the Mandatory stationed in the territory.

---

[25] In English and French; French text not printed. Ratification advised by the Senate, May 14, 1924; ratified by the President, June 5, 1924; ratified by France, July 3, 1924; ratifications exchanged at Paris, July 13, 1924; proclaimed by the President, Aug. 13, 1924.

The Mandatory shall at all times possess the right to make use of the ports, railways and means of communication of Syria and the Lebanon for the passage of its troops and of all materials, supplies and fuel.

ARTICLE 3.—The Mandatory shall be entrusted with the exclusive control of the foreign relations of Syria and the Lebanon and with the right to issue exequaturs to the consuls appointed by foreign Powers. Nationals of Syria and the Lebanon living outside the limits of the territory shall be under the diplomatic and consular protection of the Mandatory.

ARTICLE 4.—The Mandatory shall be responsible for seeing that no part of the territory of Syria and the Lebanon is ceded or leased or in any way placed under the control of a foreign Power.

ARTICLE 5.—The privileges and immunities of foreigners, including the benefits of consular jurisdiction and protection as formerly enjoyed by Capitulation or usage in the Ottoman Empire, shall not be applicable in Syria and the Lebanon. Foreign consular tribunals shall, however, continue to perform their duties until the coming into force of the new legal organisation provided for in Article 6.

Unless the Powers whose nationals enjoyed the afore-mentioned privileges and immunities on August 1st, 1914, shall have previously renounced the right to their re-establishment, or shall have agreed to their non-application during a specified period, these privileges and immunities shall at the expiration of the mandate be immediately re-established in their entirety or with such modifications as may have been agreed upon between the Powers concerned.

ARTICLE 6.—The Mandatory shall establish in Syria and the Lebanon a judicial system which shall assure to natives as well as to foreigners a complete guarantee of their rights.

Respect for the personal status of the various peoples and for their religious interests shall be fully guaranteed. In particular, the control and administration of Wakfs shall be exercised in complete accordance with religious law and the dispositions of the founders.

ARTICLE 7.—Pending the conclusion of special extradition agreements, the extradition treaties at present in force between foreign Powers and the Mandatory shall apply within the territory of Syria and the Lebanon.

ARTICLE 8.—The Mandatory shall ensure to all complete freedom of conscience and the free exercise of all forms of worship which are consonant with public order and morality. No discrimination of any kind shall be made between the inhabitants of Syria and the Lebanon on the ground of differences in race, religion or language.

The Mandatory shall encourage public instruction, which shall be given through the medium of the native languages in use in the territory of Syria and the Lebanon.

The right of each community to maintain its own schools for the instruction and education of its own members in its own language, while conforming to such educational requirements of a general nature as the administration may impose, shall not be denied or impaired.

ARTICLE 9.—The Mandatory shall refrain from all interference in the administration of the Councils of management (Conseils de fabrique) or in the management of religious communities and sacred shrines belonging to the various religions, the immunity of which has been expressly guaranteed.

ARTICLE 10.—The supervision exercised by the Mandatory over the religious missions in Syria and the Lebanon shall be limited to the maintenance of public order and good government; the activities of these religious missions shall in no way be restricted, nor shall their members be subjected to any restrictive measures on the ground of nationality, provided that their activities are confined to the domain of religion.

The religious missions may also concern themselves with education and relief, subject to the general right of regulation and control by the Mandatory or of the local government, in regard to education, public instruction and charitable relief.

ARTICLE 11.—The Mandatory shall see that there is no discrimination in Syria or the Lebanon against the nationals, including societies and associations, of any State Member of the League of Nations as compared with its own nationals, including societies and associations, or with the nationals of any other foreign State in matters concerning taxation or commerce, the exercise of professions or industries, or navigation, or in the treatment of ships or aircraft. Similarly, there shall be no discrimination in Syria or the Lebanon against goods originating in or destined for any of the said States; there shall be freedom of transit, under equitable conditions, across the said territory.

Subject to the above, the Mandatory may impose or cause to be imposed by the local governments such taxes and customs duties as it may consider necessary. The Mandatory, or the local governments acting under its advice, may also conclude on grounds of contiguity any special customs arrangements with an adjoining country.

The Mandatory may take or cause to be taken, subject to the provisions of paragraph 1 of this article, such steps as it may think best to ensure the development of the natural resources of the said territory and to safeguard the interests of the local population.

Concessions for the development of these natural resources shall be granted without distinction of nationality between the nationals of all States Members of the League of Nations, but on condition that they do not infringe upon the authority of the local Government. Concessions in the nature of a general monopoly shall not be granted. This clause shall in no way limit the right of the Mandatory to create monopolies of a purely fiscal character in the interest of the territory of Syria and the Lebanon, and with a view to assuring to the territory the fiscal resources which would appear best adapted to the local needs, or, in certain cases, with a view to developing the natural resources either directly by the State or through an organisation under its control, provided that this does not involve either directly or indirectly the creation of a monopoly of the natural resources in favour of the Mandatory or its nationals, nor involve any preferential treatment which would be incompatible with the economic, commercial and industrial equality guaranteed above.

ARTICLE 12.—The Mandatory shall adhere, on behalf of Syria and the Lebanon, to any general international agreements already existing, or which may be concluded hereafter with the approval of the League of Nations, in respect of the following: the slave trade, the traffic in drugs, the traffic in arms and ammunition, commercial equality, freedom of transit and navigation, aerial navigation, postal, telegraphic or wireless communications, and measures for the protection of literature, art or industries.

ARTICLE 13.—The Mandatory shall secure the adhesion of Syria and the Lebanon, so far as social, religious and other conditions permit, to such measures of common utility as may be adopted by the League of Nations for preventing and combating disease, including diseases of animals and plants.

ARTICLE 14.—The Mandatory shall draw up and put into force within twelve months from this date a law of antiquities in conformity with the following provisions. This law shall ensure equality of treatment in the matter of excavations and archæological research to the nationals of all States Members of the League of Nations.

1° "Antiquity" means any construction or any product of human activity earlier than the year 1700 A. D.

2° The law for the protection of antiquities shall proceed by encouragement rather than by threat.

Any person who, having discovered an antiquity without being furnished with the authorisation referred to in paragraph 5, reports the same to an official of the competent Department, shall be rewarded according to the value of the discovery.

3° No antiquity may be disposed of except to the competent Department, unless this Department renounces the acquisition of any such antiquity.

No antiquity may leave the country without an export license from the said Department.

4° Any person who maliciously or negligently destroys or damages an antiquity shall be liable to a penalty to be fixed.

5° No clearing of ground or digging with the object of finding antiquities shall be permitted, under penalty of fine, except to persons authorised by the competent Department.

6° Equitable terms shall be fixed for expropriation, temporary or permanent, of lands which might be of historical or archæological interest.

7° Authorisation to excavate shall only be granted to persons who show sufficient guarantees of archæological experience. The Mandatory shall not, in granting these authorisations act in such a way as to exclude scholars of any nation without good grounds.

8° The proceeds of excavations may be divided between the excavator and the competent Department in a proportion fixed by that Department. If division seems impossible for scientific reasons, the excavator shall receive a fair indemnity in lieu of a part of the find.

ARTICLE 15.—Upon the coming into force of the organic law referred to in article 1, an arrangement shall be made between the Mandatory and the local governments for reimbursement by the latter of all expenses incurred by the Mandatory in organising the administration, developing local resources, and carrying out permanent public works, of which the country retains the benefit. Such arrangement shall be communicated to the Council of the League of Nations.

ARTICLE 16.—French and Arabic shall be the official languages of Syria and the Lebanon,

ARTICLE 17.—The Mandatory shall make to the Council of the League of Nations an annual report to the satisfaction of the Council as to the measures taken during the year to carry out the provisions of this mandate. Copies of all laws and regulations promulgated during the year shall be attached to the said report.

ARTICLE 18.—The consent of the Council of the League of Nations is required for any modification of the terms of this mandate.

ARTICLE 19.—On the termination of the mandate, the Council of the League of Nations shall use its influence to safeguard for the future the fulfilment by the Government of Syria and the Lebanon of the financial obligations, including pensions and allowances, regularly assumed by the administration of Syria or of the Lebanon during the period of the mandate.

ARTICLE 20.—The Mandatory agrees that if any dispute whatever should arise between the Mandatory and another Member of the League of Nations relating to the interpretation or the application of the provisions of the mandate, such dispute, if it cannot be settled by negotiation, shall be submitted to the Permanent Court of International Justice provided for by Article 14 of the Covenant of the League of Nations.

Whereas the mandate in the above terms came into force on September 29, 1923, and,

Whereas the United States of America by participating in the war against Germany contributed to her defeat and the defeat of her allies and to the renunciation of the rights and titles of her allies in the territory transferred by them, but has not ratified the Covenant of the League of Nations embodied in the Treaty of Versailles, and,

Whereas the Government of the United States and the Government of France desire to reach a definite understanding with respect to the rights of the two Governments and their respective nationals in Syria and the Lebanon;

The President of the United States of America and the President of the French Republic have decided to conclude a convention to this effect and have nominated as their Plenipotentiaries:

THE PRESIDENT OF THE UNITED STATES OF AMERICA.

His Excellency Mr. Myron T. Herrick, Ambassador Extraordinary and Plenipotentiary of the United States of America to France,

AND THE PRESIDENT OF THE FRENCH REPUBLIC:

M. Raymond Poincaré, Senator, President of the Council, Minister of Foreign Affairs,

WHO after communicating to each other their respective full powers found in good and due form, have agreed as follows:

ARTICLE 1

Subject to the provisions of the present convention the United States consents to the administration by the French Republic, pursuant to the aforesaid mandate, of Syria and the Lebanon.

ARTICLE 2

The United States and its nationals shall have and enjoy all the rights and benefits secured under the terms of the mandate to members of the League of Nations and their nationals, notwithstanding the fact that the United States is not a member of the League of Nations.

ARTICLE 3

Vested American property rights in the mandated territories shall be respected and in no way impaired.

ARTICLE 4

A duplicate of the annual report to be made by the mandatory under Article 17 of the mandate shall be furnished to the United States.

ARTICLE 5

Subject to the provisions of any local laws for the maintenance of public order and public morals, the nationals of the United States will be permitted freely to establish and maintain educational, philantropic [sic] and religious institutions in the mandated territory, to receive voluntary applicants and to teach in the English language.

ARTICLE 6

Nothing contained in the present convention shall be affected by any modification which may be made in the terms of the mandate as recited above unless such modification shall have been assented to by the United States.

ARTICLE 7

The present convention shall be ratified in accordance with the respective constitutional methods of the High Contracting Parties. The ratifications shall be exchanged at Paris as soon as practicable. The present convention shall take effect on the date of the exchange of ratifications.

IN WITNESS WHEREOF, the respective Plenipotentiaries have signed this Convention and have affixed thereto their seals.

DONE in duplicate at Paris, the 4 day of April, in the year 1924.

[SEAL] MYRON T. HERRICK
[SEAL] R POINCARÉ

CONSENT OF THE UNITED STATES TO INCREASED DUTIES ON IMPORTS INTO SYRIA PENDING RATIFICATION OF THE SYRIAN MANDATE TREATY

690d.003/20 : Telegram

The Consul at Beirut (Knabenshue) to the Secretary of State

BEIRUT, *March 20, 1924—11 a. m.*

[Received 2 p. m.]

Pending conclusion convention between the United States and France in regard to mandate, French High Commission requests consent of the United States to increase customs duty on alcohol to approximately 50 percent in order to protect the local wine industry which is being injured by spurious concoctions fabricated from imported alcohol. In view of the American regulations governing export of alcohol, I recommend Department accord consent requested. Please reply by telegraph.

KNABENSHUE

690d.003/20 : Telegram

The Secretary of State to the Consul at Beirut (Knabenshue)

WASHINGTON, *March 22, 1924—5 p. m.*

Before taking action on your telegram of March 20, 11 a. m., concerning increase in customs duty on alcohol, Department desires information regarding provisions of the law in question and the attitude of nationals of other countries.

HUGHES

690d.003/21 : Telegram

The Consul at Beirut (Knabenshue) to the Secretary of State

BEIRUT, *March 31, 1924—4 p. m.*

[Received March 31—2 : 35 p. m.]

Referring to Department's telegram of March 23 [*22*], 5 p. m., French High Commission is now formulating new law increasing customs duties in general to 15 percent with few exceptions, such as certain luxuries and particularly alcohol, the latter to be approximately 50 percent. French willing fix duty on denatured alcohol at 15 percent which can only be used for medicinal purposes and not for beverages.

Other powers having accepted French mandate need not be consulted.

KNABENSHUE

690d.003/21 : Telegram

The Secretary of State to the Consul at Beirut (*Knabenshue*)

WASHINGTON, *April 2, 1924—3 p. m.*

Your telegram of March 31, 4 p. m. concerning increase in customs duty on alcohol. You may inform the French authorities that this Government consents to making effective with respect to American citizens the increased duty on alcohol for beverage purposes with the reservation of the jurisdiction of the American Consular Court in cases arising under this provision in which American citizens are concerned as of the date that this Government's consent is brought to the attention of the French authorities.

HUGHES

690d.003/23 : Telegram

The Consul at Beirut (*Knabenshue*) *to the Secretary of State*

BEIRUT, *April 9, 1924—5 p. m.*
[Received 6 : 05 p. m.]

French High Commissioner informs me that accord between the United States and France has been signed and pending ratification requests consent to new customs duties as follows: Duty to be raised from 11 percent as formerly to 15 percent on all articles with the exception of live animals, cereals, flour, rice, coffee, sugar, preserves, butter, milk, cheese, mineral water, lumber and chemical manures, the duty on all of which will remain at 11 percent. The duty on alcohol to be more than 15 percent but the exact amount not yet fixed. The above customs duties are applicable to all goods from States which are members of League of Nations and from the United States, while goods from other sources will pay 30 percent.

Please telegraph consent to new tariff as applicable to American goods.

KNABENSHUE

690d.003/23 : Telegram

The Secretary of State to the Consul at Beirut (*Knabenshue*)

WASHINGTON, *April 12, 1924—5 p. m.*

Your telegram of April 9, 5 p. m. concerning increase of customs duties from 11 to 15 per cent. You may inform the French authorities that this Government consents to making effective, with respect to American citizens, the increased customs duties with the reservations that there shall be no discrimination against American citizens or products and that pending ratification of Syrian Mandate Treaty the Consular Court shall have jurisdiction in cases arising under this provision in which American citizens are concerned. This consent shall be as of the date on which it is brought to the attention of the French authorities and on the understanding that other interested powers acquiesce in proposed increase.

HUGHES

OPINION BY THE DEPARTMENT OF STATE REGARDING JURISDICTION OVER AMERICAN NATIONALS IN SYRIA

390d.1141 Ab 8/3

The Consul at Beirut (Knabenshue) to the Secretary of State

No. 1297   BEIRUT, *February 4, 1924.*
[Received March 1.]

SIR: I have the honor to acknowledge the receipt of the Department's instruction of October 15, 1923 (File No. 390d.1141 Ab 8/–),[26] with reference to a suit brought in the local courts in Syria against Mr. Joe Abraham, an American citizen now residing in the United States. I am directed to make inquiry concerning this matter and to report thereon to the Department.

It appears from the dossier of this case that one Michel Zoghzoghy, a local subject, has brought action in the local Syrian courts against Mr. Joe Abraham, an American citizen, for alleged breach of contract. The question at issue which is of chief interest to the United States Government is, first, whether an American citizen residing in the United States can be prosecuted in the local Syrian courts for an alleged breach of contract, irrespective of whether the said breach took place in Syria, by correspondence, or in the United States; and, secondly, whether service upon the American citizen in question was effected legally in accordance with treaties, custom or usage.

In order that the situation may be made clear, it is well to review briefly the entire question of jurisdiction under the Capitulations in Syria. There are three courts in Syria which have, under varying conditions, jurisdiction in cases wherein an American citizen is either the defendant or the plaintiff:

First.—*a*) The American Consular Court in criminal cases when the defendant is an American citizen, irrespective of the nationality of the complainant.

b) The American Consular Court in civil cases when both parties to the suit are American citizens.

c) The American Consular Court in civil cases between American citizens and the citizens or subjects of other Powers enjoying capitulatory privileges, when the American is the defendant.

[26] Not printed.

Second.—*a*) The Consular Court of another capitulatory Power in criminal cases wherein the defendant is a subject of that Power and the complainant an American citizen.

b) The Consular Court of another capitulatory Power in civil cases wherein the defendant is a subject of that Power and the complainant an American citizen.

Third.—*a*) Local Tribunal (the Mixed Commercial Court) in civil cases (not arising out of landed property interests) wherein one of the parties is an American citizen and the other a local subject. Cases so heard in this Court are attended by a Dragoman of this Consulate General and two American citizens appointed by the Consulate General sit as associates with the native judges. Judgments rendered in this Court against American citizens must be referred to the Consulate General for execution. If, in the opinion of the Dragoman and the American associates, justice has not been rendered in accordance with the applicable law, the Dragoman refuses to sign the judgment and it is consequently not executed by the Consulate General, in which case a new hearing may be demanded.

b) The local tribunals, without the assistance of American associates or the presence of a dragoman, in cases arising out of landed property interests, in accordance with the Turkish law of 1867, accepted by the United States on October 29, 1874.[27]

c) Local tribunals, in criminal cases wherein the defendant is a local subject and the complainant an American. These cases are attended by a dragoman of the Consulate General.

It should be noted that in all cases in the local tribunals attended by the Dragoman of the Consulate General, the judgment must be signed by the Dragoman to make it effective. If the Dragoman refuses to sign the judgment a new case may be commenced. If the native Judge insists upon the execution of the judgment, even though the Dragoman refused to sign it, the case must be settled administratively between the French High Commission and the Consulate General.

All services in connection with cases in any of the above mentioned courts should be made upon American citizens through the intermediary of the American Consulate General.

It is my opinion that the case between Mr. Zoghzoghy and Mr. Abraham, being, as it is, an alleged breach of contract not involving real estate, should come properly in the Mixed Commercial Tribunal, and service could only be made upon Mr. Abraham through this Consulate General, irrespective of whether he resides in Syria or the United States.

Mr. Abraham has given a power-of-attorney to Mr. Kaleel Muallem to act for him and defend his interests before the local tribunal. The case has been set for hearing on February 11, 1924. It appears that the plaintiff in his action has caused the defendant's property

---

[27] Malloy, *Treaties*, 1776–1909, vol. II, p. 1344.

in Syria to be attached. Inasmuch as an attachment in a case of this kind constitutes more or less an act of execution of a judgment, which can only be effected against American citizens by the Consulate General, and inasmuch as the Consulate General was not notified by the Court in this regard, Mr. Abraham's lawyer and the Dragoman of this Consulate General will protest against the judgment at the next hearing of the case. If their protest is unsuccessful, the matter will be taken up administratively between the Consulate General and the French High Commission.

There is one more point in connection with this case and any similar cases which will be of interest to the Department. By despatch No. 1120 of August 18, 1923,[28] this office transmitted to the Department a summons for service upon Salim Ibrahim Nihra, the name by which Mr. Joe Abraham is known in Syria. In its reply of September 24, 1923 (File No. 084.90d/orig.)[29] the Department stated:

"In reply you are informed that the papers mentioned have been sent to the person to whom they are addressed with the statement that the Department is not in any sense undertaking to make service of the documents but that it is merely, without incurring any responsibility in connection with the delivery thereof, bringing the papers to his attention as of possible interest to him."

I should like to call the Department's attention to the fact that summonses issued by the Consular Courts in Syria against local subjects who are required to appear before the Consular Court must be served through the intermediary of the local Government. Reciprocally, summonses, issued by the local courts for service upon American citizens whose attendance is required before the local courts, must be served through the intermediary of the Consulate General. That being so, it would seem incumbent upon the Department to cause, on behalf of the Consulate General, the legal service of summonses transmitted to the Department for service upon American citizens residing in the United States. It is suggested that the proper procedure would probably be through the Department of Justice. I should be glad to have the Department's reconsidered opinion in this regard.

I have [etc.] P. KNABENSHUE

390d.1141 Ab 8/3

The Secretary of State to the Consul at Beirut (*Knabenshue*)

WASHINGTON, *March 14, 1924.*

SIR: The Department acknowledges the receipt of your despatch No. 1297 dated February 4, 1924, with reference to the case of Mr.

[28] Not printed.
[29] Not printed; document now filed under file no. 390d.1141 Ab 8/2.

112731—VOL. I—39——55

Joe Abraham, an American citizen now residing in the United States, who has been sued in the local courts of Syria for an alleged breach of contract.

The Department has noted your statements concerning the rights which American citizens have in respect of legal cases under the Capitulations, and particularly your statement with reference to the fact that the attachment sued out in the case of Mr. Joe Abraham constitutes, more or less, an act of execution of a judgment.

The Department is in agreement with you that, if the act of attachment is in the nature of an execution of a judgment, you should protest against the attachment and endeavor to protect Mr. Abraham's interest as an American citizen.

With reference to the question which you raised in the last paragraph of your despatch, concerning the service of summons in the United States which have been issued by local courts in Syria for service through the American Consulate, the Department may observe that it has no authority to serve judicial processes in the United States. Further, it may be stated that the general rule in the United States is that "valid service of process cannot be made upon a defendant outside the territorial jurisdiction of the court so as to confer jurisdiction over a person." (Vol. 32, Cyc. of Law, p. 455.)

In considering the question of service upon a person without the jurisdiction of the court, the United States Circuit Court of Appeals stated, in the case of *Jennings* v. *Johnson*, 148 Fed. 337, on page 339, that, "in the absence of express statutory authority, there is no power in a court to order actual personal service of process upon a defendant beyond its territorial jurisdiction."

In view of these statements of law, it would appear that processes which, by reason of extraterritorial privileges, must be served through the American Consulate Court, may not be served outside of the jurisdiction of the Consular Court, which obviously does not extend to the United States.

I am [etc.]

> For the Secretary of State:
> WILLIAM PHILLIPS

FURTHER PROTESTS BY THE UNITED STATES AGAINST THE GRANT OF EXCLUSIVE PRIVILEGES TO FRENCH ARCHEOLOGISTS FOR RESEARCH IN ALBANIA AND AFGHANISTAN[30]

875.927/5

The Secretary of State to the Minister in Albania (Grant-Smith)

No. 80   WASHINGTON, *February 26, 1924.*

SIR: Referring to your despatch No. 11 of January 5, 1923[31] and to the Department's instruction No. 17 of February 19, 1923,[32] in reply, there is enclosed for your information a copy of a letter received by the Department from the President of the Archaeological Institute of America[33] in which he protests on behalf of the Institute and of several of the larger museums of the country against the reported monopolistic concession for archaeological exploration granted by the Albanian Government to France. A copy of the Department's reply is likewise enclosed.[33]

It is desired that you bring the point of view of the Archaeological Institute of America to the attention of the Albanian Foreign Office, stating that this Government is opposed to the granting of privileges connected with permission to conduct archaeological explorations which would tend to exclude interested American individuals or societies who might wish to participate in the work.

I am [etc.]   CHARLES E. HUGHES

875.927/5

The Secretary of State to the Ambassador in France (Herrick)

No. 869   WASHINGTON, *February 26, 1924.*

SIR: With reference to the Department's instruction No. 792 of December 31, 1923[33] and to previous correspondence in regard to a monopolistic concession for archaeological exploration in Afghanistan reported to have been granted to Professor Auguste Foucher by the Afghan Government, there is enclosed for your information a copy of a letter received by the Department from the President of the Archaeological Institute of America[33] in which he protests on behalf of the Institute and of several of the larger museums of this country against this concession and against a concession for

---

[30] Continued from *Foreign Relations*, 1923, vol. II, pp. 17–21.
[31] *Foreign Relations*, 1923, vol. II, p. 17.
[32] *Ibid.*, p. 18.
[33] Not printed.

archaeological excavation granted by Albania. A copy of the Department's reply is likewise enclosed.[34]

It is desired that you bring the point of view of the Archaeological Institute of America appropriately to the attention of the French Foreign Office, stating that this Government is opposed to the granting of privileges connected with permission to conduct archaeological explorations which would tend to exclude American individuals or societies.

I am [etc.]   CHARLES E. HUGHES

875.927/8

The Minister in Albania (Grant-Smith) to the Secretary of State

No. 241   TIRANA, *March 31, 1924.*
[Received April 23.]

SIR: Referring to your instruction of February 26 last, No. 80, I have the honor to report that I did not fail to bring to the attention of the Albanian Minister for Foreign Affairs the point of view of the Archaeological Institute of America and to state that the Government of the United States was opposed to the granting of privileges in concessions with the permission to conduct archaeological explorations which would tend to exclude American individuals and societies who might wish to participate in the work.

Ilias Bey Vrioni took note of my representations in this regard and replied that, in view of the fact that the concession to the French Government, which had been negotiated to gratify M. Godart who had rendered many services to Albania, had been ratified by the National Assembly on February [*September*] 22, 1923 (as reported in the Legation's despatch No. 163 of October 1, 1923 [34]), it would, unfortunately, not be possible to modify it.

It is cause for regret that the Archaeological Institute of America did not make application for a concession in Albania early in 1923 when, there is reason to believe, it would not have been difficult to have arrived at an amicable arrangement with both the Albanian and French Governments.

I have [etc.]   U. GRANT-SMITH

875.927/7

The Ambassador in France (Herrick) to the Secretary of State

No. 4078   PARIS, *April 2, 1924.*
[Received April 12.]

SIR: I have the honor to refer to the Department's Instruction No. 869 of February 26, 1924, (File No. 875.927/5), and to previous

---
[34] Not printed.

correspondence in regard to a monopolistic concession for archaeo-logical exploration in Afghanistan reported to have been granted to Professor Auguste Foucher by the Afghan Government, to the protest made by the President of the Archaeological Institute of America on behalf of the Institute and of several of the larger museums of the United States against this concession and against a concession for archaeological excavation granted by Albania.

In reply, I beg leave to inform the Department that I did not fail to address myself to the Ministry for Foreign Affairs on the subject. In reply, I am in receipt of two Notes, one dated March 27th in regard to the concession for archaeological exploration in Afghanis-tan [35] and one dated March 28th in regard to the concession granted to the French Government by Albania.

It will be noted that the French Government is in agreement with the United States on the question of the concession in Afghanistan, but that, owing to the difficulty in amending or changing the agree-ment, it is considered advisable to leave the concession as it is. It is stated that the French Government is anxious for American archaeologists to make excavations in those localities where the French will not have explored.

In regard to the concession granted by Albania, the statement of the Foreign Office will be noted that exclusive privileges have been granted only in certain districts which are very few and closely defined.

I have [etc.] Myron T. Herrick

[Enclosure—Translation]

The French Ministry of Foreign Affairs to the American Embassy

[Paris,] *March 28, 1924.*

In its note of the 18th of this month, the Embassy of the United States was good enough to call the attention of the Ministry for Foreign Affairs to a protest made by the President of the Archaeo-logical Institute of America, in behalf of that Organization and of a great many American Museums, against the concession of a monopoly for archaeological excavations in Albania, granted recently to the French Government by the Albanian Government.

The Ministry for Foreign Affairs has the honor to inform the Embassy of the United States of America that the Franco-Albanian Convention in question, relative to excavations, does not cover all the Albanian territory. It provides only for the exclusive privilege of excavations in favor of the Government of the Republic, in certain districts which are very few and exactly delimited.[36]

---

[35] Not printed.
[36] The Department made no further representations regarding archeological exploration in Albania and Afghanistan.

DISCRIMINATION AGAINST AMERICAN SHIPPING BY FRENCH AU-
THORITIES IN REFUSING TO RECOGNIZE CLASSIFICATION AND
INSPECTION OF VESSELS BY THE AMERICAN BUREAU OF
SHIPPING

195/586

The Secretary of State to the Ambassador in France (Herrick)

No. 1000   WASHINGTON, *June 2, 1924.*

SIR: The Department encloses copies of letters dated May 13 and
May 14, 1924,[37] from the President of the American Bureau of Shipping, protesting in regard to the discrimination made by the French
Government against American vessels classed by the American
Bureau of Shipping, and requesting that the matter be taken up
with the appropriate French authorities with a view to the recognition by the French Government of that Bureau.

You are requested to present the matter to the appropriate authorities of the French Government and urge that recognition similar to
that given certain other classification societies be given to the American Bureau of Shipping, which has been recognized by this Government as its agency for classification purposes.

I am [etc.]

For the Secretary of State:
LELAND HARRISON

195/597 : Telegram

The Acting Secretary of State to the Ambassador in France (Herrick)

WASHINGTON, *July 24, 1924—6 p. m.*

243. Department instruction June 2 and telegram July 10 3 p. m.[38]
If you have not received favorable reply from Foreign Office, you
are instructed to present the following note forthwith:

"Under instructions from my Government I have the honor to
refer to my previous communications concerning the attitude of the
authorities of the French Government in the matter of the recognition of the American Bureau of Shipping, and to draw your attention once more to the importance attached by my Government to an
early favorable decision in the matter.

It is the view of the Government of the United States that the
American Bureau of Shipping is entitled to full recognition by the
French authorities on an equal footing with Lloyd's or any other
foreign classification society. This Bureau is designated by the laws
of the United States (Section 25, Merchant Marine Act 1920) as
an official classification society for the classification of vessels and

---

[37] Neither printed.
[38] Latter not printed.

for other functions in connection therewith and two members of the executive committee are designated by my Government. The inspection and certification of the Bureau are regarded by my Government as efficient and trustworthy. The high standing of the Bureau is further indicated by the fact that the London Institute of Underwriters recognizes its classification on a parity with Lloyd's. My Government, therefore, is confident that on having the facts regarding the Bureau brought to your attention your Government will accord it the recognition to which it is entitled."

For your information and guidance. Please reinforce the foregoing note with vigorous oral representations and endeavor in all proper ways to obtain prompt favorable decision. The essential fact is that France recognizes Lloyds but not the American Bureau. The refusal to recognize latter is not only important to vessels immediately affected, but has broader significance to American shipping inasmuch as greater part of American merchant marine is registered in American Bureau and any action that might be construed as reflection upon the standing of the Bureau would tend to weaken position of vessels registered therein.

The Shipping Board adopted a resolution on May 15, 1924, to the effect that the action of the French Government in this case presents a situation contemplated by Section 26 of the Shipping Act 1916 whereby it is authorized in cases of discrimination against American shipping to propose remedial measures to the President, and by Section 19 (b) of the Merchant Marine Act 1920 under which the Board is authorized "to make rules and regulations affecting shipping in the foreign trade not in conflict with law in order to adjust or meet general or special conditions unfavorable to shipping in the foreign trade." The resolution called upon the Department to communicate with the French Government, preliminary to final action by the Board, with a view to causing that Government to accept as sufficient classifications by the American Bureau of Shipping of vessels documented under the American flag in cases in which, under similar circumstances, classifications by other foreign societies are accepted.

You may informally advise the Foreign Office of the purport of the resolution at the same time furnishing it with copies of Section 26 of the Shipping Act approved Sept. 7, 1916 (See 39 Statutes at Large, page 737) and Section 19, Paragraph B of the Merchant Marine Act approved June 5, 1920 (See 41 Statutes at Large, page 995). The Department desires, of course, that a serious controversy possibly even involving consideration of recourse to retaliatory measures may be avoided.

Advise Department by telegraph of important developments.

GREW

105/598 : Telegram

The Acting Secretary of State to the Ambassador in France
(Herrick)

WASHINGTON, *August 5, 1924—5 p. m.*

254. Department's instruction of June 2 and telegrams of July 10, 3 p. m.[39] and July 24, 6 p. m.

(1) Please again call attention of Foreign Office to question of inspection of Dollar Line Steamers and, in view of urgency of situation arising from call of Steamer *President Adams* at Marseilles (now reported to arrive August 27), if you have not received reply make protest against further delay and urge early favorable action. The matter should not be allowed to drag along until the *President Adams* reaches Marseilles.

(2) Department notes statements in correspondence between Embassy and Consulate Marseilles transmitted with Consulate's despatch 974, July 11,[40] of which presumably Embassy has copy, to the effect that the United States does not recognize certificates issued by the French Government though most other leading countries do recognize them. The Department is advised by the Steamboat Inspection Service that the United States recognizes certificates of inspection issued by the French Government to French passenger vessels under reciprocal agreement with the Government of the United States.

(3) In view of paragraph 2 above, and in view of French recognition of Lloyds but not American Bureau (see Department's 243, July 24, 6 p. m.), it is difficult to understand on what grounds French authorities undertake to require Dollar Line vessels, which hold United States Government inspection certificates, to undergo inspection by French maritime officials.

Please endeavor to ascertain the grounds on which French Government requires inspection of Dollar Line vessels, consulting Consul at Marseilles if necessary, and report to Department by telegraph all particulars obtainable concerning reasons for attitude of French Government in this matter, giving references to laws and decrees on which French position is based and mailing copies if not already forwarded. Suggest you communicate with agent of Dollar Line, Paris, which is understood to be United States Lines, 1 Rue Auber, which may know or which may be able to ascertain informally from Ministry Marine precise nature of inspection in question.

Transmit copy hereof and copies of other correspondence with Department on this subject to Consul at Marseilles for his information.

GREW

195/609 : Telegram

The Chargé in France (Whitehouse) to the Secretary of State

PARIS, *August 23, 1924—noon.*
[Received August 23—8:53 a. m.]

379. My 367, August 13, 4 p. m.[41] Foreign Office has just informed me officially that pending recognition by the French Government of the American Bureau of Shipping, American vessels calling at French ports will in no way be interfered with.

WHITEHOUSE

195/611 : Telegram

The Chargé in France (Whitehouse) to the Secretary of State

Paris, *August 26, 1924—noon.*
[Received August 26—10:18 a. m.]

383. My 379, August 23, noon. In a note from the Foreign Office I am informed that the formalities to which American vessels in French ports are subjected are made necessary by article 3 of the law of April 17, 1907, and not as a result of the nonrecognition of the American Bureau of Shipping. The formalities can be waived if an agreement is concluded between the United States and France recognizing the equivalence of French and American legislation on the subject and the note concludes with a request to be informed whether the United States Government would enter into such an agreement.

I understand that the agreement can be concluded by an exchange of notes after examination by each Government of the legislation of the other on the subject.

I am transmitting by pouch a copy of the law above referred to.[41]

WHITEHOUSE

[a] Not printed.

INDEX

INDEX

Afghanistan, concession for archeological research, U. S. protest against alleged French monopoly, 753–754; French attitude, 754–755

Agreements. *See* Treaties, conventions, etc.

Albania:
Concessions:
Archeological research, U. S. protest against alleged French monopoly, 753; attitude of Albania, 754
Oil concessions, U. S. representations on behalf of American interests, 318–319
Revolutionary disturbances: Reports concerning, 306–307, 308, 309, 314–315; U. S. warship, dispatch, 306, 307, 308
Revolutionary government:
Activities and status, reports of U. S. representative, 309, 312–314, 315
Recognition: Attitude of European governments, 309, 310, 310–311, 312; U. S. maintenance of unofficial relations, 309–310, 310–312, 313
Treaty of commerce and navigation with Italy, opposition of United States, Great Britain, and Yugoslavia to certain provisions, 317–318
Treaty with United States defining relations, postponement of negotiations, 315–319

American Bureau of Shipping, French refusal to recognize its classification and inspection of vessels, U. S. representations regarding, 756–758; French position, 759

Arbitration (*see also* Boundary disputes: Bolivia-Paraguay *and* Ecuador-Peru), payment of Boxer indemnity in gold currency, possibility of submission of question to arbitration, 562, 563, 564, 569–570

Archeological research. *See* Egypt: Antiquities Law; France: Concessions.

Armament limitation (*see also* Brazil; Treaty for the limitation of naval armament; Washington Conference on the Limitation of Armament), draft treaty of mutual assistance submitted by League of Nations, U. S. unfavorable views, 79–83

Armenian and Russian refugees, U. S. acceptance of certificates of identity issued by League of Nations in lieu of passports, 83–89

Arms and munitions (*see also* China: Arms and munitions embargo), convention for the control of traffic in arms proposed by League of Nations to replace St. Germain convention of *1919:*
Conference, international, for concluding convention: Proposal by League, 75–77; U. S. favorable attitude, 76n
Negotiations. *See* U. S. cooperation with League, *infra.*
Resolution of League Assembly regarding, text, 73
Texts. *See* U. S. cooperation with League: Drafts, *infra.*
U. S. cooperation with League in drafting:
Arrangements for, 17–18
Drafts by—
Marquis Magaz, 22–25; discussion by Temporary Mixed Commission, 26–27
Subcommittee of Temporary Mixed Commission, 33–39; U. S. views, 41–50
Temporary Mixed Commission, adopted *July 12*, 55–73; consideration by Council and Assembly of League, proposed, 73–74; opinion of U. S. Secretary of War, 77–79
Private manufacture of arms, discussions concerning, 20, 21, 22, 25–26, 27–28, 29, 32, 50–52
Production of and traffic in arms, discussions on question of possible combination of subjects in one convention, 20, 21, 22, 25
Supervision of control of traffic in arms, negotiations regarding, 21–22, 26, 26–27, 28, 29–30, 47
U. S. objections to St. Germain convention, 18–20, 27, 28
U. S. representative at meetings of Temporary Mixed Commission and of its subcommittee: Instructions, 18–20, 27–28, 30–31, 40–55; reports, 20–27, 29–30, 31–32, 55; status, 18
U. S. Secretary of War, views as to inadvisability of U. S. participation in convention as drafted,. 77–79

Arms traffic convention. *See* Arms and munitions.

Army costs agreement, question of applicability of cash from liberation bonds of Austro-Hungarian succession states, 156–157

Associated American Chambers of Commerce of China. *See under* China.

Australia, concurrence in ratification of U. S.-British liquor-smuggling convention, 158*n*

Austria. *See* Austria and Hungary; Aviation.

Austria and Hungary, U. S. war claims: Agreement with United States for establishment of Claims Commission:

Commissioner to determine obligations of Austria and Hungary: Discussions concerning jurisdiction, 146, 147, 148, 149; selection of Judge Edwin B. Parker, question of, 144, 145; U. S. proposal, 143–144

Negotiations, 142–151

Similarity to U. S.-German agreement (*Aug. 10, 1922*), 143, 148, 149–150

Text signed *Nov. 26*, 152–154

Claims Commission (Mixed). *See* Agreement, *supra*.

Treaties establishing friendly relations with United States (*1921*), U. S. rights under, 142–143, 146

Austro-Hungarian succession states, U. S. interest in disposition of proposed liberation bonds. *See* Liberation bonds.

Aviation, arrangements by United States for a flight around the world by U. S. Army airplanes:

Itinerary, proposed, 231–232

U. S. communications to foreign governments regarding necessary permissions:

British Empire, 227*n*, 231–233, 245–246; responses, 229, 233, 239, 242, 244, 246*n*

China, 232*n*, 238; response, 237, 241

European countries (*see also* British Empire, *supra*), 227, 227*n*, 232*n*; responses, 228, 228–229, 236, 236–237, 238, 240

Japan, 227, 228, 229, 234, 235, 242–243, 244–245; Japanese attitude, 230–231, 234–235, 243–244, 245

Persia, 232*n*; response, 235

Siam, 232*n*; response, 236

Turkey, 232*n*, 240–241; response, 239, 243

Barton, Dr. James L., correspondence with Department of State regarding extraterritorial rights of U. S. missionaries in China, 601–604

Belgium. *See* China.

Bolivia (*see also* Boundary disputes: Bolivia–Paraguay) : Narcotics Conference, International, participation, 98, 100; request for good offices of United States for modification of Bolivian-Chilean treaty of *1904*, disinclination of U. S. Secretary of State to comply with, 320–322

Bonds. *See* Ecuador: Guayaquil and Quito Railway Co.; Liberation bonds; *and under* Dominican Republic.

Boundary disputes:

Bolivia–Paraguay:

Status of negotiations, reports concerning, 283–285, 286–287

Submission of controversy to United States for arbitration, proposed: Desire of Bolivia and Paraguay, 282–283, 284, 284–285, 286–287; draft agreement between the two countries, 283; U. S. attitude, 282, 285–286

Colombia–Panama, establishment of diplomatic relations: Agreement resulting from U. S. efforts, 287–290; boundary convention, arrangements and conclusion, 290–293

Colombia–Peru, question of Peruvian ratification of boundary treaty of *Mar. 24, 1922*:

Brazilian opposition:

Grounds for objections, and effect on Peruvian position, 296–299, 303

U. S. good offices for solution of problem, requests of—

Brazil, 304; U. S. attitude, 304

Colombia and Peru, 300–302, 303; U. S. attitude and suggestion, 302, 303

Good offices of United States (*see also* Brazilian opposition, *supra*) :

Colombian appreciation, 294; U. S. statement of attitude of impartiality, 295

Efforts of U. S. Ambassador to Peru, 293–294, 295–296, 299–300

Opinions of Peruvian Minister for Foreign Affairs, 298–299

Ecuador–Peru, protocol signed *June 21* for submission of question to arbitration in Washington, 304–305

Boxer indemnity. *See under* China.

Brazil (*see also* China: Arms and munitions embargo: Formula; *and under* Boundary disputes: Colombia–Peru), naval-building program:

Brazil, naval-building program—Contd.
Resolution adopted by Naval Committee of Brazilian Chamber of Deputies, 326–327
U. S. Naval Mission, recommendations: Nature of recommendations and plans for carrying out program, 323, 324–325; unfavorable attitude of U. S. Department of State, 323–324, 325–326; withdrawal of recommendations for revision, 326

Bulgaria (see also Aviation), extradition treaty with United States, text signed *Mar. 19*, 328–334

Cacao Growers Association. *See under* Ecuador.

Canada (see also Aviation; Liquor control):
Great Lakes, further diversion of waters, protests by Canadian Government in connection with—
Sanitary District of Chicago, proposed increase in diversion of waters, 349–351, 352–353, 353–355; U. S. replies, 351–352, 355–356
U. S. pending legislation in regard to, 350–351, 352–353; U. S. replies, 353, 355–356

Halibut fishery in the Northern Pacific, convention with United States for preservation of (*Mar. 2, 1923*): Canadian legislation in execution of, negotiations leading to amendment in accord with U. S. desire, 335–341; U. S. ratification, 341

St. Lawrence Waterway, negotiations between United States and Canada looking toward a joint project for improvement of river between Montreal and Lake Ontario: Decisions regarding Joint Engineering Board and national advisory committees, 343–349; opening of negotiations, 342–343; publication of correspondence, 347
U. S.-British liquor-smuggling convention, concurrence in ratification, 158n

Capitulations. *See under* Mandates.

Chile: Treaty of *1904* with Bolivia, disinclination of U. S. Secretary of State to offer good offices requested by Bolivia for modification of, 320–322; U. S. maintenance of informal relations with new administration at Santiago following resignation of President Alessandri, 357–360

China (*see also* Aviation; Chinese Eastern Railway):
Arms and munitions embargo:
Formula recommended by diplomatic corps at Peking approving Washington Conference resolution, with interpolation on aircraft:
Approval of Portugal, 530
Failure of U. S. and British efforts to secure acceptance: Attitude of Denmark, 534–536, 542; Netherlands, 537–538, 542; Norway and Brazil, 542; Sweden, 538–539, 542
British suggestion for formal proposals to interested governments, 531–533; U. S. reply, citing lack of unanimity among powers, 541–543
Violation by French Mail steamer, alleged: Representations to French Government, proposed, 530–531, 533–534; suggestion for negotiation of agreement between United States, France, and Great Britain prohibiting export of all aircraft to China during revolutionary disturbances, discussion, 533–534, 536, 539–541
Washington Conference resolution. *See* Formula recommended by diplomatic corps at Peking, *supra.*

Associated American Chambers of Commerce of China:
Report of annual meeting at Shanghai, *Oct. 16–17, 1923*, concerning problems of Americans in China, 580–594; U. S. consideration and explanation of policy, 594–601
Representation at Washington, desire for, 590–591
Banditry and lawlessness, observations of Associated American Chambers of Commerce of China, 583–585

Boxer indemnity:
Associated American Chambers of Commerce of China, comment, 592
Belgian preferential - t r e a t m e n t arrangement with Chinese Government (*1918*), U. S. nonparticipation in support of, 559–561, 563
Payment in gold currency, question of:
Contention of powers signatory to protocol of *1901*, with U. S. concurrence, 562, 563, 563–569; text of note to Chinese Government, 564–569

China—Continued.

Taxes, internal, observations of Associated American Chambers of Commerce of China, 581–583

Tonnage dues in Chinese ports, recommendations of Associated American Chambers of Commerce of China in regard to, 588–589

Treaties and agreements:

Agreements with Soviet Government, signed *May 31:* General principles for settlement of questions outstanding between China and Soviet Government, 495–499; provisional management of Chinese Eastern Railway, 499–501

Boxer indemnity, agreements between China and foreign powers: Protocol of *1901,* 441, 445, 446–447, 448–449, 450, 451, 458, 462, 467, 555, 559, 560, 564, 566, 567, 568; arrangement of *July 2, 1905,* 564–565, 567, 568, 569

Nine-power treaties relating to China, signed at Washington Conference: Cited, 528; delay in ratification, 425–426, 427, 431–432, 434–435, 435–436, 439, 440–441; observations of Associated American Chambers of Commerce of China, 587–588

Treaty obligations and treaty revision (*see also* Provisional Government: Recognition: Disagreement among treaty powers, *supra;* Treaties: Nine-power treaties, *supra*), 391, 394, 404, 406, 407, 431, 432, 439–440

Tsao Kun, 369, 386, 388, 389

Tuan Chi-jui (*see also* Provisional Government: Establishment, *supra*), 384, 388, 393, 394–395, 406

Unification, proposed national conference to discuss, 384, 388, 394–395, 397

Union of Soviet Socialist Republics. *See* Soviet influence *and* Soviet Russia, *supra.*

U. S. citizens (*see also* Civil war in North China: Protection of lives and property of foreigners, *supra*):

Claims against Chinese Government, 558–559, 591

Murder of American missionary (*1920*), U. S. protests against pardon and restoration to command of Chinese general held responsible for, 604–607

China—Continued.

U. S. citizens—Continued.

Treaty rights, problems involved in maintenance of:

Associated American Chambers of Commerce of China, observations and recommendations, 580–594; U. S. consideration and explanation of policy, 594–601

Missionary interests in China: Extraterritorial rights of missionaries, U. S. policy on question of ability of missionaries to surrender, 600–604; U. S. consultation with missionary boards, 599–601

U. S. consular property, observations of Associated American Chambers of Commerce of China, 585–586

U. S. diplomatic and consular services, observations of Associated American Chambers of Commerce of China, 586–587

U. S. income tax regulations, applicability to Americans residing abroad, observations of Associated American Chambers of Commerce of China, 592–593

U. S. military and naval forces, including Yangtze Patrol Force, recommendations of Associated American Chambers of Commerce of China concerning, 585, 590; U. S. attitude, 597–598

Washington Conference treaties and resolutions relating to China. *See* Arms and munitions: Formula, *supra; and under* Extraterritoriality, Tariff, *and* Treaties, *supra; also* Chinese Eastern Railway: Sino-Soviet agreements: Reservations by the powers.

Wu Pei-fu (*see also* Civil war in North China, *supra*), 373, 389, 392, 397, 398, 402

Yangtze Patrol Force, 585, 590, 597–598

Chinese Eastern Railway:

Arrests by Chinese police in railway zone, reports concerning, and activities of foreign diplomatic representatives, 510, 511–513

Bolshevik activities in railway zone, 510, 511–513

Chang Tso-lin, activities. *See* Arrests, *supra, and* Manchurian-Soviet agreement, *infra.*

Manchurian-Soviet agreement (*see also* Arrests, *supra*), reports concerning, 509–510, 510–511

Removal of seals from archives of Railway by U. S., British, French, and Japanese consuls at Harbin, 493–494, 495, 506, 507, 510

Dominican Republic:
Bond issue of $2,500,000:
  Effect on political situation, 644; on road-construction p r o g r a m, 644–645, 674, 679
  Loan contract with U. S. interests: Arrangements for, 649–651; text, 657–662; U. S. approval of contract and of proposed security, in accord with requests of Dominican Government and U. S. interests, 651–657
  U. S. approval (*see also under* Loan contract, *supra*):
    Dominican request, 643–644
    U. S. willingness to authorize issue conditional upon reservation of portion to cover purchase of Santo Domingo Water, Light and Power Co. properties, 670–671, 680, 682–683; Dominican attitude, 671–672, 683–684; U. S. Commissioner's attitude, 674, 679–680
Claim of British subject against United States for injuries suffered at hands of Dominican bandits: Memorial of claim submitted by Great Britain, 686; U. S. rejection of claim, 686–691
Constitutional reforms submitted by Provisional President, approval by Senate, 626
Convention of *1907* with United States: Citations, 627, 646, 653, 654, 655, 656, 666, 685; convention to replace, text signed *Dec. 27,* 662–666
Convention with United States to replace convention of *Feb. 8, 1907,* text signed *Dec. 27,* 662–666
Elections. *See under* U. S. control, *infra.*
Exchange of notes with United States to effect mutual unconditional most - favored - nation customs treatment, 666–670
Financial situation (*see also* Bond issue, *supra*), 645–649
Loan contract with U. S. interests. *See under* Bond issue, *supra.*
Military Governor:
  Plans for replacement, attitude of U. S. Commissioner, 624; revocation of order by Navy Department, 626
  Report on financial situation, discussion regarding, 645–646, 647–649
Minister to United States, appointment, 651, 651n
President-elect Vasquez. *See under* U. S. control: Elections, *infra.*

Dominican Republic—Continued.
Road-construction program, 644–645, 645, 674, 679
Santo Domingo Water, Light and Power Co., purchase of properties by Dominican Government:
  Bond issue, proposed, U. S. insistence on reservation of portion to cover purchase, 670–671, 680, 682–683; Dominican attitude, 671–672, 683–684; U. S. Commissioner's attitude, 674, 679–680
  Conclusion of transaction: Authorization by Dominican Congress, 684; signing of contract, 684–685; U. S. consent to necessary increase in Dominican public debt, 685
  Disagreement regarding obligations of Government under *1923* contract:
    Company's offers for settlement, 675–676, 681
    Position of Government, 671, 672–673
    U. S. efforts to bring about settlement (*see also* Bond issue, *supra*), suggested methods, 672, 674–676, 680–683; views and recommendations of U. S. Commissioner, 673–674, 676–680
U. S. control, withdrawal:
  Convention of evacuation: Plans for signature, 628–629, 630; text signed *June 12,* 631–642; transmittal to United States, 630
  Elections:
    Campaign activities, 618–623
    Election results, 623–624, 643
    Electoral registers, extension of time for completion, 622–623
    President-elect Vasquez: Cabinet appointments, 626; visit to United States, 625, 626–627, 628–629, 629–630
  U. S. Commissioner:
    Recommendations and views in regard to bond issue, 644–645, 650, 674, 679–680; controversy over obligations of Government under contract with Santo Domingo Water, Light and Power Co., 650, 673–674, 676–680; financial situation, 647–649; replacement of Military Governor, proposed, 624; U. S. policy in connection with elections, 618–619; visit of President-elect Vasquez to United States, 625, 627, 629–630
    Request for permission to return to United States, 627–628

Dominican Republic—Continued.
U. S. control, withdrawal—Continued.
U. S. Commissioner—Continued.
Suggestion to Presidential candidates regarding Policia Nacional, 618, 620
U. S. military forces, evacuation, 629, 643

Ecuador:
Asociacion de Agricultores del Ecuador. *See* Cacao Growers Association, *infra.*
Boundary dispute with Peru, protocol for submission to arbitration in Washington, 304–305
Cacao Growers Association, indebtedness:
Claim of Mercantile Bank of the Americas: Attitude of Ecuadoran President, 702–703; legislation affecting, discussion, 701–702, 704–705; U. S. representations to Ecuador regarding settlement, 703, 705–707
Payment of debts, reports concerning, 704, 705
Financial Adviser, activities, 693–694, 699
Guayaquil and Quito Railway Co., bonds, service of:
Failure of Ecuadoran Government to meet interest payments:
Efforts of U. S. Minister to bring about payment, 695–699; U. S. approval of action, 699–700
U. S. representations to Ecuador, question of advisability, 692–695
Resumption of interest payments by Ecuadoran Government, 700–701
Loan contract with British interests, status of negotiations, 693
Mercantile Bank of the Americas, claim against Ecuadoran Government for debt of Cacao Growers Association. *See under* Cacao Growers Association, *supra.*

Egypt:
American archeologists, U. S. efforts to protect interests. *See under* Antiquities Law, *infra.*
Antiquities Law of *1912*, proposed modifications:
American archeological institutions, protests and requests for U. S. support, 714–715, 719–720; U. S. efforts on behalf of, 715–716, 717, 718–719, 720–723
British and French attitude, 716–717
Egyptian position, 717, 718, 721–722, 722–723

Egypt—Continued.
Gaffir tax:
British attitude regarding collection from British nationals, 713
Collection from American nationals, question of: Egyptian attitude, and request for U. S. consent, 708–709, 711–712; U. S. position, 710, 712–714
Nature and application of tax, 708–709

Extradition:
Treaties between United States and other governments. *See under* Treaties.
U. S. negotiations with France concerning extradition from mandated territory, 730, 731–732, 734, 736–737, 739, 740

Extraterritoriality. *See under* China.

Federal Telegraph Co. contract. *See under* China: Radio communications.

Finland, extradition treaty with United States, text signed *Aug. 1,* 724–729

Fisheries. *See* Canada: Halibut fishery.

Flight around the world by U. S. Army airplanes, proposed. *See* Aviation.

France (*see also* Arms and munitions; Aviation; China; Chinese Eastern Railway; Liquor control; Mandates; Spitzbergen Treaty):
Concessions for archeological research in Albania and Afghanistan, U. S. protests against alleged French monopoly, 753–754; attitude of Albania, 754; of France, 754–755
Consular convention of *1853* with United States, question of applicability in Syria and the Lebanon, 730, 732, 734, 735–736, 739, 740
Egyptian antiquities law, attitude regarding proposed modifications, 717
Extradition treaty of *1909* with United States, question of applicability in Syria and the Lebanon, 730, 731, 732, 734, 736–737, 739, 740
Narcotics Conference, International, participation, 92, 97–98, 119n, 120, 123
Recognition of revolutionary government in Albania, attitude regarding, 309
Relief loans by United States and others to certain European nations, proposal of international coordinating agency to liquidate, 127–128; U. S. attitude, 128–129

France—Continued.
U. S. shipping, refusal of French authorities to recognize classification and inspection of vessels by American Bureau of Shipping, U. S. representations, 756–758; French position, 759

Germany (see also Aviation; Liquor control; Mormon missionaries): Agreement with United States for establishment of Claims Commission (Aug. 10, 1922), cited, 143, 148, 149–150; Lithuanian-German trade agreement, proposed, relation to Lithuania's war debt to United States, 136, 137–138

Great Britain (see also Arms and munitions; Aviation; Canada; China; Chinese Eastern Railway; Dominican Republic: Claim of British subject; Liquor control; Mormon missionaries; Narcotics Conference; Relief loans: Relief Credits Committee; Spitzbergen Treaty; Treaty for the limitation of naval armament): Egyptian antiquities law, attitude regarding proposed modifications, 716–717; Egyptian gaffir tax, attitude concerning collection from British nationals, 713; monopolies provision in Albano-Italian treaty of commerce and navigation, objection to, 317; recognition of revolutionary government in Albania, attitude regarding, 309

Great Lakes. See under Canada.

Greece:
Recognition of revolutionary government in Albania, attitude regarding, 309, 310, 312, 313
Refugee loan, American participation, 139–140
War debt to United States, U. S. informal representations concerning, 139–141; attitude of Greek Government, 141

Guayaquil and Quito Railway Co. See under Ecuador.

Gun elevation on capital ships. See Treaty for the limitation of naval armament.

Hague Opium Convention of 1912, international conference of signatory powers and members of League of Nations for further restriction of traffic in habit-forming drugs. See Narcotics Conference.

Hord, John S., activities as Financial Adviser to Ecuador, 693–694, 699

Hungary. See Austria and Hungary; Aviation.

Iceland, granting of permission for U. S. investigation preparatory to flight around the world by U. S. Army airplanes, 228

Immigration into United States, proposed legislation to restrict:
Questions under consideration; census of 1890, establishment of quota on basis of, 213–214, 218, 221–222, 225; exclusion provision, 215, 216–218; immigration certificates, 214–215, 219–221, 225–226; treaty obligations, 215–216, 223–224

Representations to United States by—
Cuba, 212–213; U. S. reply, 224
Italy, 224–226
Norway, 223–224; U. S. reply, 224
Rumania, 213–214; U. S. reply, 222
Salvador, 212; U. S. reply, 223

Views and recommendations of U. S. Secretary of State, letter to Chairman of House Committee on Immigration and Naturalization, 214–222

India (see also Aviation), Narcotics Conference, International, participation and questions affecting, 115, 116, 118, 119n, 121

Iraq, favorable attitude in connection with proposed flight around the world by U. S. Army airplanes, 242

Irish Free State, concurrence in ratification of U. S.-British liquor-smuggling convention, 158n

Italy (see also Aviation; China; Immigration into United States; Liquor control; Spitzbergen Treaty): Recognition of revolutionary government in Albania, attitude regarding, 309, 310, 310–311, 312; treaty of commerce and navigation with Albania, opposition of United States, Great Britain, and Yugoslavia to certain provisions, 317–318

Japan (see also Aviation; China; Chinese Eastern Railway; Spitzbergen Treaty): Narcotics Conference, International, participation, 102–104, 116, 119, 119n; treaty of commerce and navigation with United States (1911), cited, 215; U. S. proposed legislation to restrict immigration, 215, 216–218

Latvia, plans for opening of negotiations for refunding of war debt to United States, 138–139

League of Nations:
Convention to replace St. Germain convention of *1919*, proposed. *See* Arms and munitions.
Draft treaty of mutual assistance, U. S. unfavorable views, 79–83
Issuance of certificates of identity to Russian and Armenian refugees, U. S. acceptance in lieu of passports, 83–89
Narcotics Conference, International, arrangements for. *See* Narcotics Conference: Arrangements.
Permanent Court of International Justice, proposed modification in U. S.-Netherlands liquor-smuggling convention concerning possible submission of claims to, 202–203, 204–205, 210–211
Resolutions in regard to calling of narcotics conferences, 89–90, 91, 92; proposed convention to replace St. Germain convention of *1919*, 73
Temporary Mixed Commission. *See* Arms and munitions: Convention: U. S. cooperation with League in drafting.

Lee, Higginson & Co., loan contract with Dominican Republic: Negotiations, 649–650, 651–654, 655–657; text, 657–662

Liberation bonds of Austro-Hungarian succession states, proposed, U. S. interest in disposition of:
Applicability of cash from bonds to Army costs agreement, question of, 156–157
Recommendation of Reparation Commission regarding delivery and division of bonds, 154–155; U. S. attitude, 155–156

Liquor control under U. S. prohibition laws, conventions between United States and other governments for prevention of smuggling:
Canada: Summary of negotiations, 188; text of convention between United States and Great Britain in respect of Canada, signed *June 6*, 189–192
Denmark: Negotiations, 180–181; text signed *May 29*, 181–184
France: Summary of negotiations, 197; text signed *June 30*, 197–200
Germany: Negotiations, 161–162; text signed *May 19*, 162–165
Great Britain (*see also* Canada, *supra*): Concurrence of Dominions, 157–158; text signed *Jan. 23*, 158–161
Italy: Conversation between U. S. Secretary of State and Italian Ambassador, 184; text signed *June 3*, 185–188

Liquor control under U. S. prohibition laws, conventions, etc.—Continued.
Netherlands: Date of entry into force, question of, 206–207; exchange of notes providing for possible submission of claims to Permanent Court of International Justice in lieu of Permanent Court of Arbitration, 202–203, 204–205, 210–211; negotiations, 200–207; text signed *Aug. 21*, 207–210
Norway: Negotiations, 173–176; text signed *May 24*, 176–179
Panama: Reservation in connection with Canal Zone, 192, 196; text signed *June 6*, 192–195
Sweden: Discussions leading to negotiations, 165–168; extent of territorial jurisdiction, question of, 165–168, 168–169; negotiations, 168–169; text signed *May 22*, 170–173

Lithuania. *See under* War debts.

Loans (*see also* China: Consortium; Relief loans; *and under* Dominican Republic: Bond issue): Ecuadoran loan contract with British interests, status of negotiations, 693; Greek refugee loan, American participation, 139–140

Manchuria, agreement with Soviet Russia regarding Chinese Eastern Railway, 509–510, 510–511

Mandates:
Capitulations in Syria (*see also* Consular rights, *infra*), question of jurisdiction under, 749–750
Consular rights in Syria and the Lebanon, U. S. negotiations with France, 730, 732, 734, 735–737, 739, 740
Convention between United States and France regarding U. S. rights in Syria and the Lebanon. *See under* Syria and the Lebanon, *infra*.
Extradition, U. S. negotiations with France, 730, 731–732, 734, 736–737, 739, 740
Most-favored-nation treatment, U. S. negotiations with France, 732, 733, 738–739
Syria and the Lebanon:
Convention between United States and France to ensure U. S. rights: Negotiations, 730–740; text signed *Apr. 4*, 741–746; understanding as to most-favored-nation treatment, extradition, and consular rights, 738–740

Mandates—Continued.
Syria and the Lebanon—Continued.
Import duties into Syria, U. S.
consent to increase, pending
ratification of U. S.-French
mandate convention, 747–749
Jurisdiction over American nationals in Syria, case of Joe
Abraham, 749–751; opinion of
U. S. Department of State,
751–752
Mercantile Bank of the Americas.
See Ecuador: Cacao Growers Association.
Metropolitan Museum of Art, communications to U. S. Secretary of State
regarding proposed modifications
in Egyptian Antiquities Law of
1912, 714–715, 719–720
Missionaries. *See* China: U. S. citizens; Mormon missionaries.
Mitsui Co., 570, 571
Mormon missionaries, American, ex-
clusion from or discriminatory
treatment by certain countries:
Correspondence between S e n a t o r
Reed Smoot and U. S. Secretary
of State, 246–247, 254
U. S. representations against, instructions to U. S. representatives in—
Denmark, 248*n*; Danish attitude,
251–252, 257
Germany, 263–264
Great Britain, regarding missionaries to South Africa, **248;**
attitude of South African au-
thorities, 253, 254
Netherlands, 248*n*; position of
Netherlands Government, 251
Norway, 248*n*, 250; Norwegian attitude, 250, 252–253, 254–255
Sweden, 247, 248, 250; Swedish attitude, 247, 247–248, 248–249,
250–251, 255–256, 257
Switzerland, 248*n*, 253–254, 257–
258, 260–261; reports of U. S.
Minister as to Swiss position,
and requests for further instructions, 258–260, 261–263
Most-favored-nation policy:
Exchange of notes between United
States and—
Czechoslovakia, prolonging customs
agreement of *Oct. 29, 1923,*
615–617
Dominican Republic, to effect mutual u n c o n d i t i o n a l most-
favored-nation customs treatment, 666–670
Negotiations between United States
and France regarding man-
dated territory, 732, 733, 738–739

Munitions. *See* Arms and munitions.

Narcotics Conference, International:
Arrangements of League of Nations:
Invitation to United States and
U. S. acceptance, 91–92, 101; Preliminary (First) Conference, of
countries h a v i n g possessions
where smoking of opium is continued, plans for, 89–90, 90, 91;
Preparatory Committee, establishment, 92–93; resolutions and
plans, 89–91, 92
Negotiations looking toward agreement for further restriction of
traffic in narcotic drugs:
Attitude of delegations regarding
agreement on prepared opium
reached at First Conference,
119–120
British-Japanese controversy on exportation of raw products, 102–
103; attitude of United States,
103–104; settlement, reported,
116
Inability of conference to reach
a g r e e m e n t satisfactory to
United States, report of U. S.
delegation concerning, 120–124
U. S. suggestions presented to conference, proposed changes in
Hague Opium Convention of
1912: Reports of U. S. delegation on submittal to committees
and attitude of various delegations, 115–116, 120; text of suggestions, 104–115; U. S.-British
disagreement regarding limitation of production of raw opium
and control of traffic in prepared opium, 116–119
Preliminary (First) Conference: Arrangements for, 89–90, 90, 91; negotiations, reports concerning,
115–116, 116–117, 119–120
U. S. participation (*see also* Negotiations, *supra*):
Activities prior to assembling of
conference:
Communication of views in support of conference to Peru,
Bolivia, Turkey, and Persia,
98–100; replies, 100–101, 101–
102
Participation in work of Preparatory Committee for drafting
of program: Appointment
and instructions of delegate,
92–96; suggestions to be presented to committee, 94–96
Representations to France, 97;
French attitude, 97–98

Narcotics Conference—Continued.
U. S. participation—Continued.
Delegation:
List, 102
Withdrawal from conference:
Letter of withdrawal, 125–
1 2 6; recommendation of
chairman of delegation, 120–
124; U. S. authorization for,
124–125
Invitation from League of Nations
and U. S. acceptance, 91–92, 101
Withdrawal. See under Delegation, supra.
Naval armament limitation. See Brazil; Treaty for the limitation of
naval armament.
Naval mission to Brazil (U. S.). See
under Brazil.
Netherlands (see also China; Liquor
control; Mormon missionaries;
Spitzbergen Treaty), participation
in International Narcotics Conference, 92, 116, 119n, 119–120, 123
New Zealand, concurrence in ratification of U. S.-British liquor-smuggling convention, 158n
Newfoundland, concurrence in ratification of U. S.-British liquor-smuggling convention, 158n
Norway (see also China: Arms and
munitions embargo: Formula; Immigration into United States;
Liquor control; Mormon missionaries; Spitzbergen Treaty), treaty
of commerce and navigation with
United States (1827), cited, 223–
224

Oil concessions in Albania, U. S. representations on behalf of American
interests, 318–319
Open-door policy, U. S. protests against
alleged French monopoly on concessions for archeological research
in Albania and Afghanistan, 753–
754; attitude of Albania and of
France, 754–755
Opium. See Narcotics Conference.

Panama. See Boundary disputes: Colombia–Panama; Liquor control.
Paraguay. See Boundary disputes:
Bolivia–Paraguay.
Passports, U. S. acceptance of certificates of identity issued by League
of Nations to Russian and Armenian
refugees in lieu of, 83–89
Permanent Court of International Justice, proposed modification in U. S.-
Netherlands liquor-smuggling convention concerning possible submission of claims to, 202–203, 204–
205, 210–211

Persia (see also Aviation), participation in International Narcotics
Conference, 99–100, 100–101, 121
Peru (see also Boundary disputes: Colombia–Peru and Ecuador–Peru),
participation in International Narcotics Conference, 98, 101–102
Philippine Islands, exclusive jurisdiction of United States in question of
granting independence to, 264–266
Portugal (see also China), participation in International Narcotics
Conference, 119n, 120
President of United States (Calvin
Coolidge), message to U. S. Congress, vii
Protocols. See Treaties, conventions,
etc.

Radio communications. See under
China.
Radio Corporation of America. See
China: Radio communications:
Federal Telegraph Co. contract.
Railways. See Chinese Eastern Rail-
way; Ecuador: Guayaquil and
Quito Railway Co.; and under
China.
Refugees, Russian and Armenian, U. S.
acceptance of certificates of iden-
tity issued by League of Nations in
lieu of passports, 83–89
Reimert, W. A. (U. S. missionary to
China), U. S. protests in connec-
tion with murder of, 604–607
Relief Credits Committee. See under
Relief loans.
Relief loans by United States and
others to certain European states,
proposed establishment of inter-
national organization to liquidate:
Coordinating agency, French pro-
posal, 127–128; U. S. inability to
acquiesce, 128–129
Relief Credits Committee:
British proposal, including suggested attendance of member
of World War Foreign Debt
Commission, 129–132, 133;
U. S. consideration and rejection, 132–133, 133–134
U. S. plans to keep in touch with
work of committee, 134–135
Reparations:
Reparation Commission, recommendation regarding disposition of
proposed liberation bonds of
Austro - Hungarian succession
states, 154–155; U. S. attitude,
155–156
War debts, relation to, 136, 137–138

Resolutions:

Associated American Chambers of Commerce of China, resolutions adopted at annual meeting at Shanghai, *Oct. 16–17, 1923*, 580–594

League of Nations. *See under* League of Nations.

Radio Corporation of America, resolution regarding contracts with Chinese Government, 574–575

U. S. Congress. *See* U. S. Congress.

Washington Conference on the Limitation of Armament. *See* Chinese Eastern Railway: Sino-Soviet agreements: Reservations by the powers; *also* Arms and munitions embargo: Formula, *and* Extraterritoriality *under* China.

Rumania. *See* Aviation; Immigration into United States.

Russian and Armenian refugees, U. S. acceptance of certificates of identity issued by League of Nations in lieu of passports, 83–89

Russo-Asiatic Bank. *See* French position *under* Chinese Eastern Railway: Sino-Soviet agreements: Reservations by the powers.

St. Germain convention of *1919*. *See* Arms and munitions.

St. Lawrence Waterway. *See under* Canada.

Salvador. *See* Immigration into United States.

Sanitary convention between United States and other American republics, text signed *Nov. 14*, 266–282

Santo Domingo Water, Light and Power Co. *See under* Dominican Republic.

Serbs, Croats and Slovenes, Kingdom of. *See* Yugoslavia.

Servia: Narcotics Conference, International, participation, 121; recognition of revolutionary government in Albania, attitude regarding, 309, 312

Siam (*see also* Aviation), signature of international narcotics agreement, 119*n*

Smoot, Senator Reed, correspondence with U. S. Secretary of State regarding restrictions imposed on American Mormon missionaries by certain countries, 246–247, 254

Smuggling. *See* Liquor control.

South Africa:

Restrictions imposed upon American Mormon missionaries, reported, U. S. representations, 248; attitude of South African authorities, 253, 254

South Africa—Continued.

U. S.-British liquor-smuggling convention, concurrence in ratification, 158*n*

Spitzbergen Treaty of *Feb. 9, 1920*, proposals for adherence of Union of Soviet Socialist Republics:

French suggestion for protocol, 2; U. S. attitude and proposed draft agreement, 3, 5–6

Norwegian proposal, 1, 3–4

Attitude of France, 3; Netherlands, 4; United States, 2, 4–5

Concurrence of Denmark, Great Britain, Italy, Japan, and Sweden, 4, 4*n*

U. S. proposed draft agreement, 5–6

Sweden. *See* China: Arms and munitions embargo: Formula; Liquor control; Mormon missionaries; Spitzbergen Treaty.

Switzerland (*see also* Mormon missionaries), convention of friendship, commerce, and extradition with United States (*1850*), 253, 260

Syria and the Lebanon. *See under* Mandates.

Temporary Mixed Commission of League of Nations. *See* Arms and munitions.

Treaties, conventions, etc. (*see also under* China):

Albano-Italian treaty of commerce and navigation, opposition of United States, Great Britain, and Yugoslavia to certain provisions, 317–318

Arbitration protocol, Ecuador–Peru (*June 21*), 304–305

Armament limitation (*see also* Treaty for the limitation of naval armament), draft treaty of mutual assistance submitted by League of Nations, U. S. unfavorable views, 79–83

Arms traffic convention to replace St. Germain convention of *1919*, proposed. *See* Arms and munitions.

Army costs agreement, question of applicability of cash from liberation bonds of Austro-Hungarian succession states, 156–157

Bolivian-Chilean treaty of *1904*, disinclination of U. S. Secretary of State to offer good offices requested by Bolivia for modification of, 320–322

Boundary convention, Colombia–Panama, arrangements and conclusion, 290–293

Boundary treaty, Colombia–Peru (*Mar. 24, 1922*), question of ratification. *See* Boundary disputes: Colombia–Peru.

VOLUME II IS INDEXED SEPARATELY